# Prokofiev

# Prokofiev

ISRAEL V. NESTYEV

*Translated from the Russian by*
FLORENCE JONAS; *with a Foreword by*
NICOLAS SLONIMSKY

STANFORD UNIVERSITY PRESS: STANFORD, CALIFORNIA
1960

This book was originally published in Russian in 1957 by Gosudarstvennoe Muzikalnoe Izdatelstvo in Moscow. It is essentially an extension and elaboration of Mr. Nestyev's earlier book, an English-language version of which was published in the United States as *Sergei Prokofiev, His Musical Life* (New York: Alfred A. Knopf, 1946).

STANFORD UNIVERSITY PRESS
STANFORD, CALIFORNIA

LONDON: OXFORD UNIVERSITY PRESS

# FOREWORD

When Prokofiev played his piano compositions during his first tour of the United States in 1918, an American music critic wrote: "Crashing Siberias, volcano hell, Krakatoa, sea-bottom crawlers. Incomprehensible? So is Prokofiev." But, he warned wryly, one must be careful about premature judgment: "Prokofiev might be the legitimate successor of Borodin, Moussorgsky, and Rimsky-Korsakov."

This humorous prophecy turned out to be the truth. Within a few short years after his death, Prokofiev indeed became a Russian classic. The present biography testifies to his enormous prestige; such completeness of documentation and attention to detail are usually reserved for acknowledged masters of the classical past. Prokofiev's manuscripts, his correspondence, and other biographical materials have acquired the status of a cultural heritage, and are deposited for safekeeping in the State Archive of Literature and Art and the Central Museum of Musical Culture in Moscow.

Every biographer has the right to establish his own attitude toward his subject. Israel Nestyev takes the position that the years Prokofiev spent abroad were generally detrimental to his art, and that only after his return to Russia late in 1933 did he regain his full creative powers. Nestyev draws a dramatic contrast: happiness and productivity in Russia, distress and sterility in Paris and America. Prokofiev's associates among Russian émigrés are treated with scorn; Diaghilev is represented as a sinister snob who almost ruined Prokofiev's talent by forcing him to compose in an unnatural modernistic style to please the depraved tastes of the West; Koussevitzky's motives in championing Prokofiev's music (as both publisher and conductor) are interpreted by Nestyev as cunning commercialism.

Not every work written by Prokofiev abroad is condemned by Nestyev *a priori*. *The Love for Three Oranges,* commissioned by the Chicago Opera Company, receives his mark of approval; the celebrated March from this opera is as popular in Russia as it is in America. On the other hand, some of Prokofiev's compositions of the Soviet period are subjected to sharp criticism, although their faults are usually explained as the after-effects of Western influences.

In Prokofiev's creative evolution, as Nestyev interprets it, two forces are in conflict: realistic art nourished by the national resources of Russian folk music, and cosmopolitan modernism cultivated in the West. The danger of the realistic concept is oversimplification; the danger of modernism lies in formalistic abstraction.

Nestyev is an informed and astute writer on music, and he does not apply the dialectical yardstick literally. He knows that Soviet subject matter alone does not create realistic art. Indeed, he reserves some of his most derogatory remarks for Prokofiev's ballet *Le Pas d'acier,* produced by Diaghilev in Paris in 1927, despite the fact that it represented scenes from Soviet life. (Paradoxically, the ballet was condemned in the European press as a "Bolshevik spectacle," whereas to Nestyev it represents a travesty of Soviet reality.) Nestyev is equally critical of Prokofiev's attempt to set to music texts from the writings of Marx, Lenin, and Stalin in his *Cantata for the Twentieth Anniversary of the October Revolution,* which was never performed. In this instance Nestyev attributes Prokofiev's failure to a tendency toward "leftist" oversimplification.

A strange fate pursued Prokofiev's music written on patriotic Soviet themes. His symphonic suite *The Year 1941,* composed in response to the Nazi invasion, was quite unsuccessful; his cantata *Ballad of an Unknown Boy,* glorifying a young hero of the war, had an indifferent reception, and was never published; his opera *Semyon Kotko,* on the subject of the civil war in the Ukraine, drew some praise but was not retained in the active repertory; his *Ode to the End of the War,* scored for a huge orchestra, was found impractical for performance; his cantata on folk texts on the occasion of Stalin's sixtieth birthday received perfunctory notices but obviously added no luster to his name.

Still, it must be conceded that Prokofiev's best and most popular works were the product of his Soviet period. From this period we have *Lieutenant Kije, Peter and the Wolf,* the Fifth Symphony, the *Alexander Nevsky* cantata, the ballet *Romeo and Juliet,* and the opera *War and Peace.* Prokofiev's *Classical Symphony* was written before he left Russia, and although his Third Piano Concerto was completed in France, Nestyev points out that its main outlines had been worked out in Russia long before.

Nestyev traces Prokofiev's life and works chronologically, skillfully maintaining the parallel narrative without separating Prokofiev the man from Prokofiev the composer. He also paints the historical and social background of Prokofiev's life. In this he inevitably follows the established Soviet interpretation. The early years of the century before the Revolution are depicted as a time of political reaction and cultural decadence, with such notable exceptions as Maxim Gorky in literature, the realistic painters in art, and the Russian composers of the national school. The scene changes after the victory of the Revolution; the flowering of the arts in the Soviet Union is described with warmth and conviction. Still, Nestyev's narrative is mainly factual; only rarely does he depart from it to indulge in flights of interpretive fancy, as in the chapter on Prokofiev's return to Russia, which reports Prokofiev's exhilaration at seeing the "vibrant creative life about him, which differed so greatly from the moribund, crisis-ridden atmosphere in bourgeois Europe."

Ideology and politics are integral parts of Soviet musical life, and Nestyev's paragraphs on the subject will be revealing and sometimes fascinating for the non-Soviet reader. After all, the gigantic experiment of directing the language of music according to a set of philosophically formulated principles is unprecedented in history, and it deserves the closest study. Nestyev's book provides illuminating glances into this strange new world.

The present translation omits none of these political and ideological digressions; the tendentious descriptions of Prokofiev's years in Europe and America have also been preserved without alterations. Only one minor deletion has been made. Nestyev quotes Prokofiev's letter published in 1951 in the English-language daily, Moscow *News*, in which he voiced indignation against the alleged threats of death directed at the conductor of the Utah Symphony Orchestra in Salt Lake City by anti-Soviet American agitators because he put on his program Prokofiev's Fifth Symphony. In telling this fantastic tale, Nestyev refers to Salt Lake City as being situated "in one of the Southern states of the U.S.A." This geographical misplacement of the state of Utah has been eliminated, but the story of the letter has been scrupulously preserved.

Along with other Soviet composers, Prokofiev was condemned for modernistic and formalistic tendencies in the notorious Resolution of the Central Committee of the Communist Party of February 10, 1948. On May 28, 1958, this Resolution was officially withdrawn as unjustified; the new Resolution contained this significant passage: "Talented composers, Comrades Shostakovich, Prokofiev, Khachaturian, Shebalin, Popov, Miaskovsky, and others, were indiscriminately described as representatives of the formalist trend inimical to the people . . . Some incorrect evaluations in the Resolution reflected J. V. Stalin's subjective approach toward certain works of art."

Nestyev's book was published in Russia in 1957, before the disavowal of the 1948 Resolution, and he was doubtless constrained to pay lip service to the strictures directed against Prokofiev. He quotes a wistful letter addressed to the Union of Soviet Composers in 1948 in which Prokofiev admits some of his errors, imputing them to his "contact with certain Western trends."

Prokofiev's last attempt to write music on a contemporary subject was his opera *The Story of a Real Man,* to a libretto dealing with the exploits of a heroic Soviet flier. It was a tragic failure, and the opera was rejected after a trial performance. But this failure had a redeeming sequel, for the opera was placed in production at the Bolshoi Theater in Moscow for the 1960–61 season.

Prokofiev lived to witness the triumph of his Seventh Symphony, which was greeted by musicians and the public in the Soviet Union as a work of supreme mastery and poetic inspiration. Prokofiev's creative life, *per aspera ad astra,* was thus concluded on a happy chord.

By an ironic coincidence not mentioned in Nestyev's book, Prokofiev died on the same day as Stalin. His death was obscured by the shadow of that great event, and when it was announced in the foreign press after a delay of several days, the date was given as March 4 instead of March 5, 1953, an error that is retained in a number of reference works.

N. S.

# TRANSLATOR'S NOTE

In books translated from the Russian, dates can often be confusing, for Russians followed the Julian, or Old Style, calendar until February 1918, when the Soviet Union adopted the Gregorian, or New Style, calendar. Mr. Nestyev has given dates in Old Style throughout the first five chapters of the present book, which cover the period from Prokofiev's birth to 1918. For the sake of uniformity, I have taken the liberty of changing all the dates in these chapters to New Style.

I have tried to make the annotation of the text both useful and unobtrusive. Of Mr. Nestyev's notes, those providing primarily source or reference information are given superscript numbers in the text and are collected in the Notes section at the back of the book; on the other hand, those of intrinsic interest or of immediate relevance to the narrative are marked by asterisks and are placed at the foot of the page. In my occasional Translator's Notes, I have attempted to explain only what seemed clearly obscure or unfamiliar and to add information only when it could serve to illuminate a particularly interesting portion of the text.

In a few instances, I have used lines of prose and poetry which have already appeared in English translation. For permission to quote these, acknowledgment is due to Alfred A. Knopf, publishers of Mr. Nestyev's *Sergei Prokofiev, His Musical Life* (1946) and to Herbert Marshall, the author of *Mayakovsky and His Poetry* (1945).

I am profoundly grateful to William C. Holmes for his invaluable assistance in editing the musical analyses in this work. I also wish to thank Gene W. Tanke for his painstaking care and interest in preparing the manuscript for publication.

F. J.

# AUTHOR'S PREFACE

In this book the author has attempted to combine the biography of Sergei Prokofiev with brief descriptions of his most important works and some observations on his creative style.

Addressing his work to a wide audience, the author has insofar as possible avoided specialized musical terminology. Because of the great quantity of the material considered, it has been impossible to give more detailed analyses of the various works and the peculiarities of their musical language. This interesting task will undoubtedly be dealt with by many Soviet and foreign students of Prokofiev. The author will be happy if his work, even in some small measure, will help to popularize Prokofiev's music and to further scholarly study of it.

The biographical part of the book is largely based upon the composer's *Autobiography,* which was first published in full in the volume *S. S. Prokofiev: Materials, Documents, and Reminiscences,* compiled by S. I. Schlifstein (State Music Publishers, Moscow, 1956). Quotations from the *Autobiography* are given throughout without reference to the source.

The author has also made wide use of articles on Prokofiev published at various times in the Soviet Union and abroad, notes of conversations with the composer during the years 1940–47, and materials published in the pre-revolutionary Russian, Soviet, and foreign press between 1908 and 1953.

The comments of Prokofiev's closest friends and colleagues, N. Ya. Miaskovsky and B. V. Asafyev (Igor Glebov), have been given a special place in this book. It is the author's intention that these companions of Prokofiev's creative life should be, along with the composer himself, the *dramatis personae* of this narrative. The articles, memoirs, and letters of these outstanding musicians, as well as personal conversations with them, have been of considerable help in the writing of this book.

The author has also made use of many of Prokofiev's unpublished manuscripts (music, letters, etc.) preserved in the Central State Archive of Literature and Art, the Ministry of Internal Affairs of the U.S.S.R., the Glinka Central Museum of Musical Culture, and the personal files of I. S. Asafyeva and L. T. Atovmyan. In addition, the author has drawn valuable information from conversations with R. M. Glière, K. S. Saradzhev, V. V. Derzhanovsky, V. M. Morolev, L. V. Nikolaev, A. V. Ossovsky, S. A. Samosud, M. A. Mendelson-Prokofieva, D. F. Oistrakh, M. L. Rostropovich, S. M. Gorodetsky, V. P. Katayev, G. M. Schneerson, Ye. V. Gippius, and other intimate acquaintances of the composer.

The author wishes to express his heartfelt gratitude to all those who played a part in the creation of this book.

I. V. N.

# CONTENTS

# ILLUSTRATIONS

# Prokofiev

# ONE

# SONTSOVKA

SERGEI SERGEYEVICH PROKOFIEV was born on April 23, 1891, in the village of Sontsovka, Bakhmut district, Yekaterinoslav Guberniya (now Stalino Oblast in the Donbas).

Sontsovka, with its more than two hundred farmsteads, was situated at a distance from the railroad, near a small, winding river called the Volchya. All around stretched the limitless Ukrainian steppe, covered in the spring with brilliantly colored flowers but by June already scorched by the heat. This part of the Ukraine is distinguished by a unique beauty. The treeless plains, covered with gray feather grass, savory, and eryngium, are cut by ravines and quiet streams. In winter, winds and snowstorms rage. Spring comes early, summer is hot and arid. Ancient roads, bare burial mounds rising above the steppe, and the roughhewn stone images which from time to time catch the eye of the traveler recall the stern past of this region. Here the Scyths once roamed, and later, the Mongolian tribes. Here, in savage struggle against the Oriental conquerors, the eastern boundaries of the Slavic state were fixed.

At the end of the nineteenth century the Bakhmut district, rich in coal and salt, began to develop rapidly. It became covered by a thick network of railroads, mines, and factories. Trains laden with Donets coal passed through Debaltsevo, Grishino, and Rutchenkovo, all twenty-five to thirty kilometers from Sontsovka. Not far away, at Yuzovo station, glowed the blast furnaces of the largest metallurgical works in Russia. Trains brought crowds of ruined peasants to this region in search of work and bread.

But quiet Sontsovka remained untouched by industrial life. In their thatched clay huts the peasants still talked of taxes, of drought. Not far from the village lay the estate of the landowner Sontsov. The Sontsovs did not live in this remote and lonely place, but entrusted its administration entirely to a manager. From the beginning of the eighties, the estate was under the supervision of an agronomist, Sergei Alexeyevich Prokofiev, a tall, bespectacled man with a full, thick beard. The peasants respected and loved the agronomist Prokofiev, considering him a just and warmhearted man.

Sergei Alexeyevich Prokofiev (1846–1910) was a typical representative of the middle-class Russian intelligentsia of the sixties. The son of a small Moscow merchant of the Konyushennaya suburb, he managed to "make something of himself" by means of hard work. After graduating from the Moscow Commercial High School, where he studied at government expense, S. A. Prokofiev, like many Russian intellectuals of the sixties, turned to the study of the natural sciences. He spent the next four years (1867–71) at the Petrovsko-Razumovsky Agricultural Academy in Moscow, where such scholars as K. A. Timiryazev and I. A. Stebut were then teaching. This Academy was renowned for the revolutionary spirit of its student body, which was persecuted more than once by the Tsarist authorities; along with other students, S. A. Prokofiev was subjected to repressive measures. Being reticent by nature, he did not like to talk about this in later years. However, until the end of his life he remained a confirmed atheist, with a hatred for the gentry and the arrogance of the nobility, and a respect for the peasantry.

In Sontsovka S. A. Prokofiev set up a model farm, with studhorses and the latest agricultural machinery. Specialists who visited there from neighboring estates liked to consult him on problems of agronomy. People who knew him remember him as a good and just man, although reserved and taciturn, and always absorbed in administrative matters. He had an extensive library, to which he continually added new books.

The mother of the future composer, Mariya Grigoryevna Zhitkova (1855–1924), was an unusual person. She was born in St. Petersburg, and though her family was of modest means, she received a broad education. When she married S. A. Prokofiev, she exchanged the noisy life of St. Petersburg for the quiet, rural existence of Sontsovka. Here she became a worthy helpmeet of her husband in all administrative and communal matters. The village suffered from poverty and illiteracy, and Mariya Grigoryevna willingly devoted her leisure hours to teaching the peasant children.

A tall, stately woman with beautiful intelligent eyes, she brought tremendous energy and life into the Prokofiev home. She was good company and easily created around her an atmosphere of simplicity and warmth. A rather good pianist, she played very often, in this way relieving the monotony of country life. But not being a brilliantly gifted performer, she was shy about playing for people.

During the eighties misfortune twice befell the Prokofiev family: two small daughters born to Mariya Grigoryevna died, one after the other.

Thus, when a third child, the fair-haired Seryozha, was born, the mother and father lavished special care on him and tried to create the best possible conditions for his all-round development.

The Prokofievs' farmstead stood on a low hill outside the village. The house was whitewashed, spacious, modestly but tastefully furnished, and surrounded by a garden and outbuildings. Beneath the windows bloomed chestnut and bird cherry trees and lilacs; in the garden grew apple, pear, and plum trees. During the winter the house was quiet. In the evenings the family gathered around the lamps to read magazines and newspapers. Once in a while an acquaintance would drop in to pay them a visit. But in the summer the farmstead came to life again. Guests would arrive from St. Petersburg, the most welcome being Mariya's sister, Tatyana Grigoryevna, who brought much gaiety and youthful zest into the Prokofiev home. There were walks to neighboring estates, and bathing in the river. All shared a great enthusiasm for horseback riding, and even the women participated in this sport. Seryozha Prokofiev's first musical impressions are associated with the house at Sontsovka. Here were laid the foundations of his general and special education.

"One of my first recollections of music," the composer relates, "is the following: one evening as I lay in bed, from far off [four rooms away in the spacious country house] came the sound of a Beethoven sonata or a Chopin waltz. My mother was playing. They had put me to bed . . . but I wasn't sleepy and I lay there, listening."

When Seryozha was three or four years old, he loved to sit in an armchair in his mother's room and listen to her play. "Sometimes arguments would arise between my grandmother and me about what my mother was playing, and in these arguments I turned out to be right more often than my grandmother."

Throughout his life Prokofiev retained a feeling of profound gratitude to his mother who, from his childhood on, instilled in him a love for classical music.

Another source of Seryozha's musical impressions was the Ukrainian village with its songs, games, and dances. Seryozha was on friendly terms with the peasant children. He often drove with the grownups through the neighboring villages. In the summer the young girls sang while working in the garden around the Sontsovka house, and from far off came the singing of the peasants returning from the fields. There was a great deal of singing at all times, but even more than usual on Saturday nights and Sundays. The village singing, with its diatonic "white sound," seemed somewhat coarse and shrill to the young Prokofiev. Nevertheless, these vivid impressions left an indelible mark on his sensitive musical consciousness.

Mariya Grigoryevna began her son's musical education with great pedagogical tact. First, he was permitted to give his impressions of the pieces he had heard; then, on his own initiative, he helped her play exercises, tapping out his own countermelodies in the upper register of the piano. Eventually he began to pick out tunes by himself. At five and a half he wrote a little piece which he called *Indian Galop* because of talk he had heard about events in India. The melody was in the key of F major, but without the B flat, for the budding composer could not bring himself to tackle the black keys (FIG. 1).

FIGURE 1

Mariya Grigoryevna wrote down this first melody, but by the time he composed his next piece, Seryozha had already learned how to write notes himself. At the age of six he wrote a waltz, a march, and a rondo, and at seven, a march for four hands. In the course of two years he filled an entire notebook with his first childish pieces for the piano. Little by little his mother led Seryozha into the world of music, imperceptibly enriching his knowledge and striving to develop in him independent judgment and a real love for music.

Prokofiev himself later recalled with respect his mother's wise and correct pedagogical approach: "Above all, she considered it necessary to sustain a child's interest in music and not to alienate him with boring exercises learned by rote. Therefore, she felt that as little time as possible should be spent on scales and exercises, and as much as possible on acquainting the child with musical literature. This is a remarkable attitude which all mothers ought to remember."

Mariya Grigoryevna was continually ordering new music from Moscow. There were many piano arrangements of operas in the house, as well as music by Beethoven, Chopin, Schumann, and sets of pedagogical pieces in the Strobel and von Ark editions.

"Before giving me a piece, my mother would play it through herself, and if she felt that it was not sufficiently interesting, she would put it aside.

After I had played the pieces she approved, we would discuss them and I would tell her what I liked, what I did not like, and why. Thanks to this I early developed an independence of judgment. The ability to sight-read well and an acquaintance with a great quantity of music helped me to analyze musical works easily."*

Together with music, Seryozha also began to study Russian, mathematics, and foreign languages. Every day at a fixed hour his father instructed him in general subjects. His mother taught him French and German. Later on the family engaged a French governess, Louise Roblen, to take charge of Seryozha's general education. She was also asked to make copies of the little composer's musical manuscripts. The archives contain a number of his childhood pieces, accurately copied by Louise Roblen.

In the spring of 1900 the nine-year-old Seryozha went to Moscow with his parents. His first visits to the opera houses made a deep impression on him. He heard *Faust* and *Prince Igor* at the Solodovnikov Theater and saw *The Sleeping Beauty* at the Bolshoi. He was particularly impressed by *Faust*. The child was overjoyed when he recognized the familiar melodies of the waltz and march, which his mother had so often played in Sontsovka. Although he did not understand much of what took place on the stage, the duel and Valentine's death excited him tremendously.

These visits to the Moscow theaters did not pass without leaving a mark on the impressionable youth. On returning to Sontsovka, he began to dream of an opera of his own. At first he played theater with the village children, making up plots and acting them out before the grownups. "The plots were simple and inevitably included a duel—the result of Faust's duel with Valentin," Prokofiev recalls. Later on, in June 1900, he composed an opera, *The Giant,* based on an original plot and written in a piano arrangement without the vocal parts. The scenario of the opera, which Seryozha worked out with his Sontsovka friends, was an amusing combination of nursery tale and autobiography. The main characters, Sergeyev, Yegorov, and Ustinya, were named for the leading performers of the opera, Seryozha and his friends Yegorka and Stenya. The three very short acts told of how a terrible Giant tried to catch the little girl Ustinya, and how the daredevils Sergeyev and Yegorov, with a detachment of soldiers, valiantly rescued her. The first act took place in Ustinya's house, the second in the forest, and the third in the palace of the Good King. For the character of the Giant the

* Prokofiev points out in his memoirs certain hidden dangers in this method, for by flitting from one piece to another, he never mastered any of them. His playing became careless, and it was not until he studied at the Conservatory that he overcame this fault.

young composer employed a sharp dynamic effect (*ffff*), low bass timbre, and an angular march rhythm (FIG. 2).

The music contains many naïve descriptive details: at one point, in the forest scene, birds chirp merrily (traditional grace notes, anticipating the famous bird of *Peter and the Wolf*); at another, Ustinya writes a letter to her saviors (music depicting the process of writing); at still another the Giant sings a sinister, bravura aria ("I am Tsar and ruler over all. But there is one who has disobeyed me . . . I shall avenge myself. I shall plunge the sword into her breast," etc.). One cannot fail to note in this still completely childish composition a number of interesting characteristics

FIGURE 2

which later revealed themselves in Prokofiev's music: a bent for sharp, strong, terrifying effects, for artistic hyperbole, for striking contrasts, and for a graphic reproduction of the sounds of nature.[1]

In the summer of 1901 Seryozha and his mother visited the Rayevskys at their estate in Kaluga Guberniya (Mariya Grigoryevna's sister, Tatyana, was married to the landowner Rayevsky). They decided to produce *The Giant*. In addition to Seryozha, the performers were his aunt Tanya, who portrayed the Giant, her two sons, and her daughter, Katya. The composer himself, who was unusually excited, directed the rehearsals. Only the first act was performed. His uncle was pleased. "When your operas are produced on the Imperial stage, don't forget that your first performance took place in my house," he said jokingly.

In 1901, after *The Giant*, Seryozha wrote a second opera, *Desert Islands*, also based on his own libretto. The romantic plot, with its voyages, storms, and shipwreck, reflected the literary interests of the ten-year-old composer. True, the plot did not hang together. A ship is smashed against a rocky cliff and the heroes are stranded on a desert island. Not knowing "what to do next," the composer was forced to limit himself to the first act. The music of this act contained effects describing natural phenomena: "There was rain, expressed by gently falling notes, and there was a storm."

Mariya Grigoryevna felt that she was no longer equal to guiding Seryozha's creative efforts. In January 1902 she took him to Moscow, this time to seek advice from a prominent musician. Through the good offices of an acquaintance, Yuri Pomerantsev, a Conservatory student who later became conductor of the Bolshoi Theater orchestra, Seryozha was taken to the home of Sergei Taneyev. The revered composer treated the boy with kindness and a lively interest. After listening to parts of *The Giant* and the overture to *Desert Islands,* he advised that the boy begin a systematic study of composition. "Otherwise, he will fall into the habit of making errors which he will find it difficult to get rid of later on," he said.

" 'Above all, guard your son's gifts,' Taneyev added when we parted. And my mother often recalled this admonition."

Taneyev's diary contains some interesting entries concerning his meetings with the young Prokofiev. For example, in the entry of February 5, 1902, we read: "Seryozha played his own compositions—absolute pitch, knows the intervals, chords. From the way in which he harmonized two voices from a Bach cantata, it is obvious that he has a clear conception of

[1] Superscript numbers refer to notes at back of book, pp. 491–503.

harmony. Yusha [Pomerantsev] is to give him lessons and bring him to me once a week."[2]

Taneyev's stern, wise countenance remained indelibly impressed on Prokofiev's memory as the personification of noble, ethically pure service to art. In subsequent years, when in Moscow, Prokofiev often visited Taneyev's modest apartment in one of the narrow streets in the Prechistenka neighborhood, played four hands with him, and showed him his compositions. Taneyev often took the little composer to symphony rehearsals and, seating the boy beside him, explained "details of how to write a full score" (entry in the diary on December 3, 1902). Almost every letter from the future composer to his first teacher, Reinhold Glière, contains a request that he arrange a meeting with Taneyev. "I would like very much to visit Sergei Ivanovich—it is so long since I saw him," wrote Prokofiev on August 1, 1909. Letters from the young Prokofiev to Taneyev have also been preserved.

Taneyev and Prokofiev also met in places other than Moscow. Once, while in the neighborhood of Piatigorsk, in the Caucasus, they walked together to Mashuk mountain. On another occasion they met by chance on a train from St. Petersburg to Moscow and spent almost the entire night in enthusiastic conversation about music. Taneyev followed Prokofiev's progress attentively, helped to bring about the publication of his first works, and gave him valuable professional advice. (It was at Taneyev's suggestion that Sergei Prokofiev included in his repertory a little-known organ fugue by Buxtehude.)*

In the winter of 1902, on the recommendation of Taneyev, Seryozha began to study harmony with Pomerantsev. But the lessons in theory, divorced from living music, frightened the talented boy. "I wanted to compose operas with marches, storms, and terrifying scenes, but instead they saddled me with some sort of boring stuff."

Glière, who had the honor of being the young Prokofiev's first composition teacher, had a much more correct approach to this difficult pedagogical task. In June 1902, on the recommendation of Taneyev, Glière went to Sontsovka for the entire summer. He also spent the following summer with the Prokofiev family, seriously and systematically teaching the boy the principles of harmony, form, and instrumentation, and super-

* In 1915, when the magazine *Muzyka* proposed that Prokofiev write his reminiscences of Taneyev, who had just died, he replied, "I would be happy to reminisce about S. I. Taneyev, but I was only a little boy when I met him and consequently so unobservant that my reminiscences would turn out to be not 'Prokofiev about Taneyev' but 'Taneyev about Prokofiev.'" (Letter to Vladimir Derzhanovsky, July 8, 1915.)

vising his work at the piano. Thus, the summer months of 1902 and 1903 were devoted to giving Prokofiev a grounding in composition prior to his entrance into the Conservatory.

Glière, at that time a young composer recently graduated from the Moscow Conservatory with a gold medal, had already had some teaching experience. He still remembered vividly his classes with the remarkable teacher Taneyev, whose example he strove to follow in his own teaching. He handled his pupil with care and tact, trying to combine theory with living music. For example, when teaching the principles of three-part and sonata form, he would use classical works as illustrations, particularly Beethoven sonatas. Simultaneously, he would also take up questions of instrumentation. When a phrase occurred which suited the timbre of some particular orchestral instrument, Glière would say, "There, you see, this melody might be played by a flute. The fanfare might be given to a trumpet, and in a lower register to two French horns."

Glière considered the harmony lessons particularly important. It was necessary to clear up his pupil's confused notions about harmony, to teach him correct voice-leading.

"Our lessons in harmony went well," Glière recalls. "Seryozha very willingly did the harmony exercises I assigned him, mainly from Arensky's textbook. The boy was well-versed in musical literature, and an excellent sight-reader, with no fear of difficulties. Absolute pitch and a superb memory, remarkable harmonic sense, and rich artistic imagination helped him to master the theory of composition with ease."

The teacher and pupil played four hands a great deal—Haydn, Mozart, Beethoven, and Tchaikovsky. Glière accustomed Seryozha to improvising at the piano, he himself setting the example. Direct contact with a professional composer had a considerable effect upon Prokofiev. During these summer months Glière composed his second symphony and a sextet, and this, of course, greatly interested his eleven-year-old pupil. Even while studying theory, Seryozha was burning to compose music himself. And Glière did not restrain him, feeling that his pupil's attempts to "break loose" to free composition could only benefit him.

During the summer, as a result of his study of the three-part song form, Seryozha, under Glière's guidance, wrote two little sonatas and several piano pieces. The latter, which were called *Ditties,* were composed for various family occasions and bore personal dedications, such as "To Dear Papa," "To Aunt Tanyechka," and "To My Godfather." From then on, twelve *Ditties* a year became a "must" for Seryozha. In the five years from 1902 to 1906, five series of these miniatures were written, amounting to sixty pieces in all.

All of the *Ditties,* neatly written in thick music notebooks, have been preserved in the Prokofiev archives. The first of these begins with a musical autograph by Glière. It is interesting to trace, through them, the development of Seryozha's creative independence, from the utterly naïve, childish imitations to the completely original compositions of 1905–6, which reveal the typical Prokofiev hand. Already in the twelve *Ditties* of Series I (1902), despite the primitive harmony, one can see the little composer striving for well-defined images, sharply accented rhythms and a clearly expressed dance quality. Several of the *Ditties* are written in the style of rather crude, incisive marches, with martial fanfare-like figures, as if anticipating the opening of the March from *The Love for Three Oranges.* A good example of this is the theme of *Ditty* No. 4, Series I (FIG. 3).

FIGURE 3

In another march-like *Ditty* (No. 12, Series I), the composer uses characteristic dynamic effects. In addition to the heavy accents and fanfare-like figures, we find again *ffff* in the climax and a powerful chordal statement in the repeat. Together with the marches are *Ditties* in popular dance forms—mazurkas and waltzes. For example, *Ditty* No. 10, Series I,

FIGURE 4

is characterized by a gentle waltz theme, to which bravura chords form a contrast in the middle section (FIG. 4).

In some of the *Ditties* we find Italianate melodies reminiscent of the operatic arias of Bellini and Verdi; in others, poignant, syncopated themes in the spirit of Schumann. But especially characteristic are the echoes of the march, waltz, and polka. They obviously reflect the everyday life at Sontsovka, the mother's repertory, and also the musical impressions the young composer received while in Moscow.

Seryozha's summer studies with Glière culminated in his first attempt at a large form—a symphony. The composer recalls that his teacher initially did not agree to his undertaking such a major project. But he was insistent and determined, and "after some bargaining," Glière agreed. By the time Glière left Sontsovka, Seryozha had composed and half-orchestrated a four-movement symphony in G major, which he dedicated to his teacher. The first movement, Presto, bears traces of his enthusiasm for the Viennese classics and for Italian operatic overtures.

In November 1902, when Seryozha again went to Moscow with his mother, he showed the symphony to Taneyev. Together they played a four-hand arrangement of it, which Seryozha had prepared for the occasion. "After praising the counterpoint, which Glière had written in for me in the development section, Taneyev observed that the harmony was

A musical autograph from Prokofiev to Glière. The inscription reads: "With congratulations to dear Reinhold Moritsevich on his wonderful seventieth birthday, in memory of our first meeting in 1902. Here is the first theme of the symphony written at that time under his guidance. S. PRKFV, 1945."

much too simple, nothing but I, IV, V progressions." Later Prokofiev jokingly recalled that this remark by Taneyev had cut him to the quick and spurred him on to subsequent experiments in harmony.*

During the winter of 1902–3 there was a lively correspondence between Prokofiev and Glière. The pupil sent his teacher new pieces and harmony problems worked out according to Arensky's textbook. In the spring Seryozha composed a violin sonata, about which he proudly reported in a letter to Glière: "Even though the first movement is in C minor, I've written the Finale in C major, since I couldn't make the Presto come out in minor. Tchaikovsky's Second Symphony also begins in C minor and ends in C major."[3]

Ten years later the opening theme of the violin sonata was used in the introduction and beginning of the main theme of the cello *Ballade,* Op. 15. This theme was the earliest Prokofiev melody to be published.

In the summer of 1903 Glière returned to Sontsovka. Seryozha orchestrated his Symphony in G major, composed new *Ditties,* and began a new large work, an opera based on Pushkin's *A Feast in Time of Plague.* Thanks to Glière's help, the young Prokofiev's third opera was quite a professional work, with full score and an overture in sonata form. To be sure, the overture constituted almost half of the entire work. In the first theme the composer tried to portray dramatic passions (somber basses in unison, sharply accented *tutti* on the diminished seventh chord). The second theme, on the other hand, was distinguished by serene melody in the Italian vein. Seryozha was very proud of his opera and eagerly compared it to Cui's recently published opera of the same name. Six years later, when he was at the Conservatory, Prokofiev returned to *A Feast in Time of Plague* and completely rewrote it.

In 1903 the *Ditties* became more daring. In them can be seen the composer's striving for rhythmic and harmonic "invention": mixed meters (7/8 in *Ditty* No. 2); uncommon tonalities (seven sharps in the same *Ditty*); and capricious, whimsical rhythms (*Ditty* No. 8, *Presto,* contains hints of one of the future themes of *Sarcasm* No. 1).

The range of Seryozha's musical interests was continually widening. At the end of 1903 the first songs appeared: *Tell Me, Twig of Palestine,* to a poem by Lermontov, and *I Am No Longer the Same,* to a poem by

---

* "Eight years later, when I played the *Études,* Op. 2, for Taneyev, he said disapprovingly, 'There seem to be a lot of false notes . . .' I reminded him of our earlier conversation and Sergei Ivanovich, gripping his head with his hands, exclaimed jokingly, 'So I am really the one who pushed you onto such a slippery path!' "

Pushkin. These were still elementary and bore traces of the salon style. Not long after this he wrote two more songs: a lyrico-dramatic one, *See the Down, The Snowflakes Are Flying* (to his own words), and a little, playful parody, dedicated to Leonid Sobinov, *Oh No, Not Figner, and Not Yuzhin, Neither One Can Startle Me. You Alone My Heart Desires, Leonid, O Leonid.*[4]

Glière skillfully alternated the serious music lessons with amusing games, walks, and interesting stories. Sometimes it would be croquet, sometimes horseback riding or a duel with toy pistols. In this way Glière completely won his pupil's heart. It is to the credit of Seryozha's teachers that even while burdening him with difficult studies, they knew how to preserve his childish spontaneity and enthusiasm.

Seryozha had an avid interest in the natural sciences. For several years he kept a special record of the flowering of plants. With an important, earnest air he explained to Glière the names of the flowers and grasses. All his life he maintained this keen interest in nature, which he had inherited from his father. In addition, he collected postage stamps, organized races on stilts with the village children, and fought battles on land and sea with tin soldiers. While still a child, under the influence of books he read, he turned to writing poetry. "After the music lessons I worked on my poem 'The Count,' with adventures, shipwrecks, fights, and duels. Attached to it were illustrations—portraits of the characters— very poorly executed by me." Many of his boyish interests continued even during his first years at the Conservatory. The best compositions of the young Prokofiev strongly reflect the joy of childhood, the purity and spontaneity of a child's perception of the world.

At the beginning of 1904 there arose again the question of Seryozha's further education. At first the thought was to send him to a Gymnasium. But what was to be done about his musical studies? It was decided to choose a conservatory which also offered instruction in general subjects. In the winter of 1903–4 Seryozha and his mother lived in Moscow, and he continued to study strict style and fugue under Glière's guidance in preparation for entrance into the St. Petersburg Conservatory. With his mother he often attended the theater and symphony concerts. Visits with Taneyev, for whom he played his new compositions, were of great benefit to him.

In February 1904 Mariya Grigoryevna took her son to St. Petersburg to enroll him in the Conservatory. After listening to Seryozha, Alexander Glazunov praised his compositions and predicted a great future for him. "At the Conservatory his talent will attain its full development," said

Glazunov. "There is a chance that he may turn out to be a real artist." Glazunov presented the future Conservatory student with a score of Glinka's *Valse-Fantaisie* with the inscription, "To my dear colleague Seryozha Prokofiev, from A. Glazunov."

Later on Prokofiev was on less cordial terms with Glazunov than with Taneyev. During his years of youthful daring, Prokofiev more than once rebelled against the then director of the Conservatory, regarding him as an exponent of "dying, conservative" views. However, the discord between Prokofiev and Glazunov did not last long. As we know, Glazunov followed the young Prokofiev's progress very closely and helped to arrange for the performance of his works on the concert stage (for example, the E minor Symphony in 1908). Throughout his life, Prokofiev retained a profound respect for Glazunov, right up to the friendly meetings between them in France during the thirties.

Seryozha spent the summer of 1904 in Sontsovka, diligently preparing for the entrance examinations to the Conservatory. As before, he composed a great deal, devoting most of his attention to a new opera, *Undine*, based on Zhukovsky's translation of Friedrich de La Motte-Fouqué's poem of the same name. The libretto was written especially for Seryozha (according to a plan he had worked out) by a young poetess named Mariya Kilschtedt, with whom he had become acquainted during the winter in St. Petersburg. In May she sent to Sontsovka the text of the first act, which was completed in full score by August. Further work on *Undine* was repeatedly interrupted, and the opera was not finished until 1907.

During 1904, new *Ditties* were also composed, with richer texture, unexpected shifts of tonality, and a tendency toward sharp humor. An example of this is the playful *Vivo* (No. 8, Series III), with its mischievous grace notes and tart combinations of sounds. Together with those in a march vein, Seryozha composed *Ditties* of a rapid, étude-like nature, often in the triplet rhythm of a tarantella. A direct line runs from these to the *Études,* Op. 2, and some of the themes of the First Piano Concerto. *Ditties* in a lyrico-elegiac vein also appeared, such as *Romance* (No. 10, Series III).

At the end of the summer of 1904, when he left for the examinations in St. Petersburg, Seryozha Prokofiev bade his carefree childhood farewell.

The Prokofiev family was separated. The father remained on the Sontsovka estate, while the mother settled in St. Petersburg with Seryozha. It was decided that Sergei Alexeyevich would come to the capital two or three times a year, and the mother and son would spend the Christmas and summer vacations in their beloved Sontsovka.

# TWO

# THE CONSERVATORY

*The last duckling was very ugly. It had
no feathers, and its legs were long and
gawky. "What if it's a turkey!" exclaimed the mother duck in horror.*

Andersen: THE UGLY DUCKLING

A T THE BEGINNING of September 1904, Seryozha Prokofiev took the
examinations for the St. Petersburg Conservatory. The examinations on general subjects were followed, on September 22, by the
most important one of all, the one in special theory. Among those examined
at the same time as the thirteen-year-old Seryozha were Boris Asafyev, a student at St. Petersburg University, and other beginning composers of mature
age.

The examination required tests of the applicant's musical ear, including sight-singing in different keys, and the presentation of original compositions. The large examining board was headed by Rimsky-Korsakov,
Glazunov, and Lyadov. The spectacle of a boy armed with four operas,
a symphony, two sonatas, and a heap of piano pieces made a deep impression on them.

After listening attentively to fragments of *Undine* and the piano piece
*Vivo*, Rimsky-Korsakov exclaimed, "That's excellent!"

"The candidates awaited the results in a room adjoining the director's
office," Asafyev recalls. "In the excitement I didn't pay much attention
to anyone. But I do recall even now the bright little face of a boy who
was all dressed up. This was the thirteen-year-old Sergei Prokofiev."[1]

Finally, Rimsky-Korsakov informed the anxious Mariya Grigoryevna
that Seryozha had been accepted and was enrolled in Lyadov's harmony
class. Thus began Prokofiev's ten-year period of study at the St. Petersburg Conservatory.

In the beginning Mariya Grigoryevna lived with Seryozha in the home of her sister, Tanya Rayevskaya. Later she took a small apartment on Sadovaya Street, where the boy was given his own room. Here, with unusual diligence, he prepared his lessons, solved problems in harmony, and composed music.

When it became clear that academic subjects were taught poorly at the Conservatory, Mariya Grigoryevna arranged for lessons at home to prepare Seryozha for the examinations.

At first Lyadov took little interest in Seryozha's creative experiments, and his mother decided to turn for help to a young teacher, Mikhail Chernov. Chernov showed the boy's compositions to his friend Asafyev, and shortly afterward introduced Seryozha into the St. Petersburg musical circles which were interested in new music.

Seryozha found many things in the Conservatory disappointing. His creative aspirations received no encouragement there. At that time the St. Petersburg Conservatory, headed by the reactionary A. Bernhard, felt the deadening effect of the monarchy. Asafyev gives a graphic description of this in his memoirs:

"Compared with the University, the Conservatory seemed to me, at one moment, a gymnasium (when you entered the cheerless little classroom and sat down at the school desk!); at another moment, a monastery with its own code of rules; at still another, a narrow, provincial trade school! . . . At the Conservatory, thought had become stifled. You had to listen and obey. You were lucky if you had any contact with the greatest masters while you were still in the elementary stage of your training, if you experienced directly the influence of a great artist or composer while you were doing the prescribed work. But to 'arrive,' you had to live through the humdrum daily routine."

The fame of the St. Petersburg Conservatory rested on a few remarkable teachers—notably Rimsky-Korsakov, Glazunov, Lyadov, Esipova, Auer, and Verzhbilovich—who manifested "wonders of self-sacrifice." But most of the teachers, having no desire to encourage the creative aspirations of their students, followed the principle, "Obey, trust, and don't try anything new."

All the students in Seryozha Prokofiev's class were older than he, the oldest being past thirty. Many of them were irritated at having to study in the same class as a youngster given to mischievous pranks. A photograph taken at the time shows Lyadov with the entire group of students in his class in special harmony (Asafyev, A. Kankarovich, and others). In the right-hand corner sits a blond boy with neatly combed hair, who looks as though he had just quieted down for a minute before playing his next prank.[2]

From his very first year of instruction, conflicts arose between Prokofiev and Lyadov. "My old indifference toward problems of harmony returned," Prokofiev recalls. "I began to write carelessly, which irritated Lyadov."

The friction between teacher and pupil continued during the following years, at times breaking out in sharp clashes. Lyadov cannot rightfully be blamed for this. An excellent theoretician of the Korsakov school, a talented composer of impeccable taste and craftsmanship, he strove to inculcate in his students the sound principles of professionalism. He demanded purity in voice-leading, believing that every young composer should completely master techniques of the classical style before inventing something new.

"Perhaps you have a contempt for all these rules, but you must understand that music is based on these musical laws. You cannot destroy before something else has been created. Create a new law, and then you may break the old ones. Every violation of a law, if it is logical, at once becomes a new law."[3]

A weak point in Lyadov's method was the lack of attention to the students' free experiments in composition in the early stages of their training. Lyadov had become extremely dispirited from the long years of pedogogical drudgery which took him away from his beloved creative work.

"With an air of disgust, scarcely dropping a word, he would write out a problem and a theoretical exposition of it on the blackboard. Then, with a peculiar listless grace and a pained expression, he would play the students' exercises on the piano, inimitably catching every defect," recalls one of his pupils.[4]

But Lyadov's unique talents as a teacher and an artist shone brilliantly when he dropped his usual mask of weariness and boredom.

"Suddenly everything would begin to sparkle. He would walk up to the blackboard, carefully write out ingenious solutions to harmony problems, and then joke good-naturedly while running through our lessons at the piano."

There is no doubt that Lyadov understood very well that the unruly young Prokofiev was tremendously gifted. At the same time, even though he chafed under Lyadov's pedagogical method, Prokofiev learned a great

deal from Lyadov the composer, in his own way absorbing and trans-
forming Lyadov's characteristic fantasy, his humor, and his Russian
lyrical tunefulness.

From his first year at the Conservatory, Seryozha Prokofiev regularly
attended symphony concerts and rehearsals, often with a score in his hands.

He followed with the liveliest interest the Russo-Japanese War of 1904,
especially the naval operations. In his notebooks he carefully drew dia-
grams of naval battles and calculated the comparative effectiveness of
warships in combat.

In January 1905 the Revolution broke out, and the St. Petersburg
Conservatory seethed with student unrest. The [politically] advanced
section of the student body protested against the reactionary procedures
introduced by Bernhard, demanding autonomy for the Conservatory. These
demands were actively supported by Rimsky-Korsakov, and as a result he
was dismissed. Glazunov, Lyadov, Esipova, and F. M. Blumenfeld resigned in protest. This incident developed into a major national scandal.
The Conservatory was closed. All the young musicians became extremely
agitated. Asafyev tells of the tremendous impact the Revolution made
upon him.

"A student who had until then known man only as an idea derived
from books, I suddenly became aware of real men creating history. The
idea assumed living form."

Seryozha, who was eight years younger than Asafyev, was far from
understanding so clearly what was taking place. However, when the
students drew up a protest against the Conservatory's reactionary regime,
he signed it without hesitation. He was very much worried about what
would happen to Lyadov and Glazunov after they had left the Conservatory. He was part of a delegation which presented Lyadov with a wreath
as a token of sympathy. In a letter to Glière he asked for information
about Glazunov. ("They say that Glazunov is dangerously ill. I am very
much disturbed about his health. Do you know anything about this?")

There is no doubt that the revolutionary events of 1905 left their mark
on Prokofiev's consciousness, strengthening his natural independence, re-
belliousness, and disbelief in unshakable authority.

Upon returning to Sontsovka in the spring, Seryozha devoted no less
than five hours a day to preparing for the examinations on general subjects. As before, his studying was supervised by his father, who adhered
to a strict schedule.

"My father was methodical and strict, but he was gentle with me,"

Prokofiev relates. "All my life I have been deeply grateful to my parents for instilling in me from childhood a love for order and the ability to organize my time properly and to take pleasure in my daily occupations."

That summer Prokofiev's father opened his library to his son for the first time. Adventure novels by Mayne Reid and fantastic stories by Jules Verne (whose books Seryozha read in French) gave way to Russian classical masterpieces by Gogol, Turgenev, Ostrovsky, and Tolstoi.

"The transition to 'grown-up' literature seemed very important to me, and I began to keep a record of the things I read, grading them according to the system used in school. Turgenev's *Nest of Gentle Folk* received 5; Gogol's *Dead Souls*, 5 minus, and *Viy,* 4; Tolstoi's *War and Peace,* 5. On the other hand, I gave Ostrovsky's comedies 2's and 3's. At that time I liked neither the subjects nor the language of Ostrovsky."

In the village, Seryozha was still looked upon as the leader of the boys' games and pranks. Furious battles on stilts broke out. The combatants, hobbling about on wooden legs, knocked each other down in fierce attacks. Seryozha even developed a special tactic for use in these skirmishes and fought with great recklessness, to the horror of his mother.

The future composer was very observant and inquisitive about everything around him. Once, on a train, he wormed his way into the engineer's cab, where he inquired in detail about the mechanics of a locomotive. ("It wasn't especially comfortable in the cab, but I looked at everything around me with delight. Any fourteen-year-old boy would have envied me!") At that time Seryozha was also very much interested in photography, botany, and chess. Among his childhood manuscripts, musical sketches alternate with records of chess games.

Of course, while at home, Seryozha continued to work on his musical compositions. He composed the second act of *Undine* (in which appeared some "new harmonic ideas" and even some "discoveries") and wrote further congratulatory *Ditties,* which became increasingly original in their musical language.

One day there appeared at Sontsovka a young veterinarian, Vasily Morolev, who loved music and became a sincere admirer of Prokofiev's talent. Later whenever he visited the estate on farm matters, he always gave special attention to Seryozha. He listened to his compositions and played four-hands with him, treating him like a grownup. The boy liked the simplicity, directness, and shrewd peasant humor of this friendly man, who brought into the Sontsovka house the tart flavor of the Ukrainian steppes. Together they played four-hand arrangements of Beethoven symphonies and Rossini overtures. Morolev had Seryozha play for him Bach preludes and fugues and also some new works brought from St. Petersburg—piano pieces by Scriabin.

On one of his visits to Sontsovka, Morolev brought a piano score of Rimsky-Korsakov's *Sadko*. This was Seryozha's first acquaintance with this music. He was particularly impressed by the unexpected tonal shifts from A major to F major in the chorus, "Boundless Heavens."

Prokofiev's friendship with Morolev continued for more than forty years. The composer dedicated two works to him: the Piano Sonata in F minor, Op. 1, and the *March*, Op. 12 (composed in 1906).

 ❀   ❀   ❀

Seryozha's second year at the Conservatory was not very productive for him. He studied privately with Lyadov and attended Alexander Winkler's special piano class at the Conservatory. Asafyev, who was also studying with Winkler, protested vehemently against Winkler's pedantic teaching method and refused to make peace with his "all-leveling ruler." Prokofiev treated Winkler with more respect and even dedicated to him his piano *Études*, Op. 2 (composed in 1909). In all probability it was to Winkler that he owed the purely technical aspect of his progress on the piano.

Seryozha spent the winter of 1905–6 working on *Undine*, composing *Ditties*, attending symphony concerts, and studying harmony with Lyadov. He apparently made considerable progress in harmony, for when Lyadov returned to the Conservatory in the spring he transferred Seryozha to the third course without examination. "I think they're going to transfer two of us—a student named Asafyev and me," Prokofiev wrote Glière on April 14, 1906.

The *Ditties* of 1905 and 1906 bring to a close the five-year incubation period of the young composer's creative development. In them one can clearly see the gradual enriching of his imagination and the formation of his own distinctive creative style, especially in the sphere of harmony, rhythm, and piano texture. The last *Ditties* of 1905–6 reveal even more clearly a penchant for energetic, wildly impetuous themes, and for a witty scherzo quality. The writing becomes more complicated pian-istically, abounding in skips, hand-crossings, double thirds, and rapid passage work. The minuet *Ditty* (No. 11, Series IV) is attractive for its grace and harmonic originality. We can see in it typical features of Prokofiev's style—sharply expressive chromatic inner voices, knocking *ostinato* basses, delicately modulated backgrounds, sharply defined full cadences. These familiar devices also appear clearly in the last *Ditty*, the witty étude-scherzo *Vivo* (No. 12, Series V), composed in 1906.

The best *Ditties* undoubtedly served as studies for Prokofiev's later dance themes. From the minuet *Ditty* (No. 11, Series IV) one can draw a line to the minuets in *Romeo and Juliet* or in Op. 32; from the charming, sentimental waltz *Ditty* of May 1906 to the lyrical waltzes in *Cinderella* and *War and Peace*. The *March* (*Ditty* No. 6, Series V) was later published in revised form. The rest, which are in manuscript, still await publication.[5]

With the return of Rimsky-Korsakov and Lyadov to the Conservatory, the classes in composition were resumed. Fate brought together in Lyadov's counterpoint class a number of talented people who were to play an important role in our musical history: Prokofiev, Asafyev, Miaskovsky, the Ukrainian composer Akimenko-Stepovy, and others. Contact with older students, participation in creative discussions, and constant listening to symphonic and operatic music contributed to Prokofiev's rapid aesthetic development. He was completely immersed in the world of classical music. Among the works he liked were the suite from Rimsky-Korsakov's *Mlada,* Tchaikovsky's *Variations on a Rococo Theme* and *Romeo and Juliet*, Lyadov's orchestral pieces on Russian folk-songs, Taneyev's Symphony in C minor, Rachmaninov's Second Concerto, Beethoven's Third and Eighth Symphonies, one of the Bach suites for orchestra, Schumann's Second Symphony, Glazunov's Sixth Symphony, and Borodin's song *To the Shores of My Distant Fatherland*, in an orchestral arrangement by Glazunov ("one of my favorite songs," he noted later).

"I loved Schumann, especially his piano sonatas and *Carnaval*," Prokofiev wrote in his memoirs.

In February 1907 Prokofiev attended the première of Rimsky-Korsakov's opera *The Legend of the Invisible City of Kitezh*. Its epic power left an indelible impression on him. He was also very much excited by Rimsky-Korsakov's *Snow Maiden,* which he later called "one of my favorite operas." Imprinted in his memory was the jubilee concert (conducted by Rimsky-Korsakov) in honor of the twenty-fifth anniversary of Glazunov's debut as a composer. He listened with great interest to the first performance of Scriabin's heroic Third Symphony. In his leisure hours he studied piano scores of operas by Rimsky-Korsakov and Wagner, making a careful study of the system of leitmotivs in the latter's tetralogy, *The Ring of the Nibelungs*.

To be sure, at this time the talented youth's musical tastes began to indicate a scorn for some traditional music. He did not care for Mozart, in whom he found no "new and spicy harmonies," or Chopin, who seemed too sweet to him. As he did with books, he rated the classical works he heard according to the 5-point system. He gave a 2 to the overture to *Prince Igor*. ("However, three years later I came to really like and appreciate this opera," he writes about *Prince Igor*.)

In the fall of 1906 Prokofiev and his fellow students began to attend Rimsky-Korsakov's class in orchestration. Each session lasted four hours, during which the students' work was checked and criticized. The future composers derived enormous benefit from these meetings with Rimsky-Korsakov.

"For hours Nikolai Andreyevich would discuss work after work with exceptional care," writes Asafyev in his memoirs. "We had only to catch the precious suggestions and remarks, the advice, the keen criticisms. In these hours of analysis we were exposed to a magnetic force, to the very essence of learning. It would be impossible to draw a line between the utterances of the teacher and the observations of the composer—observations trustingly, lovingly, and lavishly conferred upon the students. The teachings of the pedogogue were continually being transformed into the creative laboratory of a distinguished master."[6]

Unfortunately, the fifteen-year-old Prokofiev did not sufficiently understand the importance of these remarkable classes. He did his assignments accurately, without taking the trouble to comprehend the creative implications of Rimsky-Korsakov's precious words. Sometimes disagreements arose between student and teacher. Schubert's marches for piano four-hands, which the students were given to orchestrate, seemed uninteresting to Prokofiev, and in turn Prokofiev's poorly thought-out, labored orchestrations irritated Rimsky-Korsakov. "Gifted but immature," he noted in one examination report. In another, in the spring of 1908, he gave Prokofiev a mark of 4 for the year's work, with the following comment: "Talented. Worked little. Progress negligible."[7]

"Only later did I realize how much I could have learned from contact with such a man as Rimsky-Korsakov," Prokofiev confessed in later years.

In September 1906 a young officer named Nikolai Miaskovsky entered the Conservatory. He attended the classes of Lyadov and Rimsky-Korsakov together with Prokofiev and Asafyev. A man with a keen analytical mind and a broad cultural outlook, a loyal friend who followed the progress of his fellow students with intense interest, he could not but win their good will. At first a friendship grew up between Miaskovsky and Asafyev.

"He had a thorough knowledge of music," Asafyev recalls. "He introduced me into the world of what was then 'modern' music (Reger, Debussy, and the neo-French in general). He was one of the first persons with whom I seriously discussed new Russian poetry, literature, and painting. But since opposites attract, he soon formed a friendship with Prokofiev which endured throughout their lives. When I was with the two of them, I always felt like a 'satellite' or a comet that had suddenly entered their orbit."

At first they seemed a strange combination—the twenty-five-year-old officer, outwardly reserved, very erudite, and unusually serious in his approach to art and the unstable, pampered adolescent with a reputation as a mischievous boy, fond of taunting. But their deep love for music drew them together and made them fast friends. Miaskovsky became interested in Prokofiev's notebook of piano pieces (which were a continuation of the *Ditties*). After seeing how "audacious" they were, he teased Seryozha good-naturedly: "What a little viper we've been nursing in our bosom!"

Thus began the close friendship of these two remarkable musicians, which continued for almost forty-five years. Prokofiev and Miaskovsky visited each other and often played four-hands together. ("I was proud," said Seryozha, "that such a grownup officer would come to visit me.") They played Beethoven's Second and Ninth Symphonies, Glazunov's Fifth, Rimsky-Korsakov's *Scheherazade,* and many other works—"with complete abandon," as Sergei put it—arguing a great deal, and discussing what they played. They continually showed each other their new compositions and consulted each other on questions of form, harmony, and orchestration. This exchange of advice continued until Miaskovsky's death. During the summer months the friends carried on a lively correspondence.

"Nikolai Yakovlevich's letters, brilliantly written and exceptionally interesting (he treated me like a 'grownup'), were very helpful to me and contributed considerably to my development," Prokofiev recalls.

One of Esipova's students, the talented pianist Boris Zakharov, and several young composers joined the music-making of Prokofiev and Miaskovsky. Sometimes they would hold composition contests. Once they all composed songs on the same text (*The Spreading Oak*); another time they wrote piano pieces depicting a Russian winter landscape. Miaskovsky portrayed "a very nasty snowstorm," Prokofiev "soft, gentle snow, falling in large flakes." The latter experiment subsequently resulted in the program piece *Snowflakes*, which has remained unpublished.

The friendship with Miaskovsky helped to broaden the young Prokofiev's musical and artistic outlook. Dissatified with the eclectic music of composers who passively imitated Glazunov and Rimsky-Korsakov, the friends avidly turned to the latest musical trends, both Russian and West European. Miaskovsky introduced Prokofiev to the very latest music of Western Europe. Of course, many of these works were either utterly devoid of content or overrefined in style. But the friends did not go very deeply into these flaws, particularly since the Conservatory frowned on modern music and "forbidden fruit" is always sweet, especially to the young. Thus their enthusiasm for Grieg, Wagner, and Rimsky-Korsakov was replaced by an avid interest in Debussy, Richard Strauss, and Reger.

In December 1906 Max Reger came to St. Petersburg to conduct a concert of his own works, among them the *Serenade* in G major. This concert marked the beginning of Prokofiev's systematic contact with the newest music.

The Russian composers of the classical school reacted very unfavorably to Reger's contrived neo-classicism. "It is simply grass," Lyadov said of his music. Rimsky-Korsakov called Reger's polyphony "horizontal nonsense." The critic Vyacheslav Karatygin, on the other hand, extolled Reger as one of the leading contemporary composers. Noting the exuberant praise of the leftist critics, the young musicians became very curious about Reger. His *Serenade* in G major was one of the first pieces that Miaskovsky and Prokofiev played together. According to Miaskovsky, this short-lived passion for Reger (the Violin Sonatas in C major and F-sharp minor, and the piano pieces *From My Diary* and *Variations and Fugue on a Theme by J. S. Bach*) exerted a certain influence on the young Prokofiev, giving him an interest in tense, agitated melodies and novel harmonies—for example, transition chords and complicated discords.

In addition to the Reger pieces, Prokofiev and Miaskovsky also played, in four-hand arrangements, Richard Strauss's tone poems *Don Juan*, *Till Eulenspiegel*, *Thus Spake Zarathustra*, and *Death and Transfiguration*.

At concerts they listened with interest to Debussy's *Nocturnes* and *Afternoon of a Faun*. They were rather indifferent to Stravinsky's early works (before *The Firebird*), but had a deep respect for the music of Scriabin. At the height of this enthusiasm, Prokofiev made a two-hand piano transcription of the first movement of *The Divine Poem*. He was very proud of it and even thought of showing it to the composer. As a token of his esteem, Prokofiev, in 1910, dedicated his symphonic piece *Dreams* to Scriabin with the inscription, "To the composer who began with *Rêverie*." Later on, however, this passion for Scriabin's music, especially for the early works, turned to scorn.

During the 1907–8 season, Prokofiev began to attend the gatherings of a modernist society called Evenings of Modern Music. As early as April 1908 he wrote to Glière, "Sometimes I go to the Evenings of Modern Music, to which Mikhail Chernov introduced me, and where my things enjoy a great success." It was here that the young composer really came to know the latest West European and Rusian music.[8]

❊ ❊ ❊

During the school years of 1906–7 and 1907–8, Prokofiev was immersed in his studies—counterpoint and fugue with Lyadov, orchestration with Rimsky-Korsakov, piano with Winkler, and score-reading with Cherepnin.* In 1908 he began to study conducting.

"This year there's such a mass of work—more than ever," he wrote Glière in February 1908.

Despite the friction mentioned earlier, Rimsky-Korsakov promoted Prokofiev to the fourth course without examination. But in Lyadov's class, the conflicts between the teacher and the most refractory Conservatory students sharpened. Obviously, the Evenings of Modern Music, which openly declared the Glazunov-Lyadov school "conservative," had much to do with this.

As a result of this dissension, the creative activity of Prokofiev and Miaskovsky took two distinct forms: on the one hand they did the required work "for Lyadov"; on the other hand they wrote music independently "for themselves."

"We did not risk showing him what we wrote 'for ourselves,' " recalls Miaskovsky, "especially since he knew that we had been contaminated by modernism (mainly Prokofiev and I)."[9]

When Prokofiev brought to the lessons exercises in counterpoint which struck Lyadov as too crude and harsh, he would either lose his temper or say sarcastically, "I guess I should be studying with you, not you with me. Go to Richard Strauss or Debussy. But for heaven's sake, don't study with me."[10]

* For the examination in score-reading in the spring of 1907 he prepared Beethoven's *Egmont,* the overture to Glinka's *Ruslan and Ludmila,* and Saint-Saëns's *Suite algérienne.*

The students repaid Lyadov with a concealed hostility and unwarranted charges that he was "reactionary." It was at this time that Miaskovsky, in jest, wrote a musical theme based on Bb-d-g#-A-c-f (B-re-gis-La-do-fa), which stood for *Beregis Lyadova* (meaning "Beware of Lyadov!").

In one of his letters Prokofiev gave an extremely unjust opinion of his teacher. "I don't show my compositions to Lyadov, for if I did, he would probably expel me from the class," he wrote Glière on February 23, 1908. "Lyadov holds firmly to the old, tranquil music and values most good voice-leading and logical progression. He rails at new music with interesting harmonies. Since my latest things fall precisely into this category, I prefer not to show them to him at all."

Prokofiev's "official" works were those in strict style, canon, double and triple counterpoint, worked out according to Lyadov's instructions. Undoubtedly the strict training in Lyadov's class was tremendously useful to Prokofiev and enriched his compositional technique. Only by going through the fire and water of Lyadov's training could he have developed his own polyphonic style, with its free voice-leading and sometimes harsh combinations of sound.

Even Miaskovsky later recalled with deep gratitude (and "horror") the difficult sessions with Lyadov. "I cannot help admitting that his extraordinarily rigid requirements (even his carping), the exceptional lucidity of his method, his unusual taste, and his extremely keen critical sense fixed our technique firmly and developed our feeling for style."

In addition to the assigned work, Prokofiev also brought to Lyadov's lessons small piano pieces, written in very simple form (mainly three-part). Among these semi-student works are to be found charming and quite mature examples of lyrical writing, as, for example, the tender, graceful Gavotte in G minor (1908), which was subsequently included in Op. 12, and the Scherzo of the future Second Sonata.

But most of the works of this period Prokofiev wrote "for himself," independently of Lyadov. In the spring and summer of 1907 the young composer returned, for the third time, to his opera *Undine*. He revised what had been written, and completed a piano score of the third and fourth acts.[11]

The romantic plot of the German fairy tale *Undine* had attracted a number of opera composers. Both E. T. A. Hoffmann (in 1813) and Tchaikovsky (in 1868) wrote operas based on it. The ancient saga of the mermaid Undine, who became the wife of the knight Hildebrand, served as the basis of the famous poem by the German romantic poet Friedrich de La Motte-Fouqué, which was translated into Russian by Zhukovsky. The poem is filled with romantic specters, terrifying visions, and motifs of doom. The fair-haired Undine, wounded by her husband's infidelity, disappears beneath the waves, and the knight Hildebrand dies in the mermaid's cold embrace.

This version of the legend offered Prokofiev's librettist, Mariya Kilschtedt, a convenient pretext for a rather unoriginal poetic exercise in the style of the decadent literature of the early twentieth century. The libretto accentuated still more the motifs of death, the other world, pessimism:

> He, who in life
> Nor use nor purpose finds,
> Steals away to peaceful cells
> And there finds rest.

The text the librettist foisted on the young composer in no way corresponded to his real interests. It was precisely this kind of melancholy, romantic despair and carrion that he was to poke fun at twelve years later in his opera *The Love for Three Oranges*.

But at that time, work on *Undine* served him as a kind of training for the mastery of operatic form; in rewriting it he tried to use what small knowledge he had acquired from studying the piano scores of Wagner and Rimsky-Korsakov.

"I'm now working on *Undine*. I'm writing everything over again, for I don't like what I wrote before. I'm now writing more seriously and using leitmotivs," he wrote Glière on May 12, 1907.

The composer's progress is clearly evident in the piano score of this opera. The development of leitmotivs and the vocal declamation are handled with greater assurance; the expressive details are carefully worked out. The recitatives indicate great attention to the text, as well as a familiarity with some of Wagner's declamatory techniques.

Among the leitmotivs there are some apt characterizations (the leaping theme of the underwater sprite Struya, Berthold's mournful theme, and Hildebrand's leitmotiv, expressing ponderous meditation). The pictorial music accompanying Undine's appearance (based on the colorful effect of a diminished seventh chord) is written in the style of Rimsky-Korsakov. The march-like theme of the wedding procession in the fourth act is in a characteristic stately manner, but with a funereal cast (Fig. 5).

By comparison with his childish experiments in opera, Prokofiev's

FIGURE 5

craftsmanship had improved considerably. However, in *Undine* there is as yet little evidence of his creative individuality. Prokofiev himself later called this music "anemic."

During the summer of 1908, while on vacation in Sontsovka, Prokofiev undertook another large work, a symphony in E minor. Miaskovsky was writing his First Symphony in C minor at the same time. The young composers earnestly consulted and advised each other in frequent letters, in which themes were carefully written out and important details of form discussed. Before the end of August, Prokofiev wrote Glière that he had completed the symphony, and planned to show it to him and Taneyev.

The Symphony is in three movements: Allegro with a slow introduction, Andante, and Finale, the coda of which contains a restatement of the subordinate theme of the first movement. Features of Prokofiev's individual style are evident in the music: in the agitated dramatic main theme of the first movement, with its melodic skips and colorful modulations, and in the gay tarantella rhythms of the Finale. Particularly successful is the slow second movement, with its profound, pensive lyricism and the wide range of its melody (so typical of the mature Prokofiev), which gradually gains in intensity as it rises to the high register (FIG. 6).

"S. Prokofiev brought his summer's work, a symphony (E minor, three movements). Fresh. Remarkable Andante," Miaskovsky noted in his diary. Nine years later, in 1917, Prokofiev included this Andante, in some-

FIGURE 6

what revised form, in the Fourth Piano Sonata. The other movements of the Symphony in E minor have remained unpublished.

During the 1908–9 season, the full score of the new Symphony was shown to Glazunov, who made a few corrections in it. " 'Well, it's certainly fiery and full of life,' Glazunov told my mother, but it was obvious that the music was alien to him."

Prokofiev tried persistently to get Glazunov to arrange a performance of the E minor Symphony by one of the St. Petersburg orchestras.

"Everything, of course, depends on Glazunov. He has entrée to the Court orchestra, and the Sheremetyev and Conservatory orchestras. But to get him to do something I have to prod him continually, and therefore I've already made more than fifteen raids on him," Prokofiev wrote Glière in December 1908.

The "raids" were crowned with success. Thanks to Glazunov's help, the Symphony was performed at a private rehearsal of the Court orchestra conducted by Hugo Warlich. "The Symphony was poorly orchestrated," the composer recalls, "and left a generally muddy impression." Glazunov was shocked at certain harmonic liberties (parallel seconds, for example). Prokofiev later discarded this work and numbered his symphonies beginning with the *Classical,* written in 1917.

In general, the young Prokofiev's individuality revealed itself more clearly in the piano miniatures than in the large forms—opera and symphony. In *Undine* and the E minor Symphony, as well as in the later symphonic works of 1909–10 (*Dreams* and *Autumnal Sketch*), his talent was still held in check either by imitation of the German romantic school (Schumann), or by the direct influence of his Russian contemporaries

(Rachmaninov, the early Scriabin). These influences can be seen in the piano sonatas of the Conservatory period—the Sonata in F minor, Op. 1, for example. On the other hand, Prokofiev's powerful and daring individual style, which had timidly broken through in the previous years, is clearly visible in the program pieces for piano of 1907–8. His acquaintance with new music, his exchange of ideas with Miaskovsky, and his persistent experimentation hastened this stylistic leap.

During the school years 1907–8 and 1908–9 Prokofiev wrote six piano sonatas. Their style has a certain motley character: completely original episodes stand side by side with moments of immature, imitative music.

"You're too anxious to give your sonatas opus numbers," said Miaskovsky, smiling. "The time will come when you'll cross this all out and write 'Sonata No. 1.'"

Miaskovsky proved to be right. Like the E minor Symphony and *Undine,* the youthful sonatas remained a kind of "prehistory" of Prokofiev's creative work. But in subsequent years he turned time and again to the "old notebooks" that were so dear to him, and extracted from them their best pages. Although the first, fourth, and sixth youthful sonatas have not been preserved, the remaining ones later led an active life. From the three-movement "Second Sonata," written in 1907, came Prokofiev's first published work, Sonata No. 1 in F minor. In 1909 he discarded the Andante and Finale, which he found unsatisfactory, and polished the first movement anew, making it a one-movement sonata.

In the F minor Sonata, Prokofiev's writing closely resembles the noble and beautiful pathos of Schumann, Rachmaninov, and the early Scriabin. Here, there are neither sarcastic grimaces nor jarring harmonies. The melodies are clear and tuneful, although not entirely original (in the subordinate theme are heard echoes of one of the themes of Schumann's F-sharp minor Sonata). The development is natural, although the expository devices and particularly a certain overabundance of figuration bespeak the composer's creative immaturity. At the same time, the Sonata is impressive in its dynamism and emotional ardor, and in some of the harmonic touches Prokofiev's own style clearly breaks through. Despite the traditional character of the themes, the Sonata reveals Prokofiev's own temperament and active relationship to the world.

Asafyev later pointed this out when he wrote, "Prokofiev is speaking of the old, but in a new way, and he expresses the new by scarcely perceptible details, digressions and effects . . . one's ear immediately senses this 'scarcely' on one's very first acquaintance with the sonata."[12]

The F minor Sonata was unsuccessful with the modernists, who considered it too orthodox. The leader of the Evenings of Modern Music, Karatygin, severely criticized it for its "coarseness, reflecting Rachmaninov's influence."[13] In the magazine *Muzyka,* another modernist critic reproached Prokofiev for the "banality" of the musical content and advised him to "make haste to sail over the surging sea of doubt and soul-searching toward 'new shores.' "[14]

The youthful Third (1907) and Fifth (1908) Sonatas played an important role in Prokofiev's later works. On looking through his folios nine years later, the composer became very much interested in these pieces and revised them. From the Third Sonata came Sonata No. 3, Op. 28. The materials of the Fifth were taken as the basis for Sonata No. 4, Op. 29 (with the addition of the Andante of the E minor Symphony as the second movement). Analyzing these two sonatas, which appeared in 1917 with the note "from old notebooks," we realize how much sincere and fervent feeling these youthful works contained. How richly they revealed the composer's emotional world, not yet dulled by tendencies toward deliberate eccentricity!

Together with the sonatas Prokofiev also wrote a number of small program pieces for piano. These were in a sense a continuation of the *Ditties,* but they no longer bore birthday dedications and were written, of course, in a more complicated style. In 1907 appeared *Reproach, Fairy Tale, Badinage, Phantom,* and *Snowflakes;* in 1908, the March in F major, *Prayer, Reminiscence, Élan, Despair,* and *Diabolic Suggestions.* Some of them remained unpublished (*Snowflakes, Prayer, Reproach*). The rest, after being polished, were incorporated in the piano pieces, Op. 3 and Op. 4, which were published by Jurgenson in 1911 and 1913. These were the pieces that the young Prokofiev considered his most daring, the pieces he could not bring himself to show to Lyadov and Glazunov. In looking through them now, we realize the profound vitality of Prokofiev's youthful efforts. The charm of some of the pieces lies in their restrained and gentle lyricism—*Reproach,* for example, with its fresh harmonies and moving melody, seems to reproduce the living intonations of human speech (Fig. 7).

Listeners are still charmed by the introspective quality (so uncommon for a young composer) of *Reminiscence* and the tender lyricism of *Fairy Tale.* There is a feeling of tranquillity in the tuneful theme of *Reminiscence,* with its brightly colored chain of altered chords. A varicolored succession of fantastic pictures forms the content of *Fairy Tale.* The prin-

FIGURE 7

cipal theme of this piece is in the typical diatonic harmony—"on the white keys"—that later became Prokofiev's favorite harmonic idiom. A line of gentle, pensive lyricism runs from *Reminiscence* and *Fairy Tale* to *Cinderella* and some of the slow movements of the later symphonies.

Another facet of Prokofiev's style is revealed in the spirited, precisely chiseled *March* in F major and the rhythmical, gay *Badinage.* Here bold harmonies—unexpected layers of sound, daring sequences of unresolved altered seventh chords—and sharply accented, extremely simplified rhythms are used to portray the ludicrous and amusing sides of life. These bitingly humorous little pieces, in which tonal complexities always give way to clear-cut cadences, are very typical of the style of the young Prokofiev.

Finally, in *Despair, Élan, Phantom,* and *Diabolic Suggestions* there are nervous, tensely dramatic images which reveal the composer's avid interest in depicting the disturbing, tragic, and sometimes terrible aspects of reality. For this he employed spare but very compelling expressive effects. In *Despair,* for example, woeful exclamations and bitter weeping heard over

*33*

an endlessly repeated chromatic phrase in the bass create a truly arresting tragic image. "It is like a fixed stare full of inexpressible torment," Miaskovsky said of this theme.[15]

The most effective of these pieces is the dynamic *Diabolic Suggestions,* which is filled with unrestrained power. Ominous tritonal harmonies and trills and somber splashes in the bass foretell something exciting and terrifying. Gradually there develops a continuously mounting, sharply expressive motion based on the endless repetition of a single bold and compelling musical phrase.

The use of tart harmonies and sharply accentuated rhythms is not here an end in itself, but serves to create an exciting, powerful, elemental image. At the same time there is no mysticism, no world beyond. The music seems to portray a violent invasion of evil fantastic forces, hostile to man. Asafyev compared the dominant image of this piece to "terrifying horsemen of the steppes, crushing every manifestation of life."[16]

Some years later, Prokofiev played *Diabolic Suggestions* for Vladimir Mayakovsky in the Moscow "Poets' Café." On hearing it, Mayakovsky drew a portrait of the composer, with the inscription, "Sergei Sergeyevich playing on the tenderest nerves of Vladimir Vladimirovich."[17] V. Kolomyitsev suggested that it be given a more specific name, such as "Wild Sabbath of Dirty-Faced Devils Dancing in Hell," or "Violent Brawl of Two Enraged Gorillas."[18]

These critics, shocked by the expressiveness of Prokofiev's music, failed to realize that it simply developed in its own way the kind of sinister fantasy found in Moussorgsky's *Night on Bald Mountain* and his "Baba Yaga" from *Pictures at an Exhibition,* or in some of the works of Rimsky-Korsakov. In pieces like *Diabolic Suggestions,* Prokofiev was in essence striving to extend the limits of the musical embodiment of negative images, the representation of forces inimical to man.

On December 31, 1908, Prokofiev made his first appearance as a composer before the musical world of St. Petersburg. This was the forty-fifth gathering of the Evenings of Modern Music, and it took place in the concert hall of the former Lutheran School. In addition to works by Grieg, Scriabin, Medtner, and Taneyev, the program included three songs by Miaskovsky (to words by Zinaïda Gippius) and seven piano pieces by Prokofiev (*Fairy Tale, Snowflakes, Reminiscence, Élan, Prayer, Despair,* and *Diabolic Suggestions*). The two young composers faced the critics of the capital for the first time. Among those present were Prokofiev's highly excited mother, Mariya Grigoryevna, and Morolev, who was on a visit to St. Petersburg. In his memoirs the latter tells of the stunning impression produced by Prokofiev's virile playing. The audience was particularly excited by *Diabolic Suggestions,* although some of those present were completely bewildered by it.

Prokofiev's first public appearance was widely noted in the St. Petersburg press. Comments appeared in the newspapers *Rech, Slovo, Novoye Vremya,* and *Peterburgsky Listok* and in the magazine *Zolotoye Runo* (under "Notes in Brief"). A number of the reviews were marked by cautious skepticism. The critic G. Timofeyev, Balakirev's biographer, noted in *Rech* that "the composer is . . . undoubtedly talented, but his harmonies contain many strange and bizarre qualities which overstep the bounds of beauty."[19] The critic of *Peterburgsky Listok* wrote evasively, "If one views all of these rather confused compositions—or, to be more exact, rough drafts and sketches—as a test for the composer's pen, then perhaps here and there one may find a trace of talent in them."

The review in *Slovo* was the most sympathetic. "In all the vagaries of this rich creative imagination, one can detect a great and indisputable talent, a talent still unstable, still surrendering to every passion, enamored of extravagant combinations of sound, yet with great skill finding a logical basis for the most hazardous modulations," wrote N. Sem (the pseudonym of one of the leaders of the Evenings of Modern Music, probably Karatygin). The critic hastened to proclaim the seventeen-year-old Prokofiev an "extreme leftist" innovator. "In daring and originality this young composer . . . who belongs to the ultra-modernist school, far outdoes the French modernists."[20]

The debut in December 1908 marked the beginning of Prokofiev's long concert career. His mother collected the newspaper reviews and pasted them neatly in a thick scrapbook. With these comments begins the literature about Prokofiev, to which every notable Russian music critic has contributed, from the venerable Nikolai Kashkin to Asafyev (Igor Glebov), who was just entering upon his career.

In 1908–9 Prokofiev finished the composition course at the Conservatory. In his fifth year, after studying fugue with Lyadov, he entered Joseph Wihtol's class in form. The Conservatory's best and most popular composition professor, Rimsky-Korsakov, had died suddenly in the summer of 1908. This intensified the young composer's feeling of dissatisfaction with his Conservatory training.

Joseph Wihtol, a distinguished Latvian composer who composed in the Rimsky-Korsakov tradition, took a more patient attitude toward Prokofiev's daring than Lyadov. But the classes with Wihtol were limited to a study of the basic compositional forms. The students had to bring to class original compositions in the various traditional forms (variation, rondo, sonata, and so on). Prokofiev and Miaskovsky often showed the teacher their old works, slightly refurbished and warmed over. Encouraged by the praise of the modernists, Prokofiev also brought to Wihtol's class new and increasingly daring pieces, among them the Sixth Sonata, which was later lost, and scenes from a new version of *A Feast in Time of Plague.*

In returning to this Pushkin subject six years after his naïve, childish effort of 1903, Prokofiev made a more serious attempt to reveal its poetic idea. What attracted him in the poem was the combination of bacchanalian motifs with images of death and cruel punishment for sinful acts. He took special pains with the final episode, in which the old priest sternly upbraids the revelers:

> Blasphemous sons of folly! Godless feast!
> With revelry and your indecent songs
> You all insult the fearful, silent gloom
> That death has spread over this mournful place!

This monologue prompted Prokofiev to search for an agitated and powerful recitative style, one with a free and harsh declamatory structure. On the composer's own admission, this scene was a stepping-stone to his later operas *Maddalena* and *The Gambler.*

While Wihtol did not discourage the experiments of his restless student, neither did he encourage them. Finding no support in the class in free composition, Prokofiev began to work with great enthusiasm in the special piano class. Apathy was alien to his ebullient nature. With the fiery passion of a sportsman he loved to surmount obstacles, engage in competition, establish better and better records of accomplishment. Now he became absolutely fascinated with the virtuoso aspect of piano playing. Among the works he studied with Winkler was Rubinstein's extremely difficult concert *Étude* in C major. His performance of it at a student concert at the end of 1908 thrilled Prokofiev more than his debut with his own works at the Evenings of Modern Music. Somewhat later he gave a brilliant performance of Schumann's equally difficult C major *Toccata.* Probably some of his specifically motoric themes (in the First and Third Piano Concertos, for example) can be traced to the influence of Rubinstein's *Étude* and Schumann's *Toccata.*

At the final examination in the spring of 1909, Prokofiev played his Sixth

Sonata and the last scene of *A Feast in Time of Plague*. Both works created a highly unfavorable impression on the examining board. "They're all bent on becoming Scriabins!" exclaimed Lyadov. "An extreme innovator with a quite one-sided technique," was Wihtol's characterization of the eighteen-year-old Prokofiev.

The young composer was nevertheless granted the title of Free Artist, though the marks in his certificate were not brilliant: for form, 4 plus; for fugue, 4 plus; for special orchestration, 4; and for the remaining subjects (piano, history of music, and aesthetics), 5. Strictly speaking, this ended Prokofiev's instruction in composition. The following year, with some difficulty, he persuaded Lyadov to accept him in the class in free composition, but the class was not a success and was soon discontinued.

Faced with the question of what to do next, the idea arose that he might continue his musical education at the Conservatory in classes in piano and conducting. On the advice of Miaskovsky and Zakharov, he decided to transfer from Winkler to Anna Esipova, the leading exponent of the St. Petersburg school of pianism.

Esipova willingly accepted the talented composer-pianist with the phenomenal technique, who had already attracted favorable attention in his appearances at student recitals.*

In May, on his way to Sontsovka, the Free Artist visited his first teacher, Glière, in Moscow. "Seryozha already looked quite grown-up," recalls Glière. "He had acquired a great deal of self-assurance. His views on modern music were characterized by a deliberate 'radicalism.' He seemed ready to dethrone any generally accepted authority. Nevertheless we parted friends."

As in previous years, Prokofiev spent the summer in quiet Sontsovka, where he composed music and worked tirelessly on a piano program for Esipova. Among the pieces he studied were a fugue by Mendelssohn and a Medtner *Fairy Tale* (Op. 8, No. 2). In a letter to Glière he asked him to find out from Medtner the program of this *Fairy Tale* so that he might know "what to concentrate on." This detail is typical of the young musician's inquiring mind, his desire to find meaning in music.

While at Sontsovka he composed the four *Études* for piano, Op. 2, and the five-movement Sinfonietta, Op. 5. The *Études* clearly reflect his predilection for a brilliant and powerful virtuoso style. Here one still notes ele-

---

* "Technical preparation exceedingly brilliant. Interpretation unique, original, but not always in the best artistic taste" was Glazunov's characterization of Prokofiev's performance at the public examination in "special piano" on May 15, 1909.

ments of the romantic pianism of Rachmaninov and Medtner (the latter's influence is quite obvious in the E minor *Étude* No. 2); but the general character of the *Études,* with their predominant trait of stormy expressiveness, is completely Prokofiev's own. Particularly rich in texture are *Étude* No. 1 (D minor, *presto energico*), with its original polyrhythmic passages, and the pathetic *Étude* No. 4 (C minor).

In the fall Prokofiev showed the *Études* to Taneyev, who, while he did not approve of certain of the composer's harmonic liberties, nevertheless recommended the pieces to Jurgenson for publication. The "primitive power and freshness" of the *Études* were highly valued by Miaskovsky, who three years later devoted a special note to them in the magazine *Muzyka.*

"In these beautiful *Études* we find now strange fantasy, now gentle but healthy lyricism, now cutting irony, now, finally, powerful impetuosity. . . . It is difficult to single out any one of them, since, though different, they are all of equal value. The massiveness of the first, tinted with moments of quiet lyricism; the ingratiating modulations of the second; the unbridled humor and mad abandon of the last; and, finally, the mysterious rustling and phantasmagoria of the third—each of them is so self-contained, so extraordinary, and at the same time so complete."[21]

After the rather unsuccessful E minor Symphony, Prokofiev worked painstakingly on a Sinfonietta in A major for small orchestra. In form and orchestration this work in five miniature movements (Allegro giocoso, Andante, Intermezzo, Scherzo, and again Allegro giocoso) closely resembles the transparent symphonic writing of the pre-Beethoven period.

"There is something very interesting about it (the cyclical Andante, fervent Scherzo)," remarked Miaskovsky in a letter to Derzhanovsky.[22]

The Mozartian "sonata style" of the first and last movements serves to set off the harmonic inventiveness and rhythmical resiliency of the Scherzo and Intermezzo. The critics later took special note of the originality of the Andante, which unfolds gradually over a strange *basso ostinato.* The composer himself was not satisfied, however, with the orchestration and harmonic polish of the Sinfonietta. ("I lacked the skill required for transparent writing," he admitted.) This work was revised twice, in 1914 and in 1929. The second revision proved to be so substantial that the composer published it as a new opus, Op. 48.

In the fall of 1909 Prokofiev again returned to the St. Petersburg Conservatory. As in previous years, his solicitous mother accompanied him and took charge of all his activities. As before, young people gathered continually in their modest apartment at 4 Pervaya Rota Street, to listen to music and argue about what they had heard.

The title of Free Artist and some experience in composition did not lessen Prokofiev's thirst for knowledge or his persistence in work. The years 1909–14 he devoted to intense study of the piano and conducting, without stopping his creative work.

Anna Nikolayevna Esipova, a world-famous Russian pianist who had been trained in the brilliant tradition of the Leschetizky school of piano playing and musical pedagogy, played an important role in Prokofiev's further artistic education. In 1908, at the age of 57, she had given up her concert career and devoted herself entirely to teaching. The young Prokofiev entered her class with a magnificently developed technique but with a persisting tendency toward careless, unpolished playing. During this period he became even more scornful of much of traditional music.

"They say that you can't give a piano recital without Chopin," he said sarcastically to his friends. "I'll prove that we can do quite well without Chopin!" He treated Mozart with similar disdain: "What kind of harmonies are these—I, IV, V!"

Unwilling to give up his careless grand manner of playing, he took too many liberties with composers' scores and often made up his own additions and corrections to the pieces he played. For example, when studying Tchaikovsky's *Scherzo à la russe,* he ruthlessly crossed out "superfluous" notes in the figurations, added octaves in the bass, wrote in *staccatos* and *accelerandos,* and even introduced additional leaps by transposing chords to a higher octave.*

Believing that Esipova was trying to "make everyone fit a standard pattern," he often ignored her requests. In the beginning, out of admiration for his unusual talent, she was tolerant with him, but later on teacher and pupil clashed frequently. The distinguished pianist would not accept his disregard for the classics, his violations of composers' scores and faulty interpretations. At the very first annual examination, in the spring of 1910, she characterized Prokofiev as follows: "Has assimilated little of my method. Very talented but rather unpolished." Yet she gave him "4 1/2"

* A copy of the *Scherzo à la russe* with Prokofiev's notations has been preserved in the V. M. Morolev archives. He also took liberties when he performed with chamber ensembles. Glazunov reproached him for this in one of the examination reports ("Many superfluous notes in the chords").

(examination report of May 17, 1910). Whenever a conflict arose, Sergei's mother always sided with Esipova and tried her best to make her unruly son see reason.

Prokofiev learned a great many works in Esipova's class, among them Schumann's Sonata in F-sharp minor and Toccata, Liszt's Sonata in B minor and a transcription from Wagner's *Tannhäuser*, Medtner's *Fairy Tales*, Glazunov's Sonata in E minor, and pieces by Tchaikovsky and Rachmaninov. His teacher also made him play Mozart, Schubert, and Chopin, demanding perfect and finely polished playing. The years of study in Esipova's class were not wasted. Prokofiev's brilliantly individual style of playing, with its clean-cut finger technique, steel-like touch, and exceptional freedom of wrist movement bore the stamp of the Esipova-Leschetizky school. Prokofiev became one of the greatest Russian virtuosos, and in his best works he enriched piano literature by altogether new means of expression.

The composer Cherepnin, Prokofiev's teacher in conducting, played a different role in his training. Among the Conservatory professors he was looked upon as a modernist. Through him, modernist ideas percolated among the youth. "He talked about innovation in such a way that I felt almost like an old-fashioned musician," Prokofiev recalls.

A violent opponent of the Belyaev School, which by this time had been discredited, Cherepnin was closely connected with the leaders of the World of Art group. (The artist A. Benois, a relative of his, designed the décor for his ballets.) In his own music (the ballets *Le Pavillon d'Armide, Narcissus,* and *The Masque of the Red Death*) Cherepnin leaned toward the French impressionists. It was natural that he should be the one professor in the Conservatory who encouraged Prokofiev's modernist tendencies.

At the same time, it was in Cherepnin's class that Prokofiev came to know the potentialities of the symphony orchestra, learning through practical experience the art of orchestration and conducting. Cherepnin devoted a great deal of attention to Prokofiev's conducting lessons. For a long time this difficult art did not come easily to Prokofiev. "You have no talent for conducting," Cherepnin told his pupil, "but since I believe in you as a composer, and I know that you will often have to conduct your own works, I am going to teach you how to conduct."

Prokofiev conducted the student orchestra regularly. Under his direction they performed Glazunov's *Poème lyrique,* Rubinstein's *Ivan the Terrible,* orchestral pieces by Dargomyzhsky, Beethoven's Seventh Symphony,

Schubert's Unfinished Symphony, and other works. He also frequently accompanied soloists in performances of such works as Tchaikovsky's First Piano Concerto, Brahm's Violin Concerto, and one of Saint-Saëns's piano concertos. Talented Conservatory students who later became famous Soviet artists, among them M. Polyakin, A. Gauk, V. Dranishnikov, and V. Tsybin, appeared with him. In the spring of 1913 Prokofiev conducted five of the eight symphonic works played at the graduation exercises. Thanks to Cherepnin, he also conducted a great deal in O. Palecek's opera class, which was of tremendous value to him, for it not only gave him practical experience in the performance of operas but also deepened his interest in this genre. In October 1913, at a jubilee concert in memory of Verdi, he conducted excerpts from *Aïda,* and on April 6, 1914, a complete performance of Mozart's *Marriage of Figaro.* His appearances as conductor received numerous (and for the most part unfavorable) reviews in the St. Petersburg press.

While encouraging Prokofiev's modernist interests in every possible way, Cherepnin at the same time fostered in him a taste for classical music, for the traditions of Haydn and Mozart, for the elegant dance forms of the eighteenth century (the gavotte and minuet), and for transparent classical orchestration. Reverence for the art of the past—with a touch of aesthetic stylization—was completely in line with the "cult of the old" that prevailed among Cherepnin's friends and colleagues, the World of Art artists. But for the young Prokofiev, who was accustomed to treat Haydn and Mozart in an offhand manner, this turning toward the music of the classic composers was exceedingly fruitful. The interest in classical music which had been fostered in his childhood was reawakened. This led to the composition of such works as the Sinfonietta (dedicated to Cherepnin), some of the pieces of Op. 12, the *Classical Symphony,* and later some of the dances of *Romeo and Juliet* and *Cinderella.* Prokofiev's talent and his fresh perception of the traditions saved him from formal, imitative stylization in these works.

Prokofiev's work in the conducting class left a considerable mark on his artistic development. Later on he made many appearances, both in Russia and abroad, as conductor-performer of his own works, capturing audiences with his forcefulness and brilliant sense of rhythm. Moreover, direct contact with an orchestra stimulated Prokofiev to write symphonic works. Finally, standing on the podium before the Conservatory orchestra, he had an opportunity to check the quality of his own orchestration.

The Sinfonietta, Op. 5, was followed in 1910 by two orchestral pieces, this time program works—*Dreams* (Op. 6) and *Autumnal Sketch* (Op. 8). *Dreams* was played for the first time on December 5, 1910, at a student concert (at the Conservatory) under the composer's direction. In 1911 and 1915 it was performed at public concerts. According to the critic Karatygin, the piece "is permeated with gloomy, joyless moods, which seem to have been transmitted to the score from a world of melancholy daydreams and phantoms. The orchestral color is deliberately lackluster (muted brasses). The pace is slow. The brighter middle section, with its mounting pathos, forms a fine contrast to the first and last sections. However, the work generally is not very characteristic of Prokofiev."[23]

In choosing the program for *Dreams*, Prokofiev probably followed the example of Scriabin, who began his symphonic writing with a short, contemplative miniature of the same kind titled *Rêverie*. Thus Prokofiev's dedication: "To the composer who began with *Rêverie*." (In the music itself, however, one does not feel the influence of Scriabin.) Later on Prokofiev sharply criticized *Dreams*, pointing out the excessive "flaccidity" and "pensiveness" of the music.

"*Dreams* is the kind of piece you can't even properly scold the composer for," he wrote to Ye. Zvyagintseva in 1915.[24] And "*Dreams* will probably be published as a posthumous work or in my old age, if by that time I shall have written myself out, or if there is nothing else to publish," he wrote much later.[25]

*Autumnal Sketch* is written in tones of contemplative, somewhat somber lyricism. On the author's admission, this "can be traced to certain of Rachmaninov's moods, mainly to *The Isle of the Dead* and the Second Symphony, to which it was related tonally (E minor)." Six years later Asafyev, writing on *Autumnal Sketch* in *Muzykalny Sovremennik*, noted in it a passivity and "submissiveness" not usual for Prokofiev.

Both *Dreams* and *Autumnal Sketch* remained unpublished. The composer revised the latter work twice and brought it to finished form only in 1934.

In 1909–10 Prokofiev, for the first time during his Conservatory years, turned to choral and song writing. First he wrote two works for female voices and orchestra to Konstantin Balmont's poems *The White Swan* and *The Wave,* hoping to perform them at one of the Conservatory concerts. But the choruses were too unusual and difficult, and were performed only once, at a private rehearsal. Neither work has been published. For a long time, simple and natural choral writing did not come easily to Prokofiev.

The choruses, Op. 7, were followed by two songs, Op. 9: *There Are Other Planets*, to words by Balmont, and *Boat Adrift*, after A. Apukhtin. Both of these works reflect the influence of the impressionist salon lyricism, with its subtly shifting harmonic fabric, exquisite piano texture, and completely declamatory, unmelodic vocal pattern. The first song—the more intimate, with its mysteriously muffled tones—is based on gently rocking lullaby rhythms. In the second, *Boat Adrift*, the composer was carried away with descriptive effects in the piano part, drawing a tragically gloomy picture of a raging sea. Careful polishing, harmonic invention, and attention to declamatory details did not save these songs from the taint of artificiality. Some years later Miaskovsky wrote that "despite certain virtues, the songs (Op. 9) do not particularly move us."[26]

Nevertheless, Prokofiev himself later confessed that "poor as it is," he continued to feel a "paternal affection" for *There Are Other Planets*.

Prokofiev did not turn to the mystical verses of the decadent Balmont as a result of fully formed aesthetic principles. Along with Balmont's symbolist work, in the same Opus 9, he also used the completely orthodox, even stylistically old-fashioned poem of Apukhtin. The decadence of Balmont's poetry was not really reflected in the sincere lyricism of the young composer. Balmont was a fashionable poet. His verses had been set to music by Cherepnin, Miaskovsky, Stravinsky, and M. Steinberg. Prokofiev, too, was attracted by the formal novelty of Balmont's poems, with their refined verbal "instrumentation."

In the winter of 1910 the musicians of Moscow heard Prokofiev for the first time. On March 6 he played his First Sonata and three of the *Études*, Op. 2, in the Synod School, at one of the "musical showcases" arranged by the singer M. Deisha-Sionitskaya. Appearing on the same program were B. L. Yavorsky, E. A. Bekman-Shcherbina, and V. N. Shatskaya. The young composer was warmly received in *Russkoye Slovo* by the distinguished music critic and friend of Tchaikovsky, Nikolai Kashkin, who noted his talent, his earnest approach to his work, and his "youthful courage."[27]

Prokofiev also continued to appear at the concerts of the St. Petersburg Evenings of Modern Music. During the 1910–11 season he played there twice. In addition to his own works (*Études* and the piano pieces, Op. 3), he also performed, for the first time in Russia, the showy, artificial piano pieces of the leader of the Austrian atonalists, Arnold Schoenberg (three *Klavierstücke*, Op. 11). During the performance of these pieces, wrote Karatgyin, "Homeric laughter broke out in the hall."[28] Nevertheless, both he and the other modernists considered Schoenberg's music brilliant, and gave him an enthusiastic reception when he appeared in St. Petersburg the following year.

It was at one of the private gatherings of the Evenings of Modern Music in 1910 that Prokofiev first met the already famous Igor Stravinsky. On that occasion Stravinsky played a piano arrangement of his newly written ballet *The Firebird*. Prokofiev did not like this music at all and made a disparaging remark about it which deeply wounded the egotistical Stravinsky ("That evening we had a 'run-in,'" recalls Sergei Sergeyevich). However, in subsequent years Stravinsky had a considerable influence on the development of Prokofiev's talent.

*❋ ❋ ❋*

Let us now draw some conclusions. In the field of composing, the period before 1911 was for Prokofiev a period when he was gathering his strength and revealing his creative potentialities. Most of the works of this early stage still bore the imprint of immaturity and therefore achieved no prominence. In the First Sonata in F minor, *Dreams, Autumnal Sketch,* and to some extent in the vocal works, there can still be noted a looking backward toward the composer's older contemporaries; echoes of the pathetic lyricism typical of early-twentieth-century Russian music can still be heard. But these works (as well as the Sinfonietta, Op. 5) reveal not only a certain imitativeness, fully understandable in a young composer, but also Prokofiev's indestructible ties to classical traditions, his predilection for lyrical images, for revealing the inner world of man. These qualities are to be found in the best pages of his piano music—in the romantic narratives (*Fairy Tale, Reminisence*); in the rhythmical pieces (G minor Gavotte, March in F major); and in the intensely lyrical, soulful themes in the Russian vein (Andante of the E minor Symphony, subordinate theme of the future Third Sonata). Among the modernists these tendencies were considered old-fashioned and seemingly untypical of Prokofiev's talent; they demanded of him "iron" themes, harmonic tricks, and grotesque distortions, always urging him on toward modernist new horizons. During the following years the young composer became ashamed of his lyricism and often felt obliged to suppress the expression of the gentler human sentiments.

At the same time, the features of Prokofiev's talent which particularly startled the audience of that day—elemental energy and turbulent dynamism, a penchant for humor, now gentle, now sarcastic, an interest in nervously expressive effects—revealed themselves brilliantly. These characteristics are evident in the piano pieces, Op. 3 and Op. 4, the *Études,* Op. 2, and the middle movements of the Sinfonietta.

Prokofiev's early piano pieces have retained their freshness to this very day. The best of the *Études* (Nos. 1 and 4) and the *Diabolic Suggestions* can still test the artistic and technical maturity of many pianists.

In 1910 a great misfortune befell the Prokofiev family: Sergei's father fell seriously ill and died soon afterward. Nineteen-year-old Sergei was now faced with making his own way in life. The visits to Sontsovka ceased. By the fall of 1910 all matters concerning the Sontsov estate were settled. Despite the difficulties that arose, the energetic Mariya Grigoryevna, who had profound faith in her son's talent, found a way to enable him to continue his studies.

# THREE

# THE BEGINNING OF RECOGNITION

T HE PERIOD DURING which Sergei Prokofiev began to win recognition was a critical one in the history of Russian culture. When the thunder of the revolutionary battles of 1905–7 had receded, there followed an ominous calm. The overwhelming majority of the bourgeois intelligentsia, who had not long before expressed sympathy for the struggling people, turned away from the democratic movement. As they grew more reactionary, decadent trends in philosophy, literature, and art began to spread. It became fashionable to malign the revolution and Marxism, to glorify individualism, mysticism, depravity. Open repudiation of realism and of the democratic traditions of the classics, flight from the present, and adherence to the cult of pure form characterized the work of many bourgeois writers, artists, and composers.

Only a small group of writers close to the working class and the Bolshevist movement, first and foremost the great humanist Maxim Gorky, continued to carry on the valiant revolutionary struggle, laying the foundations of socialist realism. Gorky wrote *Childhood, In the World,* and *Tales of Italy.* He sharply criticized the decadent trends in literature and the theater. The young Mayakovsky lifted his powerful and passionate voice, delivering angry "slaps in the face" to the hated bourgeois society.

The revolutionary tradition of Gorky was opposed in Russian culture by various reactionary trends—from the symbolists to the members of the "Change-of-Landmarks" group [*"Smena vekh"*],* from the World of Art school to pseudo-literary pornographers.

The decay and inevitable collapse of the culture of the bourgeoisie and nobility became more and more apparent. Fashions in art changed with fantastic rapidity. Intent on keeping pace with the West, imperialist Rus-

* TRANSLATOR'S NOTE: This was a group of writers, journalists, and scholars who left Russia after the Revolution of 1905. They published a "Change of Landmarks" magazine in Paris and Prague, and some of them later returned to Russia.

sia, the Russia of the Ryabushinskys and Guchkovs, produced an ever-increasing number of new and extreme schools and trends in literature and art, each of which denounced the art of its predecessors. In painting, the beautiful stylizations and decorative retrospection of the World of Art group gave way to the crude materiality and meaningless colorism of the Russian Cézannists ("Jack of Diamonds"). The young futurist groups ("Ass's Tail" and "Target") rebelled against the French orientation of the "Jack of Diamonds" and proclaimed the cult of the primitive, of the *lubok*,\* thus paving the way to abstract, nonrepresentational painting, to the "black square."

In poetry the brief domination of symbolism ended. The world of vague premonitions and capriciously elusive symbols already seemed quite old-fashioned to the young poets who appeared around 1910. Calling themselves "Acmeists," they countered the hazy phraseology of Andrei Bely and Vyacheslav Ivanov with a cult of primeval force and barbarism. Mayakovsky aptly christened the Acmeists "a pack of Adams with parts in their hair." The Russian futurists went even further in their rejection of the classical standards of art, demanding that Pushkin and other classics be thrown overboard, and turning to pure formalism, to the use of a "trans-sense" [*zaumny*] language, which was nothing but a meaningless collection of sounds.

A similar development also took place in the Russian theater: from the symbolist experiments of the Moscow Art Theater through the rage for stylization, the show booth, and the masque, to the constructivist extravaganzas of the "leftist" *régisseurs* of the twenties. And alongside this was a rejection of opera as a form allegedly out of date, and an attempt to replace it with semi-acrobatic dance movement.

All branches of modernist art followed a common path from the flaccid, refined beauty of symbolism and impressionism to simplification, coarsening, and cultivated primitivism: to cubism and sheer formalism in painting, to abracadabra and "trans-sense" language in poetry, to constructivism and deliberate cacophony in music, to the arbitrary eccentricities of the conjurer-*régisseur* in the theater. This noisy contest of the bourgeois schools of literature and art was only superficial, however, and devoid of principle. The young formalist poets who raised such a hue and cry against the refinements of symbolism took the very same attitude toward

---

\* TRANSLATOR'S NOTE: The *lubok* is a primitive Russian woodcut, a piece of folk art very popular with the common people during this period.

vital and understandable art as the symbolists had, although their anti-realism was even more daring and more extreme.

Only the strongest and most sensitive poets of the pre-revolutionary modernist schools were able to free themselves from decadent influences and take their stand for the vital, meaningful art needed by the people. Such a person was Mayakovsky, who quickly overcame the influence of futurism and became a fiery tribune of the socialist epoch. Such men were Alexander Blok and Valery Bryusov, who left the stuffy salons of symbolism for the broad highway of great, meaningful art.

The greatest artists and thinkers of the classical school voiced many sharp protests against decadent formalist art. They correctly maintained that the noble ideals of great art, which can "inflame the hearts of men with a word," do not permit the preoccupation with form for form's sake, the capricious arbitrariness of artist-aesthetes who fancy themselves the "free creators of beauty."

After the 1905 revolution Russian music followed a course very similar to that of literature, painting, and the theater. Only a few of the leading musicians remained loyal to the traditions of their teachers, the Russian classical composers, and maintained a sharply critical attitude toward decadent fads. These were the true followers of the "new Russian school" and Tchaikovsky—Glazunov, Taneyev, Lyadov, Spendiarov, Ippolitov-Ivanov, and Glière. Medtner and Rachmaninov, too, adhered to realism. The magnificent traditions of realist art also continued to develop in musical performance, both operatic and instrumental. (We have in mind the triumphs of Chaliapin and the emergence of the brilliant pianists and violinists of the Russian School.)

After the death of Rimsky-Korsakov in 1908, however, the realist school in music rapidly lost its strength. There came to be scarcely any direct reflection in musical works of the tense and critical situation then developing in the life of the Russian people. This indicated the composers' indifference to the struggle of the masses and the approaching revolutionary crisis. In many works by latter-day followers of the Belyaev and Tchaikovsky schools the traditions of the Russian classics were devitalized. It is not surprising that some of the young composers, exposed as they were to decadent influences, began to oppose all traditions, even the most progressive.

It was during these years of reaction in Russian music that modernist tendencies and groups flourished. Their interests followed the general trend of bourgeois art toward idealism, mysticism, and formal complexity.

*Above*: S. A. Prokofiev,
the composer's father.
*Left*: M. Grigoryevna-
Prokofieva, his mother.

SOVFOTO

*Above*: Prokofiev at the age of nine (*circa* 1900) with his piano score of *The Giant*. *Center*: Prokofiev at a ball held in the St. Petersburg Conservatory (1908). *Right*: Prokofiev in his last year at the Conservatory (1914).

The brilliant Scriabin moved rapidly from fits of ecstasy to subjectivism and ultra-refined forms of expression. Some of the young composers who turned away from the national traditions began to pattern their work after Western music, mainly French. It became fashionable to imitate the exquisitely scented music of the impressionists, to stylize in the manner of the World of Art school. Rebikov, Cherepnin, the young Vasilenko, and a number of others followed this trend.

This polished but imitative art was alien to the most sensitive Russian musicians. "How contrived, boring, high-flown all this is," wrote Miaskovsky of a number of new works in 1914.[1] Such composers, according to Asafyev, "do not create, they fabricate, stringing together little morsels with only one concern—that these morsels should be sophisticated and palatable to the very newest in good taste."[2]

The most typical representative of Russian modernism was Igor Stravinsky, who veered swiftly from exotic beauty to barbaric cacophony and cubistic constructions. He left Russia long before the October Revolution, subordinating his art to the demands of Western snobs. One senses in his most sensational works (*The Wedding, The Rite of Spring*) a savoring of archaic primitivism, a modernistic use of Russian folk tunes, and a striving to shock European listeners with the novel and "exotic." Disregarding the artistic perception of his listeners, he sought to impose on them his own standards of art. "As for their 'sounding barbaric,'" he wrote of his Japanese songs, "this doesn't trouble me in the least. It is a matter of convention, which, after all, is determined by habit."[3]

It is no wonder that Miaskovsky rejected the studied complexity of Stravinsky's latest works. "I'm somewhat disturbed that he's gotten himself enmeshed in intricate primitivism," Miaskovsky wrote in 1913. "And what is more, I'm repelled by the way 38,000 francs has affected his attitude toward his own composition. How unartistic, how inane!"[4]

The young Prokofiev responded with enthusiasm to the most extreme works of Scriabin and Stravinsky. He listened with great interest to Scriabin's *Prometheus* and last sonatas, comparing them with the composer's earlier works, which seemed to him stylistically old-fashioned. He eagerly followed Stravinsky's work, attended the Diaghilev performances of his ballets abroad, and spoke with enthusiasm about *The Wedding*.

However, not everything in Stravinsky's music appealed to him. For example, he found *The Rite of Spring* unintelligible and *Petrushka* full of superficial padding. Nevertheless, the provocative eccentricity of Stravinsky's music, the novelty of its form, and its inventiveness did exert a certain influence on the work of the young Prokofiev (notably the *Scythian Suite* and *The Buffoon*).

The ideological fountainhead of Russian modernism in music from 1901 to 1912 was the St. Petersburg society Evenings of Modern Music, and from 1910 to 1917, the Moscow magazine *Muzyka*. Both these circles gave their utmost support to Prokofiev's modernist tendencies.

The Evenings of Modern Music began as the musical branch of the World of Art group, adopting the basic credo of the super-aesthetes who were its leaders. Quite naturally, two of the active members of the Evenings, Alfred Nurok and Walter Nuvel, also belonged to the World of Art group and were friends and supporters of Diaghilev, D. Filosofov, A. Benois, and other leaders of Russian modernism. This group, headed by the outspoken aesthete Diaghilev, advocated the theory of a pure art, free from the "fetters" of social responsibility. Here the belief of Chernyshevsky and Stasov that art should teach was declared out of date, and the democratic traditions of the *Peredvizhniki* and the Five were ridiculed.* "I cannot understand the idea that art must serve society according to certain rigid prescriptions," Diaghilev asserted frankly.

In opposition to Stasov, who advocated the educational mission of art, Benois developed the idea of "freeing the personality of the artist from the fetters of society." The modernists had a particular aversion to the frank, easily understood emotionalism of Tchaikovsky, Rachmaninov, and Kalinnikov. In the music of Moussorgsky they approved only the novelty of form and the psychological element, refusing to acknowledge the great musician's inherent folk qualities and tendency toward social criticism.

The idea that Russian art has a distinctive national character was also declared shamefully old-fashioned. While the World of Art painters worshiped the French impressionists and the decadent art of Aubrey Beardsley and T. T. Heine, the leaders of the Evenings of Modern Music went into ecstasies over Reger and Schoenberg, Richard Strauss, and the contemporary French composers. According to Diaghilev, an orientation toward modern Western culture was "the only guarantee of progress and the only antidote to routine."

Ignatz Kryzhanovsky, physician and composer (a pupil of Rimsky-

---

* TRANSLATOR'S NOTE: The *Peredvizhniki* were a group of realistic, representational painters who flourished in the last quarter of the nineteenth century. The "Mighty" Five—Balakirev, Rimsky-Korsakov, Borodin, Moussorgsky, and Cui—led the movement toward a "national school" of music in the 1860's and 70's.

Korsakov), and the music critic Vyacheslav Karatygin played an active role in the Evenings of Modern Music. The activity of this group consisted in the presentation of seven or eight public concerts a season of the works of modern Western and Russian composers. In addition to novelties from abroad, they often presented the music of unrecognized young Russian composers. Their programs included chamber works by the French composers Debussy, Dukas, Fauré, Chausson, D'Indy, and Roussel; the German composers Schoenberg, Reger, Wolf, and Richard Strauss; and the Russian composers Scriabin, Stravinsky, Medtner, Rachmaninov, Rebikov, Senilov, Cherepnin, Gnessin, and Steinberg. From nineteenth-century music only fresh little-known works (such as Moussorgsky's song cycle *Sunless*) were presented. Famous St. Petersburg artists, among them the singers I. Alchevsky, M. Lunacharsky, N. Zabela, and A. Zherebtsova and the pianists L. Nikolayev, M. Barinova, and S. Polotskaya-Yemtsova willingly performed at these concerts. The society maintained itself on small membership fees and an equally modest entrance fee, but the Evenings were invariably noted by the critics and supplied with programs, posters, and so on. A. Benois, K. Somov, E. Lanceré, and M. Dobuzhinsky of the World of Art supported the activity of the Evenings in every possible way.

Some of the most prominent musicians of St. Petersburg, including Rimsky-Korsakov, attended the Evenings. Rimsky-Korsakov, however, vigorously opposed the fads of the modernists, who made light of Russian classical traditions and oriented the young toward the latest Western music. In his diary he refers to them rather sharply as the "impudent and earless" leaders of the Evenings of Modern Music.[5] Directly opposite to this was the position of Karatygin, the guiding spirit of the Evenings and their ideologist. In his almost daily writings in the press (mainly in the Cadet newspaper *Rech*) he persistently sang the praises of modernism of every shade, right up to the most extreme, and condemned enthusiasm for Tchaikovsky and Rachmaninov as a sign of "poor, backward taste." His writings had a strong influence upon the development of the young Prokofiev's aesthetic views.

But it would be incorrect to deny the importance of Karatygin's role in the history of Russian music, as is sometimes done, and to regard him only as the "evil genius" of the young musicians. Despite his erroneous aesthetic views, in a number of articles he evaluated various contemporary works correctly and aptly. His observations on the music of Debussy, Stravinsky, Strauss, and Schoenberg were discerning and to the point. He did not hesitate to point out the weaknesses in their music, its narrow and sometimes superficial reflection of reality. In Prokofiev, his favorite, he noted and encouraged not only the exotic "Scythianism" and grotesquerie, but also the genuine tendency toward lyricism. Some of Karatygin's brilliantly written articles on the early works of Prokofiev are still pertinent today.

It was at the Evenings of Modern Music that many compositions by the most important Russian composers of the post-Scriabin generation—Stravinsky, Prokofiev, and Miaskovsky—were given their first performance. While Miaskovsky, as he put it, "did not become one of them" [the modernists], his younger colleague Prokofiev accepted their artistic precepts for many years. They abetted and championed Prokofiev in his most daring creative plans. Those who regarded everything with cynical sarcasm, particularly Nuvel and Nurok, supported in every way the young musician's interest in formal innovation, in violating the rules of classical music.

The Moscow modernists, grouped around the magazine *Muzyka* and its editor Derzhanovsky, professed the same principles as those of the St. Petersburg Evenings of Modern Music. "Our offspring is the only bulwark of modernism in Russia," wrote Derzhanovsky of his magazine (in a letter to the composer V. Rebikov, dated December 3, 1912).

Naturally *Muzyka* maintained the same aloofness from the people's political struggle, the same exaggerated reverence for the fashionable tendencies of impressionism and symbolism, for modernist Western music. The magazine extolled the latest works of Schoenberg, Stravinsky, and Scriabin. In critical articles by L. Sabaneyev, B. Popov, and others, it ridiculed and denounced works by the composers of the realistic school. It came out against the national traditions in contemporary Russian music, against "art's serving the immediate interests and vanities of the day," against the ideological principles expounded by Maxim Gorky.*

The Derzhanovsky group had its own forum for the presentation of new works—the concert stage in Sokolniki Park, where, beginning in 1908, they offered a series of summer concerts under the leadership of the conductor Konstantin Saradzhev. Here, at the Sokolniki Circle, symphonic works by Debussy, Ravel, Dukas, Satie, Roger-Ducasse, and Florent Schmitt as well as works by the modern Russian composers S. Vasilenko, A. Krein, R. Glière, V. Senilov, and A. Yurasovsky, were performed for

* In No. 67, 1912, the magazine criticized composers who wrote "without sophistication," meaning "those who, in music, resemble Serafimovich and other apers of Gorky in literature."

the first time in Russia. Here, too, were presented such young and as yet unrecognized performers as the pianists S. Feinberg, A. Borovsky, and N. Orlov and the singer Nina Koshetz. On the recommendation of Kryzhanovsky, the young St. Petersburgites Prokofiev and Miaskovsky were also introduced into the Derzhanovsky-Saradzhev group. It cannot be denied that despite his erroneous views Derzhanovsky was a sincere and sensitive man who tried to encourage gifted young Russian musicians.*

It was in the columns of *Muzyka* that Miaskovsky, from 1911 to 1914, played a brief but fruitful role as a critic. Here too, at the very beginning of 1914, the modest St. Petersburg musician Asafyev, then pianist-accompanist of the Maryinsky Theater ballet, appeared as a critic (under the pseudonym "Igor Glebov," coined for him by the magazine's editor). These talented musicians subsequently occupied a leading place in the history of Soviet music.

The penetrating and perceptive articles of Miaskovsky and Asafyev were a departure from *Muzyka*'s cliquish tone. Dealing with real, vital problems, they contrasted sharply with the idealistic nonsense which filled the writings of the modern music experts. In 1912, for example, the magazine published a polemical article by Miaskovsky entitled "Beethoven and Tchaikovsky," in which the author voiced a daring protest against the shameful "anti-Tchaikovskyism" which had become fashionable in modernist circles. In coming out against the degrading fashion of groveling before foreign musical idols, Miaskovsky was fighting for the interests of young Russian composers.

"It seems to me that we have to dispel the mist which has befogged so many weak minds here in St. Petersburg," he exclaimed in one of his letters. "In our country, because of the fuss that is made about everything foreign, we turn away from everything of our own with truly Russian vandalism. This must be eradicated."[6]

Miaskovsky and Asafyev carried on an active struggle in *Muzyka* for public recognition of Prokofiev, contrasting his spiritual wholesomeness and youthful vigor to the spineless art of the epigoni of impressionism. These opinions sometimes ran counter to the basic principles of the magazine.

In the early years of the century new concert organizations, set up along European lines, became active in St. Petersburg and Moscow. Both of these enterprises, subsidized by wealthy patrons, courted modernist

* Witness Prokofiev's inscription on a photograph presented to Derzhanovsky, "To a Valiant Fighter for Honest Music."

circles and competed successfully with the old concert organizations (the Russian Musical Society and the Belyaev concerts), which were on the decline.

The St. Petersburg organization was established in 1903 by the famous pianist and conductor Alexander Siloti, and became particularly popular just before the First World War. Siloti, a pupil of Liszt and a relative of Rachmaninov, was married to the daughter of the Moscow merchant P. Tretyakov, a well-known art patron and founder of the famous Tretyakov Gallery. He had close connections with industrialists, among them the owners of the Triangle Rubber Factory and the sugar magnate Tereshchenko, who supported his concert activities. Siloti invited the foremost foreign conductors to direct his concerts, which included works by fashionable (and sometimes third-rate) foreign composers.

The Moscow organization was set up somewhat later by the noted double-bass player and conductor Serge Koussevitzky, a colorful personality of old Moscow. He married a millionairess of the merchant class, Natalya Ushkova, and with her financial support founded not only a concert enterprise but also his own music publishing firm, the Russian Music Publishing House. The Ushkov fortune enabled him to establish his own orchestra in Moscow and arrange a series of glamorous concerts.

A gifted conductor, trained by Nikisch, Koussevitzky became famous in Russia and later also abroad as an active exponent of new Russian music. His artistic freethinking and generous sponsorship of native talent won him praise. But the musicians associated with him often became irked by his posing and *nouveau riche* polish. Koussevitzky left Russia after the October Revolution, and later occupied a prominent place in the musical life of the United States as the conductor of the Boston Symphony Orchestra.

Neither Siloti nor Koussevitzky was averse to causing a sensation, to stunning a concert audience with the last word in musical fashion. Therefore, as soon as they were certain that Prokofiev's name had become popular with the public and the press, they both willingly promoted him.

Another enterprise which was to have a great deal to do with Prokofiev's artistic development also came into being at about this time. This was the Russian ballet company founded by Sergei Diaghilev. A leader of the World of Art group, a critic-aesthete who not long before had declared that "the artist should love only beauty" and not concern himself with "worldly cares and woes," Diaghilev became an enterprising exporter of Russian ballet, striving in every way to please the tastes of his foreign clientele. In 1909, with the financial help of various patrons, he organized a sensational tour of his company to Paris, London, and other European cities.

At first the Diaghilev productions demonstrated the brilliant art of the best masters of Russian choreography and the World of Art painters. But in response to the demands of the Western bourgeois audiences, Diaghilev gradually resorted to modernist tricks and barbaric exoticism, which were enjoying particular success in Europe. Indeed, it was the Diaghilev ballet company that gave birth to the most typical expressions of pre-revolutionary Russian musical modernism—Stravinsky's *Petrushka* and *The Rite of Spring,* Prokofiev's *Ala and Lolli* and *The Buffoon.*

The modernist leaders' cosmopolitan tendencies could not but engender a feeling of disgust among the most honest Russian musicians. Asafyev was incensed at Diaghilev's unprincipled practice of playing up to foreigners. In letters and articles, the young Miaskovsky protested vigorously against the shameless slighting of Russian national traditions, against the decadent critics' scornful attitude toward the music of Tchaikovsky, Medtner, and other composers not pleasing to them. Both he and Prokofiev spoke out against the fashionable "Frenchifying" of Russian music, against the obscure symbolist ravings which appeared regularly in *Muzyka.** But at that time neither Miaskovsky, Asafyev, nor Prokofiev was yet able to discern the true nature of Russian modernism, and they remained for many years prisoners of its harmful influences.

The general atmosphere in Russia was steadily growing more ominous and tense. The working-class movement was gaining strength. The imperialist war deepened still further the workers' resentment against the decaying bourgeois-landowner order. But the vast majority of intellectuals and artists, including musicians, seemed unaware of these historic changes.

The impending war and revolution were reflected, in a way, in the most brilliant compositions of the period, but this reflection was oblique and to a large extent distorted. Composers deliberately turned to subjects unrelated to contemporary life, expressing not so much a belief in a better, brighter future as an unconscious fear of approaching events, a foreboding of imminent catastrophe. Anxious echoes of the times were variously em-

---

* "Nothing seems to have been forgotten—neither Ormazd, nor Kant, nor Spinoza, nor anything else under the sun. Nothing is missing, it seems, except the Apocalypse and Lobachevsky's transcendental geometry," Miaskovsky wrote Derzhanovsky apropos of certain articles in *Muzyka.* Prokofiev spoke equally caustically about the hazy "profundities" which seemed accidentally to get into *Muzyka* instead of *Satirikon.*

bodied in Scriabin's *Prometheus* (1911), Stravinsky's *Rite of Spring* (1913), Rachmaninov's *Bells* (1913), and Miaskovsky's *Third Symphony* (1914). The mood of uneasy expectation also affected Prokofiev somewhat (as can be seen in the Second Piano Concerto, *Sarcasms,* and the *Scythian Suite*), although on the whole, even in those dark years, pessimism was alien to him.

This, then, was the creative atmosphere in which the young Prokofiev matured as an artist and won recognition. The aesthetic views of the St. Petersburg modernists and the Moscow *Muzyka,* set forth in articles by Karatygin and in statements by Diaghilev, turned the young musician away from the noble ideals bequeathed him by his teachers. The enthusiasm for modernism fenced him off from life and the people's struggle, and barred the way to comprehensible, democratic art. But the best that Prokofiev created during the years of his youth ran counter to the empty formalism of the modernists and revealed direct ties with the traditions of realistic Russian music.

❦   ❦   ❦

> And suddenly he grew a lion's mane,
> A lion's pointed claw,
> And skittishly the art did demonstrate
> Of touching with one's paw.
>
> V. Khlebnikov

The year 1911 was an important one in Prokofiev's career. In that year his music was first published, it was performed for the first time at a public symphony concert, and he wrote his first mature work, the First Piano Concerto, which represented a synthesis of many of his youthful efforts. His name appeared more and more frequently in the St. Petersburg press, and his performances of the First and Second Piano Concertos in 1912 and 1913 evoked wide public comment.

After his father's death, Prokofiev, who thus far had known no financial difficulties, had to make his own way. It was not an easy struggle, for young Russian composers received no encouragement from publishers, critics, or concert organizations. Miaskovsky wrote with feeling about the "really outrageous situation of talented young men who have nowhere to go." He bitterly criticized the organizers of symphony concerts for their indifference to young Russian composers. "Oh, if I were a music publisher, I would make every effort to spare poor composers the disgusting indignities to which they are so often subjected, and mainly for business reasons and to please someone's vanity," he wrote to Derzhanovsky.[7]

Miaskovsky himself endured such treatment, as did Asafyev (in connection with his ballets), Prokofiev, and others of their generation. As early as 1910 Prokofiev tried in vain to have his works published, turning now to Jurgenson, now to Bessel, now to Koussevitzky's Russian Music Publishing House. His first two works were rejected by Koussevitzky's firm. Jurgenson did not want to be bothered with the unknown composer either, despite flattering recommendations by Taneyev and Glière ("Jurgenson has replied that he is swamped with manuscripts and has no time to look through new composers," he wrote Glière).[8] Equally fruitless were his attempts to break through to the concert stage. Appeals to the conductor E. Cooper for a performance of *Dreams* and *Autumnal Sketch* brought no result. ("Three months have passed, and Cooper is still silent and has not answered my inquiries. I would like to know whether or not he will play *Dreams*. I beg you to find out. This is extremely important to me," we read in the same letter.)

Finally, when he went to Jurgenson a second time with a letter from A. V. Ossovsky, Prokofiev got what he wanted—the Moscow publisher accepted his first four works. The terms were extremely unfavorable, to be sure—100 rubles for the First Sonata and twelve piano pieces. Recalling this later, the composer wrote to his first publisher, not without sarcasm, "A few years ago, when I came to you an unwanted Conservatory student, I gave you my works without any discussion for a kopek a bushel."[9] However, "the ice was broken," and from 1911 to 1916 Jurgenson published the first two Sonatas, almost thirty piano pieces (Op. 2, 3, 4, 11, 12, 17), and the First Piano Concerto. Prokofiev had to fight stubbornly with the excessively calculating publisher for his rights (for the publication of "unprofitable" works, for fair royalties). But he had youthful impertinence, persistence, and growing fame on his side, and Jurgenson invariably yielded to his demands.

In July 1911 Prokofiev's symphonic works were performed for the first time on the concert stages of Moscow and St. Petersburg. True, these were second-class concerts—in summer parks, far from the academic concert halls. But the critics took note of them (although in a very unfriendly way), and the composer felt stimulated to go on with his creative work.

The first of these concerts took place at the Sokolniki Circle in Moscow. Here, on July 14, *Dreams* received its initial performance under the baton of K. S. Saradzhev. On August 1 *Autumnal Sketch* was presented on the same platform under the direction of A. K. Medtner, brother of the famous composer. It was Saradzhev (later to become People's Artist of the Armenian S.S.R. and Director of the Yerevan Conservatory) who was responsible for these premières. The leaders of the Sokolniki summer concerts were interested in young Russian musicians. When Saradzhev went to St. Petersburg, I. Kryzhanovsky, one of the leaders of the Evenings of Modern Music, introduced him to two promising composers—Miaskovsky and Prokofiev. As a result of this introduction, Miaskovsky's symphonic poem *Silence* and Prokofiev's *Dreams* and *Autumnal Sketch* were included in the Sokolniki concerts.

Both of Prokofiev's pieces (as well as Miaskovsky's *Silence*) received extremely unfavorable reviews. The critic for *Golos Moskvy* wrote, "It seems to me a mistake to give so much attention to this callow youth, this musical fledgling—twice in one season. For his own good it would be better to wait. In scope of talent, Mr. Prokofiev approximates Kalinnikov. I believe that he would write in much the same vein, too, were he as sincere as Borodin and other St. Petersburgites. But he is affected. He wants desperately to be a modernist, even though modernism does not become him at all."[10]

In July 1911 Prokofiev also made his debut in St. Petersburg, at a concert in the Pavlovsk Vauxhall, where *Dreams* was performed under the direction of A. Kankarovich.

The two friends, Prokofiev and Miaskovsky, accepted the critics' hostile attacks stoically. When the modernist magazine *Apollon* viciously berated Miaskovsky for his piece *Silence,* he called the criticism "amateurish stupidity." In a letter to Derzhanovsky, he warmly defended Prokofiev against the Moscow critics' attacks. "In your Moscow he has been given an unfriendly reception," he wrote, "but I dare to consider him, in talent and originality, far superior to Stravinsky. Of course, he lacks Stravinsky's stunning technique, but that can be acquired. Meanwhile, in ability to speak in his own language Prokofiev unquestionably surpasses Stravinsky."[11]

Excited by the work in the opera class at the Conservatory, Prokofiev began to write a new opera. It was his dream to produce it with the students in the class and the Conservatory orchestra and chorus. For his text he chose a one-act play, *Maddalena,* by a young St. Petersburg poetess, M. Lieven.[12] In early September he finished the piano score and showed it to Miaskovsky, who was greatly impressed with the music and reported in a letter to Derzhanovsky, "One feels how his talent has grown of late. Aside from the thoroughly unusual harmonic writing, which is at times startling in its freshness and somber power, the volcanic quality of his temperament is astonishing. In intensity of style, it calls to mind the operas of Richard Strauss, but it lacks Strauss's banalities."[13]

M. Lieven's play, written in rather mediocre verse, was a stylized melodrama in the spirit of the old Italian novella.

The scene is set in fifteenth-century Venice. The artist Gennaro is painting a portrait of the Madonna, using as his model his sweetheart, the beautiful young girl Maddalena. A passionate love scene between them is interrupted by the singing of gondoliers heard in the distance. The poetry, like that of Mariya Kilschtedt's *Undine,* reeks with cheap literary pretentiousness:

> Is it your fault that you are beautiful as the day,
> That your tresses, like fiery serpents,
> Gleam in the dark; with living coils
> Slither, caress, beckon, and intoxicate.

At the climax of the love scene, the terrifying Stenio, a learned alchemist and Maddalena's former lover, appears. The rivals engage in a duel and kill each other to the accompaniment of ominous peals of thunder. The heartless beauty, rejoicing in her freedom, looks indifferently at their bodies:

> Which of you did Maddalena love?
> Perhaps neither. A long, quiet sleep!

The young Prokofiev could hardly have been interested in M. Lieven's melodrama for the "beauty" of its language and its decadent theme. What interested him primarily in this panegyric on the fatal hopelessness of love and the cynicism of a callous hetaera was its concentrated, swiftly developing action and striking dramatic effects.

Rejecting set operatic "numbers" almost entirely, the composer constructed the whole opera on harsh, tense recitative with a harmonically well-defined accompaniment. The single melodious episode in the opera is the chorus of the gondoliers off stage. After listening to this music, Asafyev and Saradzhev, while noting its genuine dramatic qualities and the authenticity of the melodic material, pointed out its lack of warmth and tunefulness and the awkwardness of the vocal parts. According to Saradzhev, *Maddalena* was a kind of sketch for *The Gambler* in terms of the composer's free and unusual treatment of the operatic genre.

"Such a work could hardly be produced here, despite its theatrical effectiveness," Miaskovsky maintained. "I have never come across more difficult vocal parts, and as for the approval of the big shots, it hasn't got a chance."

Actually, Prokofiev did not succeed in having *Maddalena* produced, either at the Conservatory or at K. Mardzhanov's Free Theater in Moscow, where, with Saradzhev's help, a run-through was arranged in 1913. The director Mardzhanov (subsequently one of the creators of the Soviet Georgian Theater) was very much interested in it and appreciated the "dramatic intensity" of Prokofiev's music. However, the opera was not produced, for the Free Theater was closed.[14]

*Maddalena* heads the list of Prokofiev operas (*The Gambler, The Flaming Angel,* and others) which were not readily accepted for production because of their excessive vocal difficulty and the composer's flat rejection of certain important principles of operatic realism. But more will be said about this later.

While the fate of *Maddalena* was being decided at the Conservatory, Prokofiev continued to work intensely on the First Piano Concerto. This composition had originally been conceived as a modest concertino. In September 1911 Miaskovsky wrote to his Moscow friends, "Prokofiev is working on a charming, lively, and sonorous concertino for piano and orchestra. The piano part is very unusual and difficult, but the material contains a great deal that is fresh and fascinating."[15]

Working in a large instrumental form excited the composer, and the concertino gradually grew into a one-movement concerto with an extremely difficult virtuoso piano part. By winter it was finished, and he played it for friends.

"It has turned out to be a very interesting, brilliant, and sonorous piece," wrote Miaskovsky to the editor of *Muzyka*. "If you have time this summer, how about giving it a try? It might cause a sensation, but what kind no one knows, since there's much in it that is startling."[16]

Here Miaskovsky was referring to the possibility of having the Concerto included in Saradzhev's summer programs in line with Prokofiev's recent debut at the Sokolniki Circle. Miaskovsky's hopes were realized. On August 7, 1912, the Concerto had its première performance in the Moscow People's House with the composer as soloist and Saradzhev conducting. This was Prokofiev's first solo appearance with an orchestra. He had worked stubbornly on the orchestration, probably in consultation with Cherepnin, to whom the Concerto was dedicated. Miaskovsky helped

Prokofiev selflessly, participating in negotiations with the orchestra and correcting the orchestral parts.

The première went off brilliantly. The young composer captivated the audience with the power and dynamism of his playing and the freshness of his music. On August 16 he again performed it successfully at the Pavlovsk Vauxhall in St. Petersburg with A. P. Aslanov conducting.

❦ ❦ ❦

The First Piano Concerto in D-flat major was, for the young Prokofiev, something in the nature of a creative declaration. He himself considered it his "first more or less mature work, in terms of both the conception and its realization" (meaning the method of combining the piano and orchestra, and the original treatment of the one-movement, "poem-like" structure). It vividly represented Prokofiev's own distinctive piano style, combining the massive texture of chords and octaves with very difficult "acrobatic" leaps and pearly, étude-like runs. For the first time it united in a single dramatically developed structure the typical features of Prokofiev's style—the buoyancy and dynamic drive of the motor and dance themes (introduction and main theme), the nervous, tense expressiveness (subordinate theme), and the pure, dreamy lyricism (slow middle episode in G-sharp minor).

The Concerto is cast in one movement with a solemn introduction and conclusion. The thrice-repeated statement of the introductory theme (at the beginning, middle, and end of the piece) constitutes, according to the composer, the basis—the "three whales"—upon which the entire composition rests. The powerful opening phrase of the introduction, repeatedly stated in the high registers of the piano, sounds imperious, challenging (Fig. 8).

After this majestic and imperative opening the piano bursts in with a cadenza, deliberately "prosaic," in the manner of a technical exercise, but difficult, abounding in daring leaps and runs. The resilient, sharply defined pattern of the main theme in D-flat major is that of a fast dance, much like a tarantella. Here, the piano sounds metallic, resonant, and brilliant. The dialogue between soloist and orchestra creates the impression of an exciting competition of virtuosos.

When the hammering toccata-like motion reaches its climax, the subordinate theme enters (*meno mosso* in E minor). Its character is sad, almost mournful, but the unusual twists of the melody and the pungency of the orchestration endow it with a strange, fantastic quality. The second

FIGURE 8

element of the subordinate theme, nervous and agitated, sounds like the "frightening moment" of a fairy tale. Suddenly this gives way to a new, fanciful dance, which is gay, almost clownish. This theme, accompanied by complicated figurations in the piano part, is entrusted mainly to the orchestra.

At the conclusion of the exposition, the majestic theme of the introduction is heard again. This time it leads to a slow, contemplative episode (*andante assai* in G-sharp minor)—a charming oasis of intimate restrained lyricism typical of Prokofiev. Finally, after a scherzo-like development section, the recapitulation begins. It is introduced by a complicated cadenza based on the material of the first theme and a considerably modified and shortened statement of the subordinate and concluding themes. The triumphant coda restates in full the virile music of the introduction.

The entire Concerto leaves the impression of a varicolored, rhapsodic tonal canvas, in which buoyant rhythms and brilliant virtuosity predominate. The small island of lyricism in the middle of the Concerto remains unnoticed, pushed aside by the brilliance, the daring "athleticism," and a certain harshness in the principal ideas. This is one of the first works by Prokofiev in which we find the lyrical and romantic element retreating into the background under the thunderous onslaught of powerful, dynamically resilient themes.

The First Concerto called forth extremely contradictory comments in the newspapers and magazines of Moscow and St. Petersburg. The critics were sharply divided into wildly enthusiastic admirers and implacable opponents of Prokofiev.

The chief enemy of Prokofiev's music, Leonid Sabaneyev, came out with a devastating review in *Golos Moskvy*. "This energetic, rhythmic, harsh, coarse, primitive cacophony hardly deserves to be called music," he wrote. "In his search for 'novelty,' a quality that he lacks in the inner depths of his nature, the composer had definitely overreached himself. Such things simply do not happen with a real talent."[17]

The critic Gr. Prokofiev echoed Sabaneyev in *Russkiye Vedomosti*, noting in the First Concerto "harsh writing and a complete unwillingness to compromise with the listener's taste."[18]

The gutter press hastened to declare Prokofiev a madman, demanding that he be put in a "strait jacket."[19] "His professor, Cherepnin, has expressed the thought that the Concerto is madly talented. For the time being the composer's madness has gotten the better of his talent, and he has written a score which might properly be called 'musical mud,'" quipped the reactionary critic N. Bernstein.[20]

The reviewers eagerly reported that two symphonic scherzos by César Cui were also performed at the Pavlovsk concert, and that the "works of the fighting former member of the Five seemed like child's prattle" compared to Prokofiev's Concerto.

On the other hand, Florestan (Derzhanovsky) in Moscow and Karatygin in St. Petersburg praised the First Concerto unreservedly. Derzhanovsky noted in it "brilliance, wit, piquancy, and humor within a general frame of impressive splendor."[21] Karatygin, after commenting on its "rather rhapsodic form" and certain defects in the orchestration, emphasized that "the music pulsates throughout, sparkles with brilliant imagination."[22]

One critic even tried, timidly, to define Prokofiev's place in the history of Russian music: "Prokofiev may even mark a state in the development of Russian music: the first stage being Glinka and Rubinstein, the second Tchaikovsky and Rimsky-Korsakov, the third Glazunov and Arensky, the fourth Scriabin and . . . and . . . Prokofiev. Why not?"[23]

Despite the unfavorable reaction of most of the critics, the concert audiences of both capitals regarded Prokofiev with interest, admiring his youthful self-assurance and the vitality of his performance.

"His tone was hard and somewhat dry, but he played with amazing assurance and freedom," wrote one critic. "Beneath his fingers the piano does not sing and vibrate. It speaks in the stern and precise tone of a percussion instrument . . . the tone of the old-fashioned harpsichord. But it was precisely the convincing freedom of his playing and the clear-cut rhythm that won the composer such enthusiastic applause from the audience."[24]

The derisive comments did not intimidate Prokofiev in the least. On the contrary, he carefully collected all the abusive reviews, and in letters to friends bitingly ridiculed his enemies.[25] At the same time the friendly articles heartened him, strengthened his confidence in his own talent, and spurred him on to even more daring efforts.

The active support given his works by the magazine *Muzyka* played a special role in Prokofiev's creative development. Here, in 1912 and 1913, appeared Miaskovsky's discerning and enthusiastic comments on the piano pieces, Op. 3 and Op. 4, the *Études,* Op. 2, the First Concerto, and other works. In his review of the Concerto he sharply contrasted the life-affirming character of Prokofiev's music with the listless works of the epigoni of impressionism and "World-of-Artiness."

"What a pleasure and surprise it is to come upon this vibrant and healthy phenomenon amid today's widespread effeminacy, debility, and anaemia," wrote Miaskovsky.[26] He expressed the hope that Prokofiev's music, "with its freshness, power, and unusual robustness, will breathe a little life into the flaccid and often quite stuffy atmosphere of our concert life."[27]

Just over a year later Asafyev, an equally tireless advocate of the young Prokofiev's music, picked up and enlarged upon this thought in the same magazine. "There is no doubt," he wrote, "that we are face to face with real beauty, austere and a bit tart, perhaps, for our delicate taste, but no less acceptable because of this than the ultra-refined, toxic beauty of Stravinsky's tonal charms."[28]

Asafyev tried to find in Prokofiev's music signs of a new artistic *Weltanschauung,* coming to replace moribund impressionism and symbolism.

"To us, his contemporaries, his music seems strange," Asafyev asserted. "Can it be our life, our age that is reflected here? We are in a morass. On one hand we are gripped by a hysterical fear of the ominous power of fate, and on the other, we are attuned to a languid delicacy and fragility —that is, to an art for mimosas, timidly hiding from life."[29]

The writings of Miaskovsky and Asafyev, directed against the musical gourmets in their ivory tower undoubtedly had a progressive purport.

Their views, we must remember, ran counter to the basic viewpoint of the journal *Muzyka*. At the same time it could hardly be said that Miaskovsky and Asafyev were fighting for Prokofiev from consistently realistic positions. In their excitement over the novelty and freshness of his music, they failed to consider the perils that lay in wait for the young composer in his striving toward new shores, and above all, the danger of being cut off from classical traditions, from the spiritual and intellectual bases of progressive Russian art.

The editors of *Muzyka* persuaded Prokofiev to try his hand at music criticism. He wrote some critical notes on the works of Miaskovsky, Stravinsky, and Stanchinsky, and a few brief analyses of his own works. "I don't think that I'd make a bad critic, but I'd be a real beast," he remarked caustically in his diary.

The young Prokofiev's articles clearly reflected the aesthetic opinions he held at that time. An eager desire for originality and a deep-seated contempt for all imitativeness, for the "beaten path"—this was the budding critic's basic position. He severely criticized performers who were afraid to play new works.

In his review of Miaskovsky's First Piano Sonata we read, "When I drew the attention of one pianist to the new sonata, he replied, 'What? No, thank you. I had better learn all the Beethoven sonatas before tackling something new.' Very commendable but utterly hopeless. For this pompous attitude, so typical of our pianists, is dictated not by lofty feelings for old idols but by a fear of the tastes of the mob, by a laziness about tackling something new, and, most important, by an appalling ignorance of what is good and what is bad. And what if it is not good?! The more complicated a thing is, the more our conforming pianists shy away from it and the closer they stick to the beaten path of Peters's and Litolff's editions."[30]

In the young composer's observations there is both a suggestion of disrespect for old idols and a scorn for the backward tastes of the general audience.

Like his friend Miaskovsky, Prokofiev came out in defense of the national honor of Russian musicians and against the humiliating worship of everything foreign. On Stanchinsky's piano *Sketches* he wrote, "The composer loves to ape the French. He is ashamed of his Russian origin. At least he cannot bring himself to sign his name in Russian to his own Russian compositions!"[31]

The young critic was equally severe and outspoken in condemning lack of originality and passive borrowing. In an unpublished note on Sabaneyev's piano pieces he accuses the composer of slavishly imitating Scriabin. "A limited store of native talent has forced Mr. Sabaneyev to draw from outside sources, particularly from Scriabin's broad stream. In certain pieces the borrowing is so obvious that they cease to have any value."[32]

At the same time, works in which the musical style (above all, the harmony) was striking evoked Prokofiev's keenest interest and unqualified praise. He expressed a special admiration for Stravinsky's *Three Little Songs for Voice and Piano.* In these subtly stylized miniatures on Russian folk themes, he was attracted by the "piquant" combination of an "artlessly simple" vocal part and "complex accompaniment." "Though the accompaniment is really clear and simple in design, it often pricks the ear with its unusual harmonies."

While strongly disapproving the use of simple and traditional melodic patterns as a manifestation of banality, Prokofiev was ready to forgive composers this sin provided the harmonies were fresh. Thus, in one of Stanchinsky's *Sketches* he was disappointed in the "simple Rubinstein-like theme, which is not free of stereotyped figures." However, the "complex harmonies and a certain dramatic quality save the piece from triteness."

Prokofiev's critical comments reveal, on the one hand, his avid interest in novel, piquant harmonies, which "nip the listener's ear," and on the other hand, a dread of traditional melodic patterns, of lyrical communicativeness, which he considered "banality." These predilections, so typical of the young Prokofiev, become more and more apparent in his works of 1912–13.

In the intervals between his Conservatory studies with Esipova and Cherepnin, and between frequent appearances at student recitals, Prokofiev worked continuously. Most of his time was spent on piano compositions —experimenting, inventing, seeking original means of expression. An interest in sharpening the harmonies and enriching the texture of virtuoso passages can be seen more and more frequently in his works of this period.

In the spring of 1912 he composed the very difficult piano *Toccata,* Op. 11, which startled audiences with its daring harmonies and impetuous rhythms. In verve and intensity this was a direct continuation of the most brilliant piece in Op. 4, *Diabolic Suggestions.*

In a letter dated April 24, 1912, Miaskovsky wrote, "Not long ago S. Prokofiev composed a little thing that I am absolutely mad about—a piano toccata. It is devilishly clever, biting, energetic, and typical. The themes are extremely simple and original. It may seem strange that I should write a whole dithyramb to a piece of some ten or twelve pages, but I cannot refrain from shouts of rapture. So far this is one of his best, and, in any case, it is a most mature work."

A few years later Asafyev also wrote about this tempestuous *perpetuum mobile*: "When one speaks of kinetics in music—that is, of the embodiment in music of motion in some stage or other—and of the disclosure of the purely dynamic nature of tonal material, one thinks immediately of Prokofiev's beautifully constructed, resilient, and powerful piano *Toccata*."

Indeed, rhythmic drive, abandon, and sweep of motion are powerfully presented in this *Toccata*. Seemingly bursting all dikes, the uncontrollable torrent gushes forth. There is a feeling of heroic strength, and youthful, exultant laughter, suddenly giving way to moments of gentle reverie. The essence of a ceaseless rhythmic race is set forth in strangely fantastic tones through the use of pungent and percussive timbres, harsh suspensions, and contrapuntal devices.

Apparent in the *Toccata,* as in both the *Études,* Op. 2, and the bravura passages of the First Concerto, is Prokofiev's passion for motive power, for "common forms" of motion. This predominance of motor images, of pure rhythm over melos, we shall also encounter many times in Prokofiev's later toccata-like works, right up to the Fifth Concerto [1932] and the Seventh Sonata [1940]. At the same time both the *Toccata* and the *Études,* Op. 2, contain moments of vivid, realistic descriptiveness. Toccata devices proved extremely useful to the composer in a number of his works for the theater, especially for depicting headlong pursuits, dramatic skirmishes, and clashes of hostile forces. Two examples of this are the "brawl music" in *Romeo and Juliet* and "Severyan's Pursuit of the Mistress" in *The Stone Flower.* In these instances the bewitching element of rhythm served to reproduce faithfully the disturbing pages of life.*

In the same year that he composed the *Toccata,* Prokofiev wrote the charming piano *Scherzo* in A minor; this was another virtuoso piece abounding in passage work, but otherwise different from the *Toccata*—gentle, lacy, and romantically picturesque, with an elegant, mock-lyrical middle section and subtle interplays of rhythm in the recapitulation. Here inspired poetry overshadows daring construction. This was one of Prokofiev's first pieces to interest concert pianists. As early as 1916 Alexander Borovsky played it successfully at one of his concerts.[33]

* The *Toccata,* Op. 11, has remained in the Soviet concert repertoire (E. Gilels, L. Oborin, and others).

Prokofiev spent the summer of 1912 in Kislovodsk, where his mother usually went for the cure. He combined reading and hikes in the mountains with persistent creative work. Here he completed his most important composition of 1912, the Second Piano Sonata, Op. 14 (begun in March, finished on September 10).

This sonata was not conceived all at one stroke. In those years Prokofiev still originally thought in terms of small pieces, and it was only in the process of composition that larger forms took shape. Thus the First Piano Concerto had grown out of a youthful concertino, and the First Violin Concerto out of a violin concertino. It was approximately in this way, too, that the Second Piano Sonata developed from a one-movement sonatina. At first the sonatina grew into a romantic sonata allegro. To this was later added a scherzo (originally composed in Lyadov's class) and two more movements. Compared with the purely propulsive *Toccata,* the Second Sonata is far more imaginative and broader in emotional range.

The Piano Sonata No. 2, Op. 14, is one of young Prokofiev's finest achievements. Compared with the First Sonata, which is stylistically immature, it represents a great step forward; it is the work of a completely mature creative personality.

"In the Second Sonata," Asafyev observed, "the wings of the imagination have grown so strong that at each step one can sense Prokofiev's willful and stubborn striving. One can hear him say, 'Thus I wish it. Thus let it be!' "[34]

The four movements of the Sonata—Allegro, Scherzo, Andante, and fast Finale—differ sharply in mood, though linked organically by a common conception and even at times by common melodic material. In the almost ceaseless flow of contrasting images and moods, the hand of the future dramatist makes itself felt. Just as in an intensely dynamic play or motion picture, frame replaces frame and scene replaces scene swiftly and naturally. All the episodes are set forth concisely and succinctly, without lengthy bridge passages and transitions.

A very important element in the basic construction of this work is its piano texture, which is closely related to that of Mozart and Beethoven. Spare, two- or three-voiced exposition and clearly accented, non-legato playing predominate. Flexible rhythms, gay runs, and vigorous technical passages endow the Sonata with buoyancy, health, and youthful exuberance. In addition to the typically pianistic, sharply accented passages, there are tender, lyrical episodes in the first and third movements. Throughout the

Sonata the minor mode, enriched by a complex use of alterations and modulations, is employed in a fresh and modern manner.

From its very first measure, the first movement, Allegro ma non troppo, captures the attention with its tense forward drive (combining a bass in triplets with a melody in duple meter) and soaring crescendo culminating in a sharply-defined, clipped cadence. This romantic surge of energy is interrupted by the second element of the first theme—a repeated "knocking" phrase—which applies a brake, as it were, to the initial motion. Then once again the impetuous theme is heard.

While the texture and rhythm are extremely simple and classical, the harmonic scheme is strikingly novel. The dominant is avoided; passing tones are subtly used; the counterpoint is fresh; and the use of deceptive modulations—sudden transitions to distant keys with free-flowing returns to the tonic—is original.

The agitated, soaring first theme gives way to a whirling, scherzo-like bridge passage. In sharply defined and measured motion, built on a single endlessly repeated descending phrase, a melancholy motiv enters, anticipating the melody of the second theme. When the measured motion subsides, the tender, wistful melody of the second theme appears—one of the best melodies in the Sonata (Fig. 9).

FIGURE 9

The contemplative, static quality of this theme is relieved by richly developed harmony, a beautiful succession of pure triads. The entire exposition is brought to a close in a strong cadential manner. Once again the brief, distinctive descending phrase of the bridge passage is heard.

A gradual retardation of the rhythm accentuates still more its provocative playfulness.

The development section proceeds in a fresh and unusual way. Here, too, contrasting "scenes" replace one another freely, as in an opera or a ballet. The charming second theme of the exposition returns in a new tonality, like a simple love song or a ballet adagio; this is followed by the appearance of the playful, whirling phrases of the bridge passage. And finally, in the middle of the development section the three elements are combined contrapuntally—the second theme (expanded), the "knocking" phrase of the first theme, and the descending figures of the bridge passage. The interweaving of these themes sounds natural, vivid, and exciting, and not at all like a contrived contrapuntal trick. This new cycle of motion leads to a strong climax, culminating in a series of powerful cadences. Then follows the recapitulation, which repeats the familiar material almost exactly, and a brief coda based on the material of the first theme.

This dramatic scene, in which romantic impulses alternate with a love dream or sly jest, is followed by the lively Scherzo. Here we find a direct continuation of the playful element of the first movement. The Scherzo is constructed on two sharply delineated themes. The first is an energetic, well-defined *perpetuum mobile*. Sharp exclamations are heard now and then over a ceaseless staccato. The swift tempo, the rhythmical precision of the leaps, the hand crossings, and the biting accents create the image of an exciting and lively youthful game. The energetic first theme gives way to a gay, rhythmical second theme. This is virtually a genre scene, depicting in a few ironic tones the motion of some sort of popular dance (calling to mind the swaying rhythms of Rachmaninov's *Polka*). Unexpected modulations and the static quality of the pedal point in the bass invest this dance episode with a special color. There is a notable similarity between the amusing theme of the dance and the descending octave phrases of the first movement. The three-part Scherzo concludes with a restatement of the opening *perpetuum mobile*, which mounts gradually from timid, scarcely audible "tapping" to powerful chordal passages.

The third movement of the Sonata is the most serious and profound. The twenty-year-old composer here demonstrated his ability not only to amuse and play merry tricks but also to observe intently the world about him. Over a smoothly swaying lullaby figure unfolds a prominent melody in declamatory style, which mounts gradually from quiet meditation to almost tragic pathos. Here the texture is thicker and richer than in the first two movements; the melody appears in combination with an intricate pattern of figurations. The second theme of the Andante, in 7/8 time, emerges like a tender recollection over a flowing chromatic line in the inner voice and a pedal point in the bass. Later the two themes of the Andante are repeated in modified form.

When the third movement ends in gloomy reflection, it suddenly gives way to the mischievous music of the Finale. At first the theme of the Finale seems to resemble the main theme of the first movement (the same whirling, tarantella-like motion in D minor), but soon lively, playful themes gain the upper hand. Humorous episodes flash by swiftly, as in a film. Festive garlands of gaily rushing descending passages lead into a provocative buffoon's dance. Once again sharp accents and biting percussive sounds are heard. But the frolicsome dance gradually subsides, and the lyrical theme of the first movement appears like a tender vision, sounding even more pensive and sweet. However, it is abruptly cut off by a new buffoon's dance with amusing grimaces; the composer, as if fearful of becoming too sentimental, here seems to break in on his poetic reverie with a rather coarse jest.[35] Later the playful themes whirl round and round as if in a fantastic vortex. This motion continues throughout the sharply dramatized development and the recapitulation, which repeats almost literally the material of the exposition. Then follows the coda, in which the two themes of the Finale are skillfully combined. The Sonata ends in a bacchanalia of laughter, dance, and energetic virtuosity.

Even now, forty years after it was written, the Second Sonata charms listeners with its theatrical concreteness—its bold juxtaposition of youthful excitement, dreamy lyricism, and infectious laughter. Some pianists have emphasized its grotesque, eccentric, and humorous features, but their interpretation violates the true spirit of Prokofiev's music. Unquestionably, it is the willful romantic impulse, the tireless force of life and youth that predominates here; the humor and lyricism only serve to emphasize this. More sensitive musicians, when speaking of the Second Sonata, recall the young Beethoven—his powerful "lion's grip," his daring virtuosity, and his plebeian humor.

The Second Sonata was followed immediately by a new instrumental work, a one-movement *Ballade* in C minor for cello and piano. It was written at the request of the amateur cellist N. P. Ruzsky, with whom Prokofiev played now and then. The young composer used as the main theme of this work the opening melody of the violin sonata he had written in

Sontsovka in 1903. This naïve, purely string theme, which appears several times as a refrain, proved to be the best melody of the *Ballade*, suiting perfectly the singing qualities of the cello.

The second theme, an agitated, rhythmically pronounced pizzicato over dry, percussive piano chords, is quite different in character. It has a gloomy and fantastic quality. The remaining themes of the piece are less expressive. They abound in contrived, angular figures which prove to be quite unidiomatic for the cello. The form of the piece, a broadly developed rondo, suffers from a looseness unusual for Prokofiev. The over-all mood, predominantly somber and restless, closely resembles that of the Second Piano Concerto, which appeared the following year. Prokofiev himself pointed out that the dramatically agitated passages of the *Ballade* were related stylistically to *Maddalena*.

Miaskovsky expressed great enthusiasm for this piece, maintaining that "it seems as though it had been written especially for Casals."[36] At the same time he also noted the melodic weakness of some of its themes. Karatygin was more severe in his appraisal. After commenting on certain "highly interesting moments," he noted that "on the whole, this piece is long-winded and poorly suited to the technical resources and possibilities of the cello."[37]

The *Ballade* was given its first performance by the Moscow cellist E. Belousov at a chamber recital of the Evenings of Modern Music on February 5, 1914.

✸   ✸   ✸

The success of the First Piano Concerto inspired Prokofiev to more radical experiments. Late in 1912 he composed some instrumental miniatures which revealed his interest in musical grotesquerie. These were the playful *Scherzo* for four bassoons and the first of the pieces which were later called *Sarcasms*. Like the *Toccata,* Op. 11, these works demonstrated the composer's predilection for piquant and daring harmonies. For the eccentric *Scherzo* for four bassoons, the composer chose a pertinent epigraph from Griboyedov's *Woe from Wit*: "that croaker, that strangler, the bassoon."* The piece is characterized by a deliberate combination of primitive rhythms and harsh harmonies. "One feels that the composer is trying too hard to be amusing," remarked Asafyev in one of his notes.

---

* The *Scherzo* exists in two versions: for piano solo (Op. 12, No. 9) and for an ensemble of four bassoons. In 1954 the Bolshoi Theater included it in the score of the ballet *The Stone Flower* as an inserted number (the comic "Dance of the Ram and the Goat" in the fair scene).

The growing refinement of Prokofiev's style manifested itself even more clearly in the Second Piano Concerto, also begun late in 1912. In this work the composer seemingly declared his right to an even more complex musical language and a more dramatic content than he had aspired to in the D-flat major Concerto, with its superficial bravura and athletic vigor. "The charges of surface brilliance and a certain 'football' quality in the First led me to strive for greater depth of content in the Second," the composer himself remarked.

His work on the Concerto progressed rapidly. Early in April 1913 Miaskovsky wrote to Moscow, "Serge Prokofiev is finishing his Second Piano Concerto in four movements. It is very fresh and interesting, and in a more intimate vein than the First, but also more difficult. He played some of it for me—there are wonderful bits, quite novel and most intriguing."[38] The new Concerto was included in the summer symphony concerts at Pavlovsk.

Indeed, the Second Concerto differs sharply from the First. Whereas youthful bravado predominates in the First, the Second is filled with uneasy agitation and dramatic outbursts. In the First the piano and orchestra are equal partners, but in the Second the piano dominates. Instead of using the concise, one-movement structure of the First Concerto, the composer chose to cast the Second in four movements: a stormy, romantic Andantino; an exciting, furiously dynamic Scherzo; an extremely "barbaric" Intermezzo; and a Finale in which grotesque images are juxtaposed with a singing theme in a Russian vein. In the Second Concerto gentle, soulful lyricism with a suggestion of fairy-tale narration clashes with an exaggerated expressiveness verging on frenzy.

The beautiful first theme of the opening movement is a majestic epic melody against the background of a rhythmically swaying triplet figure (Fig. 10). This broad, flowing theme (marked *narrante*) suggests a quiet, serious tale in the vein of a romantic legend. The austerity of the harmonic coloring is relieved by surprisingly warm and sweet-sounding modulations. The second theme has a different quality. It is a fanciful image, veiled in mystery—a rather dance-like theme suffused with ceremonial grace but adorned with capricious accents and light splashes of piano runs. This theme is given a complex development. The central place in the first movement is occupied by the dramatically heightened development section, which is set forth in the form of a magnificent cadenza. Here the music suggests a gloomy landscape charged with elemental power. The tones are steely and harsh, evoking pictures of turbulence in nature—surg-

FIGURE 10

ing waves, black storm clouds. The piano writing is in the grand manner, with large strokes predominating. And at the end of the first movement, as in a tale told by a bard, the opening epic melody is heard again.

The highly complicated Scherzo (second movement) consists of continuous passage work in the piano combined with extremely simplified rhythms in the orchestra, in the spirit of a primitive dance. The Intermezzo (third movement) has a sinister, fantastic coloration. The harshly exaggerated tonalities, the deliberately coarsened orchestral effects, and the absence of melodic clarity prefigure the expressionistic excesses of Prokofiev's style in the twenties. The images of archaic barbarism evoked by these sonorities call to mind certain passages in the *Scythian Suite* and in Stravinsky's *Rite of Spring.*

The same suggestion of untamed primordial forces dominates the extremely angular main theme of the Finale, which is veiled in complicated figurations and unusual leaps. Following this, we have once again the simple, romantic fantasy of the first movement. This lyrical Russian melody, accompanied by sadly swaying lullaby rhythms, recalls the lyricism of Moussorgsky. Like the second theme of the first movement, this lullaby theme undergoes very complex variation (comparable to that later found in the second movement of the Third Piano Concerto). The Finale concludes with a restatement of the main theme which is startling in its suggestion of cosmic power and savagery.

The unusual progressions, rhythmic tricks, and harsh polytonal combinations (such as the simultaneous use of G major and A major triads in the coda of the Finale)—all these compositional artifices and excesses bear witness to the young composer's desire to startle his listeners.

The exaggerated stylistic effects of the Second Concerto were noted even by Prokofiev's sincere admirers. Asafyev, although generally enthusiastic, drew attention to "a certain coarseness" in it and observed that some passages, especially in the Intermezzo, left "a tart aftertaste." ("The persistent attempt to startle with all sorts of devilish intervals annoys the ear.") And Karatygin, who was delighted by the Concerto, spoke of the "painful impression" left by the final coda: "The listener is frozen with fright, his hair stands on end, when the brasses sound the final chords of the concerto."[39] Both Asafyev and Karatygin criticized the composer severely for the artificiality of his orchestration and for his failure to think it through adequately.[40]

❦ ❦ ❦

The incongruity between style and content in the Second Concerto was in many respects symptomatic; as Prokofiev gained maturity, his work echoed more and more clearly the anxieties of the time. It will be recalled that just on the eve of the First World War pessimism and despair were common themes in Russian art. Motifs of gloom appeared in the poetry of the symbolists and in certain works by Rachmaninov and Miaskovsky.

"I have felt so morbid lately that if it were not for work, I would hang myself," exclaimed Miaskovsky in a letter in 1913. That same year another very close friend of Prokofiev, the young pianist Max Schmidthof, committed suicide. (Prokofiev dedicated the Second Piano Concerto to his memory.) However stoutly Prokofiev's healthy nature tried to withstand it, the oppressive atmosphere of the times forced its way into his life and work. Thus, in the Second Concerto (and in *Sarcasms* as well) one senses, along with lofty romanticism and fairy-tale imagery, traces of nervousness and morbidity. Later Asafyev correctly discerned a reflection of the ominous prewar atmosphere in the music of the Concerto, which he called "not so much brilliant as emotionally condensed, 'compressed' to the point of suffocation."

It was natural that this Concerto proved to be Prokofiev's ticket of admission to the highest circles of Russian modernism, bringing him success and the recognition of Diaghilev and Stravinsky.

❦ ❦ ❦

In the summer of 1913 Prokofiev left Russia for the first time. He visited London and Paris, and vacationed for a while in a small town in the Auvergne. While in Paris he heard Stravinsky's *Petrushka* for the first time.

Upon returning home, he diligently set about preparing for his important concert in Pavlovsk. On July 15 Miaskovsky reported in a letter, "He has just begun to memorize his astounding concerto."

On September 5 Prokofiev's name once again attracted the attention of St. Petersburg's musical circles. The occasion was the première of the Second Piano Concerto, which took place at Pavlovsk under the baton of Aslanov. The Concerto left the audience in a state of open bewilderment. Miaskovsky, who attended the concert, reported that the audience "hissed and often did not behave quite properly."[41]

The gutter press of St. Petersburg, delighted with the musical "incident," spared no words to make their account of it spicy. "The debut of the piano cubist and futurist has excited universal interest. On the train to Pavlovsk before the concert one heard on all sides, 'Prokofiev, Prokofiev, Prokofiev.' 'Here is a new piano star,'" exclaimed the feuilletonist of *Peterburgskaya Gazeta* in a detailed report of the sensation at Pavlovsk. "On the platform appears a youth with the face of a Peterschule student. It is Sergei Prokofiev. He seats himself at the piano and begins to strike the keyboard with a dry, sharp touch. He seems to be either dusting or testing the keys. The audience is bewildered. Some are indignant. One couple stands up and runs toward the exit. 'Such music is enough to drive you crazy!' 'What is he doing, making fun of us?' More listeners follow the first couple from various parts of the hall. Prokofiev plays the second movement of his Concerto. Again the rhythmical collection of sounds. The most daring members of the audience hiss. Here and there seats become empty. Finally the young artist ends his Concerto with a mercilessly discordant combination of brasses. The audience is scandalized. The majority hiss. Prokofiev bows defiantly and plays an encore. The audience rushes away. On all sides there are exclamations: 'To the devil with all this futurist music! We came here to enjoy ourselves. The cats at home can make music like this!'"[42]

Most of the critics could not find words to describe this violator of musical canons. Of the twelve reviews in the press, eight were sharply negative. Yu. Kurdyumov called the Concerto "a Babel of insane sounds heaped one upon another without rhyme or reason."[43] N. Bernstein found it "a cacophony of sounds that has nothing in common with civilized music. . . . Prokofiev's cadenzas, for example, are unbearable. They are such a musical mess that one might think they were created by capriciously emptying an inkwell on the paper."[44]

The enraged critic of the Black Hundreds newspaper, *Novoye Vremya* (probably M. Ivanov),* declared that "the young Prokofiev has outdone Mr. Scriabin, the 'man of reason and illumination.' . . . Mr. Prokofiev's Concerto is a torrent of murky, muddy water."[45]

The hostile reaction to Prokofiev's Concerto is easy to understand. To the Pavlovsk audience and the critics who reflected its tastes, this music was a tonal "slap in the face," an impertinent, anarchic assault. Exactly the same reaction was evoked by the daring utterances of the young futurist poets, who maliciously mocked their listeners. At just about this time the Moscow "cubo-futurist" poets Mayakovsky, Kamensky, and Burlyuk were causing a similar sensation at literary evenings in various Russian cities. The bourgeois press's comments on their tour were very similar to the hostile reviews of Prokofiev's performance at Pavlovsk. It is not surprising that the critics called Prokofiev a "futurist." Three years later, one of them, in a desire to irritate him for the defiant nature of his performances, bluntly accused him of "aping Mayakovsky."[46] And there may have been a grain of truth in this accusation, for the young Prokofiev's *épatage* was actually closely related to the "ultra-leftist" revolt which was developing in Russian poetry and painting.

Only one St. Petersburg critic defended Prokofiev's Second Concerto unreservedly. This was Karatygin, whose reviews appeared almost simultaneously in several publications (*Rech, Teatr i Iskusstvo*, and *Apollon*). Despite the opinions of most of the critics, he predicted a brilliant future for the young composer. "The public hissed. This means nothing. Ten years from now it will atone for last night's catcalls by applauding unanimously a new composer with a European reputation."[47]

Karatygin praised all the modernist excesses in the Concerto, enthusiastically pointing out the "extreme, 'hyperaesthetic' sensitivity of the harmonic nerves of the artistic organism." The leader of musical modernism thus bestowed his blessing on Prokofiev's future modernist audacities.

After the performance at Pavlovsk the tireless composer set about re-

---

* TRANSLATOR'S NOTE: The Black Hundreds were an unofficial group of ultra-conservatives who banded together during the Revolution of 1905 in opposition to any change in the autocratic system of government. *Novoye Vremya* was not actually an organ of the Black Hundreds, but as the leading conservative newspaper of the time, it often expressed views similar to those of that group.

vising *Maddalena,* in the expectation that it would be produced at K. Mardzhanov's Free Theater. Remembering his friends' criticisms, he made many changes in it. "Prokofiev is now furiously tearing his *Maddalena* to pieces. He has already revised two scenes, but as much again still remains," Miaskovsky reported on September 21, 1913.

Miaskovsky's chief concern was whether his friend would achieve the necessary vocal naturalness in the opera. ("We shall see how he handles the voices," he wrote.) In another letter he called the revision of *Maddalena* "superb in all respects," and added, "If he sustains this to the very end, it will be a magnificent opera. . . . Now the voices really sing!" But the Free Theater closed, and *Maddalena* was never produced. Only two of its four scenes were orchestrated. Prokofiev's return to this opera in 1913 clearly shows that he had not lost interest in his favorite genre.

Among Prokofiev's interesting works of 1913 was the cycle of ten piano pieces brought together in Op. 12. Half of the pieces in this collection were composed that year; the rest were partially revised versions of old compositions. The diversity of genres and styles represented here further confirms the dualism in the young Prokofiev's creative tendencies. Although strongly attracted to modernist innovations, he was still firmly tied to the classical traditions instilled in him since childhood. The most radically modern of these pieces were the eccentrically comic *Scherzo* for four bassoons [piano version] and the somewhat contrived *Mazurka* (1909), written almost entirely in parallel fourths. ("The prank of a spoiled youth, flaunting his fearlessness by defying the precepts of generally accepted musical taste," Asafyev called it.)[48] On the other hand, there is sincere, tender feeling in the lyrical pieces—the pensive, epical *Legend* (the best of the ten pieces, according to Prokofiev), the graceful *Capriccio,* and the very melodic *Gavotte* in G minor (the first version of which had been written in 1908 for Lyadov's class). The *Gavotte,* the ponderous *Allemande,* the engaging *Rigaudon,* and the gaily rippling *Prelude* with its broken chords and glissandi are all typical of Prokofiev's classical style, which later revealed itself so brilliantly in the First Symphony and in the dances of *Romeo and Juliet* and *Cinderella.* These traditional pieces also display the composer's characteristic humor, his love for elegant, slightly ironic dances, and even his favorite diatonic key of C major (*Rigaudon, Prelude*), which we find in dozens of his later compositions.[49]

Prokofiev's classicism has nothing in common, however, with the stylized imitation that characterized the snobbish "neoclassicism" which was so widespread in Western music during the twenties. Prokofiev was striving to express completely fresh, contemporary content in traditional forms. His gavottes, minuets, and rigaudons convey vividly the genial, gentle humor of a modern Russian artist. In the *Gavotte* and especially in the *March* in F minor (composed in 1906 as a congratulatory "ditty" for V. Morolev) we also hear echoes of the charming and gay "poetry of childhood," which Prokofiev's works always retained despite their terrifying modernist excesses. Incidentally, on returning to the childhood *March* seven years later, Prokofiev changed it considerably, primarily by developing and enriching the harmonic texture. By comparing the original version of 1906 (Fig. 11) with the final one (Fig. 12), we can see some of the typical devices of modern harmony that Prokofiev used.

FIGURE 11

FIGURE 12

The artless, naïvely clear theme, scarcely altered, is enriched by suspensions, passing notes, and colorful juxtapositions of chords which add a touch of buoyant, joyful humor. Was it not this piece that Mayakovsky had in mind when he spoke of his liking for the "crude, spirited marches" of the pre-foreign Prokofiev?

The ten pieces of Op. 12 clearly demonstrate how unjust it was of the critics to regard Prokofiev as a futurist and a musical lawbreaker. Most of these pieces express simple human emotions; the lyricism is natural and the humor unforced. These same qualities appear later in the Third and Fourth Sonatas, the First Violin Concerto, and the *Fugitive Visions,* and they become firmly established in the best works of his Soviet period.

✸ ✸ ✸

By now the young Prokofiev's personality was clearly defined. While he was persistent, searching, and unusually diligent, he was also spoiled, impudent, and unwilling to submit to any authority whatsoever. Many ill-wishers could not forgive him for what they called his defiant behavior. Everything smooth, sleek, and correct sickened him. He hated stereotypes, in life as well as in art. Rebelling against them, he strove to be completely original, not only in his creative work but also in the way he lived, in his manner of expressing himself, and so on. At about this time, for example, he developed a special style of handwriting (bold and angular, like the old Slavonic ligature) and an unusual method of spelling—without vowels. A typical example of this is his signature, "S. Prkfv." The letters of his youth are filled with amusing neologisms and witty stylizations, now "like a peasant," now "like a foreigner," now in the old-fashioned style of a petty government official. He struck at his enemies with derisive nicknames, and good-naturedly gave his friends amusing ones; for example, he called Miaskovsky "Nyam" [from his initials, N. Ya. M.], "Miaskutsius," and "Niamusënochek." One is reminded of the epistolary frolics of Moussorgsky and his friends of the Mighty Five.

Striving for greater efficiency in the technical aspects of composition, Prokofiev revised the system of score-writing. Once, while still in Cherepnin's class, he grew tired of trying to analyze a Berlioz score ("I would spend three minutes trying to make out a chord, only to find that it was nothing but a C major triad"). This gave him the idea of discarding the complicated practice of transposition and of writing all the instruments in his scores in the key of C, just as they sound on the piano. The only clef he retained, apart from the treble and bass, was the alto (for viola, trombone, and English horn). The tenor clef was dispensed with altogether (the treble and bass clefs serving for the bassoons and cellos). All of Prokofiev's scores, beginning with the First Piano Concerto, were written according to this considerably simplified system.

The young composer openly expressed his scorn for the works of Rachmaninov, Medtner, the early Scriabin, and even his teacher Cherepnin. For example, when refusing to perform the Scriabin Piano Concerto, he wrote, "I don't like the Concerto at all. I would really begrudge the time to learn this lackluster piece." He considered the popularity of Rachmaninov a sign of "poor taste," agreeing in this with Karatygin. The music of Cherepnin's ballet *Narcissus* he sarcastically called "an excellent lesson in scoring." As for the hostile critics, who irritated him with their attacks, he denounced them in the strongest possible language.

Prokofiev impertinently accused the Moscow publisher Jurgenson of "hopeless timidity," niggardliness, and an undeviating tenderness toward the untalented. The young musician voiced his daring protest against routine hack work in these words: "You have published scarcely a single genuine composer since Tchaikovsky. As if by a decree of fate, all the best names are to be found somewhere else. On the other hand hundreds of scribblers, whose names appear neither on programs nor even in the musical calendar, fill the shelves of your warehouses, like dependable lodgers. To be sure, you can pay them in small change, but after all, you are the head of a first-class publishing firm, not a sanctuary for failures."[50] At about this time Prokofiev sent a similarly denunciatory letter to Siloti for refusing to include Miaskovsky's Third Symphony in his concerts.[51]

Naturally enough, the young composer was almost completely absorbed in music. His friend V. M. Morolev once said, "You begin to talk with him about literature and he shifts the conversation to music." Indeed, he took little interest in contemporary poetry, with all its modernist "revelations" and conflicting tendencies—which may explain why he turned his attention to Balmont and later to Anna Akhmatova but failed to notice such a brilliant and powerful writer as Alexander Blok. The musical modernists acquainted him with the latest works of the "leftist" painters who had brought to Russia the style of Cézanne and Matisse, and he liked the sharply defined quality of their works.

Along with music Prokofiev was extremely enthusiastic about chess. He frequented the chess club in St. Petersburg, spending hours on simultaneous games and seeking opportunities to play with formidable opponents. He also took some interest in sports, and for a while he regularly attended the gymnastic drills of the Sokol. This led him to write a sports march, which the society published.

The young musician had a real passion for traveling. He always left St. Petersburg during vacation periods, going to the Caucasus, the Crimea, and Finland. And he did not forget his native Yekaterinoslav. In the summer of 1913, with Max Schmidthof, he visited the Ukrainian town of Nikopol, where Morolev and his family lived.

Prokofiev's circle of friends was extremely wide, as we can see from his dedications of the pieces in Op. 12—*Scherzo humoristique* to Professor Cherepnin, *March* to Vasyusha Morolev, *Allemande* to M. Schmidthof, *Scherzo* in A minor to Volodya Deshevov, *Gavotte* to Boryusya (the pianist Boris Zakharov), *Mazurka* to Kolyechka Miaskovsky, and so on. Here, too, we can see intimations of the first awakening of love in the dedication of the *Capriccio* to Talya Meshcherskaya and the *Prelude* to the young harpist Eleonora Damskaya, a Conservatory student.[52]

The year 1913–14 was Prokofiev's last at the Conservatory. During that season the number of his public appearances as conductor and pianist increased. He was literally swamped with academic and concert work. In the opera class he was given the assignment of preparing Verdi's *Falstaff* for performance. On April 6, 1914, he conducted Mozart's *Marriage of Figaro*. It is reasonable to assume that contact with these masterpieces of comic opera subsequently had some effect on his own work (*The Love for Three Oranges* and, more particularly, *The Duenna*).

At the end of November 1913 Prokofiev met Claude Debussy, who had come to St. Petersburg at the invitation of Koussevitzky. Debussy conducted a concert of his own works and also participated in a chamber recital arranged in his honor by the editors of the magazine *Apollon*. On this occasion Prokofiev played his *Legend*, Op. 12, and three of the Études of Op. 2. Debussy praised and congratulated him. Prokofiev, however, was not deeply impressed by the French composer's works. At that time he felt that impressionist music was "not sufficiently meaty." It was not until much later, when he lived in Paris, that he came to appreciate the new French music.

During the winter of 1914 Prokofiev made two appearances with new chamber works—on February 5 in Moscow, in the Small Hall of the Conservatory, and on February 20 in St. Petersburg, at the Evenings of Modern Music. The entire second half of each concert was devoted to Prokofiev, and it was on these occasions that the Second Sonata, the *Ballade* for cello, and a number of the piano pieces in Op. 12 were given their first performance.

These concerts evoked considerable interest, and musical Moscow began to receive Prokofiev more favorably than it had before. Along with abusive reviews by L. Sabaneyev,* K. Eiges, and others there was a very friendly

---

* Sabanayev wrote of the Second Sonata: "Crude, leaping, and absurdly artificial, it gives a true picture of the modern 'football' generation. There is something about it that is stupid, inane, and blockheaded." (*Golos Moskvy*, February 6, 1914.)

article in *Russkiye Vedomosti,* in which the Moscow critic Yu. Engel described Prokofiev's music as "powerful primarily for the play of musical ideas, the energy of the creative will; it has a kind of angularity, harshness, and coldness, but at the same time a genuine freshness."[53] The critic O. von Riesemann of the Moscow German newspaper made an interesting prediction about Prokofiev's future: "One can hardly believe that in this fair-haired, inoffensive youth there lies hidden such musical devilishness as he displayed this evening. . . . We cannot be sure that this fiery young composer who recklessly casts aside all the precepts of artistic tradition . . . will not eventually develop into a Scriabin or a Debussy. Young wine has to age. There is reason to hope that a similar metamorphosis will take place in Prokofiev's creative work."[54]

By now, performing at chamber recitals and occasional appearances at summer concerts no longer satisfied Prokofiev. The doors of the major concert organizations—the Siloti, Koussevitzky, and Sheremetyev orchestras and the Russian Musical Society—still remained tightly closed to him. All attempts to persuade Siloti to include the Second Piano Concerto in his programs ended in failure; Siloti refused on the grounds that Prokofiev "had not yet found himself." "I cannot invite Prokofiev to play the Second Concerto because then I should have to conduct, and that is beyond my strength. The music of Debussy gives forth a fragrance, but this gives off a stench," said Siloti maliciously in the circle of his intimate friends. To the same group he described Prokofiev as a "white Negro."

Siloti's attitude roused the just anger of Miaskovsky, who saw in it a shameful neglect of the achievements of young Russian composers.* With true national pride he stood up for his friend Prokofiev. During the 1913–14 season *Muzyka* published two articles by Miaskovsky (signed "Misanthrope")[55] bitterly accusing Siloti and also the directors of the Belyaev concerts of indifference toward young composers.† The second article, entitled "St. Petersburg Fogs," caused a sensation. Angrily denouncing Siloti's behavior, Miaskovsky wrote, "Only recently he grace-

---

* An invitation to the French composer Roger-Ducasse to perform his mimed drama *Orphée* at the Siloti concerts led Miaskovsky to comment caustically, "If I come to know him [Siloti] better, I shall try to make him understand that such enthusiasm is more appropriate for a Russian work than for foreign rubbish. I shall never forgive him for Prokofiev." (Letter to Derzhanovsky dated January 8, 1914.)

† TRANSLATOR'S NOTE: The Belyaev Concerts were instituted in 1885 by the businessman Mitrofan Belyaev for the purpose of presenting music by Russian composers. The initial group of composers whose music he promoted, which included Rimsky-Korsakov, Borodin, Lyadov, and Glazunov, is sometimes called the "Belyaev circle."

fully dodged an opportunity to include in his programs Prokofiev's wonderful Second Piano Concerto (which, as is known, has one quality that no one disputes—powerful individuality) with a vague promise to consider the composer when he has 'found himself.' Glory to the sensitive ear and keen insight of Mr. Siloti!" And at this point Miaskovsky reminded the conductor of the behest of his teacher, Liszt—to encourage all the best musical talent in Russia.

The articles in defense of Prokofiev did not go unnoticed. It was not long before all the leading concert organizations of St. Petersburg and Moscow were obliged to recognize him. In February 1914 he was invited to perform at one of Koussevitzky's subscription matinees, where he played his First Concerto with success. Even Siloti gave way.

In the spring of 1914 Prokofiev completed his courses in conducting and piano at the St. Petersburg Conservatory. The final examination in conducting went off extremely well. Cherepnin, who had long since discerned the tremendous originality of Prokofiev's talent, characterized him as follows: "Outstanding talent in composition. Has acquired a rather sound technique in conducting, which will prove useful when conducting his own works. Has a terribly thankless and heavy hand. Capacity for work is exceptional."

That spring Prokofiev set himself a task—to complete the piano course with honors and to win the Rubinstein First Prize. "While I did not particularly mind the poor rating I received in composition," he recalls, "this time ambition got the better of me and I was determined to finish first in piano." His teacher Esipova being seriously ill, Prokofiev had to prepare for the examinations on his own.

The spirit of competition took complete hold of the young musician. He chose his program with cold calculation. Instead of the customary fugue from Bach's *Well-Tempered Clavier,* he prepared a little-known one from the *Art of Fugue*; for the classical concerto he substituted his own Piano Concerto No. 1. He completed the list with a Liszt transcription from *Tannhäuser,* which would give him an opportunity to display his virtuosity. For the preliminary examination A. K. Glazunov, the Director of the Conservatory, gave Prokofiev's playing a very high, though rather ambiguous, appraisal: "Original virtuoso of a new type, with an extraordinary technique. Tries to evoke from the modern piano effects beyond its capacity, often to the detriment of beauty of tone. Tiresome affectation, not always sincere." At the same time Glazunov gave him the highest mark, 5 plus.

The directors of the Conservatory did not consent at once to the inclusion of Prokofiev's little-known concerto in the program of the competitive examination. This was not according to the regulations. The composer persisted, however, and they finally agreed on the condition that each examiner be given a copy of the concerto a week before the competition so that he might familiarize himself with it. Even this obstacle did not stop Prokofiev. He besieged Jurgenson with requests that he print the piano score in time to meet the requirement. "I earnestly beg you to have the concerto ready by April 23 at the latest, for if it is not, I may have serious trouble—I may even be barred from the examination," he wrote the publisher.[56] His entreaties produced the desired effect, and the score was printed in time. The young composer himself distributed the copies to all twenty members of the jury.

"When I came out on the stage," he recalls, "the first thing I saw was my concerto spread out on twenty laps—an unforgettable sight for a composer who had just begun to be published."

Prokofiev's performance at the examination on May 5, 1914, once again startled his audience with its powerful virtuosity and masterful vigor.[57] However, the examining professors were divided into two sharply opposed camps: Esipova's group and the young professors (Kalantarova, Drozdov, Vengerova, Lemba, and Medem) were in favor; the influential academic group (among them Liapunov, Lavrov, and Dubasov) was opposed. The most vehement objection came from Dubasov, who protested against encouraging "harmful" creative tendencies. Nevertheless, the Conservatory could not but recognize the outstanding talent of its unruly student, and Prokofiev, by a majority of votes, was awarded the Rubinstein First Prize, a Schroeder piano. Glazunov, who had just voted against Prokofiev himself, announced the results of the contest.

On May 24, 1914, the First Concerto was played at the graduation exercises with an orchestra under Cherepnin's direction. The entire press of St. Petersburg reported Prokofiev's success, with photographs and an interview with him. This marked the beginning of Prokofiev's recognition by most of the music critics and concert organizations. Even his enemies were now compelled to reckon with his talent.

# FOUR

# REBELLION

*Then I replied that I was a heretic and
a barbarian . . . and that I cared nothing for all these Archbishops, Cardinals,
Monseigneurs, and so on.*
Dostoyevsky: THE GAMBLER

IN THE SUMMER OF 1914, after his triumphant graduation from the
Conservatory, Prokofiev had definitely arrived. His name appeared
more and more frequently in the newspapers of the capital, he was
received in St. Petersburg's art salons, and theatrical circles began to show
an interest in him.

This period in the composer's life coincided with a grave period in
the history of Russia, the beginning of the First World War. The events
of the war cast a gloomy shadow over every aspect of Russian life. Material conditions became increasingly difficult.

"I have no means of support whatever except my capacity for work,"
Prokofiev wrote Jurgenson. "My mother, who has some means, has supported me in the past, but the general financial difficulties caused by the
war have also affected her affairs, and as a result she can now offer me
no more than room and board."[1]

The war engendered a spirit of chauvinism in some Russian artists and
intellectuals. The bourgeois poets began to glorify the idea of "defending
the motherland against the German barbarians," thereby fanning the flames
of official patriotism. The young Prokofiev, however, remained indifferent
to these tendencies. High-flown rhetoric and pseudo-patriotism were alien
to him. The sharp impressions of the war years served only to intensify
the agitated and expressionistic qualities in his work.

The outbreak of the war separated Prokofiev and Miaskovsky. Miaskovsky was sent to the front as a sapper officer, while Prokofiev, as the
only son of a widowed mother, was granted a deferment. Being quite
unaware of the true significance of the war, Prokofiev drew even closer

to modernist circles and rebelled even more openly against classical traditions.

During 1914–15 the composer became acquainted with the literary-philosophical circle of the poet Boris Verin, born Boris Nikolayevich Bashkirov, the son of a rich St. Petersburg flour merchant. Every Monday evening Bashkirov-Verin had an "at home" for young poets, philosophers, artists, and musicians. Among those who attended were the critic Karatygin, the philologist B. Demchinsky, and the singer A. Zherebtsova-Andreyeva. Lectures were given on the philosophies of Kant, Aristotle, and Socrates, new poems were presented, and musical compositions were played. An atmosphere of unrestrained adulation for idealist philosophical trends and modern decadent poetry prevailed here. The host wrote dilettante poetry, which he printed at his own expense. One of his poems, "Trust Me," written in cheap drawing-room style, was set to music by Prokofiev in 1915. Asafyev, who knew Bashkirov personally, characterized him as a representative of foppish merchant modernism.

Prokofiev, too, attended the Bashkirov "Mondays" and sometimes performed his new works there. In this salon he came into further contact with fashionable philosophical fads and the latest innovations in modernist poetry. Half in jest, he even joined in the poetry-making, writing a few triolets of parody. To his credit, however, these enthusiasms were only transitory, and the discussions on vague philosophical subjects left no deep mark on his clear and sober mind.[2]

After his graduation from the Conservatory, Prokofiev, eager to apply his talents to a large-scale work, was drawn again to his favorite genre, opera. For several years both he and Miaskovsky had toyed with the idea of writing operas based on Dostoyevsky's novels, literary sources thus far neglected by the great Russian composers of opera. During these critical times Dostoyevsky was the rage among Russian intellectuals. "Even today it is contemporary and very dear to the Russian heart," wrote Miaskovsky of one of Dostoyevsky's works.[3] Dramatizations of *The Brothers Karamazov, The Possessed,* and *The Idiot* were presented at the Moscow Art and Nezlobin theaters. This turning to works "likely only to disturb still more a society already disturbed enough" called forth an angry rebuke from Gorky.* It is not unlikely that these theatrical experiments influ-

* See Gorky's articles "On Karamazovism," and "More on Karamazovism," *Russkoye Slovo,* October 5 and November 9, 1913. Both articles had enormous repercussions. All the bourgeois critics, including such pillars of the World of Art as Benois and Filosofov, rose up in arms against the author.

enced Prokofiev's decision to write an opera based on *The Gambler* and Miaskovsky's plan to write one based on *The Idiot*.

But Prokofiev's idea for a new opera was not immediately realized, for his interests turned in another direction. In June 1914, on the eve of the war, he went to London for the opening of the Diaghilev ballet season. On this trip he was accompanied by W. F. Nuvel, a typical St. Petersburg Bohemian, a snob and cynic who ridiculed the "preconceptions" of classical art. Nuvel took it upon himself to introduce the young composer into the circle of the supreme arbiter of Russian modernism, Sergei Diaghilev.

The Diaghilev company, which was touring the major European cities, included in its repertoire Rimsky-Korsakov's *Golden Cockerel,* Stravinsky's *Nightingale* and *Petrushka,* and Ravel's *Daphnis and Chloe.* The brilliant inventiveness of the choreographer M. Fokine, the magnificent décor of Benois and other artists of the World of Art, and the masterly performances of the Russian ballerinas, headed by T. Karsavina, were creating a sensation. The jaded bourgeois audience was no longer content with Russian classical music. It wanted new thrills, and Diaghilev was striving in every way to oblige it with exotic modernist productions.

The mastermind of this entire venture was a cultured, imperious businessman of the familiar European type. "He was a self-assured aristocrat," said Asafyev of Diaghilev, "sophisticated, intelligent, and very elegant in his impeccable full dress. With his associates he was charming, and with patrons, on whom he seemingly depended, he was rather haughty. It was as though he were thinking, 'I am the leader, I have the intellect and taste, and you—the money!' "[4]

Diaghilev strove to dazzle the public with barbaric splendor *à la russe.* His open catering to the tastes of foreign snobs incensed many prominent Russians. Asafyev, who attended the Diaghilev performances in Paris in May 1914, angrily denounced the impresario and his associates for their commercialism and lack of principle. "All their empty talk about art— what has this to do with art, when all they are concerned about is pleasing the Parisians with this, the Londoners with that, and the Berliners with something else. . . . For what and for whom all these efforts are made I don't know, but it's not for Russian art."[5]

In the summer of 1914 the Diaghilev company presented a ballet version of Rimsky-Korsakov's *Golden Cockerel.* In this sensationally formalistic production, an eccentric ballet was performed to the singing of a chorus and soloists seated in tiers on the stage. The social implications of the satirical fairy-tale opera were thus completely obliterated. "In my opinion *The Golden Cockerel* is a travesty, a mere farce," wrote Asafyev.

Experiments of this kind arose largely from the anti-operatic tastes of Diaghilev, Benois, and other leaders of modernism. They considered the operatic genre too realistic and earthly; believing that its day had passed, they thought it should give way to the more capricious and fanciful genre of ballet. They felt that ballet, with its naïveté and spontaneity, would usher in a new era in theater art.[6]

It was said that after producing *Scheherazade* and *The Golden Cockerel,* Diaghilev planned to stage Scriabin's *Prometheus* until the composer rejected this venturesome idea.

In the course of a single month Prokofiev attended the London theater and heard Stravinsky's *Firebird* and *Petrushka,* Ravel's *Daphnis and Chloe,* a performance by Chaliapin, and symphony concerts under the direction of Richard Strauss.

To be sure, he did not accept the new works without reservations. "Their vitality, inventiveness, and 'trickiness' interested me tremendously," he relates, "but I found them lacking in real thematic material." He noted some padding even in the score of *Petrushka.* Nevertheless, an intimate knowledge of the music of Stravinsky and other modern composers was bound to influence the impressionable young Prokofiev.

Nuvel introduced Prokofiev to Diaghilev, who consented to listen to the Second Piano Concerto. Greatly impressed by Prokofiev's talent, the foremost spokesman of Russian modernism immediately invited the composer to work with his theatrical enterprise. Prokofiev mentioned his plan to write an opera based on *The Gambler,* hoping to receive a commission for it, but Diaghilev flatly rejected this idea, declaring categorically that opera was out of date and that the present called for ballet and pantomime. There was even some talk of producing the Second Concerto in the form of a ballet. (Diaghilev had in mind using the second theme of the Finale to portray some fairy-tale hero, like Lel in *The Snow Maiden.*) The negotiations ended with Prokofiev receiving a commission for a ballet "on a Russian fairy tale or prehistoric theme." Diaghilev suggested that Nuvel and Karatygin put the composer in touch with one of the modern poets, someone like Sergei Gorodetsky, who had not long before won fame with his book *Spring Corn.*

Thus began the long business relationship between Prokofiev and Diaghilev which continued until the latter's death in 1929. Throughout these many years Diaghilev fostered in every way the development of ultra-aesthetic views in Prokofiev. He chided the composer for his love for diverse musical styles. "In art you must know how to hate. Otherwise your own music will lose its identity," he taught Prokofiev, thus nourishing his lack of respect for the "obsolete" democratic traditions of classical music.

Diaghilev won the admiration of young people with his impelling personality, his ingenious and paradoxical observations, and his display of erudition in all matters of art—from painting to music and choreography. Prokofiev was captivated by him. As a matter of fact, the young composer was so carried away by his experiences in London that, on his own admission, he barely missed being caught in the impending European war, and arrived in St. Petersburg only a few days before the fighting broke out. In compliance with Diaghilev's instructions, he laid aside his plans for *The Gambler* and with Karatygin's help arranged for Gorodetsky's collaboration on the ballet. While the poet was gathering material for the scenario, Prokofiev reorchestrated and partially revised the Sinfonietta, Op. 5, which was to be performed at the Siloti concerts.[7]

The young poet Gorodetsky, a member of the Acmeist group, based his scenario on material from ancient Slavic mythology, some of which he had used in his book *Spring Corn*. He treated the images of the myths—sun-worshiping, veneration of the perpetual alternation of light and darkness, heat and cold—in an ultra-aesthetic manner, and gave the pagan gods stylized names, such as Chuzhbog, Ala, and Lolli.

The plot of the ballet *Ala and Lolli* was briefly as follows: The ancient Slavs are worshiping Veles, the sun god, and Ala, a wooden idol personifying the creative powers of nature.[8] The ballet was to open with primitive ritual dances of the Scyths ("Worship of Veles and Ala"). Opposing the friendly gods is the crafty Chuzhbog, protector of the destructive forces of evil, and his seven loathsome subterranean monsters; in the second scene they perform the frenetic "Dance of the Evil Spirits." One night Chuzhbog, with the aid of the evil spirits, tries to abduct Ala. His spell, however, works only in absolute darkness; the light of the moon renders him powerless. The fairy moon-maidens descend from the heavens to comfort Ala on this dread night. Later, when Chuzhbog threatens her again, the Scythian warrior Lolli comes to her rescue. An unequal struggle ensues. Just as Lolli is at the point of death, the all-powerful sun god, Veles, smites Chuzhbog with his scorching rays.

Neither Gorodetsky nor Prokofiev knew very much about ballet dramaturgy and they had difficulty with the scenario. On the whole, Prokofiev approved the poet's scenario, and while impatiently awaiting new pages of it, he very quickly sketched fragments of the music. Excited by the quest for pungent harmonic effects, he demanded of the poet the most terrifying barbaric images possible, images that would stun the audience. "It is all much too pretty," he told Gorodetsky on one occasion.

Prokofiev was particularly fascinated with the scene of the evil spirits' frenzied orgy, in which he imagined all sorts of fantastic monsters and subterranean creatures. Differences arose between the coauthors. The poet, who dreamed of flowing, tuneful music in the style of Rimsky-Korsakov, was shocked by Prokofiev's noisy improvisations. The two authors met almost every day, and yet their work on the ballet dragged on through the fall of 1914 and into the winter of 1915.

In a letter to friends in Moscow, Prokofiev tried to justify the enthusiasm that had caused him to give up his opera temporarily and accept the Diaghilev commission. "My interest in *The Gambler* has never waned—it is stronger now than ever—but first I must do the ballet. About three-fourths of the music is already written and I'll be orchestrating it all spring. If you have an idea that writing for the ballet is composing of a lower order, may God forgive you for not understanding anything. When I finish the ballet, I'll tackle my dear *Gambler,* if I don't feel the urge to take a rest from big things and dash off a few trifles."[9]

The theme of the "Scythian" ballet *Ala and Lolli* was a very typical one for modernist art on the eve of the Revolution. Bored with the languor of the boudoir and aesthetic self-adulation, artists and writers began to glorify the animal wisdom of primitive man. "Poets wore themselves out trying to roar like wild animals," K. Chukovsky recalls. "The craze for the savage, the primitive, and the beast of the forest became the outstanding feature of the epoch."[10]

In verse after verse poets rang all the changes on Adams, Scyths, and Huns. The worship of brute force was combined with an unaccountable fear of the advent of the "future Hun," who was to shatter and destroy all bourgeois civilization. The Acmeists, who appeared around 1910, tried to counter the nervous refinement of the symbolists with "savageness" and a synthetic joy of living. "As Adamists we are to some degree beasts of the forest. In any case we will not give up the beast in us in exchange for neurasthenia," declared the Acmeists' leader, N. Gumilyov.[11]

Glorification of prehistoric man, with his savagery, his superstitions, and his fear of the forces of nature, was also expressed in the works of the World of Art painter Nicholas Roerich ("Idols" and "Slavs on the Dnieper," among others). These stylized paintings reflected a yearning to escape from the turbulent events of the day, a presentiment of impending catastrophe. Finally, the same theme of Scythianism, the same glorification of barbaric instincts, appeared in Russian music—for example, in V. Senilov's symphonic poem *The Scythians* (1912) and Stravinsky's *Rite of Spring* (1913), which caused a sensation. Stravinsky's turning to the theme of *The Rite of Spring* was not without significance. Surfeited with the delicacies of impressionism, he was seeking to artificially rejuvenate his prematurely aging muse by resurrecting primordial forces, by reviving barbaric, pagan instincts.

*The Rite of Spring* did not evoke any enthusiasm among Prokofiev's closest friends. "*The Rite of Spring*—there's a monster for you!" exclaimed Miaskovsky. "To me *Spring* at times seems exceedingly poor in inventiveness," he remarked in another letter.[12] At the beginning of 1914 *The Rite of Spring* was performed at one Koussevitzky's concerts. Although Prokofiev said he "did not understand" it, this extremely harsh and dissonant music undoubtedly left an imprint on his memory. It seemingly had some effect upon the style of *Ala and Lolli.*

Of course Prokofiev viewed Scythianism differently from Stravinsky, without any philosophical complexities. For him the subject suggested by Gorodetsky was only a convenient opportunity to give rein to his harmonic daring, to "try his hand at something big," something monumental. His stormy temperament, which had sought an outlet in *Diabolical Suggestions,* the *Toccata,* and the most extreme episodes of the Second Concerto, now fully revealed itself. Finding little to satisfy him in the static scenario of *Ala and Lolli,* he directed all his creative ingenuity to inventing acrid harmonies, archaic melodies, and crude pagan rhythms—everything that he thought would suit the Scythian subject.

Late in the winter of 1915 he finished a rough draft of the piano score of the ballet. On hearing the music, Diaghilev's plenipotentiaries in St. Petersburg, Nuvel and Nurok, were somewhat taken aback by its confused sound. Nuvel lost no time informing Diaghilev that "Prokofiev has written something absurd to an absurd plot." Shortly after this the composer was asked by Diaghilev to come to Italy to discuss the fate of the new ballet.

In terms of the modernism of its musical language, *Ala and Lolli* might be compared to Prokofiev's piano cycle *Sarcasms,* completed in 1914. In these five short pieces (the first written in 1912, the second and third in 1913) are embodied the most extreme manifestations of Prokofiev's "grotesquerie." Here elements of mischief, of devilish skepticism, predominate. The composer seems to be poking fun at his listeners, jeering at their ingrained musical habits. While the odd-numbered pieces are filled with violent, unbridled emotions, a fantastic, almost eerie atmosphere pervades the even-numbered ones. In the first *Sarcasm,* which was written before the Second Piano Concerto, furious, teasing images, rhythmically exaggerated, give way in the middle section to soft, dreamy passages. Altogether different is the impressionistic second piece, abounding in broken runs and spicy harmonies. In the third *Sarcasm,* another impetuous piece, an ominous, persistent *basso ostinato* is suddenly interrupted by powerful chordal outburst. At this point a surprising harmonic trick is exhibited: the right-hand part is written in F-sharp minor, while the left-hand is in B-flat minor. This is not a polytonal device, however, for on careful analysis the piece proves to be in B-flat minor with a typical *ostinato.* Even more surprising is the middle section of this piece, tender and lyrical, akin to Tchaikovsky in its soulfulness. The fourth *Sarcasm* (marked *Smanioso*) takes one aback with its fancifulness, compounded of intricate, clownish melodies with strange skips and distortions. And finally, there is the profoundly tragic fifth *Sarcasm,* based on a very noteworthy philosophical idea akin to the "laughter through tears" theme of Gogol's *Overcoat* and *Dead Souls*: "Sometimes we laugh maliciously at someone or something, but when we look closely, we see how pitiful and wretched is the object of our laughter, and then we begin to feel uncomfortable—the laughter rings in our ears, but now someone else is laughing at us."

The musical ideas of this amazing piece unfold in keeping with the above program: first, a fast-moving section of coarse, boisterous laughter ("as though a sensation-seeking crowd had broken loose," as Asafyev aptly remarked); then, hobbling, hesitating music with pitiful sobs and wailing; and finally, the first idea again, radically changed—the theme of laughter sounding muffled, bitter, almost ominous in the lower registers of the piano.

It is indicative that in *Sarcasms* the derisive images, which had long attracted Prokofiev, at times acquire a dark and sinister quality. In all likelihood the composer was seeking to express moods somewhat related to the ironically Mephistophelean images of Scriabin. It was precisely this tendency of his to embody moods of nervous refinement and affected torment in daring, harshly exaggerated sonorities that received the greatest encouragement from his friends, the modernists.

This is not surprising when we recall that the members of this circle were inordinately fond of sarcasm, skepticism, and the habit of speaking ironically. Diaghilev himself was such a person, as were Nuvel and his inseparable friend, the art critic Nurok, one of the strangest figures of the World of Art group, a person who seemed to have stepped straight from the pages of E. T. A. Hoffmann. Even Nurok's appearance, according to one of his contemporaries, was utterly grotesque. "Tall, emaciated, with a bald head and an angular profile. He wanted very much to appear frightening and cynical—this was his pose."[13]

These people delighted in whatever was most sophisticated, elegant, and snobbish in modern Western art. They supported and encouraged everything in Prokofiev's musical experiments that appealed to their jaded tastes. "Nurok has fought all his life for new music, and now in his old age God has sent him Prokofiev," said Cherepnin. And it must have been these "friends" of Prokofiev that the magazine *Muzykalny Sovremennik* had in mind when it remarked rather maliciously that "all kinds of aunts and uncles of art draw warmth for their old bones from the pranks of the healthy rising generation."[14]

It was natural that Prokofiev's odd-sounding *Sarcasms* should particularly appeal to Nurok and Nuvel. It was they who conceived the title, feeling that the composer's original title, *Sarcastic Pieces,* sounded too banal. Karatygin raved about *Sarcasms,* fully satisfied that here at last, "all ties with classicism have been broken." He considered the pieces a deliberate gibe at "the transient conventions of artistic language." It delighted him that the "devils of Prokofiev's unbridled imagination have given themserves up to an orgiastic dance over the graves of the 'principles' of musical beauty."[15]

Asafyev reacted quite differently to these pieces, finding in them "repressed horror" and devils "frightened by their own cold, malicious, mocking tone, their own contempt for spirituality."[16] "It is sinister and terrifying music," he wrote later. "The five *Sarcasms* are five of the most caustic and penetrating expressions of the dark forces of life, its evil, its poison."[17]

One cannot but agree with Asafyev's view that the music of the *Sarcasms,* with its exaggerated harshness sometimes bordering on tonal anarchy, should have been regarded at that time as a bitter attack on the hot-house prettiness of impressionist music and "World-of-Artiness."

"Sergei Prokofiev, I recall, played his explosive *Sarcasms* brilliantly at the dazzling opening of a very elegant World of Art exhibit," Asafyev relates in his memoirs. "The aesthetic elite of St. Petersburg was there. And I thought, 'It's a good thing that when you listen, all you hear are titillating sounds. Were Khlebnikov and Mayakovsky to come here with their poems, you either would hiss them off the stage or would have them ejected, or you yourselves would run away.' Prokofiev's *Sarcasms* are more taunting, more trenchant than the verses of the early Mayakovsky, and the horror of

them is more terrifying and powerful. Yet you just sit there in your impervious and insensitive aestheticism, drinking in the spicy, acrid chords."[18]

Thus, the *Sarcasms,* and later *The Gambler* and some of the songs, Op.
23, not only represented anarchical extremes of musical style but also expressed the young composer's bitter mockery of aspects of life and art that
were alien to him.

In sharp contrast to the *Sarcasms* and *Ala and Lolli* was a very remarkable work which Prokofiev completed in the fall of 1914 during a temporary
suspension of work on the Scythian ballet.

"As for my vocal music, this fall I have written a large piece of about
fifteen pages based on Andersen's fairy tale *The Ugly Duckling,*" he wrote
Derzhanovsky.[19] From this letter it is clear that the composer had a longing
to return to composition for the voice, a form of writing which had been
interrupted by the Diaghilev commission. His turning to *The Ugly Duckling* was prompted by more than a need for relaxation from the strain of
his quest for new forms; this wonderful example of Prokofiev's vocal lyricism represents an expression of the humanist tendencies which continued
to unfold in his work despite all the temptations and enticements of modernism. (This was the "inconsistency," the love for different kinds of music,
for which Diaghilev had reproached him.)

While the predominant features in the music of *Ala and Lolli* were decorative and pictorial—representations of pagan rituals and steppe scenes—
in *The Ugly Duckling* warm human lyricism asserts itself against a fairy-
tale background.

The entire fairy tale is presented in the form of a uniquely conceived
*scena,* a narration of Andersen's prose text somewhat abridged by the composer. Further developing Moussorgsky's operatic technique of prose declamation, Prokofiev found remarkable means for setting ordinary Russian
speech to music. The entire work is constructed on a combination of melodic recitative (based on the inflections of ordinary speech) and a vividly
descriptive piano accompaniment, which follows the text without interruption.

The declamatory line subtly conveys the emotional undertones implicit in
the tale of the little swan who was hatched in a duck's nest and experienced
the bitterness of universal scorn. At one moment the vocal part expresses
the distress of the narrator as he relates the woes of the young swan; at
another it reproduces with remarkable naturalness the exclamations of the
animal characters ("What if it's a turkey?"). The flexibility of the vocal
line is in no way inhibited by the use of a prose text. On the contrary, the

melodic recitative, unimpeded by the restraints of verse rhythms, sounds freer and more natural.

The descriptive episodes of the piano part parallel the vocal declamation continuously, as in a motion picture, frame after frame. For these Prokofiev found a great number of suitable expressive devices without stooping to naturalistic extremes. The music draws concrete, almost visible images—a lazy summer day, a frozen winter scene, an amusing procession of newly hatched ducklings, fearsome dogs chasing the ugly duckling. Upon hearing the amusing chords embellished by grace notes that subtly imitate the sounds of the bird kingdom, one cannot but recall the descriptive mastery of Moussorgsky in "The Ballet of the Unhatched Chickens."

Using the *durchkomponiert* or through-composed technique, Prokofiev skillfully avoided formlessness or dramatic looseness. By restating the most important melodies and leitmotivs he was able to maintain a strong musical logic throughout the entire work. Thus, the music characterizing the summer day (gaily flitting, colorful, arpeggiated grace notes) both introduces and concludes the fairy tale. In the opening section of the work the comically pompous theme of the duck brood predominates as a refrain. Later on, the theme of the duckling's pitiful wanderings and the particularly expressive, woeful phrase which becomes the leitmotiv of his suffering are repeated (FIG. 13).

FIGURE 13

*The Ugly Duckling* reveals an important aspect of Prokofiev's talent, an aspect which in his Soviet period was to develop in a rich and interesting manner. This was his spontaneous and vital sense of childhood, his understanding of children and their naïve perceptions of the world. This sensitivity manifested itself both in the astonished exclamations of the little duckling (such as, "How big is God's world!") and in the sympathetic portrayal of the bird kingdom. At the same time, in Prokofiev's interpretation the fairy tale becomes the story of wonderful, inspired Man victimized by stupid Philistinism and hidebound convention. Those who sought grotesquerie and buffoonery in this music were hopelessly misled. *The Ugly Duckling* is a fresh, truthful story of life.

This was how it struck Asafyev, when he heard its première in Petrograd.[20] He called it "a fairy tale about S. Prokofiev as told by himself." "Prokofiev's *Ugly Duckling*—a delight! Fresh, bright, and convincing. It is a pearl among the soporific music offered by the modernists."[21] Asafyev persistently contrasted the freshness of this work with the lifeless music of the numerous epigoni of impressionism.

"Once again, with his Concerto and *The Ugly Duckling,* Prokofiev has proved to be far above all the scribblers. One has only to listen to these modernists. How dull! How boring! It is not only I that feel this, but also people of their very own group. Suddenly you hear music that is real, sincere, bright, joyful. How can you help responding! And how can you keep from saying over and over again, right and left, that our hope lies in Prokofiev, that he is no monster but simply a powerful, though erratic talent."[22]

*The Ugly Duckling* drew friendly praise from all the Petrograd critics, even the conservative ones. *Russkaya Muzykalnaya Gazeta,* which had vilified Prokofiev not long before, now declared that *"The Duckling . . . is not at all ugly. It is inventive and imaginative, and Mr. Prokofiev's customary harshnesses seem to be considerably softened."*[23]

Karatygin correctly pointed out a certain kinship between Prokofiev's skillful methods of musical illustration and Moussorgsky's song style. However, both Asafyev and Karatygin commented on the inadequate musical conclusion of the tale, where the text, relating the duck's transformation into a swan, requires more plastic, more poetic music.[24]

"Who knows, perhaps the end of the tale did not quite come off because his own transformation into a swan—that is, the full flowering of his talent and self-knowledge—is yet to come," asserted Asafyev in his review. He expressed this same thought in a letter. "The end of *The Duckling* falls short of success because Prokofiev himself has not yet been transformed into a swan."

❦   ❦   ❦

Prokofiev's performance of his Second Piano Concerto at the Russian Musical Society early in 1915 was a noteworthy event.[25] The very fact that a musical rebel was invited to play before this Society, which was considered the capital's most conservative musical institution, testified to Prokofiev's increasing fame.

The composer's closest friends spoke of this with satisfaction. "If only you had been there to see how pleasant it was," wrote Asafyev. "Prokofiev plays with a triumphant air at the R.M.S.?! And his lovable smiling phiz gazes indifferently at the giggles, hisses, etc. Splendid!"[26]

The concert evoked a new flurry of interest among the Petrograd public. "No end of talk and argument!" reported Asafyev. "Some are for, some against, but everyone senses the presence of power and talent, and whoever doesn't like it—let him get out! The pedants are howling quite a bit. They stubbornly refuse to take the trouble just to listen attentively, without bias— all they do is call names."

The press, which was rather generous in its coverage, was more restrained than it had been after the première of the Concerto. This time even those who disapproved tried to find some justification for Prokofiev's creative audacities, often explaining them as reflections of a complex "transitional epoch" in history. "The young artist is unquestionably endowed with great talent. It is, however, still in a state of ferment. But then our entire epoch is in ferment, as the present terrible war clearly shows," wrote one critic.[27]

Another critic, after pointing out the merits of the Concerto (beautiful themes, sharply defined rhythm, verve, and earthy power), expressed the hope that the young composer would "soon overcome the itch for eccentricities."[28] Only the reactionary M. Ivanov of *Novoye Vremya* again heaped abuse on the composer.

With unconcealed polemical fervor Asafyev came to the defense of Prokofiev in the magazine *Muzyka*. Praising his friend's "glittering talent" and "fiery performance," he sharply contrasted him with "all the rigidly orthodox musicians."[29] Thus Asafyev declared his intention to champion modernism against all other trends in art.

On February 19, shortly after this sensational appearance with the Russian Musical Society, Prokofiev left for Italy to meet Diaghilev, taking with him the piano score of the Scythian ballet. Because of the war, he had to travel by an unusual route, through Rumania, Bulgaria, and Greece. Thirsty for new impressions, he visited Bucharest, Athens, Rome, and Naples. He was charmed by the beauty of Italy. "Here the sky is blue, the sun scorching, and the weather simply paradise," he wrote to Moscow from Sorrento.[30]

Prokofiev's next meeting with Diaghilev took place in Milan. After looking through the music of *Ala and Lolli,* the impresario flatly rejected it. He found the plot contrived and static, the music not very interesting ("à la Cherepnin!"). It was decided that Prokofiev should write a new ballet. As compensation for rejecting *Ala and Lolli,* Diaghilev arranged for Prokofiev to give a concert of his works in the Augusteo, one of the most important concert halls in Rome. The Italian press carried advance notices of this event.

"The musical circles of Rome are awaiting this concert with particular curiosity.... After the enthusiasm with which the Russian Igor Stravinsky was received at the Augusteo two weeks ago, the twenty-three-year-old Prokofiev will certainly find the public ready to give his music the approval it deserves."[31]

This concert, held on March 7, 1915, was Prokofiev's first appearance abroad. He played his Second Piano Concerto and several of the pieces from Op. 2 and Op. 12. The noted Italian conductor Molinari conducted. Public reaction here, as in Petrograd, was divided. Almost the entire press (*Tribuna, Concordia, Giornale d'Italia,* and others), after paying due respect to the young Russian's virtuosity, severely criticized the Second Concerto ("nightmarish," "tricks," "meaningless piano exercises"). "We had expected to find a new Stravinsky, tart and interesting, but on the contrary we found an artist still lacking individuality and wandering between the old and the new," wrote one of the modernist critics.[32]

Prokofiev was not greatly disturbed by this cold reception from the critics. He avidly attended concerts and plays, and through Diaghilev he met Italian poets and artists. In his letters to Moscow friends he told of the Italians' great interest in Russian music and the sensational success of Stravinsky's *Petrushka* ("The composer, who was present, received a tremendous ovation, but there were also some catcalls").[33]

At Diaghilev's home Prokofiev met Stravinsky and the Italian futurists Marinetti and Balla, who had been invited to discuss a ballet based on Neapolitan carnivals. This time Prokofiev treated Stravinsky with great respect, and despite Diaghilev's apprehensions the meeting went off without any disputes. Stravinsky praised the Second Concerto. At Diaghilev's request the two composers played a four-hand arrangement of *Petrushka* for the Italian guests. This was the beginning of a relationship between Prokofiev and Stravinsky which, despite occasional breaks caused by disagreements in principle, continued for many years.*

* This meeting is mentioned briefly in Stravinsky's autobiography: "During this stay I had an opportunity to enter into closer relationship with this remarkable musician, whose worth is now universally recognized." Stravinsky, *An Autobiography,* p. 89.

The Italian futurists, whose leader was the inveterate formalist Marinetti( later one of the troubadours of Fascism), aroused neither deep interest nor personal sympathy in Prokofiev. Their overrefined urbanist ideas were alien to him. He well remembered hearing the vociferous and pretentious Marinetti pompously discuss modern art. "I even experienced a feeling of pride at associating with such a terribly 'advanced' man, but his theories left me cold," the composer recalls.

The futurists demonstrated for Diaghilev and his friends the latest noise instruments, which they believed would replace the obsolete violin and piano. Prokofiev found nothing appealing in this "music of the future," as can be seen from his matter-of-fact description of it in an article entitled "The Musical Instruments of the Futurists." "The futurists, who worship speed, also glorify modern machines," he wrote. "They maintain that there is a beauty of noises—for example, the distant noise of a rushing train, or the singing of a propeller. In their search for beautiful noises, they are inventing new musical instruments. Even apart from the question of technical deficiencies, the resources of these instruments are too meager for them to play any independent role."[34]

Obviously, foreign urbanist fashions had no particular attraction for the young Prokofiev. As we know, Mayakovsky's literary group also completely dissociated itself at this time from the imperialistic theories of Marinetti, denying that its work was influenced by the "Italo-futurists."[35]

Despite the war, Diaghilev tirelessly continued working out plans for his troupe's foreign appearances. He planned performances for Monte Carlo and prepared such sensational novelties as Stravinsky's *Wedding* and a ballet to music by Scarlatti.

While Prokofiev was in Italy the subject of his new ballet was chosen and its plot outlined. Diaghilev, who had sensed elements of the Russian national style in the Second Piano Concerto, pressed the composer for "Russian exoticism." Accordingly it was decided to replace the rejected Scythian ballet *Ala and Lolli* by one on a Russian folk-tale theme.

Diaghilev was swift and insistent in his decisions. Looking through Afanasyev's collection of Russian folk tales, which Stravinsky had brought for them, he and Prokofiev selected two humorous stories from the Perm region [in the Urals], from which they worked out a ballet scenario in six scenes. The future ballet was given the rather long and fanciful title, *The Tale of the Buffoon Who Outwitted Seven Buffoons.*

The negotiations between Prokofiev and the entrepreneur concluded with the signing of Prokofiev's first real contract, for three thousand rubles. The composer left for home, inspired by the new creative idea and Diaghilev's farewell advice. Charmed by Diaghilev's daring views and ingenuity, he did not examine too closely what the impresario meant by "national tendencies."

Of course, Diaghilev's interest in the Russian style in music and in folk tales had nothing in common with the progressive national ideals which had inspired the Five and the *Peredvizhniki*. In folk art he was seeking not a reflection of the real life of the Russian people but only bizarre subjects and situations likely to amuse European aesthetes.

Both of the Perm tales on which Prokofiev's new ballet was based were rooted in life, and their humor is tinged with social satire. Their hero is a gay village wag, a clever rogue somewhat like Pushkin's Balda. In the original tales, published by Afanasyev, the buffoon exemplifies the freedom-loving, anticlerical tendencies of the peasant masses. He is a mischievous mocker who adroitly dupes the priest, the priest's wife, and the rich merchants.[36] In one of the versions of this tale, there is also a landowner whom the buffoon throws into an ice-hole.

Diaghilev was not at all interested in social satire, however; the audiences which filled the theaters of London and Monte Carlo did not demand it. Therefore, in adapting the Perm tales, Diaghilev carefully deleted all the satirical, anticlerical implications. The priest and his wife, the principal characters in the tales, were completely eliminated. The buffoon was transformed into a caricature of an eccentric mischief-maker who plays amusing pranks. All sorts of brawls, murders, and antics were introduced, apparently to entertain the Western audiences with the Asiatic ignorance and boorishness of the Russian peasant.

The "Russian style" that Diaghilev was striving for was completely alien to the realistic principles of Russian national art of the nineteenth century. Lovers of Russian exoticism expected from the Diaghilev company skillfully contrived stylizations in the manner of the popular print, the *lubok*. Such were the deliberately simplified "Russian" canvases of the young modernist artists of the "Ass's Tail" group (for example, Goncharova and Larionov), who copied the crude, primitive style of the *lubok*. Fashionable artists of this group were engaged by Diaghilev to design his new ballets. Stravinsky's *Renard* and *L'Histoire du Soldat,* composed two or three years later, had the same quality. *The Buffoon,* too, was conceived in this style.

On returning to Petrograd, Prokofiev applied himself with characteristic fervor to the music for the new ballet. He was deeply interested in the Diaghilev commission, excited by the idea of searching for his own national style. Catering to the tastes of foreign audiences was alien to his nature.

"The Russian material was composed with great ease," the composer recalled. "It was as though I had come upon unbroken land or sown virgin soil and the new earth had yielded an unexpected harvest."

Of course, the derisive tone of the scenario directed the composer's imagination toward caricature and eccentric effects. The Russian dance melodies, which he composed without quotations or ethnographical research, were almost invariably modernized in an affected manner by the use of exaggerated, harmonic harshness and a deliberate sharpening of the melodic line. And yet, despite the fact that Prokofiev's task was to produce a fashionably stylized work, the music of *The Buffoon* did contain pages of genuine lyricism.

During the summer, Prokofiev finished the piano score of the six scenes of the ballet. He then considered going to Italy again in order to work with the choreographer on the completion of *The Buffoon*. Since by this time the spread of the war had made it impossible to travel through the Balkans, Prokofiev worked out an incredible itinerary via Archangel, Iceland, and Bordeaux. ("Although it is roundabout, there won't be any mines," he wrote his friends.) But this trip did not take place and Prokofiev had to send the manuscript to Diaghilev.

Recalling this period, Prokofiev wrote, "The main thing was that on my scales, Russian interests outweighed foreign ones." By "Russian interests" he meant work on the *Scythian Suite,* which he composed from the music of the ballet *Ala and Lolli,* and the opera *The Gambler,* of which he continued to dream despite Diaghilev's anti-operatic views.

Prokofiev's friends followed his growing participation in the Diaghilev enterprises with regret and misgivings. For example, in a letter from the front, Miaskovsky severely criticized him for the inconstancy of his aesthetic principles, for having so easily fallen under the impresario's influence. "Naturally Diaghilev had no difficulty getting around him," Miaskovsky wrote Derzhanovsky.[37]

On the other hand, the contract with Diaghilev greatly increased Prokofiev's opportunities in the commercial world of music. Concert organizations vied with one another for performances by a composer who had become famous abroad. "During the past year, I have achieved a solid and definite success with the public, musicians, critics, and concert organizations," Prokofiev wrote Jurgenson. "I see reasons to expect it to increase in the future, and no reasons for it to diminish."[38]

Prokofiev repeatedly attacked those who controlled Russian musical life, demanding attention for his music. He no longer pleaded with his publisher Jurgenson, as he had three years before. Now he himself dictated the terms, insisting on his rights.

With characteristic persistence he also fought for the rights of Miaskovsky, who was at the front. When Siloti refused to include Miaskovsky's Third Symphony in his programs on the pretext of wartime difficulties, Prokofiev attacked him vigorously. "The affair with Siloti has reached the point of sixteen-inch shells," he told his friends, promising to rebuke his adversary in an open letter.

During 1915 Prokofiev's name appeared more and more frequently on Petrograd concert programs. In addition to the First Piano Concerto, which by now had become popular, three old works of his Conservatory days—*Dreams, Autumnal Sketch,* and the Sinfonietta, Op. 5—were also played. The Sinfonietta was specially revised and reorchestrated for its première at one of Siloti's regular concerts. On April 26 Prokofiev played his Second Piano Concerto with the Court Orchestra under the baton of Hugo Warlich. On June 9 he appeared at the summer symphonic concerts in Sestroretsk (*Dreams* and the Second Piano Concerto, conducted by N. Malko), and on July 20 in Pavlovsk (*Dreams* and the First Piano Concerto, conducted by G. Fitelberg). The Sinfonietta was performed at Siloti's concerts on November 6, and *Dreams* was played in Moscow on December 20 at Koussevitzky's concerts, under the direction of G. Fitelberg. Asafyev praised the new orchestration of the Sinfonietta saying, "He had made excellent progress in scoring, which pleased me exceedingly."

As a "fashionable" musician, Prokofiev was also invited to perform at various charity and jubilee concerts. On May 17 he played five pieces from Op. 12 at an evening in memory of Scriabin held at N. Dobychina's studio. On November 28 he played his First Piano Sonata at a concert for the benefit of wounded soldiers; I. Yershov, V. Kastorsky, I. Tartakov, and other popular artists also participated in this program.

There was a marked change in the Petrograd public's attitude toward the young composer. "Only three years ago," wrote Karatygin, "most of our music lovers saw in Prokofiev's compositions only the excesses of a mad anarchism that threatened to overturn all Russian music. Now they won't let him leave the stage until he has played numerous encores."[39] "A huge success. The public likes him," remarked Asafyev after the Pavlovsk concert.[40]

Obliged to abandon the second trip to Italy, Prokofiev worked intensely throughout the summer of 1915, alternating concert appearances with composing and laboriously checking music proof sheets for the Jurgenson publishing house. "I spend the time now being bored, now being bellicose, and in between I groan under Jurgenson's proofs and work a bit on the new ballet," he wrote on May 30. "I've called off my trip abroad and am staying within the limits of the Petrograd area. I'm hard at work on the new ballet, and I'm making an orchestral suite from the old one," he said in another letter.[41]

Thus, while working on *The Buffoon* Prokofiev also made a symphonic suite from the music of *Ala and Lolli*. Not agreeing with Diaghilev's devastating judgment of it, he carefully looked through the sketches of the ballet which he had prepared the year before and decided that "if some of the uninteresting bits are discarded, the music is worth saving." The four-movement *Scythian Suite* incorporated the principal material of *Ala and Lolli*, presented in the same order as the four scenes of the rejected ballet.

With *Ala and Lolli* began Prokofiev's practice of creating symphonic suites out of material from his ballet, opera, and theater music. In the decades that followed, more than twenty suites were composed from such works as *The Buffoon, Le Pas d'acier, Cinderella, The Duenna,* and *The Stone Flower.* The best of them (the suites from *Romeo and Juliet*) achieved wide popularity.

✳ ✳ ✳

While in *The Buffoon* Prokofiev was absorbed in a search for his own national style, in the *Scythian Suite* he was concerned mainly with questions of orchestration. He conceived a score of unprecedented color and magnificent sonority. Thus far his writing for orchestra had amounted to the comparatively simple accompaniments of the first two piano concertos and the immature scores of *Dreams, Autumnal Sketch,* and the Sinfonietta. The *Scythian Suite* was his first large-scale, independent orchestral work.

"By this time I had sufficient mastery of orchestration to tackle a large orchestra and to try to carry out a number of ideas," he recalls. "The first two movements were orchestrated very easily. I spent much more time on the last two, and as a result they are more interesting in texture. I spent almost as much time on the closing sunrise as on half of the Suite."

The *Scythian Suite* impresses one primarily with the elemental power of its rhythm and the stunning color of its orchestration. Under the immediate impact of these effects, the melodic element recedes into the background, at times utterly engulfed in a torrent of deafening sounds.

The work is scored for an enormous full orchestra with a large number of additional instruments, including the rarely used alto trumpet. Brasses (including eight French horns) and percussion instruments play a decisive role in the orchestration. On the other hand, descriptive sound effects, such as tremolos and wailing chromatic passages, are often allotted to the strings. An important place in the score is assigned to the twanging timbres of the piano, celeste, and harp, which in a number of cases provide additional decorative background.

The score abounds in superimpositions of orchestral groups and complicated combinations of simultaneously sounding *ostinato* figures. Very complicated *divisi* and unusually bold color combinations are widely employed. This excessive use of massive orchestral resources, as well as the method of scoring itself, prefigured many extremes of the formalist music of the twenties. The arbitrary piling on of sounds produces an abundance of harsh polytonal combinations. The combination of harmonic dissonance and deafening tonal effects at times transforms the music into a naturalistic din in which the germs of melodic phrases disappear.

Unlike Prokofiev's concertos and sonatas, the Suite is not based on classical forms but on a drama-like succession of scenes and episodes. There are no leitmotivs to link the movements of the Suite, and only in the middle two movements can one clearly sense the design of a closed three-part construction. These peculiarities of form, as well as the harshness of the harmonic idiom and the reduced role of melody, unquestionably make the *Scythian Suite* difficult to grasp.

The first movement, "Worship of Veles and Ala," opens with frenzied invocatory phrases coming from various sections of the orchestra over a rumble of percussion instruments. The tempo is swift and energetic. This invocation is followed by a new and even more propulsive phrase, which is endlessly repeated in a primitive rhythm by all the strings and winds. The effect here is that of heavy stamping. The sonority grows even thicker and denser, and over the stamping is heard the shrill whistle of the woodwinds. At the climax of this episode eight French horns and four trombones carry the theme in parallel, harshly dissonant chords, in the same savage rhythm. Then, as the stamping gradually dies down, the second and more transparent section of the movement begins, apparently portraying the goddess Ala. The melody of the flute, against a background of gently swaying rhythms from the celeste and the harp, sounds exotic in its Eastern languor.

After the softly fading conclusion of the first movement, the second movement, "Chuzhbog and the Dance of the Evil Spirits," sounds martial and menacing. The music suggests a fierce enemy raid. Against the mechanical rhythm of footsteps there bursts from the French horns a vigorous signal theme, filled with primitive power (FIG. 14).

FIGURE 14

Later this march-like music gives way to a frenetic dance in complicated rhythm (an interchange between the bassoon and the English horn over the dry, deathlike timbre of the strings playing *col legno*). The dance of the evil spirits become wilder, the rhythms become more and more pronounced, and at the very end the somewhat altered opening phrase of Chuzhbog rings out like a call to battle. In this movement, particularly in the opening section, one can see a kinship to Borodin's Polovtsian Dances; we find here the same evocation of primitive life on the steppes, of barbaric nomads and supernatural forces.

In the third movement, "Night," the purely decorative element predominates. This "steppe nocturne" opens and closes with a diatonic melody in the familiar vein of the composer's lyrical themes, constructed "on the white keys." But later on, the melodic clarity disappears and sheer color comes to the foreground: rustling and buzzing in the strings; soft, ringing sounds in the celeste and the harp; and vague, elusive phrases in the flutes and oboes. The music impressionistically paints an exquisite "stage set," a steppe scene immersed in gloom. In the middle section of this movement, the tranquil mood is overthrown by sharply accented, angular phrases, as if a savage enemy raid had shattered the peacefulness of the night. Toward the end, the emotionally restrained, decorative phrases of the nocturne return.

At last there unfolds the dazzlingly sonorous music of the Finale, for which the composer chose a gigantic orchestral "armada." In essence, most of the Finale (a continuous succession of fantastic episodes suggestive of marches and pagan dances) serves as a preparation for the concluding section, "Sunrise." This short coda consists of a colossal, continually mounting crescendo. New groups of instruments are added in succession to the swelling din, above which are heard the penetrating—one might say scorching—sounds of five trumpets. Although the melodic element all but disappears, the compelling combination of brilliant tone color and simple but full-sounding harmonic effects (a chain of chords over a ceaseless pedal point of B-flat major triads) is truly captivating. In this climax, the composer achieves a triumph; by the use of novel techniques resembling those of poster art, he creates a brilliantly dynamic image of the sunrise. It is this movement of the Suite that produces the greatest effect, an effect somewhat like that of the finale of Scriabin's *Poem of Ecstasy*.

Thus, despite the vacuousness of its original conception, oriented as it was toward "barbaric exoticism," and despite its exaggerated harmonies and tonal effects and its neglect of the melodic element, the *Scythian Suite* has its strong points, particularly in the second movement and the coda of the Finale. In his evocation of natural scenes and mysterious forces inimical to man, Prokofiev enriched the descriptive resources of music. The "rhythms of invasion" at the beginning of the second movement were helpful to the composer years later, in the 1930's, when he composed his music for the "Battle on the Ice" section of the *Alexander Nevsky* cantata.

Even before the *Scythian Suite* was completed, Prokofiev was invited by Siloti to include it in the programs of the 1915–16 season, and to conduct it himself. "I don't know which is better: to conduct it myself, or to just sit and listen," Prokofiev wrote as he dreamed of soon hearing his colossal score played.[42] On September 15, 1915, the newspapers reported that the *Scythian Suite* had been completed and was to be included in the Siloti programs.

❈   ❈   ❈

In the intervals between composing large-scale commissioned works calculated to overthrow traditions, Prokofiev snatched time to express his lyrical inclinations. After the anarchic audacities of *The Buffoon* and the *Scythian Suite,* he was glad to return to the pure, simple, profoundly human lyricism which had attracted him since his youth. Early in 1915 he conceived the idea for a violin concertino, but after composing a serene, flowing melody in D major (the future first theme of the First Violin Concerto) he put this work aside. The same year he wrote a number of amazingly fresh and charming little piano pieces, either as sketches for larger works, or merely as records of fleeting impressions. Here, as in the Second Piano Sonata, the pieces of Op. 12, and *The Ugly Duckling,* one is struck by the colorful combination of lyricism and lively humor. These pieces were later included in Op. 22, which was given the title *Fugitive Visions.* Numbers 5, 6, 10, 16, and 17 (possibly the best ones) were written in 1915. It is difficult to believe that these delicate and touching pieces, as well as the lovely, sunny melody of the D major Violin Concerto, were created at the same time as the frightening complexities of the *Scythian Suite* and *The Gambler.*

During the same troubled summer of 1915, Prokofiev once again turned to the vocal genre. "I've now plunged into writing songs," he reported in a letter on September 1. The five new songs, which constitute the vocal cycle Op. 23, demonstrate the instability of the young Prokofiev's poetic tastes. Alongside the ultra-aesthetes Balmont (*In My Garden*) and Gippius (*The Gray Dress*) stands the dilettante Verin, feebly aping the symbolist poets (*Trust Me*). In these three songs, especially the meditative *Trust Me* and *In My Garden,* one senses little of Prokofiev's individuality. He is completely the captive of this decadent and affected poetry; hence the contrived quality of the harmonies and the unnatural brokenness of the vocal declamation. Decadent motifs are particularly evident in Gippius's poem *The Gray Dress.* The image of the "wicked little girl in the gray dress," with vacant eyes and cotton-like braids, symbolizes Parting, the Daughter of Death. The unwholesome mysticism of these poems could hardly have had any deep appeal for Prokofiev, who in his best lyrical works strove so eagerly to express spiritual purity and love of mankind. No wonder that when he worked in the song idiom he turned to purely surface description and overrefined harmonies. It is important to point out that these poems were not chosen by the composer himself. *The Gray Dress* was suggested by Derzhanovsky, and *Trust Me* apparently was given him by Verin, to whom the song was dedicated.

Prokofiev used poetry of a completely different kind in the songs *Under the Roof* (by V. Goryansky) and *The Wizard* (by N. Agnivtsev). The authors of these poems were contributors to the popular humorous magazine *Novy Satirikon*. The prosaic lyricism in Goryansky's poem about city slums and the bitingly satirical tone of Agnivtsev's tale of the Wizard contrasted sharply with the pretentious symbolist works of Balmont and Gippius. The young Prokofiev's interest in the works of the *Satirikon* poets is revealing. While *Novy Satirikon* was not distinguished for political daring, it was the most anti-government humorous magazine of that period. Together with the clever stories of A. Averchenko (which, it is true, rarely overstepped the bounds of cautious liberalism) appeared the satirical "hymns" of the young Mayakovsky, which exposed the loathsomeness and rottenness of bourgeois society (*Hymn to Dinner, Hymn to the Judge,* etc.). The caustic tone of *Novy Satirikon* seemingly corresponded completely to the views of Prokofiev, who liked to poke fun at all sorts of "old, used stuff" in life and in art.

The poetry of Goryansky and Agnivtsev offered an opportunity for a kind of vocal lyricism unusual for that time and for a type of satirical song neglected since Moussorgsky's day. It also provided a basis for formal experiments very much related in style to the *Sarcasms*. The composer himself points out that the songs in Op. 23 bore a certain relationship to the *Sarcasms*. This was particularly so in the case of the bitingly grotesque song *The Wizard*. The poem tells the story of a strange hermit who creates for himself an "ideal" woman—dutiful, submissive, virtuous. But soon afterward he hangs himself, unable to endure his unleavened "family happiness." With devastating sarcasm, Prokofiev's music draws the portrait of a dull, boring "ideal woman." Despite the deliberate harshness of its harmonies, the piece is a daring musical caricature, a challenge to Philistine notions of beauty and well-being. Prokofiev was working in a genre untouched in Russian vocal music since the days of Moussorgsky's *Classicist* and *He-Goat*.[43]

The song *Under The Roof,* like *The Wizard,* is noteworthy in many respects. In deliberately prosaic and unpoetic verse, Goryansky expressed a poet's sympathy for the common people of a capitalist city, who retain a touching love of life and nature despite oppressive poverty and toil:

> . . . It was a week ago that someone told me
> I was blind and knew not life's joys,
> That I was all sunk in working and sweating,
> That my children were sin's ugly toys. . . .

But that's not so, now! Really not so!
My children have all the graces!
But I'm poor, and that's why they starve and are famished,
What gives them such pinched little faces.
I see the wide world through my one tiny window,
My soul is not blinded to light.
Oh, I see the sun climbing higher and higher,
Through banks of clouds and the night.

And at the end the cheerful and serene conclusion:

Who said that I live not knowing nature
Affronted me, spoke in vain.
No! I have felt fair nature's glad smile! . . .

It may be that the sentiments in this poem were close to those of the young Prokofiev, who retained a genuine love for life and nature despite all the ugliness of surrounding reality. In composing *Under the Roof,* the composer, as he put it, "took the greatest pains to convey in the music every nuance and thought and feeling expressed in the text." But the deliberately prosaic, unmusical nature of the poetry led him to extreme angularity in the melodic line. This lack of melodiousness in the vocal part, together with an accompaniment constructed on exaggerated *ostinato* figures, severely weakened the effect of the song.

After the warm lyricism of *The Ugly Duckling,* the songs, Op. 23— especially *The Gray Dress, Trust Me,* and *In My Garden*—were an open concession to the vogue of decadence. Is it not strange that Prokofiev himself, captivated by the quest for new forms, considered these songs more modern than the simple and earthy *Ugly Duckling?* "The Little Girl is more subtle and more advanced than the Duckling," he asserted in one of his letters. "The Duckling is simpler. On the other hand, thanks to its text, it has more variety."[44]

The five songs in Op. 23 did not impress the critics. Even Prokofiev's admirers (including Karatygin) were very restrained in commenting on them. *"Under the Roof* was the only thing that Karatygin did not understand," the composer remarked somewhat reproachfully.

Karatygin's criticism was well founded, however. "It must be admitted that Prokofiev's vocal music is less convincing than his piano music," he wrote. "The accompaniment, which is supposed to illustrate the text, often suits it poorly. Each detail in it lays claim to distinctiveness. There is no 'neutral' music. This continuous variety, besides not fully corresponding to the text, in the end produces monotony."[45] Derzhanovsky expressed a similar thought about Prokofiev's songs: "The composer has not as yet completely mastered the forms of vocal music. The word, I think, tends to inhibit him, and is not always completely realized in the music."[46]

These criticisms might be enlarged upon, of course, for most of Prokofiev's early vocal works do lack the melodic element and a natural cohesion of words and music. However, such songs as *The Wizard* and *Under the Roof* (to say nothing of *The Ugly Duckling*) revealed not only the composer's formal innovation but also traces of a critical attitude toward contemporary bourgeois morality. This attitude manifested itself even more clearly in the opera *The Gambler,* to which the songs of Op. 23 were direct steppingstones.

Of course, the social criticism in these early works was in no way connected with consciously formulated political views. Prokofiev was, as before, very far removed from politics. But the atmosphere around him was becoming more and more tense. As Lenin wrote, "Like every crisis, the war has sharpened the antagonisms deeply hidden underneath, bringing them to the surface, tearing off the cloak of hypocrisy, rejecting all conventionality, destroying all discredited and partially discredited authorities."[47]

Prokofiev could not remain impervious to the discontent and indignation of many of the people around him. Feelings of this kind were expressed, for example, in Miaskovsky's letters from the front. Miaskovsky's friends Asafyev, Derzhanovsky, and Prokofiev read these letters with alarm. "Everyone is fed up with the war, especially with the outrageous confusion, shallowness, ignorance, and other charms that reign here," wrote Miaskovsky in April 1915. "Oh, how they lie, cheat, swindle, etc. All these Dmitrievs, Nik. Nik., Ivanovs, and others—these shameful incompetents who cannot foresee what is apparent even to simple combat officers."*

During the same summer of 1915, Mayakovsky wrote a poem of violent protest, *A Cloud in Trousers,* and castigated the bourgeois system in his "hymns," published in *Novy Satirikon.* Skepticism, disillusionment with authority of every kind, and contempt for hypocrisy and philistine complacency spontaneously broke through even in some of Prokofiev's works (in the songs, Op. 23, for example, and especially in the opera *The Gambler*).

In 1915 Prokofiev was faced with a call to military service. His friends, who felt Miaskovsky's absence, were deeply worried that the war might now remove still another highly talented Russian musician from creative

---

* Letters to Derzhanovsky, April 14 and May 30, 1915. These are references to the Russian high command. "Nik. Nik.," for example, means the Grand Duke Nicholas Nikolaevich, who held the post of commander-in-chief.

work. In order to obtain a deferment Prokofiev re-entered the Petrograd Conservatory in September 1915, this time in the organ class.

The deferment made it possible for him to begin work on his long-planned opera, *The Gambler*. Production of *The Buffoon* was postponed until the end of the war, and Prokofiev's connections with the Diaghilev company were temporarily broken. On the other hand, the Director of Imperial Theaters, V. Telyakovsky, unexpectedly took an interest in him.

During the pre-revolutionary years the directorate of the Maryinsky Theater began to permit the performance of some modern novelties. Modernist *régisseurs* such as Vsevolod Meyerhold were engaged, and the latest works by contemporary Western composers were staged, or at least rehearsed (Strauss's *Elektra,* among others). The Theater's marked shift toward modernism was prompted by a desire to satisfy the demands of the highest bourgeois and aristocratic circles, and also by a determination not to lag behind Diaghilev. The success of the Diaghilev company had awakened a feeling of envy in the Russian bourgeoisie, for by exporting his Russian novelties to the foreign market, Diaghilev was preventing them from being performed in Russia. The bourgeois press was outraged at so arbitrary a thwarting of the Russian public's interests.

"It seems that even though the war ought to halt the sale of new Russian works abroad, Prokofiev's new ballet, commissioned by S. P. Diaghilev, is going to be presented not on a Russian stage, but on a foreign one, and as before, for the thousand and first time, we shall watch the same ballets in the Maryinsky Theater that not only our fathers but our grandfathers watched," wrote one Petrograd newspaper apropos of *The Buffoon*.[48]

Repeated criticism of this kind forced the Maryinsky Theater to give more attention to the works of modern Russian composers. This new policy was actively supported by the young conductor Albert Coates.[49] Coates was gradually replacing the aged Napravnik, who had almost ceased to conduct. The influential Siloti introduced Prokofiev to Coates, who immediately encouraged him. "'Write your *Gambler*,' he said, 'and we'll produce it!' It would be difficult to imagine a more fortunate combination of circumstances," Prokofiev relates.

The composer again reread Dostoyevsky's novel and began to draft the libretto. The finished product was straightforward and almost entirely conversational prose, without a single aria, chorus, or ensemble. In an attempt to bring the operatic action closer to that of the usual dramatic play, the composer rejected generally accepted operatic forms. In one of his interviews he said, "I consider the custom of writing operas to rhymed texts an utterly ridiculous convention. In this instance, Dostoyevsky's prose is more vivid, more graphic, and more convincing than any verse."[50]

Thus the libretto consisted of Dostoyevsky's original dialogue, greatly abridged by the composer, and a small amount of new material necessary to maintain continuity in the action. Only in the next-to-last scene, which depicts the feverish roulette game, did Prokofiev find it necessary to depart from the original and write a new text based on situations in the novel's plot. The coauthor of this scene (the most difficult one dramaturgically) was B. N. Demchinsky, a dabbler in philosophy and art and a regular guest at Bashkirov-Verin's salons.

The operatic principles on which *The Gambler* was based were not altogether new or surprising in Russian music. It was this type of "dialogue opera," constructed entirely on the original prose text of a literary work, that Moussorgsky had chosen for *The Marriage*. Moussorgsky considered his experiment an attempt at direct "artistic reproduction of human speech in all its finest shades." But he himself soon became convinced of the limitations of this method, which leads to an impoverishment of the melodic richness of opera, to "uniformity of intonation" (which he called "the worst of sins in so capricious a thing as *The Marriage*"). *The Marriage* remained an unfinished experiment in the creative work of the brilliant reformer of Russian opera. But Prokofiev saw no such limitations. In *The Gambler* he not only adopted Moussorgsky's method as an aesthetic principle, but carried it to even greater extremes.

The revival of this very daring experiment was by no means the result of conscious imitation. Nowhere do we find any indication that Prokofiev wished to continue Moussorgsky's experiments. However, Asafyev, who knew Prokofiev intimately during these years, noted that in his vocal music he "clearly and repeatedly" (even if not consciously) followed the path marked out by Moussorgsky (in *The Marriage* and *Sunless*). It will be recalled that in 1909, after forty years of oblivion, *The Marriage* was given its first performance at one of the public concerts of the St. Petersburg Evenings of Modern Music. Karatygin was very enthusiastic about it. In all likelihood the young Prokofiev, too, responded very keenly to this opera, the most "anarchical" of Moussorgsky's works.

Prokofiev applied himself with enthusiasm to *The Gambler,* a work he had dreamed of for almost three years. For him, turning to opera was a highly principled act—an act, moreover, of the utmost significance in his creative life. In writing opera he was going against the stream, for most of his teachers and immediate predecessors—among them Glazunov, Lyadov, and Scriabin—had shunned the writing of opera for one reason or another, and many modernists of the Diaghilev-Benois school were predicting the imminent death of Russian opera. Nevertheless, Prokofiev turned eagerly toward this most interesting genre, which had attracted him since his youth.

In an interview given at that time, he stressed the desirability of intensifying the dramatic element in opera. "I believe that Wagnerian grandeur had a disastrous effect upon the development of opera, as a result of which even the most advanced musicians came to consider opera a dying form," he said. "However, given an understanding of the stage, flexibility, freedom, and expressive declamation, opera should be one of the most vibrant and compelling of the scenic arts."[51] Unfortunately, weaknesses in the content of his libretto and (above all) the modernist extremes of his musical style prevented Prokofiev at that time from creating a truly realistic Russian opera.

Work on *The Gambler,* begun in November, progressed with incredible speed. The entire piano score was written in five and a half months. The first act was completed on December 21, 1915; the second on February 10, 1916; the third on March 29; and the fourth in the middle of April. The composer worked as though possessed, striving to complete the opera in time for the coming theater season.

"I'm spending all my time on the opera. I'm very tired, but am already dashing through the third act," he wrote on February 22. "I'm hurrying to finish the piano score by May (there is still an act and a half to be done), and the full score (not yet begun) by October," he reported in a letter on March 15.[52] Even in these early years Prokofiev was amazingly well organized in his work and unusually good in the matter of completing projects on time.

Proceeding from the modernist principle that traditions must be defied, the young composer made the musical language of the opera as complicated as possible. He strove to stun the audience with harmonic superimpositions and unusual declamation. The entire structure and character of the music is the very antithesis of classical opera. The enthusiasm of the modernist critics for the *Scythian Suite* and the Second Piano Concerto played no small part in urging him to these extremes. "Encouraged by the interest aroused by the *Scythian Suite,* I chose the most radical language possible for *The Gambler,*" the composer recalls.

On his own admission, these extreme devices were suitable primarily for the expression of intense nervous emotion and bitter mockery. But the rest of the music contained, as he put it later, "a great deal of tiresome modernist padding which added nothing and simply confused the vocal line."

No wonder the dissonances of *The Gambler* frightened and irritated even his closest supporters—including his mother, who until then had patiently endured all her son's excesses. "Do you really understand what you are pounding out on that piano of yours?" Mariya Grigoryevna once exclaimed on entering the room where the opera was being composed. "We were at odds for two days," Prokofiev recalls.

❈   ❈   ❈

As we know, Prokofiev had become interested in Dostoyevsky's *Gambler* while still in the Conservatory. He considered it the "least Dostoyevskian" of all the writer's works. What excited him in the novel was its dynamic plot, which offered possibilities for sharply expressive development of action, and its stinging satire, so congenial to his own creative purposes at that time.

Unlike the story of *The Buffoon,* the libretto of *The Gambler* was completely plausible. A retired Russian general is amusing himself at a fashionable foreign health resort noted for its gambling houses. He is surrounded by a crowd of idlers like himself: a Marquis, a cunning businessman who lends him money; an Englishman, Mr. Astley; a seductive demimondaine, Mlle. Blanche. Having long before gambled away all his money, the General is impatiently awaiting the death of a rich grandmother in Moscow, whose wealth he hopes to inherit. But suddenly Babulenka, the grandmother, unexpectedly arrives at the resort. Not only does she lay bare the General's cynical plans and refuse to give him any money, but she, too, becomes infected with the pernicious passion for roulette. After losing a fortune she leaves for home, completely shattering the General's hopes. In a parallel plot, the libretto deals with the passion of a young tutor, Alexei, for the General's young stepdaughter, Polina. Polina is faced with marriage to her father's creditor, the Marquis, whom she does not love. In order to rescue her from this situation, Alexei vows to win the money for her at roulette. He has fantastic luck—he breaks the bank. But when he brings the money to Polina, she flings it in his face, crying that money is an insulting payment for love. The opera ends with Polina in hysterics and Alexei raving mad.

In the course of the opera (particularly in the first three acts) the characters engage in little action, appearing on the stage only for brief dialogues. Whatever action there is takes place at the end of each act, where the most dramatic situations are concentrated. The composer tried to draw a line of mounting tension from the beginning to the end of the opera. The fast-moving scene of Alexei's lucky game, with the hero surrounded by a crowd of frenzied gamblers (Act IV), constitutes the climax of the whole work.

As we have seen, it was not only the dynamic quality of the intrigue that attracted Prokofiev in this story, but also the social censure. In the libretto he gave special emphasis to the passages showing Alexei's mad and provocative behavior, Babulenka's cutting outspokenness, and the greed and shamelessness of the General and his friends. We see Alexei jeering at the haughty German baroness (end of Act I), Babulenka lecturing the General and his hangers-on with the bluntness of a peasant, Alexei denouncing the morality of a burgher family that virtually worships the power of money. It is interesting that when Prokofiev began to compose *The Gambler,* he started with the text of this denunciation. One of the most important moments in Alexei's part, it is typical of the tone of the libretto:

"The virtuous father, the obedient family, a stork on the roof, flowers in front of the house. All work like oxen and hoard money: money, money, money. The daughter is an old maid; she was given no dowry. The youngest son was sold into servitude and the money added to the capital. At last enough money is accumulated to enable the forty-year-old son to marry. The father gives him his blessing, weeps, moralizes, hands over his capital, and dies. And on and on it goes, until six generations later there is the solid, respectable firm of Hoppe & Co."

The satiric motif found in this monologue is clearly evident in other passages of the libretto as well. Take, for example, the derisive remark of the English gambler in the roulette scene, "The percentage of rogues in our Manchester is lower, considerably lower"; or the irate General's remarks to Alexei (a sort of caricature in the manner of Saltykov-Shchedrin): "We in Russia have authorities. In our Empire, there's guardianship . . . In our country we make such old women knuckle under! Knuckle under!" These details show that during the pre-revolutionary years, a tendency toward social satire was not alien to the young Prokofiev.

On the whole, however, what predominates in this libretto is not the wholesome laughter of a strong man who is certain of his own ideals, but cynical ridicule. All the leading characters are cynics—false, spiritually bankrupt people poisoned by a passion for gain. Even the "positive characters," Alexei and Polina, are no exception—their moral depravity and hysteria make them repulsive. ("There is pleasure in utter degradation and humiliation," Alexei declares bluntly in a duet with Polina.) The most normal person in the opera is Babulenka, whose Russian forthrightness is delightful, but in the end even she submits to the power of blind passion.

Despite its satiric notes, the libretto of *The Gambler* is on the whole very pessimistic, and lacking in morality and faith in man. The music accentuates these qualities. The repudiation of classical traditions is clearly evident in all the components of the opera—in the complete rejection of accepted operatic forms, in the ignoring of rounded-out vocal melody as the principal means of expression, and in the grotesque exaggeration of the harmonic and orchestral writing.

The composer based the form of the opera on the principle of continuous declamation (complicated by the deliberate prose style of the text), combined with an expressively descriptive orchestral accompaniment. It cannot be denied that in a number of episodes the young composer, who had already acquired some experience in writing opera (*Maddalena*) and songs (*The Ugly Duckling*), revealed a keen sense of the intonations of human speech. The opera contains a number of sharply effective declamatory details, which fix individual traits of the characters—the deceitfulness and stupid pomposity of the General, the sham coquetry of Mlle. Blanche, the ugliness of Mr. Astley, and so on. Despite their caricatural quality, some of the characterizing leitmotivs are quite effective—for example, the awkward, broken leitmotiv of the Englishman Astley (FIG. 15).

FIGURE 15

The love scenes between Alexei and Polina contain germs of sincere lyricism, restrained and spare, in the typical Prokofiev manner. Unfortunately these lyrical melodic phrases (mainly in Polina's part) are drowned in a torrent of exaggerated vocal declamation.

The continuous recitative, for the most part high-strung and unrelieved by a single arioso passage, inevitably becomes monotonous. However ingenious the recitative, an opera cannot succeed without melody. But in the entire opera there is not a single aria, not even an ensemble—only innumerable prose dialogues. The composer rejected choral episodes, explaining in an interview on *The Gambler* that in general the operatic chorus is "not flexible and not good theater."[53] Only in the scene in the gambling house are there a few choral and ensemble bits, in a purely declamatory vein. The declamation of *The Gambler* abounds in eccentric and grotesque effects which verge on buffoonery, such as the Baron's grunt in the finale of Act I, the General's stammering prattle when Babulenka first appears, and his heart-rending howl at the end of Act III.

The composer's inherent keenness of observation reveals itself in a number of the orchestral episodes (notably in the tense, dynamic portrayal of reckless gambling).

But the orchestral construction of the opera is kaleidoscopic; the composer very seldom returns to familiar themes or leitmotivs. This leads to a feeling of formlessness. The orchestral part often amounts to a repetition of rather mechanical *ostinato* figures, which, instead of illustrating the action, create a general atmosphere of tension or derision. Moreover, like most of the music of the opera, these orchestral passages abound in complicated polytonal harmonies and intentionally colorless chords which accentuate the caricatural quality of the work.

According to the composer's plan, the music associated with Babulenka was to stand in sharp contrast to the basic musical characteristics of the opera. In fact, many of Babulenka's phrases do have a clearly Russian flavor, but even in her part the typically Russian song element is distorted by grotesque harmonization. Typical in this respect is the Russian theme, which recurs now and again as if to remind the opera's heroes of their distant homeland (FIG. 16).

In short, despite many interesting details which reflect Prokofiev's genuine dramatic sense, the opera as a whole leaves an impression of monotonous jesting and mockery.

*The Gambler,* with its exaggerated recitatives and dissonant orchestral music, to some degree paved the way for the expressionist extremes of the modernist operas of the twenties. Work on this opera may have given Prokofiev some experience in the technique of declamation and may have sharpened his own innate dramatic sense. But at the same time it was precisely *The Gambler* that fixed in his mind those one-sided musico-dramatic principles which later became a serious obstacle to his efforts at operatic realism. The tendency toward completely declamatory, "conversational" forms of opera, toward expressionistic excesses—both in contrast to the

FIGURE 16

moral directness of the classical Russian opera—also made it difficult in later years for the composer to work successfully in this most important musical genre.

❋   ❋   ❋

While working on *The Gambler,* Prokofiev made a few concert appearances. On November 6, 1915, he conducted the première of his Sinfonietta at Siloti's subscription concert in the Maryinsky Theater. This piece "was not given a very friendly reception."[54] However, most of the critics noted a certain freshness in it, as well as clever harmonic invention, especially in the middle movements.

On January 29, 1916, the composer also conducted the première of the *Scythian Suite* at Siloti's seventh subscription concert in the Maryinsky Theater. Never had Prokofiev's music stirred up such a storm of indignation and enthusiasm, such noisy and contradictory criticism in the press. Even before the première, the newspapers reported that the rehearsals had been "accompanied by incidents" because members of the orchestra could hardly bear the Suite's strident, dissonant sounds. This was corroborated by the composer, who noted in his memoirs, "In the orchestra there were feeble attempts at obstruction." According to a newspaper report, "The Suite calls for an orchestra of a hundred and forty members. What is more, Mr. Siloti had to spend seven full rehearsals on it."[55]

The diversity of styles offered at the concert was astonishing. Together with the *Scythian Suite* and other modernist novelties, the program included excerpts from Cherepnin's choreodrama *The Masque of the Red Death,* Glinka's *Kamarinskaya,* Grieg's Piano Concerto (with Siloti as soloist), and arias from Tchaikovsky operas.

The audience was extremely shocked by the *Scythian Suite.* "The first movement was received in silence; the last called forth both applause and stormy protests. Despite this the composer, who had conducted his own 'barbaric' work, took a number of bows," reported *Birzheviye Vedomosti.*[56]

All of musical Petrograd was in the hall that evening. Glazunov, whom the composer himself had invited to the concert, left several measures before the end of the Suite. This furnished rich food for the newspaper gossips, who played up the incident in every possible way.

Prokofiev was quite content with the fact that the Suite had caused such a sensation. "Last night I conducted Ala, which went off with a tremendous hullabaloo," he reported to his Moscow friends.[57] Far from discouraging him, the uproar created by the Suite only intensified his desire to stun the bourgeoisie with his modernism.

The highly unfavorable reaction of a part of the audience in the Maryinsky Theater was widely reflected in the Petrograd press. "It is simply incredible that such an utterly meaningless piece could be performed at a serious concert. . . . A hodge-podge of bold, impertinent sounds, expressing nothing except infinite braggadocio," wrote Yu. Kurdyumov in *Teatralny Listok.*[58] "Only Nasreddin, the late Shah of Persia, would consider such works to be music," wrote the critic of *Novoye Vremya* in an attempt to be witty.[59] "Hair-raising musical rowdyism," "A novel way of smudging music paper," "Horse racing"—the music critics stopped at nothing in their attempt to sting the young composer.

Even *Muzykalny Sovremennik,* which was considered the organ of progressive art circles, carried an openly derisive article on Prokofiev's Suite. Comparing it with *The Rite of Spring,* the magazine sharply contrasted the style of the "aristocrat and gourmet" Stravinsky, whose works are "permeated with culture," with the coarser, cruder style of the young Prokofiev. "He is not troubled by any perceptible spiritual doubts, not encumbered by an overly refined cultural heritage. He is as wholesome as a country boy, and young with that playful youthfulness which feels at home in any circumstances and in any attire so long as it is not tight." While taking note of Prokofiev's gifts, his fiery temperament, and the richness of his orchestration, the magazine at the same time pointed out tartly that the composer's talent was very "one-sided."[60]

The sharp controversy over the *Scythian Suite* increased public interest in it, and Siloti decided to perform it again at the beginning of the following season. On this occasion, a non-subscription concert on November 11, 1916, Prokofiev appeared on a program with Rachmaninov, who played his own Second Piano Concerto. According to Karatygin, the Suite "was received quite differently this time. At its performance last season there was more indignation than praise for this tempestuous and provocative novelty. This time the composer was called out four times."[61]

However, the evening did not pass without an exchange of abuse between Prokofiev's adherents and his opponents. "The battle ended in Mr. Prokofiev's favor," remarked Igor Glebov [Asafyev], "for the majority supported the daring composer, even though Mr. Rachmaninov preceded him."[62]

In contrast to the rest of the Petrograd press, Karatygin gave the highest praise to the stylistic extremes of this "barbaric" score. He declared the *Scythian Suite* to be "one of the most important and valuable examples of Russian musical modernism."[63] The leader of the Evenings of Modern Music was particularly enthusiastic about Prokofiev's pungent harmonies, which he said make the listener "shudder and tremble."

Karatygin not only tried to justify these harmonic exaggerations, but even declared them to be a kind of "norm" in modern music. He defined the polytonal use of harsh superimpositions and arbitrary chordal combinations as "neo-heterophony," which, unlike classical polyphony, ignores the laws of traditional harmony, replacing them with the principle of dissonance, "the superimposition of one pattern on another without any particular relation between the two." In his enthusiasm for the audacities of the *Scythian Suite,* this critic was ready to consider them a good means for further "refreshing" the musical language. Karatygin's articles, obscured by complicated phraseology, summoned young composers to tonal anarchy, to a rejection of the functional bonds of traditional harmony.

Asafyev, who was also stunned by the novelty and power of the *Scythian Suite,* approached it from a different point of view. He tried to relate it to Borodin's most elemental, pagan music, the Polovtsian Dances. "It seems to me that the initial impression created by Borodin's music, with its striking individuality, power, and rich flavor of the broad, rolling steppes, must have been very like the impression we now receive when we listen to the music of Prokofiev." He contrasted the hard, chiseled character of the *Scythian Suite* with the hothouse delicacy and thematic poverty of modernist music in general, with "its doting on ultra-refinement, its sucking on sweet candies, particularly of foreign manufacture, its infatuation with sound for sound's sake." Asafyev forgave the composer of the Suite for its stridency, unevenness of style, and metrical monotony, arguing that these defects were outweighed by its merits. Its chief merit lay in giving expression to a "turbulent will," and a "thirst for life—healthy, strong, bold, and stopping at nothing."

Asafyev sensed in the images of the *Scythian Suite* forebodings of the social upheaval toward which Russia was steadily moving. "Prokofiev's music, revealing to us as it does the free will's exultant drive toward creative becoming, is profoundly contemporary," he wrote, "for the entire country is right now consumed with a thirst for active life, a thirst for real work, a belief in a bright future. Surely it depends upon the people themselves to shape their own destiny."[64]

These lines were written just one year before the monarchy was overthrown. One cannot but be amazed at the insight of this eminent musician and thinker, who sensed, in his own way, the approach of significant social changes. Of course, Asafyev highly exaggerated the topicality of the *Scythian Suite*. Actually this Suite, with its barbaric, primitive exoticism, in no way reflected a conscious understanding of the impending revolutionary storm. (If anything, the images of the Suite constitute something in the nature of a refraction of the horrors of the First World War.) Nevertheless, the effect produced by this turbulent music, coming as it did only a few months before the beginning of the Revolution, proved symptomatic indeed. Those who were socially sensitive perceived it through the prism of their own anxieties, endeavoring to hear in it the voice of an explosive epoch, a kind of portent of the impending storm.

# FIVE

# CROSSROADS

*In the thorny-crown of revolution*
*I see nineteen-sixteen emerge.*
                              Mayakovsky

D URING 1916 there were visible signs that the crisis in Russia was
coming to a head. The war was spreading incalculable misery
among the people. Economic difficulties multiplied. It became increasingly clear that the tsarist government was on the verge of collapse.
The Bolsheviks, under the leadership of Lenin, led the masses in their
movement against the hated war. The great Russian writers Gorky and
Mayakovsky lifted their voices against the horrors of the world holocaust.
In his poem "A Cloud in Trousers" and in other works, Mayakovsky expressed eager anticipation of the Revolution.

On the eve of the storm, Prokofiev found himself at something of a
crossroads. The social unrest, which was clearly beginning to produce
changes in the life of Russia, was bound to affect his artistic consciousness.
At about this time he met Gorky, grew closer to Asafyev, and attended one
of Mayakovsky's stirring public readings. The temporary break in his association with Diaghilev was beneficial to his creative development. In the
works composed during 1916–17, buffoonery and superficial extravagances
disappear, and warm humanity, clarity, and depth of musical thought
predominate.

But having neither clearly formulated political ideals nor a sense of the
historic significance of current events, Prokofiev remained isolated in a
world of narrowly professional interests, unable to see a role for himself
in the developing social struggle.

During 1916 Prokofiev was chiefly occupied with orchestrating *The
Gambler,* which was given an audition at Telyakovsky's house and accepted
for production. Attending the audition were the conductors of the Maryinsky Theater headed by Coates, the chief *régisseur* I. Tartakov, and Siloti,

acting as a consultant. Coates arranged for the audition to take place in the absence of Glazunov and Cui (both permanent members of the repertory commission), who would be certain to reject the modernist music of *The Gambler*. As it happened, even Telyakovsky did not approve of the opera, but yielding to the enthusiasm of the younger conductors, he agreed to "take a chance" and signed a contract with the composer. The opera was included in the repertory for the coming 1916–17 season.

As if to tease the opera's future audience, Prokofiev stated in a newspaper interview that the music of *The Gambler* would be extremely simple and clear. He said: "In my deep concern for the theatrical aspect of the opera, I have done everything possible not to burden the singers with unnecessary conventions, in order to afford them freedom in the dramatic realization of their parts. For the same reason the orchestration will be transparent, so that each word may be heard." And to the reporter's anxious question, "But won't there be any extravagances in your *Gambler*?" Prokofiev replied flatly, "None whatever. I am aiming only for simplicity."[1]

Shortly after this interview the casting took place at the Maryinsky Theater. Alexei was to be sung by I. Yershov and I. Alchevsky, Polina by Ye. Popova, the General by G. Bosse, and Babulenka by Ye. Zbruyeva. N. Bogolyubov was appointed the *régisseur* and Coates the conductor.

Newspapers hostile to Prokofiev reported that the singers were quite unhappy about the difficulty of their parts. "Apparently the directors of the Imperial theaters are trying to imitate Mr. Diaghilev," sneered one critic. "We can only sympathize with the subscribers, who will be forced to listen to a futurist opera whether they want to or not."[2]

Prokofiev spent the summer of 1916 on the Gulf of Finland not far from the estate of Ilya Repin. "I am at present staying in Kuokkala. My primary occupations are tennis and scoring the opera," the composer wrote friends on June 29. Mariya Grigoryevna, who always accompanied her son, boasted to friends about his unusual skill in scoring.* The summer ended with a trip to Georgia, where Prokofiev visited with interest the picturesque spots around Borzhomi.

During the 1916–17 concert season Prokofiev made a number of successful appearances. On October 21, 1916, he conducted *Autumnal Sketch* at a Siloti concert; on November 11 he participated in the second performance of the *Scythian Suite* at the Maryinsky Theater; on December 1 he

---

* Prokofiev recalled in his memoirs: "My mother once asked Cherepnin how many pages he usually scored in a day. 'Oh, sometimes a chord,' he replied, playfully showing off how meticulously he worked. 'But my son does as many as eighteen pages a day,' mother said proudly."

played the First Piano Concerto at a concert of the Russian Musical Society in Kiev, with Glière conducting; and on February 15, 1917, he gave a piano recital of his own works in Saratov. It was during this season that provincial audiences first heard Prokofiev's music. At this time, too, the British press reported a performance of the *Scherzo* for four bassoons in a concert by the London Philharmonia.[3]

The heated controversy about Prokofiev continued. On December 19, 1916, Siloti's third chamber concert (in the Small Hall of the Petrograd Conservatory) created tremendous excitement, for this time he devoted the entire concert to Prokofiev's works. Presented for the first time were *Sarcasms,* the songs of Op. 23, the *Toccata,* the bassoon *Scherzo,* and the cello *Ballade.* The singers on this occasion were I. Alchevsky and Ye. Popova. Once again the Petrograd press became noisy and contradictory. *Zritel*'s feuilletonist N. Shebuyev, after acknowledging Prokofiev's music to be brilliant and witty, expressed his belief that the composer was "hampered by mischievousness, childishness, and his aping of Mayakovsky."[4] This was a typical reference to Mayakovsky; apparently Prokofiev's "shocking" concerts reminded some critics of the equally provocative appearances of the Russian futurists.

Approximately the same chamber program was given in Moscow on February 18, 1917, at the second Evenings of Modern Music concert in the Small Hall of the Conservatory. Participating in this concert with Prokofiev were the cellist Ye. Wolf-Israel and the singers Z. Artemyeva and O. Butomo-Nazvanova. The audience included the most prominent Moscow musicians, among them Rachmaninov and Medtner, who at that time did not approve of Prokofiev's music. According to Asafyev they both laughed openly, and it was on this occasion that Medtner passed the famous remark that was soon quoted by one of the critics, "If this is music, then I am no musician."[5] Rachmaninov, however, "within a short time began to take Prokofiev more seriously, as a musician of striking talent."[6]

The February 18th concert called forth an extremely irritated review from the critic Yevgeny Gunst, who expressed the opinion of the Moscow Scriabinists.[7] According to Gunst, Prokofiev's works "left the painful impression of being a kind of ugly growth on Russian music." This critic found the melodic material "extremely insipid," the harmony "kind of a crazy quilt," the content "dull, indifferent, worthless," and even the rhythm "for all its power and verve, unaesthetic." It is noteworthy that A. D. Kastalsky, in contrast to many Moscow musicians of both the academic and modernistic schools, "warmly rejoiced at the new phenomenon."[8]

In December 1916 Prokofiev was presented with an unexpected opportunity to avenge himself on an old enemy, the critic Sabaneyev (who still maintained that Prokofiev's music reflected his "heart of stone" and "the poverty of his spirit."[9]

On December 25, the Moscow première of the *Scythian Suite,* scheduled for that day, was canceled. Unaware of this, Sabaneyev hastened to publish in the Moscow newspaper *Novosti Sezona* the review he had already prepared. Describing the concert in great detail, the critic ridiculed Prokofiev's "cacophonous" music and concluded with the statement that "the composer himself conducted with barbaric abandon."[10]

Prokofiev lost no time delivering a counterblow to the critic "who, with his own hand, has dug his own grave." Both the newspaper *Rech* and the magazine *Muzykalny Sovremennik* carried an open letter from the composer which tersely stated that the concert Sabaneyev had denounced had not taken place and added that the *Scythian Suite* could not possibly be known to him since the composer possessed the single manuscript copy of the score. The disgraced critic was compelled to leave the editorial boards of *Muzykalny Sovremennik* and several newspapers. This shameful episode was long remembered by Russian musicians as an outstanding example of the corrupt practices of the bourgeois press.

A controversy over the works of Prokofiev, Miaskovsky, and other young composers caused a split in the editorial board of *Muzykalny Sovremennik,* which was published jointly by Andrei Rimsky-Korsakov, son of the composer, and the rich sugar manufacturer and music lover P. P. Suvchinsky. Some of the editors strongly disapproved of Prokofiev and refused to support his work. This outraged Asafyev, who was one of the magazine's leading writers. In January 1917 a sharp dispute broke out in connection with a concert of the Russian Musical Society, at which Prokofiev's First Concerto, Miaskovsky's Second Symphony, and Stravinsky's *Petrushka* were performed. Asafyev gave this concert a glowing review, but the editors categorically refused to print it.

"My article on Miaskovsky, Prokofiev, and Stravinsky was ridiculed in a professorial tone, and that started the fireworks," Asafyev relates. "A lot of caustic remarks were passed about the music of Miaskovsky and Prokofiev, about their insignificance as composers, and so on. How I controlled myself and kept from showing them up for what they are—inferior, imitating scholastics—I don't understand."[11]

As a result of the conflict Asafyev left *Muzykalny Sovremennik,* taking with him Suvchinsky, who declared that he agreed with Asafyev and that the magazine could not possibly be published without him. "This has caused an uproar here in Petrograd—in Siloti's group, in the Conservatory, and in the salons," reported Asafyev triumphantly. In opposition to the moderately academic *Muzykalny Sovremennik,* Suvchinsky and Asafyev founded a new magazine called *Melos.*[12] Turning to Derzhanovsky for support, Asafyev wrote, "Despite everything we shall march together, and our banner will bear the names Prokofiev, Miaskovsky, Kastalsky, and all those who will share their views in the future, perhaps even some new luminaries!"

A considerable obstacle to the popularization of Prokofiev's music was the reluctance of publishers to accept it. For a long time Koussevitzky's Russian Music Publishing House rejected everything, and the cautious Jurgenson accepted mainly piano pieces, not wanting to take a chance on expensive scores. The Second Piano Concerto, *Scythian Suite,* Sinfonietta, *The Buffoon,* and *The Gambler* were still unpublished.

Late in 1916 Prokofiev decided to break with Jurgenson and go to the Gutheil publishing house. Actually, this firm belonged to Koussevitzky, who had acquired it from the Austrian Gutheil after the latter left Moscow at the beginning of the war. Convinced of Prokofiev's growing popularity, Koussevitzky finally opened the doors of his publishing house to him. The songs Op. 9, 18, 23, and 27, *Fugitive Visions,* and the Third and Fourth Piano Sonatas were accepted and published.

Thus began Prokofiev's business relationship with the Gutheil publishing house, which lasted for almost twenty years. More will be said later about the extent of this relationship and the composer's long financial dependence on the publishing activities of Serge and Natalya Koussevitzky.

In October 1916 Prokofiev finished orchestrating *The Gambler,* confident that the première would take place not later than February or March of 1917. After creating the music of crazed passion and violent uproar in *The Gambler,* he was once again drawn to gentle lyricism, to that restrained expression of deep, inner feeling so natural to him. Gorky's words about the young Mayakovsky, "Somehow he spoke in two voices—one purely lyrical, the other bitingly satirical," might also be applied to Prokofiev.

While the lovers of the "truly modern"—Diaghilev, Nurok, and Nuvel —admired most the grotesquerie and pungent harmonies in Prokofiev's music, Asafyev and Miaskovsky pointed with approval to the singular charm of its restrained but profoundly human lyricism. Karatygin also wrote of this; he, too, was able to discern behind the tumult of the barbaric episodes, which captivated him, the gentle charm of the lyrical passages.

"The Andante of the Second Sonata, the Andante of the Sinfonietta, surely this is the purest lyricism—stern and harsh, to be sure, but genuine, sincere, and moving. With these pieces, Prokofiev has for the first time let us come close to the lyrical side of his soul," wrote Karatygin in an article entitled "Prokofiev's Art." At the same time he expressed a hope: "It is in the further development of the innate poetry of his art, in the enrichment and deepening of his tonal lyricism that I would hope to see the further evolution of Prokofiev's brilliant talent. Will my hope be realized?"[13]

Prokofiev himself resented the critics' attempts to picture him as a barbarian and a boor devoid of warm, human feeling. When A. Koptyayev ridiculed the lyricism of the Second Sonata, seeing in it "the hideous grin of malice," the composer was stung to anger. "He outdoes both Igor and Leonid. 'The hideous grin of malice.' This is my lyricism. Oh!" exclaimed Prokofiev in one of his letters.*

In 1916, after finishing *The Gambler* (Op. 24), the composer added to his list of compositions the names of two projected major works—the *Classical Symphony,* Op. 25, and the Third Piano Concerto, Op. 26. A skilled and methodical craftsman, he was able to plan large works several years in advance. For example, both the *Classical Symphony* and the Violin Concerto, Op. 19, a rough draft of which was begun as early as 1915, were deliberated over a long period of time. By this time the principal themes of the Third Piano Concerto had already been outlined, although the work itself was not completed until five years later, in 1921. Finally, while engaged in all of these works the composer wrote some new *Fugitive Visions* (Nos. 2, 3, 7, 12, 13, and 20).

Toward the end of the year, after delivering the score of *The Gambler* to the theater, Prokofiev decided to "relax" by writing some light chamber music. "In one breath" (from November 13 to November 16) he composed the vocal cycle, Op. 27, a fresh and interesting example of his youthful lyricism. The composer himself pointed out the considerable softening of mood in these songs, a great change from the stridency of *The Gambler* and the *Scythian Suite.* "After these songs [Op. 27] many people believed, for the first time, that I really could write lyrical music."

The song cycle, Op. 27, was based on five poems by Anna Akhmatova: "The Sun Fills My Room," "True Tenderness," "In Remembrance of the Sun," "Greeting," and "The Gray-Eyed King." In her poems, this fash-

---

* To Derzhanovsky, August 7, 1915. Attached to this letter is Koptyayev's review from *Birzheviye Vedomosti.* "Igor" and "Leonid" refer to Igor Glebov and Leonid Sabaneyev.

ionable Acmeist poetess employed deliberately simple and concrete images to convey the refined and sometimes morbid feelings of a woman of the upper classes. These poems were much simpler and more modest than the high-flown "cosmic" verses of Balmont, but alongside warm, lyrical feelings they exhibit traces of unwholesome eroticism and gloomy sorrow. What attracted the young Prokofiev was the combination of an almost prosaic concreteness with a gentle feminine quality in Akhmatova's poetic images. For example:

> The sun filled the room
> With a yellow, transparent dust.
> I awoke and recalled:
> Darling, today is your birthday.

Warm and tender lyricism predominates in the music of this cycle. Despite the extremely laconic style in which they are written, these songs are appealing for the naturalness of their vocal declamation and the simplicity and transparency of their accompaniments, which are good examples of Prokofiev's bright diatonic harmony (especially the third song, *In Remembrance of the Sun*). The composer skillfully combines agitated *ostinato* figures in the accompaniment with expressively melodic vocal lines. Some of the melodies are particularly charming in their purity and warmth of feeling; these delicate themes, which suggest bright dreams of love, seem to anticipate the finest female characterizations of the later Prokofiev (certain lyrical sections of the opera *War and Peace,* for example).

At the same time, the affected torment in Akhmatova's poetry, with its motifs of death and bitter disillusionment, gave rise to somber contrasts in the music, such as the eerie, almost mystical passages found in the endings of the second and fourth songs and in the middle section of the third. In *Greeting* (No. 4), for example, a moving theme gives way to nervous recitative and ominous tritonal harmonies (FIG. 17).

Particularly characteristic in this respect is the last song, *The Gray-Eyed King.* ("Welcome art thou, unappeasable pain"), which is tinged with tones of resignation and submissiveness in the face of death. Thus, despite Prokofiev's tendency toward bright, sunny, and human lyricism, this music to Akhmatova's poetry is permeated with the morbid characteristics of decadent art. Although the lyricism of *The Ugly Duckling* is unquestionably more cheerful and more wholesome, these songs are nonetheless an artistic expression of the young Prokofiev's lyrical bent.

The first performance of the songs, Op. 27, took place at a Concert of Modern Music in Moscow on February 18, 1917, with Z. Artemyeva as

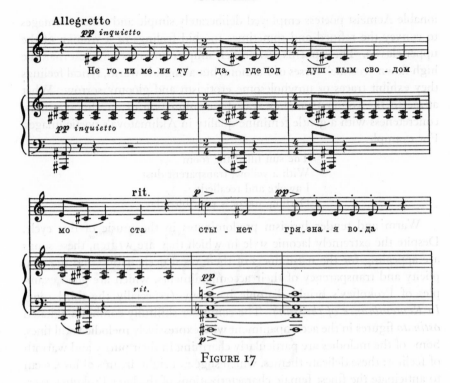

**Allegretto**

Не го-ни ме-ня ту - да, где под душ-ным сво - дом мо - ста сты - нет гря-зна-я во-да

FIGURE 17

soloist. The critics hailed Prokofiev's turn toward pure lyricism. "One hardly expects to find tenderness, warmth, emotion, or in short, lyrical charm in Prokofiev's music. Some say that the young composer has none of it. But after hearing the songs set to Akhmatova's words (especially *In Remembrance of the Sun*), it is difficult to agree with this," wrote Yu. Engel.[14]

Later both Miaskovsky and Asafyev warmly praised the songs. In 1923 Miaskovsky wrote, "These songs are so charmingly delicate, so transparently bright, and so completely expressive that they leave an indelible impression. The harmonic style is finely polished, the melody infinitely tender and eloquent, and the exposition utterly simple while nevertheless expressing each thought to the full."[15]

The year 1917 found Prokofiev deeply involved in work—composing, attending rehearsals of *The Gambler,* and giving concerts in Petrograd and the provinces. His time was strictly scheduled for several months to come: "January 22, beginning of orchestral rehearsals of *The Gambler*; the 27th, concert at the Russian Musical Society; from the 28th on, Acts II and III of *The Gambler*; February 15, Saratov; the 18th, Moscow; late February to the beginning of March, performances of *The Gambler*."[16]

The excitement in the press about the forthcoming opera première did not cease. Rumors were published that Dostoyevsky's widow had protested the operatic production of *The Gambler* and was demanding royalties. Then it was reported that the *régisseur* N. Bogolyubov had refused to work on the opera and had turned over the production to Meyerhold and the artist A. Golovin. A cartoon in one newspaper showed Meyerhold "shelving" the manuscript. Despite all this, Prokofiev clung to the belief that his *Gambler* would soon be performed.

Even in this busy time he began searching for a subject for a new opera. One libretto offered to him proved so ludicrous that he promptly returned it to the authors. "I received . . . a very stageworthy libretto in which Hindus most curiously speak the language of the Gospel. I have returned it with thanks," he wrote to Derzhanovsky.[17]

At the suggestion of Meyerhold, Prokofiev began to consider the idea of an opera based on Carlo Gozzi's theatrical tale, *The Love for Three Oranges*. This witty comedy, as well as other plays by the Italian playwright, had captivated the leaders of the modernist trend in Russian theater. They were fascinated not only by the thoroughly stylized nature of Gozzi's plays, which were intended for improvised performance in the manner of commedia dell'arte, but also by their pervasive element of grotesque parody. As used by Gozzi to express distaste for Goldoni's plays of everyday life, parody was now declared to have an immediate significance in Russian theater. The ideologists of theatrical modernism sought to use the old Italian comedies to ridicule the clichés of the contemporary classical theater and also to experiment with improvised performances constructed on the basis of a purely formalistic "theatricality." The admiration for Gozzi on the part of the theater people grouped around Meyerhold was so strong that as early as 1914 they began to publish a little magazine called *The Love for Three Oranges* (*Journal of Doctor Dappertutto*). The very first issue, which boldly proclaimed the cult of pure form and rejected all realistic traditions, contained a scenario based on Gozzi's comedy. This little magazine, in a gay yellow cover, fell into Prokofiev's hands.

On reading Gozzi's comedy, Prokofiev quickly became fascinated with it, giving little thought to the meaning of the struggle between theatrical schools which constituted its subtext. He immediately began to visualize images of Truffaldino's merry entertainments, of noisy processions, games, and festivities. He shared his ideas with his friends.[18] "We are already talking about the next opera," he reported to Derzhanovsky on April 9, 1917.

During this time Prokofiev was also working feverishly on instrumental compositions which he had begun in previous years. In the spring of 1917 he added nine piano pieces to the eleven composed in 1915–16 to form the piano cycle *Fugitive Visions*. These boldly experimental, vividly expressive little compositions are something like entries in a diary. Or perhaps more accurately, they are like experiments from a laboratory, a store of materials to be used in the future large works of a composer always eager to increase the scope of his art. The title of the cycle was taken from Balmont's lines:

> In every fugitive vision I see worlds,
> Full of the changing play of rainbow hues.

The twenty *Fugitive Visions* vary widely in mood and imagery. The composer arranged them in a contrasting sequence, alternating the lyrical pieces with the dramatic or gay, dance-like ones. There are wildly dynamic pieces suggesting the clash of hostile forces; among these are No. 14 (marked *feroce*), in which nervous excitement unexpectedly gives way to serene dreaminess, and No. 4, which is constructed on sudden tonal contrasts and alternating registers. Asafyev found No. 4 to have much in common with the last two *Sarcasms,* in which he perceived "mirthful clowning" give way to a cold "atmosphere of torpor."[19] The pieces seem like sketches for opera or ballet scenes, illustrating either eccentric contrast or the tense atmosphere of a dramatic conflict.

Some of the *Fugitive Visions* are fanciful, vividly descriptive, and filled with unexpected harmonic tricks. In these the composer seemed to be experimenting with harmony, rhythm, and piano texture. An example of this is the exquisite No. 7 (subtitled "Harp"), in which textural and harmonic inventions completely overshadow the melodic thought. Equally delicate are No. 12, in slow waltz rhythm, and No. 2, with its suggestions of gloom and mystery. At times, however, the studied nature of the devices leads the composer into dull and affected thematic patterns (Nos. 13 and 15).

The best works of this cycle are those in a predominantly playful and lively lyrical vein. Nos. 3, 5, 6, 10, and 11, bursting with youthful zest and without a trace of mockery or sarcasm, are among the most brilliant and fresh examples of Prokofiev's humor. In these little scherzos one is attracted by the unexpected combination of extremely simple, even primitive, rhythms (typical of children's play songs) and unusually daring harmonic sequences. No. 5 is a gaily mischievous piece constructed on freely shifting major triads. No. 10, a kind of comic dance full of amusing leaps and accents, evokes the image of a prankish boy. It is characteristic of Prokofiev to shift suddenly, in a short piece, from sparkling humor to the tenderest lyricism. Thus in No. 11, in the midst of carefree, playful romping there suddenly emerges a touching melody in the Russian vein. On the other hand, in No. 3 a lullaby rhythm suddenly gives way to a furious dance in the spirit of the *Scherzo* for four bassoons.

This cycle is also distinguished by its more thoroughly lyrical pieces, which have the purity of feeling and peculiar naïveté of a Russian fairy tale. These pieces (Nos. 1, 8, 16, 17, and 20) became the source of *Tales of the Old Grandmother* and many more of Prokofiev's later works in a fairy-tale, lyrical vein. Here, as in the songs of Op. 27, extremely simple diatonic melodies are combined with colorful harmonies (sequences of unresolved seventh chords). Such is No. 1, which suggests a naïve child's pleasant dream. In these lyrical sketches a special role is played by the transparent C major, the "music of the white keys" which Prokofiev used so subtly in the songs, Op. 27. (See, for example, No. 6 and the middle sections of Nos. 8 and 16.) Soft, melancholy sounds, lilting rhythms, and moods of sadness predominate in Nos. 16 and 17 and occur in parts of the last piece, No. 20. It was no accident that the composer placed the most serene and transparent lyrical pieces at the beginning and end of the cycle; their subdued images, so unusual for the composer of the *Scythian Suite,* set the tone of the whole cycle.

The best of the *Fugitive Visions* have deservedly been accepted as Russian piano classics. Karatygin was correct when he saw in this cycle a turn on the part of the young Prokofiev toward a more profound revelation of the stirrings of the soul. "In these twenty miniatures, which the composer has aptly called *Fugitive Visions,* along with echoes of his earlier tonal naturalism one also hears something new," wrote Karatygin. "Now and then amid all kinds of flashy effects, screeches, bustle, and commotion, suddenly something tender, gentle, and sweet wafts over us. Prokofiev and tenderness—you don't believe it? You will see for yourself when this charming suite is published."[20]

Six years later Miaskovsky spoke even more pointedly and warmly about the *Fugitive Visions.* He, too, was delighted with Prokofiev's turn toward more varied lyrical expression: "In *Fugitive Visions* one clearly senses a kind of organic deepening, an enrichment of the composer's soul. One feels that the composer has already passed the stage of running at top speed and is now beginning to slow down and look around, to notice that the universe reveals itself not only in furious vortexes but that even while in continuous motion it has moments of repose and quiet which soothe the soul." According to Miaskovsky, this forceful revelation of genuine lyricism, previously an insignificant element in Prokofiev's work, made it necessary "to regard Prokofiev as the rightful successor of the brilliant group of geniuses who recently passed into the history of our young music."[21]

Along with the *Fugitive Visions,* Prokofiev continued to work on the Violin Concerto, Op. 19, and the *Classical Symphony,* Op. 25. In that same spring of 1917, while looking through his old notebooks from the Conservatory years, he discovered two sonatas he had written for Lyadov's class in 1907–8. He found in them much that was worth reworking, and his rewritten and enriched versions of them later became the Third and Fourth Piano Sonatas.

His meeting with Maxim Gorky was a memorable occasion for the young composer. This took place on February 25, 1917, at a literary and musical evening held in conjunction with an exhibition of paintings at N. E. Dobychina's studio. Appearing on the program were Gorky (who read for the first time excerpts from *Childhood*), the violinist Jascha Heifetz, and Prokofiev, to whom the entire second half of the program was devoted. The composer's *Scherzo* for four bassoons, *Études,* Op. 2, *The Ugly Duckling,* and *Sarcasms* were performed. Gorky showed great interest in Prokofiev. He laughed heartily over the bassoon *Scherzo* and listened attentively to *The Ugly Duckling,* in which he noted autobiographical overtones ("but this he has written about himself!"). While acknowledging Prokofiev's enormous talent, Gorky felt that his pieces represented a somewhat pampered art.

Dobychina, who had arranged the evening, introduced the composer to Gorky. After embracing the youth warmly, Gorky strolled with him through the hall for a long time, questioning him in a friendly way about his work. After this, according to Dobychina, Gorky would always ask, "And what new thing has Prokofiev written?"

Prokofiev's acquaintanceship with Gorky continued for many years. During the period of the Kerensky government, the writer arranged Prokofiev's exemption from military service. "We are not so rich," said Gorky, "that we can shoe the soldiers' boots with gold nails." And in the summer of 1917, it was the newspaper *Novaya Zhizn,* headed by Gorky, that printed Asafyev's enthusiastic article on Prokofiev's music. Later Gorky and Prokofiev also met abroad.

Like most others in his circle, Prokofiev greeted the February revolution with joyous excitement. "During the revolution, I was in the streets of Petrograd, hiding from time to time behind house corners when the shooting became hot," the composer recalls. He saw the Revolution as some kind of grandiose and elemental event, the expression of mighty but chaotic forces. Under the immediate impact of the February street battles, he wrote one of the pieces later incorporated in *Fugitive Visions* (No. 19, *Presto agitatissimo*) (Fig. 18). According to the composer, this agitated, vigorous music depicts "the excitement of the crowd rather than the inner essence of the revolution."

Figure 18

Is it not strange that so observant an artist, one so thirsty for impressions, was not stirred to the depths of his soul by the romantic revolutionary events of 1917? How could it have happened that he did not hear the true music of the Revolution, that his works bear no trace even of the fiery rhythms of the revolutionary songs which filled the air of Russian cities at that time?

The primary reason for this was the political apathy of the bourgeois intellectual circles in which he had moved in recent years. In these groups the very possibility of a relationship between art and politics was considered unthinkable. At meetings of writers and artists in the spring and summer of 1917, many outstanding representatives of the arts stubbornly asserted art's independence from the influences of the Revolution. Most of Prokofiev's friends would have interpreted any attempt to respond directly to the events of the Revolution as a betrayal of the principles of pure art. Even the democratically-minded Miaskovsky (who in his letters of 1917 had openly expressed a desire that "all emblems be tossed away" and the war put to an end) considered it a sign of banality for a composer to respond creatively to immediate events.[22] As for Prokofiev, he was so absorbed in his music that he failed to grasp the meaning of what was happening and was therefore unable to define his place in the revolutionary struggle. His primary concern was the fate of his own music. "The question is: how has *The Gambler* fared under all these overthrows?" he anxiously asked Derzhanovsky.[23] Nevertheless, the feverishness of Prokofiev's activity in 1917 and the character of some of his works written in that year do suggest that he was not wholly unaffected by the historic events then unfolding.

The year 1917 was one of the most productive in Prokofiev's career. In the course of a few months, he completed a whole series of major compositions: the Violin Concerto, Op. 19, the *Classical Symphony,* the Third and Fourth Piano Sonatas, and the "Chaldean Invocation" *Seven, They Are Seven.* To this year also belong the sketches of the Third Piano Concerto and the plan of the opera *The Love for Three Oranges.*

Some of these works are examples of Prokofiev's fully mature, deeply meaningful art. In composing them, he seemed to have rid himself of many of the extremes of his creative youth. The powerful, life-asserting images of the Third and Fourth Sonatas and the Third Piano Concerto, the serene lyricism of the Violin Concerto, and the gay irony of the *Classical Symphony* give evidence of the young composer's striving for greater simplicity, clarity, and nobility. And in this turn toward simplicity, coming so shortly after the stunning complexities of the *Scythian Suite* and *The Gambler,* one cannot but perceive the spirit of the times, with its general democratic trend. (No wonder one critic, writing in early 1918, noted traces of "Bolshevist accessibility" in Prokofiev's music.)[24]

Thus, while not fully grasping the essential nature of the Revolution, Prokofiev intuitively sensed the vital, invigorating atmosphere of this unforgettable time and reflected this in his own way in the sunny, joyful images of his music of 1917. His favorite barbarisms—the dark, fantastic images—do reappear, however, in the cantata *Seven, They Are Seven.*

❉  ❉  ❉

Shortly after the February events, a revolt took place in the Maryinsky Theater against the production of *The Gambler*—the singers and the orchestra flatly refused to perform it. "The prevailing sentiment among the artists is that Prokofiev's opera *The Gambler* should be dropped from the repertory," reported the press, "for while this cacophony of sounds, with its incredible intervals and enharmonic tones, may be very interesting to those who love powerful musical sensations, it is completely uninteresting to the singers, who in the course of a whole season have scarcely managed to learn their parts."[25]

Siloti, whom the provisional government had appointed director of the theaters, could not induce the theater artists to relent, and shortly afterward *The Gambler* was removed from the repertory. Throughout the summer Prokofiev carried on negotiations for a production of the opera at Moscow's Bolshoi Theater, but even with the help of friends he was unsuccessful.

During the spring and summer of 1917, Prokofiev again played his First Piano Concerto in Petrograd and the provinces. By now this had become his most popular work; the critics called it "a magnet for the public." He played it on June 1 in Pavlovsk, on July 23 in the Petrograd Theater of Musical Drama (under the direction of G. Fitelberg), and on August 25 at the Kislovodsk Kursaal (under the direction of V. Berdyaev). Meanwhile he was working on other compositions, with a view to performing them during the 1917–18 concert season. A Prokofiev program, which was to include the Violin Concerto, the Third and Fourth Sonatas, and the *Fugitive Visions,* was planned for the Siloti concerts in November 1917.

In the spring of 1917 he also completed his revision of the Third Sonata, Op. 28. (The one-movement Sonata in A minor written at the Conservatory in 1907 had been marked No. 3.) The composer lovingly retained the general construction and basic thematic material of the youthful piece; then he sharpened the harmonic details, made some revisions in the development and recapitulation, and, most important, improved the piano writing, casting it more in the grand manner (this is particularly noticeable in the magnificent coda, which was thoroughly repolished).

※ ※ ※

The Third Piano Sonata proved to be one of the finest of Prokofiev's piano compositions. While exuberant laughter and vigorous virtuosity played an important role in the Second Sonata, more dramatic images predominate in the Third. There is no mischievous taunting here, but rather a powerful impetuosity which builds up continuously throughout the short one-movement piece. "Its basic qualities," wrote Miaskovsky, "are infectious, captivating élan and fervent passion, through which shines with great clarity the serene freshness of a young self-asserting will."

In its thematic material and in the character of its exposition the Third

Sonata resembles the Second. It shows the same predilection for agitated triplet rhythms and has the same sculpturally expressive virtuoso devices (wide leaps, strong accents, toccata-like figures alternating with energetic passage work, and pages of beautiful *cantilena*). There is also basically the same harmonic treatment (transparent diatonic harmonies combined with freely employed alterations and with harsh dissonances and counterpoint). But on the whole the Third Sonata is more "symphonic," more unified in character. There is no kaleidoscopic shifting of episodes as in the earlier work; its dramatic impact is achieved through the complicated development of two or three basic themes.

The Sonata opens with a mighty cascade of sound in a rapid, toccata-like motion. Like a signal horn, a powerful ascending phrase replies to the opening bars. The dialogue between these two passages forms the brief introduction. The first theme is filled with an explosive inner power. Its design is broad—wide leaps, now an octave above, now in sevenths below —and its rhythm is disturbed and uneven, owing to rests and sharp dotted figures.

The motion of the agitated bridge passage reminds one of the spinning of a top. Each time the ascending figure dashes forward, it meets a sharp rebuff in the form of concise descending motivs. Finally the second theme appears, a simple, moving melody stated in a uniquely treated alternate key; it remotely resembles the opening bars of Tchaikovsky's *Troika* (FIG. 19).

FIGURE 19

The exposition concludes with a tenderly swaying melody, *diminuendo,* which is purely diatonic in character.

Suddenly, like a gust of wind, the opening phrases of the development section burst forth. Here the ascending signal-like phrases of the first theme take on a martial sound. The tensely beating rhythms, the nervous ascending and descending runs, and the sharp accents are in striking contrast to the preceding mood of gentle languor.

In the development section the familiar phrases of the first and second themes are subjected to radical alteration. The second theme is transformed from a tender melody into an angry shout, and the swaying coda of the exposition becomes agitated. Midway through the development, the melody of the second theme returns like a reminiscence, this time over an agitated and breathless accompaniment. Still later this lyrical theme is changed again, and becomes more angular and pointed, leaping from the lowest registers to the highest. Finally, the exciting development section concludes with a mighty climax, like an orchestral tutti, brimming with exertions of defiant power and will. All that remains of the final bitingly dissonant chord is a single gradually diminishing sound; out of this emerges the soft hum of a reiterated short phrase. This is the recapitulation.

Here, unlike the precise recapitulations of the Second Sonata, the composer achieved an interesting dramatic development. The main theme, which was used extensively in the development section, is omitted. The recapitulation begins immediately with the bridge passage, which is developed and supplemented by new material. When the long-awaited melody of the second theme finally appears, it is hardly recognizable. It has lost its singing quality and has become percussive and strangely restless (combined with an agitated "hunt rhythm" in the bass). This treatment of the theme is coda-like in character. Now, at last, the long-restrained heroic forces burst forth, and the Sonata ends with a powerful passage which seems to assert the triumph of a daring youthful will. In the final measures of the coda, phrases of the second theme are heard for the last time, loudly and heavily, in a spirit of triumph and affirmation.

Many critics paid glowing tribute to the Third Sonata. Asafyev more than once praised the powerful dynamism of this composition and the unity and impetuous drive of its development, comparing it to "the whirring trail of an arrow flying through the air."[26] Miaskovsky considered the Third Sonata one of Prokofiev's most effective piano pieces. "In order to convey the entire range of Prokofiev's colors, the performer must possess a finished technique, indomitable temperament, profound insight, and, finally, the gift for sincere yet wholesome lyricism. Prokofiev's Third Sonata is indispensable to the concert stage."[27]

Almost simultaneously with his work on the Third Sonata, Prokofiev was working enthusiastically on the First Violin Concerto in D major, the main theme of which he had conceived in 1915. For nearly two years work on *The Gambler* had prevented him from devoting his attention to this composition, of which he was very fond. "I often regretted that other work prevented me from returning to the pensive opening of the violin concertino," he relates.

The modest plan of the concertino gradually developed into a concerto in three movements, which are presented in an unusual sequence—the first and third are predominantly tender and melodic, while the second, instead of being the traditional Andante, is a fast, grotesque, and mocking scherzo. Having explored the resources of the violin while working on symphonic scores, Prokofiev attempted to include in this concerto passages that would give free rein to the expressive possibilities of this instrument—from the lyrical *cantilena* to giddy scale passages and complicated shifts from *pizzicato* to *arco,* from the extremely harsh *marcato sul ponticello* to transparently clear harmonics. On questions of bow markings and other technical details the composer consulted the famous Polish violinist Paul Kochanski, who was then teaching at the Petrograd Conservatory. It was planned to have Kochanski give the first performance of the Concerto in November 1917.

The Concerto was completed in piano score by summer, but owing to the situation in Petrograd the première did not take place in the fall of 1917. It was not until more than five years later, in Paris, that the Concerto received its first performance.

Everything in the Violin Concerto, Op. 19, was fresh and original, from the virtuoso effects to the unusual contrasts of musical ideas. Unexpectedly for Prokofiev's music, a tenderly melodious, lyrical theme predominates in the first movement (and is restated in the coda of the finale). It is almost impossible to find in any of Prokofiev's early works a melody so simple and clear, so soulful and warm. The singing qualities of the violin are most effectively employed, and the subtle nuances produced by the polyphonic dialogue between violin and orchestra intensify the effect of this pensive theme (FIG. 20).

This melody is typical of Prokofiev's lyricism—serene, contemplative, and devoid of emotional stress or psychological complexities. Incidentally, the composer himself cautioned performers against excessive sentimentality, demanding of them the utmost simplicity and restraint. ("The main

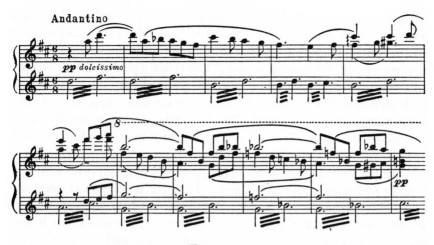

FIGURE 20

theme must not be dragged; it must by all means be *andantino* and not *andante*," he pointed out in one of his letters).[28]

Throughout the Concerto the solo violin is given the interesting role of one of the leading members of the orchestral ensemble, the "first among equals." This becomes apparent in the very first statement of the main theme. The critic I. Yampolsky was correct in pointing out that "the solo violin is not set against the orchestra, but rises from within to dominate it. This is a unique modern treatment of the *violino principale* role found in the pre-classic violin concerto."[29]

After a bravura passage, abounding in difficult runs and trills with continuous modulations, the second theme appears. Odd and fanciful, compounded of chromatic twists, leaps, *tirate*, and grace notes, it contrasts sharply with the warm, flowing main theme. This eccentricity suggests the comical hobbling of some fantastic little creature like Grieg's Kobold or the Gnome in *Pictures at an Exhibition*. What is more, the rocking rhythm and vivid harmonic contrasts of the accompaniment endow the entire image with a narrative tinge (making it rather like a child's fantastic dream after hearing a fairy tale).* The exposition of the first movement ends with violin pyrotechnics *con brio* over dryish *pizzicato* phrases in the double basses, which are derived from the main theme.

---

* Prokofiev did not intend this theme to be mocking or grotesque. "Play it as though you are trying to convince someone," he told David Oistrakh, stressing the theme's narrative character.

The composer expended a great deal of creative thought and imagination on the music of the development section. Here, the two themes of the exposition are substantially transformed by the powerful energy of a continuously accelerating motion. The lyrical opening theme becomes unrecognizable; it is sharpened, mechanized, and then dissolved in swift scale passages. Phrases taken from this theme move upward in fourths with a nervous, biting sound. The fairy-tale quality in the melody of the second theme is also radically transformed as it dissolves into continuously moving violin figurations.

The last section of the development, *poco piu mosso,* is permeated with a spirit of negation and biting irony. Here the lyrical theme undergoes still further modification. Transferred to the orchestra and accompanied by an *ostinato* bass and harsh *pizzicato* chords in the solo violin, it loses its original character. The feeling of distortion and edginess is also heightened by harmonic means, particularly the polytonal combining of figurations in A major with a continuously repeated fragment of the B major scale in the bass. It is as though dark and sinister forces were opposing the principal bright and sunny images of the Concerto. This devilish grimace (in the spirit of the composer's *Sarcasms*) recalls the Romantic tradition of grotesque distortion of lyrical themes (illustrated, for instance, in the famous Mephistophelean episodes of Berlioz's *Symphonie fantastique,* and in Liszt's *Faust Symphony* and B minor Sonata). But this demonic mockery cannot destroy the beautiful human dream, and toward the end of the development it gradually gives way to a serene passage based on material from the concluding section of the exposition. In the recapitulation which follows, the enchanting melody of the first theme returns once again with an even greater inner warmth. Now it is given to the orchestra (*dolce*) while, in its highest and tenderest register, the violin plays muted passages which glitter softly like morning sunlight. The recapitulation is very brief, for the second theme and concluding section are omitted. Joyful love of life and nature triumph completely over evil.

The whole gamut of scherzo-like moods and images, so attractive to the young Prokofiev, is presented in the second movement, a sparkling virtuoso *vivacissimo.* In its general character, the Scherzo is related to the wonderful scherzos of the Second Piano Sonata and Second Piano Concerto. Here, the same *perpetuum mobile* and sparkling, sometimes mischievous humor predominate. This movement is in the form of a five-part rondo. The first theme, based on an ascending chromatic figure in very pronounced, sharply accented rhythm, is filled with youthful zest. Light, whirling runs, mocking accents, and *pizzicato* to *arco* shifts in the violin all seem to tell of merry amusements, of swift pursuits and adventures.

In the two middle episodes of this miniature rondo, the gay mood is abandoned. Here, as in the development section of the first movement, images of sneering sarcasm and sinister forces predominate. In the first episode this mood grows from unusually harsh sounds in the solo violin (*staccato marcatissimo*), and in the second episode it becomes even more prominent under the purely orchestral effect of playing near the bridge (*sul ponticello*). In the second episode, the portrayal of the evil, soulless images reaches its climax. In these grotesque episodes, for all their daring inventiveness, one senses a certain kinship to the classical traditions. Taunting and biting irony are not rare in either Russian folklore or the works of the classical composers (Mussorgsky's song *The Urchin* or the scene of the Simpleton and the boys in *Boris Godunov,* for example).

In the third movement serene lyricism once again prevails. In its general mood and harmonic structure (colorful interplay of triads and seventh chords at the distance of a whole tone or a third), the main theme of the finale is related to the introductory theme of the first movement. Just as at the beginning, the violin sings in a full voice of the beautiful and lofty feelings of man. In the middle section of this movement, the mechanical motion of rapid runs and the image of a sardonic smile again appear, but this time they are clearly relegated to the background. The finale is in typical three-part form and ends in an enormous coda, which is actually an extended conclusion for the entire work. After a lengthy introductory statement based on the quiet narrative theme which opened this movement, the coda proper begins—and it is one of the most interesting sections in the entire Concerto. Here the two lyrical themes are masterfully combined: the theme of the finale played by the orchestra, and the sunlit theme of the first movement played by the solo violin and a group of the first violins. The result is a wonderful tonal effect, evoking in the listener's imagination the picture of a joyous spring landscape bathed in sunshine.

Prokofiev's inventiveness in the field of tone color deserves a separate analysis, for in this area he unquestionably contributed new modes of expression to violin playing. Some of his contemporaries, even those favorably disposed toward him, could not accept the unusual technical innovations in his Concerto, maintaining that they were not congenial to the resources of the violin. Thus, in a review published in 1923 in *K Novym Beregam*, K. S. Saradzhev pointed out "certain moments of little interest in a specifically violinistic sense" and suggested that the solo part be revised. This suggestion drew a sharp rejoinder from Prokofiev: "I should like to inform the gentlemen who consider the Violin Concerto ungrateful to the soloist that in Paris the Concerto did not achieve as much success as its performer. . . . In the performance with the orchestra, the concluding section of the first movement in 6/8 and the *ponticello* in the second sounded best." The composer also reminded his critics of the mistake of Leopold Auer, who in his day had "reduced to ashes" Tchaikovsky's Violin Concerto.

Certainly the concert history of the First Violin Concerto, with the remarkable interpretations given it by the best violinists of today (Szigeti, Oistrakh, and others), has decisively proved the value of Prokofiev's technical innovations.

Compared with the first two concertos for piano, the First Violin Concerto reveals a greater maturity in Prokofiev's art, a broadening in the range of his artistic inclinations. Its dominant characteristic is neither the rhythmic element, which pervades the First Piano Concerto, nor masses of sound, which are so abundant in the last two movements of the Second Piano Concerto. The musical ideas unfold clearly and confidently; the themes are more clear-cut, simple, and human. The grotesquerie is not used for its own sake, but only as a contrast to the predominating lyrical images. The principal theme, which stretches like a rainbow from the beginning of the Concerto to the final coda, glorifies the indestructibility of human happiness.

❊ ❊ ❊

Prokofiev spent the summer of 1917 in a small country house near Petrograd. Living alone (his mother had gone to the Caucasus to take the cure), he was busy composing music and working hard on orchestration. Still, he gave some time to reading. "During 1916–17 I read quite a bit of philosophy, although rather haphazardly," he said. "I read Kant and Schopenhauer. What interested me most in Schopenhauer's philosophy were the maxims of practical behavior, not the apologia for pessimism and avoidance of choice."[30] This interest in philosophy probably grew out of Prokofiev's attendance at Bashkirov-Verin's literary Mondays. An acquaintance with the theories of Kant was later reflected in the title of the piano pieces *Things in Themselves* (Op. 45, 1928). In general, however, more than a passing interest in the abstract categories of idealist philosophy was alien to the composer's sober nature. During these summer months he devoted most of his attention to scoring the Violin Concerto and the *Classical Symphony*.

The idea for this gay, transparent symphony stemmed from Prokofiev's classical interests, which had been stimulated in Cherepnin's conducting class. A kind of Mozartean quality had already emerged in some of the pieces of Op. 12 (*Rigaudon, Caprice, Gavotte*) and to a certain extent in the Sinfonietta, Op 5. But now the composer conceived the idea of a whole symphony in a style similar to that of the Viennese classics: "It seemed to me that if Haydn had lived into this century, he would have retained his own style of writing while absorbing certain things from newer music. I wanted to write the kind of symphony that would have such a style."

Prokofiev's intention was to combine the modest texture and transparent orchestration of Haydn and Mozart with "a touch of new harmonies." In 1916 he composed his popular D major Gavotte, which became the third movement of the symphony, and in the same year he made sketches of the symphony's first and second movements.

The authorized program note for the first performance of the symphony stated that "The composer's aim was to resurrect the 'good old days' of strong traditions, the days of hoop skirts, powdered wigs, and queues." But although this symphony evokes the past, it has absolutely none of the qualities of a restored museum piece. It has innocent lightheartedness, a zest for life, and a smiling, slightly ironic tone accentuated by piquant harmonic contrasts and amusingly awkward melodic leaps—all quite typical of the young Prokofiev, in the spirit of *The Ugly Duckling* and *Fugitive Visions*.

Aside from the task of creating fresh and original musical material, the plan for the new symphony involved mastering a technical problem that was new for the composer. For the first time, he decided to compose a major work solely on the basis of memory and imagination, without the aid of a piano. He purposely did not take his piano to the country, in order to avoid the temptation of improvisational, "finger" composition. As he explained, "before this I had always composed at the piano, but I began to notice that thematic material composed without the piano was often better in quality. Transferred to the piano, it often sounds strange at first but after one has played it through a few times everything falls into place." Following this plan, Prokofiev conceived the thematic material and composition of the symphony during walks in the country. He also discarded the sketches of the finale he had made in 1916, and rewrote it entirely.

As if to challenge those who persisted in calling him a futurist, Prokofiev called his new symphony the *Classical Symphony*. Speaking of his reasons for this choice, he said, "First of all, because it was simple. And secondly, out of mischief—to 'tease the geese'—and also in the secret hope that it would be accurate if, in the course of time, the symphony really did turn out to be a classic."

The secret hope, as we know, was fulfilled. This symphony was among the first of Prokofiev's works to win universal acclaim and it has long been regarded as a classic.

The *Classical Symphony* in D major is written in the traditional four-movement form: Allegro, Larghetto, Gavotte, and Finale. The composer retained the composition of the Haydn orchestra, including paired wind instruments without trombones. After the overpowering sonorities of the *Scythian Suite*, the pure tone colors of the solo instruments—the gay trills of the flute, the crochety grumbling of the bassoon, the scarcely audible *spiccato* of the violins—came as a welcome delight to music-lovers. Throughout the entire symphony one encounters the traditional Viennese device of sudden shifts from limpid *piano* to *tutti fortissimo*. The seemingly clipped phrases and periods are in complete conformity with Prokofiev's style of precise and well-defined cadential writing.

Almost all the thematic material of the Symphony was inspired by the general spirit of the pre-Beethoven symphonic style. Here, too, are the scale-like and arpeggiated figures, octave leaps, elegant trills, and grace notes. But throughout the Symphony the composer found it possible to sharpen familiar phrases with playful exaggerations of the melodic line or colorful juxtapositions of harmonies (although nowhere are stridence and buffoonery permitted).

The first movement of the Symphony is a clearly constructed, miniature sonata allegro. The pace is quick and light, and cadences are loudly exclaimed by the full orchestra. The first theme, with its scales, trills, and interruptions, would sound entirely like Haydn or Mozart were it not for the capriciousness of the harmonic scheme (the sudden shift to C major at the beginning of the second statement and the equally free return to D major).

A slight suggestion of irony runs through the second theme. Enormous two-octave leaps, amusing grace notes, the modest way in which the violin is combined with the staccato accompaniment of the bassoon—all this creates a blend of dance-like elegance and quaint awkwardness. In the development section the two themes are subjected in turn to rather simple treatment. However, the second theme becomes more ponderous when given to the basses; "the elegantly playful theme" is transformed, as Asafyev aptly put it, into "the lumbering strides of a giant."

The second movement, in the style of a stately minuet, is charmingly graceful. The principal theme, in the very high registers of the violins, sounds tender, almost wistful. Mincing pauses and capricious "curtsies" at the ends of the phrases are combined with a sedate, measured accompaniment. The style of the exposition, especially the rhythm and harmonic coloring, clearly anticipates certain dances in *Romeo and Juliet* (the widely known "Dance of the Maids from the Antilles," for example).

In the third movement, a witty Gavotte, Prokofiev's individual style is particularly evident in the parallelism of the octave leaps, in the freely juxtaposed pure major triads (D, C, B), and in the deceptive cadences (when the key of C sharp is expected, D major suddenly appears). In the middle of the Gavotte, a traditional musette over a drone bass, one hears echoes of a Russian folk tune. The elegant, well-defined quadruple meter of the Gavotte was very much to Prokofiev's liking; in addition to the Gavotte of the *Classical Symphony,* there are the well-known piano gavottes of Op. 12 and Op. 32, and others in the music for *Hamlet* and in the *Cinderella* ballet.

The Symphony ends with a gay and lively finale. The first theme returns, with its simple ascending and descending arpeggios and scale passages, and its amusing, repeated short phrases in the violins. Also restated is the witty sceond theme, with its crisp motiv in the woodwinds. The concluding theme in A major is a bright, typically Russian melody very closely related to one of the themes of Rimsky-Korsakov's *Snow Maiden* (Fig. 21).

FIGURE 21

Here the classical images of eighteenth-century music are refracted, as it were, through the prism of Russian song.

The Symphony is much more than a semi-ironic stylization of Haydn's music or an evocation of the mannered life of the eighteenth century in the spirit of the World of Art painters. One senses in it, above all, the original and powerful personality of the composer, striving by means of Haydn's techniques to sing of the simple joys in life.

Early in the fall of 1917 the new Symphony was completely orchestrated (the score was completed on September 10). The composer dedicated it to his old friend Asafyev, to whom he was particularly close during these years. Prokofiev's work on the *Classical Symphony* proved useful to him in later years. His fondness for old dance rhythms and the modest texture of pre-Beethoven instrumentation subsequently manifested itself in many episodes of his ballet music (the court dances in *Cinderella,* a number of dances in *Romeo and Juliet*), as well as in certain chamber pieces (among them the Flute Sonata, Op. 94). An actual musical reminiscence was to link the *Classical Symphony* to the score of *Romeo and Juliet.* At the end of the first act, the famous Gavotte from this symphony was introduced in somewhat altered and expanded form. Thus, after twenty years, the composer returned with paternal affection to one of the freshest and most characteristic creations of his youth.

❋   ❋   ❋

While Prokofiev was working on the scores of the *Classical Symphony* and the Violin Concerto, his name again appeared several times in the Petrograd press. As before, the hostile critics wrote abusively of his summer performances of the First Piano Concerto.

On July 26, 1917, the Social-Democratic newspaper *Novaya Zhizn,* founded and edited by Gorky, published an article on Prokofiev entitled "The Road to Joy." Written by Asafyev (under his usual pen name, "Igor Glebov"), it tried to prove a spiritual kinship between Prokofiev's music and the Revolution. According to Asafyev, this article had been suggested by Gorky and Mayakovsky, who shared the idea of publishing a piece on the reflection of the Russian Revolution in contemporary music.[31] Before the article appeared there were long and heated discussions in the editorial offices of the newspaper, to which Mayakovsky was a regular contributor until August 1917. The poet was mistrustful of Asafyev, whom he regarded as a "dry-as-dust pedant," a guardian of the music of the past.

"What do your Beethovens mean to us? I'd give up all the old music for one Prokofiev!" roared Mayakovsky angrily.[32] He also told Asafyev, "Only Prokofiev's music excites me now. No sooner do the first sounds ring out than life bursts in—not a form of art, but life, a rushing mountain stream, such a torrent that you feel like jumping under it and shouting,

'Oh, how wonderful! More, more!' "[33] Obviously, by this time Mayakovsky knew Prokofiev's music and was enamored of it.*

Asafyev's article expressed the views of those modernists who believed that Prokofiev, with his strong, earthy art and his joyous affirmation of life, was the musical prophet of the approaching revolutionary storm. Asafyev considered the Revolution as abstractly synonymous with universal joy and the free unfolding of man's creative powers and tried to find these qualities in the music of the *Scythian Suite*.

"Joy as consciousness of one's vast creative power, as faith in a better future, as a moving force of exceptional immediate import," he wrote, "burst forth in the final movement of Sergei Prokofiev's suite *Ala and Lolli*." According to Asafyev, in this finale "one perceives the first intimation in Russian music that a path has been found to the sun, to that unrestrained happiness and overflowing joy that comes when one realizes the infinitude . . . of mankind's creative energy." And of music's role in the Revolution he said, "Contemporary Russian music has sensed and foretold the coming of the changes now taking place in the country, the coming of the sudden shift toward an affirmation of voluntarism and a yearning for free creative development."

Several months later Asafyev developed the same ideas in another article entitled "The Road to the Future," which was printed in the second issue of the magazine *Melos* for 1918. In this article he again tried to establish a kinship between Prokofiev's music and the Revolution. "In him we have the only true representative of our day, one in whom life is perceived as creation and creation as life!" he wrote. Unfortunately, however, the composer's development in the 1920's did not confirm Asafyev's analysis.

After completing the *Classical Symphony* and proving to himself that composing without the piano could be both fruitful and fascinating, Prokofiev toyed with the idea of writing a miniature Russian symphony in a similar vein. But this idea was never carried out. It gave way, during this ominous summer, to "a desire to compose something big, something cosmic." Sensing the grandeur of impending events, the composer sought suitable forms in which to express these feelings.

"The revolutionary events that were shaking Russia penetrated my subconscious and clamored for expression," he later recalled. "I did not know how to do this, and my mind, paradoxically, turned to ancient themes.

---

* Prokofiev had similar feelings about Mayakovsky's poetry. In the spring of 1917 he attended one of Mayakovsky's readings in Petrograd and noted the "powerful impression" produced on him by the poet's verses.

The fact that the thoughts and emotions of those remote times had survived for many thousands of years staggered my imagination."

For his text Prokofiev chose Balmont's poem "Seven, They Are Seven" from the book *Voices of Antiquity*.[34] This poem, which was filled with overdrawn fantastic images, was based on a Chaldean invocation engraved in ancient Assyro-Babylonian cuneiform on the walls of an Akkadian temple. The sinister mood of the poem could not possibly have been more at odds with the feelings and yearnings of the revolutionary masses at this decisive moment in Russian history.

The text of the ancient inscription, which had been deciphered by orientalists, gave Balmont the basis for his portrayal of seven terrible giants who ruled the world:

> In the deep abyss
> Their number is seven;
> In the azure sky,
> Seven, they are seven.
> When they arise in the west,
> They are seven.
> When they loom in the east,
> They are seven!
> Sitting enthroned, in the deep shadow,
> 'Tis their voice that rises, mutters, and roars
> And 'tis their shape that fills immensity from heaven to earth.
> Seven, they are seven! Seven, they are seven! Seven, they are seven!

Prokofiev abridged and slightly rearranged this poem, adding a quatrain of his own which contained a veiled allusion to contemporary events:

> They cause heaven and earth to shrink.
> They confine, as behind doors, whole countries.
> They grind nations as nations grind corn.
> Seven, they are seven! Seven, they are seven! Seven, they are seven!

Thus the terrible Chaldean giants apparently symbolized for Prokofiev the dread force that had plunged mankind into the abyss of war and devastation.

But in the decadent Balmont's poem this sinister force rules the world, and it is opposed by nothing more than savage pagan incantation, the violent exorcism of a shaman, the mystic invocation: "Oh, thou Heavenly Spirit! Curse them! Curse them! Curse them!"

And so into the sunlit world of Prokofiev's art, which had just brought forth such joyful creations as the Third Sonata, the *Classical Symphony*, and the Violin Concerto, there entered once more the poisonous stream of decadence. Balmont's poetry, with its unrestrained glorification of evil and delight in archaic savagery, once again lured the composer from the pursuit of realism.

Of course, Prokofiev could not take the mysticism of Balmont's poem seriously, and later he could joke about the devilry of the "seven spirits" ("Swear by the score of *Seven, They Are Seven.* If you won't, I'll let all seven of them loose on you," he wrote to Derzhanovsky).[35] What seems to have interested him in this poem was what he had sought several years before in the libretto of *Ala and Lolli*: first, hyperbolic imagery, which he could illustrate by exploiting to the full the dynamic effects of the orchestra, and second, sinister fantasy, which would afford him a pretext for sharply dissonant harmonies and deafening timbres. The music of *Seven, They Are Seven* resembles in many respects such savage-sounding parts of the *Scythian Suite* as "Worship of Veles and Ala" and, particularly, "Chuzhbog and the Dance of the Evil Spirits." But although the *Scythian Suite* has the virtue of containing vibrant dance rhythms, which at times actually suggest the dances of the steppe nomads, *Seven, They Are Seven* is totally unrelated to any nationally defined genre or even, for that matter, to the music of the East.

This was Prokofiev's first work in a vocal-symphonic genre giving a chorus the leading role. *Seven, They Are Seven* is a one-movement cantata for dramatic tenor, mixed chorus, and full orchestra with an amplified percussion section. Despite these characteristics, the composer flatly rejected the "old-fashioned" designation "cantata," giving his piece the unusual subtitle "Chaldean Invocation."*

As he later described it, his plan was to write the entire score in three stages: "The first stage: make a rough skeleton of the whole text (working without the piano); mark the climaxes and anticlimaxes; determine how each section is to be expressed; jot down fragments of melodies, phrases, accompaniments, and ideas for orchestration. Having the text, I was able to set it entirely, measure by measure, and with such exactness that that aspect of it was finished. The second stage: detailed work on the music,

---

* When, in 1922, the Music Department of the State Publishing House printed the score with the subtitle "Cantata," the composer protested vigorously. On December 18, 1922, he wrote to Derzhanovsky: "Who ever hit on the idea of calling it a 'cantata'? The word 'cantata' suggests something draggy and quite at odds with the impetuosity of 'Seven.' It must be called 'Seven, They Are Seven: Chaldean Invocation for Orchestra, Chorus, and Tenor Solo,' and not 'cantata.'" To be sure, this rejection of the term "cantata" was but a manifestation of the young composer's nihilism. Twenty years later he did not hesitate to call one of his best works (*Alexander Nevsky*) a cantata.

at the piano, in accordance with the skeleton—the skeleton acquires flesh. The third stage, again without the piano: scoring."

In only one week in early September, at the country house near Petrograd, Prokofiev worked out the general plan and outlined the main themes. While working on the music, he "imagined certain passages so vividly" that he was "breathless with excitement," as he put it.

*Seven, They Are Seven* is a typically expressionistic score, overloaded with frenzied, sinister images. In an attempt to keep his music exactly parallel to the text, Prokofiev constructed the cantata according to the principle of kaleidoscopic development, that is, without literal repeats or recapitulations. The one-movement work is divided into seven or eight short, sharply contrasting episodes. Several times a thunderous, raging orchestral *tutti* gives way to a mysterious muffled *piano* episode. In the opening measures, the listener is assailed with a tumult of deafening sounds, vividly depicting some kind of cosmic catastrophe. Here, as elsewhere, the score is startling for the density of its harmonies; as in the *Scythian Suite,* Prokofiev uses the device of contrapuntal layers of different descriptive effects—clashing trills in the brasses, a menacing rumble in the basses, harps *glissando,* passage-work in the strings, and a roll in the percussion which rises and falls off like gusts of wind. Just as this terrible tempest seems to be raging and seething over the entire universe, the orchestral storm suddenly abates, and the tenor soloist begins the narration in a loud whisper. The male chorus repeats this ominous whisper, and the orchestral accompaniment is reduced to a rumble in the percussion and a scale-like surge from the muted cellos. This is followed first by an even louder, more clamorous *tutti,* which drowns out the spare responses of the chorus, and then by another vocal episode—this time a tenor solo with *ostinato* phrases in the chorus.

After a third violent *tutti* begins the furious climax, typically marked *feroce.* The rhythm grows more agitated, the tempo becomes livelier, and the sonority of the combined orchestra and chorus reaches a state of frenzy. Suddenly the tumult subsides, and the tenor, who has been silent for some time, pronounces his invocation with tremendous intensity. The frenzied shrieks of the chorus and the roar of the full orchestra do not subside until near the end of the cantata; at that point, they give way to a mood of quiet supplication in which the soft, weary psalmody of the soloist and chorus floats across a background of scarcely audible, sustained orchestral sounds. This music (also marked by barbaric dissonant harmonies) could only leave the impression of some incredible mystic vision.

A number of unusual effects are employed in the score of *Seven, They Are Seven*: the whispering of the chorus at the beginning; the *col legno* tapping of the full string section; the rising *glissando* of the full chorus, which sounds like the anguished wailing of a crowd; and, finally, just before the coda, the barbaric episode for percussion alone, suggestive of a pagan rite.

Quite obviously, all these devices were used solely for coloristic purposes, to intensify the atmosphere and terrify the listener. Descriptive tonal and harmonic effects clearly predominate over melodic expressiveness; melody is limited to brief invocatory phrases or spare, deliberately archaic psalmody. These brief phrases, intoned alternately by the tenor and the chorus, degenerate into *ostinato* figures, repeated endlessly like the exorcism of a shaman:

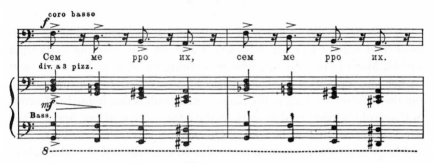

FIGURE 22

In several places the vocal line is given only a minor coloristic role. This instrumental treatment of the chorus—as the performer of the complicated, nonmelodic declamatory part—reappears many times in Prokofiev's later vocal-symphonic works (right up to the *Ballad of an Unknown Boy* in 1943).

On the whole, the "Chaldean Invocation" *Seven, They Are Seven* proved to be one of the most extreme manifestations of Prokofiev's pre-foreign modernism; it stands in a direct line with such expressionistic compositions of the twenties as the Second and Third Symphonies and the opera *The Flaming Angel*.

This cantata, written in the very thick of revolutionary events, reflected not only the persisting and unwholesome influences of bourgeois decadence on Prokofiev's taste, but also his own narrow, superficial understanding of the great events of 1917. While sensing some sort of universal significance in the revolutionary storm that had broken out in Russia, Prokofiev perceived in it not the purifying joy of liberation (as Asafyev thought he had), but only the chaos of destruction and the power of elemental cataclysms. In its mood of rebellion and ecstatic excitement the cantata is related to such pre-revolutionary works as Rachmaninov's *Bells* and Scriabin's *Prometheus.*[36] Indeed, like his distinguished predecessors, Prokofiev embodied here only a tremendous nervous excitement at sensing the work of incomprehensible forces shaping great historical events.

*Seven, They Are Seven* was first performed in 1924 in France, where it was regarded as no more than another example of Russian barbaric exoticism. It was never performed in Russia, and its importance now is only as evidence of the difficult processes which took place in Prokofiev's consciousness on the very eve of the great Revolution.

☀  ☀  ☀

In September the situation in Petrograd became acute. The city was threatened with a German advance. Upset by the alarming newspaper reports, Mariya Grigoryevna, who was taking the cure at Essentuki, sent for her son. Prokofiev prudently packed his manuscripts in a suitcase and sent them for safekeeping to the Koussevitzky publishing house in Moscow. In Essentuki he continued to work on the *Classical Symphony, Seven, They Are Seven,* and the Fourth Sonata, Op. 29.

He spent the days of the Great October Revolution in Kislovodsk, where he read the local newspaper reports of the formation of "the government of Lenin" in Petrograd. "The news was exciting, but . . . contradictory and distorted," the composer recalls. He had to remain for more than half a year in this resort town far from the capital. His attempts at returning to Petrograd to play in the Siloti concerts were unsuccessful because the North Caucasus had been cut off from Russia by the Kaledin uprising on the Don. As he said, "Kislovodsk became a trap from which it was impossible to escape." Prokofiev did not waste the time, however. He continued to compose, and he also made appearances at two chamber music recitals and one symphony concert in Kislovodsk.

The music of the Fourth Sonata took shape easily and naturally from material in youthful manuscripts. The composer utilized the first movement and the unfinished finale of his Fifth Sonata and the second movement, *Andante assai,* of the youthful E Minor Symphony (both written at the Conservatory in 1908). He carefully polished the harmony and piano texture (particularly in the second movement) and completed the finale of the early sonata; but the basic themes and general structure of the first two movements he left unchanged.

Unlike the fiery and exciting Third Sonata, the charm of the Fourth Sonata lies in its thoughtful, restrained, narrative tone. Here we find neither mirthful gaiety nor nervous frenzy; although an agitated feeling prevails in the first movement, it is not intensely dramatic, but restrained, in the manner of Medtner's *Fairy Tales*. The melodic outline and harmony are austere and even, to some extent, in the Schumann-Brahms tradition. However, certain pungent details—notably, the novel part-writing, with its moving basses and countermelodies, and such distinctive harmonic devices as complex suspensions and clipped cadences—reveal the composer's familiar style.

In the opening movement after the epic-like first theme, one is charmed by the delicate lyricism of the colorful bridge passage, which evokes images later to be found in *Tales of the Old Grandmother*. The second theme has the same narrative quality, with a touch of whimsy in its creeping chromatic basses and strange splashes of ascending *tirate*. The development section, which is characterized by a rich use of polyphonic techniques, is devoid of powerful emotional outbursts. In the recapitulation the lyricism becomes even more restrained, suggesting a recollection of things past.

It is not the narrative first movement which is the most effective, however, but rather the contemplative Andante, which is one of the most beautiful pieces of Prokofiev's lyricism. Over a background of steadily repeated thirds in the bass, there arises a beautiful, broad melody expressing profound meditation and reflection on life (see Fig. 6, p. 30). Here the composer approached that heroic and noble lyricism which was to engage his interest time and again, right up to the slow movement of the Fifth Symphony and the second theme of the first movement of the Seventh Symphony.

The Andante, which is in binary form, is constructed on two themes: the first is severe and stately, and the second very tender and lyrical. In the modest lyricism of its melody and the diatonic transparency of its harmony, the second theme recalls the most touching moments in *Fugitive Visions* and also, to some degree, the *Songs*, Op. 27. Paradoxical as it may seem, one senses in this theme a certain similarity to Rachmaninov's lyricism—not to the gloomy or anguished passages, but rather to the moments of quiet contemplation found in some of his songs (*Lilacs* and *The Little Isle*, for example) and in the most transparent of his preludes. Here are the same rippling triplet figures beneath a typically Russian diatonic melody, fresh as a forest spring.

The Andante is charming for the richness of its internal development, which leads to noble outbursts of dramatic expressiveness, for its full-bodied texture, enriched by a thick fabric of figurations, and for the expressive polyphony of its countermelodies. The movement ends with the two themes masterfully combined contrapuntally.

The exultant finale contrasts sharply with the introspective Andante. After the searching reflection of the preceding movement, the music of the finale creates the impression of "an outburst of long pent-up emotion" (Asafyev). The impetuous character of the rhythm (continuous racing figurations in the bass) and the ebullient, sharply accented melody, with its accentuated dissonance, evoke images of a merry and vigorous game. One is reminded here of the energetic race of the themes in the First Piano Concerto and the *Études,* Op. 2 (see, for example, the middle C major section of *Étude* No. 1). The middle section of the finale (a rondo-sonata) contrasts wonderfully with the brilliant dynamism of the main theme; this simple, serene melody, reminiscent of the lyrical *Ditties* of Prokofiev's childhood, is filled with an innocent, spontaneous awareness of life.

After completing the Fourth Sonata and *Seven, They Are Seven,* Prokofiev found himself without further plans. His enforced residence in the boring town of Kislovodsk began to depress him, and in letters to his friends in Petrograd he eagerly asked for news of musical events.

In Kislovodsk the people began to form local Soviets of Workers' and Peasants' Deputies to fight the counterrevolution. The White officers used the Grand Hotel, where Prokofiev lived, as their headquarters. One night armed workers surrounded it and began a search for White Guards. On learning that Prokofiev was a musician, they treated him in a friendly way. For the first time he realized that the Soviet "man with a gun," while merciless toward his enemies, valued and respected the true representatives of culture.

But the prevailing sentiment in Kislovodsk was hostile to the Revolution, and this poisoned Prokofiev's mind. People who hated the new regime whispered in his ear that Soviet society "did not need art," that no one in Russia was thinking about music now, and that it would be better for him to go to America, where he could "see and be seen." "I did not have the slightest idea of the scope and significance of the October Revolution," Prokofiev admitted later. "I did not yet realize that, like any other citizen, I, too, might be useful."

It was not until March 1918, when the Kaledin front collapsed, that the composer succeeded in leaving Kislovodsk with a safe-conduct pass from the local Soviet of Workers' Deputies. The journey from Mineralnye Vody to Moscow took eight days.

In Moscow the Gutheil firm (owned by the Koussevitzkys) was still operating as a private business, although the owner was actively cooperating with the new government and had even accepted an appointment as head of the first State Symphony Orchestra. When Prokofiev offered to sell Koussevitzky a number of his unpublished works, Koussevitzky accepted with alacrity. For a pile of "Kerensky paper," which soon lost its value, he obtained the publication rights to almost all of the composer's large-scale works (*Scythian Suite, The Buffoon, The Gambler,* etc.). The advance of 6,000 rubles which Prokofiev received in Moscow was the first link in the chain which bound him for many years to the Koussevitzky publishing firm.

During his stay in Moscow Prokofiev became friendly with a group of futurist poets headed by Mayakovsky. These poets, as well as other leftist artists, poets, and actors, frequented the Poets' Café in Nastasyinsky Pereulok; at this café, one of the centers of Moscow artistic life, Mayakovsky declaimed his poems. Prokofiev, long an admirer of Mayakovsky's poetic innovations, was also drawn into this circle.

"Once the young composer Sergei Prokofiev mounted the platform and played one of his new things," V. Kamensky, one of Mayakovsky's fellow poets, relates in his memoirs. "His brilliant performance, his virtuosity, and the originality of his composition captivated all of us. . . . While Prokofiev was playing, Volodya drew an excellent portrait of him in his sketchbook."[37]

During this period Mayakovsky and Prokofiev had many discussions about art, and once, as a mark of friendship, the poet presented the composer with a copy of his poem "War and Peace" with the amusing inscription: "To the World President for Music from the World President for Poetry. To Prokofiev [signed] Mayakovsky." The two artists also met in later years, both abroad and in Moscow.

After a few weeks in Moscow Prokofiev returned to Petrograd, which he had not seen for nine months. The great city, the first to raise the victorious banner of the October Revolution, was living through historic days. The old state apparatus was being broken up, and the workers' government was confiscating large private fortunes. However, some bourgeois newspapers were still being published and private concert organizations were still in existence.

In the middle of April Prokofiev succeeded in arranging three concerts of his own music. On April 15 and 17, at recitals given in the hall of the former Tenishev School, he played for the first time the Third and Fourth Sonatas and the *Fugitive Visions*. He conducted the former Court Orchestra in the première of the *Classical Symphony* at a symphonic concert in the hall of the former Court Chapel. Advance newspaper notices also mentioned among Prokofiev's new works the Third Piano Concerto, which then existed only in preliminary sketches. The music critics called these days "Prokofiev Week."

Even though the halls were not completely filled, all three concerts were enormously successful. The one in the Tenishev School was attended by "many scientists, artists, and writers, who were most enthusiastic," reported A. Koptyayev in *Novoye Vedomosti*.[38] The serene lyricism and clarity of these works, especially the *Classical Symphony,* compelled even Prokofiev's opponents to acknowledge his triumph. "No more grimaces, no more outrageous discords. It is all chaste and pure, clear, simple, and reminiscent of the best youthful inspirations of Haydn and Mozart," the critic Dzbanovsky wrote of the *Classical Symphony*.[39] A third critic, V. Kolomyitsev, quite justly noted ". . . Mr. Prokofiev's striving to give up his artistic flippancy and buffoonery, his attempts to settle down, to delve more deeply, to become more serious, even if it should imperil his reputation for originality, that is, for grotesquerie."[40]

The Petrograd critics also unanimously approved the Third and Fourth Sonatas. "The latest sonata, the Fourth, is characterized by an unusual clarity, preciseness, and sincerity," noted *Vecherneye Slovo*'s critic.

In his last article on Prokofiev (April 1918) V. Karatygin wrote, "Except, perhaps, for the brilliant but somewhat superficial finale, the Fourth Sonata enables us to say with certainty that Prokofiev's talent is deepening and penetrating into a psychological and emotional world he has heretofore disregarded. The marvelous Andante of this Sonata even bears a certain kinship to Chopin."

A few days after the first performance of the *Classical Symphony,* Gorky and Benois introduced the young composer to A. V. Lunacharsky, People's Commissar of Education, who had attended the première. At that time the commissar had his office in one of the rooms of the Winter Palace, which had been restored after the October fighting. At this meeting, Prokofiev told Lunacharsky of his desire to go abroad. Lunacharsky was astonished that Prokofiev should want to leave Russia in these tense, stirring days of historic change. The commissar asked Prokofiev the purpose of his trip.

"I have been working very hard, and I would like to get a breath of fresh air," Prokofiev replied.

"And don't you find that we have enough fresh air here now?"

"Yes," said Prokofiev, "but I would like to breathe the physical air of the seas and the oceans."

Lunacharsky thought a bit and then replied amiably, "You are a revolutionary in music, we are revolutionaries in life. We ought to work together. But if you want to go to America, then I will place no obstacles in your way." Apparently the commissar thought Prokofiev was filled with naïve dreams of a "foreign paradise," which would be dispelled as soon as the composer came into contact with life in the capitalist world.

Thus, with the permission of the Commissariat of Education, Prokofiev received a passport for travel abroad and a document stating that he was going "on matters of art and to improve his health." The decision to leave Russia was a bitter and irreparable mistake for the young musician, for nothing could ever compensate for his prolonged separation from his motherland, which had entered upon the path of revolutionary reconstruction. "In vain one wise man said, 'You are running away from events, and events will not forgive you. When you return, you won't be understood.' I did not heed his words," Prokofiev recalls.

Before his departure the composer became acquainted with the new works of his old friend Miaskovsky, who had just returned from the Army and had finished his Fourth and Fifth Symphonies. Prokofiev thought highly of the Fifth Symphony, especially its charming Scherzo on Galician themes.

On May 7, 1918, Prokofiev left Petrograd for Vladivostok. His baggage consisted mainly of music, including the scores of the *Scythian Suite,* the First Piano Concerto, the *Classical Symphony,* the piano score of *The Gambler,* and a number of piano pieces. He also took with him his sketches for the Third Piano Concerto, a plan for a string quartet, and the scenario for the future opera *The Love for Three Oranges.*

✳ ✳ ✳

The spring of 1918 separates the pre-revolutionary period of Prokofiev's career from the subsequent foreign period.

During the years 1907–17 the composer finished more than thirty works, among them a considerable number of masterpieces. As we have seen, however, far from all of these early works won a place in the concert repertory. *The Gambler, The Buffoon, Seven, They Are Seven,* and the First Violin Concerto were not even performed in pre-revolutionary Russia;

being closely tied to modernist influences, they were alien to the interests of the Soviet audience and were not performed until much later, in other countries. The *Classical Symphony,* the Third and Fourth Piano Sonatas, and *Fugitive Visions* were played only once before the composer's departure.

The fame of the young Prokofiev rested mainly on his piano works—the concertos, sonatas, and miniatures. Of the pieces included in his numerous performances of his own music, he played the First Piano Concerto most frequently. Of the symphonic pieces, the most noticed and discussed was the *Scythian Suite*. It was this suite and, perhaps, the Second Piano Concerto—both of which revealed the young musician's striving to overthrow the academic principles of art—that aroused the sharpest controversies. Despite the controversies, however, it became clear to most people that a composer of great stature and striking individuality had appeared in Russian music.

The distinctive stylistic features that make Prokofiev's music immediately recognizable—like the music of Liszt, Grieg, Borodin, or Scriabin—emerged very early. Prokofiev's music is an unusual combination of the simple and the complex—simple, well-defined rhythms combined with fresh, pungent harmonies, impeccable classical form and texture with daring invention. In many respects, these stylistic features violated the aesthetic principles of the fashionable schools of impressionism and symbolism. In place of ultra-refined emotions and semi-mystical signs and portents, we find in Prokofiev a somewhat coarse dynamism; in place of deliberately enigmatic images and nebulous other-worldliness, a straightforward logic; in place of vague, diffuse forms, a classical precision and simplicity. This simplicity, however, was itself distinctly new. The young composer at times shied away from any easily recognized sort of simplicity, which he considered banal and too reminiscent of well-known, traditional music. He strove in every way possible to combine logic and clarity of form, texture, and rhythm with harsh, unusual harmonies and timbres. He created his own distinctive melodic design, in which simplicity of line is combined with unusual twists and angularities, and his own harmonic idiom, in which transparently diatonic harmonies (much like old folk harmonies) alternate with sharp polytonality. Finally, he made great use of vigorous, clear-cut rhythms, inspired by elements of the march, the dance, and human gesture.

During these years Prokofiev's creative genius manifested itself most forcefully in his two favorite spheres—music for the piano and music for the theater.

From the composer's early youth, the piano had been his favorite instrument, the principal medium through which he revealed his creative personality and his stylistic experiments. Rejecting the intimate style of the impressionists, he often used the piano as a means for delivering thunderous musical orations—for such was the impression created by his virile performances of the First and Second Piano Concertos. Needless to say, this did not prevent him from infusing a genuine tenderness and pensiveness into many of his piano miniatures and the lyrical episodes of the Sonatas.

In contrast to his distinguished predecessors (such as Glazunov, Lyadov, Scriabin, and Medtner) who did not work in the operatic genre, Prokofiev composed *The Giant* when he was nine years old and continued throughout his career to test his powers in opera, and later also in ballet. In discussions with modernist leaders he stubbornly insisted on the value of composing opera. The possibility of creating concrete images inspired by life or literature excited him. Many of his early piano works (for example, *Diabolic Suggestions, Despair,* some of the *Fugitive Visions,* and the numerous dance pieces) as well as some of the early songs (Op. 27 and *The Ugly Duckling,* for instance) were almost like sketches for future theatrical scenes. It was not by chance that a substantial part of his symphonic music, from the *Scythian Suite* to the Third and Fourth Symphonies, stemmed directly from music written for the theater.

The acute contradictions of the times nourished an undeniable dualism in Prokofiev's stylistic tendencies. Listening carefully to his early works, we can discern in them very diverse images, which came into being as a result of quite different and, at times, contradictory creative aspirations. Some of these images are lifelike, truthful, and charmingly human; others are contrived, distorted, and superficially eccentric. Sometimes both appear within a single work or cycle.

The aesthetic principles of the classical tradition, instilled in the young composer by his teachers, often fell before the temptation to follow the modernist vogue. When this happened, the young artist resorted to the bizarre and the eccentric, to superficial originality; he suppressed his romantic impulses, stepping (as it were) on the throat of his own song.

As we know, modernism's basic weakness was its antihumanist orientation. Artists of the modernist school considered it old-fashioned to treat the natural feelings of the ordinary man or to reveal his moral and spiritual goodness. Grotesque dolls, marionettes, and mechanical freaks began to replace people in art. When these artists did portray a living man, they sought to emphasize his base, unwholesome, and offensive traits. In such works as *The Gambler* and *The Buffoon,* the image of man is distorted into a caricature. In *The Buffoon,* the characters are more like grotesque dolls than gay Russian peasants; in *The Gambler,* they are either over-drawn conventional types or people with sick, tormented souls. In the *Scythian Suite* and *Seven, They Are Seven* the representation of man's spiritual world is obscured by decorative effects and a contrived use of bar-baric, primitive images. Echoes of these frightening sound-images can be heard also in a number of Prokofiev's non-programmatic instrumental works, from the Second Piano Concerto to certain compositions of the thirties and forties.

These stylistic tendencies, we repeat, were determined in large measure by Prokofiev's nihilistic attitude toward the art of the past—particularly toward the style of the late romanticists and impressionists. It was as if he were saying to these predecessors, "You have languished long enough in perfumed tendernesses and precious refinements; to shake your little world, I'll sing of buffoons and coarse Scyths, I'll show you unprecedented cosmic explosions and cataclysms." This attitude also reflects the desire for supercharged art, for exaggerated expressiveness, which was so charac-teristic of the time. It was fashionable to shock and bewilder the listener with the massive, the unusual, the eccentric.

The *Scythian Suite, The Buffoon,* and the Second Piano Concerto will doubtless be performed many times in various countries and their color, dynamism, or ingenious invention will still arouse interest. But it is not likely that such music will ever replace the simple and human lyricism found in the *Fugitive Visions,* the Third and Fourth Sonatas, and *Romeo and Juliet.*

At the beginning of the twentieth century, many young poets and painters strove for eccentric effects by distorting traditional artistic methods. They defiantly rejected the accepted criteria of art without ever clearly revealing the value of their own aesthetic principles. Rejecting the ex-quisite prettiness of late romanticism and impressionism, these leftist artists went to the other extreme—deliberate anti-aestheticism. Unconcerned with perspective, young painters covered canvases with coarse, greasy smudges. Defying all poetic traditions, young futurist poets fractured the rhythms of verse, used crude, unpoetic images, and gave their volumes such flashy titles as *The Sickly Moon* or *The Milkers of Emaciated Toads.*

A tendency toward anti-aestheticism, toward a deliberate debasement of images, also appeared here and there in the works of Prokofiev. It revealed itself chiefly in a shocking grotesquerie, a bitter caricaturing of reality. Both the leftist artists and theatrical *régisseurs* were carried away by grotesqueness for its own sake. Stanislavsky called this modernist craze "the offspring of satiety." In the grotesque images of Prokofiev, melodies were sharply exaggerated; they acquired an artificial, angular character. Harmonies were distorted and sometimes deliberately incongruous with the melodies. Rhythms became mechanical or took on the character of a primitive dance. Perfect examples of Prokofiev's grotesquerie can be found in *The Buffoon,* in many passages of *The Gambler,* in the *Sarcasms,* and in certain other early works.

Some of the early vocal works are based on quite unpoetic, conversational texts, which would seem completely unsuited to musical treatment. The results of such a combination are readily apparent in *The Gambler* (and later, in *The Love for Three Oranges*). In vocal works of this sort the singer was often transformed into an eccentric mime who, instead of singing beautiful arias, was obliged to demonstrate the most diverse and eccentric vocal effects. In addition to grotesquerie and caricature, the composer also became interested in terrifying, repellent images of primitive savagery and barbarism. To Prokofiev, sinister and terrible emotions called for the harsh harmonies and timbres and the nervously distorted melodies which abound in both the *Scythian Suite* and *Seven, They Are Seven.*

Finally, Prokofiev's modernist experiments led him to the frequent use of motoric images. His earlier concertos contain whole pages of mechanical motion in the form of runs and toccata-like passages. His use of them, however, was more effective than the usual striving for bravura effects. At times these supercharged toccata-like figures acquired an almost graphically machine-like character, reflecting, in a way, the influences of contemporary urban life. Speaking of his enthusiasm for motoric images, the composer himself later admitted, "This element is probably the least important."

It was the grotesquerie, the deliberately prosaic vocal music, the barbarism, the exaggerated machine-motion—all the purely original aspects of Prokofiev's music—that immediately struck the critics and caused some of them to take Prokofiev as a kind of musical bugbear, a paragon of insensitivity. But such critics were not acutely perceptive. Behind the mask of the Scyth and rebel stood a warm and vibrant Russian artist, a man in love with life and striving in his own way to communicate its beauty and complexity. Modernist distortions could not destroy this love for life and nature, this interest in man and his emotions. Even in Prokofiev's early art, warm humanity breaks through all the artifices of fashion—sometimes in spite of the composer's own efforts (as in certain lyrical moments in the *Sarcasms* and even in *The Buffoon*).

Even in these early years one could hear clearly in Prokofiev's music his other "I," his lyrical "double," singing with warmth and genuine tenderness. This double often remained in the background, behind the screen of eccentricity. At times the composer himself hid it from his listeners for fear of being accused of simplicity and eagerness to communicate. But the lyrical spirit of the true Russian musician revealed itself more and more clearly in his best works: in the contemplative, melodic pages of the piano sonatas and concertos; in the best of the *Fugitive Visions* and the songs, Op. 27; in the principal themes of the First Violin Concerto; and, somewhat later, in *Tales of the Old Grandmother* and the songs without words of Op. 35.

Prokofiev's lyricism—restrained and chaste, free of exaggerated sentiment and superficial pathos—sounded strange and unfamiliar to many people. Tender, singing melodies were combined with colorful modulations and a transparent diatonic harmony that was distinctly Prokofiev's own. Sometimes this contemplative lyricism flowed from the world of serene reminiscences, of "grandmother's tales" and fantastic legends. For all its distinctiveness, this lyricism bears a relationship to the tranquil images of Rimsky-Korsakov and Rachmaninov, to the fragile fairy-tale world of *The Snow Maiden* and Vasnetsov's *Alenushka,* and to the restrained emotions of Moussorgsky's lyrical heroes (*On the Don*). It is somewhat surprising that the majority of the critics failed to recognize Prokofiev's lyrical gifts, noting in his music only crude impulsiveness or bitter mockery.

In addition to this lyricism, Prokofiev's best works sparkle with wholesome and infectious humor, which ranges from good-natured smiles to biting sarcasms. This element of humor is not revealed in the aesthetically distorted grotesquerie found in such works as *The Buffoon,* which reflects life as in a carnival mirror, but rather in sparkling wit, ringing youthful laughter, and a witty scherzo quality. The bright good humor of *The Ugly Duckling* and some of the *Fugitive Visions* has nothing in common with grotesquerie. Gentle humor also colors those works in which the composer sought to resurrect the style and texture of eighteenth-century classicism (the *Classical Symphony* and a number of the pieces, Op. 12, for instance).

The logic underlying Prokofiev's juxtaposition of images in his instrumental cycles is very indicative. He strives to achieve bold and striking contrasts, to combine seemingly incongruous images and moods in a single cyclic work. Thus the alternation of sharply contrasting ideas in the First Violin Concerto, in which a sunny musical landscape touched with tones of tender dreaminess is darkened by a sinister, fiendish devilry. The Second Piano Sonata presents a world of romantic transports, seething energy, and live and saucy laughter; an equally rich and broad sense of life permeates the Third and Fourth Sonatas and the Third Piano Concerto. But however complex and entangled the musical exposition becomes in such works, however far the digression from the dominant images into sardonic humor or strange fantasy, Prokofiev invariably returns to a healthy and powerful affirmation of the joy and beauty of life. In the end, it is this optimism which prevails in the First Violin Concerto, the Third Piano Concerto, and the wonderful early sonatas. After all sorts of digressions into the realm of fiendish grotesquerie and gloomy expressionism, this final affirmation sounds even more confident and convincing.

Prokofiev did not always heed the call of fashion. Again and again he returned to humane and meaningful music. Thus, even while working on the *Scythian Suite* he composed the sincere and touching parable of the ugly duckling, and after employing clever craftsmanship in *The Buffoon* he created the singing lyricism of the Violin Concerto. Prokofiev the modernist proved to be utterly inconsistent in his wanderings from the traditions of realism. In this respect he "lagged behind" his older contemporary Stravinsky, who proceeded from bold experiments in the Korsakov tradition straight to the cold impasse of ultra-refinement. Not until he had lived through another fifteen years of infatuation with various formalistic techniques would Prokofiev be able to set himself deliberately in pursuit of the realism bequeathed him by his distinguished teachers.

Much in the music of the young Prokofiev might be compared with the poetry of the young Mayakovsky: the combination of hyperbolic images and gentle lyricism; the daring, *épatant* tone; the well-defined rhythms and fervent oratory; the striving to counter the salon refinement of symbolism with an art that was thunderous, impulsive, and earthy. It is not surprising that these two superb Russian artists felt a strong affinity for each other.

But in many respects, this similarity in artistic tendencies was only superficial. Prokofiev's works lacked the political fervor and the profound understanding of social processes that were so powerfully expressed in

Mayakovsky's early poetry. Both artists maintained a bitter hatred of Philistine well-being, satiety, and complacency, of cheap beauty and clichés in life and in art. But Prokofiev could not, like Mayakovsky, rise to a conscious rejection of all decadent bourgeois culture. Both of them, in their best works, strove to glorify the beauty of life and the spiritual nobility of man. But unlike Mayakovsky, Prokofiev did not sense the approach of the new socialist order and did not sing the triumph of the Revolution.

After 1917 the lives of these two artists took very different turns. Mayakovsky at once took an unconditional stand with the builders of the new Soviet culture. Prokofiev, failing to comprehend the grandeur of what was taking place in his motherland, set out to win world fame and remained for a long time cut off from the soil that had nourished him. Only on returning to his native land in the early thirties did he see open before him the path to a great realistic art imbued with progressive ideals.

# SIX

# YEARS OF WANDERING

*"Whither, madman?"*
*"To seek the three oranges."*
*"But they are in Creonta's castle!"*
*"I do not fear Creonta."*

GOZZI: THE LOVE FOR THREE ORANGES

PROKOFIEV'S JOURNEY from Petrograd to Vladivostok took eighteen days, for the Trans-Siberian line was jammed with troop trains carrying Czechoslovak war prisoners. As a matter of fact, Prokofiev was on the last train to complete this trip before the Czechoslovakian front was formed in Siberia. Fighting had already flared up between Red Guard detachments and Ataman Semyonov's bands. The postcards Prokofiev sent to his friends Miaskovsky and Asafyev in Petrograd did not reach them for almost a year.

Thus began the composer's journey around the world—traveling across a country in the throes of civil war. He was doubtless filled with romantic thoughts of foreign lands and burning with an ambition to achieve world fame. Indeed, he must have been obsessed with these thoughts to leave revolutionary Petrograd, his country, and friends at such a time.

By June 1 he had arrived in Tokyo. He had planned to leave shortly for South America, hoping to be there in time for the winter concert season, but the boat for Brazil had just sailed and his plans were frustrated. He remained in Japan for two months waiting for a visa to the United States.

As luck would have it, he arrived in Japan shortly after the publication of a book on modern music by M. Otaguro, which had a chapter devoted to Prokofiev's work.[1] Japanese managers became interested in him and arranged three recitals of his works, two at the Imperial Theater in Tokyo and one in Yokohama. These recitals were publicized in advance by the Tokyo newspapers, some of which even printed portraits of Prokofiev and facsimiles of his music. In addition to his own music, Prokofiev played pieces by Chopin (*Ballade* No. 3, a mazurka, and an étude) and Schumann (among others, *Novelette* and *Warum*). Unfortunately, the recitals were poorly attended. In Tokyo the audience was predominantly Japanese, in Yokohama European. "Neither audience understood much of the music, but I must admit that I found it more enjoyable to play for the Japanese. They listened attentively, sat amazingly still . . . and applauded the technical passages," he wrote to the magazine *K Novym Beregam*.[2]

The composer sailed from Yokohama to San Francisco by way of Honolulu. He was struck by the natural beauty of the tropics, and he later recalled with delight his "wonderful stopover in Honolulu." During the long voyage across the Pacific, he jotted down new themes for the White Quartet (so called for its completely "white," or diatonic, style) which had been conceived in Russia, and he also worked on the plan for the opera *The Love for Three Oranges*.

In San Francisco he had his first (and not too amiable) encounter with American authorities. Taking him for a "Bolshevist agent," they did not want to permit him to disembark, and he spent three days on an island [Angel Island] as a "suspicious" foreigner. As recorded in his memoirs, his replies to questions from the immigration officials were often derisive in tone:

"Have you ever been in jail?"
"I have."
"That's bad. Where?"
"On your island!"
"Oh, you like to joke, don't you!"

When he was finally allowed to enter the United States, he was penniless. Some people he had met on the boat lent him a small sum of money, and early in September 1918 he arrived in New York. At first he stayed with the Russian dancer Adolph Bolm, a former member of the Diaghilev company. On learning of his arrival, the New York reporters lost no time informing their readers that "the most promising Russian composer since Stravinsky" was now in the United States.[3]

Prokofiev soon discovered that the conquest of America of which he had dreamed was not going to be so easy as he had expected. American concert audiences at that time showed little interest in new music; the United States had no outstanding composers of its own, and the only modern works accepted were those that bore the stamp of European approval. The average American was mainly interested in famous performers, and even then only if their programs were light and free from "experiments." Furthermore, Prokofiev realized that he would have to compete with the most brilliant piano virtuosos, and that the critics would not excuse any technical lapses. Music in America was then, as it is now, a commodity in which enterprising managers carried on a brisk trade (in collaboration with the noisy bourgeois press). Armed with neither money nor connections, Prokofiev was at the mercy of the American music-business machine.

His first performance in the United States attracted little attention. He played at a Russian concert given in connection with the opening of an exhibition of works by Boris Anisfeld, a St. Petersburg artist formerly connected with the Maryinsky Theater. The concert took place on October 19, 1918, in the Brooklyn Museum. The program included Russian singers and the dancer Bolm, who presented choreographic études to the music of the *Fugitive Visions,* performed by the composer. The tender lyricism of the *Fugitive Visions* and the pieces, Op. 12, proved rather disappointing to the New York critics who had expected modernist excesses. "Prokofiev may well be the lion of the musical revolutionists, but yesterday that lion roared as gently as the gentlest dove. We waited in vain for those manifestations of musical extremes for which he is so famous," complained one critic.[4]

Prokofiev's first solo recital, given in Aeolian Hall on November 20, 1918, attracted more attention. Music-lovers with a taste for the sensational displayed a keen interest in "this strange Russian." "The very character of the audience which filled Aeolian Hall to the last seat was indicative of the respect in which Prokofiev is held, for many of the city's prominent musicians were there."[5]

Fearful that he might startle his listeners too greatly, Prokofiev included on the program, along with his own works, Scriabin études and preludes by Rachmaninov (who was present at the performance).

This concert was a success, and scores of reviews appeared the next day under incredibly sensational headlines. "A piano titan," "Russian chaos in music," "a volcanic eruption at the keyboard," "carnival of cacophony," "Godless Russia," "Bolshevism in art"—such were the lengths to which the American reviewers went in taking advantage of the current public interest in revolutionary Russia.

Opinion on Prokofiev was sharply divided. Just as before in St. Petersburg, the critics either maligned him or praised him to the skies. "Personally, I cannot imagine how any musician of sane mind could write so many formless and impressionistic vaporings spontaneously," wrote the reviewer for *The New York Herald*. "The recipe for this sort of composition is as simple as that for boiling an egg. Write anything that comes into your head, no matter how commonplace. Then change all the accidentals, putting flats in the place of sharps, and vice-versa, and the thing's done," said *The New York World*.

On the other hand, the farsighted critics were in raptures. "He is one of the most stimulating composers that the Land of Unlimited Trouble has sent us in many moons," one of them declared in *The New York Tribune*.

Most of the critics did not take the trouble to make a serious analysis of Prokofiev's music. One found influences of Chopin, Wagner, and Beethoven in it, another maintained that Prokofiev "derives from Scriabin," and a third called Prokofiev a "Mendelssohn with false notes." "Take one Schoenberg, two Ornsteins, a little Satie, mix thoroughly with some Medtner, a drop of Schumann, a liberal quantity of Scriabin and Stravinsky—and you will brew something like a Serge Prokofiev, composer," wrote the critic of *Musical America*. One prominent critic found that "the finale of the work evoked visions of a charge of Mammoths across some vast, immemorial Asiatic plateau." "When the dinosaur's daughter graduated from the Conservatory of that epoch, her repertoire must have included Prokofiev," commented another.

Prokofiev's style of playing was spoken of as mechanical and devoid of nuance: "Steel fingers, steel wrists, steel biceps, steel triceps. . . . He is a tonal steel trust." After hearing of this testimonial the Negro elevator operator in Prokofiev's hotel (taking the composer for a famous boxer) politely asked to feel his muscles.

Despite the ballyhoo in the newspapers, this first recital in Aeolian Hall barely covered expenses. However, the composer had attracted public attention. A pianola firm invited him to record a number of his compositions on player-rolls, and two New York publishing firms offered to buy some new piano pieces from him. The publisher's offer led him to compose the four miniatures, Op. 31, entitled *Tales of the Old Grandmother* and the Four Pieces, Op. 32 (*Dance, Minuet, Gavotte* and *Waltz*). These two small cycles, which later won popularity, are among the best of Prokofiev's early works in the classical style. In lyrical depth, humor, and originality of conception they resemble the most interesting of the *Fugitive Visions*.

❈   ❈   ❈

*Tales of the Old Grandmother,* a cycle of four program pieces, was given the following poetic epigraph by Prokofiev: "Some recollections had become half erased from her memory; others will never be erased."

All of these pieces are leisurely and calm in character, bearing such markings as *con una dolcezza, sostenuto, tranquillo,* and *cantabile.* In their melodic structure they closely resemble Russian folk songs, but in the refinement of their harmony, which is by turns severely archaic (on the white keys) and delicately chromatic, they reveal Prokofiev's individual style. Tender, soulful lyricism is combined in all these *Tales* with traces of fairy-tale narration and a scarcely perceptible grotesquerie. Their deep, somber basses and peculiar twists of melody, full of melismas and strange turns, convey echoes of terrifying and fantastic tales heard in childhood.

All of the *Tales* are in three-part form and contain expressive internal contrasts. In the first piece, a fussy staccato melody, seemingly portraying the outward appearance of "the old grandmother," gives way to an angular and somewhat eerie second theme. The second piece, with its tender, sad melody and delicate timbres, is unusually touching. Indeed, its poignant, unaffected sentiments make it one of the most deeply moving examples of Prokofiev's lyricism. The composer who was considered by many an exponent of "coarseness and mischief," here revealed an inner warmth that proved him a direct heir to the best traditions of Russian national lyricism.

The third *Tale* has the graphic quality of a drawing of some enchanted scene. Its basic theme, moving over a somewhat heavy and cumbersome staccato bass, was probably inspired by the music of Bydlo in *Pictures at an Exhibition.* In the fourth *Tale* one is struck by the contrast between the first theme, which is in the spirit of a slow, flowing Russian song, and the second, which is light and gay.

The music of *Tales of the Old Grandmother* is related in many ways to the vivid characterizations of Moussorgsky's *Pictures at an Exhibition* and Lyadov's charming miniatures. Prokofiev continued to develop the Russian narrative quality which pervades the *Tales,* and it occurs in works as late as the First Violin Sonata (1938–46) and the ballet *The Stone Flower* (1948–50).

Like some of the *Fugitive Visions,* the *Tales of the Old Grandmother* reveal the typical traits of Prokofiev's early piano style. Asafyev characterized this style as follows: ". . . the overcoming of thick, ponderous harmony and virtuoso effects for their own sake. A line of rich melody runs throughout. It is at once supple, lively, resilient, gay, and deeply expressive; every part is sharp, clear, and appropriate, as if drawn by the steel point of an etcher."[6]

*171*

The four dance pieces, Op. 32, are also quite representative of this early style. The best of them, the famous *Gavotte* in F-sharp minor and the *Minuet,* were a direct continuation of Prokofiev's "classicism," faintly tinged with good-natured irony. In the middle section of the *Gavotte* one hears again a clearly expressed Russian lyricism very like that of the *Tales of the Old Grandmother.* But the *Dance* and particularly the *Waltz* contain traces of artificial ornamentation and harmonic thickness.[7]

The *Tales of the Old Grandmother* soon won a permanent place in the repertory of Soviet pianists. In 1923 the magazine *K Novym Beregam* hailed it in these words: "It is probably safe to say that within ten years these *Tales* will be played and enjoyed wherever there is a piano, even in the smallest provincial towns."[8]

After seeing the *Tales* and Opus 32, the New York music merchants began to entangle Prokofiev in a complicated web of encumbering commitments. "I immediately ran into a whole maze of contracts, conditions and agreements," the composer recalls. At first he managed to maintain his independence. When a publisher offered him very little for the pieces in Op. 31 and Op. 32, he rejected the offer. His obstinacy and professional pride, nurtured in Russia, exerted themselves just as strongly in America. Anticipating an early return home, he stubbornly refused to bind himself to contracts. In offering him a two- or three-year contract, one concert manager said, "I know that I will lose on you the first year, but I hope to make it up the second." "But I was so certain that I would be going home soon," Prokofiev writes, "that I did not want to be bound by a long-term commitment."

Prokofiev was very much disappointed in his meeting with Walter Damrosch, one of America's leading conductors. Damrosch displayed so little understanding of the First Piano Concerto that the composer did not even show him the *Scythian Suite.* After hearing the *Classical Symphony,* the conductor exclaimed, "Charming! Just like Kalinnikov." This immediately convinced Prokofiev that Damrosch knew nothing about modern music. Recalling the incident, Prokofiev wrote, "I left indignant, but it turned out that he had intended this as a compliment—Damrosch had toured all over America with Kalinnikov's Symphony."

In December Prokofiev made several concert appearances—twice in Chicago (on the 6th and 7th with the First Piano Concerto and the *Scythian Suite*), and twice in New York (on the 10th and 11th with the First Piano Concerto, the *Classical Symphony,* and some piano pieces). The New York concerts were with the orchestra of the Russian Symphony Society.

Modest Altschuler, founder of the Russian Symphony Society in New York, was regarded as a champion of Russian music. It was under his baton that works by Scriabin and Rachmaninov, among others, were first performed in the United States. Unfortunately, Altschuler was distinguished neither for great talent nor for devotion to principle; he had once aroused Rimsky-Korsakov's indignation by his butchering of Russian music to please the uncultivated elements of the American public.

Prokofiev's symphonic debut with Altschuler's orchestra, on December 10, was a failure. The New York press severely criticized both Prokofiev and his music. "A worse riot of considered or ill-considered, wanton eccentricity as was displayed in this concerto I am free to say I never heard," wrote the critic of *The New York Herald*. Concerning the performance of the First Concerto, *The New York Times* declared, "The composer handled the keyboard—handled is the precise word—and the duel that ensued between his ten flail-like fingers was to the death: the death of euphony. The first descending figure . . . is persistently affirmed in various nontonalities by the orchestra till the slow mood, the piano all the while shrieking, groaning, howling, fighting back, and in several instances it seemed to rear and bite the hand that chastised it. . . . He may be the Cossack Chopin for the next generation . . ." There was also the usual lying in the American press. In an abusive article, *The New York Tribune*'s critic ascribed S. Vasilenko's *Flight of the Witches* to Prokofiev. In the next issue of the newspaper the critic admitted that, having glanced at the program in the semi-darkness of the hall, he had confused the composers' names. Thus began the protracted discord between Prokofiev and the New York critics.

The composer was given a much friendlier reception in Chicago, in part owing to the good offices of the art patron Cyrus H. McCormick. In the summer of 1917, while in Petrograd with the Root Mission, McCormick had met Prokofiev and promised him his support.* When the composer came to Chicago, McCormick introduced him to the leaders of the musical life there: Frederick Stock, conductor of the Chicago Symphony Orchestra, and Cleofonte Campanini, director of the Chicago Opera Company. Stock, who was well versed in modern music, was not afraid to perform the *Scythian Suite*.

The Chicago performance of the *Suite* (December 6, 1918) caused a considerable sensation; but the Chicago critics, apparently in deference to

---

* TRANSLATOR'S NOTE: Elihu Root headed a U.S. diplomatic mission sent in an attempt to keep the Russians fighting for the Allies.

the tastes of local leaders of music, gave Prokofiev a much warmer reception than he had found in New York. A few writers even ventured into historical and aesthetic generalizations and contrasted the virility and incisiveness of Prokofiev's music to the effeteness of French impressionism. In the December 1918 edition of *Current Opinion,* one critic wrote: "Russia, it appears, will furnish us the long-awaited antidote to the musical impressionism of France, to that delicate, perfumed twilight which pervaded the music of Western Europe before the war . . . Russia . . . seems to have produced a new, brutally realistic psychology, which in politics has produced Bolshevism and in music a materialism equally as ruthless and inconsiderate of precedents."

Prokofiev was also taken as a personification of the spiritual grandeur of the Russian nation. The *Chicago Evening American* called him "the glittering hope of future Russia." At the same time, many critics, attempting to equate Bolshevism with anarchy and the destruction of traditions, spoke of the "Bolshevist" nature of the *Scythian Suite.* "The red flag of musical anarchy raged tempestuously in staid old Orchestra Hall yesterday afternoon, while Bolshevist tunes rose fleetingly to the surface of a sea of tone, only to be submerged again by an overwhelming cacophony," reported the Chicago *Herald-Examiner.* Considering that it was written in 1919, the review in the Chicago labor paper, *New Majority* (October 25), is even more interesting. Naïvely hailing Prokofiev as a representative of revolutionary Russia, this paper proclaimed, "He is an artist-revolutionary. Workers should listen to his music. In it breathes freedom."

After attending the Prokofiev concerts, the directors of the Chicago Opera Company approached the composer with the idea of producing one of his operas. Prokofiev first suggested *The Gambler,* but he had only the piano score to show, the full score having been left behind in the library of the Maryinsky Theater. Then he mentioned *The Love for Three Oranges,* the plan of which he had carefully worked out on the trip from Russia. "Gozzi! Our dear Gozzi! Wonderful!" exclaimed Campanini, delighted with the idea of a gay opera on a classic Italian theme. In January Prokofiev signed a contract with the Chicago Opera Company to deliver the full score by October of that year. This was the first time in the United States that a foreign composer had been officially commissioned to write a new opera.

On January 7 at the Society for Contemporary Music in New York City, Prokofiev gave the first American performance of *Tales of the Old Grandmother.* On February 17 he played Tchaikovsky's Sonata in G major at a concert in Aeolian Hall commemorating the twenty-fifth anniversary of the composer's death. When an advance payment on the commissioned opera made possible a temporary rest from his exhausting concert activity, he turned with enthusiasm to composing *The Love for Three Oranges.* Prokofiev himself wrote the libretto of the new opera using the text of the comedy by the same name, which had been written by K. Vogak, Vs. Meyerhold, and Vl. Solovyov from Carlo Gozzi's scenario.[9] He was also concerned with making the music more intelligible. He said in his memoirs, "Bearing in mind American tastes, I chose a simpler musical idiom than that of *The Gambler,* and the work went easily."

In the midst of his work he fell ill with scarlet fever and diphtheria. An abscess in his throat almost cost him his life. ("I thought that you were dying—that's why I sent you those roses," an American lady admitted to him later.) After a month and a half of illness he applied himself to the opera with renewed enthusiasm. "Once I began to recover," he said, "I could hardly wait for the doctor's permission to continue my work. . . . The illness refreshed me, if that's possible, and by June all the music was composed." He devoted the summer of 1919 to orchestrating the opera, and on October 1 (exactly on time) the full score was submitted to the theater in Chicago.

Shortly after completing the opera, Prokofiev easily and quickly composed a new chamber work which soon won success. This was the *Overture on Hebrew Themes,* Op. 34, for clarinet, string quartet, and piano. It was written at the request of a group of former fellow students at the Petersburg Conservatory, whom the composer had met in New York that fall. The group, which had formed an ensemble called "Zimro," gave concerts of chamber pieces by Jewish composers, but they had difficulty making ends meet. They asked Prokofiev to write a work with parts for all six members of their ensemble and gave him a notebook of Jewish folk themes. At first he refused, for at that time he considered it "bad form" to compose music on borrowed themes. However, he gradually became fascinated with the folk tunes. Once, "to while away the time," he leafed through the notebook his friends had given him, "chose a few charming melodies, began to improvise at the piano, and suddenly noticed that somehow whole sections began to take shape." "I worked all of the following day," he relates, "and sketched out the entire overture."

This was Prokofiev's first work based on authentic folk material. It is constructed on two contrasting tunes: a rhythmically precise dance, playful with a slight touch of sadness (main theme), and a plaintive and sustained lyrical melody (subordinate theme). These are ingeniously combined to form a laconic sonata allegro with a strong folk element. In the entire piece there is neither buffoonery nor harmonic eccentricity. The faint humor emerges from the very nature of the first theme, and it is sharpened only slightly through rhythmic accents. The instrumentation, in which the singing or harsh timbres of the strings are contrasted with both the vivid color of the clarinet and the somewhat dry timbre of the piano, has an original and specifically Hebrew flavor. Listeners have long been charmed by the various interesting ways in which the thematic material is treated in this composition—such as the amusing crescendo in the coda, which is constructed on an endlessly repeated phrase taken from the basic dance tune.[10]

In the *Overture on Hebrew Themes* Prokofiev displayed an unexpected ability for handling folk themes reverently without sacrificing his own creative individuality. Although he did not attach any special importance to this overture, having composed it almost by chance, it nevertheless proved far more viable than many other works of his foreign period. Soviet audiences always listen to this piece with interest.

The Zimro ensemble gave the first performance of the *Overture* in New York on January 26, 1920. In 1934 the composer scored it for a small symphony orchestra, but some of the special folk flavor of the original instrumentation was thereby lost.

✳    ✳    ✳

The production of *The Love for Three Oranges* had been scheduled to take place late in 1919. The directors of the Chicago Opera Company had allotted a substantial sum for the settings, which had been ordered from Boris Anisfeld. The press lost no time in reporting that the California and Florida orange kings had become interested in the new opera as a possible advertising gimmick. It was said that the California firm of Sunkist Oranges was willing to supply the opera's entire cast with free oranges, and that this famous purveyor of orange juice would pay almost any price for permission to hang a placard in the theater's lobby reading, "This succulent and healthful brand inspired Prokofiev and is used exclusively by him in this opera and at home."[11]

Prokofiev's hopes for a production of the new opera were not to be realized so soon, however. Campanini, who had been warmly disposed toward the Russian composer, died suddenly in December, and the première was postponed until the following season. Having lost his connections with the concert world during the nine months he was writing the opera, Prokofiev found himself without money or work. Publishers who had not long before considered his music sensational, and hence capable of bringing in a quick profit, now turned away from him. With difficulty he succeeded in arranging a few concerts, but the managers insisted that he play as few of his own works as possible in order to avoid disturbing the audiences.

Accordingly, his programs included one of Bach's French Suites, Beethoven's *Contredanses,* Schumann's *Carnaval,* Moussorgsky's *Pictures at an Exhibition,* and even Scriabin's *Feuillet d'album* and *Désir.* At a concert in Carnegie Hall he played Rimsky-Korsakov's Piano Concerto. Only at the end of his regular program did he have an opportunity to play his own compositions (usually the most popular ones, such as the *Gavotte* and *Scherzo* of Op. 12 and *Diabolic Suggestions*). At one of the concerts (on April 8, 1920) he played for the first time a transcription of the Scherzo from *The Love for Three Oranges.*

A concert tour of Canada early in 1920 brought Prokofiev neither spiritual nor material satisfaction. He was deeply depressed by the conservatism of American audiences, and also somewhat resentful of the success of the popular virtuosos who had found an easy path to the listeners' hearts.

Despite the unfortunate fate of *The Love for Three Oranges,* Prokofiev did not, of course, cease composing. And even though it seemed almost impossible to get his operas produced, he was again drawn toward opera.

"Actually, my interest was not altogether timely," he admits. "I had begun *The Love for Three Oranges* with a contract in my pocket, and nothing came of it. To begin another large work then, without any prospects, was rather foolish. Possibly the stubborn streak in my nature was asserting itself: one opera did not go, so I would write another."

In looking for a subject for the new opera, Prokofiev came across Valery Bryusov's "historical novel" *The Flaming Angel,* which had first appeared in 1907–8 in the symbolist magazine *The Scales.* According to the composer, this was "one of the few really artistic Russian books" he was able to find in America. Intrigued by the gloomy, high-strung characters of Bryusov's story, he wrote the libretto and first two acts of the opera in a very short time. "This absorbing activity filled the void created by the cancellation of the *Oranges,*" he writes.

The story by Bryusov which caught Prokofiev's interest was typical of the decadent trend in Russian literature. It is filled with the images which so fascinated the Russian modernists: medieval mysticism, eroticism combined with religious ecstasy, morbid visions, and hallucinations. What is more, Bryusov had performed a complicated stylistic feat. To mystify the reader, he had brilliantly reproduced the style and mood of German literature of the sixteenth century, the epoch of Dürer and the Counter-Reformation. The full title of the story ran: "A Truthful Narrative, in Which the Story Is Told of a Devil Who More Than Once Appears to a Young Maiden in the Form of a Fiery Spirit and Tempts Her to Commit Various Sinful Acts; of Godless Dealings in Magic, Astrology, and Necromancy; of the Trial of the Young Maiden Conducted by His Grace the Archbishop of Trier; And Also of Meetings and Conversations Between a Knight and the Triune Doctor Agrippa von Nettesheim."

The entire story is told in the first person by the knight Ruprecht, humanist and skeptic, traveler and warrior, a stranger to mystical prepossessions. But the central character in the novel is Renata, Ruprecht's sweetheart, who is subject to religio-mystical paroxysms and is a victim of the Inquisition.

The autobiographical style of the story gave the composer great difficulty in writing the libretto. He later corresponded about this with Demchinsky, the coauthor of *The Gambler,* who was living in Leningrad. But even Demchinsky's dramaturgical ingenuity could not save the libretto from looseness and a certain static quality.

For Prokofiev the chief attraction of the story lay in its emotional intensity, so akin to his own artistic temperament. This was in every respect the antithesis of *The Love for Three Oranges.* While *Oranges* is a rich mixture of satire, banter, and amusing fantasy, *The Flaming Angel* is a dramatic representation of the cruel and horrible aspects of life. The scenes portraying the work of the Inquisition and Renata's hysterical fits in the convent are set to music of heightened expressiveness.

Like *The Gambler,* the new opera was based on vocal declamation (at times exaggerated) and a complex symphonic fabric. The composer used leitmotivs, clearly delineated in his own trenchant manner, to distinguish the principal themes of the drama—Ruprecht's theme, the convent theme, and Renata's agitated love theme (FIG. 23).

Renata's theme, the convent theme, and certain others were taken from sketches of the unfinished White Quartet. Several years later these themes returned to the domain of instrumental music when the composer used them in his Third Symphony (1928).

The complexity and exaggerated expressiveness of the vocal parts, as

FIGURE 23

well as weaknesses in dramatic conception, were serious obstacles to any production of *The Flaming Angel*. Aware of these shortcomings, the composer struggled with the opera intermittently for the next eight years (1919–1927); nevertheless, prolonged negotiations for its production with both American and European theaters ended in failure (save for a concert performance of some excerpts at one of Koussevitzky's Paris concerts in June, 1928).[12]

In the spring of 1920 Prokofiev finally became convinced that America had nothing to offer him. All his hopes had been dashed by the callousness, indifference, and commercial cynicism of American music merchants. He wrote of that time: "I wandered through the enormous park in the center of New York, and looking up at the skyscrapers bordering it, I thought with a cold fury of the wonderful American orchestras that cared nothing for my music; of the critics who were repeating for the hundredth time, 'Beethoven is a great composer,' while balking violently at new works; of the managers who arranged long tours for artists playing the same hackneyed programs fifty times over . . ."

He now felt that he had made an irreparable mistake in leaving Russia to seek "triumphs" in America, and he thought of returning home; but the young Soviet Republic was still cut off from the world by the prolonged imperialist blockade, and the idea of returning had to be put aside.

During these days that were so difficult for his homeland, Prokofiev more than once demonstrated his sympathy toward revolutionary Russia. He participated in a concert arranged by the Friends of Soviet Russia.

Exposing the lies of reactionary newspapers, he stated in an interview, "The Bolsheviks are patrons of art and are doing everything possible to foster its development. . . . It is my belief that there is a great future for music in Russia."[13]

In April of 1920 Prokofiev left the inhospitable United States for Western Europe. His subsequent visits to America were sporadic, only for concert appearances. The two years in the United States left no mark on his artistic taste or interests; he remained completely indifferent to the general craze for jazz, and he shunned the cheap lures of entertainment music. All his musical ideas of these years had their real origins in Russia and were closely tied to pre-revolutionary art.

On leaving America Prokofiev went to Paris, which was then considered the spiritual headquarters of modern Western art. Here he was to meet again the old supporters of his modernist tendencies, Diaghilev and Koussevitsky. During the following years, these leaders in voluntary exile strove actively to hitch Prokofiev more securely to the musical chariot of the bourgeois West. Diaghilev had revived his ballet enterprises after the war; in London and later in Paris, he received the composer with his usual condescension.

Prokofiev was soon introduced into the Paris art world. He met, among others, Pablo Picasso, Ernest Ansermet, and Maurice Ravel. Later he fondly recalled the musicale at the Parisian salon where he first met Ravel. This was in 1920. Prokofiev was struck by the distinguished composer's spiritual purity and unassuming manner. ("Oh, please don't call me *maître!*" Ravel had said to him.) Throughout his life Prokofiev retained a high regard for the music of this French master, considering him "one of the most important musicians of our time."[14]

In the spring of 1920 Diaghilev was preparing new surprises for his European clientele. He resumed negotiations with Prokofiev for a production of *The Buffoon*. Once again Prokofiev was captivated by Diaghilev's enterprise, caustic wit, and inexhaustible fund of ideas.

*The Buffoon* had not been produced in 1915 on account of the war, but the piano score was still in Diaghilev's files. On looking through it, Diaghilev felt that changes should be made in several places. When he pointed these out, Prokofiev considered his judgment sound and readily agreed to make the required alterations and additions. It was decided, for example, that five symphonic entr'actes should be added so that all six scenes of the ballet could proceed without a break. Certain passages were discarded, and the final dance entirely rewritten. Stravinsky, who was still collaborating with the Diaghilev company, also became very much interested in the ballet and offered suggestions, mainly concerning orchestration. ("At this spot it might be better to give it to the tuba." "Here give the double bass a sharp *arco* instead of *pizzicato*.")

Prokofiev completed the score in Mantes, near Paris, where he was spending the summer. Keeping in mind the taste of foreign audiences, he also enlarged his concert repertoire with a number of piano transcriptions, taking care to select only fresh, unhackneyed material from traditional music. Recalling a suggestion once made to him by Taneyev, he unearthed a little known Buxtehude organ fugue in D minor and arranged it for piano. Stravinsky suggested that he use Schubert waltzes and *ländler*. Selecting a number of his favorite pieces, he combined them in a suite, scarcely changing the original texture. In 1923 he revised this suite for two pianos, this time making some harmonic and contrapuntal additions. Asafyev praised it warmly, finding that stylistically it "surpassed the pianism of Liszt." Much later, waltzes appeared in many of Prokofiev's works (from *Cinderella* and *War and Peace* to the *Pushkin Waltzes* and *Winter Bonfire*).

❄ ❄ ❄

Prokofiev's second visit to the United States, in the fall of 1920, also proved unsuccessful. The production of *The Love for Three Oranges* was postponed again, this time because the composer demanded compensation for the previous year's breach of contract. "I decided that even if the opera were not produced, I would not let them make mincemeat of me," he wrote. When the directors of the Chicago Opera Company rejected his demand, Prokofiev was obliged to begin an extensive tour as a pianist, which included a month and a half in California. Again his programs included a large amount of classical music: his transcriptions of the Schubert waltzes, Beethoven's A major Sonata, Op. 101, Chopin études, and pieces by Lyadov and Rimsky-Korsakov.

The concerts attracted little attention and brought Prokofiev no satisfaction whatsoever. He had to share the limelight with other touring artists, mostly singers, and the American newspapers referred to him only as a pianist, ignoring his accomplishments as a composer—the caption of a photograph in *Musical America* read, "Composer Stravinsky and pianist Prokofiev."

In December, during the California tour, Prokofiev wrote five songs without words for voice and piano in a refined lyrical style. A direct development of the delicate, feminine lyricism of the Akhmatova songs, these five vocalises are charming for their purity and earnestness of mood, so unusual for the young Prokofiev. Though wordless, these songs evoke a singularly pure impression of romantic reverie and the transports of love. All this is communicated by spare vocal declamation and capricious harmonies — sometimes transparently diatonic, sometimes complicated through the use of unexpected passing tones. The composer's favorite technique of sudden modulations and shifts to distant tonalities is used here not for mockery, but to convey subtle nuances of feeling. While marked by a general unity of lyrical style, the songs nevertheless present contrasts. In the second and fifth the dominant mood is tender reverie, but in the third it is fervent feeling, and in the fourth, gentle humor. Occasionally there appear images delicately oriental in character, with a touch of impressionist coloring (the middle episode of the second song, for example).

Considering the time and place of composition, it is significant that Prokofiev chose to write a cycle of deeply emotional songs without a text. Evidently, he was unable to find poetic material suited to his rich fund of musical ideas, the alien milieu being in no way conducive to the realization of serious artistic ideas.

The five songs without words were performed for the first time in March 1921 by the Russian singer Nina Koshetz, at one time an eminent interpreter of Rachmaninov (Prokofiev dedicated this cycle to her). In 1925 with the aid of the violinist Paul Kochanski, the composer rewrote these songs for violin and piano.

In the spring of 1921, with a change in the management of the Chicago Opera Company, the question of the production of *The Love for Three Oranges* was finally settled. The new manager, Mary Garden, celebrated as the creator of the role of Mélisande in Debussy's opera *Pelléas et Mélisande,* was known for her sympathetic attitude toward modern music. On her insistence, Prokofiev's opera was included in the repertoire for the following season. His aim achieved, Prokofiev returned to Europe to help in the production of *The Buffoon.* The rehearsals were held in Monte Carlo, the temporary haven of the Diaghilev company.

At this time an unexpected rivalry developed between the two exporters of Russian art, Diaghilev and Koussevitzky, over which one would introduce Prokofiev to the Paris public. Both expected a tremendous sensation, and for some time neither would yield. Koussevitzky finally won and presented the *Scythian Suite* on April 29, 1921. The Paris critics gave it an enthusiastic reception. "It is impossible to resist such a combination of skill and freshness," declared the newspaper *L'Eclair* on May 9.

Diaghilev opened his season on May 17 with the première of *The Buffoon*. Since the fate of a ballet could be determined by its reception in Paris, then considered the absolute arbiter of artistic fashion, Diaghilev always took great pains to make his Paris productions as elaborate as possible. The première of *The Buffoon* was no exception. The sets and costumes, by Larionov, were designed in a deliberately exaggerated futurist style, which combined features of the show booth and the primitive *lubok*. The program carried a pencil sketch of Prokofiev, specially ordered from the celebrated painter Matisse. The composer himself was to conduct, and the all-powerful press had been mobilized for the occasion.

Diaghilev displayed his usual commercial attitude toward art and deference to foreigners. This was bound to provoke a feeling of resentment in Prokofiev, who had always taken a respectful and serious approach to his work. Diaghilev's approach to art is clearly revealed in Prokofiev's report of an incident that occurred during the dress rehearsal of *The Buffoon* in London: "Noting, while conducting, that something was wrong, I stopped the orchestra. Diaghilev immediately rushed up to me and whispered angrily, 'I've assembled the cream of London for this rehearsal and now, by stopping, you have ruined the whole effect. Please, just go on, no matter what happens.' "

※　※　※

Let us pause for a brief description of *The Buffoon*.

As previously mentioned, the ballet is composed of six highly compact scenes which proceed without interruption, being linked together by five symphonic entr'actes. The action develops swiftly and energetically, without pausing for contemplation or psychological probing. The composer abandoned the ballet solo and *pas de deux* traditionally used to express the moods and feelings of principal characters. His aim was conciseness, a tightening of musical style. Brief, dynamic episodes of pantomime flash by in swift sequence, only now and then giving way to complete dance numbers ("Dance of Laughter," "Dance of the Buffoons' Wives," "Dance of the Buffoons' Daughters," the ritualistic "Dance of the She-Goat," and so on).

The distinguishing features of the plot are trenchant humor and mischievous clowning. A crafty village prankster (the Buffoon) sells seven of his fellow villagers a "wonder-working" whip, by means of which the dead can be resurrected. To prove this, he stages before his customers the "murder" of his own wife, whom he then and there restores to life by means of the magic whip. The seven buffoons, duped by this performance, buy the whip for three hundred rubles and then proceed to test it by killing their wives. But the whip proves to be powerless—the wives fail to come back to life. The enraged buffoons want to square accounts with their swindler, but before they can find him the Buffoon manages to disguise himself as a young peasant woman (Molodukha, supposedly his own sister). Unable to catch the offender, the seven buffoons take Molodukha to their house as a cook. Then an incredible thing happens: a rich merchant appears to select a wife from among the buffoons' seven daughters; naturally, he chooses the cook. The "young bride," terrified by this time, is brought into the amorous merchant's bedroom. But once again the wily mischief-maker devises a ruse: he feigns illness, goes out for an "airing," and slips a goat into the bedroom as his substitute. The distressed merchant, deciding that his bride has turned into a goat, pushes and tosses the poor animal about until it dies. At this point the Buffoon enters, accompanied by seven soldiers, and demands three hundred rubles from the merchant as payment for his dead "sister."

On the basis of this plot, Prokofiev created one of his most eccentric scores, a striking expression of that nihilistic grotesquerie which had appealed to him so strongly in his youth. In its exaggerated *lubok* style this theatrical tale (all of the characters appear in stylized, caricatural masks) bears a certain relationship to Rimsky-Korsakov's *Golden Cockerel*. Even though Prokofiev's characters are more unreal, stylized, and grotesque, the duped buffoons and the amorous merchant have something in common with such musical personages as King Dodon and the Voivode Polkan.

But it would be fruitless to seek in *The Buffoon* the spirit of satire found in *The Golden Cockerel*. Whereas in Rimsky-Korsakov's opera bold and biting political satire plays the decisive role, in *The Buffoon* the authors (Prokofiev and Diaghilev) confined themselves to contriving superficial eccentric effects, to provoking laughter for its own sake. The underlying satire of the old folk buffoonery, which glorified the intelligence, shrewdness, and wit of the simple Russian peasant (his superiority to the rich and idle), was completely emasculated. If comparisons are to be drawn, it is rather the eccentric *lubok* works of the young Stravinsky that come to mind.

The dominant motifs of *The Buffoon* are pointless mischief and meaningless cruelty—brawls, fights, murders, and malicious clowning. The humor is consistently gruesome and mocking, as in the two funeral processions (one for the seven wives and one for the goat). It is indicative that whereas in the original folk tale the merchant, the priest, and the landowner were objects of scathing satire, in *The Buffoon* the most "lyrical" character in the motley collection of grotesque mimes is actually the amorous merchant, who is musically portrayed with perceptible flashes of human feeling.

To match the emotional tension engendered by the ballet's rage, terror, and vicious taunting, Prokofiev employed thick, dissonant harmony. The murder of the seven wives and the beating of Molodukha take place to the accompaniment of the most jarring harmonies and strident orchestral timbres.

The score contains a number of leitmotivs, most of them in a Russian national vein. Among these are Molodukha's theme, the merchant's theme, the theme depicting the noisy band of seven buffoons, and the theme of the Buffoon himself, which reappears in all five entr'actes. Some of these leitmotivs, like those of the merchant and Molodukha and the main theme of the final dance, resemble melodies of Russian peasant songs. But the composer tends to burlesque the folk song melodies by means of exaggerated harmonies and melodic ornamentations (grace notes, *tirate,* and leaps), as if to depict the grimaces and gestures of the puppet-like characters in the ballet. After creating a tune in typical folk style, he deforms it by exaggerated leaps or deliberate chromaticism; the national quality of the melody is retained, but in caricatured form.

Some of the dance themes are decidedly primitive in the manner of children's ditties and rhymes; two examples of this are the "Dance of the Buffoons' Daughters" and the motiv of the quarrel between the Buffoon and the merchant (FIG. 24).

FIGURE 24

The rigid, mechanical quality of the rhythm and the repetition of the melodies in combination with eccentric harmonies give such themes a puppet-like quality.

Scattered throughout the score are bits of musical parody, such as the caricatured fugue in the scene where the buffoons kill their wives, and the unexpected quotation from the introduction of Tchaikovsky's song "If I'd Only Known," which is introduced when the seven buffoons' daughters look through the window to see the merchant arriving.[15] At times, as in the introduction, the music acquires the character of naturalistic noise, constructed on strange sound effects and lacking any melodic meaning. The composer himself described this episode as "whistling and rattling, as if dusting the instruments in the orchestra."

Almost all the music of the ballet is in strict duple meter with heavily accented strong beats. This simplification of the rhythm, although it compensates somewhat for the harshness of the harmonies, creates a certain monotony. Most of the dance episodes remind one rather more of the action of mechanical dolls than of emotionally vital folk dance.

The mechanical quality of the music is heightened by the biting, graphic orchestration, with its almost continuously hammering phrases in the piano and percussion. The many striking orchestral effects (muted trumpets, strings *sul ponticello*) and various descriptive devices (*glissandi, tirate,* etc.) accentuate the puppet-like, burlesque character of the whole work.

On studying the score of *The Buffoon* today, one regretfully notes its lack of meaningful content; it is a far cry from the democratic folk traditions of advanced Russian art. The grotesquerie in *The Buffoon* is essentially an end in itself. Folk life and folk art are refracted through the prism of modernist eccentricity. As a consequence, despite its seeming gaiety, the work is fundamentally pessimistic.

Nevertheless, for all the grotesque and eccentric effects in the music of *The Buffoon,* it would be a mistake not to see in it certain manifestations of a keen and vital talent. For there are moments when the grimacing and mechanical monotony of the music are suddenly broken by passages of soulful lyricism. Such, above all, is the theme of the Buffoon, which runs through all five entr'actes. Its melody has a warm, human quality and its harmonies are exquisitely beautiful and expressive (FIG. 25).

One can easily find similarities between this theme and those in *Tales* of *the Old Grandmother.* Moments of genuine feeling also appear in the lyrical themes of Molodukha and the merchant. At such moments, the prevailing puppet-like quality which characterizes most of the composi-

FIGURE 25

tion suddenly retreats into the background, and behind the buffoons' masks one can discern the features of real people.

In the music of *The Buffoon,* Prokofiev revealed his ingenuity as a composer for the theater; he demonstrated a remarkable ability to portray with a single stroke, in one swift rhythmic and melodic gesture, the typical movement and outward appearance of a character, and thus the essence of his action and behavior.

Now enters the noisy band of buffoons, arms insolently akimbo; now the clever Buffoon and his wife merrily frisk and frolic concocting the next prank; now the buffoons' daughters dance, with wooden grace and stony faces. Although these characters and their actions are sharply caricatured, they are based on the composer's observations of the comic aspects of life. He develops the basic themes of the ballet in conformity with the action; it is interesting to note the various modifications of Molodukha's theme and the ingenious development of the Buffoon's theme at the moment his wife is resurrected. All these descriptive details reveal the composer's inherent sense of the theater and his mastery of the mimetic qualites of sound.

\* \* \*

To the fashionable circles of Paris, sated with the hothouse spices of impressionism, *The Buffoon* was simply another serving of the Russian exoticism that so pleasantly titillated their jaded appetites. But most of the critics were in raptures: "a cascade of ideas, an inexhaustible fund of color, rhythms, melodies." Characteristically, the modernist critics, who demanded only exotic side shows *à la russe* from the Diaghilev ballet, were not altogether satisfied with *The Buffoon,* finding the few somewhat human elements in it disconcerting. "The production is not quite consistent. The grotesquerie and doll-like movement are not sustained throughout. Two figures—the young Buffoon and the Merchant—strike a jarring note with their realism," complained one critic.[16]

While, on the whole, *The Buffoon* was warmly received in Paris, which had long been accustomed to Diaghilev's excesses, its première in London on June 9, 1921, caused a major scandal. Almost all the English newspapers sharply criticized the composer. ("About 120 reviews, of which 119 were abusive," notes Prokofiev.) This was almost an exact repetition of what had happened in Petrograd five years before, following the première of the *Scythian Suite.*

One critic labeled *The Buffoon* a ballet absurdity; another called it stupid and puerile music. A third, representing an almost non-existent minority view, considered it a "revelation of musical genius" (*Daily Graphic,* June 16, 1921). One reviewer advised, "stuff your ears so as not to hear this music"; another compared the ballet to jazz and futurism. Diaghilev answered one of the English critics in a long and sharply worded letter, in which he defiantly asserted the right of contemporary artists to a modernist "revitalization" of art (*Daily Telegraph,* June 16, 1921).

In later years performances of *The Buffoon* continued to provoke hostile attacks on Prokofiev. After a performance in Belgium in 1928, *La Gazette de Liége* pronounced, "This music . . . declares war on all laws, scorns all rules, overthrows all methods, plunges us into an abyss of dissonances, into a tempest of raucous, disconnected, wild, shrieking sounds. It is mad!"

*The Buffoon* has been produced only once in the Soviet Union. In January 1928 it appeared (under the Ukrainian title *Blazen'*) at the Kiev Theater of Opera and Ballet, with the ballet master M. S. Dyskovsky as producer and A. S. Orlov as conductor. According to *Zhizn Iskusstva,* this production, designed by the young artist Armashevsky-Kurochka, was "in the style of a primitive print."[17] Since the theater did not have the full score, the music had to be reconstructed from the symphonic suite of the ballet; the orchestral entr'actes were omitted, and this resulted in prolonged intermissions. The Kiev production was given a laudatory review in the modernist magazine *Sovremennaya Muzyka,* Ya. Yurmas calling it a "living musical pantomime, a far cry from the stale classical choreography."[18] Nevertheless, *The Buffoon* met with little response among the people of Kiev and was soon withdrawn.

Repeated attempts to have the ballet staged at Moscow and Leningrad theaters ended in failure. When, in 1925, Asafyev thought of giving it at the Leningrad Maryinsky Theater with an antireligious intermezzo in the style of folk comedy, the composer flatly rejected the idea. "What kind of comic, antireligious episode in *The Buffoon* are you talking about? I, of course, have no intention of permitting any such insertions or digressions," Prokofiev wrote Asafyev.[19] The music of *The Buffoon* has been performed often in the Soviet Union, but only at symphonic concerts.

The ballet proved to be the most typical expression of Prokofiev's grotesquerie. Lunacharsky gave a perceptive explanation of Prokofiev's early predilection for the grotesque: "His rich individuality, set in the midst of a mechanized world, feels lost. This is why buffoonery plays so large a role in his music. After all, the buffoon is the plaything of society."[20]

After the première of *The Buffoon*, Prokofiev settled down for the summer of 1921 on the coast of Brittany. Here he completed the Third Piano Concerto, which he had begun while still in Russia. Most of the thematic material of this work had been composed several years earlier: the wonderful E minor theme of the variations (second movement) dates to 1913; the first two themes of the first movement and two of the variations date to 1916–17; and the first and second themes of the finale were taken from the unfinished string quartet conceived in 1918.[21] The difficult passage of parallel triads in the recapitulation of the first movement had been put in reserve as far back as 1911, when, in addition to the D-flat major concertino, Prokofiev had planned a large piano concerto "full of virtuoso passages."

Adding a few themes that were lacking (the subordinate theme of the first movement, the third theme of the finale) and combining everything into a harmonious three-movement design, Prokofiev created one of his finest works, a worthy climax to many years of experimentation in the field of piano composition.

The vivid contrasts of musical ideas so typical of the young Prokofiev are presented in the Third Piano Concerto with the greatest clarity: the soulful Russian lyricism, the good-naturedly grotesque fantasy, and, most of all, the dynamic and powerful virtuosity. The composer daringly juxtaposes contrasting ideas even within single movements. These sharp and unexpected juxtapositions take the place of complicated development sections; a broad, flowing melody in the reeds gives way to lavish cascades of runs or oddly angular, fantastic themes; a sustained singing melody is replaced by impetuous, energetic rhythms.

The Third Piano Concerto is more serious, more profound, and more mature than the First Concerto. At the same time, its emotional content leaves a far brighter, more joyful impression than the somber, almost stuffy atmosphere of the Second Concerto. The best aspects of Prokofiev's genius are clearly shown here: the spare and noble lyricism (in the opening theme of the first movement, the theme of the variations of the second movement, and the middle episode of the finale), and the powerful, robust energy (in the main sections of the first and third movements). The bravura texture is extremely varied, abounding in fine, smooth runs in the early classical style, resilient, ringing toccata-like passages, and complicated chordal progressions. The most difficult bravura effects often serve to express the irrepressible vigor of youth. Coming after rather dry scale passages and percussive staccato figurations, the singing, lyrical episodes are especially captivating.

At times, however, the music seems to have a certain artificiality, a somewhat calculated eccentricity; such moments occur during some of the variations in the second movement and in the grotesque episodes in the first, with their mechanical rhythms and lifeless, brittle tone color (recalling the puppet-like, strangely colorless images of *The Buffoon*). The composer sometimes seems overly interested in markedly unemotional, étude-like runs. Despite the richness and fullness of the predominantly diatonic harmonies, exaggerated harmonic devices do appear in certain variations of the second movement and in the recapitulation of the finale.

But these characteristic tonal audacities do not prevent the triumph of the Concerto's best elements—buoyant energy and diatonic clarity of melody and harmony.

An important feature of the Third Concerto is its clearly defined national quality. Here the Russian national style is vividly and poetically expressed, but in a fresh and novel way. While not rejecting the warmly expressive melodic element, the composer strives to invigorate the style with a certain active dynamism.

The introductory theme of the first movement is a kind of poetic epigraph to the Concerto. This melody, announced by the solo clarinet, is reminiscent of a broad, flowing folk song or the piping of a shepherd (Fig. 26).

This serene melody gives way to impetuous running passages, out of which emerges the energetic and buoyant main theme, stated in a spare two-voice passage by the piano. This theme is probably derived from the introductory tune, but in place of the clarinet's sustained, flowing melody,

FIGURE 26

clear-cut rhythms are the dominant feature. A vigorous dialogue of running passages between piano and orchestra leads to the lyrical, narrative second theme. This is one of those storybook themes in a semi-grotesque vein which occur so frequently in Prokofiev's cyclical compositions, from the subordinate themes of the First Piano and First Violin Concertos to the final theme in the first movement of the Seventh Symphony. Here this serene Russian theme is given a strange coloration through angular twists and figurations, a rigid, mechanical rhythm, and sharpened harmonies and orchestration; thus transformed, it conjures up vague images of the fantastic characters in old folk tales.

A new statement of the singing theme of the introduction plays the major role in the short development section. Here this beautiful melody sounds even richer and more full-bodied; tinged with the unique flavor of Prokofiev's diatonic style, it seems to sing of the sunny expanses and beloved distances of Russia. In the recapitulation the material of the exposition is considerably changed: while the passage-work becomes even more complicated and entangled, the second theme acquires more distorted, rather macabre features (dry, brittle, knocking chords). In the coda, the even, étude-like runs triumph again, culminating in a sharp final chord.

The second movement (*Andantino*) is constructed in the form of a theme with five variations and an extended coda. This charming theme, announced by the orchestra, is perhaps the finest melody of the entire Concerto. Naïvely melodic, in graceful rhythm, it is in the spirit of some of the early dance pieces (the G minor *Gavotte* of Op. 12, for example). The composer's treatment of the variation form is strikingly imaginative and free. He alters the original theme so radically that it becomes almost unrecognizable: now subjecting it to a kind of grotesque distortion, now dissolving it into exquisitely colorful impressionistic sonorities, now entangling it in a network of cleverly conceived figurations. In some of the variations the theme becomes elusive, dispersed into tiny fragments; only the beautiful and full-sounding plagal cadences, repeated in almost every variation, recall the unity of the thematic material.

Of the five variations, only the first preserves the melodic contour of the theme, adorned by graceful ornaments. The second is marked by grotesquerie in the spirit of *The Buffoon* and certain episodes of the First Violin Concerto. The third is a kind of intermezzo, filled with brilliant virtuoso passages. The fourth is slow and fantastic, with a suggestion of the lifeless iciness of *The Kingdom of Kashchei*. And, finally, the fifth is in the character of a broadly burlesqued march. In the coda the opening theme of the movement is restated in its original form by the orchestra, accompanied this time by light, staccato chords in the piano.

In the finale (*Allegro ma non troppo*), just as in the first movement, swift, ceaseless motion prevails. The main theme, with its diatonic coloring and characteristically Russian turns, has something in common with the opening theme of the first movement. But here the melodic element is more thoroughly subordinated to a sharply accentuated dance rhythm.

The main theme is developed to some extent in the exposition by means of sudden tonal shifts, and complicated by grace notes, leaps, and *glissandi* which further intensify its resilient dynamism. After this comes the captivating middle section of the finale (*meno mosso*). This passionate, singing theme, enriched by wide intervals and a colorful inner modulatory scheme, is filled with the joy and optimism of youth; in this, it prefigures many of Prokofiev's later lyrical themes, such as the life-affirming theme of the Mistress in *The Stone Flower* and the best themes of the Fifth and Seventh Symphonies.

But here, too, the lyrical outpouring of song is suddenly interrupted by a short interlude in the spirit of the humorous *Fugitive Visions,* like the appearance of some droll, grimacing character from a fairy tale. This image is quickly replaced by an extended statement of the lyrical theme, now richly ornamented. Eventually this lyricism gives way to the resilient motion of the first theme. The recapitulation is altered in many ways and becomes charged with dynamism and action. The second theme is not restated, and the first theme is sharpened, peppered with accidentals and chordal superimpositions. The rhythm and brilliant virtuosity keep mounting until the very end of the Concerto, generating an overwhelming, almost hypnotic, power.

❄ ❄ ❄

The Third Piano Concerto very quickly achieved world-wide recognition. It was first performed on December 16, 1921, in Chicago, with the composer as soloist and Frederick Stock conducting. The following January Prokofiev played it again in New York (under Albert Coates), and in April in Paris and London. He subsequently performed this Concerto in many other countries and also recorded it. The American public, according to Prokofiev, "did not quite understand" the Concerto and the New York newspapers received it with complete indifference. The press in France, Poland, and other European countries, however, praised it highly, pointing out the composer's turbulent imagination and the boldness of his ideas. In the spring of 1925 Prokofiev referred in a somewhat sardonic vein to his performance of the Third Concerto at "the citadel of academic music—the Paris Conservatory." "This is the oldest and most conservative concert institution in Paris, hence a certain piquancy," he reported in one of his letters.

The Third Concerto quickly achieved acceptance in the Soviet Union, too. In the fall of 1923 the pianist S. E. Feinberg played it for the first time at one of the evenings arranged by the International Book Association in Moscow. This première particularly pleased the composer. "I was happy to learn of the success of the Third Concerto in Moscow. Please convey my gratitude to the performers, Feinberg and Saradzhev," he wrote to his Moscow friends.[22]

Asafyev noted that the Concerto "sounds unusually bright; it has a real Russian sweep to it, even though it contains neither folk themes nor deliberate stylization." "What is important," he pointed out in another article, "is that Prokofiev has still not cut himself off from his own country. His work throbs with its strength, and radiates the Russian understanding of art's meaning and value."[23]

In more recent years the Third Concerto has been performed frequently by Soviet pianists, among them Lev Oborin, Emil Gilels, and Yakov Zak. It has rightfully become part of the golden treasury of modern Russian music.

Among Prokofiev's papers is a sonnet entitled "The Third Concerto," written by Balmont after the first performance of this work in France (September 1921). Balmont's poem, although marked by symbolist pretentiousness, is interesting as a unique attempt by a listener to convey his impression of this Concerto through the medium of poetry:

> An exultant flame of a crimson flower,
> A verbal keyboard sparkling with flames
> That suddenly leap forth in fiery tongues.
> A raging stream of molten ore.
> The moments dance a waltz, the ages a gavotte.
> Suddenly a wild bull, startled by foes,
> Bursts his chains, halts, his horns posed to strike.
> But once again the tender sounds call from afar.
> From tiny shells children fashion a castle.
> An opaline balcony, beautiful, finely wrought.
> But all is dashed by a foaming wave.
> Prokofiev! Music and youth in bloom,
> In you the orchestra yearns for summer's ecstasies
> And the indomitable Scyth strikes the tambourine-sun.

Prokofiev had met Balmont in the summer of 1921, when the poet was also staying at a place on the coast of Brittany. Now faded and seedy, Balmont tried to bask in the light of the talented composer's glory. He dashed off some verses dedicated to Prokofiev and also offered him several texts for songs. Thus, almost simultaneously with the Third Piano Concerto, Prokofiev composed the Five Songs, Op. 36: *An Incantation for Fire and Water, The Voice of the Birds, The Butterfly, Think of Me (A Malayan Incantation),* and *The Pillars.*

Once again Prokofiev's music echoed the savage incantations, the stylized, mystical exorcisms of Balmont's poetry. All five songs (but especially the last, *The Pillars*) are gloomy and despondent in mood. They possess elements of the overrefined chromatic style of French impressionism and traces of the florid, oriental primitivism of Gauguin—features not at all consonant with his own true style. It is indicative that whenever he undertook to write music to symbolist poetry, the composer began searching for "piquant" and exotic sounds; thus it had been with the songs of Op. 23 (Balmont's *In My Garden,* Verin's *Trust Me*), and so it was again.

The creative collaboration with Balmont did not last long. The émigré poet soon turned his pen against his "suffering homeland" (as he called it), and the coauthors gradually drifted apart.

The song cycle, Op. 36, was dedicated to the young Spanish singer **Lina Llubera,** whom Prokofiev had met in the United States. Within a short time Lina Llubera, who had spent her childhood in Russia (her mother was half-Russian), would become his wife and the mother of his two sons.

❋   ❋   ❋

The première of *The Love for Three Oranges* was scheduled for the fall of 1921 in Chicago. In October Prokofiev went to America for the third time, to participate in the production of the opera. During the rehearsal period he made a number of concert appearances; he performed in Chicago with Nina Koshetz at a concert arranged by the Friends of Soviet Russia under the slogan "In Defense of Soviet Russia."

In Chicago Prokofiev's abilities as a *régisseur* were revealed for the first time. He not only conducted the orchestra, but also familiarized himself with the sketches of the sets and worked with the singers and the stage director, Coini. Coini proved to be completely devoid of creative imagination. "At first I only grumbled at his lack of ingenuity," Prokofiev recalls, "but after a while I went backstage and explained the roles to the singers, and later I even went out on the stage and showed the chorus what to do. Finally Coini lost his temper and asked, 'Strictly speaking, who is in charge here, you or I?'" To which Prokofiev retorted, "You—to carry out my wishes!" On the other hand, the composer was completely satisfied with Boris Anisfeld's sets and with the cast, which included Nina Koshetz in the role of the witch Fata Morgana.

As an artistic creation, *The Love for Three Oranges* was unrelated to anything in contemporary American art; both the idea and the musical embodiment of the opera originated in the Russian pre-revolutionary modernist theater. The turning of Vs. Meyerhold and his colleagues to Gozzi's comedy was highly symptomatic; they took a satirical tale which ridiculed the eighteenth-century Italian theater and used it to make a burlesque of all traditional theatrical clichés. The authors of the Russian scenario added an allegorical prologue to Gozzi's play, in which they depicted a desperate struggle among the representatives of various theatrical schools and genres: Tragedians, Comedians, Lyricists, and Empty Heads. The Tragedians wanted *Weltschmerz,* misery, and murders; the Comedians demanded wholesome, joyous laughter; the Lyricists argued for "romantic love, moons, tender kisses"; and the Empty Heads insisted on "entertaining nonsense, witty double-entendres, fine costumes." Against absurd and old-fashioned standards the authors place the superficially brilliant but empty art of the Ridiculous People, the art of pure form, the baring of theatrical devices. In the plot of *The Love for Three Oranges* everything is stylized, ironic, unreal; the audience is shown not a real drama but a parody, deftly performed by gay mimes. But while ridiculing the clichés

of the old theater the authors opposed them only with mischievous grimacing and refined buffoonery constructed on the purely formal effects of
theatrical convention.

In working with this comic conception, it was certainly not Prokofiev's
conscious intention to condemn or ridicule traditional art. "The mixture
of fairy tale, humor, and satire in Gozzi's play, and especially its theatrical
qualities, had a strong appeal for me," Prokofiev recalls. In this sense the
Italian comedy corresponded fully to the composer's creative tendencies of
that time, his bent toward the ironic, the grotesque, and the ludicrous.
Later on, critics in many countries tried to guess whether the object of the
parody was old operatic forms or lachrymose, decadent art. "They tried
to determine what I was laughing at—the audience, Gozzi, operatic convention, or those who cannot laugh. They found in *Oranges* a chuckle, a
challenge, and grotesquerie." According to the composer himself, his aim
was simpler and more modest: "All I tried to do was to write an amusing
opera," he confesses in his memoirs.

Indeed, the plot of the opera abounds in lively intrigue and amusing
parody. The King of Clubs, ruler of an imaginary kingdom, suffers a great
sorrow: his son, the young Prince, has fallen into a state of incurable
hypochondria. Besides this, two wicked conspirators, the King's niece
Clarissa and the Prime Minister Leandro, are plotting to poison the Prince
and seize the throne. In addition to the real personages, the cast of characters includes sorcerers—the good magician Celio, the King's protector, and
the evil witch Fata Morgana, Leandro's protectress. The doctors declare
that there is only one cure for the Prince's malady—laughter. The jester
Truffaldino is summoned to organize festivities to amuse the Prince. All
his efforts fail, but finally, when the old woman Fata Morgana tumbles
down and turns a somersault, the Prince bursts out laughing. Enraged,
the old witch puts a terrible curse on him: he must travel to distant lands
in search of three magic oranges. After exciting adventures, the Prince
and Truffaldino find three enormous oranges in the castle of the sorceress
Creonta; one of the oranges contains the charming Princess Ninetta, with
whom the Prince falls in love. After overcoming a number of obstacles, the
enamored Prince takes Ninetta to his father's palace and marries her. Fata
Morgana and the enemies of the Prince vanish into the nether regions.

On the basis of this plot Prokofiev worked out an operatic spectacle in
four acts and ten scenes. The brief scenes follow each other easily and
swiftly. There is no psychological probing. Indeed, the composer seems
to delight in theatrical conventions and unreal situations: the magician

Celio and Fata Morgana furiously playing cards to the sinister howls and fiendish dancing of The Little Demons; The Monsters with enormous heads arriving at the royal festivities followed by droll Gluttons and Drunkards, who start a wild brawl; the fierce Cook (though female, sung by a *basso profundo*) who guards the magic oranges threatening to kill the Prince and Truffaldino with a soup ladle. All the characters of the opera are portrayed in an ironically exaggerated style: the Prince, perpetually sick, groaning and whining; the King, grieving inconsolably; the mock-romantic operatic villains Leandro and Clarissa, with their wicked scheming; the sorcerers and Little Demons, illuminated by the magic glow of the footlights.

The character who best suited the composer's purposes was the jester Truffaldino, "a person who knows how to make people laugh." His rollicking themes closely resemble those in *The Buffoon* and in many of Prokofiev's scherzos. Every time a traditional operatic situation arises (such as the traitorous plotting of Clarissa and Leandro, or the "tragic" clash of the King and the Prince), the overjoyed Tragedians, Lyricists, or Empty Heads rush out onto the stage, for they love these customary theatrical clichés. Intrusions of this kind naturally heighten still more the burlesque quality of the opera.

As he had done in *The Gambler,* Prokofiev completely shunned arias, ensembles, and choral episodes. The entire opera is written in a purely declamatory style, with a continuously unfolding descriptive orchestral accompaniment. The dialogue of the characters is terse, witty, and lively. Instead of extended vocal numbers such as monologues and arias, there are brief remarks in recitative or equally concise leitmotiv phrases in the orchestra. Such, for example, is the clownish, tripping leitmotiv of Truffaldino, so akin to many of the young Prokofiev's scherzo themes (FIG. 27). The Prince's love theme, the theme of "regal stateliness," the theme of the King's suffering, and a number of others have the character of brief orchestral leitmotivs. The choral parts throughout are reduced to phrases as

FIGURE 27

terse as recitative, to sharp dynamic exclamations; the only exception to this is the comical chorus of the Doctors at the beginning of the first scene of the opera, which, although more extended, is in a declamatory style somewhat like that of Moussorgsky.

The musical characterizations of the principal characters (Truffaldino, for example) have a dance-like rather than a song-like quality. The most important moments of the action, those requiring musical generalization, are expressed not in arias or ensembles, but in dances, processions, or pantomimes. Examples of this are Truffaldino's comic dance at the beginning of the fourth scene, the festive march in the same scene, the choruses and dances of the Little Demons in the card game episode (second scene), and the dance of the Courtiers on the occasion of the Prince's recovery. At times the whole spectacle creates the impression of a kind of hybrid opera-ballet.

As a whole, the music of this opera is in a lighter, simpler, more transparent style than that of *The Gambler* or *Ala and Lolli*. The music evokes images of two contrasting worlds—the world of theatrical make-believe, with witches, devils, and magicians, and the world of real, though caricatured, people. Such a juxtaposition of the imaginary and the real is found in many classical operas, but in Prokofiev both the fairy-tale characters and the real people are presented in an exaggerated, ironic manner.

In the themes characterizing the fantastic characters—Fata Morgana, the demon Farfarello, the Little Demons—the composer employs many complicated harmonic effects, among them polytonality, fanciful chains of seventh and ninth chords, and whole-tone progressions. The melodic element is shackled and shoved into the background by an abundance of sharp harmonies, which at times seem to become an end in themselves; typical of this is the moment of Fata Morgana's oath in the finale of Act II, where we find the combination of C major and F sharp major triads—the "chord of terror" used by Stravinsky in *Petrushka*. Grotesque harmonization with incidental, false-sounding counterpoint is used in the scene of the festivities, where the music accompanies the caricatured procession of the Monsters and Gluttons. The harshest orchestral effects are concentrated in the fantastic episodes, reaching the point of thunderous outbursts in the magic oaths of the evil forces.

The music portraying the court life and the Prince's romantic adventures has a different character. Here, the harmonic and orchestral language is clearer, simpler. In place of complicated, artificially constructed harmonies are the customary major and minor, made somewhat spicy in the manner of Prokofiev's early scherzos. Melody plays a considerably larger role, both in the descriptive themes of the orchestra and in the declamatory phrases of the singers. Most important are the themes and images associated with the various diverting extravagances, comic entertainments, and adventures—the themes of Truffaldino and the Ridiculous People, the laughter scene in the finale of Act II, and so on. It is in this gay, lively manner that the two most fully developed and memorable orchestral episodes of the opera are written: the festive, theatrical March in Act II (repeated later at the end of Act III) and the impetuous Scherzo in tarantella rhythm which accompanies the Prince's journey in search of the three oranges (entr'acte, also appearing twice in Act III). Both of these episodes later entered the concert repertory in the form of symphonic excerpts and piano arrangements. The famous March, full of buoyant energy and gay mockery, became particularly popular. "To write so original and fresh a march in this day of countless marches," wrote Asafyev later, "is the mark of a truly gifted composer, one equally dear and understandable to all."[24]

Prokofiev delineated the characters of the Prince, the King, Leandro, Clarissa, Pantalone, and other personages of the opera with spare, sharp strokes. The success of these characterizations is due in part to the composer's frequent use of aptly caught speech inflections, which are sometimes subjected to good-natured caricature and at other times used realistically to reproduce peculiarities in Russian speech. The vocal parts of the opera contain many ingenious details which reveal Prokofiev's sensitivity to the nuances of human speech and his ability to embody it in musical declamation.

The recitative of the opera is exceedingly varied, ranging from expressive melodic phrases to dry psalmody and including such purely eccentric devices as the howling "vocalise" of the Little Demons, the moaning *glissando* of the sick Prince, and the hoarse bass of the ferocious Cook.

The few lyrical passages occupy significant places in the opera: the Prince's love theme, heard soon after Fata Morgana's curse, the episodes of the appearance of the three thirsty princesses, and the amorous declarations of the Prince and Ninetta. As if fearful of excessive sentimentality, the composer quickly interrupts the Prince's love scene with the intrusive jesting of the Lyricists, who have at last seen "romantic love and tender kisses."

It was undoubtedly the combination of fast-moving comedy, expressive recitative, clever orchestral effects, and colorful staging that attracted and amused audiences. In turning to witty and lively operatic action, Prokofiev was seeking an antidote for the static heaviness of Wagnerian and impressionist opera. Asafyev, an enthusiastic apologist of new music, wrote of his effort: "One could hardly imagine an opera more antithetical to Wagnerian opera than *The Love for Three Oranges*. Here, instead of endless stretches from word and reflection to action, we find adventure, theatrically formulated and tersely characterized in music; instead of long, drawn-out lyrical outpourings and contemplation, a noisy poster; instead of complicated dramatic clashes, the improvisation of masques; instead of the romantic and the mystical, a good-natured theater magic, which deceives no one."[25]

Despite its subtle irony and witty inventiveness, *The Love for Three Oranges* has not become a part of the standard repertory. One reason for this is the composer's emphatic rejection of any kind of positive ideal—the lighthearted nihilism in *The Love for Three Oranges* is devoid of any social orientation, and thus an end in itself. While laughing at old romantic art, the composer did not reveal his own beliefs. At times this brilliantly devised parody seems nothing more than negation for the sake of negation. Belinsky long ago asserted that "every negation, to be vital and poetic, must be made in the name of an ideal." Satire devoid of purpose leads an artist to cold skepticism.

Another reason for the opera's failure to achieve wide and lasting popularity has to do with the peculiarities of Prokofiev's operatic style. The listener's attention is easily distracted by a host of details, witty remarks, and eccentric or comic effects. Except for the March and the Scherzo, the opera lacks well-developed musical generalizations; and even these two generalizations are realized by orchestral and not by vocal means, which are the essence of the operatic genre. These factors have made *The Love for Three Oranges* a work of limited appeal.

Naturally, Prokofiev's work on this comic opera did not pass without leaving its mark on him. His interest in theatrical buffoonery and lighthearted satire reappeared many years later in two comic pieces which he wrote in the Soviet period—the ballet *Cinderella* and the opera *The Duenna*. But in these later works, this interest expressed itself quite differently. The satire in *Cinderella* is more gentle and humane, and the buffoonery in *The Duenna* is more realistic and purposeful; in both works grotesque marionettes are replaced by real people with real emotions.

*  *  *

The première of *The Love for Three Oranges* on December 30, 1921, was warmly received by the Chicago public. Although the Chicagoans understood little of the subtle parody of the Gozzi tale and even less of the unusual music, they were flattered by the fact that a new, specially commissioned opera was having its première in their theater. The reviews were extremely favorable.

In New York, however, where the Chicago company performed the opera in February 1922, the critics were extremely hostile. "It was as though a pack of dogs had broken loose and were tearing my trousers to shreds," the composer remarks in his memoirs. While Chicago people were disposed to take some civic pride in "their" production, the New Yorkers had no such interest and criticized it mercilessly, as if to say, "You wanted to show us something that we didn't think of producing ourselves? Well, this is what we think of it!" Indeed, the New York critics could not find words devastating enough for the opera. One critic wrote, "The cost of the production was $130,000, which is about $43,000 for each orange, but the opera fell so flat that a repetition of it would be a financial fiasco." A similar fate befell the first American performances of the Third Piano Concerto: after a successful première in Chicago (December 16 and 17, under Frederick Stock) it was severely criticized in New York (December 26 and 27, under Albert Coates).

Prokofiev once more realized that his works would not receive the support he had hoped for in the United States. His hopes that the Chicago Opera Company would produce *The Flaming Angel* with Mary Garden as Renata were dashed when Miss Garden resigned as director of the company. "The American season, which had begun so brilliantly, completely fizzled out," writes Prokofiev. "I was left with a thousand dollars in my pocket, an aching head, and a longing to get away to some quiet place where I could work in peace."

Prokofiev left America and in March 1922 settled in Ettal, a quiet, picturesque little village in the Bavarian Alps, three kilometers from Oberammergau. With him were his wife and also his mother, who had recently come from Russia. After four years of continuous wandering, the composer felt the need to rest and review the feverish activities in which he had been engaged. For the following year and a half he made Ettal his home, leaving it only occasionally for concerts in various European cities.

In April 1922 the première of the Third Piano Concerto took place in Paris (under Koussevitzky) and London (under Albert Coates). In June *The Buffoon* was revived in Paris. In January 1923 the *Scythian Suite* was performed in Brussels, where it was received with "whistling, applause, indignation, enthusiastic letters, and invitations to play it next season."[26]

In the spring of 1923 Prokofiev played in Barcelona, Paris, Antwerp,

Brussels, and London. Postwar Germany, which was experiencing great material difficulties, took little interest in new Russian music. The performance of the *Overture on Hebrew Themes* and excerpts from *The Love for Three Oranges* passed unnoticed.

Prokofiev's work on *The Flaming Angel*, begun in America, progressed rapidly in Ettal. The Bavarian town of Oberammergau was famed for its medieval Passion play, and it seemed to Prokofiev that the witches' sabbaths described in Bryusov's story must have taken place somewhere in the vicinity. In Ettal he also composed the Fifth Piano Sonata (1923), prepared for publication the piano scores of *The Buffoon* and *The Love for Three Oranges*, arranged a symphonic suite from *The Buffoon*, and rewrote and reorchestrated the Second Piano Concerto, the score of which had been lost in Petrograd.[27] "I have so completely rewritten the Second Concerto that it might almost be considered the Fourth," Prokofiev informed his Moscow friends in a letter on December 4, 1923.

While living in Bavaria, he once again established connections with the Koussevitzky publishing house, which had moved from Russia. The noted conductor had left the Soviet Union in 1920 for a "holiday" and had not returned. In Germany he found the equipment of his Russian Music Publishing House intact. He transferred the firm to Paris, converting it into a corporation under the former name of "A. Gutheil" in order to maintain its artistic reputation.

Thus Koussevitzky resumed his publishing activities, which were oriented toward the latest works of Stravinsky, Prokofiev, and Rachmaninov. In 1924 his reputation as an outstanding conductor won him his appointment as conductor of the Boston Symphony Orchestra; but until 1930 he continued to conduct his own symphony concerts in Paris, at which he introduced the latest Russian novelties. Over a period of years the Koussevitzky publishing firm, which was directed by experienced businessmen (first G. Eberg, later Paichadze), kept Prokofiev entangled in a spider web of contracts and financial agreements. Prokofiev often quarreled with Koussevitzky, whose pose as an art patron irritated him, but his contracts prevented him from leaving the powerful publishing firm.

While living in Ettal Prokofiev was almost continually occupied with preparing scores for publication and correcting proofs. The Gutheil firm had a virtual monopoly of the publication of his works: in 1922–23 they published nearly everything he had written during the previous decade (Op. 15 through Op. 38, with the exception of *Sarcasms, The Gambler,* and *The Flaming Angel*).

In the summer of 1922, after the revival of *The Buffoon,* Prokofiev met Stravinsky again in Paris. After hearing Prokofiev play some of the music from *The Love for Three Oranges,* Stravinsky sharply criticized it and refused to listen to more than one act; he was shocked by the "simplicity" of the harmony and by the declamatory devices, which sometimes seemed reminiscent of the Moussorgsky style. This quickly provoked a disagreement, and Prokofiev in turn expressed his dislike for the cold "neo-Bachism" of Stravinsky's latest works—the Piano Concerto and the Sonata.

Somewhat later Prokofiev shared his impressions of Stravinsky's music with Asafyev. "Stravinsky's Concerto continues the course taken in the Finale of the Octet—that is, stylization of Bach," wrote Prokofiev. "I disapprove of this, for although I love Bach and find nothing wrong in composing according to his principles, I don't think one should write stylized imitations of him. For this reason I find the Concerto less valuable than *The Wedding* or *The Rite of Spring,* since, generally speaking, everything which is imitative, like *Pulcinella* or my own *Classical Symphony,* has less value. Unfortunately, Stravinsky thinks otherwise. He does not feel that this is aping, and now he has written a piano sonata in the very same style. He even believes that this is creating a new epoch."[28] Critical observations of this kind indicate that Prokofiev was unwilling, in principle, to yield to the Western vogue of neo-classicism.

Also in 1922, while on a visit to Berlin, Prokofiev spent several memorable evenings with Mayakovsky, who had come there from Moscow. On one of these occasions Mayakovsky engaged in an argument with Diaghilev and a group of his collaborators. The poet sharply attacked expressionist painting and Stravinsky's music; to Stravinsky's art, which was alien to him, he opposed the work of Prokofiev. Although Diaghilev tried to refute the criticisms with his characteristic eloquence, Mayakovsky finally carried the evening with an impassioned reading of his latest poetry.

In a letter written after his meetings with Russian musicians abroad, Mayakovsky again expressed his strong dislike for Stravinsky's music. "I feel closer to the Prokofiev of the pre-foreign period, the Prokofiev of the crude, dashing marches," he wrote.[29] This is perhaps the only positive allusion to music to be found in all of Mayakovsky's writings.

The differences with Stravinsky and a temporary break with Diaghilev, who had disdainfully rejected *The Love for Three Oranges,* coincided with Prokofiev's growing interest in Soviet musical life. In 1922 he resumed contact with his Soviet friends. Through a lively correspondence with Miaskovsky, Asafyev, and Derzhanovsky, he was informed in detail about the musical activities that had been revived in Moscow and Petrograd since the termination of the civil war. Prokofiev sent his works to Miaskovsky and Asafyev, carefully noting their suggestions and comments.

Beginning in 1923, interest in Prokofiev's music mounted steadily in the U.S.S.R. The Music Department of the State Publishing House began to publish his compositions. In the fall of this year, the International Book Association in Moscow presented some of his new works at its "Musical Showcases"; it was here that the *Tales of the Old Grandmother,* the *Overture on Hebrew Themes,* the songs of Op. 36, and the Third Piano Concerto were first performed in the Soviet Union. A year later the Leningrad Evenings of New Music also presented some Prokofiev compositions. In April 1923 the magazine of the Association for Contemporary Music, *K Novym Beregam,* devoted a considerable portion of its first number to the music of Prokofiev (articles by "Igor Glebov," S. Feinberg, and others). To be sure, the leaders of the ACM, who set the tone in Soviet musical life at that time, extolled the most extreme, modernist, and radical of Prokofiev's works. *K Novym Beregam,* for example, gave its highest praise to *The Buffoon,* while the first work put out by the Music Department of the State Publishing House was the score of *Seven, They Are Seven.*

An editorial entitled "Window Into Europe," in the 1924 New Year's issue of *Zhizn Iskusstva,* spoke of the eminent Russian musicians, among them Prokofiev, who had been stranded abroad: "However wide we have thrown open our 'window into Europe,' nothing will compensate us for the protracted absence from Russia of some of her finest musicians. In the coming year we shall await news of the repatriation of our 'foreign' composers."

But Prokofiev did not understand the Soviet journal's appeal. The composer himself says of this period: "At that time I had not yet fully grasped the significance of what was happening in the U.S.S.R. I did not realize that these events required the cooperation of all citizens—not only men of politics, as I had thought, but men of art as well. Moreover, I was tied down by the routine of the life I was leading: publishing music, correcting proofs, giving concerts. . . . Family affairs also played no small part: my mother's protracted illness, her death, my marriage, the birth of my son."

The composer's mother died in France at the age of 69. She had always maintained a lively interest in her son's work, and in her memoirs she gives a detailed account of his childhood.

Prokofiev's Bavarian sojourn brought forth a work which sums up, in a sense, his earlier creative endeavors. The Fifth Sonata, Op. 38, the only work written there (excluding considerable work on *The Flaming Angel*), rests on the borderline between his earlier style, associated with the Petersburg period, and his new "foreign" style. Prokofiev's move from Ettal to Paris in October 1923 marked the beginning of a new period in his work, perhaps the least productive of all.

In terms of Prokofiev's career as a composer, what is the significance of the first five years (1918 to 1923) of his wanderings abroad? In general, this period was one in which Prokofiev drew his inspiration from the past. The powerful surge of his creativity in the years 1916–17 seemed to continue on its own momentum; he had not yet exhausted the fund of musical ideas and impressions accumulated during his youth, and his creative imagination was still excited by artistic ideas first generated in Russia.

The Third Piano Concerto and *The Love for Three Oranges,* conceived and begun in Russia, were in a direct line with his earlier efforts, as were the wonderful piano pieces of 1918 (*Tales of the Old Grandmother* and the four pieces, Op. 32), the brilliant *Overture on Hebrew Themes,* and the five songs without words, Op. 35. One can safely say that the Third Concerto, the *Overture,* and the *Tales* are among the classics of Prokofiev's early work. Also during these years he prepared for publication *The Buffoon,* the First Violin Concerto, and the Second Piano Concerto, all of them begun in Russia.

Prokofiev's successful appearances both as a pianist and a conductor consolidated abroad the renown he had won by his earlier attainments in Russia. His bold and powerful piano virtuosity shocked academic audiences in the West just as it had in St. Petersburg. At the same time, many foreign listeners sought to hear in his best works a poetic expression of the historic changes at work in contemporary Russia.

In all important respects, then, Prokofiev's foreign period began not in 1918, the year he left Petrograd, but rather in 1922–23, when the creative resources he had accumulated in his homeland were finally exhausted. The Fifth Sonata (1923) is the first work that belongs entirely to the new, foreign period.

But the impetus of the past could not operate forever. Having cut himself off from the country that had nourished him for so long, he found no new or potent creative stimuli in the West. From 1924 on, his separation from Russia began to tell more and more on his work.

# SEVEN

# CRISIS

*And you*
*In Europe,*
    *Where every citizen*
*Reeks with complacency,*
    *Gorging*
        *Lucre!*
*Is not our air*
    *Purer,*
        *Cleansed twice*
*By the storm*
    *Of two revolutions?*

Mayakovsky

I N OCTOBER 1923 Prokofiev moved to Paris, where he lived for the next ten years. He was already known in the French capital as the composer of the *Scythian Suite, The Buffoon,* and the Third Piano Concerto, which had been successfully performed there.

The Paris art world of the twenties differed but little from the noisy bourgeois market place, with its indifference to real art, so vividly described by Romain Rolland in *Jean-Christophe.* Only the names had changed: the craze for Debussy had given way to the cult of Stravinsky, and the fragile refinements of Monet and his imitators had been replaced by the senseless constructions of the cubists, suprematists, and other coteries. The prevailing attitude toward traditional aesthetic standards, particularly those concerned with meaning and content, became cynical and defiantly anarchic.

The music of Ravel, Dukas, Roger-Ducasse, and other composers of the older generation, considered fashionable on the eve of the First World War, was already regarded as "dated." The modernist critics were vigorously pushing to the fore a young group known as *Les Six* (Milhaud, Honegger, Auric, Poulenc, Durey, and Tailleferre), who resorted to all the latest devices of polytonalism, constructivism, exotic barbarism, and the *style méchanique*. "Victorious France also wanted to be the victor in music," Prokofiev wrote in his memoirs. "Hence the extraordinary attention given 'Les Six' . . . an attention which 'Les Six' could not quite live up to."

Composers rushed from one extreme to another in search of convenient pretexts for sensational experiments—from the roar of a locomotive to primitive dances, from biblical and ancient subjects to modern jazz. This was the unprincipled approach to art which Rolland so aptly described in *Jean-Christophe*: "Composers searched doggedly for new combinations of chords to express—does it matter what? . . . Novelty at all costs! They had a morbid fear of anything that 'had been said before.' The best of them were paralyzed by this fear."

The postwar modernist schools in painting, music, and poetry strove to overthrow, once and for all, every known aesthetic canon. Whereas the subjectivity of impressionist art was based on some perception of reality, the new expressionist schools broke even this last connection with the real world and carried subjectivity to an extreme. Objective reality ceased to exist for the artist. Nothing mattered except his own inner impulse, his own artistic license. Turning his back on observable nature, the artist expressed only his own most personal and idiosyncratic ideas—fabricating them, breaking them up into their component parts, distorting them in any way he pleased. Considering himself capable of understanding and communicating "the hidden essence of things," the artist portrayed an object not as he saw it in life but as he felt it with his own "special" sense. As a result, his work lost not only reality but also meaning and content. Its value was measured solely by the ingenuity and originality of the artist, whose perception of the world was governed by laws which he alone understood. In painting this formalistic approach expressed itself in an absurd nonobjectiveness, in chaotic combinations of incomprehensible lines and constructions put together with no regard for the principles of drawing and perspective. In music, clear melody degenerated and the functional relationship of harmonies disappeared, giving way to arbitrary and unrestrained cacophony.

A great number of seemingly contradictory groups and trends sprang up in the bourgeois art of postwar Europe. While constructivism and cubism, with their cult of pure form and deliberate unemotionalism, were flourishing in France, Austria and Germany nurtured expressionist groups (especially Schoenberg and his school) notable for their morbid excitability, which was strangely combined with formalistic methods of serial composition. Basically, however, one common trait characterized the art of all these groups and schools—a complete lack of meaning and content, the result of their isolation from life and the struggle of the masses.* Such was the state of art in Western Europe, the atmosphere in which Prokofiev's music developed during his years in Paris.

In addition to his contacts with the French modernists, Prokofiev also associated with the leaders of Russian émigré art—Stravinsky, Diaghilev, and certain other composers, artists, and actors. Cut off from their homeland, these men eventually lost their national identity and became out and out cosmopolites. Diaghilev's case is typical; the productions of his company gradually lost vitality, and he finally yielded completely to Western demands. According to Lunacharsky, who visited Paris in the early twenties, the public was rushing as eagerly as before to the Russian ballet theater in the hope of finding artistic surprises. And Diaghilev, "in response to the continuous demand for something a little new, a little tart, a little witty, began to 'oblige'—with the result that he has degenerated into a jester who, in the name of our noble Russian art, will grimace for anyone with a few hundred francs to throw away."[1] P. Suvchinsky, the former publisher of *Muzykalny Sovremennik,* wrote with bitterness and shame about the "émigré Russia" that flourished in Western Europe. And in 1925 Prokofiev wrote: "This 'Russia abroad' is not worth much. Each year its break with the stream of Russian history becomes more and more evident. Besides, contemporary Europe, too, has become spiritually impoverished; whether its *Untergang* will be catastrophic or gradual, it is inevitable. And the new is certainly not being created here."[2]

Indeed, there was much in contemporary Western art that repelled Prokofiev. Of contemporary Western music he wrote to Asafyev, "I think that you attach more importance to it than it deserves."[3] In other letters he observed that "of late there have been no interesting books on music. There aren't any interesting American composers in sight either," adding later, "In England, I believe, there's nothing at all."[4] In a number of articles and letters he also spoke ironically about the vacuousness of the latest bourgeois

* Only in the mid-thirties, under the influence of the mass anti-fascist movement, did the most talented French composers (particularly former members of the Six) turn to more immediate and meaningful art.

*Above*: Prokofiev at age twenty (1919). *Right*: Prokofiev and Boris V. Asafyev on Lake Geneva (1928).

Prokofiev (1933)

music being performed in Paris. He found Kurt Weill's Violin Concerto "passionless, cadaverous," and he called the American music played by Koussevitzky "a boring wasteland."[5]

Prokofiev was astounded and chagrined at the concert situation in Paris, where a few private orchestras competed desperately among themselves, "not letting each other live." He spoke of the starvation wages paid to orchestral musicians at the famous Paris Opéra, which was dragging out a miserable existence under the control of rich businessmen.

Finally, he was outraged at the lack of principle of certain modernist composers who vacillated between constructivist complexities and amusing superficiality. In a letter to Derzhanovsky he reported, "Of late they've begun to say in certain Parisian circles, 'We have had enough tragic and emotional music. Give us something entertaining, like the music of the good old days of Rameau. And if it has to be a little trite and vulgar to be entertaining, that's all right, too, as long as it's amusing and to the point.' Curiously enough, even Stravinsky indulges a bit in these practices."[6]

While living abroad, Prokofiev did not personally participate in any of the festivals arranged by the International Society for Contemporary Music in Salzburg. He was not present, for example, when his *Overture on Hebrew Themes* was performed in the summer of 1923.

Even though he was not in sympathy with many aspects of contemporary modernist art in the West, Prokofiev was drawn into the vortex of Parisian musical life. Without support, the healthiest tendencies of his early years gradually withered and succumbed to new, extremely negative influences.

At about the time Prokofiev moved to Paris, the première of his Violin Concerto took place. This work, finished in 1917, had awaited performance for more than five years. Several famous violinists (including Huberman) refused to learn it, apparently finding it too unusual. Finally, the concertmaster of the Koussevitzky orchestra, Marcel Darrieux, was asked to play it, and on October 18, 1923, it was presented at one of the Koussevitzky concerts. The Paris critics received the Concerto very coldly. To people enamored of the ultramodern, the lyricism of Prokofiev's Violin Concerto seemed old-fashioned. For the first time, the composer found himself criticized by modernists, for writing music that was too lucid and not sufficiently complex. Among those who did not like the Concerto were the composers Nadia Boulanger, Georges Auric, and the Russian critic Boris de Schloezer. Auric found traces of artificiality and "Mendelssohnism" in it.

Thus very shortly after his arrival in Paris, Prokofiev felt the pressure of the most extreme modernist circles. The warm and human quality in his work, that quality which asserted itself in his music despite the formal radicalism of the modernists, found no favor with the sophisticated Parisians. Stravinsky frankly expressed this attitude toward Prokofiev's art in a conversation in 1927. After condescendingly praising Prokofiev's talent, the Parisian *maître* added that there was "something" in Prokofiev that he did not like: "a certain instability in his cultural make-up, some indefinable quality in his musical gift, *precisely that quality, incidentally, which is now making him a success in Russia.*"[7]

It was only after its brilliant performance by Joseph Szigeti in the summer of 1924, at a festival of new works in Prague, that the Violin Concerto won the fame it deserved. Szigeti's subsequent performances of it in many cities (among them Berlin, Cologne, Geneva, Lausanne, London, Amsterdam, Stockholm, Budapest, Warsaw, Moscow, and Leningrad) contributed much to its world-wide popularity. By the 1924–25 season the best Soviet violinists were playing the Concerto with success.

The Parisians were also unimpressed with the Fifth Sonata (C major, Op. 38), which Prokofiev played there in March 1924; according to the composer, they received it with restraint. Still the least played of Prokofiev's nine sonatas, it clearly shows the composer moving away from the vitality of his early piano compositions toward a cold, formal speculation.

The most lucid of the three movements of this sonata, the one bearing the closest resemblance to Prokofiev's early style, is the first, *Allegro tranquillo*. The main theme, in a bright C major with characteristically colorful digressions, is charming in its naïve, Schubertian ingenuousness and classical clarity; this is the fresh and youthful quality of the pieces, Op. 12, and the *Classical Symphony*. Quite different in feeling, however, is the descriptive second theme, which is somewhat in the spirit of Rimsky-Korsakov's *Kashchei the Immortal*. Here, and in the development section that follows, the music becomes more complex and assumes a trace of sombre grotesqueness.

The second movement, *Andantino*, is a scherzo in mechanical triple rhythm, tinged with sinister sarcasm. The persistent hammering of the *ostinato* phrase is like an evil *idée fixe* or the memory of a nightmare, and throughout the movement are heard strange embellishments, recalling one of the most frightening pages of Russian music—the scene of the Countess' death in the fourth act of *The Queen of Spades*.

The main theme of the finale (*Un poco allegretto*) is forced and artificially complex. The polytonal combination of the theme and the unchanging bass sounds deliberately harsh, and the twists of the melody seem derived from some kind of geometrical construction. The narrative second theme, which suggests sad recollection, does not change the general impression of the music of the finale, in which abstract invention predominates over genuine feeling.

In his memoirs, the composer himself mentions the "intricate" style of the Fifth Sonata and its resemblance to his "most chromatic" works (the Quintet and the Second Symphony), which were also written under the influence of bourgeois art in Paris. In attempting to resurrect this Sonata many years later (1952), Prokofiev wrote a new, somewhat simplified version and listed it as Op. 135.

While the Fifth Sonata passed unnoticed, two premières, presented in the spring of 1924 on the Koussevitzky series, once again brought Prokofiev's name before the Paris public. On May 8 the new version of the Second Piano Concerto was performed by the composer, and on May 29 the cantata *Seven, They Are Seven* was given its first performance. As a matter of fact, the cantata was played twice that evening. "The audience was somewhat piqued when Koussevitzky repeated *Seven, They Are Seven,* for what he thought would be their greater edification," Prokofiev writes.

The Second Concerto was received coldly, but the savagely mystical "Chaldean Invocation" quite suited Parisian tastes. This time, however, the composer was accused of using old works to win success. Irritated by this charge, he decided to show the Parisians that he could write a piece of music as modernistic as anything done by the Six. Thus arose his plan for a new symphonic work "made of iron and steel"—the Second Symphony in D minor, on which he spent the entire fall and winter of 1924.

"Unlike the Third Concerto," he wrote of his new symphony, "it is chromatic and ponderous, but this does not mean that I have said goodbye forever to the diatonic style. In form the symphony resembles Beethoven's last piano sonata, that is, an austere first movement followed by a theme and variations as the second and final movement."

The main theme of the first movement is characterized by an artificiality and angularity of melody, an abundance of strange leaps, a harshness of sonority, and a general atonal coloring. Everything here seems contrived to shock and stun the listener (FIG. 28).

FIGURE 28

Employing the harsh constructivist devices of the *Scythian Suite* (the simultaneous movement of various *ostinato* figures in different registers of the orchestra), and utilizing deafening sonorities, the composer created an extremely overloaded score, whose barbaric clamor was not this time justified by the basic material.

"After the energetic first movement," says the composer, "I wanted to relieve the tension, at least at the beginning of the second, which I conceived as a theme and variations. For this I used a quiet theme which I had composed in Japan." But this diatonic theme (originally sketched, it seems, for the unfinished White Quartet) also smacked of a certain artificiality and affected simplicity, and the variations lacked the rich diversity which was so enchanting in the variations of the Third Piano Concerto. The development of the musical idea was sacrificed to noisy effects and contrapuntal intricacies. On the whole, the Symphony is a strange combination of chaotic barbarism and the *style mécanique.*

Works abounding in forced and artificial effects invariably cost Prokofiev a great deal of effort, while those that were unaffected and warm almost always came freely and easily. Like *Ala and Lolli* and *Seven, They Are Seven,* the Second Symphony was composed with difficulty, and there were times when the composer himself doubted the value of these monstrous undertakings. The letters he wrote while composing the Second Symphony are filled with statements to that effect: "I'm working as hard as I can, but because of its complexities, it is creeping along," he said in one; in another, "I'm immersed in the symphony, but the end is nowhere in sight"; and to Asafyev he admitted, "I'm afraid this symphony won't reach the heights you have set for me." Finally, after its première under Koussevitzky on June 6, 1925, the composer observed self-critically, "Neither I nor the audience understood anything in it."[8] "It was too thickly woven. There were too many layers of counterpoint which degenerated into mere figuration."

Even the sophisticated Parisians found the Second Symphony something of an oddity. Almost all the critics denounced it, expressing disappointment in Prokofiev's talent (of 28 reviews, 25 were abusive and only one laudatory). "The majority were horrified by my symphony," Prokofiev reported. "Even though I still have some ardent admirers, the others are now grieving over my downfall."[9]

While working on the Second Symphony Prokofiev composed the music for a short ballet, *Trapeze*—"to earn some money," as he put it. This was commissioned for the traveling company of the ballet master Boris Romanov, who had studied under Fokine and had at one time worked at the Maryinsky Theater in St. Petersburg. Although the plot of the new ballet dealt with circus life, Prokofiev completely rejected the idea of using descriptive, programmatic devices; he apparently regarded this commission as a pretext for writing an abstract instrumental chamber piece. He recalls that the music contained "some impractical rhythms, such as one number in 10/8 $(3 + 4 + 3)$, which gave the choreographer a great deal of trouble." Since the Romanov company could not afford an orchestra, it was decided to score the work for a modest chamber ensemble (oboe, clarinet, violin, viola, and double bass). *Trapeze* was performed several times in Germany and Italy, but it was soon forgotten. The music was later incorporated in the six-movement Quintet, Op. 39, where the intricate, chromatic style, the contrived angularity of the themes, and the complicated technique of simultaneously developed melodic lines were all just as evident as they had been in the Second Symphony. It is no wonder that even in Paris no one was willing to perform it.

Summing up the works of 1923–24 Prokofiev wrote: "The Fifth Sonata, the Quintet, and the Second Symphony, continuing the line from *Sarcasms* through the *Scythian Suite* and *Seven, They Are Seven,* were the most chromatic of all my works. The atmosphere of Paris had something to do with this."

The failure of the Second Symphony and a certain weakening of interest in him on the part of the Paris critics forced Prokofiev to give serious thought to his artistic future. "It occurred to me that I might be destined to become a second-rate composer," he confesses in his memoirs. Indeed, Paris could just as easily forget a fashionable name as praise it to the skies. "A vogue did not last long, and an idol inevitably awoke one fine morning to find himself in the rubbish heap" (*Jean-Christophe*).

Poverty, disillusionment, the lot of the deposed idol threatened Prokofiev. His Soviet friends watched the gradual decline of his European fame with anxiety. As one Russian journalist said, "Paris is adamant: Stravinsky, Stravinsky, Stravinsky! No wonder Prokofiev's star is setting on that horizon and art circles speak of him as though he were dead. Prokofiev does not exude the stench of ripe cheese so dear to the nostrils of the Paris bourgeois."[10]

Meanwhile, Prokofiev continued to make concert appearances. On December 5, 1924, he gave a recital in Paris, playing the Second, Third, Fourth, and Fifth Sonatas. On January 24, 1925, he played his piano pieces for the first time in Berlin. In March he went to Cologne for the European première of *The Love for Three Oranges,* which was conducted by Eugen Szenkar. The production designed and directed by Strohbach was less lavish than the one in Chicago, but was much better integrated. "On the whole the Rhenish people were excellent, and the production was fine," the composer wrote to Asafyev. "Both the conductor and director put a great deal of love and imagination into this work. The audience responded well, but the press even better, particularly the Berlin press, who came to Cologne for the première."[11]

During this period Prokofiev's connections with the Soviet Union were growing steadily, and he was delighted with the increasing popularity of his music there: "I'm surprised and happy about the successes of my music in Moscow," he wrote Derzhanovsky.[12]

In the summer of 1925, he carried on negotiations with I. Ekskuzovich, the director of the Leningrad State Theater of Opera and Ballet, concerning a production of *The Love for Three Oranges* in Moscow and Leningrad. "This conversation seems to have opened up the broadest possibilities for contact with the academic theaters," he wrote Asafyev on August 14. During the same year there were also negotiations with B. B. Krasin, the representative of the Soviet Philharmonic Organizations, concerning an extended concert tour of the Soviet Union. "I was longing to go to Russia," Prokofiev later wrote Asafyev.

But just at this critical stage in the composer's career, his former patron Diaghilev, who had turned away from his no longer fashionable ward, suddenly remembered him. Shortly after the performance of the Second Symphony, he proposed to Prokofiev that they work together on a new ballet. In Prokofiev's memoirs we read, " 'But I cannot write in the style you approve of,' I said, taking a poke at the rather banal stuff Auric and Milhaud were composing for him."

This time, however, Diaghilev had an idea that astonished Prokofiev—a ballet depicting life in Soviet Russia. The shrewd impressario sensed that a Soviet theme might prove popular in the West. The capitalist powers were then beginning to recognize the Soviet Union, and interest in the new Russia was growing everywhere; a "Bolshevist" ballet might very well be a success. Prokofiev accepted the idea in all sincerity, as a way to regaining a spiritual rapprochement with his homeland. "I could not believe my ears. It was as though a fresh breeze had blown through my window, that breeze of which Lunacharsky had spoken," he recalls.

Work on the new ballet began at once. Ilya Ehrenburg, who was then living in France, was first considered as a possible librettist, but the job finally went to the Soviet constructivist artist Georgi Yakulov, who had only recently had an exhibit in Paris. He and Prokofiev worked out the scenario together. It was decided not to present a sustained plot, but rather a number of scenes depicting the chaos of the Civil War period and the reconstructive labor of the Soviet workers. The first scene was to take place in a railway station during the period of "war communism" and show meetings, speeches by commissars, and a train full of food speculators. The second scene was to show the beginnings of socialist construction by depicting a Soviet factory, machines and steam hammers, yesterday's sailor turned worker, and so on. Yakulov, with his passion for constructivist ideas, urged the composer to glorify "the poetry of the machine." As the creators visualized it, the ballet was to show the motion of transmission belts and flywheels, flashing light signals, and even dancers imitating machines at work. Thus the "Soviet ballet" was conceived from the very beginning in terms of urbanistic tricks.

In writing the music, Prokofiev resolved first of all to give it a truly Russian flavor, and secondly to reject the chromatic intricacies of the Quintet and the Second Symphony in favor of returning to a strict, purely diatonic style. The work progressed rapidly. "Having taken the bit in my mouth, I dashed off the new ballet in no time," he reported to his friends in Moscow.[13] In the fall of 1925 the piano score was given to Diaghilev, who accepted it for production and gave it the pretentious title *Le Pas d'acier* (The Steel Leap).

In the winter of 1925–26, while working on the orchestration of the ballet, Prokofiev made a long tour of the United States. This time he was received as a recognized master. The American bourgeoisie, which not long before had closed its ears to Prokofiev's music, now regarded it as an honor to attend his concerts. He gave half of his fourteen concerts with the Boston Symphony Orchestra, whose new conductor was his old patron Koussevitzky. He played the Third Concerto in a number of cities.

American interest in the celebrated Russian composer was for the most part superficial. In his memoirs Prokofiev recalls, with some irony, the stiff formality with which he was introduced to the members of the Society for Contemporary Music: "After the concert all three hundred members of the Society wanted to shake hands with us. . . . A member of the Society approached the Secretary and said, 'I am Mr. Smith.' The Chairlady turned to me and said, 'Permit me to present Mr. Smith.' I shook hands and said, 'Delighted, Mr. Smith.' Mr. Smith said, 'Delighted, Mr. Prokofiev,' and proceeded to my wife. Then Mr. Jones, and so on three hundred times."

During this concert tour Prokofiev worked out the unique method of orchestration which he followed in scoring most of his later works. Since he had to spend many days on trains, traveling from city to city, he wanted to find a way of using this time for scoring *Le Pas d'acier.*

"The jolting made it difficult to write out a full score," he relates, "so I decided to do all the preliminary work on the train—not only to plan which instrument should play a certain melody or accompaniment, but also to work out each measure down to the most minute detail: to each doubling, to the allotment of instruments to the chords, and to the last bow marking, accent, and nuance." Between the braces he left an extra stave on which he could insert additional voices. He also wrote out on separate sheets the most complicated color combinations—complex interlacings or unusual string chords. After all the preliminary markings had been written in pencil on the piano score, there remained only the task of transcribing all the orchestral voices to the full score pages, a purely mechanical job that could be entrusted to a highly skilled assistant. This method of scoring spared Prokofiev a great deal of tiresome technical work; with the exception of *Alexander Nevsky,* most of his compositions written after 1925 were scored in this way.[14]

In the spring of 1926 Prokofiev gave a number of concerts in Italy. In Naples he had a very cordial meeting with Gorky; after an afternoon concert, the writer took Prokofiev to his villa in Sorrento, where they had a long, friendly talk which lasted far into the night. "Gorky was in good form, and we had an exceptionally pleasant evening," Prokofiev recalls.

In 1926 performances of *The Love for Three Oranges* once again drew attention to Prokofiev's name, both in Europe and in the Soviet Union. At this time, too, the Moscow Persimfans (the first conductorless orchestra) began to popularize Prokofiev's music. Bruno Walter also became interested in him and offered to produce *The Flaming Angel* at one of the Berlin theaters.

*The Love for Three Oranges* was the only one of Prokofiev's early theater works to achieve a certain popularity. In those years, the March from the opera was performed everywhere; in 1926 the Moscow Persimfans played it at a concert in the Red Barracks, on a program that also included Grieg's *Peer Gynt* and Rimsky-Korsakov's *Dubinushka*.

On February 18 of the same year, the opera had its première at the Leningrad State Theater of Opera and Ballet (formerly the Maryinsky Theater) under the baton of V. Dranishnikov, once a fellow student with Prokofiev at the St. Petersburg Conservatory. The *régisseur* of this production was S. Radlov, the artist V. Dmitriev, and the ballet master L. Vainonen. Asafyev was also closely associated with the production. The principal performers included I. Yershov, G. Bosse, and M. Maksakova. While noting a certain incongruity between the somewhat heavy splendor of the production and the light irony of the music, the Soviet critics nevertheless gave the opera a very warm reception. Prokofiev deeply regretted that he was unable to attend the première. "I have waited ten years for my opera to be staged at the Maryinsky Theater, and now that this has finally happened I'm on the other side of the globe," he wrote Asafyev.[15]

On October 9, 1926, *The Love for Three Oranges* was performed at the Berlin State Opera, with Leo Blech conducting. According to the composer, the production was "solid and impressive, in the Prussian manner, but it lacked hot Italian blood. Nevertheless, the hall rocked with laughter, and it was a success."[16] This success proved short-lived, however. "As I was walking across the stage a quarter of an hour before the curtain went up," Prokofiev recalls, "I heard an old stagehand remark, 'Just think of how much good German money has been spent on these sets, and after a couple of performances, everything will be thrown out.' I thought, 'Well, we'll see about that!' But the stagehand was not far wrong. The opera lasted only eight performances."

The composer blamed this on the director's lack of ingenuity and the conductor's highly stilted and pedestrian interpretation. However, the primary reason for the opera's brief run lay in the peculiarities of its content and musical style. True, it received scores of laudatory reviews in the German press, virtually all of which remarked on the originality of the orchestration and the composer's lively imagination and sparkling wit. But the Communist newspaper *Die Rote Fahne* pointed out that Prokofiev's "musical harlequinade," while poking fun at traditional opera, conveys no idea of what modern opera should be. "While turning opera into a circus, a review, an entertaining show where not a single word or character can be taken seriously, Prokofiev, with great brilliance, achieves unrestrained merriment," the newspaper wrote. "But the Russian Prokofiev is not one of the musicians of the new revolutionary Russia. His music does not spring from the depths of the Revolution, nor is it intended for the masses."[17]

On May 19, 1927, the opera was given its first performance at the Bolshoi Theater in Moscow. The best artists were involved in this production: the conductor N. Golovanov, the director A. Diky, and the artist I. Rabinovich; the leading roles were sung by A. Nezhdanova (Ninetta), V. Petrov (the King), and N. Oboukhova (Clarissa). This time the critics praised the music highly, but charged the theater with an excessive interest in surface effects and an inability to interpret correctly the elegance and liveliness of Prokofiev's declamatory style. Much was said regarding the social purport of the opera ("Who is Prokofiev laughing at?"), and a number of critics expressed serious doubts about the ideological depth of the work. A. Drozdov wrote in *Muzyka i Revolutsiya*: "For all its originality and entertaining features, the opera will never really appeal to the masses and can never become the definitive operatic achievement of our time, first, because there is not a quiet moment in the entire work (which makes it difficult to grasp the music), and secondly and most important, because the subject, while charming, is meaningless, and this necessarily dooms the opera to remain only a brilliant humoresque. True, it sparkles with subtle artistry and inspiration, but these qualities, after all, are only tangential to the art of music and not its core."[18]

Unfortunately, the critic's prediction proved correct. While the opera enchanted a relatively limited circle of sophisticated connoisseurs, it did not appeal to the general Soviet audience. In 1929, after a few dozen performances, it was dropped from the repertory in both Moscow and Leningrad. (A revival at the former Maryinsky Theater in 1934 was also short-lived.)

Generally speaking, the Paris theaters did not take to *The Love for Three Oranges* either, apparently considering it not sufficiently modern. A symphonic suite drawn from it was coldly received when it was first played there on November 29, 1925. This suite, written in 1924, consisted of six numbers: (1) "The Ridiculous People," (2) "Scene in Hades," (3)

"March," (4) "Scherzo," (5) "The Prince and The Princess," and (6) "Flight."

During the summer of 1926 Prokofiev orchestrated and revised *The Flaming Angel* and also worked on the B-flat major Overture, Op. 42, which had been commissioned by a New York music firm. This overture, written in a deliberately spare chamber style for an ensemble of seventeen performers, is interesting not so much for its musical content as for the unusual combination of instruments called for in the score: two pianos, doubled by harps; a celesta; five solo woodwinds, supported by two trumpets and a trombone; two cellos, a double bass, and a few percussion instruments—no violins or violas. Such experiments with chamber groups, fashionable in the twenties as a kind of reaction to the massive orchestras typical of the newest music, were for the most part contrived and ephemeral.

The "American" Overture, Op. 42, written in a comparatively simple harmonic idiom, has the character of a festive dance sprinkled with pleasant lyrical episodes, some contemplative and others stirringly poetic. One might have thought that the composer had abandoned the stylistic excesses of his Paris period were it not for the deliberate eccentricities in some of the episodes (for example, the unwarranted, rather incongruous intrusion of the percussion in the main theme, obviously intended to break what the composer thought an overly commonplace flow of the music).[19]

❈    ❈    ❈

During these years Prokofiev's ties with Soviet musical circles were growing ever stronger. After having been dropped so abruptly by the Parisians, he found numerous reasons to be convinced that people in the Soviet Union were taking a sincere interest in his music.

In addition to the lively response evoked by the Moscow and Leningrad productions of *The Love for Three Oranges,* much interest was aroused by S. Feinberg's performance of the Third Concerto (under Saradzhev in Moscow, March 22, 1925), Szigeti's performance of the Violin Concerto, the first Moscow performance of the *Scythian Suite* (by the Persimfans orchestra), and numerous performances of the March and Scherzo from the *Three Oranges* (under Oscar Fried). While the West regarded Prokofiev only as an interesting foreigner and honored him with little more than fleeting curiosity, Soviet music circles considered him one of the outstanding representatives of contemporary Russian music. In the spring of 1926 Lunacharsky spoke warmly of his work: "The freshness and rich imagination characteristic of Prokofiev attest to his exceptional talent. . . . It is pure lyricism that gives him his tremendous significance. Stravinsky has, to a marked degree, already succumbed to glittering artifice. For Prokofiev to fully realize himself he must return to us, before the evil genii of Americanization have stifled him."[20]

During his travels in America and Europe in 1926, Prokofiev decided to go back to the U.S.S.R. In January 1927, after an absence of nearly nine years, he returned to his native land. "You can imagine how excited and elated I was," he writes of these days.

His stay in the Soviet Union proved to be a triumph the like of which he had never before experienced. He was overjoyed to meet his old friends and fellow musicians again—Miaskovsky, Asafyev, and Saradzhev, among others—and he began to acquaint himself with the work of Soviet composers.* The eight concerts he gave in Moscow were an unprecedented success. Witness a reviewer's description of the one given on January 26: "This was not a concert, it was an event. Individual voices were drowned out by the unanimous acclaim. It was as though a spell had been cast over the hall, and indeed, the composer himself played that evening with a special *élan,* which was quite natural considering that this audience could not but be particularly near and dear to him."[21]

Prokofiev was happy and moved when he visited familiar places, especially Leningrad, where he had spent his youth. "In the intervals between concerts I roamed the streets and embankments," he relates, "recalling with affection the city where I had spent so many years."

In one of his interviews he spoke with gratitude of the friendliness of Soviet audiences: "The public response has been simply amazing, unlike anywhere else. I find myself here in an exceptionally happy situation. They have received me as one near and dear to them, as their own. It is particularly gratifying to be greeted like this in your own home."[22]

He was delighted with the Leningrad production of *The Love for Three Oranges.* "This was its first real production—brilliant and lively, many times superior to the productions in Chicago, New York, Cologne, and Berlin," he remarked shortly afterward. Lunacharsky, who was with him at the opera, compared the music to a glass of champagne.

After Leningrad, Prokofiev visited Kharkov, Kiev, and Odessa, giving two piano recitals in each city. On his return to Moscow he appeared in

---

* In subsequent years Prokofiev made a considerable effort to popularize abroad the music of Miaskovsky, Shostakovich, Shebalin, Khachaturian, and others. On one of his American tours he played, together with his own compositions, Miaskovsky's *Whimsies.*

three more concerts, one of them a benefit performance to aid homeless children. His Quintet for winds and strings, Op. 39, was performed for the first time at one of these concerts, and at about this time the Overture, Op. 42, also had its première in Europe.

Soviet musical life at this time was characterized by serious internal conflicts. The forces of the realistic school were still artistically weak and not very productive. On the other hand, extremely unhealthy modernist trends were flourishing, with strong support from the leaders of the Association for Contemporary Music. One after another, the modernist operas of Krenek, Schreker, and Alban Berg were produced in the opera theaters, especially in Leningrad; the philharmonic organizations, too, promoted the ultra-modern novelties of the West. The ACM gave its wholehearted encouragement to young modernist composers, praising in their critical articles anything they considered "advanced," that is, at variance with classical traditions.

The Moscow magazine *Sovremennaya Muzyka* (the organ of the ACM) devoted two special issues (Nos. 19 and 20, 1927) to Prokofiev's visit to the U.S.S.R. in which it extolled the works he had conceived in Paris, precisely the ones that revealed an incipient crisis in his art. The Quintet, Op. 39, and the Overture, Op. 42, were mentioned in laudatory articles, and the leadership of the ACM urged immediate performances of the Second Symphony and *Le Pas d'acier*. At this time even Asafyev's position was not entirely correct. With his unreserved, ecstatic praise of the Fifth Sonata, the Quintet, and the Overture, he sanctioned his friend's modernist tendencies. It is to his credit, however, that he constantly reminded his readers of the lyrical aspect of Prokofiev's talent, which was yet to be fully revealed. "It seems to me that Prokofiev, turbulent and fiery as he is in his conceptions of external phenomena, is utterly transformed the moment he ventures into the sphere of intimate feeling," Asafyev wrote early in 1927. "He has not yet fully revealed himself in this sphere; here there is still a great potential.[23] And indeed, the subsequent years, especially those after Prokofiev's final return to his homeland, brought an unusual flowering of his lyrico-romantic inclinations, which had not found full expression for so long.

In 1927, of course, Prokofiev still felt completely identified with the modernist tastes of his Moscow and Leningrad friends. In the new Soviet art which he had occasion to see and hear, he responded most quickly to works which seemed to reflect his own aesthetic views. He praised Meyerhold's constructivist productions, expressed his satisfaction with the "advanced" repertory of the opera theaters (which now included many modernistic novelties), and gave his approval to the most radical works of the young composers (such as Shostakovich's First Sonata and G. Popov's Septet).

Most Soviet audiences, however, could not accept extreme modernism. They responded with enthusiasm to the earlier Prokofiev sonatas, the *Classical Symphony,* The Third Concerto, and the March from the *Three Oranges,* but they turned away perplexed from the Quintet and the Overture, Op. 42. "The audience was nonplused by the American Overture, Op. 42. They did not understand it," the composer recalled later.

The critics who were not contaminated by the extreme views of the ACM wrote quite candidly about this. For instance, after remarking on the skillful counterpoint in the Quintet and the Overture, *Muzyka i Revolutsiya* asserted that "the themes of these works are not so vivid and impressive as Prokofiev's themes usually are, and despite the complexity of these compositions, they do not strike one as very significant."[24] "There are features in his music that are foreign to us, that alienate us from his art," the same magazine observed. "We have in mind his subjects, his avoidance of profound and meaningful content, which we believe is an essential element of all truly great art. His *Oranges* is brilliant, his *Buffoon* witty and amusing, but to us the themes dealt with here are quite trifling and unimportant. These are no more our subjects than are the subjects of his Balmont songs and his *Flaming Angel.* And it is probably these works which most clearly reveal the West's influence on Prokofiev."[25]

Later, as the struggle between trends in Soviet music sharpened, criticism of the negative aspects of Prokofiev's work became even more severe.

❄ ❄ ❄

Although Prokofiev left Moscow filled with vivid impressions and enriched by new ideas gathered from many interesting meetings, he was not yet ready to sever his ties completely with the West. The Diaghilev première of *Le Pas d'acier* was in the offing, and there was a possibility that *The Flaming Angel* might be produced in Germany. Aside from his interest in these performances, many ties still bound him to the music business of Western Europe. One of his most serious commitments was his contract with the Gutheil publishing house, which gave Gutheil the right to sue him if his works were reprinted in the Soviet Union or even performed there without payment in foreign currency. Thus, despite his

Soviet passport, Prokofiev continued to be a "Parisian" for another six years.

On June 7, 1927, *Le Pas d'acier* finally had its sensational première in Paris. On July 4 Diaghilev risked presenting the ballet in London before the highest social circles of Britain (even the Prince of Wales was present). Critics in both countries were astonished at the evolution of Diaghilev's productions from lush exoticism to mechanistic asceticism.

"Of all the ballets, this is the least pleasing to the eyes," wrote one French critic. "We do not find here the splendor of *Scheherazade* and *The Nightingale*. Against a bare background, two raised platforms: this seems to suggest the severe deprivations of the Soviet people during the years of chaos and civil war."[26] Another critic pointed out that Yakulov's sets "are in the constructivist style introduced by Meyerhold. The element of pure decorativeness is completely lacking. All the construction is utilitarian, supporting the movement of the performers like the apparatus of a circus artist."[27] Modernist critics raved about the dissonance of the music, which captivated them with its "spontaneity and fullness of sound."

The British critics, also greeting the spectacle as a sensation, flaunted their approval of the "Bolshevist" ballet. "To one familiar with the Russian ballet . . . Prokofiev's Bolshevist ballet was something of a shock. . . . [But] if the 'Red' composer writes better music than Stravinsky, then by all means let us hear it," wrote the *Daily Telegraph* on July 5, 1927. "Writers and orators have been telling us about this for years, but Prokofiev's ballet expresses the spirit of modern Russia better than all of them put together" (*Empire News*). "Prokofiev travels through the civilized world, but in his mode of thinking, he refuses to belong to it" (*Daily Mail*).

Some critics were puzzled: was this simply another bit of fantasy from the inexhaustible imagination of the famous impresario, or was it Bolshevist propaganda? "A strange work from start to finish. Can it possibly be intended to replace *A Life for the Tsar*?" queried one Paris newspaper. "Do you think that the public was scandalized? Not in the least. Snobs, casting their eyes upward, said *'charmant,' 'épatant,' 'rigolo,'* and called out the authors seven times at the end of the performance."

White Russian émigré newspapers, regarding *Le Pas d'acier* as Communist propaganda, flew into a rage. They called Diaghilev an "out-and-out Kremlin entrepreneur" and the ballet "repellent Soviet stuff," and "an achievement of the Commissar of Education!" These papers also took the occasion to put forth their usual predictions of the imminent downfall of the Soviet government: "In his Soviet rejuvenation, Diaghilev will vanish from the theatrical scene just as speedily as the Bolshevists themselves are presently vanishing from the international scene."

This indignation from reactionary circles was misguided, of course, for *Le Pas d'acier* in no way reflected real Soviet life or thought. The ballet was only another Diaghilev extravanganza, portraying for the Paris snobs their own idea of "Bolshevist exoticism." It presented such fanciful characters as a sailor tattooed from head to foot with an earring in one ear and a single felt boot, cigarette and candy venders gaily turning somersaults, and a former countess in ragged dress peddling her possessions. In the second scene, dancers in overalls diligently went through the motions of machines to an ear-splitting musical imitation of steam hammers.

The music is written in a thoroughly constructivist style closely related to that of Stravinsky's *Rite of Spring* and *The Wedding*. In keeping with the idea of a Soviet ballet, Prokofiev made an honest effort to compose distinctly Russian melodies. Thus, the diatonic theme with which the introduction opens even recalls the well-known refrain of an old factory song (FIG. 29). But unfortunately, these Russian themes lost their national

FIGURE 29

character when subjected to artificially coarsened harmony (such as *ostinato* figures in the form of harsh chords), which was not in keeping with their simplified melodic patterns. The musical characterizations of the commissars, the orator, the sailor with the bracelet, and the working woman were written in a stylized descriptive manner and invariably distorted by harsh counterpoint. It was only in the episode of the candy and cigarette venders, written in the style of one of his typical mischievous scherzos, that Prokofiev achieved some degree of success.

It appears that the composer gave most of his attention to the second scene (particularly the episodes of "the factory" and "the hammers"), where he made lavish use of dissonant and deafening orchestral effects to reproduce the noise of machines. The Russian melodies woven into this rattle and din are imperceptible. This roaring music, although very similar to the most extreme examples of modernist art, was not appreciated even by such a lover of powerful sensations as Stravinsky, who frankly told Prokofiev that he did not like the clatter of the "steam hammers."

This music in no way conveyed the essence of the revolutionary transformations taking place in Russia. Indeed, knowing nothing about Soviet life, the composer could hardly have been expected to achieve this. The images of Soviet people in *Le Pas d'acier* were in fact contrived, distorted. Only at rare moments in this music, moments when we find a fresh, unblemished Russian theme (like the A minor theme accompanying "The Train of Speculators"), do we realize that the composer had not completely forgotten his native language.

※　※　※

Besides *Le Pas d'acier,* several of Prokofiev's other works were performed in 1927, both in the Soviet Union and abroad. On May 7 a ballet called *Die Erlösten* (The Redeemed), set to the music of the *Scythian Suite,* was presented at the Berlin State Opera. The Moscow première of *The Love for Three Oranges* took place on May 19. On October 11 another ballet to the music of the *Scythian Suite* was given in Buenos Aires, and early in January 1928 *The Buffoon* was performed in Kiev.

Prokofiev considered the Berlin production of *Die Erlösten* (by the choreographer Max Tempis) unsuccessful and, above all, stylistically false. "They bungled it without me. If I had been there, I never would have permitted them to use the *Scythian* music for a Dante theme," he wrote to his Moscow friends.[28]

These performances of music for the theater reawakened the composer's old interest in opera, toward which Western theaters were quite indifferent. But as before, all of his efforts to have his new operas produced proved futile. In the summer of 1927 he completed the score of *The Flaming Angel,* which he had begun eight years before, and made a number of changes in the libretto. However, although the Berlin Opera had accepted it, the opera was not produced. In June 1928 a few excerpts from the second act were played at one of the Koussevitzky concerts in Paris.

Having completed this opera, Prokofiev resumed work on *The Gambler,* the manuscript of which had been preserved in the library of the former Maryinsky Theater. Many things in this opera, written eleven years before, now struck him as unnecessarily complex. He now saw quite clearly that certain passages were simply padding disguised by terrifying chords. Accordingly, he considerably simplified a number of episodes, discarding everything that encumbered the vocal parts. This work produced the second version of *The Gambler,* which was performed on April 29, 1929, at the Théâtre Royal de la Monnaie in Brussels. The opera was carefully produced, but most of the audience did not understand it, and it was soon dropped from the repertory.[29] Somewhat later, in 1931, Prokofiev used material from this opera as the basis for a symphonic suite.

Time and again Prokofiev's desire to compose was blocked by the insistent demands of impresarios and concert managers. When, at the end of 1927, he decided to stop concertizing for a while in order to devote himself to composing, "this caused pandemonium among various presidents and directors of musical institutions, though everyone knows that these gentlemen don't care a fig for composers as long as their little shops are doing business."[30]

During these years abroad, Prokofiev produced much less than he had in the extremely productive 1916–17 period. Except for the "American" Overture, Op. 42 (written on commission), and the revised version of *The Gambler,* he actually composed nothing new in either 1926 or 1927. In 1928, however, a certain creative upsurge yielded the most important works of his Paris period, the Third Symphony, Op. 44, and *The Prodigal Son,* Op. 46.

When it became clear that *The Flaming Angel* would not be produced, Prokofiev decided to use the music from it for a symphonic suite. During the summer of 1928, however, the suite blossomed into a large four-movement symphony (the Third). Although this symphony is based on themes from *The Flaming Angel,* it is an independent non-program work and not a symphonic embodiment of the opera's story. In a statement published several years later, the composer vehemently protested against the tendency to regard this symphony as a program work, pointing out that the principal themes of the opera were originally conceived as instrumental themes and that the symphony only returned them, as it were, to the domain of pure instrumental music.[31]

The Third Symphony is the most dramatic of Prokofiev's four early symphonies. After the witty and elegant *Classical Symphony* and the harsh, constructivist Second compounded of "iron and steel," Prokofiev created a symphonic drama, very complicated in its musical language and filled with hauntingly expressive images.

In the first movement, a sonata allegro with an introduction, three sharply contrasting themes are developed: the first two are those of Renata's mental anguish in *The Flaming Angel*—the chromatic *ostinato* theme of the introduction (her despair), and the agitated melody of the main theme (the leitmotiv of her love for Madiel, shown in Fɪɢ. 23). Completely different in character is the quiet, confident subordinate theme (the theme of Ruprecht the Knight in the opera). The development section, filled with darkly raging sounds, repeats almost entirely one of the opera's entr'actes. The suffering and pain in this music are presented with expressionistic emphasis in strident dissonances and complex counterpoint.

In sharp contrast to the first movement is the mystical, other-worldly, Andante, with its archaic, diatonic quality (taken from one of the episodes in Act V of *The Flaming Angel* depicting Renata's emotions in the convent).

According to the composer, the tempestuous motion of the demonic Scherzo (the third movement) was suggested by the finale of Chopin's B-flat minor Sonata. But here the image of a terrible whirlwind is intensified many times by a chaotic torrent of orchestral sounds, which give an overpowering energy to this frenzied music. Only in the middle section do we find a more peaceful theme, echoes of which are heard later in the reprise.

The finale brings back the dark world of medieval mysticism with images of suffering, torture, and monstrous exorcisms. Funereal rhythms contrast with tense, piercing themes. The calmest of the finale's three themes is related to the music of the Andante. In the recapitulation the composer returns to the subordinate theme of the first movement, combining it with the basic theme of the finale.

"I believe that in this symphony I succeeded in deepening my musical language," Prokofiev wrote some years later. Indeed, the seriousness and depth of his artistic intentions is indicated partly by his dedication of the Third Symphony to Miaskovsky, one of the most confirmed symphonists of our time.

The first performance of the Third Symphony took place in Paris on May 17, 1929, under the direction of Pierre Monteux. It has been played several times in the United States (under Leopold Stokowski),[32] and also in the Soviet Union (under Dranishnikov, Gauk, and the composer himself). However, its complex musical style and overabundance of somber, frenzied expressionistic images prevented it from winning the favor of Soviet audiences.

※　※　※

While the Third Symphony was something of an "echo of the past," being made up of materials dating from 1918–19, *The Prodigal Son* represented a new departure in Prokofiev's music.

This was Diaghilev's last commission to Prokofiev. Having tantalized the Parisians with the modern "Bolshevist exoticism" of *Le Pas d'acier,* the indefatigable impresario suggested a new subject to the composer, this time one taken from the Gospel according to St. Luke. As we can see, there was no limit to Diaghilev's ingenuity; in seeking themes for fashionable entertainments, he moved with ease from scenes of industrial construction in Russia to the Biblical parable of the prodigal son. Inasmuch as the fifteenth chapter of the Gospel according to St. Luke is not exactly suitable for a ballet libretto, Diaghilev and his librettist B. Kochno used it simply as the basis for a general scenic outline, supplying other details themselves. The one act ballet consists of three scenes—the Prodigal Son's departure from home, his adventures in foreign lands, and his return. After leaving his father's home, the Prodigal Son meets some friends, who make him drunk and then rob him, after which he returns home, beaten and humbled. Diaghilev introduced a romantic element by including a meeting between the leading character and a certain Beautiful Maiden. The scene with the envious elder brother, which carries the moral of the Biblical story, was discarded, and the Prodigal's sisters and his wicked friends were added. The fable ended, as in the Bible, with the Prodigal's repentance and the complete absolution of his sins.

Diaghilev's choice of a Biblical theme was symptomatic of the times. Many French artists, weary of the excesses of cubism and the emptiness of contemporary art, began turning to classical or Biblical themes, resurrecting antique subjects and art forms. After his subjectless cubistic designs, Picasso went back to Ingres; after *Mavra* and *L'Histoire du soldat,* Stravinsky wrote *Oedipus Rex* and later the *Symphony of Psalms,* paving the way for a mannered neo-classicism. Surfeited with mischievousness and anti-aestheticism, bourgeois art tried to become intellectually subtle and profound. In seeking "eternal themes," in turning to artistic devices of the remote past, the artists of the West sought to save themselves from the complete intellectual and artistic degeneration toward which their rootless experimentation was inevitably leading.

Diaghilev's *Prodigal Son* was conceived as an exquisitely stylized spectacle. The noted artist Rouault was engaged to do the settings, and Serge Lifar, a dancer of the Diaghilev school, was assigned the role of the Prodigal. The idea of a "Biblical" ballet appealed to Prokofiev. After the grotesque complexities and eccentricities of his recent works, he was drawn to more serious themes, especially ones with moral significance. The experiences of the Prodigal, who left home and returned repentant, offered him an opportunity to portray deep emotions and meaningful actions. Pro-kofiev wrote the music for the ballet with ease, and with a feeling of pleasure and achievement as well. "My sojourn in Paris has given me an opportunity to complete the new ballet, which will undoubtedly be one of my most successful works," he informed his Moscow friends.[33]

The choreographer George Balanchine invested *The Prodigal Son* with elements of refined neo-classicism. The action seemed to take place outside time and space; neither the score nor the production in any way suggested locale, epoch, or nationality of characters. In keeping with this scenic con-ception, the composer carefully avoided giving the least suggestion of time or place; there are no ritual dances or sunny landscapes, as in *Ala and Lolli,* no stylized folk dances, as in *The Buffoon,* no sketches of everyday life and sound effects, as in *Le Pas d'acier.* Sharply contrasting emotional states and scenes succeed each other swiftly and laconically: the brashness of the Prodigal Son leaving his father's home, the grief of the parting, the im-petuous "Meeting with Friends," the tender lyricism of the portrait of the Beautiful Maiden.

Prokofiev's old predilection for tense, sharply drawn images again re-vealed itself in such scenes as "The Meeting with Friends," "The Carousal," "The Robbery," and "The Division of the Spoils." Particularly character-istic are "The Robbery," a persistent scherzo in 6/8 time with harsh poly-tonal layers, and "The Meeting with Friends," constructed on an energetic *ostinato* in the bass (similar to that found in the *Étude,* Op. 2, No. 4).

Not infrequently the music is marred by the arbitrary harshness of the polyphonic and harmonic devices and the lack of real development: a number of very lean melodic phrases are carried over without change from one episode to another.

The music actually contains few of the elements of pure dance. The only finished dance number in the entire score ("Men's Dance," No. 4) is probably the weakest episode in the ballet. All the other musical scenes are designed mainly for pantomimic action, often with acrobatic elements.

Despite the abstract and stylized conception behind *The Prodigal Son,* Prokofiev expressed in it a striving toward something new. This was the first large-scale stage work in many years in which he placed a major emphasis on purely lyrical episodes. Here and there, in such passages as "The Beautiful Maiden," "The Return," the love scene, and the episode of awakening and repentance, tender lyrical themes emerge; these have a charming purity of feeling, and Prokofiev's subtle modulations make them expressive of fine emotional nuances. In a way, these themes are forerunners of the captivating melodies of *Romeo and Juliet,* although many of them here are still constrained by mannered harmonic devices. The best character of the ballet, the Beautiful Maiden, is drawn in delicate, somewhat faded colors (FIG. 30).

FIGURE 30

In the Beautiful Maiden there begins to emerge a new Prokofiev character, one destined to be a favorite of his—a fragile young girl with a sad, exquisite grace. Her emotions are far more modest and restrained than the unbridled exaltation of Polina in *The Gambler* or Renata in *The Flaming Angel.* She is the prototype of Juliet, Cinderella, and Natasha Rostova.

Prokofiev avoided a complicated harmonic idiom in composing the lyrical passages of the ballet. A theme is sometimes heard in unison or at the octave without chordal support. Emotional nuances are expressed by means of scarcely perceptible alterations and modulations; this too indicates the composer's striving for orchestral means new for him—something like a transparent, almost colorless "pencil" drawing with the lone and delicate timbres of the flutes, oboes, and clarinets. After the fiery sonorities of the *Scythian Suite* and the stinging timbres of *The Buffoon,* this palette seemed deliberately ascetic.

The best pages of *The Prodigal Son* were evidence of the fact that Prokofiev had wearied of eccentric complexities and that his great talent intuitively gravitated toward the human and profound. But this tendency could not possibly find satisfactory expression in Diaghilev's ballet, which was a mixture of modernistic craftsmanship and pretension to aesthetic discoveries. The modest lyricism of the ballet remained unnoticed and unappreciated, lost in the overly stylized production. It was not until seven years later, in the inspired music of *Romeo and Juliet,* that Prokofiev was able to fully reveal his lyrical gifts and his talent for daring innovation in the sphere of ballet composition.

The première of *The Prodigal Son* took place in Paris on May 21, 1929;

Stravinsky's *Renard* was on the same program, and each composer conducted his own work. Although Prokofiev felt that most of the choreography was rather poor, he found the final repentance scene (a mime scene in which the Prodigal Son crawled on his knees toward his forgiving father) quite impressive. The ballet was well received by the Paris critics, as it was by Rachmaninov, who attended the première. Diaghilev soon presented it in Berlin and London, where it was given very favorable attention by the press.

This was Diaghilev's last production. Two months after its première, the impresario died suddenly in Venice. One of the threads that had so long bound Prokofiev to the West was broken.

Like many other Diaghilev productions, *The Prodigal Son* was soon forgotten. Prokofiev subsequently included a number of the ballet episodes in a symphonic suite (Op. 46-bis) and in the Fourth Symphony. Several of his piano pieces, Op. 52, are also based on material from this ballet.

*　＊　＊　＊*

Prokofiev's efforts at developing new melodic techniques are apparent not only in *The Prodigal Son* but also in a number of piano works written in the late twenties and early thirties. In the summer of 1928, which he spent in a village near Paris, Prokofiev composed two small piano pieces which he called *Things in Themselves* (Op. 45). This was his first piano music since the Fifth Sonata, written five years earlier. The coldly intellectual piano style which he had developed in Paris was far removed from the healthy, virile style which had delighted listeners in his youthful works.

*Things in Themselves* was followed by a whole series of piano miniatures, all similar in genre and style: two sonatinas, Op. 54, one in E minor (1931) and one in G major (1932); three pieces, Op. 59, entitled *Promenade* (1934), *Landscape* (1933), and *Pastoral Sonatina* (1934); and finally, three pieces called *Thoughts* (1933–34). It was difficult to recognize the old Prokofiev in any of these pieces. Rhythmic resilience and clarity of thought had vanished. Intense emotion and impulsive youthful vigor had given way to dull, rational speculation, and rich tone color had faded into colorless outlines. The composer had even given up his old predilection for the dance, the song, and theatrical action.

Thus a composer whose whole inspiration seemed to come from the excitement of the concert stage and the theater suddenly plunged into a world of rationalistic constructions, a sphere utterly foreign to his nature. It is not difficult to guess the reasons for this radical metamorphosis. First of all, the latest bourgeois art, with its emphasis on rationalism and a severe "purist" approach, could not but have affected his work. Most important, however, was the sad fact that Prokofiev had lost touch with the living sources of his art. Lacking the external stimuli favorable to the creation of music reflecting some aspect of reality, he retired into a narrow world of pure abstractions. The same composer who in his youth had rebelled against the aloofness and contemplative intimacy of modernist piano music had now arrived at a typical salon style, a style appreciated only by a small circle of connoisseurs.

Like the lyrical passages of *The Prodigal Son,* the new piano pieces revealed the composer's persistent attempts to achieve greater depth by becoming more introspective and by rejecting external effects. But what he had conceived as an expression of philosophical principles, as a music of pure contemplation (*Thoughts, Things in Themselves*), most listeners regarded as an artificial combining of sounds.

During the remaining years before his final return to the Soviet Union, the crisis in Prokofiev's work became more and more evident. Life abroad failed to provide him with fresh ideas and inspiration. But since even under these circumstances he could hardly stop composing, he turned more and more frequently to his earlier compositions, revising them and fabricating new opus numbers in the form of arrangements and transcriptions. As he later admitted in his memoirs, this gave the Parisians occasion to smile and think "the composer is grinding out new opus numbers."

Thus in 1929 he made a new version of his youthful Sinfonietta, Op. 5. In an effort to refurbish this old work, he complicated the score with burdensome harmonic details and somewhat reduced the form of the second and fourth movements. This version of the Sinfonietta was published as Op. 48.

By adding two new numbers to another two extracted from the ballet *Trapeze* (commissioned by the Romanov company in 1925) Prokofiev created the *Divertissement* for orchestra, Op. 43. Of the four movements of this work, the first and third ("Moderato" and "Dance") are from *Trapeze,* while the second and fourth ("Nocturne" and "Epilogue") were newly composed in the summer of 1929. The composer was especially fond of the second movement, which is one of the most typical examples of his experimentation with lyricism.[34] In 1938 he made a piano transcription of the *Divertissement*. Neither the orchestral nor the piano version won a permanent place in the concert repertory.

From the music of *The Prodigal Son* came several piano transcriptions:

*Intermezzo,* from the first scene of the ballet; Rondo, from the themes of the Beautiful Maiden; and *Étude,* which repeated in full the episode in which the Prodigal is robbed. These transcriptions, together with three others (the Scherzo from the Sinfonietta, one of the Songs Without Words, Op. 35, and the Andante from the String Quartet, Op. 50), were published in 1931 as Op. 52. Prokofiev dedicated these pieces to the outstanding pianists of the time—Artur Rubinstein, Vladimir Horowitz, Nicolai Orlov, and Alexander Borovsky.

Prokofiev continued to long for Russia. He was deeply upset by the cancellation of his second trip there, which he had planned for 1928. "You had already whetted my desire to see the dear places again, and to tell the truth, I am immensely upset by this cancellation or postponement," he wrote Derzhanovsky in February 1929. He asked his Soviet friends for details about a proposed production of *The Gambler* at the Maryinsky Theater with Meyerhold directing.

In the fall of 1929 Prokofiev made a second brief visit to the Soviet Union. Owing to some trouble with his hands, he gave no recitals. His only musical effort was to conduct excerpts from *The Love for Three Oranges* on a radio concert, which also included his Violin Concerto and Sinfonietta, conducted by K. Saradzhev.

Because of their modernism, the new Prokofiev works played in Russia in 1928—music from *Le Pas d'acier* (conducted by V. Savich) and the Second Symphony (conducted by V. Dranishnikov)—were not well received by their Soviet audiences. Even the composer's close friends (Miaskovsky, for one) did not like the Second Symphony. "The enthusiasm and idolization of Prokofiev are changing to coolness," remarked the magazine *Proletarsky Muzykant,* reviewing a Prokofiev program presented by the Persimfans orchestra. "An atmosphere of apathy and cold indifference prevailed at the concert."[35]

At this time the notorious Russian Association of Proletarian Musicians began to play an active role in the leadership of musical life. The leaders of RAPM pursued a policy of bureaucratic control, attempting to force their own ultramodern "principles" on composers of other tastes and tendencies. In their articles and in conversation they characterized Prokofiev as an enemy of Soviet culture, maintaining that there was no hope of directing him toward socialist realism. Such severe attacks could hardly draw the composer closer to Soviet musical life.

A bitter controversy developed over the projected production of the ballet *Le Pas d'acier.* The Association for Contemporary Music fully endorsed the idea, hailing the work as "the precursor of a revolution in ballet." After negotiations with Prokofiev, the directorate of the Bolshoi Theater included the ballet in its repertory plan, hoping to interest Meyerhold in directing it. "The machine age has probably never before been expressed with greater power," wrote the ACM magazine *Sovremennaya Muzyka.* "What predominates here is a strange mechanical precision, a suggestion of inexorable cogwheels created by the ceaseless rhythms (which occasionally overlap each other)." The article concluded with the naïve assertion that "in the very near future, *Le Pas d'acier* will be included in the repertory of every theater in the U.S.S.R."[36]

With the composer present, the directorate of the Bolshoi Theater carried on a stormy discussion about the ballet. The leaders of RAPM, who set the tone at this conference, placed all kinds of obstacles in the way of its production. Shortly afterward, the magazine *Proletarsky Muzykant* published two articles on *Le Pas d'acier,* one of which was written "on instructions from the Plenum and Council of RAPM." In these clamorous, abusive articles Prokofiev himself was severely criticized, and his ballet was characterized as "a flat anti-Soviet joke, a counter-revolutionary and all but Fascist work."[37]

In the heat of this controversy, *Le Pas d'acier* was withdrawn from the Bolshoi repertory while still in rehearsal. In itself this decision was fully justified, for the handling of the ballet's theme, based on constructivist principles, only cast discredit on contemporary Soviet life. Nevertheless, the composer's attempt to treat the Soviet theme unquestionably deserved support. What he needed was friendly help in finding the correct means of solving his artistic problem.

In early 1930 Prokofiev made an extended tour of the United States, giving twenty-four concerts with the major orchestras. The "American crush," as he called it, completely exhausted him. "I am terribly worn out, running from trains to rehearsals, from concerts to trains," he wrote to Derzhanovsky. His return to Europe brought no relief. "I thought that I would rest after America, but nothing of the sort," he reported in another letter. "Yesterday I waved and played through the sixth concert (Brussels, Turin, Monte Carlo, Milan), and in all, there will be thirty-three concerts this season. If this continues, goodbye Moscow until the fall."[38] This same letter, dated April 21, 1930, contains a brief but sorrowful postcript: "I am deeply grieved about Mayakovsky" (the great poet died on April 14, 1930).

As a result of the American tour, Prokofiev received some new commissions. For the fiftieth anniversary of the Boston Symphony Orchestra he wrote the Fourth Symphony, and for the Library of Congress in Washington he composed his first string quartet.[39]

The Quartet in B minor, Op. 50, is somewhat unusual in form. It is in three movements: an Allegro in sonata form, a Scherzo, and slow, lyrical Finale. As in *The Prodigal Son,* the music here is predominantly introspective. This mood prevails in the subordinate theme of the first movement, the introduction to the Scherzo, and finally, in the most important movement of the entire work—the quiet, mournful Andante, which reveals Prokofiev's growing inclination toward a typically Russian melodic style. The composer himself considered this Andante one of his finest achievements.

The classical main theme of the first movement (one of the prototypes of the main theme in the Second Violin Concerto), and the sparkling semi-dance melody of the Scherzo are typical of Prokofiev's individual style. The music is encumbered, however, by a few needlessly complicated polyphonic effects. The composer took special pains with this work; before starting it, he carefully studied the scores of Beethoven's quartets in an effort to master the peculiarities of quartet composition.

Miaskovsky, who attentively followed his friend's progress, responded very warmly to the string quartet.[40] Delighted with the deepening lyricism of Prokofiev's style, he shared his impressions with Asafyev: "First of all, the composition is completely free of effects, something quite surprising for Prokofiev. Secondly, there is true profundity in the sweeping melodic line and intensity of the Finale. This movement strikes deep. . . . How marvelous it would be if this tendency in him were to become firmly fixed."[41]

Like the Third, the Fourth Symphony (first performed in Boston on November 14, 1930) is based on Prokofiev's theater music. Its first and fourth movements were newly composed on themes from *The Prodigal Son,* but the remaining two were taken almost without change from the music of the ballet (the second movement from the Prodigal's return, and the third movement from the description of the Beautiful Maiden). This Symphony was not well received in Soviet Russia, owing to its general lifelessness and to insufficient contrasts in the music. In 1947 the composer revised the work, renumbering it Op. 112.

In the summer of 1930 Prokofiev also received a commission from the Paris Opera for a ballet. The creative history of this work, originally called *On the Dnieper,* provides an excellent illustration of the intellectual and spiritual crisis the composer suffered during his last years abroad. The scenario and choreography were worked out by the ballet master Serge Lifar, formerly one of Diaghilev's closest collaborators. Gaston Monmousseau, a leader of the French Communist Party, once said of this fashionable dancer who had adopted his teacher's tastes, "He is nothing but a pretentious theatrical corpse, put on a pedestal by the French bourgeoisie."

Neither Serge Lifar nor the directors of the French Opera were concerned about the content of the ballet, and the composer shared this attitude. "In planning this ballet," Prokofiev wrote in a letter, "Lifar and I began by constructing the choreographic and musical framework, regarding the subject of the ballet as secondary."

Lacking the stimulus of a subject, the composer wrote abstract music in conformity with a purely conventional plan of "passionate climaxes" and "lyrical moments." Where and when the action was to take place, what sort of heroes were to be portrayed—such things were immaterial. All that existed was a general skeleton of the piece, worked out in conjunction with the ballet master: a lyrical *pas de deux* in one place, a fast variation in another, a contemplative mood here, a passionate outburst of emotion there. When this skeleton plan was clothed with music, a more or less suitable story was to be worked out for it. Could an artist possibly go further in rejecting the natural creative process?

The story supplied for the music was extremely simple. A soldier falls in love with a peasant girl, and this is presented in tender love scenes and sentimental *pas de deux*. But the father wants the girl to marry someone else. The dramatic climax of the ballet occurs when the rejected soldier comes to the betrothal, duels with the fiancé, and is seized and tied to a tree. In the finale he is set free by his sweetheart, to the accompaniment of soft, tender music. That the action should take place on the Dnieper was decided only at the last minute (probably at the insistence of the Russian artists Larionov and Goncharova, who were to design the sets). Because of the difficulty the French had in pronouncing the word "Dnieper," the Slavic name of the river was replaced by its ancient Greek name, Borysthenes, and the ballet called *Sur le Borysthène* (Op. 51).

In this ballet Prokofiev repeated the experiment of *The Prodigal Son*, with its stylized and abstract action. There was no question of introducing any Ukrainian color into the music. The lyrical images were less human than those of the earlier ballet and the characterizations less poignant and dramatic. It is clear that this lack of real subjects of the kind that have always inspired composers of dramatic music had its effect on Prokofiev's music.

*Sur le Borysthène* was the last work for the theater Prokofiev wrote while abroad. He finally seemed to realize that in the bourgeois West, it was impossible for him to work successfully in his favorite field, musical drama. No one was interested in his operas. *The Flaming Angel* could find no producer, and it was useless to write new operas if no one would produce them. In any case, he could find no subjects, no fertile ideas for opera. "It very often seems," he wrote, "that one subject is just as meaningless as another."

While working on the Quartet, Op. 50, Prokofiev also composed the symphonic suite *Portraits,* Op. 49, based on the opera *The Gambler.* Making use of *The Gambler* was a complex and difficult task. It was impossible for him to extract anything resembling finished instrumental passages from among the intricate patterns of the purely declamatory music. He had to write entirely new orchestral episodes on the basis of phrases and motivs in the operatic parts. His method of doing this was unique. After spreading the pages of the piano score out on the floor, where he could readily compare them, he began selecting the thematic germs he needed from the parts of the leading characters. The individual motivs began to coalesce, forming distinct units of instrumental music. In this way five symphonic fragments were derived from the opera: "Alexei," "Babulenka," "The General," "Polina," and a final episode entitled "Dénouement." According to the composer, a great deal of time and effort was expended on this Suite. "It was not easy to put together and bridge passages had to be added, but the condensation seems to have made the character portraits more vivid," he wrote Asafyev.[42]

Prokofiev soon realized that the music of *Portraits,* artificially constructed from operatic declamation, was quite unintelligible. A year later he wrote to Moscow asking that this Suite not be played on the same program as *Le Pas d'acier.* "Side by side, *Portraits* and *Le Pas d'acier* would cancel each other out," he said.[43]

On commission from the one-armed pianist Paul Wittgenstein, he wrote the Fourth Piano Concerto for left hand alone. Wittgenstein was then enjoying considerable popularity, and concertos had already been written for him by Richard Strauss and Maurice Ravel. As we know, the Ravel Concerto was a success and entered the repertory of many pianists, including Gilels. But Prokofiev's Concerto, which was extremely contrived and complicated, did not appeal to the pianist; "Thank you very much, but I do not understand a single note of it and I shall not play it," he wrote to the composer. This work, which was not performed until 1956, is written in four movements; the first and fourth abound in virtuoso passages, while the second is an Andante and the third a sonata allegro. For a long time the composer intended to revise the Concerto for two hands, but this was never done.

In the summer of 1931 Prokofiev became interested in motoring and spent two weeks driving through all of Southern France, from Savoie at one end to Toulouse at the other. During the trip he happened to meet Glazunov, who showed him one of his latest works written in France, a ballade for cello and orchestra.

During this period Prokofiev kept in touch with his Soviet friends. He attentively followed the new works of Miaskovsky. "I am very happy that Miaskovsky has again burst into riotous creativity," he wrote Derzhanovsky.[44] While helping Asafyev collect materials for his ballet *The Flame of Paris,* he made a serious study of the music of the French Revolution. He also read new Soviet books. "Could you send me Leonov's *Sot* and some little novel of N. Ya. M's choice?" he asked Derzhanovsky on February 2, 1931.*

Prokofiev also formed friendships with leaders of Soviet culture who traveled abroad, among them the playwright Alexander Afinogenov and the film director Sergei Eisenstein. He met French progressive leaders, too, and in the fall of 1932 he visited at the country house of the well-known Communist critic Georges Sadoul. Although he sometimes felt that the grandiose scale of Soviet construction must leave the Soviet people no time for music, he still hoped that he could soon free himself from his commitments abroad and finally return home.

The last works Prokofiev composed in Western Europe belong entirely to the instrumental genre: the Fourth and Fifth Piano Concertos, Two Sonatinas for piano, Op. 54 (1931–32), the Sonata for two violins, Op. 56 (1932), the *Symphonic Song,* Op. 57 (1933), and the Cello Concerto, Op. 58 (begun in 1933). None of these works ever became popular.

Early in 1932 the composer informed Asafyev: "While traveling about through various cities, I have almost completed sketches for a new piano concerto, which, by the way, I would like to call 'music for piano and orchestra.' What do you think of this? In addition, two piano sonatinas are

---

* "N. Ya. M." stands for Nikolai Yakovlevich Miaskovsky.

on the horizon."[45] The concerto, however, outgrew the composer's original plans. "Unfortunately, the music for piano and orchestra is turning out to be rather difficult for the pianist, although I had really hoped to get by with something light but effective," he wrote Asafyev.[46]

This work, the Fifth Concerto, once again revealed Prokofiev's proclivity for experiments in virtuoso writing. Piano virtuosity, which he had neglected since the Third Concerto, now acquired meaningless, complicated forms. The machine-like, athletic, "toccata" element of his early piano style—full of wide leaps and daring hand-crossings à la Scarlatti—was carried to the extreme. Sheer piano acrobatics completely dominate the principal movements of this work—the first, third (Toccata), and fifth (Finale). In the precipitate Toccata, the dynamic quality degenerates into mere mechanical motion, and the orchestral sounds are like the metallic clamor of some huge machine. There are a few episodes of bright lyricism, however, which afford some relief from the predominantly harsh, urbanistic style of this work—the subordinate theme of the first movement (in the spirit of the lyrical theme of *The Prodigal Son*), the gavotte-like theme of the second movement, and the lullaby theme of the fourth movement and the beginning of the Finale.

❦   ❦   ❦

Prokofiev worked for more than two years to secure a production of the ballet *Sur le Borysthène*. Although it had been commissioned and accepted by the Paris Opéra in 1930, the general economic depression of the time made new productions difficult to finance. "I waited a whole year with my *Dnieper*, but the Paris Opéra was in no position to stage new productions," the composer wrote. "The French government failed to grant an adequate subsidy, and the director, tired of supplementing it out of his own pocket, resigned. And since it turned out that he made all the contracts in his own name and not in the name of the theater (that is, the government), those who work at the Grand Opéra became considerably alarmed."

It was not until December 16, 1932, in Paris, that *Sur le Borysthène* was given its first performance, together with two other new ballets. Response was lukewarm, and it was soon withdrawn from the repertory. The same evening also saw the première of Prokofiev's Sonata for two violins; this was held at the inauguration of Triton, a society for the performance of new chamber music, whose membership roll included Milhaud, Poulenc, Prokofiev, and other modern composers. The Sonata was played by the violinists Robert Soetens and Samuel Dushkin.

Late in 1932 Prokofiev made his sixth concert tour of the United States. He played the Third and Fifth Piano Concertos under Frederick Stock, Bruno Walter, and other well-known conductors. He himself also conducted an orchestra of unemployed musicians at a concert at the Metropolitan Opera House. "There were many people in the huge Metropolitan, and when I came out, the orchestra stood up. The performance had a considerable (but not extraordinary) success," he wrote Derzhanovsky on January 12, 1933. Some of Prokofiev's extremely complex new works proved bewildering even to the most blasé American concert-goers. Following the performance of *Portraits,* an American sitting in a box next to Prokofiev's said loudly, "I'd like to meet that guy [meaning the composer]. I'd tell him a thing or two!" "I hastily took my leave," the composer wrote with obvious amusement.

Meanwhile, important events were taking place in Soviet musical life. The Communist Party resolution of April 23, 1932, brought about a radical reorganization of literary and artistic groups. The harmful sectarian policy of the Russian Association of Proletarian Musicians was ended, and the association itself dissolved. The RAPM, the ACM (which had disintegrated earlier), and other small art groups were replaced by the Union of Soviet Composers. These events stimulated musical activity and generated a tremendous creative upsurge. The happy news from his Moscow friends hastened Prokofiev's return to his homeland. In August 1932 the Moscow City Committee of Composers invited him to the U.S.S.R. In November of that year he arrived in Moscow with the intention of joining his fate once and for all to that of the Soviet Union.

This sound decision had been maturing over a long period of time. Like other Russian artists whose fate had separated them from their homeland, Prokofiev had become increasingly nostalgic. Although he thought little of politics and lacked a deep understanding of world events, he nevertheless felt a keen sympathy for the great transformation which was taking place in the Soviet Union. He was especially attracted by the prospect of regaining direct contact with his old friends and fellow-artists, whom he trusted implicitly. Finally, he was bitterly disappointed over the unfavorable reception of some of his latest works. He recognized clearly that continued residence in alien lands would only aggravate the crisis in his creative work.

In the reminiscences of the French critic Serge Moreux, who was friendly with Prokofiev during those years, we learn of an interesting conversation he had with the composer in Paris in 1933. Concerning the decision to return to the Soviet Union, Moreux quotes Prokofiev as saying: "The air of foreign lands does not inspire me because I am Russian, and there is nothing more harmful to a man than to live in exile, to be in a spiritual climate incompatible with his race. I must again immerse myself in the atmosphere of my homeland—I must once again see real winter and spring, I must hear Russian speech and talk with the people dear to me. This will give me what I lack here, for their songs are my songs. Here I'm restive. I'm afraid of falling into academism. Yes, my friend, I'm going home!"[47]

❋   ❋   ❋

In our assessment of Prokofiev's foreign period, we may begin with the year 1923, because until that time his genius was still nourished by what he had absorbed from life and art during his youth in Russia. After 1923, however, he lost touch with these sources of inspiration and succumbed more and more frequently to the devitalizing effects of an alien environment. His creative output dropped sharply, and his list of opus numbers began to include more rearrangements of old compositions and all kinds of adaptations of music originally written for the theater.

The most striking examples of the effect of formalistic influences on Prokofiev are the Second Symphony and the Quintet for winds and strings, both of which drew sharp disapproval even from his warmest admirers. In his new ballets, the dance element became emasculated and clearly defined national character disappeared.

During the ten years after 1923 Prokofiev did not compose a single new opera or vocal work. This is understandable, for there was nothing for him to sing about. The music he had loved since childhood, music which originated in the living intonation of Russian speech, no longer aroused his interest because all around him foreign languages were being spoken. His piano style for the most part acquired an intimate, salon flavor and even became somewhat pallid and anemic. His virtuoso works (the Fourth and Fifth Concertos) revealed a rejection of realism in favor of sheer virtuosity.

While striving to withstand the influence of fashionable trends, which he often strongly opposed, Prokofiev nevertheless felt the pressure of the aesthetically overrefined tastes of the bourgeois West. His statements in letters and newspaper interviews are clear evidence of this.

As before, Prokofiev believed that art must have nothing to do with politics. "As I see it, music and politics are mutually antagonistic," he once remarked in a letter. He believed that there could be "pure musicians," interested in their art as a thing in itself.[48] He considered it wrong for a composer to strive after popularity and even reproached Tchaikovsky for having done so. The main purpose of his own work, he felt, was to search for new means of expression, to break through traditions and laws to the discovery of new standards, which would achieve acceptance only in future years. As if teasing his readers, he declared in one newspaper interview: "The classical composer is a madman who composes things that are incomprehensible to his own generation. He discovers a certain logic as yet unknown to others, and therefore these others cannot follow him. Only after some time has passed will the courses he has charted, if correct, become understandable to everyone else." The idea that a great composer is necessarily unintelligible to his contemporaries is obviously incorrect.

During these critical years, Prokofiev sought new means of expression not so much by reflecting images of reality as by combining sounds in an abstract, rationalistic manner. He wondered why the general public and even the professional musicians, particularly in the Soviet Union, did not understand some of his works (such as the Quintet, Op. 39, and the Overture, Op. 42). He attributed this lack of appreciation to bewilderment at his "new melodic designs," which were deliberately different from the familiar ones: "Unable to grasp a new melodic design at once, the listener passes it by without noticing it. It is exactly the same with melody itself. If it follows a familiar pattern, it will be easily understood but just as easily tossed into the wastebasket. A melody with an unaccustomed design is at first not accepted as a melody at all, because it consists of turns and motivs not previously considered melodious. But if the composer is right, he will have extended the range of melodic possibilities, and the listener will inevitably follow him, if only at a respectable distance."

It is no wonder that by experimenting with melody he often perplexed his audiences, for he made frequent use of themes to which listeners were not attuned. Only during the Soviet years, in his best works of the thirties and forties, was he able to overcome this tendency and to create melodies which were not only original but also completely understandable.

More evidence of Prokofiev's modernist tastes during the years of his wandering is to be found in his sharp disapproval of the music of Tchaikovsky, Rachmaninov, and Medtner. In one of his letters he chides a Soviet magazine for its partiality toward the music of Scriabin and Medtner: "But that's Moscow, and nothing can be done about it. Perhaps I'm the one who's wrong, with my foreign coating. Here I'm used to the fact that no one is at all interested in them," he wrote. In another letter he criticized Miaskovsky for not dropping "Glazunovisms."[49]

Life abroad greatly constricted the circle of the composer's intellectual interests. "I have no ideas," he exclaimed in one letter. "I know not my forebears and care not where I'm going," he confesses in another. This attitude probably explains his vacillations between expressionistic frenzy and salon anemia, between the constructivist excesses of the Second Symphony and *Le Pas d'acier* and the pale, rationalistic abstractness of the new piano pieces.

At the same time, as he grew older and more mature, he began to strive for greater seriousness in his art, for a more profound lyricism. After *The Buffoon* and *The Love for Three Oranges,* he abandoned grotesque grimaces and pointless jesting; he protested repeatedly against the tendency of certain critics to see this quality as the chief characteristic of his style and thus to affix the label "grotesque" to all his works.

For a long time he persistently sought an outlet for his lyrical tendencies; hence, the experiments in a new lyrical style which found expression in the best pages of *The Prodigal Son,* the string quartet, and some of the piano miniatures. Also apparent in his music was a strong gravitation toward Russian folk melody (seen in his 1931 adaptation of the folk songs *White Snowflakes* and *Guelder-Rose on the Hill*) and an unexpected affinity to the style of Moussorgsky (in the Andante from the Quartet, Op. 50). But these tendencies found no support in the alien environment. His attempts to develop a lyrical melodic style were purely experimental, for they were not borne up by powerful ideas or clear and meaningful subject matter.

The year 1933–34 marked a sharp dividing line in Prokofiev's work: it was the end of the critical Paris period and the beginning of a brilliant new efflorescence.

# EIGHT

# RETURN

IT GIVES ME the greatest joy to be home again in the Soviet land," Prokofiev told Moscow newsmen late in November 1932, while on his third concert tour of the U.S.S.R. This tour, which took place in November and December, proved decisive. In conversations with leaders of the Commissariat of Education and the Union of Soviet composers, he expressed a deep desire to settle permanently in the Soviet Union and to participate actively in building its musical culture.

He was exhilarated by the vibrant creative life about him, which differed so greatly from the moribund, crisis-ridden atmosphere in bourgeois Europe. "The Soviet Union's gigantic achievements on the material and cultural fronts have impressed me tremendously," he stated in his interview. "I hope to reflect the fervor and enthusiasm that have made this possible in one of my future symphonic works."[1]

Having successfully completed the first Five-Year Plan in four years, the Soviet Union was now preparing for great new advances. The magnificent contours of the Socialist system were emerging in the scaffolding of new factories, the vast stretches of the collective farms, and the growing prosperity of the Soviet people. The buoyancy of this young country, rushing eagerly toward a happy future, could not fail to excite Prokofiev, who had grown weary of wandering in foreign lands. He looked forward to the day when he would be free of concert commitments and would have time to travel in the U.S.S.R., to visit the new cities and constructions, and above all to engage in new creative work. Among other things, he planned to visit Dneprostroi and to take a long trip through Transcaucasia.

At that time a new upsurge began to manifest itself in the literary and artistic life of the Soviet Union. The period of confusion that had formerly marked the work of the artistic organizations was now ended; the small groups and associations which had advocated formalist aesthetic principles in literature and art no longer existed. At the very beginning of the thirties, with the withdrawal of Miaskovsky, Shebalin, and other leading

244

composers, the notorious Association for Contemporary Music had disintegrated.

The Communist Party resolution of 1932 put an end to the cliquish, ultra-leftist activity of the Russian Association of Proletarian Musicians, which had long impeded the development of music, especially during the period from 1929 to 1932. The dissolution of RAPM and the formation, in the summer of 1932, of a single Union of Soviet Composers revitalized musical creativity.

By advancing the method of Socialist Realism as the basic method of Soviet literature and art, the Party equipped writers and composers with extremely valuable theoretical tools. The First All-Union Congress of Soviet Writers, held in the summer of 1934, played an important role in defining the principles of Socialist Realism. These aesthetic principles also strengthened music criticism and helped to expose the error of those who insisted that the necessary prerequisite for "revolutionary progress" in music was a formal, technical "rearmament" along modernist lines. And even though modernist influences continued to manifest themselves for a long time in the work of many gifted composers (including Prokofiev), the struggle against these influences was now carried on from more clearly defined theoretical positions.

Prokofiev could clearly see that many prominent musicians, among them his old friends Miaskovsky and Asafyev, had begun to turn away from modernism. Miaskovsky, for example, had begun to search for clearer and more classical means of expression, for meaningful and relevant themes, in his Twelfth Symphony (the "Kolkhoz"), which was first performed in 1932. That year also saw the première of Asafyev's ballet *The Flame of Paris*. In a foreign press interview, Prokofiev expressed a great liking for both of these works.[2]

During the years 1932–34 the tendency to reflect reality through the use of contemporary Soviet themes manifested itself in various ways in a number of works, among them Steinberg's "Turksib" Symphony, Knipper's Third and Fourth Symphonies, Kabalevsky's Second Symphony, and Shostakovich's music for the film *The Encounter*.

Soon after his arrival in Moscow Prokofiev became part of the large and friendly community of Soviet musicians; these men sought to interest him in various kinds of creative work that were new to him, deeply confident that his great talent and contact with Soviet life would help him overcome his past errors. Plans were projected for him to write Soviet operas, film scores, and incidental music for the theater. The Commissariat of Education suggested that he direct the training of advanced composition students at the Moscow Conservatory.

Although he was still extremely busy with concerts, Prokofiev found time to establish new professional contacts with composers in Moscow and Leningrad. "At a meeting with Leningrad composers," reported the newspaper *Sovetskoye Iskusstvo,* "Prokofiev gave his impressions of the state of music in Western Europe. According to him, the European composer is presently writing whatever he is paid for, and as a consequence his work is losing integrity and direction. Further, he emphasized the phenomenal growth of musical composition in the U.S.S.R. and his desire not only to popularize Soviet music in the West, but also to work in the same spirit that animates it."[3]

It was not easy for Prokofiev to re-establish contact with Russian audiences. The concerts he gave in December of 1932 were not well received. Though brilliantly performed by the composer himself, the Fifth Concerto proved disappointing. This was also the case with the *Portraits* from *The Gambler* (conducted by N. Golovanov) and the latest chamber compositions (the Sonatina, the Sonata for two violins, and the Quartet for strings, Op. 50). Audiences found these works totally unrelated to their own experience and devoid of that *joie de vivre* which had so impressed them in the best of the composer's early music. Despite this general reaction some critics praised these works unreservedly; others, however, tactfully noted a "certain experimental quality" in the music and the "cold, unemotional character" of Prokofiev's performance. Even such a staunch admirer as Miaskovsky was not happy with the new works of the "Paris period," finding them lacking in the earlier vitality. "Prokofiev sent me a sonata for two violins—it is rather strange," he noted in his diary on October 3, 1933. Of the Fourth Piano Concerto he wrote, "Interesting but somewhat dry"; and of the Fifth Concerto, "First and third movements not very pleasing, but the fourth and fifth very good."[4]

In 1933 and 1934 Prokofiev became more and more actively involved in Soviet cultural life. Besides completing works begun abroad, he boldly undertook new projects, striking deeper roots into the fertile Soviet soil. He spent the greater part of these two years in the U.S.S.R., although he did make occasional trips abroad, including visits to his family in Paris and a tour of the United States.

In April 1933, following his rather extended American tour, he once again returned to his homeland, where he participated in a series of concerts of his own works in Moscow and other major cities. The programs included the Third Symphony, the Third Piano Concerto, and the *Scythian Suite*. By the time this tour reached Tblisi, however, he decided that the program was overloaded with the complicated novelties which had been so coolly received in Moscow. "It is dangerous to present an entire program of my works—neither the orchestra nor the audience can cope with them," he remarked in a letter.[5] At the same time he shunned easy success, refusing to limit his performances only to familiar works. "I would not like the Soviet listener to judge me only by the March from the *Three Oranges* and the Gavotte from the *Classical Symphony*," he declared in one article.[6]

Prokofiev was seriously interested in writing a new opera, an undertaking which he had been unable to realize for many years while abroad. In an effort to find material for a libretto, he read several books by Soviet writers. He flatly rejected the suggestion that he write an opera exposing the dregs of life in Paris. "Such a piece would be negative and destructive," he wrote. "I am interested in Soviet themes. I am seeking and hope soon to find a sound, wholesome plot based on Soviet life."[7]

On another occasion he went into greater detail. "What kind of subject am I seeking? Not a caricature ridiculing the shortcomings, the negative features, of our life. At the present moment this does not attract me. What interests me is a subject asserting a positive principle. The heroism of construction. The new man. The struggle to overcome obstacles. These are the moods and emotions with which I should like to fill large musical canvases."[8] He encountered great difficulties in trying to realize these aspirations, however. Lacking an intimate knowledge of Soviet reality, he failed more than once in attempting to use contemporary Soviet themes in his music.

In December the composer promised the leaders of the Commissariat of Education that he would begin teaching in the school for advanced composition at the Moscow Conservatory. "I want to help Soviet youth as much as I possibly can," he declared in a letter to friends. During the 1933-34 school year he kept his word. Miaskovsky, who had long been engaged in teaching, gladly introduced his friend into this new and unfamiliar field.

Needless to say, young Soviet musicians were excited at having an opportunity for personal contact with this famous Russian composer. As far back as the twenties this younger generation of composers had thrilled to Prokofiev's music; even then, their frequent imitation of Scriabin's harmonic refinements and capricious texture was beginning to be replaced by incisive rhythms and slightly coarse, "grotesque" harmonies in the style of the early Prokofiev. The young Shostakovich was not immune to this influence.* Traces of it are to be found in the Scherzo of his First Symphony, in the popular *Fantastic Dances,* and in several of his piano preludes. The enthusiasm for Prokofiev is also evident in some of V. Deshevov's early works (in his *March,* Op. 1, for example, which he dedicated to Prokofiev).

"You can easily imagine our excitement when one day in 1933 Nikolai Yakovlevich [Miaskovsky] told us that Prokofiev was coming to the Conservatory and that he wanted to hear the students' compositions," recalls Aram Khachaturian. "Exactly at the appointed hour, the tall figure of Prokofiev appeared at the director's office. He entered briskly, in animated conversation with Miaskovsky, scarcely noticing our stares, our burning curiosity, and our poorly controlled excitement." On that day Prokofiev heard works by K. Makarov-Rakitin, Yuri Biryukov, Evgeny Golubev, N. Makarova, T. Khrennikov, and Khachaturian. Concerning the performance of his Trio for violin, clarinet, and piano, Khachaturian says, "I recall that all his remarks were friendly, specific and to the point. . . . He liked my trio and even asked me for a copy to send to France."

During the following two or three years Prokofiev gave lessons in practical composition to young composers at his home. Among those who attended these sessions at various times were A. Spadavekkia and N. Makarova. Prokofiev's comments, aimed at developing creative imagination and artistic daring to the utmost, are very interesting. When Khachaturian showed him a sketch of the second movement of his piano concerto, Prokofiev (referring to the oversimplified piano part) caustically remarked, "Here your pianist will be twiddling his thumbs." Then he told Khachaturian, "It is very difficult to write a concerto. One has to be inventive. I advise you to jot down all the ideas as they occur to you, without waiting for the whole thing to mature. Write down individual passages, interesting bits, not necessarily in the correct order. Later on you will use these 'bricks' to build the whole." Prokofiev's passionate interest in his own creative plans eventually led him to give up teaching.

During the years in which he was tutoring young composers, he also studied persistently. After carefully reading the works of Lenin in 1933 and 1934, he became interested in the possibility of writing a large-scale musical composition on Lenin's actual texts. With this in mind, he copied

---

* Shostakovich played Prokofiev's First Piano Concerto in Leningrad and introduced several changes in the composer's orchestration.

the following passage from *What Is To Be Done?*: "We are marching in a compact group along a precipitous and difficult path, firmly holding each other by the hand. We are surrounded on all sides by enemies and are under their almost constant fire."[9] He later used these lines in one of the sections of the *Cantata for the Twentieth Anniversary of the October Revolution*.

To compose—tirelessly, every day—was now the composer's sole objective, and to further it he sharply reduced the number of his concert appearances. As early as December 1932 he had said, "Continuous concertizing is hardly conducive to serious creative work. I hope to begin such work as soon as I am settled in the U.S.S.R."

Prokofiev received a number of commissions from Soviet film organizations, Moscow theaters, and the All-Union Radio Committee. After years of intellectual and spiritual drifting, without vital subjects to draw on, his creative imagination was stimulated by projects which dealt with interesting programmatic material.

In 1933 the Leningrad director A. Feinzimmer asked the composer to write music for the film *Lieutenant Kije*, based on Yuri Tynyanov's story of the same name.

Nothing could have better suited Prokofiev's talent, his natural predilection for concrete, visual images, than the dynamic and many-faceted art of the motion picture. Loss of contact with living nature had at times caused his imagination to flag, to turn wearily to a dismal search after all sorts of abstract "things in themselves"; but now it was quickened not only by a delightful subject, but also by newly completed film sequences in which typical, real people were presented. One could hardly imagine a more suitable stimulus for Prokofiev's imagination. And indeed it was the Soviet cinema which inspired the creation of such brilliant examples of Prokofiev's art as the music for *Lieutenant Kije, Alexander Nevsky,* and *Ivan the Terrible*. He regarded composing for films not as wearisome day-labor, but as interesting and truly creative work. "I still consider the motion picture the most modern art," he maintained in a letter to his close friend, the film director Sergei Eisenstein.

With his characteristic directness, he asserted the rights of the composer in the cinema, sharply criticizing the "anti-musical" tendencies of culturally underdeveloped directors. "Because the motion picture is a new art, we have not yet learned to assess its component parts, and we regard music as an incidental adjunct unworthy of any special attention." In the films on which Prokofiev worked, music fulfills an important dramatic function. This certainly is true of the music of *Lieutenant Kije,* his first film score and the first test of his pen in the Soviet Union.

It was not by mere chance that this subject was suggested to Prokofiev; the satirical quality of Tynyanov's story had much in common with the composer's caustic humor. The plot of the story springs from a simple device: a military clerk, through a slip of the pen, enters in the rolls the non-existent name "Lieutenant Kije." Owing to the rigidity of military bureaucracy, Lieutenant Kije, who exists only on paper, acquires an illusory life—he receives a new assignment, marries, and dies. The film wittily portrays the barrack-like atmosphere of early nineteenth-century St. Petersburg under the half-mad martinet Paul I. A group of gifted actors, including M. Yashin, E. Garin, and S. Magarill, created memorable characterizations.

In the music the composer had to convey not only the quaintly satirical tone of the film, but also the atmosphere of the epoch. For the first time since the *Classical Symphony* he undertook to recreate, in his own way, an old style; this time, however, it was not "Viennese classicism" but "early Empire" St. Petersburg. He solved this interesting task brilliantly. Even though Tynyanov's story, and indeed the film itself, afforded ample opportunities for comical musical effects, Prokofiev resisted the temptation and tried instead to reproduce the spirit of the age. In brief tonal fragments he created memorable vignettes of the St. Petersburg of Paul I, with its formal, Prussian-style parades and dashing Hussars. A Russian snow scene gives way to a dull ceremonial march, a slightly parodied sentimental romance to a reckless coachman's song and the jingling bells of a dashing troika. After the contrived abstractions of the *Thoughts,* Sonatinas, and piano pieces, Op. 59, Prokofiev created a film score as vividly descriptive as an engraved illustration.

The score was completed quickly and delivered to the Leningrad Belgoskino Studios where, late in 1933, the sound track was successfully recorded by an orchestra under I. O. Dunayevsky, who was just beginning his career as a film composer.

On July 8, 1934, Prokofiev completed a five-movement symphonic suite based on fragments of the film music. In composing *Lieutenant Kije,* Op. 60, the composer had to make substantial revisions in the original form and orchestration of the various episodes. The transparent scoring of the suite calls for a full orchestra supplemented by instruments used for specific coloristic purposes: a cornet for military effects, a tenor saxophone for parody, and *sonagli* bells on a horse's harness to imitate the sound of a troika. The composer supplied two versions for both Movements II and IV ("Romance" and "Troika"): one version for baritone solo and orchestra, the other an alternative setting for orchestra alone.

The first movement, "The Birth of Kije," with its subtly parodied parade-drill motivs, sets the basic mood for the entire suite. From off stage is heard a cornet fanfare, which acts as an epigraph for the whole piece, suggesting the limitless expanses and strange, spectral tales of Russia. This is followed by an amusing, marionette-like march given out by the piccolo over the mechanical roll of a military drum. A characteristic feature of the piccolo melody is the use of the Lydian mode (an E natural in the key of B-flat major), which emphasizes the fictitiousness of the situation and the slight irony of the music (FIG. 31).

FIGURE 31

This rather silly melody, constructed on persistently repeated notes in descending sequential patterns, is followed by a soulful Russian tune. This phrase, the most important leitmotiv in the suite, is the theme of Lieutenant Kije. In the trio of the march the fanfares of the brasses are combined with the cannon-like booming of the bass drum.

The second movement, "Romance," has a completely different coloring. Its theme is patterned on *The Little Gray Dove is Cooing,* a sentimental ballad after the well-known poem by I. Dmitriev. The composer did not use the original tune, however, but composed a melody of his own in the spirit of this popular early nineteenth-century song. Here again the melody is modal, this time in the natural minor, with a melancholy, guitar-like accompaniment played by the harp.

Unlike Stravinsky's *Mavra,* with its caricatural stylization based on artificial combinations of harmonies, *Lieutenant Kije* contains no grotesque exaggerations; quite to the contrary, it is a gently humorous interpretation of the style of bygone days, based on essentially the same principle of semi-ironic "resurrection of the old" that Prokofiev had followed in the *Classical Symphony.*

The third movement, "Kije's Wedding," opens with rather heavy, pompous music in the style of a welcoming chant. This gives way to the lilting tune of a wedding song, to which the somewhat shrill timbre of the cornet adds a faint touch of mockery. The familiar "Kije leitmotiv" returns in the middle section of this movement, but here it acquires a slightly more sensuous quality from the throbbing tone of the tenor saxophone. The movement ends with a restatement of the gay wedding tune and the pompous opening phrase.

A rakish Hussar song constitutes the main theme of the fourth movement, "Troika." Its rapid accompaniment, colored by the percussion instruments, piano, and harp, suggests a dashing troika with bells jingling and hoofs clicking. A variation of the familiar theme of Kije recurs as a ritornello between the couplets of the song.

Finally, in the symphonically developed finale, "The Burial of Kije," the principal themes of the entire suite are interwoven. This movement opens and closes with the familiar cornet epigraph. Kije's theme is first stated in the somber low register of the clarinet to the accompaniment of doleful, funereal rhythms. Then follows the melody of *The Little Gray Dove is Cooing,* which here sounds sad and heavy, played alternately by the solo tuba and by the strings, which give out a mock moaning in the inner voices. The make-believe sadness soon is broken by a highly amusing contrapuntal combination of the song melody and the wedding tune of the third movement, this time abounding in sudden, comical modulations. Later this tune slyly intrudes on a mournful statement of the Kije theme. At the end of the finale the Kije leitmotiv gradually fades away in the scarcely audible tones of the flute. All that remains is the distant sound of the cornet over a faint roll of the drum.

The orchestration of this suite, with which Prokofiev took special pains, reveals the hand of a true master. "Kije is a devilish job," he remarked in a letter to friends, "but what gay music!"[10]

The *Lieutenant Kije* suite at once brought Prokofiev back to his favorite sphere, the theater, revealing with new force the distinctively Russian character of his art. The entire work is delightful for its subtle national flavor. This quality runs through the many Prokofiev works which contain material taken from Russian life—from *Lieutenant Kije* right up to the Hussar scene at Dolokhov's in *War and Peace* and the fair scene of *The Stone Flower*.

Almost concurrently with his work on *Lieutenant Kije*, Prokofiev composed the music for a theatrical entertainment called *Egyptian Nights*, on a commission from the Kamerny Theater in Moscow. The productions of this theater, which was headed by A. Y. Tairov, often revealed a tendency toward superficial aestheticism. Traces of surface originality were also present in *Egyptian Nights*, which was drawn from three texts: Pushkin's *Egyptian Nights*, Shakespeare's *Antony and Cleopatra*, and Bernard Shaw's *Caesar and Cleopatra*. This was Prokofiev's first encounter with the grand passions and fiery heroes in Shakespeare, and it was Shakespeare's tragedy that emerged as the main ingredient in this concoction. ("Old Shakespeare smothered Bernard Shaw," joked Prokofiev.)

The music for the play was written almost a year and a half before its première. At the Kamerny Theater, Prokofiev was happy to meet again the conductor A. K. Medtner, brother of the composer, who many years before (in the summer of 1911) had given the first performance of his youthful piece *Autumnal Sketch*. But Tairov's production, first given in April 1935, was contrived and cumbersome and proved a failure.

In the music of *Egyptian Nights*, decoratively descriptive episodes alternate with brief but powerful portraits of the leading characters. In contrast to the transparent score of *Lieutenant Kije*, somber, nocturnal colors prevail here, and although the orchestral forces are relatively modest, the coloristic effects are thick and solid. The musical style is more refined than that of *Lieutenant Kije*; the harmonies are severe and at times strangely archaic, and the melodies are more fragmentary.

In the summer of 1934 Prokofiev made a symphonic suite (*Egyptian Nights*, Op. 61) from this music. Of the seven movements of the suite, four are purely decorative episodes originally intended to accompany the stage action: the first movement, "Night in Egypt," a brief tonal landscape in the impressionist style; the third, "Alarm," written for percussion alone;

the fourth, "Dances," in a highly sophisticated pseudo-oriental vein; and the seventh, "Roma militaris," filled with stern, fierce power. The three remaining movements (No. 2, "Caesar, the Sphinx, and Cleopatra"; No. 5, "Antony"; and No. 6, "The Decline of Cleopatra") portray the emotions of the principal characters—Antony's resoluteness and nobility and Cleopatra's sensuousness. In the last two movements one can see the composer's striving for more dynamic dramatic development. "The Decline of Cleopatra" closes with the somber sounds of twilight, and just before the end of "Roma militaris" we hear a reminiscence of the opening movement, with its musical description of a close and oppressive tropical night. This latter episode is followed by the awesome music of the finale, which evokes the grandeur of victorious Rome. The composer himself considered "The Decline of Cleopatra" the best movement in the Suite. He felt that the third movement ("Alarm") could be omitted, and one must agree, since music for percussion alone, while admissible as a decorative element in a play, is utterly ineffective in the concert hall. In the fourth movement ("Dances") the composer approximated "oriental" tone color in a typically original way: in an effort to avoid the cloying sweetness of traditional "orientalism," he turned to harsh, archaic sonorities.

*Lieutenant Kije* and *Egyptian Nights* head the list of Prokofiev's works of the Soviet period. These were followed by the ballet *Romeo and Juliet,* the Second Violin Concerto, the piano pieces for children, and a number of mass songs [for large groups of singers]. This turning toward new themes and a new style did not proceed without serious contradictions, however; more time was needed for Prokofiev to overcome completely the enthusiasms he had developed during his foreign period.

It is hard to believe that during the very period he was writing the transparent and witty music of *Lieutenant Kije* (1933-34), Prokofiev also composed the piano cycle *Thoughts,* Op. 62, which bears the imprint of the earlier, crucial period in his development. These three short pieces abound in gloomy moods of withdrawal, apathy, and introspection. The noble, plaintive melodies which open the first and third pieces are soon lost in a labyrinth of contrived, arbitrary constructions. The harmonic development is artificially restrained, the melodic design fragmented, and the rhythms amorphous and weak. Several other works composed in 1933-34, primarily in Paris, bear a close stylistic resemblance to the cycle *Thoughts*: sketches for the Cello Concerto, Op. 58; the three piano pieces of Op. 59 (*Promenade, Landscape, Pastoral Sonatina*); and the *Symphonic Song,*

Op. 57. During this same time the composer also put together a symphonic suite from the ballet *Sur le Borysthène*. These works were in the nature of a summing-up of the Paris period.

Prokofiev conceived the *Symphonic Song* as a complex philosophical piece expressing three successive states—obscurity, struggle, and achievement. The three movements, which proceed without interruption (*Andante assai, Allegro,* and *Andante*), were constructed according to this conception. But the exposition and development of the musical ideas proved exceedingly vague and the lyricism studied and abstract, much as in the piano pieces *Thoughts* and *Things in Themselves*. Even Koussevitzky, an enthusiastic advocate of Prokofiev's most modernistic works, was puzzled by this score.

The première of the *Symphonic Song* in Moscow on April 14, 1934 (on a program including *Portraits* and the First Piano Concerto), was met with complete indifference by the public. "There were literally three claps in the hall," Miaskovsky recalls. *Sovetskaya Muzyka* (No. 6, 1934) criticized the work severely, noting in it traces of weariness and morbid depression. In the opinion of the magazine, the excellent craftsmanship of the *Song's* orchestration did not compensate for its vacuousness and the oppressive preponderance of disembodied, melancholy arabesques. "Prokofiev's *Symphonic Song* does not sing; it is not a song at all in our sense of the word," asserted the author of the article. "We regard it as a symphonic monologue for the few, a sad tale of the decline of the fading culture of individualism." The gist of the article was that a continuation of the tendencies displayed in the *Symphonic Song* would be ruinous to the talented composer and completely unacceptable to Soviet audiences.

Prokofiev was not yet fully aware of the complete artificiality of such contrived music. "I do not understand why 'lyricized' music should be unconvincing to Soviet musicians," he wrote to Asafyev. "Why, melody is the basic element, the most acceptable and most desired. Those who do not understand this should be taught."[11]

But melodies like those in *Things in Themselves* were not felt to be an expression of human emotions, but rather the result of a contrived combination of sounds. At times such melodies even baffled the composer himself. "Sometimes I would forget a work that I had written during this period and had not seen for a number of years," he wrote later. "Then I would play it and wonder, 'What in the world is this?' I would play it through once, twice, three times—and suddenly out of the darkness would emerge the outlines of a real face." It is hardly surprising that music which puzzled the composer should prove confusing to the majority of his listeners.

In line with Prokofiev's thinking at this time was a view which he expressed in an article published in *Izvestia* on November 16, 1934. Here he spoke of the need for two distinct categories of music: one for "connoisseurs" and another for average listeners; on the one hand, "great music," capable of "posing problems even to leading musicians"; and on the other, "serious light music," comprehensible to the masses coming into contact with art for the first time. Appraising his own recent works according to this system, he placed his *Symphonic Song, Sur le Borysthène,* and the Third and Fourth Symphonies in the first category, and *Lieutenant Kije, Egyptian Nights,* and the mass songs which he was then writing for the radio in the second.

These views, which were unquestionably related to the modernist approach to art, account for the duality in Prokofiev's music of 1933–34. We shall find that the composer later overcame this duality and created works that appealed equally to "connoisseurs" and to the general public.

During his trips abroad in 1933–34 Prokofiev was an active advocate of Soviet music. He was eager to see new Soviet music performed in France, England, and Italy, and he discussed this with foreign composers and conductors. On his recommendation the gifted Greek conductor and pianist Dimitri Mitropoulos was invited to tour the U.S.S.R.

Musicians abroad continued to maintain a high regard for Prokofiev, and they followed his development with interest. In early 1934 he was elected an honorary member of the Academy of St. Cecilia in Rome.

"The Roman Academy has just made me an honorary member and so—alas, poor me—the cycle is complete; from attacking the foundations of academism to being made an academician," he reported, tongue in cheek, to his Moscow friends.[12]

Prokofiev spent the summer of 1934 in Bugry near Maloyaroslavets, not far from Moscow, at the country house of his friend, the artist P. Konchalovsky. Here Konchalovsky painted a large portrait of the composer seated in an armchair against a background of trees and foliage. During this summer Prokofiev worked hard on the orchestration of the *Lieutenant Kije* suite. Even so, he found time for walks through the picturesque countryside. "He would rise very early," relates Konchalovsky, "and before morning coffee would disappear for a long time, taking his regular four or five kilometer walk. He was an excellent walker."

In the fall Prokofiev became excited about a new creative project; the Leningrad Theater of Opera and Ballet had suggested that he write a ballet on the theme of Shakespeare's *Romeo and Juliet*. The management of the Moscow Bolshoi Theater also became interested in this idea. Indeed, during that period many Soviet theaters competed in producing Shakespeare's plays: *Romeo and Juliet* was presented at the Theater of the Revolution, *Hamlet* at the Vakhtangov Theater, *Romeo and Juliet* and *Othello* at the S. Radlov Studio Theater, and *King Lear* at the Jewish State Theater.

Prokofiev's volatile imagination caught fire as it had in the best years of his youth. In the spring of 1935 he spent many hours with the director Radlov, carefully working out the scenario of the future ballet. Rough sketches of the musical themes and characterizations began to emerge, and at the end of May he showed them to Miaskovsky. Prokofiev waited impatiently for the summer, when he might devote himself entirely to the music for *Romeo and Juliet*.

Almost simultaneously with the new ballet, Prokofiev began to work on the Second Violin Concerto. During one of his visits to Paris, a group of French musicians had commissioned him to write a concert piece for their friend, the talented violinist Robert Soetens. By agreement, Soetens was to have exclusive performance rights to this music for a year after its première. First conceived as a concert sonata for violin and orchestra, this piece developed into the three-movement Violin Concerto, Op. 63. The main theme of the first movement was composed in Paris early in 1935, and the entire work was completed in the U.S.S.R. later that year during intervals between other compositions and concert appearances.

About two years after his return to the U.S.S.R., Prokofiev was joined by his wife and two sons, Sviatoslav and Oleg. By this time he was firmly established in the musical life of his homeland; his name was more and more frequently mentioned in the Soviet press, often in connection with the activities of the Union of Soviet Composers. In early 1935 he was one of the judges in a competition for the best work written for the Tenth Congress of the Young Communist League, and in the same year he himself participated in two similar contests—one for the best march for the All-Union Spartakiad, and another for the best mass song.

This was a brilliant period in the history of the Soviet song. The beautiful songs of Isaac Dunayevsky, Alexander Alexandrov, Lev Knipper, and Dimitri and Daniel Pokrass were just appearing and becoming popular. For the first time symphonic composers such as Miaskovsky, Shostakovich, and Anatole Alexandrov also began to write songs. And although most of their songs did not win wide popularity, they afforded their composers some good training in the contemporary melodic style. This was also true of Prokofiev. His writing of the mass song *Partisan Zheleznyak* only a year after the rationalistic music of *Thoughts* indicated a strong desire on his part to tackle new creative problems. The mass-song genre did not permit artificial experimentation; it called for clear and extremely logical melody in the popular idiom, a kind of writing against which Prokofiev had only recently rebelled.

In the summer of 1935 he wrote four mass songs for a song competition arranged by the newspaper *Pravda*: two of them, *My Country is Growing* and *Through Snow and Fog*, to words by the playwright A. Afinogenov (with whom he had become friendly while abroad); *Partisan Zheleznyak*, to a poem by Mikhail Golodny, published in *Pravda*; and *Anyutka*, to the words of a popular *chastushka*.*

The song competition of 1935 evoked a tremendous response. In addition to 120 professional composers, a whole army of amateurs participated. As a result of these efforts, about 4,500 lyrics and more than 2,000 musical compositions were submitted, including something like 400 different settings of the poem *Partisan Zheleznyak* alone. No first prize was awarded. Prokofiev's *Anyutka* won second prize, and *My Country is Growing* received an honorable mention.

All four of Prokofiev's songs are interesting, each in its own way. The most viable has proved to be *My Country is Growing,* the touching, lyrical reflection of a man taking leave of his departing youth. All around him Soviet construction is in full swing. People are working, growing older, and maturing; the young years are passing, leaving as a parting gift a "graying temple":

> Farewell, comrade youth.
> At this cross-road,
> Beloved, we'll part,
> As friends, you and I.
> Comrades, friends,
> We still are very young,
> We'll still be happy,
> Even tho' our temples are gray.

* TRANSLATOR'S NOTE: a *chastushka* is a two- or four-line folk verse, usually humorous and topical, sung in a lively manner.

Prokofiev based his song on the alternation of two contrasting melodies: the first and dominant one tinted with a cheerful smile, and the second one expressing serene sadness. The melodic writing reveals a love for the meaning of every line of the poem—hence the convincing repetition of words and phrases, the subtle changes of dynamics and tempo. Years later, in the 1950's, this charming song was given many successful performances by the singer Nina Dorliak in her concerts with the pianist Richter.

*Partisan Zheleznyak* and *Through Snow and Fog* are closer to the traditional style of the Soviet marching song. In *Partisan* we recognize the typical turns of a marching song in a minor key, with its expressive alternation of strong accents and rests; only the colorful harmonies reveal the composer's distinctive touch. *Through the Snow and Fog* is a compact dramatic ballad which tells of a skirmish between Far Eastern partisans and Japanese samurai. The form, unusual for a mass song, consists of three parts with a contrasting dramatic middle section. The rhythm is also unusual: a cumbersome, march-like triple meter in the first theme, followed by 6/8 in the second. At the climax of the middle section the even flow of the song is interrupted by lines of expressive recitative over a purely descriptive accompaniment. Both songs contain some interesting features, even though the composer's individuality is not very apparent in them.

Prokofiev's distinctive style is more evident in the song *Anyutka,* the humor of which he underscored by characteristic accents, amusing exclamations, and repeated musical phrases. Nevertheless, this song has a rather stylized character. Although he used a *chastushka* text, the composer unfortunately ignored the melodic wealth of the modern Russian *chastushka,* with the result that *Anyutka* has the quality of a village song of earlier years.

Though these songs (like those of Prokofiev's later years) were no match for the best Soviet songs and did not become part of the popular repertory, nevertheless the composer gained valuable experience in the writing of them.

During this same year (1935) Prokofiev also composed the *March for the Spartakiad,* his first work for brass band. As we know, he had been interested in sports since the days when he attended the gymnastic drills at the Sokol society. In 1910 the St. Petersburg critics had talked interminably about the "athletic" character of the First Piano Concerto. Now Prokofiev envisaged millions of Soviet athletes for whom he could compose a spirited, festive march. He was completely successful. The march was truly "youthful"—buoyant, gay, and lively. The basic march melody—

triumphant and exhilarating—contrasts well with the tuneful alternate melodies in the Russian national vein. Save for some harsh chords in the cadences, the harmonies are bright and firm throughout. The march is in a complicated and original three-part form, with each section built on the principle of a rondo.

The Soviet musicologist V. Zuckermann warmly praised this work. "The march belongs to that category of Prokofiev's works," he wrote, "in which, while using a popular idiom, he does not sacrifice those elements of his individual style which are so dear to him, particularly his characteristic pungency."[13] Moreover, this critic took note of the march's clearcut form, with its exact reprise. "In this," he added, "one also senses something typically Prokofievan (if you violate principles, violate them completely; if you follow them, follow them exactly)." It is regrettable that this excellent work is seldom played on the radio and is not utilized at our sports festivals.

Prokofiev spent part of the summer of 1935 at a rest home in Polenovo, near Tarusa in the wonderful Oka country. The modest landscape of central Russia was conducive to inspired work, and in Polenovo were written *Romeo and Juliet*, the small piano pieces later entitled *Music for Children*, and parts of the Second Violin Concerto. "I've now been here two weeks," Prokofiev wrote to Moscow on July 14. "I'm taking full advantage of the quiet of my secluded little house, and I'm working at top speed. I'm very eager to finish off Juliet and the concerto as soon as possible." Indeed, the work progressed very rapidly. By the end of July he reported, "Juliet is tripping through the third act."

Such rapid progress was made possible by the composer's meticulous preliminary planning of all the details in the ballet and his preparation of musical themes and sketches. The procedures he had followed in Paris when he wrote the ballets *Trapeze* and *Sur le Borysthène* now seemed ridiculous to him. Music for the theater must be written on the basis of concrete subject matter, not according to abstract "emotional schemes."

"When I am asked to write music for a play or film, I rarely consent immediately, even if I know the text of the work, for it takes me from five to ten days to 'see' it, that is, to visualize the characters, their emotions, and their actions in terms of music," he wrote in 1936. "While I am thinking it over, the main themes usually begin to take shape."[14] This is precisely the manner in which Prokofiev worked on *Romeo and Juliet*. And the finished composition showed him to be not merely a designer of music for hastily contrived ballet plots, but a true musician-dramatist.

Prokofiev's scenario for the ballet *Romeo and Juliet* shows how carefully he read Shakespeare and how deeply he thought through every nuance of the protagonists' thoughts and feelings. Here are some of his notes for the scenario: The ball at the Capulets': "Juliet dances with Paris stiffly and perfunctorily. Romeo watches her admiringly . . . Madrigal. Romeo, loving; Juliet, playful. Romeo more passionate than before. Juliet again playful. Together, tender. Juliet frees herself and runs away playfully." The heroine's visit to Friar Laurence's cell. "Laurence admits Juliet, dressed in pure white, the personification of virginity." The encounter between Tybalt and Mercutio: "They look at each other like bulls, their blood boils." The duel between Romeo and Tybalt: "unlike the duel between Tybalt and Mercutio, in which the antagonists were not aware of the seriousness of the situation and fought from pique, here Romeo and Tybalt fight furiously, to the death." Juliet's bedroom, the lovers' farewell: "To evade the ticklishness of the situation, the composer has tried to make the music pure, transparent." The introduction to Act III: "Music recalling the Duke's power over Romeo's fate." Regarding the orchestration of Act III, the composer writes: "Unlike the preceding act, which took place in the square, the third act is laid indoors. Therefore the scoring of the music is more chamber-like in style." Notes of this kind indicate how profoundly Prokofiev pondered all the complexities of the tragedy he was translating into music.

The second act of the ballet was completed in piano score on July 22, the third act on August 29, and the entire work on September 8. In 1939, while the ballet was in production, the composer added several important numbers to the original version.[15]

Early in October, the music of *Romeo and Juliet* was given its first performance in the Beethoven Hall of the Bolshoi Theater. Commenting on it, the newspaper *Izvestia* spoke favorably of Prokofiev's "new realistic language." However, a controversy immediately developed over the plans of the librettists and choreographer to add a happy ending to Shakespeare's tragedy: Juliet was to be restored to life, and the ballet was to end with a joyous dance of the lovers. Most of the critics flatly opposed such a distortion of a classical work, and the play's original ending was restored.

The ballet was not accepted for production immediately. Many people in the theater considered the music so complex as to be virtually incompatible with the requirements of the dance. "There is no tale of greater woe than Prokofiev's music for *Romeo*," one listener remarked.[16] It was not until the 1939–40 season, after the music had been enthusiastically received by the public at symphonic and chamber concerts (in the form of two orchestral suites and a set of piano pieces), that the ballet was produced successfully at the Kirov Theater in Leningrad. In December 1946, it was finally presented at the Moscow Bolshoi Theater, adding luster to an already brilliant ballet repertory.

While at Polenovo, Prokofiev found relief from the psychological complexities of the ballet in sketching the twelve small piano pieces which comprise the collection *Music for Children* (Op. 65). Like the children's pieces of Schumann and Tchaikovsky, these were given titles relating to childhood impressions and experiences. There were summer landscapes (*Morning, Rain and Rainbow, Evening, Moonlit Meadows*); fantastic vignettes (*Fairy Tale, Parade of the Grasshoppers*); little scenes from the everyday life of a child (*Walk, Tag, Repentance*); and finally, dance pieces (*Waltz, March, Tarantella*). "My old love for the sonatina style reawakened," the composer recalls.

These little pieces are striking for their clear and expressive melodies, which are free of surface exaggeration. The best of them—the lyrical sketches *Morning, Evening, Repentance,* and *Waltz*—closely resemble the traditional types of children's music. Listening to the pensive melody of the second section of *Morning,* or to *Evening,* with its serene Russian lyricism, or to the touching and plaintive phrases of *Repentance,* one can clearly see that Prokofiev here achieved that essentially melodic kind of writing which only masters of the realistic method can achieve. These little pieces also reveal the typical features of Prokofiev's piano style: the skips and hand-crossings (in *Morning, Walk,* and *Fairy Tales*); amusing harmonic combinations (in *Rain and Rainbow*); and organ points and *ostinato* figures. All these, employed in a form accessible to children, enhance the pictorial imagery. It is also interesting to note both the Russian folk-song character of the best pieces and the realistic quality of the landscape episodes, which seem to have been sketched from nature. According to Prokofiev, the last piece, *Moonlit Meadows,* was inspired by a nocturnal landscape at Polenovo.

In contrast to the abstract outlines of *Landscape* (one of the three pieces of Op. 59), these little scenes from nature are charming for their genuine poetic quality and almost tangible concreteness. No technical tricks could possibly simulate such pure and artless spontaneity of perception; it is as if the wonderful purity of feeling that once marked the little Sontsovka boy, who composed birthday *Ditties,* had come to life again.

After the twelve pieces of Op. 65, Prokofiev went on to create a whole series of remarkable works for Soviet children. It was not long before hundreds of children in the music schools of the Soviet Union were playing the *March, Waltz, Fairy Tale,* and other pieces. The composer himself returned more than once to these pieces. For example, he used seven of them (*Morning, Tag, Waltz, Repentance, March, Evening,* and *Moonlit Meadows*) in a symphonic suite entitled *Summer Day,* Op. 65-bis. The scoring gave the music a rather heavy quality, however. *Waltz* and *Evening* were used in *The Stone Flower,* the theme of *Evening* becoming one of the most important lyrical leitmotivs of the ballet.

The Second Violin Concerto (Op. 63) was finished at about the same time as *Romeo and Juliet.* In its lyrical passages, it bears a close resemblance to the ballet. In May 1935, after hearing the sketches of the Concerto, Miaskovsky wrote in his diary, "Superb!" Part of this work was written while the composer was on tour; besides Polenovo, one part is marked Paris, another Voronezh, and a fourth Baku. The score was finally completed in Baku, the capital of Azerbaijan, in August of 1935.

According to the previous agreement, the new work was given to the violinist Robert Soetens, with whom Prokofiev made a concert tour in the winter of 1935–36, visiting Spain, Portugal, Morocco, Algeria, and Tunisia. Besides Prokofiev's pieces, they performed sonatas by Beethoven and Debussy.

The trip to Spain made a deep impression on Prokofiev. The country was then in the throes of a mighty revolutionary upsurge—it was the eve of the historic victory of the Republican People's Front. The composer crisscrossed the entire country. He was delighted with the love of music shown by the people of Madrid, Barcelona, and St. Sebastian, and he was deeply affected by their warm interest in the Soviet Union and its new culture. "Wherever I played," he recalls, "after every concert, whether in a café or during supper in a restaurant, they would ask me thousands of questions about the Soviet Union, about Soviet music. The Spaniards were particularly interested to hear about our unions of creative artists, composers' contracts, and the centralization of our concert institutions and orchestras." Prokofiev's performances in Madrid were the occasion for vehement demonstrations in honor of the Soviet Union. "When I came out on the stage, the orchestra and entire audience stood up and hailed me as a Soviet artist visiting Spain."[17]

The first performance of the Second Violin Concerto was given in revolutionary Madrid on December 1, 1935. The Spaniards were very proud of the fact that the première was held in their capital, and a special delegation visited Prokofiev to express their gratitude to him.

Together with *Romeo and Juliet,* the Second Violin Concerto marks an important turning point in Prokofiev's creative activity. It was significant that he should return, after so many years, to writing for the solo violin; seemingly convinced of the utter futility of formalist experimentation, he renewed his youthful striving to express genuine human emotions, choosing for this effort one of the most singing of all musical instruments.

The Second Violin Concerto is more serious, more philosophical than the First, which was written twenty years before. Here we no longer find those mocking, grotesque effects which had so astonished listeners in the development section of the first movement and, particularly, in the Scherzo of the First Concerto. There are fewer harsh timbres and harmonies, and a more restrained and gentle play of tone colors. The Second Concerto is written in a simpler, more intimate style, which is not surprising, since the composer had originally planned it as a sonata. The virtuoso writing is also more modest, containing fewer unusual technical innovations, even though this time the composer did use some very complicated technical figurations with biting accents.

As we know, the First Concerto was built on a closed three-movement form, with a pensive opening movement, a lively scherzo in the middle, and a lyrical finale. In the Second Concerto the images are presented in a different sequence, proceeding from profound meditation and romantic outbursts in the first two movements to a colorful dance-like motion in the finale.

What is new in the Second Concerto is a clearly expressed Russian national flavor, especially evident in the main theme of the first movement, and a more noticeable connection with classical antecedents, which can be heard, for instance, in the echoes of Beethoven and Brahms in the contemplative Andante. Typical of the composer's classical tendencies is the rich use of polyphony, the beautiful imitation in the dialogue between the violin and orchestra.

The two themes of the first movement are appealing in their loftiness of feeling and breadth of melodic line. Though similar, each has its own distinctive character. The main theme, stated first by the unaccompanied solo violin, is reminiscent of a flowing, meditative Russian song. This impression is created not only by the pattern of the melody but also by the inner variation in the melodic line, which is accomplished by a shifting of the strong beats. This music evokes an image of the snow-covered plains of Russia, and immediately suggests parallels with certain themes of Moussorgsky and Tchaikovsky (in the latter's First Symphony, "Winter Day-dreams"). But the free tonal shifts and subtle modulations at once betray Prokofiev's hand. The second theme, in B-flat major, evokes a different image; its delicate modulations and broad intervals giving way to sensuous chromatic turns endow it with traces of the passionate romanticism found in the love themes of *Romeo and Juliet*. This second theme is one of the mature Prokofiev's most felicitous melodic revelations (Fig. 32).

FIGURE 32

In the bridge passage, at the conclusion of the exposition, and again in the development section, the two principal themes are interwoven with colorful passages and sustained in a light and playful manner.

The tranquil second movement, permeated with a feeling of happy communion with nature, would have been unusual in Prokofiev's early works. The singing theme of the violin, which emerges over a triplet figure as in Beethoven's *Moonlight Sonata,* recalls the contemplative melodies of a classical Andante. This movement is developed in a classical manner, with strict variation technique, beautiful ornamentation, and polyphonic interweaving of simultaneously flowing melodic lines. The charming middle section is tenderly pensive, in the style of Prokofiev's earlier lyricism.

Only in the rhythmically resilient music of the finale (*Allegro ben marcato*) does the long pent-up force of Prokofiev's stormy temperament burst forth. The rich triads of the violin's basic dance theme are ponderous and cumbersome, their strong beats sharply emphasized. The fiery motion of this rather coarsely accented, triple-beat dance continues throughout almost the entire finale. The more melodious second theme and the agitated, sad theme of the middle episode, both sandwiched in between the lively scherzo-like passages, provide a contrast to the prevailing dance theme. In the recapitulation the principal dance theme becomes even more energetic and vigorous. The composer seasons it with a fairly good dose of harmonic "pepper" in the form of harsh-sounding chordal superimpositions.[18] All this endows the conclusion with aspects of a wild and turbulent bacchanal.

The Second Violin Concerto is similar in many respects to *Romeo and Juliet*. The lyricism of the concerto's first two movements is closely related to the lofty emotions of the love Adagios, and in its finale one seems to hear the defiant laughter of Mercutio and echoes of the gay carnival festivities.

A year after its première in Madrid, the Second Violin Concerto was played in Moscow by B. Fischmann. In 1937 it was performed in the United States by Jascha Heifetz, who recorded it; David Oistrakh took a great liking to it and played it widely in the U.S.S.R.

While the fate of *Romeo and Juliet* and the Second Violin Concerto were being decided, Prokofiev was already immersed in a very complex new project. On a commission from the All-Union Radio Committee he was preparing the monumental *Cantata for the Twentieth Anniversary of the October Revolution*.

❦   ❦   ❦

> *Shakespeare's* ROMEO! *Mon dieu,*
> *what a subject! Everything in it*
> *seems designed for music.*
>
> Berlioz

The writing of *Romeo and Juliet* marked a truly "revolutionary leap" in Prokofiev's artistic development, a leap from cold experimentalism to a consistent affirmation of realism. Never before had the composer achieved such a truthful portrayal of life in all its diversity, such a profound communication of humanist ideas. Here we find no trace of surface inventiveness, grotesquerie, or expressionistic hyperbole, and none of the anemic, intellectual abstractions of his Paris period. The music recreates with extraordinary power and compassion the transports, passions, and dramatic conflicts of Shakespeare's immortal characters. The form of the work is characteristically fresh and original, but dramatic and musical innovations are subordinated throughout to an expressive unfolding of the story.

To many people, the thought of putting Shakespeare's great tragedy on the ballet stage seemed little less than blasphemous; it would be impossible, they thought, to express the subtle psychological nuances, the entire range of feelings expressed in the tragedy, without the power of the poetic word.

History seemed to support this opinion, for although many attempts had been made, no ballet representation of Shakespeare had ever achieved a greatness commensurate with the play upon which it was based. There had been a production of *Othello* by the Milanese choreographer Salvatore Vigano at the beginning of the nineteenth century. Even earlier, in Venice, ballets had been staged on the themes of *Hamlet, A Midsummer Night's Dream,* and *Macbeth.* But in all of these presentations the music was of the trite, "divertissement" variety, and the only relation to Shakespeare's original plays was a superficial adherence to the plot. In the ballet on *Romeo and Juliet* performed in Copenhagen in 1811 with music by Schall, the plot was so simplified that the theme of the enmity between the Montagues and Capulets was omitted entirely. Equally abortive was the attempt by the English composer Constant Lambert to create a ballet on this subject in the 1920's. This version portrayed the backstage life of English actors during a production of *Romeo and Juliet.* According to Asafyev, Lambert's music is "watery, and at times sounds like a poor imitation of Stravinsky's *Pulcinella.*"[19]

While history has not left us a single ballet classic based on one of Shakespeare's plays, magnificent operas and symphonic works have been composed on them, and particularly on *Romeo and Juliet.* Even today audiences throughout the world thrill to Tchaikovsky's Fantasy Overture *Romeo and Juliet* and Berlioz' dramatic symphony with chorus on the same subject. In the history of music there have been fourteen different operas based on *Romeo and Juliet,* among them the inspired one by Gounod, which is performed on the Soviet stage. Thus, in turning to *Romeo and Juliet,* Prokofiev faced the challenge of past failures by ballet composers and great achievements by illustrious composers of symphonies and operas. Nevertheless, he succeeded in meeting the challenge, approaching Shakespeare from a contemporary point of view.

The composer's erstwhile opponents, who had regarded him only as a crude violator of academic standards, would never have believed him capable of handling so lofty a theme. "To each his own," the critic V. Kolomyitsev had written in 1916. "To one it is given to sing of the love of Romeo and Juliet, to another to depict the frenzied screeches and comical capers of monkeys," he wrote, referring to the shrill timbres of the *Scythian Suite*. And now, twenty years later, the incredible had happened: the "boor" Prokofiev sang with true poetry of the love of Romeo and Juliet. This was done under new conditions, after the composer had joined his fate with the humanist Soviet culture.

*Romeo and Juliet* presents a striking contrast to the ballets Prokofiev composed in Paris. When he wrote *The Prodigal Son* and, especially, *Sur le Borysthène,* he had no vital material to fire his imagination, nothing to stimulate his talents for portraiture, dramaturgy, and poetry. How could the incorporeal characters of *The Prodigal Son* stir his imagination when they lacked not only dramatic characterization but even names? Perhaps even more constricting was the method arranged for working on *Sur le Borysthène,* which amounted to providing a musical accompaniment for an entire ballet which had neither plot nor characters.

Unlike Prokofiev's Paris ballets, *Romeo and Juliet* was conceived as a richly developed choreographic drama replete with clearly defined musical portraits, vividly realistic scenes, and psychologically motivated action.

The scenario recreates the Shakespearean tragedy concisely and convincingly, retaining all of its principal characters and presenting the scenes in their original sequence. Owing to the particular requirements of ballet dramaturgy, however, the play had to be abridged, and accordingly, certain scenes and episodes were omitted, among them the ones presenting Romeo's love for Rosaline and his duel with Paris in the churchyard. At the same time the creators of the ballet skillfully expanded other aspects of the drama that lent themselves to choreographic treatment. For example, most of Act II takes place against a background of the merrymaking and street dancing of a folk festival. This lively action, lacking in Shakespeare's play, serves to heighten the contrast between the gaiety of the crowd and the bloody events that follow. The episode following Juliet's drinking of the sleeping potion is ingeniously worked out: at this point, a transparent "Morning Serenade" and graceful "Dance of the Young Girls with the Lilies" to relieve the psychological tension of Juliet's solo scene. A true sense of the theater is also evident in the climactic scene of Act II—Mercutio's death and the funeral cortege bearing Tybalt's corpse—which was also an original addition to Shakespeare's plot.

These examples demonstrate the special nature of musical dramaturgy, which precludes any exact reproduction of a literary text on the stage. It was no accident that precisely those episodes which the authors read creatively and worked out in terms of their particular art form proved to be the most stageworthy and the most effective. This is especially evident in the finale of Act II.

Prokofiev drew the musical portraits of the leading characters, especially Juliet, with the sensitivity of a true realistic dramatist. For example, in interpreting Shakespeare's portrait of the heroine, he added a new dimension to the mischievous little girl ("lamb," as her family called her) by subtly depicting the first stirring of her love. This serves to heighten still more the dramatic intensity of the later scenes. Equally perceptive was the composer's delineation of the important character Friar Laurence, the scholar, humanist, and protector of the lovers. In this characterization there is neither churchly sanctity nor mystical remoteness; the music underscores the Friar's wisdom, spiritual nobility, and kindly love of people. The musical portrait of Romeo corresponds completely to Shakespeare's conception of the hero, seized at first with romantic yearning and later displaying the flaming passion of a lover and the valor of a warrior.

Prokofiev correctly realized that *Romeo and Juliet,* more than any other of Shakespeare's tragedies, contains comic elements. Punctuating the woeful progress of events in the tragic love story are Mercutio's mirthful escapades, the Nurse's rather coarse jests, and other examples of Shakespeare's salty, plebeian humor. This side of Shakespeare was in close harmony with the temperament of a composer who had always shown a penchant for the humorous. One might venture to say that not one of the composers who had previously interpreted the theme of Romeo and Juliet caught and expressed so well the tragedy's light and playful moments, the aspect that endows it with fresh contrasts and sharply defined chiaroscuro effects.

This lighter side of the play is given a particularly rich and buoyant ring in the first two acts of the ballet, which present the merrymaking in Verona's streets, the Masker's dance, Juliet's amusing pranks, and the droll, swagging, old-womanish theme of the Nurse. And finally, there is the most typical personification of Prokofiev's humor—the gay, lighthearted Mercutio. His musical portrait, drawn in two or three well-developed thematic episodes, is charming for the richness of its melodies, the jauntiness of its rhythms, and the sweep of its emotional range, from merry taunting to pugnacious braggadocio. Mercutio's principal theme (in A-flat major) is all motion, a gay shifting of accents and leaps. Listening to this music, one can almost see the figure of the scrapper and scoffer and hear his ringing laughter.

The musical portrait of Mercutio calls to mind Truffaldino in *The Love for Three Oranges* as well as many nameless characters of Prokofiev's instrumental scherzos. But in the ballet the element of mockery takes a greater variety of forms and is much more vividly and sharply outlined. To realize this, one need only recall one of the ballet's most gripping scenes —the duel between Mercutio and Tybalt, with Mercutio's tragic death. Here one of Mercutio's rollicking themes (from the Masker's dance) acquires somber, morbid overtones, as though the last bitter jests were falling from his dying lips. In this scene Prokofiev showed himself to be a true musical dramatist, capable of treating themes boldly to fit the action.

In striking contrast to the merry world of youthful pranks is the second most important element in the dramatic development of the ballet—the bitter enmity between the Montagues and Capulets, the blind hatred and medieval bigotry which drive Romeo and Juliet to their tragic end. We often encounter contrasts between exuberant humor and expressive tragedy in Prokofiev's instrumental works, but here the contrast is justified by the real clash of conflicting forces in the drama. The theme of feudal strife is presented in the sharply defined and energetic "motiv of enmity," expressed in a terrifying unison of the basses; in the heavy "Dance of the Knights," with its incisive rhythms; in the musical portrait of Tybalt, the personification of evil, arrogance, and class haughtiness; in the swift-moving, tensely dramatic episodes of the skirmishes and duels (Acts I and III); and in the ominous sonorities of the Duke's theme, constructed on harsh, lifeless chords in the brasses.

The forces inimical to the love of Romeo and Juliet are presented in a variety of ways: in genre-dance episodes which reproduce the solemn ceremony of aristocratic life ("Dance of the Knights"); in the vividly descriptive passages which accompany the bloody skirmishes; and finally, in the more abstract themes symbolizing the cruelty of fate.

In the dramatic climaxes of Acts I and III the masterfully developed themes are so convincingly combined with the unfolding events that life itself, in the full complexity of its passions and actions, seems recreated before the viewer-listener. Few composers have achieved in music alone, without the aid of a sung or spoken libretto, so concrete and realistic an embodiment of life.

But it is neither the spirit of playful jesting, of masquerades and merry pranks, nor the motif of the family feud which constitutes the main theme of this amazing choreographic poem. For the first time in a major stage work by Prokofiev, the dominant theme is a lyrical one, the theme of a lofty and noble love victorious even in death. Never before had the composer succeeded in treating a lyrical theme so profoundly, so seriously; never before had he handled such a theme without subjecting it, at some point, to grotesque or decadently complex distortion. This is why *Romeo and Juliet* holds a place of particular significance in Prokofiev's creative development. It is in this work that the inspired images of human feeling and romantic passion which the young Prokofiev had so often shied away from, which he had tried to smother with buffoonery or intense expressiveness, finally flowered in a profusion of emotional colors.

The composer portrayed the emotions of the young lovers with unusual lavishness. More than ten themes, most of them developed and richly melodic, convey the various nuances of their feelings—the first vague awakening of love, the shy and gentle smiles of the first rendezvous, the fiery passion, and the bitter sorrow of parting. Particularly rich and full is the portrayal of Juliet, who gradually develops, before the very eyes of the audience, from a carefree, playful young girl into a strong, selfless, and loving woman. Three alternating themes appear in "Juliet— The Little Girl": the first two are markedly dance-like and filled with mischievous action; while the third, which announces the first stirrings of emotion, is pensive, timid, and lyrical. Typically, this third theme is in Prokofiev's favorite diatonic harmony, "on the white keys." Also characteristic is the way in which many of the lyrical themes are entrusted to the tender tones of the solo flute in the high, "celestial" register with very thin melodic support. Timbre, register, texture, and free, pensive rhythm— everything here is subordinated to the dramatist's aim of drawing a tender, soulful portrait of a girl.

Of an entirely different character are the themes representing the growth of mature passion. Here the pure diatonic style gives way to a complicated alternation of subtly chromatic progressions and broad, singing passages. These themes are colored by rich harmonic effects: beautiful modulations into distant keys, and subtle, unusual suspensions and passing tones. These characteristics can be easily recognized in the richly colored theme of Romeo's passion or in the principal "theme of love" with its characteristic use of descending sixths (Fig. 33).

In these themes the timbres are thicker and darker, the rhythms more

FIGURE 33

pulsating and agitated (as in the particular love theme of Romeo's which is constructed on a nervous, throbbing rhythm).

The musical dramaturgy of *Romeo and Juliet* is very interesting, especially for the method of symphonic development the composer employed. The ballet contains almost no inserted illustrative dance numbers. Virtually the only set dances in the entire score are the street dances in the first and second acts, the elegant ballroom dances in the first act, and the sad, graceful "Dance of the Young Girls with the Lilies" in the last act.

After having rejected the use of genre elements for so many years, Prokofiev now returned to traditional dance forms. The strikingly original treatment of these dances makes them live in one's memory: the fast tarantella, the spirited "Dance with the Mandolins," the slow, exquisite "Dance of the Young Girls with the Lilies," and the rather ponderous minuet. At the end of Act II, the composer presents a new version of his own D major gavotte from the *Classical Symphony,* as if to declare a return to his old classical tendencies. But these dances are in no way related to the traditional divertissement type of dance number; each one is an integral part of the drama, supplying the realistic background for specific parts of the play.

The remaining music either portrays characters or depicts specific moments of stage action in a series of freely constructed episodes of either a descriptive or psychological nature. This music, developed according to symphonic principles, is designed for the complex alternation of mimed action and dramatically expressive dance. This alternation of pantomime and dance bears some resemblance to the musical fabric of Prokofiev's operas, in which freely developed declamation alternates with melodically rounded-out passages. But whereas the recitatives in his early operas were often deliberately prosaic and melodically spare, in *Romeo and Juliet* all the music accompanying mimed scenes is rich in expressive melody—as in such lifelike episodes as the betrothal in Laurence's cell or the scene of Mercutio's death.

Leitmotivs describing the heroes or their emotions are widely used in the ballet. These are not brief, abstract germ melodies but, for the most part, fully developed episodes, which sometimes constitute independent parts of the entire musical form. Take Romeo and Juliet's "theme of love," for example, a broad, flowing theme, bright and full of hope. This, the principal musical theme of the ballet, appears many times, in either full or fragmentary form. There are also the sinister, ponderous theme of death, somberly intoned by the tuba and contrabasses, and the despondent theme of doom.

Far from being used in any restricted way, fastened like labels on the characters, these leitmotivs are developed with the degree of generalization which is characteristic of symphonic thought. They are freely treated, at one moment portraying a hero, and at another expressing an emotional or dramatic idea. Thus, one of Juliet's themes sounds at one moment like a theme of amorous yearning, and at another like a portent of doom; Mercutio's leitmotiv becomes a theme of merriment and youthful challenge; the theme of the obdurate, swaggering Capulets symbolizes the brute forces of enmity and hatred which stand in the way of the lovers' happiness. The supercharged music depicting the clash between the Montagues and Capulets in the first act is repeated almost in its entirety in the scene of the duel between Romeo and Tybalt. This treatment of the themes underscores the dramatic connection of events and contributes to the musical unity of the work. In a number of the climactic scenes the leitmotivs are radically altered. For example, the theme of Juliet as a young girl, the theme of the knights, and Mercutio's theme are all broadly developed, dramatized, and intensified. Here the composer used the proven methods of symphonic thematic development.

The mature Prokofiev's most typical stylistic devices appear here in all their diversity. His harmonic language is classically clear and spare in the lyrical scenes, but abounds in dissonance in the scenes depicting the bloody skirmishes and the terror of the crowd. A similar contrast is found in his orchestration, which is sometimes transparent, reduced to the thin line of a flowing solo melody and the most delicate, silvery tints (flute solo, violins *concertante*), and at other times harshly expressive, characterized by bold, poster-like strokes or a daring interweaving of the thick and strident voices of the orchestra. Pure texture and clearly defined melodies supported by simple accompaniments prevail in the music, however.

The charm of Prokofiev's melodic inventiveness increases with each new hearing of this music. Classically symmetrical lines are combined here with the twists and turns so distinctly the composer's own. Prokofiev's heightening of the melodic element may at first seem odd to the listener unfamiliar with it; after the exquisitely passionate chromaticism of the love themes of Liszt and Wagner, the extreme economy of this lyricism (its simple two- or three-part writing and spare harmonic backgrounds) could at first seem somewhat cold and passionless. But as one grows accustomed to this music, its poetic quality and the depth of emotion it expresses become clear. However, as several writers pointed out after its first performance, certain aspects of the ballet's musical construction are open to criticism.[20] For example, the use of a montage technique in treating the leitmotivs and episodes often leads to a mechanical transference of the same themes from one scene to another. As a result, there is almost no new music in the last four scenes; this somewhat weakens the dramatic tension in the final scenes, in which most of the music sounds like an echo, or sometimes even an enfeebled repetition, of what has gone before.

In this ballet Prokofiev refrained almost completely from using local and historical elements to describe sixteenth-century Italy. This self-imposed limitation demonstrated the wisdom of the composer, whose primary aim was not to present an exotic and colorful picture of Renaissance life, but rather to communicate the principal ideas of Shakespeare's tragedy.

The composer might have chosen another, more tempting method: he might have strung together, in divertissement fashion, a succession of Italian folk dances (tarantellas, saltarellos, etc.) or even literally resurrected sarabandes, pavannes, and other old aristocratic dances. But this method, so widespread in ballet dramaturgy, would have diverted him from his lofty poetic conception and led him into the realm of surface description. Only in the tarantella rhythms of the "Folk Dance," which opens the second act, are there echoes of an authentic Italian dance. Except for this, Prokofiev—as always, brilliantly original—proceeded from his own conception of Shakespeare's play. As for the pictorial representation of life in Renaissance Verona, this task he left to the *régisseur* and scenic designer. It is interesting to note that in certain passages Prokofiev's music has a somewhat Russian flavor, as do the program works of Tchaikovsky which were inspired by Western literary classics (the lyrical theme of his *Francesca da Rimini,* for example). And this is natural, for the great Russian artist perceived and interpreted in his own way the images of Shakespeare's great classic.

# NINE

# EFFLORESCENCE

*It was meet that we should make merry,
and be glad: for this thy brother was
dead, and is alive again; and was lost,
and is found.*

THE PARABLE OF THE PRODIGAL SON

Y THE BEGINNING of 1936 a complicated situation had developed in
Soviet music. The four years that followed the dissolution of the
Russian Association of Proletarian Musicians and the formation of
the Union of Soviet Composers had been fruitful ones, marked by intensive
creative work and some interesting and daring efforts at musical realism.
Nevertheless, even under the new Soviet conditions the struggle between
artistic schools which had begun in the twenties had not ceased.

On one hand, the trend toward a new realism had grown markedly
stronger. Some beautiful patriotic songs were written. The repertory of
the musical theaters was enriched by such operas as I. Dzerzhinsky's *Quiet
Flows the Don* and V. Zhelobinsky's *Kamarinsky Peasant,* and by Asafyev's
ballets *The Flame of Paris* and *The Fountain of Bakhchisarai.* These
works clearly showed the determined effort of their composers to master
and carry forward the realistic traditions of the classics.

During this period composers also began to collaborate actively with
film producers. Among the brilliant examples of film music produced
were Shcherbachev's score for *Thunderstorm,* Shostakovich's for *The
Golden Mountains* and *The Encounter,* Prokofiev's for *Lieutenant Kije,*
Kabalevsky's for *St. Petersburg Night,* and Dunayevsky's songs for popular comedies.

An earnest desire to imbue the musical language with honest emotion
and national character began to manifest itself in the symphonic genre.

Eloquent examples of this are Miaskovsky's Fourteenth, Fifteenth, and Sixteenth Symphonies, Khachaturian's First Symphony and Piano Concerto, and Kabalevsky's Second Symphony and Second Piano Concerto.

On the other hand, modernistic tendencies were still strong, and with the encouragement of some critics, they were even becoming quite assertive. Modernism in Soviet music was a stubborn and persistent malady. The spurious notions that classical traditions were antiquated, that a "formalistic technical rearmament" along modernistic lines was necessary, continued to poison the thinking of many musicians. Typical results of these misconceptions included G. Popov's First Symphony, Shostakovich's Fourth Symphony, and V. Shebalin's Third Symphony, the "Lenin."

Opposing tendencies, seemingly mutually exclusive, sometimes appeared even in the works of the same composer; for examples of this we need only compare Miaskovsky's Thirteenth and Fourteenth Symphonies, composed almost simultaneously, or Shostakovich's *Lady Macbeth of Mtsensk* and his film music. As we know, Prokofiev's music also contained traces of dualism. Unfortunately, the new works (such as *Romeo and Juliet* and the Second Violin Concerto) which gave evidence of a change in his artistic thinking were not at once widely played, while those of the critical Paris period were often performed. But as the works of 1934–35 clearly demonstrate, Prokofiev was gradually recovering from his artistic crisis; he had planted both feet firmly on Soviet soil and had begun working mainly in the realistic spirit of Soviet music.

The healthy tendencies in Prokofiev, which were in complete accord with the life around him, found further encouragement in certain memorable statements against formalism and naturalism made by Soviet art critics in February 1936.

Naturally during the years when socialist culture was advancing, when more and more workers and peasants were beginning to enjoy the treasures of mankind's cultural heritage, it was quite impossible to accept the modernistic distortions which appeared now and then in music, poetry, painting, and architecture. These distortions could only seem offensive and incomprehensible anachronisms in the pure and beautiful world which the Soviet people were creating. Early in 1936, *Pravda* printed two articles ("Confusion Instead of Music" and "Ballet Counterfeit") which provoked a sharp and widespread discussion of formalism and soon initiated a public movement against the remnants of decadence in various branches of Soviet art.

The editorial articles in *Pravda* against decadent influences in music, the ensuing statements by leading musicians, writers, and artists, the severe criticism of the work of such modernist *régisseurs* as Meyerhold and Tairov —all this could not but have exerted the most serious influence on Prokofiev's creative thinking. After the almost continuous praise of modernist critics, who had urged him on to bolder and bolder excesses, the composer for the first time heard stern voices raised against formalism and in defense of the realist principles of music. After studying the newspaper and magazine articles, he carefully played through the score of the opera *Lady Macbeth of Mtsensk* in an effort to clarify and judge for himself the nature of Shostakovich's errors.

Of course, Prokofiev did not accept unreservedly all the articles and speeches denouncing musical formalism. ("Formalism is sometimes the name given here to that which is not understood on first hearing," he said.) But he did become more deeply aware of the need for clear, meaningful, and beautiful music, music which would embody the noble artistic ideals bequeathed to him by his teachers. Later, surveying the path he had traveled, Prokofiev emphasized that the *Pravda* articles of 1936 had helped him to define his own aesthetic views more clearly. "After *Pravda*'s exposure of the formalistic mistakes in Shostakovich's opera," he recalled, "I thought a great deal about my own creative methods and arrived at the conclusion that such a path was incorrect. This led me to search for a clearer and more deeply meaningful language."[1]

The evolution of Prokofiev's thought was accelerated by personal meetings with several outstanding leaders of Soviet culture. Of particular interest is his last talk with Gorky, which the composer recorded in one of his notes: "I asked him what kind of music one should write now. 'You ought to know that yourself,' Alexei Maximovich replied, smiling. 'Everyone says that our music ought to be cheerful and vigorous to match our new life,' I said. 'But it must also be warm and tender,' Alexei Maximovich added."

Prokofiev gave a great deal of thought to what music ought to be like in the country of socialism. In his articles and notes of 1936–37 he more than once wrote of his striving for clarity and melodiousness, at the same time deploring the tendency of some composers to use unnecessarily difficult, "trans-sense" language and the willingness of others to pander to "vulgar" tastes.

❋ ❋ ❋

On returning to Moscow after his tour of Spain and North Africa, Prokofiev once more devoted himself to composing. During this period he worked on songs to texts by Pushkin, several pieces and songs for children, a large symphonic overture on Russian themes, and music for new theatrical productions.

In the summer of 1936 Prokofiev and his family moved into a new apartment on Zemlyanoi Val (later Chkalov Street). After the many years of wandering in foreign lands, of living in hotels and chance apartments, the composer finally found himself settled, and in an atmosphere conducive to a consistently creative life. His relations with concert organizations, theaters, directors, poets, and librettists now became more firmly established. As before, his old friends—Miaskovsky, P. A. Lamm, Derzhanovsky, and others—followed his work with warm interest.

The composer's first new work of 1936 was the symphonic tale for children *Peter and the Wolf,* written on commission for the recently opened Central Children's Theater. The composer himself wrote the text of this tale, which he first called *How Peter Outwitted the Wolf.* It was a simple story about a Pioneer named Peter who displayed the adroitness of a hunter in capturing a bloodthirsty wolf.* The tale is constructed on a continuous interweaving of recitation and symphonic music. This is not "recitation to music," however, but a free alternation of musical episodes and short fragments of narration.

This was an entirely new departure for Prokofiev: a brief lesson in instrumentation designed to acquaint young listeners, in an interesting way, with the sounds of the various orchestral instruments. In his foreword to this work the composer wrote: "Each character of this tale is represented by a corresponding instrument in the orchestra—the bird by a flute, the duck by an oboe, the cat by a clarinet staccato in a low register, the grandfather by a bassoon, the wolf by three horns, Peter by the string quartet, and the shots of the hunters by the kettledrums and the bass drum. Before the performance it is advisable to show these instruments to the children and to play the corresponding leitmotivs. In this way the children will easily learn to recognize the sonorities of the instruments during the performance."

Thus, twenty-two years after *The Ugly Duckling,* Prokofiev once again created a series of apt and amusing animal sketches as vivid as any drawn from nature by an artist. The music describes the carefree chirping of a bird, the languorous purring and furtive leaps of a cat, the angry growling of a wolf, and the quacking of a duck as it lazily waddles along. In addition

* TRANSLATOR'S NOTE: The Pioneers are a Soviet organization for children between the ages of ten and fourteen.

279

to the animals, the music portrays the dauntless Peter, his grumbling old grandfather, and the hunters.

Remembering the simplicity of a child's perception, the composer did not hesitate to use the most traditional descriptive devices—clear grace notes and delicate figurations of the flute to portray the chirping of the birds, deafening blows on the kettledrum and drums for the hunters' rifle-shots. The music conveys the anxious cries of the bird as it tries to save itself from being caught, the sudden leaps of the pursuing cat, and even an occasional duck quack from the depths of the wolf's belly. This music is never merely imitative, however, for the melodies are well developed and fantasy is interwoven with reality.

Unlike *The Ugly Duckling,* in which the decisive role is played by recitative accompanied by brief, descriptive piano passages, this work abounds in flowing, strikingly melodic leitmotivs, any one of which could have been made into a piano piece or ballet episode. Such, for example, is Peter's broadly developed theme, the principal musical refrain of the entire tale, which is repeatedly stated in various tonalities and textural alterations (Fig. 34).

FIGURE 34

The dance-like theme of the cat, the marching of the hunters, and other episodes are equally well developed.

The charmingly naïve tale of *Peter and the Wolf* was actually intended more for kindergarten children than for Pioneers. The fearless Peter, warned against danger and led away by his grandfather, is closer to the little heroes of K. Chukovsky or A. Barto than to the real Pioneers of A. Gaidar or L. Kassil. Prokofiev's music presents a charming and realistic picture of the enchanted world of early childhood, the world in which fantasy is interwoven with reality.

In this highly original composition, the composer achieved unity by skillfully following the principle of thematic repetition. The tale opens in a novel manner: at the very beginning, before the unfolding of the dramatic events which follow the appearance of the wolf, the composer introduces the leading characters and sets the stage for the action. Here the music suggests the idyllic atmosphere of summer in the country. The dominant theme of Peter alternates with the themes of the bird, duck, cat, and grandfather. Here, too, the first "secondary conflict" occurs—the cat tries to grab the bird while it is busy quarreling with the duck, but it narrowly escapes when Peter warns it of the danger.

The middle section of the tale, its "development section," contains the most exciting episodes: the sudden appearance of the wolf, its pursuit of the duck, the duck's disappearance into the jaws of the wicked animal, and finally the daring action of Peter, who with the help of the bird skillfully lassoes the enemy. Only two new themes appear here, those of the wolf and the hunters, while the themes of Peter, the bird, and the cat are subjected to various kinds of modification.

Finally, the brief "recapitulation" opens with the victorious procession of the brave Peter and his hunter friends leading the captured wolf away. At this point, while all the principal characters pass before the listener, Peter's theme is transformed from a light, carefree tune into a pompous, sharply accented march. The "reprise quality" of this part is heightened not only by the restatement of the main themes but also by the return to the original tonality of C major.

Thus, the composer constructed a complex, three-part work with developmental elements in the middle section and a vigorous, lively recapitulation. Nowhere, however, was he inhibited by academic rules of composition. On the contrary, he consistently underscored the dependence of the musical action on the literary text. As a consequence, the musical material is developed not according to stereotyped methods, but by means of subtle combinations and superimpositions of the main themes. Examples of this are the blending of Peter's theme with the texture and timbre of the bird's theme and the contrapuntal treatment of the themes of the grandfather and the cat.

It would be rewarding to analyze fully the musical language of this tale, for it presents in a classically pure and polished form the melodic and harmonic style of the mature Prokofiev. Let it suffice here to mention the many skillful, fresh-sounding modulations within Peter's C major theme (the shift up a minor second, for example) and the use of harmonic "terror effects" (simultaneously sounding C and F sharp triads). These and the rest of Prokofiev's characteristic devices were so deftly handled that the music proved completely understandable even to the youngest listener.

Prokofiev wrote *Peter and the Wolf* in a single week, completing it in piano score on April 15, 1936. He completed the orchestration on April 24, and the work was first performed, under his own direction, on May 2, 1936, at a matinee concert arranged for children by the Moscow Philharmonic Organization.* Since then *Peter and the Wolf* has won the love of young and old alike both in the Soviet Union and abroad. It is, without exaggeration, one of the classics of Soviet music.

Asafyev spoke with great enthusiasm about this work: "What could be more commonplace than what happened to a certain Peter in *Peter and the Wolf*? Yet everything in the music, every detail of the behavior of the child, the duck, the bird, the cat, and the wolf sounds as though it were all happening for the first time on earth. And you ask yourself, do we not have here the elements of a new Soviet symphonic style free from both intellectual self-analysis and a tragic view of reality?"[2]

The composer's keen interest in bringing music to children was not confined to the writing of *Peter and the Wolf*. At a concert for children on April 11, 1936, he played for the first time the easy piano pieces of Op. 65. At about this time he also wrote two little songs which were gay vignettes from the life of Soviet children—*The Chatterbox*, to words by A. Barto, and *Sweet Melody*, to words by N. Sakonskaya. The first of these, a monologue reminiscent of an episode from a comic opera, is the more interesting. The words of the song are those of a little school girl named Lida, who is chattering about her homework. The entire little scene is made up of passages in a gay patter style which alternate with a tender melodic refrain. In this song the composer laughs at the little chatterbox, but with the gentle laughter of a mature man who delights in the enthusiasms and tribulations of children. This music is strongly reminiscent of Moussorgsky's song cycle *The Nursery*, which also expresses the perceptiveness and sympathy of an artist who seems to be enjoying the naïveté of children.

*Sweet Melody* is not so effective as *The Chatterbox*, mainly because of its text, which sounds like a jingle written as an advertisement for a candy factory. In 1939, another song was added to these two—*The Little Pigs*, set to a poem by L. Kvitko, translated by S. Mikhalkov. Like *The Chatterbox*, it is also a miniature scene, this time presented in the form of a dialogue between the strict Anna Vanna and two small children who want to look

---

* TRANSLATOR'S NOTE: This is a state concert organization concerned primarily with arranging performances of serious music.

at the little pigs on a collective farm. The dialogue is Prokofievan in its terseness, but the declamation is apt and expressive and the melodic material is in Russian folk song style. These three children's songs, of which the best known is *The Chatterbox,* were published as Op. 68.

These works for children notwithstanding, Prokofiev was chiefly occupied during 1936 with projects inspired by the works of Pushkin. The country was preparing to commemorate the hundredth anniversary of the great poet's death; plans were afoot for the production of plays and films on Pushkin themes and also for the composition of romances and songs to his poetry. Almost simultaneously Prokofiev received three very interesting commissions: from the movie director M. Romm, to write incidental music for the film *The Queen of Spades,* and from the Meyerhold and Kamerny theaters to create music for *Boris Godunov* and a dramatic presentation of *Eugene Onegin,* respectively, the latter in an adaptation by S. Krzhizhanovsky. In June 1936, the composer reported in the press on the work he planned for *Eugene Onegin* and *The Queen of Spades.*

Prokofiev could not have chosen a better traveling companion on his journey to realism than the immortal Pushkin, who had inspired every major Russian composer for a century. He had not turned to this great poet's works for almost thirty years, since his youthful experiment with the opera *A Feast in Time of Plague.* In modernist circles, particularly in the West, Pushkin themes would have been considered quite old-fashioned. As we know, when Stravinsky used a Pushkin subject for his comic opera *Mavra* in 1922, he transformed it into a cynical caricature of early nineteenth-century Russian life.

In 1936, such an approach would have been completely out of the question for Prokofiev. Carefully and thoughtfully reading Pushkin's poetry, he found much in it that touched a responsive chord. It was no accident that the first song he set to a Pushkin text, *Pine Trees,* took on an autobiographical meaning, for it expressed something of his own joy at returning to his homeland:

> Ten years have passed since then—and much
> Has changed in life for me,
> I, too, obedient to life's laws,
> Have altered—but here again
> The past enfolds me in its arms.

What attracted Prokofiev in Pushkin's poetry was its clarity of thought and emotional restraint, qualities which were highly compatible with his own artistic temperament. As a matter of fact, Miaskovsky once called him "the Pushkin of music," referring to his tremendous emotional restraint, his ability to sheathe the most powerful feeling in a stately suit of armor.

In turning to Pushkin themes, which both Tchaikovsky and Moussorgsky had treated so brilliantly, Prokofiev once again revealed his exceptional boldness and daring. His decision to risk comparison with the composers of the greatest Russian classics was not a sudden one. The artist Konchalovsky tells how, a year before, he had tried to persuade the composer to write new music for *Eugene Onegin*. "No, after Tchaikovsky it would be rather awkward," Prokofiev had replied at that time. When he later changed his mind, he selected parts of Pushkin's *Eugene Onegin* which were not included in Tchaikovsky's opera. "I think it will be unusually interesting to see Lensky arguing heatedly with Onegin over a bottle of Ay, Tatyana visiting his empty house, or Onegin on the banks of the Neva," wrote the composer. "It is my intention to adhere as closely to the original as possible," he added.[3]

Isolating himself for the summer in his beloved Polenovo, he immersed himself in the world of Pushkin's poetry. He reread *Eugene Onegin, The Queen of Spades,* and *Boris Godunov* and composed musical sketches for them. "I enjoyed writing the music very much and felt that I had succeeded in finding some true images," he wrote of these days.

Prokofiev took special pains with the music for *Eugene Onegin,* for which he composed a series of characterizations of the principal characters and a number of poetic scenes depicting life on a country estate. He composed a few themes for Onegin and three lyrical themes for Tatyana, which were supposed to express the gradual development of her passion. He considered particularly successful the music depicting the rustic quietude of the Larin estate and a few dance fragments for the ball at the Larin's (a waltz, a polka for two pianos, etc.).

Prokofiev also found much that appealed to him in *The Queen of Spades,* particularly the tragic, high-strung character of Hermann. This story bears an obvious resemblance to *The Gambler,* which also treats the game of chance as symbolic of the cruelty of fate.

*Eugene Onegin, Boris Godunov,* and *The Queen of Spades* were never produced; although Prokofiev's incidental music for them remained unpublished, it was included in the list of his compositions (*The Queen of Spades* and *Boris Godunov* under Op. 70, *Eugene Onegin* under Op. 71). The composer frequently returned to these brilliant musical fragments.

Five years later, for example, he used a number of the sketches for *Eugene Onegin* in the opera *War and Peace*. The waltz for the Larin's ball became the waltz for Ellen Bezukhov's ball (Scene 4 of the opera), and the theme of Tatyana's budding love became Andrei Bolkonsky's principal lyrical leitmotiv. From the fragments for *Boris Godunov* which depicted the battle between the Russian soldiers and those of the false Dimitri, Prokofiev created the theme of the German invasion in the opera *Semyon Kotko*; Liza's leitmotiv from *The Queen of Spades* he transformed into one of the opening themes for the first movement of the Eighth Sonata.

Prokofiev's work on the Pushkin subjects in many ways served to perfect and ennoble his art, and it also proved of value in his search for a Russian national style (which he continued later in such works as *Alexander Nevsky* and *War and Peace*).

The list of Pushkin works composed in 1936 also includes the three songs, Op. 73—*Pine Trees, Roseate Dawn,* and *In Your Chamber.* These songs are very different in mood. *Pine Trees* is a reflective elegy, *Roseate Dawn* a delicate pastorale, and *In Your Chamber* a love song with a faint tinge of sadness. Much in this music seemed quite unusual for Prokofiev. Miaskovsky, on hearing the songs, noted a "surprising sensibility" in them.[4]

The moods of Pushkin's poems, which range from philosophical profundity to light playfulness, are faithfully embodied in these miniatures. In these songs Prokofiev made excellent use of subtle modulatory techniques to convey all the nuances of feeling, and the melodic writing is characteristically fresh and original throughout.

Nevertheless, the songs of Op. 73 lack the simplicity and naturalness of vocal melody which characterize the classical examples of Russian lyricism. For example, the beautiful melody of the third song has a purely instrumental character. Complicated harmonies and an abundance of shifting tonalities make certain passages (especially in the middle sections of the second and third songs) difficult to understand. It is probably for this reason that these songs have never become popular.

In 1936 the list of Prokofiev's works was also increased by the *Russian Overture,* Op. 72, and two symphonic suites from *Romeo and Juliet.* The suites comprise the most self-contained and brilliant episodes of the ballet. No effort was made to preserve the original plot sequence of the numbers, for each suite has its own inner dramaturgical design. Four of the seven movements in Suite No. 1 are genre-dance episodes which recreate the background of the drama: (1) "Folk Dance," (2) "Scene," (4) "Minuet," and (5) "Masks." Contrasted to these are two lyrical love episodes, (3) "Madrigal" and (6) "Romeo and Juliet," and the bitterly tragic final episode, "The Death of Tybalt."

Suite No. 2, which has become the more popular one, includes three musical portraits of the leading characters, (1) "The Montagues and the Capulets," (2) "Juliet—The Little Girl," and (3) "Friar Laurence," plus the two most important dramatic episodes, (5) "Romeo and Juliet before Parting" and (7) "Romeo at Juliet's Grave."

The première performance of Suite No. 1, given by the Moscow Philharmonic Orchestra on November 24, 1936, prompted many musicians to begin speaking of Prokofiev's sharp turn toward realism. "Fresh, bright, sonorous, expressive," wrote Miaskovsky in his diary. "Stormy success, music of the highest order."[5]

During the summer of 1936, while working on the incidental music to Pushkin's works, Prokofiev also composed the *Russian Overture* for symphony orchestra. He had first thought of writing a large symphonic piece on Russian themes as early as 1916, when he was composing the *Classical Symphony,* but only now did he set himself to work on the idea. Before beginning the composition he pored over volumes of Russian folk songs. His gravitation toward a clearly defined national style, dormant during the Paris period and reawakened in *Lieutenant Kije,* now became more clearly apparent than ever.

The *Russian Overture* is based on the traditional juxtaposition of two elements in Russian folk music—the lively dance and the smooth-flowing lyrical song. Most of the themes in the piece closely resemble authentic folk tunes, and the two dance melodies in the first section are direct quotations from folk music. At the same time, the composer's own themes in the Russian national style are easily recognized by their expanded intervals, characteristic modulations, and sharp rhythmic irregularities. Here folk melodies are no longer altered for purposes of caricature and derision, as they were in *The Buffoon,* but used instead to heighten the emotional quality of the images. In this writer's opinion, the best themes in the overture are one of the dance melodies of the first section (marked *brusco*), which has an exhilarating rhythm and dash, and the broad, sweeping melody of the middle section (FIG. 35), which is reminiscent of exuberant girls' songs like *I Was at a Feast.*

The overture is constructed in the form of a rondo-sonata, without a development section. The exposition follows a dance-song-dance sequence; the middle section is a somewhat colorless lyrical intermezzo; and the

FIGURE 35

recapitulation repeats the material of the exposition. Within each section, the composer merely linked the themes together, as in a ballet scene, without making any attempt to develop them. To compensate for this lack of symphonic development, he frequently changed the tonality and also periodically introduced new, contrasting images. For example, what seems to be a merry folk festival is interrupted several times by harsh shrieks and exclamations from the brasses. In the long and swift-moving coda, the familiar phrases and melodies are presented in kaleidoscopic alternation, as though caught in a violent vortex.

The best passages of the Overture are delightful both for the expressiveness and national flavor of the melodies and rhythms and for the exuberance and drive of the dance themes, which seem to suggest the unrestrained merriment of a crowd.

Despite its considerable realism, this music does not convey the feeling of present-day Russian life. Apparently fearing that it might sound overly traditional, the composer often resorted to deliberate tonal harshnesses and many-hued coloristic effects. A studied coarsening also appears in the orchestration, which at times grows extremely noisy and thick from the use of all kinds of unusual effects (slightly out-of-tune, "accordion-like" chords and thunderous bellowing in the brasses) which often disturb the merry flow of the music. Natural development of the musical material is replaced by a play of purely impressionistic orchestral colors. All of these devices are in the spirit of "World-of-Art" exoticism, reminiscent of the florid canvases of Malyavin, with boisterous fairs, garish side shows, and wild revels. Later, in the ballet *The Stone Flower,* Prokofiev was once again to portray this kind of intoxicated Russian life in a colorful fair scene, but this time with fewer tonal excesses, and the images of brutish forces, as personified by the steward Severyan and his underlings, would be justified by the story itself. A year later the composer revised the overly thick orchestration of the *Russian Overture,* scoring it for a smaller orchestra.[6]

As before, Prokofiev showed all his latest composition to Miaskovsky. The two friends were often together at the piano, going over each other's sketches or completed new works. Miaskovsky sought Prokofiev's advice regarding the pianistic writing in some of his new pieces; at Prokofiev's suggestion he made revisions in the score of his Sixteenth Symphony. Prokofiev consulted him about the Second Violin Concerto, the sketches of *Romeo and Juliet,* and the plan for his cantata based on the writings and speeches of Marx, Lenin, and Stalin.

Of considerable interest is Prokofiev's review of the first performance of Miaskovsky's Sixteenth Symphony, which had glowing praise for the work's originality and austere style. "This is truly great art," said Prokofiev, "which does not strive for superficial effects or seek to curry favor with the public. Here there is no cloying naïveté, no reaching down into the graves of dead composers for the material of yesteryear." He also praised Miaskovsky for his spiritual kinship to the Russian classical tradition, referring specifically to the lyrical theme of the second movement in which "one catches a glimpse of Glinka's smile."[7]

Late in 1936 Prokofiev made his next to last concert tour of Western Europe and the United States. The West followed the composer's new works with undiminished interest. The scores of *Lieutenant Kije* and *Egyptian Nights* were published by the Koussevitzky Publishing House. The American critics were obliged to acknowledge the great progress in the creative work of the famous Russian composer who had returned to his homeland. Following the performance of the first suite from *Romeo and Juliet,* the New York magazine *Modern Music* observed, "Prokofiev has written music for the masses and at the same time has attained extraordinary nobility in expressing the idea."

While on tour in the West, Prokofiev became more and more convinced of the enormous superiority of the new socialist culture to bourgeois culture. Somewhat later, he described in a Soviet newspaper article the indignities suffered by gifted young musicians in the West: "There they have to give cheap lessons and have only the worst hours of the day for their own work. They dream of finding patrons, playing for them in the evenings and listening to their criticism, which is sometimes stupid. Even in a country like the United States, which is noted for its musical organizations, music depends entirely upon the millionaires' beneficence toward performers and composers. How fortunate our musicians are that they are spared all this."[8]

During the summer of 1937 Prokofiev completed the jubilee cantata, Op. 74, for the coming twentieth anniversary of the October Revolution. The September issue of *Sovetskaya Muzyka* reported that Prokofiev was "finishing a large work for chorus and orchestra to texts from articles and speeches by Lenin and Stalin." The plan, which had interested the composer for a number of years, was grandiose in conception but of doubtful artistic soundness.

"Lenin's language was so graphic, colorful, and convincing that I did not want to use any versified exposition of his ideas," the composer declared. "I wanted to go right to the source and use the leader's actual words." In the cantata, the texts from the works of Marx, Lenin, and Stalin were arranged in chronological order—from the *Communist Manifesto* and the first documents of the Bolshevik Party to materials connected with the new Constitution of the U.S.S.R.

The idea of setting documents of the Communist movement to music was not new. The oratorio by the Czech composer Erwin Schulhoff to the text of the *Communist Manifesto* and works by the German composer Hanns Eisler and others are well known. A similar attempt was made in the Soviet Union by A. Krein, in the symphonic dithyramb *USSR, Shock Brigade of the World Proletariat*; in this work, musical episodes were combined with parts of Stalin's speech "On the Tasks of Managerial Workers."

Because they forewent poetic generalizations and underestimated the importance of melody, the composers of such works were invariably unsuccessful despite the complete sincerity of their intentions. It was no different with Prokofiev, whose cantata also reflected the vulgar leftist tendencies prevalent at that time in the works of certain revolutionary artists of the West.

*The Cantata for the Twentieth Anniversary of the October Revolution* consists of ten parts:

Part One: orchestral introduction (the epigraph to this is the phrase from the *Communist Manifesto*: "A specter is haunting Europe—the specter of Communism")

Part Two: *Philosophers* (chorus to a text taken from Marx's theses on Ludwig Feuerbach)

Part Three: orchestral interlude

Part Four: "We are marching in a compact group along a precipitous and difficult path" (chorus to a text from Lenin's *What Is To Be Done?*)

Part Five: orchestral interlude

Part Six: *Revolution* (chorus)

Part Seven: *Victory* (orchestra and chorus to texts from Lenin's works)

Part Eight: *Stalin's Vow* (chorus)

Part Nine: *Symphony* (for symphony orchestra and accordion orchestra, on the theme of Socialist construction)

Part Ten: Chorus (dedicated to the new Constitution of the U.S.S.R.).

The *Cantata* was intended for a huge number of performers, no less than five hundred people: two choruses, professional and amateur, and four orchestras—symphony, brass, percussion, and accordion.

Despite the grandeur of its artistic conception, the *Cantata,* Op. 74, was little more than an unsuccessful experiment. It was never performed and has remained unpublished. The chief reason for this failure was the composer's obviously forced method of handling the Revolutionary texts, which underestimated the importance of melody.

Brilliant and graphic as the utterances of the leaders of the Revolution may have been, they were never intended to be set to music. Transferred to the realm of choral singing, these texts lost much of their oratorical power and only encumbered the melodic idiom. As a result, the principal choral episodes of the *Cantata* were contrived and unmelodic. The strictly prosaic character of the texts led to a predominance of dry recitatives unsuitable for singing. The best parts of this work were the orchestral interludes, in which the composer tried to convey his own ideas of the Revolution. Here he succeeded in creating a few images which expressed the inner joy of seeing the success of the Revolution (Part Seven, for example, which portrays the radiant and confident calm of the victors).[9]

Along with the *Cantata,* Op. 74, the list of Prokofiev works written in 1937 includes a large number of mass songs. "In the music written during this productive year, I have striven for clarity and melodiousness," the composer wrote in *Pravda.* "But at the same time I have not tried to get by with hackneyed harmonies and melodies. This is what makes it so difficult to compose clear music: the clarity must be new, not old."

In searching for texts for mass songs, Prokofiev turned to contemporary folklore—Russian, Belorussian, and Ukrainian. At that time current folk poetry was being collected on a wide scale in the Soviet Union. On Gorky's initiative, folklore expeditions were recording great numbers of wonderful tales and songs about the motherland, the Party, and socialist labor. In 1937 the best of these were published by *Pravda* in an anthology entitled *Folk Arts,* dedicated to the twentieth anniversary of the October Revolution. Among the songs which originally appeared in *Pravda* were the Ukrainian *Two Falcons,* the Russian *From Border to Border,* and the Belorussian *Good Health to You!* Several Soviet composers used these texts (some of which were translated by M. Isakovsky) to create many famous songs. Prokofiev also became interested in them and composed his own music to *From Border to Border, Good Health to You!* and *Golden Ukraine.* "I have used my own melodies but tried to keep close to the national style. I hope that they will be easy to understand and remember," the composer wrote in an article.

In addition to these songs on folk texts, he composed a number of others to verses by Soviet poets: *Brother for Brother* and *Lullaby* by V. Lebedev-Kumach, *Over the Bridge* and *Girls* by A. Prishelets, and *The Twenty-Year-Old* by S. Marshak. In combination with the folk songs, these formed a suite of eight songs for soloists, chorus, and orchestra. The new suite, entitled *Songs of Our Days* (Op. 76), was performed early in 1938 by the chorus and orchestra of the All-Union Radio Committee with the soloists F. Petrova, G. Abramov, and V. Zakharov under the direction of A. Gauk.

In *Songs of Our Days* various aspects of Soviet life are presented: the heroism of border guards, the enthusiasm of the young girls who went to the Far East to participate in the new construction there, the selflessness of a Young Communist who saved children from a fire, and the life of collective farmers. Some of these songs are highly dramatic. Such a one, for example, is the ballad *Brother for Brother,* unquestionably the most successful song in the suite. The composer was doubtless moved by this poem, which concerns a young border guard who took the place of his brother killed at his post. An agitated march theme in a narrative vein runs like a refrain through the entire song. Two episodes in particular, the ones relating the mother's grief on learning of the heroic death of her elder son and the younger son's oath, are very expressive. In this song Prokofiev displayed his ability to find suitable means for conveying the text. *Brother for Brother,* of course, is not a mass song, but rather a work in the style of a ballad, and it has an appropriately simple and convincing dramatic quality.

The modest *Lullaby,* which is ingenuous and warm, might well have served as a sketch for the inspired *Lullaby* of the oratorio *On Guard for Peace. The Twenty-Year-Old,* Prokofiev's first setting of a Marshak text, is written in the breathless tempo of a patter song. Although it is quite original, one senses in it a kind of studied simplicity, which unfortunately weakens its effectiveness.

Apparently it was not easy for Prokofiev to find the new simplicity he was seeking. In some of the new songs, especially the lyrical ones, he used excessively primitive melodic patterns and harmony. Nondescript melodic material, remoteness from the current folk song idiom, and lack of emotional depth prevented such songs as *Golden Ukraine,* and *Good Health to You!* from becoming genuine mass songs. "To be simple and at the same time remain himself proved too difficult for the composer. Much in the cycle is pale and lacking in individuality," the critic V. Vasina-Grossman correctly wrote of *Songs of Our Days.*[10] This opinion was shared by the average listener.

Despite their general lack of success, these songs provided the composer with valuable training in the vocal idiom. In former years he had limited himself exclusively to the declamatory style, and nowhere, neither in his operas nor in his songs, had he employed true melody. In writing these songs, he finally attempted to master this very difficult sphere of musical composition. Without the mass songs of 1935–37 (Op. 66 and Op. 76), Prokofiev could hardly have achieved that classic purity of melodic line which was to prove so captivating in the Russian choral melodies of *Zdravitsa (Hail to Stalin)* and *Alexander Nevsky.*

In 1937 Prokofiev also composed some marches for brass band: *Lyrical March, Marching Song,* and *Cavalry March,* which contains the chorus, "Over the Bridge," taken from the *Songs of Our Days.* At about this time, on a commission from a Leningrad theater under Radlov's direction, he also composed incidental music for Shakespeare's *Hamlet.* Of the eight pieces he submitted to the theater, those which attracted the most favorable attention were the three songs of Ophelia, the funeral march, and particularly the gavotte (the fourth of Prokofiev's gavottes), which was shortly afterward published by the Koussevitzky Publishing House.

Finally, in the same year, Prokofiev responded to continued interest in the music of *Romeo and Juliet* with ten piano transcriptions of the best episodes of the ballet. The entire cycle was written in a very simple style, with no virtuoso effects; actually, the pieces are parts of the original piano score, carefully edited for concert performance. All the pieces are completely pianistic, and despite their simplicity, they quickly won the interest of many Soviet pianists with the richness of their thematic material.

During the second half of November, shortly after the celebration of the twentieth anniversary of the October Revolution, the first Festival of Soviet Music was held in Moscow. Among the works performed at the festival were Shostakovich's Fifth Symphony, Miaskovsky's Sixteenth and Eighteenth Symphonies, and Khachaturian's Piano Concerto. A special concert devoted to the works of Prokofiev included the Fourth Symphony, the Second Violin Concerto (played by B. Fischmann), and the second suite from *Romeo and Juliet*. While the Fourth Symphony was received coldly, the *Romeo and Juliet* suite won the acclaim of both the audience and the critics.

On December 31, 1937, *Pravda* carried an interesting article by Prokofiev entitled "The Flowering of Art." In this article we no longer find him speaking of two categories of music, one for connoisseurs and one for ordinary men; instead he speaks of the relation between musical innovation and continually growing spiritual demands of the Soviet people.

"The search for a musical language in keeping with the epoch of socialism is a difficult but noble task for the composer," he wrote. "In our country music has come to belong to the masses of people. Their artistic taste, the demands they place upon art, are growing with incredible speed, and the Soviet composer must take this into account in each new work. This is something like shooting at a moving target. Only by aiming at the future, at tomorrow, will you not be left behind at the level of yesterday's demands. For this reason I consider it a mistake for a composer to strive for simplification. Any attempt to 'play down' to the listener represents a subconscious underestimation of his cultural maturity and developing tastes. Such an attempt always has an element of insincerity. And music that is insincere cannot endure."[11]

The best and most truly innovatory works that Prokofiev wrote during the Soviet period confirmed these views. It was not condescension to the "poor" tastes of Soviet listeners but rather confidence in their continuing artistic growth that ensured the success of his works.

In the early part of 1938, the composer once again undertook a long concert tour which took him to Czechoslovakia, France, England, and the United States. This was his last trip abroad. Progressive circles in the United States greeted him warmly, like an old friend. While in Los Angeles, he visited the movie studios in Hollywood, where he made a careful study of film music techniques with the thought of applying them to his own future work on Soviet films. In press interviews he told of the exceptionally favorable conditions under which Soviet composers work.

❈ ❈ ❈

In May 1938, soon after returning from abroad, Prokofiev had an opportunity to apply the valuable knowledge he had acquired from observing the American film industry—he was asked by the film director Eisenstein to write the score for the film *Alexander Nevsky*.

The work of Sergei Eisenstein, creator of the classic film *Potemkin*, had long interested Prokofiev, who had a high regard for the great director's exceptional artistic erudition and creative daring. Eisenstein, in his turn, greatly admired Prokofiev's music. Having exchanged their views on art at several previous meetings, both abroad and in the Soviet Union, the two artists had been hoping for an opportunity to work together. "Having long been an admirer of Eisenstein's remarkable talent, I was delighted to accept his suggestion," the composer relates.

The subject of *Alexander Nevsky* required that Prokofiev make a careful study of historical materials and acquaint himself with the Russian culture and Catholic hymns of the Middle Ages. "I derived enormous pleasure from working on the music for *Alexander Nevsky*," he recalls. "The fascination of the subject, the richness of the images, Eisenstein's great artistry, and the creative collaboration of the whole group engaged in making the film proved extremely stimulating."

The composer was definitely set against an antiquarian approach to composing the music. "I thought that it would be best to write the music for the Teutons not as it actually sounded at the time of the Battle on the Ice, but as we now imagine it. I adopted the same approach in working on the Russian music. It is cast in a modern mold rather than in the style of seven hundred years ago."

Working at the Mosfilm studios, where he could develop an intimate acquaintance with the techniques of sound recording, gave Prokofiev many fruitful ideas and awakened his old passion for experimentation. He noted, for example, that when too powerful a sound is directed straight into a microphone, it damages the tape and produces a distorted ringing or scratching noise when played back. It occurred to him that perhaps this imperfection in the apparatus might be used to achieve some desirable descriptive effects. The idea was a good one. When the music characterizing the German crusaders was being recorded, the composer had the musicians play the fanfares directly into the microphone; the result was a harsh, snarling sound which sharpened and exaggerated the themes of the Teutonic Knights.

Prokofiev also experimented with the seating arrangement of the orchestra. He placed the more powerful instruments, such as the trombones, far back in the studio, and the weaker ones like the bassoon right next to the microphone. This created an original effect unattainable in the ordinary symphony orchestra.

Excited by the varied possibilities of the sound film, Prokofiev personally took part in the recording of his music. The film people expressed admiration for the unusual exactness with which he worked. Eisenstein himself recalled this in one of his articles. "We leave the small projection room," he wrote, "and even though it is now midnight, I feel completely calm. For I know that at exactly 11:55 A.M. a small, dark blue car will come through the gate of the film studio. Sergei Prokofiev will get out of it. In his hands will be the next piece of music for *Alexander Nevsky*. At night we look at a newly filmed sequence. In the morning the new musical sequence will be ready for it."

The completed film sequences, which Eisenstein always showed him, excited his imagination. The vivid, sculpturesque quality of the scenes and the swift pace of the action inspired him to create boldly defined musical images. As each musical sequence was completed, it would be played for Eisenstein, who would then offer suggestions and criticisms to the composer. The director was so taken with Prokofiev's brilliant music that at times he would adjust the action of the film to take advantage of the rhythm and melody of a musical sequence.[12] In this way the collaborators preserved the original structure of the music and achieved a natural fusion of music and film action.

Prokofiev suspended his work on *Alexander Nevsky* for a two-month visit to the Caucasus, where he prepared the songs of Op. 76 for publication and worked on a plan for a new opera. On his return to Moscow in the fall, he completed the music for the film.

On December 1, 1938, *Alexander Nevsky* was shown for the first time on the Soviet screen. Thanks to the superb artistry of Sergei Eisenstein and the cameraman Eduard Tisse, the interesting scenario by P. Pavlenko, and the performances of such outstanding actors as N. Cherkasov, N. Okhlopkov, A. Abrikosov, and D. Orlov, the film achieved a great and lasting success.

One of the most unusual features of the film was its use of music as an integral part of the drama. The slow, meditative orchestral prelude and first chorus form a fitting background for the unhurried pace of the opening episodes ("Russia under the Mongol Yoke," scenes of life in Novgorod) which are set forth in the manner of a *bylina*. As the chorus sings a majestic song of the past exploits of Alexander Nevsky, the bleak panorama of the north comes into view, with fishermen in flaxen shirts pursuing their peaceful labors. The action quickens in the ominous scene of the enemy's violence against the unfortunate people of Pskov; the screen shows a city in flames, and the brutish glares of the Teutonic invaders. The Teutonic trumpeters blare the call to battle and pillage, while the chorus and orchestra resound with the sanctimonious Catholic chorales of the invaders. As the Novgorod peasants rise to defend their homeland, walking fervently but calmly with axes in their hands, they are accompanied by the stirring, heroic song "Arise, Ye Russian People."

The pivotal and longest episode of the film is the famous "Battle on the Ice." Here each new page of the narrative finds a brilliant echo in the music: the frozen, misty landscape at dawn, with the armies tensely awaiting the hour of battle; the sinister, mechanical rhythm of the advance of the mounted Teutonic Knights; the gay tunes of the *gudok**  players; and the valor of the Novgorod champions, lustily slashing the hated foreigners. The climactic episode of the catastrophe on Lake Chud is followed by a night scene, which shows a Russian girl walking about the battlefield, torch in hand, seeking her sweetheart among the fallen. As she walks, she sings a beautiful lament. This episode thus suggests an epic opera scene. The film ends with the triumphal entry of the Novgorod warriors into their redeemed city, to the festive ringing of bells. The victorious warriors walk proudly, with the Teutonic prisoners trudging behind them, glancing from side to side like captured wolves. The people of Novgorod watch the funeral procession of their fallen heroes in mournful silence. The final scene of the city's merrymaking is accompanied by the music in Russian folk style that had been heard earlier in the film.

The musical expressiveness of the film was due in large measure to the exceeding care with which the director treated Prokofiev's music. Each musical fragment was finished simultaneously with the corresponding film episode, and the result was a unique counterpoint of tonal and visual images, full of brilliant effects. For example, even while the Russian warriors silently await the attack of the Teutons, we hear the "invasion theme"

* TRANSLATOR'S NOTE: A *gudok* is a primitive Russian viol instrument with three strings.

foretelling the impending danger; and later, as the panic-stricken Teutonic leaders rush wildly about their camp, sensing imminent defeat, the victory theme of the Russian horsemen resounds triumphantly. Thus the visual and tonal images are used contrapuntally to complement and intensify each other.

*Alexander Nevsky* is interesting for more than its artistic innovations, however. Much of its power derived from its clear political relevance. In the bestial Teutonic Knights, Soviet spectators saw the modern fascist instigators of war who were threatening mankind. In 1938 they witnessed the Munich provocation, the Austrian Anschluss, and the events at Lake Khasan. Hitler's machine of destruction was being prepared to embark upon its bloody campaign. The "Battle on the Ice" episode reminded the people of the heroism and valor of Russian patriots and of the criminal nature of modern fascism, the "Teutonic order" of our time.

❦   ❦   ❦

After finishing the music for *Alexander Nevsky,* Prokofiev turned to the cello concerto he had sketched in Paris in 1933. "The first sketches did not satisfy me," he wrote. "I clearly felt 'seams' between the various episodes, and not all the music was of equal value. After the long interruption I revised the concerto, adding some new musical material."[13]

The three movements of the concerto follow a rather unusual sequence. The first movement is an Andante; the second and most important is a fast *Allegro risoluto* in toccata style; and the third is a theme and variations. The composer tried to enrich the cello technique by using unusually high registers and by introducing virtuoso effects which are more characteristic of the violin. But these innovations could not save the work from a certain dryness and melodic inflexibility. This is not difficult to understand when one recalls that the principal material was composed at approximately the same time as the *Symphonic Song* and *Thoughts.*

The first performance of the Cello Concerto, by L. Berezovsky, during the second Festival of Soviet Music in late November 1938 was coldly received and the work was soon judged a failure. "It lacks the soaring melody, the broad, expressive cantabile quality, which characterizes Prokofiev's Violin Concertos," commented the critic I. Yampolsky. Even the composer's close friends were disappointed in it. "First-rate music but somehow it doesn't quite come off," Miaskovsky noted in his diary.

An attempt by *Sovetskoye Iskusstvo* to build sympathy for the Concerto before it was performed was sharply criticized by the other organs of the press, and a controversy developed which was hardly beneficial to the work.[14] For a long time the composer did not agree with the criticisms leveled at the Concerto. "The critics remained indifferent out of sheer obtuseness," he said. "The Concerto is very much like the Second Violin Concerto!" Later on, however, he felt the need to make radical revisions in it. Heeding the criticisms of Miaskovsky, who pointed out substantial flaws in its form, Prokofiev introduced a number of changes into the score, including a cadenza. In 1940 the Concerto was performed in the United States by the famous cellist Gregor Piatigorsky.

The failure of the Cello Concerto and *Songs of Our Days* at the music festival in 1938 was partly compensated for by the enthusiastic reception given the Second Piano Concerto, performed by the pianist M. V. Yudina with A. Melik-Pashayev conducting. The romantic loftiness of the first movement and the irrepressible dynamism of the Scherzo captivated the audience in the Great Hall of the Moscow Conservatory. At this time, too, the composer received the happy news from Czechoslovakia that the ballet *Romeo and Juliet* had been produced successfully in Brno.

Toward the end of 1938 Prokofiev made sketches for the Violin Sonata in F minor, Op. 80. In a few days he composed the opening of the first movement, the exposition of the second, and the principal themes of the third. In all these themes one can discern elements of the Russian epic style; apparently the epic images which had filled his imagination while he was composing the film score for *Alexander Nevsky* sought an outlet in the realm of instrumental chamber music. The sketches for the sonata had to be laid aside, however, for early in 1939 the composer became involved in other major projects: a cantata based on material from the film *Alexander Nevsky,* and a new opera on a Soviet subject.

Composing the *Alexander Nevsky* cantata required a tremendous amount of additional work. Prokofiev had not only to select the most important material from the film's musical sequences, but also to arrange it in a well-balanced vocal-symphonic structure. The orchestral episode with which both the film and the cantata open ("Russia under the Mongol Yoke") and certain vocal episodes ("Song of Alexander Nevsky," "Arise, Ye Russian People," and "The Field of the Dead," which form the second, fourth, and sixth movements respectively) were left virtually unchanged. On the other hand, the orchestral sequences employed in the film scenes "The Battle on the Ice" and "Alexander's Entry into Pskov" (the fifth and seventh movements in the cantata) had to be substantially reconstructed. In reshaping these two movements the composer employed a method he had not used in the film, that of combining various themes contrapuntally,

as he had done in the finale of the *Lieutenant Kije* suite. The third movement, "The Crusaders in Pskov," was constructed in three-part form. Some
of the film score's descriptive episodes, such as the one illustrating Alexander's combat with the master of the Teutonic Knights and the one containing the mournful music in the triumphal scene of the entry into Pskov,
were completely discarded. Since the original score, which contained certain unique effects that could only be achieved through sound recording,
would not have sounded well in the concert hall, the entire cantata had
to be reorchestrated. The composer worked with special care on the new
score, and in February 1939 he reported in *Sovetskaya Muzyka,* "I am very
happy to have completed this work, dedicated to one of the most glorious
episodes in the history of the Russian people, on the eve of the Eighteenth
Party Congress."[15]

The *Alexander Nevsky* cantata is a unique example of a large-scale
vocal-symphonic composition based entirely on a film score. Prokofiev
displayed a fine sense of form when, instead of stringing together a number
of episodes, he created an integrated seven-movement work with its own
inner logic. The general structure of the cantata has certain features of
the sonata form. The first four movements represent the introduction and
exposition of the main themes, and the fifth, in which the contrasting
themes are contraposed and combined contrapuntally, is in the nature of a
development section. These are followed by a lyrico-dramatic intermezzo
(the sixth movement). The last movement, in which the principal themes
of the second and fourth movements are restated, serves as a recapitulation.
Thus, while not actually using the sonata form, the composer did follow
its structural principles—a contrast and struggle of conflicting musical ideas
and a restatement and reaffirmation of the principal themes.

Dramatic tension is built up in the cantata primarily through the conflict of two sharply opposed images: the Teutonic Knights and the patriotic
Russian people. This antagonism is conveyed in the music by means of
contrasting styles. The Teutonic invaders are portrayed by ponderous mechanical rhythms, harsh polytonal harmonies, and colorless timbres (heavy
brasses, percussion, and the lifeless sonorities of church chant); the Russian
patriots are portrayed by the warm, tender colors of the strings, by the
chorus and a mezzo-soprano solo, and by beautiful melodies in the folk
style.

Stylistically there is much in this cantata that was completely new for
Prokofiev. Some of his earlier works, such as the *Scythian Suite,* had contained tonal landscapes and episodes of dramatic action, but none of them

had contained such a convincing and integrated embodiment of simple, tuneful vocal episodes with roots in the national tradition of Russian song and classical opera. Even the fundamental conception of the work is original. The daring combination of vividly descriptive instrumental passages and richly melodic vocal episodes produced a novel fusion of genres, a unified whole combining elements of program music with almost operatic choral episodes.

Of the seven movements, the first, "Russia under the Mongol Yoke," is the shortest and least developed. It is an orchestral prelude, a kind of introduction to the entire cycle which establishes the grim and hopeless mood in Russia during this epoch. It conveys what the writers of the scenario (Pavlenko and Eisenstein) prescribed for the opening scenes of the film: "Woeful traces of the ravages wrought on Rus by the Mongols— heaps of human bones, swords, rusty lances. Fields overgrown with weeds and ruins of burned villages."

The very first melodic figure, with its rather weird *appoggiaturas,* evokes the spirit of the bleak medieval atmosphere. A woeful melody sung in unison by the oboe and bass clarinet responds to it. The combination of the very high and very low registers of these instruments, moving in unison four octaves apart, creates an unusual tonal effect which heightens the feeling of a vast and desolate Russian landscape. The composer later employed a similar effect in other mournful episodes depicting scenes of ravaged Russia (for example, the theme of the national disaster in *War and Peace* and the introduction to Act V of *Semyon Kotko*). Out of the desolation and stillness arises a plaintive melody played by the oboe over an agitated hum of the violins *tremolo.* The movement ends in a mood of hopelessness and despair.

The epic "Song of Alexander Nevsky" (second movement) serves as the main theme signifying Russia in the cantata, the musical expression of its stern grandeur and invincible might. The words of this song, "They who march 'gainst Rus shall meet their death," might well have served as an epigraph for the entire work. There is an obvious relationship between the principal melody of this chorus and the traditional Russian *byliny* with their calm assurance and inner strength. Harmonic devices and orchestral effects, such as the wide use of plagal harmonies and the imitation of a *gusli** by the harp, are here employed in a manner similar to that of the classical Russian composers; but Prokofiev's individual style is evi-

* TRANSLATOR'S NOTE: A *gusli* is a rudimentary Balkan instrument having a round, concave body, parchment soundboard, and one horsehair string.

dent throughout in the clipped cadences and the heavy rhythmic accents, which suggest the mighty tread of epic heroes. The lively middle section of the song, which tells of Alexander's victories over the Swedes, forms a striking contrast to the stately melody with which it opens and closes. Here a battle atmosphere is suggested by the use of the martial sonorities of the percussion; this section was meant to convey not so much a concrete image of a battle as the memory of battles long past, which is evoked by the narration.

The music of the third movement, "The Crusaders in Pskov," is permeated with icy horror. Its opening chords, acrid and jarring in the stentorian timbres of the brasses, at once introduce a world of cruel, inhuman images. Biting harmonies are employed, such as a C-sharp minor triad with a simultaneously sounding B sharp.[16]

The opening chords are followed by the main themes of the Teutonic invaders. First we hear a Latin chorus sung in the manner of Catholic chant, expressing the hypocritical righteousness of the Crusaders. After this a coarse, snarling motiv in the low basses, based on a minor third, tells of their bestial dullness. Finally, an ominous fanfare played in unison by the four horns represents, by its abrupt and soulless quality, their military aggressiveness. The brief Latin text of the chant *("Peregrinus expectavi pedes meos in cymbalis")* expresses the warlike spirit of the knight-conquerors, ready to wipe the enemy from the face of the earth. The sacred quality of their unctuous chant is somewhat marred by harshly exaggerated counterpoint.

In the middle episode of this movement the mood changes radically. The brasses and chorus become silent, and the harsh dissonances give way to a sad Russian melody in the style of a folk lament. This beautiful theme, sung by the strings, expresses the painful sufferings of the people of Pskov, exhausted by the enemy invasion. The feeling of lamentation is heightened by an intricate combination of the strings *divisi* and an abundance of "sobbing" suspensions in the harmonies. Here we have an eloquent, realistic representation of the people's sorrow. Suddenly the martial fanfare of the Teutonic Knights breaks in upon the Russian theme of weeping in an ominous counterpoint. Once again the soul-chilling theme of the enemy's brute force is repeated, accompanied by the hypocritical chanting.

Like the second movement, the fourth, "Arise, Ye Russian People," is a choral piece in the Russian tradition. But while the second movement told of days long past, this is a vigorous call to battle, a summons to expel the hated enemy. Proceeding from the traditions of Russian folk music and nineteenth-century opera, Prokofiev here created a magnificent heroic song with a strikingly national character. In its harmonic structure, which alternates between C minor and E-flat major, it is quite akin to Russian folk song; the principal melody is also traditional, but Prokofiev enlivens it with a vibrant spirit of daring and valor, principally through the use of march-like accents. In the middle section of the choral exposition Prokofiev's characteristically colorful modulations add pungency to the melody. The central episode in D major ("In our beloved Rus no foe shall live"), sung by the altos alone, serves as a beautiful poetic contrast to the opening melody. Here the prevailing mood is gentler and brighter, the rhythm smoother and more fluid, and the timbre more transparent. This heroic lyrical theme, one of the most captivating in the entire score, expresses filial love for the motherland and delight in its austere beauty.

The principal events related by the choral-symphonic drama, those of the encounter between Alexander Nevsky's warriors and the Knights, are concentrated in the fifth movement ("The Battle on the Ice"), the central and most fully developed part of the work. In this mighty scene is revealed Prokofiev's extraordinary sweep of imagination as a painter of battle scenes. This movement is neither a reminiscence nor a summons to action; it is action itself, expressed with almost visual reality. The world's musical literature contains few battle scenes of such power and authenticity. This movement is the only one in the cantata in which episodic exposition of the themes takes precedence over the overall structural unity. The alternation of the episodes here is determined by the sequence in which the film's scenes appeared and not by any formal musical scheme. But even in this free-flowing arrangement one senses a certain unity; this manifests itself in the close resemblance between the quiet, placid music of the introductory and concluding sections, as well as in the rondo-like alternation of Teutonic and Russian themes in the central battle episode.

The panorama of "The Battle on the Ice" opens with an almost pictorial introduction portraying the misty morning landscape of the frozen Lake Chud. The restless tremolo in the cellos and the harsh sounds in the violas *sul ponticello,* which suggest the ominous screeching of birds, create a mood of anxious expectation. This is followed by the mechanical rhythm of the Crusader's invasion, which gradually mounts and gains speed. The dull *ostinato* figure given out by the basses conveys the impression of the relentless, iron tread of the enemy host. Against this background arises the familiar leitmotiv of invasion from the third movement; at first it is intoned as if from a distance by a muted trombone off stage, but later it is transferred to the heavy, bellowing tuba and other brasses. According to the composer himself, "since the sound of their trumpets must have been unpleasant to the Russian ear," he used deliberately harsh orchestral and harmonic means. After this the chant episode from the third movement is repeated in the same C-sharp minor tonality and by the same choral combination of altos, tenors, and basses.

The invasion episode, constructed almost entirely on familiar leitmotivs, gives way to the episode of the encounter between the Crusaders and the Russians. The singing of the Knights, to the words *"Vincant arma cruci-fera! Hostis pereat!"* becomes increasingly frenzied and alternates with the brief themes of the Russian warriors ready for battle. The orchestra plays the heroic phrase of the song "Arise, Ye Russian People"; this is followed by a lively tune over an *ostinato* figure in the bass. After this episode of the encounter, the music of the Teutonic invasion returns once again, in the manner of a refrain—the same cloying chorale in C-sharp minor, accompanied by furious battle cries in the brasses.

Finally, the episode of the counter-attack of Alexander Nevsky's forces unfolds, to form a striking contrast. The D major theme signifying the Russian attack (FIG. 36) sounds light and swift; its combination of melodic clarity, lively rhythm, and transparent major tonality calls to mind certain themes of Glinka.

FIGURE 36

This music evokes an image of the unconquerable Russian host rushing swiftly against the enemy. Here the theme of attack alternates with the victorious melody of the chorus "Arise, Ye Russian People."

The final section of the great battle scene is a unique synthesis, in which the constantly reiterated leitmotiv of the Teutonic invasion is combined with the themes of the Russian attack and of the chorus "Arise, Ye Russian People." Prokofiev boldly superimposes the C-sharp minor theme of the Teutonic battle cry on the theme of the Russian attack, which appears alternately in the keys of D major and B-flat major. These polytonal superimpositions create a harsh but convincing pictorial effect. The theme of the Teutonic battle cry is subjected to substantial modification by the introduction of descending intervals of the augmented fourth and seventh. The theme loses its triumphant ring, and no longer sounds as brazen and menacing as it did before. Once an arrogant call to attack, it now becomes the sound of panic, the savage shout of a routed army.

Next there follows the purely decorative episode of the catastrophe on the ice of Lake Chud, which is probably the least effective portion of the entire work. Here melodic imagery gives way to purely descriptive, deafening chords in the brasses and stormy passages in the strings and winds. Only toward the end does an ascending dramatic theme recall the just and stern retribution which befalls the enemy troops.

The fifth movement concludes with a poetic coda. In the tender high register of the violins *con sordino* emerges the lyrical theme of the fourth movement's middle section ("In our beloved Rus no foe shall live"). This music calls to mind the Russian heroes who have fallen in battle for their motherland.

The serene mood of this transparent coda is sustained in the sixth movement, "The Field of the Dead," which contains the mournful song of a Russian girl searching for her lover on the field of battle. Here the same soft colors of the muted strings, the same doleful quiet prevails. After the terrible, shattering images of the bloody battle, the lament of the mourning girl, sung by a mezzo-soprano, is affectingly unadorned and full of anguish. One can hardly believe that this severely classical Russian aria, reminiscent in character of Yaroslavna's lament in *Prince Igor,* was written by a composer who had persistently rejected the traditional aria form. One is captivated by the aria's opening melody, with its severity of line and singing folk quality. The harmonization is simple but forceful; certain effects, such as the minor chord on the sixth degree of the scale, are highly expressive. In the middle section of the aria we recognize the theme of the Russian lament from the third movement. This, the only solo aria, introduces an element of warm and tender feeling, of deep personal emotion.

The seventh and concluding movement, "Alexander's Entry into

Pskov," is based almost entirely on the Russian themes heard earlier. It opens and closes with the epic melody of the "Song of Alexander Nevsky," with sopranos added to the chorus for more brilliance and the resounding, triumphant pealing of bells introduced into the fuller-sounding orchestra. In this movement, only one new theme makes its appearance—"Rejoice and sing, our beloved Rus," which has the character of a festive dance. In the middle section the lively tune from the fifth movement is skillfully combined with the theme of native Russia (from the chorus "Arise, Ye Russian People"). The contrapuntal combination of this playful tune and the majestic patriotic song creates a vivid, lifelike image. Toward the end of the finale a wave of victorious sounds overwhelms the listener.

The *Alexander Nevsky* cantata has many features connecting it to the traditions of Russian classical music—the patriotic nature of its subject matter, the folk character of its themes, and the masterful depiction of landscape and dramatic action. Images from Russian nature form the background for almost every scene of this vocal-symphonic drama: the bleak panorama of ravaged Russia in the first movement; the frosty pre-dawn mist, in the style of a Surikov painting, at the beginning of "The Battle on the Ice"; the gloomy, nocturnal hues in "The Field of the Dead." Against these scenes from Russian nature emerge semi-fantastic images of war and destruction, recalling medieval frescoes.

The orchestral means and techniques used in the cantata are rich and varied. The composer used with equal skill the delicate colors of an aquarelle (achieved by a very subtle use of the strings *divisi*) and the broad and sweeping strokes of a fresco. His very interesting use of a contrapuntal "dual-plane action" brought the dynamic techniques of film montage into the realm of symphonic music. (The best example of this is in "The Battle on the Ice," in which the triumphant theme of the Russian horsemen and the distorted theme depicting the rout of the enemy are skillfully combined.)

But the most striking feature of this cantata is the amazing timeliness it had for contemporary Russia. Its images of the thirteenth century were refracted through the prism of contemporary events, and thus gained modern political significance. The mechanical tread of the Teutonic hordes seemed to presage the iron march of Hitler's tank columns, which were already poised to attack Russia. The patriotic call "Arise, Ye Russian People!" might have been addressed to the Soviet people, who were preparing to repulse a vicious enemy invasion.

The *Alexander Nevsky* cantata was given its first performance on May

17, 1939, at a concert of the Moscow Philharmonic Orchestra, with the composer as conductor and V. Gagarina as soloist. Repeated in the fall of the
same year at the Third Festival of Soviet Music, the cantata was justly
acclaimed as a major achievement of realistic art. At about this time two
other large choral works on historic themes were also performed for the
first time: Yuri Shaporin's symphonic cantata *On the Field of Kulikovo*
and Marian Koval's oratorio *Yemelyan Pugachev*. All three compositions
have attained a permanent place in the repertory of both concert organizations and radio programming.

A few years later Asafyev called the *Alexander Nevsky* cantata "the
finest lyrico-epic embodiment of Russian history in contemporary music."
Asafyev saw in this work not only a vitalization of the Russian national
style, but also a new treatment of realism in symphonic form: "Note the
wicked, cruel tread of the Teutonic Knights and you will realize that no
historical narrative in words could possibly make one feel so strongly and
visualize so clearly the character and appearance of these enslavers and
oppressors. It is in such music that one must seek the elements that can
bring about a revitalization of the traditional symphonic principles and
forms which, while estimable, continue to be bound by many academic,
pedagogical rules. And to achieve this one must start first with truthful,
concrete musical imagery and from this advance to structural design and
architectonics."[17]

❈ ❈ ❈

The success of the cantata inspired Prokofiev with a desire to compose
on contemporary Soviet themes, and he dedicated all of his work in 1939
to this noble purpose. He soon decided to write a Soviet opera, fully aware
of the difficulties involved. "It is one thing," he wrote, "to make heroes of
the past, people in wigs, velvet waistcoats, and buckled pumps sing arias.
In this case, the conventions of the operatic style present no special difficulties to the modern composer. But when you portray in opera a hero of
today, one of us, speaking the language of today, and perhaps even talking
on the telephone, you may easily slip up and sin a bit against artistic
truth."[18]

The composer spent a long time trying to find a subject for his new
opera, and he eventually turned to Alexei Tolstoi for advice. The writer,
who had an excellent feeling for music, suggested Valentin Katayev's story,
*I, Son of the Working People,* which had been published in 1937. It was
thought that Meyerhold, then head of the Stanislavsky Theater, might
produce the new opera.

The romantic story of Semyon Kotko, a partisan in the Civil War and the hero of Katayev's tale, was indeed a promising subject for an opera. What attracted the composer to this work were the dramatic situations, the vivid "Gogolesque" descriptiveness, the combination of tender lyricism and folk humor, and the colorful language full of Ukrainian colloquialisms.

"Katayev showed a great understanding of operatic style and undertook to write the libretto for our opera himself," Prokofiev relates. But differences arose between the composer and librettist over the treatment of the operatic form. Katayev envisaged the work as a typical Ukrainian folk opera, with many arias, songs, and dances. But Prokofiev flatly rejected this approach. Again, as in his earlier operatic works, he decided to write a dialogue opera based on prose, with a minimal use of formal arias. "I don't need rhymes and arias," he told Katayev.

At Prokofiev's request, Katayev made the dramatization, retaining many of the original prose dialogues. There was virtually no need for poetic texts, aside from a few verses to be used for songs based on Ukrainian folk melodies. Katayev realized that a preponderance of recitative would prevent the opera from winning popular success. "Wouldn't you like your opera to live on the stage as long as Bizet's *Carmen*?" he asked his co-author. But Prokofiev firmly defended his operatic method, considering it truly modern. "At least if you made the sailor Tsarev dance the *yabloch-ko*. After all, he is a sailor!" Katayev argued. But to the composer such a "banal" device was an utterly unacceptable compromise.

Work on the new opera proceeded according to a strict timetable. Precisely on the specified dates, Prokofiev would ask the librettist for the next sections of the text and show him the music he had written.

In undertaking this work, Prokofiev faced a complicated problem and one that was entirely new to him—giving a musical portrayal of actual scenes from the life and struggle of the Russian people during the years of the Civil War. He began his work by selecting a number of texts and melodies from collections of Ukrainian folklore. For the arioso of Semyon's young sister Frosya, for example, he chose the popular folk tune *Oh, Don't Be Afraid of the Little Toy Pistol,* which Tchaikovsky had also used for Vakula's aria in the opera *Cherevichky*. At Katayev's suggestion, the libretto contained the texts of Taras Shevchenko's *Commandments,* the comic folk song *All Is Ahum and Abuzz,* and a few traditional wedding songs. The composer later wrote his own melodies to these texts.

The Ukrainian setting of Katayev's novel awakened in Prokofiev memories of his childhood in Sontsovka—the village children, the friends old and young, the Ukrainian songs sung by the Sontsovka girls. Musical themes for the opera came easily and naturally to the composer, and his work progressed rapidly. The scene of Semyon's meeting with his fellow villagers (Act I, Scene 2), with which he began writing the opera, was completed on March 26. After that he finished Act II on April 8, Act I, Scene 1, on April 15, Act III (the most important one) on May 5, Act IV on June 16, and the entire opera on June 28.

In the summer of 1939, while living in Kislovodsk, Prokofiev worked persistently on the orchestration. Meanwhile S. G. Birman, who was to produce the work, was familiarizing himself with the completed vocal score in preparation for rehearsals at the Stanislavsky Theater.

As soon as he had orchestrated a section of the vocal score, Prokofiev would send it to his assistants P. Lamm and V. Derzhanovsky, who would immediately begin deciphering his markings (written on an expanded piano score) and preparing the final score. By this method the opera was completely orchestrated in two months and was finished on September 10, 1939.

While still in the midst of his work on *Semyon Kotko,* Prokofiev was asked by Eisenstein to write music for a new film entitled *Sands and Waters.* This time the composer had to decline. "At present I'm up to my ears in an opera which the cast has already begun to learn," he wrote to Eisenstein on July 30, 1939. "As soon as I've finished it, rehearsals will begin. At the same time I'll be busy with the production of *Romeo and Juliet* when the Leningrad company comes to Moscow. I can't possibly take on such a large task as you propose. After all, I can't be both here and there—not even in thought."

However, Prokofiev did interrupt his work now and then to write some mass songs. For the People's Commissariat of Light Industry he composed the song *Stakhanovite Girl* (to words by A. Blagov), and to a collection of songs for workers in the water transport industry he contributed *Over the Arctic Ocean* (to words by M. Svetlov). He also wrote two songs on texts taken from *Folk Arts—Down the Road* and *Send-off,* the latter of which evenutally became one of the principal episodes in the cantata *Zdravitsa.* Most of the songs written in 1939 (included in Op. 79) suffered from the same shortcomings as *Songs of Our Days*—dull, and colorless melodic material. The composer still seemed unable to express a contemporary theme successfully in the simple and accessible forms of the mass song.

After completing work on the opera, Prokofiev undertook to write some piano sonatas, a genre which he had long neglected. He planned a cycle of three large sonatas (the Sixth, Seventh, and Eighth) and began to make sketches for them, at once adding them to his list of opus numbers as 82, 83, and 84. Their principal themes and most fully worked-out parts he then "laid in store" with the intention of completing them sometime in the future.

Prokofiev had long followed this method of storing up themes. His collected papers contain many sketch books filled with themes, harmonizations, contrapuntal combinations and endings, and even structural outlines for future works. These raw materials were specially numbered to facilitate their later use. In the notes for the Sixth Sonata we read, "To finish the sixth—alternate the first theme of the fourth movement and the first theme of the first." Whenever a melody came to him, whether he was walking, traveling, or even lying in bed during a prolonged illness, he would immediately jot it down. "A theme is an elusive thing—it comes, it goes, and sometimes it never returns," he said in one of his interviews. "Some of my critics might say, no doubt," (his eyes twinkled) "that the more themes of mine that never return, the better."[19]

The three piano sonatas begun in 1939 were not finished until much later. Work on the Sixth Sonata slowed down as the original modest idea began to grow larger and more complex, and it was not completed until the spring of 1940. The other two sonatas in this cycle were finished during the war, the Seventh in 1942 and the Eighth in 1944.

In the fall of 1939, Prokofiev laid aside the piano sonatas to accept a commission from the music section of the All-Union Radio committee for a cantata in honor of Stalin's sixtieth birthday. The composer himself put together the text from a number of contemporary folk songs in which he had long been interested. The cantata, entitled *Zdravitsa* (Hail to Stalin), was very quickly written, orchestrated, and presented to the Radio Committee.

❈　❈　❈

*Zdravitsa* was based on the texts of folk songs of several nationalities—Russian, Ukrainian, Belorussian, Kumyk, Kurd, Mari, and Mordovian. The varying character of these songs gave the composer an opportunity to present several scenes from contemporary Soviet life and achieve a certain rhythmic diversity. In these folk verses, a feeling of love and respect for the Communist Party is interwoven with thoughts about the new socialist life.

The tone of the whole work is set by the opening lines, which express the joy of free kolkhoz labor:

> Never have our fertile fields such a harvest shown,
> Never have our villagers such contentment known,
> Never life has been so fair, spirits been so high,
> Never to the present day,
> Never to the present day grew so green the rye.

Later the words paint poetic portraits of the people of a kolkhoz. One of them is a young Ukrainian peasant woman, rocking her baby to sleep:

> Ah, how white the cherry blossoms!
> White as mists of morn.
> Life has blossomed like the cherries the sun has born.

Also portrayed is an aged Mari woman, sadly dreaming of all the good deeds she would perform if she were younger. Finally, there is a genre scene showing Belorussian collective farmers giving a send-off to their most outstanding worker, Aksiniya, who is going to a reception in the Kremlin. Before the triumphant conclusion, a few lines recall the former wretched existence of the oppressed Belorussian peasantry.

Prokofiev chose for his one-movement cantata the flexible, well-defined rondo form, which enabled him to arrange frequently changing scenes within a single monolithic structure. The dominant role in this seven-part rondo is played by the refrain, which expresses its prevailing and basic sentiment. This refrain is a broad, flowing Russian melody in Prokofiev's typical C major, adorned with beautiful modulations (Fig 37).

FIGURE 37

The whole theme radiates a bright and serene confidence, a deep love of life. The intricate scheme of modulations within the key of C major gives it emotional variety and a wealth of lyrical nuances; furthermore, a genuine feeling of optimism is achieved here without artificial effects or pompous fanfares. All in all, this is one of the most expressive themes that Prokofiev created during his Soviet years. The orchestral introduction is built on this refrain, which returns twice in the middle sections and finally appears triumphantly at the end, in rhythmically expanded form and fuller orchestration.

The remaining melodic material, which alternates with the refrain, is written mainly in the Russian folk manner, although colored by Prokofiev's individual style. Such is the exultant theme of the first chorus, also constructed on a colorful juxtaposition of keys (A-flat major to C minor and A-flat major to B major. The melody of *Lullaby* is modest and tender, in the style of a Ukrainian lyric. The song about Aksiniya's send-off is a broad melody in 6/8 time. The gay, festive chorus which opens and closes this episode calls to mind the traditional tune of a Russian *chastushka*.

The cantata is unmelodic at only one point—the bridge passage leading into the coda, which tells of the sorrowful events of the distant past. To describe these events the composer used agitated scale passages. Both the melodic pattern of the scales and the polyphonic "relaying" of the melody from one voice part of the chorus to another create a feeling of excitement and tension. Nevertheless, this device does not save the episode from a touch of artificiality.

The melodic richness and deeply national quality of the principal themes of the cantata are clear evidence of Prokofiev's increasing mastery in writing songs, particularly songs based on modern folk texts. In all probability, the contemporary songs of the peoples of the U.S.S.R. which he had heard sung by choral groups in concerts and on the radio had left an imprint on his memory.

In this work, Prokofiev demonstrated a keen feeling for the color resources of the chorus. Skillfully employing the techniques of opposing choral groups, he highlighted the distinctive timbre of each section. Examples of this can be heard in the shift from the female to the male groups in the first chorus, the alternation of the sopranos and altos in *Lullaby,* and the pure color of the altos in the "monologue of the old woman." The carefully conceived tonal plan (C major, A-flat major, C minor, D-flat major, and B major, with C major predominating) gives the work an aura of formal unity.

The chief virtue of the cantata is its sincere and sensitive embodiment of the feelings of the Soviet people, rejoicing in the fruits of their freely given labor. Only a long and complex evolution in Prokofiev's creative thought can account for his progress from the distorted, stylized Russia of *Le Pas d'acier* to the genuinely contemporary Soviet images of *Zdravitsa*.

The cantata was performed with tremendous success in the Great Hall of the Conservatory in Moscow on December 21, 1939. Since then, as is the case with the best-loved mass songs, recordings of it have been played many times on popular radio broadcasts.

❋　❋　❋

The 1939–40 season presented Prokofiev with his first opportunity in many years to work closely with musical theaters. In the past his love for opera had received virtually no encouragement from theatrical circles; he had been especially disappointed by this during his years abroad. To be sure, this was due not only to the conservatism of the theaters but also to the character of his operas, which were intended for a relatively limited audience. His attempts to interest Soviet theaters in his old operas *The Love for Three Oranges* and *The Gambler* ended in failure. It became clear that only new works created in collaboration with the Soviet theaters would enable the composer to realize his old dreams of achieving success with operas and ballets.

Rehearsals of *Romeo and Juliet* at the Kirov Theater and *Semyon Kotko* at the Stanislavsky Theater took place almost concurrently in the fall of 1939. Prokofiev participated actively in these rehearsals. He took a keen interest in the plans of the director, the choreographer, and the stage designer. While the ballet was in production he composed some additional musical episodes for it and also made a number of revisions in the orchestration.

*Romeo and Juliet* had its long-awaited Soviet première in Leningrad on January 11, 1940. It was justly acclaimed one of the supreme achievements of the Soviet musical theater. Glowing tributes were paid to the work of the choreographer L. Lavrovsky and the stage designer P. Williams, and especially to the masterly performance of Galina Ulanova as Juliet.* Among the other dancers who performed successfully were K. Sergeyev

---

* It is interesting that Prokofiev did not share the critics' enthusiasm for the production of *Romeo*. "I did not agree with the high praise of Lavrovsky (the staging was often at odds with the music) and Williams (a slick-haired and finicky artist)," he wrote the present author in June 1941. These criticisms indicate the high standards of the composer, who expected of his collaborators even greater brilliance and imagination than they had shown.

as Romeo, A. Lopukhov as Mercutio, R. Gerbek as Tybalt, E. Biber as the Nurse, and L. Shavrov as Paris. The conductor was I. Sherman. In the spring of 1940 the ballet was presented in Moscow during the Festival of the Leningrad Theaters, and once again it was enthusiastically received by both the public and the press. The critics noted the unusually felicitous union of Prokofiev's inspired music and the choreography and dancing, especially that of the superb Ulanova. They also pointed out the significance of the choreographic innovations, which presented Shakespeare's play in a profoundly realistic manner by combining elements of the classical dance with inspired pantomime.

On September 20, 1940, several months after the first performance of *Romeo and Juliet,* the opera *Semyon Kotko* was given its première at the Stanislavsky Theater in Moscow. The conductor was M. Zhukov, the director S. Birman, and the scenic designer A. Tyschler. The leading roles were performed by M. Voskresensky (Semyon), N. Panchekhin (Tkachenko), K. Malkova (Sofia), and N. Averkieva (Frosya).

* * *

Like the recently performed *Alexander Nevsky* cantata, the opera *Semyon Kotko* was an important landmark in Prokofiev's work, another clear indication of his desire to create realistic images of contemporary life. More than twelve years had passed since he had finished his last opera, *The Flaming Angel.* The artistic success of *Romeo and Juliet,* the *Alexander Nevsky* cantata, and other works of the thirties had undoubtedly reawakened his interest in music for the theater, and especially in the musical portrayal of real human characters.

However, the subject of *Semyon Kotko* presented the composer with new and extremely difficult problems. The techniques he had used in composing *The Gambler* and *The Love for Three Oranges,* which included the rejection of traditional operatic forms and the use of eccentric effects and grotesque parody, were not at all suitable for the writing of a contemporary folk drama. To portray the heroic struggle for Soviet power, to depict scenes from everyday life, the composer had to seek basically different, realistic means of expression. While his efforts were successful in many respects, his former approach to operatic composition clearly hampered his creative imagination.

The theme of *Semyon Kotko* was the complete antithesis of the themes of Prokofiev's earlier operas. After the scourging satire and nervous hysteria of *The Gambler,* the stylized parody of *The Love for Three Oranges,* and the mysticism of *The Flaming Angel,* the composer now undertook to depict Civil War heroism and life in a Ukrainian village. The characters of Katayev's *I, Son of the Working People* are natural, historically authentic, and brilliantly representative of their living counterparts.

The action of this story takes place in the southern Ukraine in the spring of 1918. Semyon Kotko, a young artilleryman, returns to his native village after four years at the front. The Soviet government gives him land and cattle. He is in love with the young girl Sophia Tkachenko, whose father, once a sergeant major in the Tsar's army and now a rich peasant, tries in every way to prevent their marriage. During the betrothal ceremonies, German soldiers invade the village and brutally murder the village patriots; they also burn down the Kotkos' hut and mercilessly beat Semyon's mother and little sister Frosya. Semyon manages to escape, however, and joins the partisans in the steppes. Thus, having only recently returned from the front, he once again becomes a fighter. Learning that Tkachenko has arranged to marry Sophia to the landowner Klembovsky, Semyon returns to the village, bursts into the church where the wedding is in progress, and after stunning those present with a hand grenade, kidnaps the bride. The young fighter falls into the hands of the enemy and is about to be executed when a band of partisans arrives to save him.

This plot deals with the conflict between two hostile groups: the ordinary people striving for peace and happiness (Semyon, Sophia, Frosya, Mikola, and the Bolsheviks Remenyuk and Tsarev), and the enemies of the Revolution (the kulak Tkachenko, the landowner Klembovsky, and the German occupiers and Ukrainian counterrevolutionaries). This prompted the composer to employ contrasting musical materials: warm lyricism, sly humor, and elements of folk song for portrayals of the Russian heroes; coarse harmonies, harsh orchestration, and caricatural devices for portraits of the enemies.

Many of the characters of Katayev's story were perfectly suited to Prokofiev's artistic inclinations, particularly Frosya and Mikola, the mischievous adolescents, and Nikanor Tkachenko, who provided an excellent target for his satire. The dramatization suffered from a number of defects, however. As we mentioned earlier, the libretto was written in complete conformity with the composer's wishes and hence reflected his own peculiar approach to opera. Not only was the text overloaded with naturalistic details and prose filled with local slang, but the action seldom stopped long enough to allow time for musical commentary in the form of arias or songs. Furthermore, Katayev's central theme, the theme of the people's heroism, was completely overshadowed by the comic and romantic scenes and the tragic episodes. Finally, the abrupt happy ending was naïve and quite implausible.

In terms of operatic style, however, there was much in the music of *Semyon Kotko* that was definitely new for Prokofiev. For example, the melodic element was unquestionably given greater emphasis than in his earlier operas. The melodies were also more natural, the themes suggested by the dramatic situations more poetically inspired. Though still quite undeveloped and brief, whole melodic episodes (absent in his earlier operas) did appear—for example, Semyon's arioso at the beginning of Scene 1, Frosya's little song in Scene 2, her account of the sorrow she endured, and Sonya's description of her terrible dream. And choral episodes, once completely rejected by Prokofiev, played a considerable role—the choruses of the young people at the betrothal and the funeral chorus at the grave of the executed Psarev, among others.

The themes in the lyrico-romantic vein, those expressing the pure and lofty feelings of Semyon and Frosya, of the sailor Tsarev and his sweetheart Lyubochka, contain some of the best melodies of the entire opera. In melodic design and modulatory scheme, these moving themes closely resemble many of the earlier examples of Prokofiev's lyricism. It is regrettable that they appear only as brief remarks or sometimes only in the orchestra and are not more fully developed. The inspired nocturne in the scene between Semyon and Sophia at the beginning of Act III is more fully developed than the other melodic episodes and contains what is probably the most appealing lyrical theme in the opera (Fig. 38). Its tenderness is heightened by the subtle coloristic play of light and shade (A-flat major and A-flat minor). One senses Ukrainian folk elements in this melody which relate it to the wedding choruses of the preceding act. As a matter of fact, many of the themes in this opera contain elements of Ukrainian folk songs, always bearing, of course, the stamp of Prokofiev's individual style. This can be heard both in the broad, flowing melodies (the theme of Semyon's sadness, the main theme of the funeral chorus, the wedding choruses of Act II, Frosya's song with its quotation from an authentic Ukrainian song), and in the recitatives of Tkachenko, Frosya, the old men, peasant women, and so on.

One of the most successful aspects of the opera is the aptness of its musical characterizations. There is no doubt that in his ability to portray a human being in a few strokes, to combine telling declamation with

FIGURE 38

appropriate orchestral characterization, Prokofiev approximates the style of Moussorgsky.

The most successful characters in the opera are those drawn in a lyrical vein (Sophia and Lyubochka), in a lyrico-comic vein (Frosya and Mikola), and in a satirical vein (Tkachenko). The best of the musical portraits are presented in continuous development—witness Tkachenko, now sadly reflecting on the vicissitudes of life, now coarse and despotic, now smooth-tongued and hypocritically polite, or Frosya, at first carefree and mischievous, but later matured by her first experience of bitter grief.

Freely constructed scenes in a declamatory style predominate over those in set operatic form. The heroes are shown in action, in continuous inter-relation or conflict. Particularly noteworthy is the episode of the match-making (Act II), in which the music corresponds to the dual action taking place on the stage. While the ceremony of the matchmaking is going on in the sitting room on one side of the stage, Sophia and her mother, Khivrya, in the bedroom on the other side of the stage, are feverishly getting ready for the meeting with the matchmakers. In the musical portrayal of this dual situation, each member of the ensemble retains his individual traits. The listener catches, in the swift flow of the action, the excited exclamations of Sophia, the lamentations of the distraught Khivrya, the shouts of Tkachenko, and the arguments of the matchmakers. The same method is also used at the end of Act II, where the German soldiers are disarmed against the background of the exultant wedding chorus.

The music of the second scene of Act I (Semyon's meeting with his fellow-villagers) has a natural, lifelike quality. Here running dialogue, brief solos, and duets succeed each other with cinematographic speed. There are interesting little duets between Frosya and the third old woman ("Run to Tkachenko's Sonya") and between Semyon and Frosya (the conversation about the matchmaking); in both instances a gay and lively orchestral part is skillfully combined with merry patter. On the whole, the music portraying the village people is rollicking and dance-like, as is the carefree, tripping theme of Frosya and Mikola, for example, or the accordion-like tune which characterizes the sailor Tsarev.

There is much that is new and instructive in the opera's recitatives, in which Prokofiev once again showed his sensitivity to the natural inflections of human speech. Here one finds tuneful declamation approaching arioso (Semyon's monologue at the beginning of Scene 1, Tkachenko's monologue at the beginning of Act II), semi-comic or agitated patter, and dry *parlando*. The composer attempted musical settings of the most prosaic texts (for example, the German command's requisition for food and the lesson on the construction of a cannon). Unfortunately, however, the abundance of recitative, particularly of the most unmusical, conversational variety, at times outweighs the more melodic aspects of the work.

Leitmotivs are widely employed throughout the opera. In some cases they amount to purely instrumental formulas, whereas in others they develop out of characteristic vocal remarks. Noteworthy, for example, is one of the love themes of Semyon and Sophia, which grows out of a tender farewell sung in recitative ("And so, 'till we meet again!"). The orchestral leitmotivs of the enemies, such as the themes of the German invasion, the counterrevolutionary nationalists, and Klembovsky, are incisive as well as melodically and harmonically exaggerated.

The dramatic finale of Act II, the climax of the entire opera, contrasts sharply with the gentle playfulness and romantic loftiness of the opening scenes; here and at the beginning of Act IV the composer concentrated the most horrible scenes of the enemy's brutality and the people's suffering. The finale of Act III, which depicts Tsarev's execution, the madness of his sweetheart Lyubochka, the conflagration, and the grief and terror of the people is particularly powerful. However, though there is much in the music that is gripping, the abundance of dissonant sounds, the harsh orchestration, the repetition of the mad Lyubochka's heart-rending phrases, and the swift succession of terrifying scenic effects—all unrelieved by a single broadly developed chorus—give this scene a tense, expressionistic quality. The following scene of Tsarev's funeral has a heavy, gloomy coloration; the rather dry "choral declamation" seems incongruous with the singing lines of Taras Shevchenko's *Commandment*.

The theme of heroism is poorly realized in the opera. The portrayal of the hero, Semyon Kotko, is kept too strictly within the bounds of everyday life; his ideological growth, his transformation into a conscious fighter for the Revolution, is reflected neither in the action nor in the music of the opera. The Bolsheviks Remenyuk and Tsarev also lack heroic stature. There are no musical themes which express the selfless struggle for Soviet power. Particularly disappointing in this respect is the finale, with its idyllic song, which in no way expresses the pathos of the Civil War.

On the whole, *Semyon Kotko* left an ambivalent impression. It was undoubtedly the defects we have noted in its dramatic conception and the lack of variety of its musical style (particularly the minimizing of vocal melody) which prevented it from becoming popular with Soviet audiences.

At the same time the work is interesting for its truthful portrayal of life and human characters, its brilliant lyrical, comic, and satirical episodes, and the ingenious way in which the recitatives and leitmotivs are handled. In this sense *Semyon Kotko* was an important steppingstone to Prokofiev's later stage works, and above all to the opera *War and Peace*. We can also hear echoes of the lyrical and dramatic themes of this opera in the composer's instrumental works, for example, in the poetic Andante of the First Violin Sonata, in certain pages of the Eighth Sonata, and in the Sixth Symphony.

Although he did not achieve his principal aim, the creation of a Soviet opera on a heroic theme, Prokofiev did solve a number of artistic problems in *Semyon Kotko*; he enriched the possibilities of the operatic form and found new, flexible expressive means. It would be wrong to put this opera down as an unequivocally formalist work and thus disregard what was new and valuable in it.

In contrast to the almost unanimous acclaim given the ballet *Romeo and Juliet*, *Semyon Kotko* evoked a sharp controversy in the musical world. While some musicians considered it a noteworthy achievement in Soviet realism, others charged Prokofiev with distorting reality and reverting to modernism. The discussion continued in the magazine *Sovetskaya Muzyka* for half a year. Some of those who took part in the controversy compared the opera to Khrennikov's *Into the Storm,* which was produced the same year, finding that work more intelligible and appealing to the general audience. Later, in December 1940, the discussion was reopened at the All-Union Opera Conference. Once again, as in the early years of his career, Prokofiev found himself at the center of a musical controversy.

Miaskovsky, who attended almost every performance of *Semyon Kotko,* firmly supported it. "Its impact grows stronger and stronger. Extraordinary music," he wrote in his diary the day of the première. In another entry, on May 4, 1940, he expressed dissatisfaction with the staging and the artists but called the third and fourth scenes "stupendous."

Somewhat later, in 1947, Asafyev made a number of interesting observations on *Semyon Kotko* in articles published in the book *Essays on Soviet Musical Works.* In these years the distinguished scholar took a somewhat more critical attitude toward the music of his old friend than he had shown twenty or thirty years before. On various occasions he spoke of the contradictions in Prokofiev's operas. He pointed out that on the one hand, the music of *Semyon Kotko* was "surcharged with tense, nervous emotion and bold, vivid reflections of reality" and that like many other Soviet operas it revealed the traditional Russian tendency toward an artistic "recreation of simple truth." On the other hand, he felt that the opera lacked emotional straightforwardness and failed to depict the people's thoughts and feelings through strong characters who are "moved by the ultimate ideals" of the Revolution. One cannot but agree with these observations.

In 1941 *Semyon Kotko* was dropped from the repertory and has not been revived since.

❋　❋　❋

During the winter of 1939–40, while *Semyon Kotko* was still in rehearsal, Prokofiev was working on the Sixth Piano Sonata (Op. 82), which he completed on February 11, 1940. On April 8 he played this technically complicated piece for the first time during the course of a radio recital, and in November of the same year Sviatoslav Richter, always a staunch exponent of Prokofiev's music, performed the Sonata brilliantly in public concert.

Unlike the ten piano pieces from *Romeo and Juliet,* the Sonata in A major, Op. 82, once again demonstrated the composer's penchant for piano virtuosity. In it he employed a variety of virtuoso devices: difficult, sharply accented leaps in the first movement; full-sounding chordal writing and rich figuration in the third movement; and rapid finger technique in the finale. The irrepressible demons of Prokofiev's temperament, which had raged so furiously in his earlier works, reappear in this Sonata. Miaskovsky commented on the "power and daring" of this music and also the novelty of its style, which he called "a mixture of the old and the new Prokofiev." Indeed, certain familiar features of Prokofiev's earlier writing, such as rigid rhythms and "barbaric" harmonies (first movement) and light texture in the style of Scarlatti (finale) are strangely combined here with profound lyricism and mature emotion (middle movements).

This Sonata is interesting for the unusual complexity of its content and the extreme sharpness of its contrasts. For all its complexity, one can sense a hidden program in the arrangement of its musical images, which range from the frighteningly harsh to the delicately lyrical.

The music of the first movement (Allegro moderato) is almost devoid of simple human emotions; instead, cruel and terrible forces are in command. In the listener's imagination arise either archaic images of raging monsters or recollections of devastating military invasions.

The opening theme, a warlike march which seems to convey shouts and signals, is permeated with coarse power. Dissonant harmonies and mechanical rhythms give it a brutal, soulless quality, which continues in the following bridge passage. This music has much in common with certain pages of the *Sarcasms* and the early *Toccata,* Op. 11, in which sheer motion was combined with sinister mockery.

A completely different world is presented in the strange and melancholy second theme. Here Prokofiev's restrained and delicate lyricism is brought to its extreme limits. The theme is set forth in a spare, severe manner, and its diatonic melody, with a minimum of harmonic support, seems deliberately achromatized and devoid of all emotion.

These two themes, subjected to substantial alternation, clash in the complicated development section, which contains harsh, polytonal passages. Here various contrapuntal devices, such as imitations at the augmented fourth and thematic augmentation, are employed. It is chiefly the second theme that is developed; it loses its constrained lyrical character and is considerably coarsened. It is accompanied by restless, hammering *ostinato* figures in the bass and persistent signal-like motivs derived from the main theme. The climax of the development section acquires a mood of unrestrained fury, which is intensified by the use of such percussive piano devices as *glissandi* and blows of the fist (marked *col pugno*). Toward the end of the development, the nervous fury gradually subsides and gives way to a languid passage almost detached in its inactivity. The lifeless, descending chords here recall passages in the music of Scriabin's late period, particularly the opening theme of his Ninth Sonata. In the contracted recapitulation the march-like main theme is followed by a brief statement of the second theme, which is altered. In the coda the spirit of wrath and fury once again takes precedence.

After the demonic, expressionistic images of the first movement, the listener gratefully welcomes the engaging gaiety of the dance-like second movement (Allegretto). In its rhythmic grace, sparkling harmonic colors, and charming melody (alternately pensive and playfully ironic) this movement recalls some of Prokofiev's early dances—those of Op. 12 and Op. 32, for example. Here the three-part form is skillfully combined with inventive variation techniques.

The third movement, a lyrical nocturne in the rhythm of a slow waltz (*Tempo di valzer lentissimo*), is equally appealing. In the sensuous yet austere play of its harmonic colors and in the fresh lyricism of its melody, this music resembles the romantic passages of *Romeo and Juliet,* suggesting a theatrical scene filled with clandestine trysts and lovers' sighs.

The rich and vivid harmony, with its wealth of polyphonic writing in the inner voices, sharply differentiates the two middle movements from the terrifying clashes of sound in the first.

The exposition and development section of the finale displays delightfully gay and lighthearted qualities. We recognize in this playful Vivace the familiar characteristics of the youthful Prokofiev—his love of vigorous movement and impetuous running passages. The thematic material here is light and carefree, not at all reminiscent of the terrors of the first movement.

But in the recapitulation of the finale a dramatic change suddenly occurs. The merry melody of the first theme is suddenly interrupted by a restlessly hammering motion in the bass. The martial signal cries of the main theme in the first movement and the descending chords of its development section return like the remembrance of some terrible nightmare. This fantastic reminiscence introduces a feeling of nervousness into the otherwise carefree atmosphere of the finale. In fact, the feeling of lighthearted gaiety never returns, for when the principal themes are restated in the recapitulation, they are adorned with sinister overtones and stripped of their light coloration. This becomes particularly noticeable at the very end of the finale, where the harmonies are subjected to still harsher treatment. Reminiscences of the signal motiv of the first movement are heard and the main theme is accompanied by furious exclamations, *glissando* flights, and nervously hammering figures in the spirit of Beethoven's *Appassionata* Sonata.

The frenzied images of evil, temporarily displaced by the warm lyricism and gentle humor of the middle movements, again triumph at the end of the finale, and the Sonata concludes on a note of gloom and unconcealed anxiety.

The Sonata called forth extremely contradictory reactions. The two middle movements, which have the character of interludes, were greeted with interest and much of the finale was found commendable. But the deliberate barbarisms of the first movement were seen as a reversion to the composer's earlier expressionist tendencies.

The critics spoke favorably of the Sonata's broad conception, the earnestness of the composer's intentions, and the natural emotion expressed in the two middle movements. But at the same time they pointed out that the music tended to assault the listener with its coarseness; as one critic said, "many passages in the first movement were excessively brutal."[20]

It was not piano music, however, but opera and ballet that engaged Prokofiev's interest during 1940–41. After finishing *Semyon Kotko,* he set to work on *The Duenna,* a lyrical comic opera based on Sheridan's comedy of that name.* The idea of writing the new opera was suggested to him by the young poetess Mira Mendelson, who had just graduated from a literary institute in Moscow.

While at the institute, Miss Mendelson had collaborated with a fellow student on a translation of Sheridan's play. Prokofiev was very taken with it and decided to write an opera on it. He himself wrote the libretto, while Mira Mendelson supplied the rhymed texts for several numbers. The collaboration thus started was to continue for many years. In 1941, following Prokofiev's divorce from Lina Llubera, Mira Mendelson became his wife and a true helpmeet in all his later work.

*The Duenna* was completed and orchestrated during the summer and fall of 1940. The dramatic material, which corresponded splendidly to Prokofiev's artistic purposes, fitted easily into an operatic frame. The composer retained the comedy's original plot, witty dialogue, and principal characters, but he modified some of the scenes, taking advantage of the

---

* TRANSLATOR'S NOTE: Prokofiev's *Duenna* has also been called *Betrothal in a Monastery.*

special musical possibilities afforded him by the subject. For example, at the end of the first scene he introduced a large ballet sequence depicting a carnival, and in the sixth scene he had the entire action take place against the background of a comic love trio. In this opera he also attempted to avoid unrelieved recitative and to employ more set vocal pieces. "The structure of Sheridan's play, with its abundance of songs," he wrote, "gave me an opportunity to introduce many formal vocal numbers—serenades, ariettas, duets, quartets, and large ensembles—without interrupting the action."[21]

The company of the Stanislavsky Music Theater prepared this gay opera for production in the summer of 1941. Several private showings were given at the theater during May and June, but the outbreak of the war prevented the public première.

❦ ❦ ❦

In the spring of 1941, in connection with Prokofiev's fiftieth birthday, the editors of *Sovetskaya Muzyka* suggested that he write some brief auto-biographical notes. Prokofiev readily agreed. The "notes" grew into a rather lengthy autobiographical sketch in which the composer revealed a brilliant literary gift, a lively sense of humor, and an earnest desire to evaluate his entire creative development. Characteristic of Prokofiev was his attempt to define the principal lines along which his work had developed. He mentioned five such lines: first, "classical" (the use of classical instrumental forms or imitation of the classical style); second, "innovatory" (the search for new harmonic idioms, and later, for a medium through which "to express powerful emotions"); third, toccata (an interest in rapid, rhythmically precise motion); fourth, lyrical; and fifth, scherzo-humorous. The composer gave special emphasis to his lyrical quests, saying that he had given them "more and more attention" as time went on. He also objected strenuously to the exaggerated emphasis placed on the "grotesque" in his music, suggesting that this plaguing term be replaced by the words "jest," "laughter," or "mockery."

The first chapters of this autobiography were published in *Sovetskaya Muzyka* (No. 4, 1941 and No. 4, 1946). These memoirs unquestionably constitute one of the most valuable contributions to the written history of Russian music.

On April 23, 1941, the musical world celebrated Prokofiev's fiftieth birthday. Since Miaskovsky had reached the age of sixty on April 20, *Sovetskaya Muzyka* devoted a special edition to these two luminaries of contemporary Russian music.

Early in February 1940 Prokofiev was elected vice-chairman of the

Board of the Moscow Union of Soviet Composers. Together with Shebalin, Shaporin, and other leading composers, he participated regularly in the meetings of the Union's advisory commission, where new works were given a hearing. In his comments he was always precise, straightforward, and intolerant of hack work and dilettantism.

During this time he was a frequent and welcome guest at the Central House of the Composers. In February 1940 he played there at a reception in honor of the famous polar fliers (A. Liapidevsky and others); in June he performed his Sixth Sonata at one of the composers' concerts; and in December he participated in a discussion of Shostakovich's Piano Quintet.

But Prokofiev devoted most of his inexhaustible energy to composing, giving fewer and fewer performances as time went on. When one admirer asked why he would not arrange a recital of his works, he replied, "I can't —it would cost me half a sonata." He had planned to appear as a guest conductor of the New York Philharmonic Orchestra in the winter of 1940, but this trip was made impossible by the outbreak of the war.

At the beginning of 1941 Prokofiev was completely immersed in a new work for the Kirov Theater in Leningrad, the three-act fairy-tale ballet, *Cinderella.* "I conceive it as a classical ballet with variations, adagios, *pas de deux,* and so on," the composer reported to the press. "I see Cinderella not only as a fairy-tale character, but also as a real person, feeling, experiencing, and moving among us."[22]

Vakhtang Chabukiani was named producer of the new ballet and Galina Ulanova was assigned the title role. While living in Sochi during March and April of 1941, Prokofiev finished the second act of the ballet. At the same time he planned an eight-movement symphonic suite based on material from the opera *Semyon Kotko* (1. Introduction, 2. "Semyon and His Mother," 3. "The Betrothal," 4. "Southern Night," 5. "The Execution," 6. "Village in Flames," 7. "The Funeral," and 8. "Our Men Are Back").

In June of 1940 Prokofiev and his wife were living in the country at Kratovo, not far from Moscow. The composer was busy working on *Cinderella.* The beauty of the countryside, the clear summer weather— everything was conducive to work. Prokofiev was also attending rehearsals of *The Duenna* at the Stanislavsky Theater; the rehearsals were in the final stage and the première promised to be an interesting musical event.

"On the warm sunny morning of June 22, I was sitting at my desk," relates the composer, "when suddenly the caretaker's wife appeared, looking terribly upset, and asked me whether it was true, as they were saying, that the Germans had attacked us and were bombing our cities. We were stunned at this news. We hurried over to see Sergei Eisenstein, who was living nearby. Yes, it was true."

On June 22, 1941, the first salvos of the Great Patriotic War shattered the peaceful life of our country. The war imposed new demands on all the Soviet people, Sergei Prokofiev among them. The composer now entered upon a new and significant stage in his creative life.

# TEN

# THE GRIM YEARS

*And legend marches in step with him.*
*She grows and ever walks beside him.*

P. Antokolsky: BALLAD OF AN UNKNOWN BOY

THE GREAT PATRIOTIC WAR lasted almost four years. The Soviet people displayed unprecedented valor, giving all their strength to the task of defeating the enemy. Like the fighting forces at the front and the toiling people at home, Soviet writers, artists, and composers also played a heroic role. Shostakovich's great anti-fascist Seventh Symphony and the whole series of books and scores which Asafyev wrote in the midst of the horror of besieged Leningrad were brilliant examples of the spiritual strength of the Soviet intelligentsia. The best songs and marches written by Soviet composers served as a great inspiration for the people at war.

Prokofiev, too, worked with intensified energy during these grim years. Although as a young composer he had failed to reflect in his works the tragic events of the First World War, in his maturity the great Soviet artist now faced the raging conflict with great patriotism, like a true citizen of his country. Like all Soviet artists, he was eager to dedicate his talent to the common cause of defending the motherland. The terrible ordeals of the Soviet people deepened still more his love for Russia and drove him to work even more forcefully and consciously at developing the national character of his art.

The war immediately pushed aside the gay and carefree themes of *Cinderella* and *The Duenna*. Life now presented demands for entirely different subjects and themes. Like all Soviet composers, Prokofiev turned to writing songs and marches for the Soviet Army. In July 1941 he composed the *Symphonic March*, Op. 88, and the March in A flat for brass band. At that time he also composed two mass songs—*Admiral Trash,* to words by Mayakovsky, and *The Song of the Brave,* to words by A. Surkov.

An air battle which he saw in Kratovo left an indelible impression on the composer. "Although this country place was not a military objective," he wrote, "enemy planes often circled above us at night and lit up the whole area with flares to get their bearings. The skies were flooded with glaring searchlight beams. These shafts of light, the green tracer-bullets of the pursuit planes, and the Germans' yellow flares created a scene of ominous beauty."

At the beginning of 1941, Prokofiev and Mira Mendelson had begun thinking of an opera based on Tolstoi's novel *War and Peace*. With the outbreak of the war this idea assumed immediate relevance. In July, after laying *Cinderella* aside for future completion, the composer worked out the plot and libretto of the new patriotic opera. Turning to Tolstoi's novel was Prokofiev's way of responding to the spiritual challenge of the times. He felt that the outbreak of war had brought this great epic especially close to the hearts of the Soviet people, "since it told of the Russian people's struggle against Napoleon's armies and of the expulsion of the enemy from Russian soil."

"The more deeply I delved into the material," wrote Prokofiev, "the more I realized how difficult my task was going to be; it also became clear that the emphasis would have to be placed on the events closest to 1812, and that the first part of the novel would have to be omitted. In the opera I tried to present the principal events and characters of the novel."[1]

Certainly, it was a very difficult task to bring together in the opera both the personal drama of Natasha and Andrei and scenes of the Russian people's historic struggle against the Napoleonic invasion. The Committee on the Arts was very eager that the patriotic theme should be highlighted and that the opera should contain mass scenes.

During July the contours of the libretto began to take the shape of a coherent whole. Prokofiev once again used the original text extensively in his libretto, making only a few necessary additions or insertions in verse. "My librettist and I strove to preserve the spirit and language of Tolstoi's novel," the composer explained. "In places where the novel was lacking in dialogue, we drew on Tolstoi's text and characterizations in writing our own. In addition to the novel we availed ourselves of the notes of the poet-patriot Denis Davydov and also used the texts of songs sung by the people during the War of 1812." Also in July, while working on the libretto of *War and Peace,* Prokofiev conceived the plan for a programmatic symphonic suite entitled *The Year 1941.*

Early in August, a group of leading artists and musicians, representatives of the "old guard," among them Prokofiev, was evacuated to the town of Nalchik in the Northern Caucasus.[2] When the composer left Moscow, he took with him many partially completed compositions, including sketches for the Seventh and Eighth Sonatas, the Violin Sonata, Op. 80, two acts of *Cinderella,* and the almost finished libretto of *War and Peace.*

During his three months in Nalchik Prokofiev worked continuously, finding life in this quiet little town conducive to creative activity. "Let us hope that the return to Moscow is not far off," he wrote his friends. He did not know that he would not see the capital again for almost a year and a half.

In the Caucasus, as before, he spent a great deal of time with Miaskovsky. Almost every day the friends discussed their ideas and plans and played sketches of new works for each other. Miaskovsky was then working on his Twenty-second and Twenty-third Symphonies and Seventh Quartet, and Prokofiev was composing *War and Peace,* the Second String Quartet, and the suite *The Year 1941.*

In Nalchik Prokofiev also formed a close friendship with the oldest actress of the Moscow Art Theater, O. L. Knipper-Chekhova. The musicians and actors frequently gave performances in the theater at Nalchik and also went to the army hospitals to perform for the wounded soldiers.

By the middle of November, Prokofiev had written the first two acts of *War and Peace* and completed the score of *The Year 1941.* The program of the latter work clearly shows Prokofiev's concern with current events; its three movements are entitled "In Battle," "Night," and "For the Brotherhood of Peoples." As the composer himself described it, "The first movement is a scene of heated battle, heard by the audience sometimes as though far away and sometimes as though on the actual battlefield; the second is a poetic night scene disturbed by the tension of impending conflict; the third is a triumphant lyrical hymn to victory and the brotherhood of peoples. "

The first performance of *The Year 1941,* given a year and a half later in Moscow, was coldly received. *Sovetskaya Muzyka* later noted in it a certain "superficiality in the musical material which does not correspond to the grandeur and significance of the theme," concluding that "The music of the Suite, while at times very poetic, does not penetrate to the core of the events which are indissolubly associated, in our minds, with the tragic year of 1941."[3] Shostakovich also spoke unfavorably of the work, finding it "insufficiently thought through and developed."[4] The suite remained unpublished.

In Nalchik Prokofiev thrilled to the stern beauty of Mt. Elbrus and the majesty of the surrounding panorama. He became interested in the fresh and little explored musical folklore of Kabarda, and he was soon listening to performances by folk musicians and studying recordings of Kabardinian folk songs.* He was impressed by the fact that many years before Taneyev had traveled through this area and made a special study of the music of the Kabardinians and mountain Tatars.

Prokofiev decided to write a string quartet based on the folk songs and instrumental tunes of this region. The result was the String Quartet No. 2 in F major, Op. 92, most of the themes of which were taken from Kabardinian and Balkar folk music. Among the materials used were the spirited song *Getigezhev Ogurbi,* the lyrical love song *Syuilyaklik Zhir,* and the popular *lezhinka Islambey.* Begun on November 2, the piano score of the Quartet was finished a month later, on December 3.

In Nalchik Prokofiev also wrote two mass songs, *Son of Kabarda* and *The Tankman's Vow* (to words by Mira Mendelson), which he dedicated to the famous infantryman Taubekov and the tankman Khakim Depuyev, respectively. Somewhat later three more songs (also to words by his wife) were added to these: two lyrical songs, *A Soldier's Love* and *The Soldier's Sweetheart,* and a satirical one, *Fritz.* Together with *Admiral Trash* and *Song of the Brave,* these songs were incorporated in Op. 89.[5]

None of these songs can be counted among the composer's more successful efforts. The critics correctly noted their "excessively elementary style" and the absence of melodies that would appeal to the masses. The best of the songs, *A Soldier's Love* and *The Soldier's Sweetheart,* are characterized by serene, lofty lyricism and pure, restrained feelings. But even these melodies are rather colorless and unmoving. None of these songs has been widely performed.

On November 23, 1941, when the battle lines were stretching toward the Caucasus, Prokofiev and the entire group of evacuated artists were transferred from Nalchik to Tbilisi, the capital of Georgia. Prokofiev was enchanted by this picturesque southern city and deeply impressed by the new buildings, the fine embankment of the Kura, and the Botanical Gardens situated on the hill not far from the old cemetery.

Despite wartime difficulties, the musical life of the Georgian capital re-

---

* During this time, on commission from the government of the Kabardino-Balkar A.S.S.R., Miaskovsky was working on his Twenty-third Symphony, which was based on folk themes of the Northern Caucasus. Works on Kabardinian themes were also written by Anatole Alexandrov, Samuel Feinberg, and Alexander Goldenweiser.

mained vigorous. K. Igumnov, V. Kachalov, A. Gauk, S. Feinberg, and A. Dolivo appeared in concerts there. Prokofiev conducted a program of his own works and also gave several recitals in Tbilisi, Baku, and Yerevan. (These proved to be his last appearances as a pianist, for poor health soon compelled him to give up concertizing.) He frequently attended concerts, as well as performances at the Georgian theaters and opera house. He was particularly impressed by a production of *Othello* at the Rustaveli Theater.

Life in Tbilisi was far from easy, however. "I must confess that life is rather difficult, as prices are very high here," Miaskovsky wrote to Moscow. "Besides, this is an unusually cold winter. . . . But even though it is difficult, we are living, and many are also working."[6]

It was in Tbilisi that Prokofiev finished the opera *War and Peace*. At the beginning of March he reported to Moscow that his work on the piano score was nearly finished. By the end of the month, all eleven scenes of the first version were completed and sent to the capital. While anxiously awaiting word about the opera, the composer worked ceaselessly on new compositions. In May of 1942 he finished the Seventh Piano Sonata, which he had started in 1939, and immediately after this he began working on other projects.

In Tbilisi, as in Nalchik, Prokofiev was surrounded by friends who took a lively interest in his work. In his letters to Moscow, Miaskovsky gave his impressions of the new compositions which he heard. "S. S. Prokofiev has done a lot of work here—the suite '1941' (which I don't particularly care for), the Second Quartet on Kabardinian and Balkar themes (magnificent music) and, finally, eight of the eleven scenes of 'War and Peace,'" he wrote on February 21, 1942.

Miaskovsky spoke reservedly about the opera. "The work is at times magnificent, but it is in his usual style: for the most part, the singers 'talk' to the accompaniment of wonderful orchestral music. But the music is first-rate throughout, and here and there very powerful." In another letter from Tbilisi he wrote, "Prokofiev has finished 'War and Peace.' Even though the music is exceptional, the opera probably won't come off. It's the same thing all over again—scene after scene after scene (like a play), endless talk and almost no singing. Besides, there are many superfluous episodes. Still, there are some stunning scenes, for example, at the old aunt's (Natasha Rostova's despair), Prince Andrei's death, and the end of the scene in Moscow (fires, executions, funerals)." Miaskovsky's criticisms proved to be apt and well-founded. In subsequent years Prokofiev had to make substantial revisions in the opera.

In Tbilisi Prokofiev conceived the idea of a large composition on a war theme, a cantata on P. Antokolsky's poem *Ballad of an Unknown Boy*. But he put this idea aside, for in the spring of 1942 he was invited by Eisenstein to come to Alma-Ata to work with him on *Ivan the Terrible*, a film they had planned before the war. Prokofiev was very happy at the prospect of working again with the great film producer, with whom he had collaborated so fruitfully four years before. "Your letter arrived at precisely the right moment," he wrote Eisenstein. "I have just finished writing the last bars of 'War and Peace,' and therefore I will very soon be ready to bend to your yoke."[7] He asked the director to send him the scenario as soon as possible so that he might begin to study it.

At the end of June in 1942 Prokofiev and his wife left Tbilisi and set out for Alma-Ata. "On the 29th the Prokofievs left us for Alma-Ata. We are very sorry. We feel orphaned," Miaskovsky wrote to Moscow. Before his departure, Prokofiev played the Seventh Piano Sonata for his friends. In a letter to Derzhanovsky, Miaskovsky called it "superbly wild."[8]

The journey to Alma-Ata by way of Baku, the Caspian Sea, Krasnovodsk, and the Turkmenian steppes was long and difficult, but Prokofiev wasted no time during the trip; even while on the Caspian steamer he managed to continue scoring *War and Peace*.

❦ ❦ ❦

While living in the Caucasus during the first year of the war, Prokofiev had written, besides the rather unsuccessful mass songs and *The Year 1941*, three major works: the opera *War and Peace*, the Second String Quartet, and the Seventh Sonata.

The deep feelings and emotions aroused in Prokofiev by the shattering events of the war were clearly reflected in the Seventh Sonata, the new Quartet, and particularly in the epic pages of *War and Peace*. At times, the composer's reaction to wartime events gave rise to tense, hyperbolic music. In parts of the Seventh Sonata (first movement) and the Quartet (development section of the first movement) we hear once again strident, furious sonorities, images of dark and evil forces. The *Ballad of an Unknown Boy* and the music for the film *Kotovsky* presented caustic sketches of the German militarists. So strong was the composer's predilection for portraying negative characters that it sometimes led him away from the principles of Soviet art, whose principal hero and subject, even during this terrible time, was the ordinary Soviet man, who was displaying unparalleled fortitude in the struggle against fascism.

The Second String Quartet, Op. 92, is one of Prokofiev's few works based almost entirely on folk material. His treatment of Kabardinian song and dance melodies was completely original. The whole tonal structure of this tart, harsh-sounding piece constitutes a kind of rejection of the stereotyped "oriental" style found in much Western music. What Prokofiev accentuated in the music of the Northern Caucasus was its severity and primitive power. Turning his back on the artificial ornamentation sometimes found in music on oriental themes, he at times went to the other extreme and pointed up the wild, purely primitive qualities of the music. Obviously such treatment could scarcely reflect the new life being created in the republics of the North Caucasus at that time.

After hearing the Kabardinian folk music played in the place of its origin, Prokofiev tried, as the young Glinka and Balakirev had done, to reproduce its peculiar harmonies and timbres. But in doing so, he often exaggerated the original folk idiom. His aim, as he himself put it, was to achieve "a combination of virtually untouched folk material and the most classic of classical forms, the string quartet," at the same time using "unhackneyed harmonization." Carried away by his fondness for concise, clearcut melodies and harsh, primitive-sounding chords, however, he sometimes made excessive use of "barbaric" harmonies and strident timbres (particularly in the first movement).

The Quartet is in classical form, with three carefully worked-out movements. The themes, based on folk songs, are very logically arranged to form contrasts between the vigorous, rhythmical passages and those that are lyrical, restrained, and somewhat melancholy.

Menacing, warlike images of the ancient Caucasus appear in the opening measures of the first movement. The persistent, stubbornly reiterated melody, moving in a well-defined rhythm, seems a typical product of Prokofiev's style. Actually, however, it is an authentic folk melody which the composer has accompanied by a harsh-sounding chord built on a series of open fifths (Fig. 39).

Here the chords in the strings sound hard, edgy, and metallic. These harsh diatonic harmonies, combined with abrupt dynamic effects, sound especially strange when performed by a string quartet. This theme is followed by the contrasting subordinate theme, a bright round-dance melody, which has a certain kinship to one of the episodes in *Zdravitsa,* although here the diatonic harmonies are treated more gently, more transparently. The jubilant concluding section of the exposition, in which the opening phrases of the movement are handled in a new way, is a natural continuation of the main theme.

FIGURE 39

In the development section the principal themes of the first movement undergo various modifications, entwining and clashing with each other. They acquire a sinister quality from an abundance of tritonal chords and contrapuntal superimpositions that verge on polytonality. It seems as though the "eyes of a Shaitan" (Lermontov) are glittering with an evil light in the darkness of a mountain landscape. The opening section of the first movement is repeated almost exactly in the recapitulation.

An utterly different world of sound is revealed to us in the lyrical second movement (Adagio), which is a charming nocturne. Here, too, national color is suggested by the character of the themes, the peculiarity of their design, and the tender folk quality of their diatonic style, which contains elements of the Phrygian mode and the natural minor. The first theme, introduced in the warm tones of the cello, is interlaced with scarcely audible figures in the accompaniment. Later, the rhythmic pattern of the accompaniment becomes more elaborate and is transformed into an intricate embellishment, seemingly an imitation of the strumming of a Caucasian bowed instrument of the *kemange* family.* "It was a sly trick, in a way, to transform the motiv of a *lezghinka* into an accompanying ornament," the composer later recalled, explaining that he had thought a traditional treatment of the dance tune might sound "dull, even banal."[9]

As surprising as a contrasting scene in a musical play is the middle

---

* This melody is based on the Kabardinian dance tune *Islambey,* which was also used by Miaskovsky in the third movement of his Twenty-third Symphony. It is possible that this is a variant of the melody used by Balakirev in his *Islamey.*

episode of the second movement, a graceful, rhythmic melody reminiscent of a Spanish serenade. This new theme is related to the opening melody of the Adagio, but here it is radically altered and acquires a sharp, ringing sonority from a change of rhythm and a skillful combination of *pizzicato* and *arco*. Thus the pensive, tender theme with which the movement opened is transformed into a capricious and elegant dance-serenade.

The Quartet has an interesting finale, constructed in rondo-sonata form with two subordinate themes and a slow episode in place of a development section. The whole movement is dominated by a joyful, vigorous theme in the syncopated rhythm of a mountain dance. This is the popular Kabardinian dance tune *Getigezhev Ogurbi,* which was also used by Miaskovsky in the first movement of his Twenty-third Symphony. One might suppose that the theme itself would have prompted the composer to write the finale in the form of a festive dance movement. But Prokofiev took a different and more complicated course, choosing to create new dramatic conflicts in the finale. The first subordinate theme in E-flat minor, anxious in character and with a nervous rhythm, recalls the agitated recitatives of Prokofiev's operas. The second subordinate theme, on the other hand, sounds roguish and jaunty, like a witty folk tune. Finally, the slow section of the finale, which opens with a dramatic cello cadenza, is based on a restless song theme and is accompanied, as in the Adagio, by capricious, embellished figures. In the recapitulation the familiar fast themes are presented in reverse order; first come the two subordinate themes, and then the rather coarse, gay, dance theme of the refrain, which brings the movement to an end.

In this work Prokofiev once more demonstrated his ingenuity in working with timbres, the care and logic with which he could distribute tonal effects. Some of these effects imitate Caucasian folk instruments, as the previously mentioned ornamental passages, for example, or the sharp, knocking devices of *pizzicato* or *col legno,* which represent the timbres of percussion instruments. Here the composer appears once again in the role of an innovator, this time enriching the resources of the string quartet. Asafyev wrote enthusiastically about this, pointing out "the brilliance of the quartet scoring, the power and freshness of expression, and the novelty of the rhythmical development."[10]

Nevertheless, the harsh polytonality of certain passages in the Quartet, particularly in the first movement, unduly distorts the structure of Kabardinian folk music and thus brings about a certain stylistic duality in this generally interesting work.

Approximately the same contradictions that exist in the Second String Quartet are found in the Seventh Piano Sonata. Here, too, strident dissonances and nervous excitement predominate, particularly in the first movement. In harshness and fury this is the most radically modern of Prokofiev's piano sonatas, surpassing in this respect even the Sixth Sonata, with its fierce raging and moments of almost mystical aloofness. We know that the composer planned the Seventh Sonata as early as 1939, at the same time as the Sixth, and even made sketches of its principal themes. But according to him, he did not succeed in completing the new sonata at that time and had to lay it aside several times. Finally, in the spring of 1942, the work "finished itself" very quickly, in the course of a few days.

This sonata is in three movements; as the composer described them to this writer, "the first movement unfolds in fairly rapid tempo [*Allegro inquieto*]; the second is a lyrical andante, at one moment tender, at another tense; the finale is in 7/8."[11]

The first allegro creates the impression of a fiendish scherzo, filled with swirling motion. This feeling is heightened by all of the elements of the music—the restless pattern of the melody, the unrelieved persistence of the *ostinato* phrases in the bass, the bare rhythmic construction, and mainly the dissonant harmonic texture, which the composer himself described as "atonal." Again one recalls such driving pages of Prokofiev's music as the *Toccata,* Op. 11, and the Toccata of the Fifth Piano Concerto. The most high-strung episodes of his operatic music also come to mind—the scene in Napoleon's headquarters in *War and Peace,* for example. Here melody clearly becomes secondary in importance to the blend of spare texture, dissonant harmony, and sharply accentuated mechanical rhythm (FIG. 40).

FIGURE 40

*335*

This harmonic language is actually quite different from a cerebral aton-alism, however, for the tonal centers (B-flat major and B-flat minor in the first movement) are clearly evident in the strong cadences, although the composer has disguised the tonality by means of polyphonic superimposi-tions, blocks of chords, and so on.

The turbulent first theme gradually subsides, like the rumble of a receding storm, and is followed by the melancholy second theme. Here the complexity of the harmony and the twists of the melodic line create a feeling of unreality and secrecy. This contrasting theme temporarily relieves the tensions created at the beginning of the movement, but a gradual accelerando eventually brings back the unrestrained emotions of the opening theme. In the development section, these emotions become even more powerful. The lyrical second theme reappears only briefly in the recapitulation, where it is followed by a strong and definite restatement of the agitated opening theme, which gives the entire movement a quality of expressionistic overstatement.

The melodic unity of the first movement is worthy of note. The restless, knocking figure, which resembles the "fate motiv" of Beethoven's Fifth Symphony, reappears frequently in the principal theme and the bridge passage, and later, in a slower tempo, it ushers in the second theme.

A beautiful singing theme in the baritone register forms the basis of the second movement. Here everything is in direct contrast to the high-strung music of the first allegro: the soft outlines of the lyrical theme, the unhurried tempo, bright tonality (E major), and rich harmonic texture. As in the case of the lyrical movements of the Sixth Sonata and the Second Quartet, one cannot but draw a comparison here with the romantic, pensive episodes of Prokofiev's operas. In the middle section of the Andante there appears an austere theme in the bass, which briefly suggests a mood of sober contemplation. This new theme is varied and becomes entwined with an intricate network of figurations; it is then developed, and grows more and more restless. Finally, the opening lyrical theme returns, like a bright vision; the most peaceful and serene theme in the entire Sonata, it strikes one as the embodiment of a bright and happy dream.

The third movement is the most impressive. It is a dynamic Russian toccata in fanciful 7/8 time, which calls to mind the heroic images of Borodin's music. The massive chords, thumping *ostinato* basses, and cease-lessly flowing rhythm which seems driven on by the strong accents—all seem chosen to suggest a martial procession of legendary giants. Just as in the first movement of the Sonata, melody is here overwhelmed by ele-

*Above*: Prokofiev and N. Ya. Miaskovsky (1941). *Below*: S. A. Samosud, M. A. Mendelson-Prokofieva, and Prokofiev (1946).

Caricature of Prokofiev by N. Radlov

mental rhythm, a growing volume of sound, and heavy, dissonant chords. This powerful, relentless onslaught continues, in strictly sustained rhythm, throughout the finale. Against this rhythmic background are heard the anxious phrases of the bridge passage and the scarcely audible, yearning lyricism of the second theme. Here, in contrast to the frenzied first movement, a clearer, more harmonically stable tone prevails until the very end, when the tonic key of B-flat major is firmly stated. This music evokes an image of tremendous heroic forces aroused to victorious struggle. The freedom of its metric pattern and the peculiarities of its melodic structure make it resemble somewhat the tunes of the Russian *byliny*.

At the same time, one can see in this Sonata a certain "aestheticizing" of antiquity, an attempt to endow epic images with arbitrarily distorted features. Despite the boldness and stunning power of the composer's unusual manner of writing, it is here so exaggerated as to make it difficult for the listener to perceive any features of Soviet reality in the music. The overdrawn tension in the first movement and the primitive elements found in the finale give this work a certain stylized quality.

Like the Second Quartet, the Seventh Sonata was hailed by the critics. They asserted that it fully expressed "the Soviet man's wholesome and positive sense of life," that in its commanding tones one hears the "voice of the motherland." These evaluations were obviously exaggerated, for they failed to take into consideration the questionable aspects of the work, which prevented it from becoming a genuine expression of national feeling during the terrible year 1942.

❈   ❈   ❈

Prokofiev's best works were widely performed during the war, inspiring the Soviet people in their struggle against the enemy. Most effective of all was the wonderful music of *Alexander Nevsky,* which now resounded with new power in the movie houses, on the radio, and in the concert halls. It was brought to the cities of Central Asia by the State Symphony Orchestra of the U.S.S.R. and was received everywhere with tremendous enthusiasm. On the seven hundredth anniversary of the Battle on the Ice, it was performed in full by the Sverdlovsk Philharmonic Orchestra. On this occasion, excerpts of Konstantin Simonov's poem *The Battle on the Ice* were read during the breaks between the third and fifth movements. The cantata, especially its patriotic choruses, was often played on the radio.

The film *Alexander Nevsky* was shown many times throughout the winter and spring of 1942 for the soldiers and sailors defending Sevastopol. During the difficult days of enemy bombing and shelling, it was presented in underground shelters and caves in the most advanced sections of the defended areas. One of the participants in the defense of Sevastopol wrote of this: "The song 'Arise, Ye Russian People' produced an overwhelming impression. Intensified by the resonance of the cave, it powerfully gripped the soul."[12]

During these years there was also a growing interest in Prokofiev's music abroad, especially in the United States and England. The common struggle against fascism strengthened the cultural ties between the U.S.S.R. and these countries, and Soviet music in general became increasingly popular.

"At the present time Russian music is more popular in England than it has ever been," Sir Adrian Boult, the conductor of the B.B.C. Symphony Orchestra, wrote to the Union of Soviet Composers.

During the early years of the war, the *Alexander Nevsky* cantata scored a brilliant success both in England and the United States. It was performed in New York on March 7, 1943, by the N.B.C. Symphony under Leopold Stokowski, with Jennie Tourel and the Westminster Choir. The critics abroad all pointed out how perfectly this music accorded with the Soviet people's heroic struggle.

"The work has singular and dramatic appositeness to the situation today in Russia," maintained Olin Downes, the critic of *The New York Times*. Reminding his readers of the rout of the Teutonic Knights by the forces of Alexander Nevsky, Mr. Downes confidently stated that "now it would seem that history is about to repeat itself. A certain process, calculated to put the dream of eastern domination forever to rest, is now in order."

Critics also heard an echo of the times in the Seventh Sonata, which was successfully performed by Vladimir Horowitz, one of the greatest pianists of the United States. "In its own way this piece is just as characteristic of the staggering war of Russia as Shostakovich's Seventh Symphony," remarked the critic of the *Chicago Sun*. "Something in the inexorable rhythm of the finale gives a suggestion of the heroic inflexibility of a people who are not to know defeat."

Audiences abroad also responded with increased interest to such Prokofiev works as the *Classical Symphony,* the *Scythian Suite, Peter and the Wolf, Lieutenant Kije,* the suites from *Romeo and Juliet,* and the Sixth Sonata.

✹ ✹ ✹

In June of 1942 Prokofiev took up residence in Alma-Ata, which lies at the foothills of the Altai Mountains in Central Asia. He liked this green city, with its broad avenues lined with flowering trees. "I'm scribbling a lot of different kinds of music here, and completing the orchestration of 'War and Peace,'" he wrote to Moscow in September 1942. He spent almost a year in this Central Asian city, more than three thousand kilometers from Moscow. A small room in the House of the Soviets hotel served as his workroom.

The Moscow and Leningrad film studios had been evacuated and were now located in Alma-Ata. Prokofiev became one of the main composers of the Central Soviet Film Studio. While preparations were being made for the filming of *Ivan the Terrible,* he wrote music for the films *Tonya* (directed by A. Room) and *Kotovsky* (directed by A. Feinzimmer). The music for *Kotovsky* contained some trenchant characterizations of the German soldiery. In addition to these two films, he also worked on the score for the biographical picture *Lermontov,* which had been started before the war began. For this he wrote the *Contredanse* and *Mephisto Waltz,* transcriptions of which were later incorporated in the set of piano pieces, Op. 96.

But he was most interested in starting work on *Ivan the Terrible.* Eisenstein had given him a detailed account of the scenario, and he was impatiently awaiting the filming of the picture. Indeed, he was so excited by Eisenstein's scenario of the new film that he began making musical sketches for it even before the actual shooting began. Thus, by November 1942 he had already written the chorus "The Vow of the Oprichniki," which was later used in Part II of *Ivan the Terrible.*

Prokofiev's work on the music for this film was to be a further development of the heroic-epic element of his style, which had begun to manifest itself in *Alexander Nevsky* and in a number of scenes of *War and Peace.* In the midst of the war, the film's theme was certain to be especially meaningful.

During the summer and fall of 1942 momentous battles raged in the south and southeast of the Soviet Union. The fascist armies were pushing toward the Volga and the Caucasus. The places where only a year before Prokofiev had worked on an opera and a quartet were now bloody battlefields. Tbilisi, from which Miaskovsky and his other friends had been evacuated farther east, became a front-line city. This situation caused Prokofiev a great deal of anxiety. "I have had no news from N.Ya.M. for a long time, and I don't even know where he is," the composer wrote anxiously to Moscow in September 1942.[13] A month later he received the sorrowful news of the sudden death of Derzhanovsky in Moscow. "I deeply mourn my dear old friend," he wired Derzhanovsky's widow.

During the summer months of 1942, Prokofiev worked on the one-movement cantata *Ballad of an Unknown Boy.* In October he wrote to Moscow that he had finished the piano score of this work. By April of 1943 he had completed the orchestration of *War and Peace.*

❄ ❄ ❄

The horrible experiences of the war were to some degree reflected in the music of the *Ballad of an Unknown Boy* (to verses by P. Antokolsky). "The central theme of the cantata," wrote the composer, "is the moving story of a boy whose mother and sister were killed by the fascists and who avenges their death by hurling a hand grenade into a fascist staff car during the enemy's retreat. The name and fate of the boy remain unknown, but word of his heroic deed spread far and wide, inspiring others to feats of heroism. . . . I have endeavored to make this cantata a swift-moving, dramatic composition."[14]

What particularly attracted Prokofiev in this subject was the caricatural depiction of the fascist soldiery:

> That night the storm troopers
> Entered the Soviet city B,
> And there, when the shooting had subsided,
> Barked their first "Heil Hitler."

In his portrayal of the Hitlerites, Prokofiev employed the same trenchant expressionist means, the same kind of fearsome "barbarisms" he had used in depicting the Knights' invasion in *Alexander Nevsky,* the enemy's atrocities in *Semyon Kotko,* and still earlier, in certain episodes of the *Scythian Suite* and *Seven, They Are Seven.* The theme of the invasion in the *Ballad* is expressed by a terrifying march with clipped cadences and in Prokofiev's typical harmonic style (FIG. 41).

FIGURE 41

In its general color, this caricatured march has something in common with the famous invasion theme of Shostakovich's Seventh Symphony, although that theme is more vivid and sharply defined. In the *Ballad of an Unknown Boy,* the theme of the invasion is given descriptive details which seem at one moment to express the groans of the tortured victims, and at another the exultant shouts of the enemy reveling in their own brutalities. (The composer marked one of the orchestral phrases "Like a Roar.")

One would naturally expect to find, as a contrast to these repellent "themes of the enemy," resounding heroic themes portraying the invincible Soviet people risen in struggle against fascism. It would have been fitting here to introduce simple, tuneful melodies similar to those of the songs in *Alexander Nevsky.*

Unfortunately, the composer failed to find simple and graphic musical means even for depicting the *Ballad*'s central character, the young hero of the war. The fragile theme of the Boy, in the familiar diatonic style with subtle harmonies and colorful modulations, closely resembles many of Prokofiev's contemplative melodies. But the characterization of the heroic partisan called not for contemplative, lyrical themes but rather for heroic and dramatic ones. These are totally lacking in this work. The principal leitmotiv, repeated again and again by the orchestra, conveys the general anxiety of the war years rather than resoluteness and fighting spirit.

The composer's limited use of the resources of the cantata form only makes one feel more keenly the absence of a positive heroic image. The leading role is assigned not to the voices, but to the orchestra, which continuously illustrates Antokolsky's text. Both the soloists (a dramatic soprano and a dramatic tenor) and the chorus are given melodically spare declamatory phrases, which are clearly subordinated to the themes of the orchestra. What is more, the work is weighed down with prosaic textual material, which is awkward for singing and at times crudely naturalistic (for example, "He wandered through the deserted farms that smelled of death and dung"). All this only served to make the cantata difficult to perform and understand.

The rich experience Prokofiev gained from working on such realistic cantatas as *Alexander Nevsky* and *Zdravitsa,* in which the melodic vocal element plays a decisive role, was not brought to bear in this new work. Instead, the composer once again resorted to superficial illustration and ineffective kaleidoscopic techniques, as he had previously done in the unsuccessful Chaldean invocation *Seven, They Are Seven.*

It is hardly surprising that the cantata did not meet with a sympathetic response. The reception of its single performance in Moscow in February

1944 was more than restrained.[15] The composer himself expressed apprehension about its fate when he sent the work to Moscow. "I'm only afraid that without me they won't make head nor tail of it," he wrote. "Last January N.Ya.M. only mumbled something about it politely through his moustache."[16]

Indeed, while acknowledging the sincerity of the conception, as well as the power and expressiveness of certain episodes, Miaskovsky criticized the vocal writing in the cantata: "The singers are given isolated bits of melody—quite unrewarding for performance." ("I'm afraid it won't take," he noted in his diary.) The work was also justly criticized by Shostakovich in his report to the Plenary Session of the Organization Committee of the Composers' Union in March 1944. "Prokofiev possesses an amazing gift for apt musical illustration of a text," he said, "but this also gives rise to a serious flaw in his creative work: in his enthusiasm for illustration he neglects the organic unity of musical form. The music in the *Ballad* lacks a solid, constructive base. I feel it as a series of separate, unconnected musical episodes. It seems to me that it is impossible to create a large-scale work by a method of this sort."[17]

For a long time Prokofiev did not agree with the unfavorable appraisal of the cantata: "*The Boy,* I am sorry to say, has been trampled to death," he told the present author. The *Ballad* was never performed again and has remained unpublished.

＊　＊　＊

While living in Alma-Ata, Prokofiev developed a great interest in the national culture of Kazakhstan. Kazakh folk music was widely performed on the radio, in the theater, and at concerts, and the composer attended several Kazakh operas and plays. Actually, this interest was not a new one for Prokofiev. The fresh and tuneful melodies of the Kazakh songs had attracted his attention as far back as 1927, when he first became acquainted with A. Zatayevich's *1000 Songs of the Kirghiz People.* At that time, after studying this famous collection, he had made five arrangements of Kazakh songs for voice and piano: *Kanafiya, Manmanger, Kare Kyz, Shama,* and *Yek Kugarai.* Now he conceived the idea of writing a comic opera based on Kazakh folklore.

After reading a great many Kazakh tales, legends, and proverbs, Prokofiev and Mira Mendelson finally chose as the theme of the projected opera a charming story about a young shah whose forehead sprouted horns, a symbol of his regal majesty of which he was both proud and ashamed. The work was tentatively given the title *The Shah Has Horns* (*Khan Buzai*). In gathering musical material for it, the composer selected authentic folk melodies from Zatayevich's three-volume collection. "I am planning to write the opera according to a new method: by dividing the libretto into separate episodes, like scenes in a film, and then selecting what seems to me the most suitable music for each scene," Prokofiev reported in one of his articles.

Work on the new opera, begun in Alma-Ata, was repeatedly interrupted by other more pressing duties. The composer planned to finish it after *War and Peace* and *The Duenna* had been produced, but new creative plans prevented him from returning to the Kazakh opera. All that remains of this work is a large quantity of thematic material, carefully arranged according to his new method.

In December 1942 Prokofiev went to Moscow. On the way he stopped in Semipalatinsk, where the Ukrainian film industry was temporarily located, in order to deliver the score for the film *Partisans in the Ukrainian Steppes* (directed by I. Savchenko). This score incorporated material from the suite *The Year 1941* and also included the theme of the popular Ukrainian song *Oh You, Galya.*

In Moscow Prokofiev gave a private performance of *War and Peace* (in piano score) and the new Seventh Sonata for members of the musical community. Shortly after this, Sviatoslav Richter began to prepare the Sonata for concert performance. Prokofiev was overjoyed to see Miaskovsky again and played a number of his new works for him, among them the *Ballad of an Unknown Boy.*

On returning to Alma-Ata the composer resumed work on several unfinished compositions.

"I have completed the orchestration of *War and Peace* and have begun to look through *The Betrothal,* into which I'm introducing some changes," he wrote to his friends. "In the very near future I plan to finish the symphonic suite from *Semyon Kotko,* for which I already have sketches, and also to complete the Eighth Piano Sonata, one movement of which is already finished."[18]

Prokofiev also prepared two sets of piano transcriptions in Alma-Ata: three pieces from the ballet *Cinderella,* Op. 95 (*Intermezzo, Gavotte,* and *Valse lente*), and three pieces, Op. 96 (*Waltz* from the opera *War and Peace,* and *Contredanse* and *Mephisto Waltz* from the music for the film *Lermontov*). While scarcely altering their original themes and inner construction, he introduced complicated pianistic figurations into these arrangements. He later transcribed ten more pieces from *Cinderella* to form Op. 97. The four-movement Sonata for flute and piano, Op. 94, begun in September 1942, was also written in Alma-Ata.

While in Kazakhstan Prokofiev attentively followed the reception of his new works in Moscow. Despite the increasingly frequent enemy air raids, concert life continued in the blacked-out capital. As a matter of fact, on the very evening that Prokofiev's "Kabardinian" Quartet was given its first performance (September 5, 1942), there was an air-raid alert and the concert began late. The Quartet was played by the Beethoven State Quartet in the Small Hall of the Conservatory and was favorably received by the press. During the same season, on January 18, 1943, Sviatoslav Richter gave the première of Prokofiev's Seventh Piano Sonata. On April 19, *The Year 1941* was performed at a concert of Soviet music in the Great Hall of the Conservatory, with N. Rakhlin conducting.

In July of 1943 Prokofiev had the great joy of being awarded the Order of the Red Banner of Labor for his outstanding contribution to Soviet music. At about the same time he was also given the title of Honored Artist of the R.S.F.S.R. Similar recognition was also given the oldest Russian composers—S. N. Vasilenko, N. Ya. Miaskovsky, A. N. Alexandrov, Yu. A. Shaporin, and V. V. Shcherbachev. "I was especially pleased for N.Ya.M. He should have been honored ten years ago," wrote Prokofiev.[19] Somewhat earlier, in March 1943, the composer had been awarded the Stalin Prize, second degree, for the Seventh Sonata.

When the filming of *Ivan the Terrible* was postponed for an indefinite period, Prokofiev found no reason to remain in Alma-Ata. It was at about this time that he was invited by the Kirov Theater of Leningrad to come to the city of Molotov [Perm] in order to finish his ballet *Cinderella*. He looked forward to a sojourn in the beautiful Ural region. "The south is fine, but still the northern summer is better," he remarked in one of his letters from Alma-Ata.

In June of 1943 Prokofiev and his wife moved to Molotov, where they lived for about six months. Here he completed *Cinderella* and put the finishing touches on the flute sonata that he had begun in Kazakhstan (although the main themes of this work had been sketched before the war). "It's very pleasant to be in the north again," he wrote his friends. "The theater is taking care of our everyday needs, and my work is going quite well." The severe beauty of the Urals and the forest-covered banks of the Kama remained indelibly imprinted on Prokofiev's memory.

By the end of the summer of 1943 Prokofiev had completed the charming Flute Sonata, the sunniest and most serene of his wartime compositions. "The Sonata for flute is almost finished," he wrote L. T. Atovmyan on August 12. "I still have to polish the recapitulation of the finale. It has turned out to be quite bulky, with four movements and about forty pages."

The idea of composing a transparent, graceful piece for the flute had interested Prokofiev years before in France, where the art of woodwind playing is highly cultivated. He still spoke with respect of the "heavenly sound" of one of the best French flutists, Barrère. Once again the composer attempted to revive, in the contemporary musical idiom, the simplicity of the classical instrumental style, with its unaffected melodic clarity. After the harsh and intense sonorities of the Seventh Sonata, the "Kabardinian" Quartet, and the *Ballad of an Unknown Boy,* this was a natural emotional release. It was in such a way, many years before, that the serene lyricism of the *Fugitive Visions* and the *Classical Symphony* had followed the daring outbursts of the *Scythian Suite* and *The Gambler.* The character of the sonata's principal images—the quiet, gentle lyricism of the first and third movements, the capricious merriment of the second movement, and the playful dance quality of the finale—suited the transparent tone color of the flute splendidly.

In this Sonata, as in the best of his early works and later in *Romeo and Juliet* and the *Music for Children,* Prokofiev reveals to the full his inexhaustible gift for melody. He easily and naturally unfolds before the listener a series of simple and appealing images, ranging from dreamy lyricism to gentle, frolicsome humor. In the clarity and purity of its ideas and the classical precision of its style, this Sonata closely resembles certain examples of Prokofiev's children's music and his earlier works in the classical vein. But despite its clarity of form, miniature scale, transparent texture, and even the use of certain specifically classical devices, this work is not merely a re-creation of the late eighteenth-century style. On the contrary, it is completely modern and typically Prokofievan in its harmonic thinking, its intricate interweaving of figures and passages, and its distinctive lyricism. The style of this piece is derived chiefly from its blend of simple melodies, resilient rhythms, subtle modulations, and colorful contrasts of harmony.

The main theme of the first movement (*Moderato*) somewhat resembles the opening theme of the First Violin Concerto. Here we find the same pensively lyrical melody, progressing in fourths, the same sparkling key of D major, and the same gentle interplay and changes of harmonic color, which seem to suggest shifting shadows. Only the characteristic "chirping" figure in the second measure and the gay embellishment at the end of the first phrase add a touch of playfulness, a hint of a smile (FIG. 42).

FIGURE 42

The graceful second theme is in the typically Prokofievan dance manner. Here the combination of sharp dotted rhythms and a charming play of modulations calls to mind certain dances of *Romeo and Juliet.* In the concise, fragmentary development section the themes are presented not in conflict but alternately, in a new harmonic treatment without complicated counterpoint or harsh dissonance. The recapitulation is in strict classical style, repeating almost exactly the material of the exposition.

The second movement (*Presto*) is a light and carefree scherzo in which the principal themes complement each other. The first theme consists of gay running figures with cleverly displaced rhythmical accents, while the second is in the manner of a strictly rhythmical, semifantastic dance. In sharp contrast to these themes is the pensive melody of the middle section. The rather static quality of the piano accompaniment in open fifths as well as certain subtleties of the melody itself, such as oscillation between major and minor and Lydian coloration, endow this theme with a rather naïve fancifulness. But this theme once again gives way to a statement of the principal scherzo themes, which are repeated almost without change. Only at the very end does the composer darken the bright colors of this movement with a few shades of harmonic tartness.

After the involved Scherzo, the lyrical Andante sounds simple and artless. Here we find the same pensive quality as in the first movement, and also the same delicate, colorful harmonic development, in keeping with the character of the simple, song-like melody (for example, the sudden shift from the tonic F major to the sad-sounding F-sharp minor at the end of the first statement). The active voice-leading and distinctive character of the cadences reveal the typical Prokofiev hand. The middle episode abounds in complicated passage work of rather intricate design. The recapitulation is constructed on a novel combination of the opening theme in the piano and figured patterns from the middle section in the flute.

The Sonata concludes with a lively finale (*Allegro con brio*) in the spirit of eighteenth-century classicism, which is particularly evident in the character of the main theme, with its grace notes, ornamentation, and well-defined 4/4 rhythm. In its exuberance and wit, as well as in its combination of traditional forms and piquant harmonies, this movement closely resembles the fast movements of the *Classical Symphony*. This similarity can be seen in the playfully active theme of the bridge passage, which recalls the amusing melodies of the Italian opera buffa. Unexpected humor also appears in the second theme, which bears a close resemblance to the mechanical piano exercises of Hanon (one is reminded of similar Hanon-like passages in the First and Third Piano Concertos). It is only in the middle episode of this rondo-sonata that the desired contrast occurs and the merriment gives way to a lyrical recollection, to that kind of contemplative lyricism which later appears in *War and Peace*.

The Sonata ends with a joyous, resounding statement of the principal phrase of the finale, in which a feeling of bright optimism prevails.

❈ ❈ ❈

While living in Molotov Prokofiev also worked on the piano score of the ballet *Cinderella,* which he had begun for the Kirov Theater early in 1941. He was happy to have the opportunity of working closely with the company of this theater, which had brought forth such an inspired production of *Romeo and Juliet.* In putting the finishing touches on the new ballet, Prokofiev worked with the gifted dancer K. Sergeyev (creator of the role of Romeo) and the librettist, N. Volkov. Together the composer, the ballet master, and the librettist discussed each detail of the music and staging. Their work was made easier by the fact that most of the music had already been written. At this time, however, some of the themes of the final act were revised. The composer did not complete the orchestration of the work since the première, with Ulanova in the title role, was postponed until the end of the war. There was some discussion in Molotov about producing *The Buffoon,* but this idea was soon abandoned.

In the late summer of 1943 Prokofiev was invited to Moscow to conduct a concert of his works. But he now had little interest in conducting. "As for your wish that I conduct my concert," he wrote to L. T. Atovmyan, "I beg you to take into consideration that it is much more important for me to listen to 'Kotko' and '1941' from the hall, for there I can hear how they sound and decide on any retouching that might be required before publication. For this reason I should like someone else to conduct."[20]

Meanwhile, Prokofiev's return to Moscow was delayed by requests from Alma-Ata that he come there to complete work on the music for *Ivan the Terrible.* "I'm waiting to see what my tormentors in Alma-Ata want— I believe they need me in October," he wrote in one of his letters. But he did not go to Alma-Ata, and in October 1943, after a two-year absence, he and his wife returned to the capital.

The musical season 1943–44 was an extremely busy one for Prokofiev. With many other Moscow composers he participated in a contest for a national anthem. The versions of his anthem were added to the list of his compositions as Op. 98, in which four versions of an anthem for the R.S.F.S.R. were later included. On January 8, 1944, the government expressed its gratitude to Prokofiev and the other composers and poets who had taken part in creating the new anthem. During this period Prokofiev also wrote the *March* for military band, Op. 99, a very spirited work with a gay main theme and a broad flowing baritone solo in the Russian style. This *March,* which contained novel modulatory effects and a number of difficult bravura passages, was intended more for concert performance than for the parade field.

Several times during the season Prokofiev attended concerts in which his works were performed. He was present, for example, when the flutist N. Kharkovsky and the pianist S. Richter introduced the Sonata, Op. 94, in the Small Hall of the Conservatory on December 7. The work was very well received.

At about this time, after consulting David Oistrakh, Prokofiev arranged this Sonata for violin and piano. The new version, listed as Op. 94–bis, differed considerably from the original, containing such typical violinistic devices as double stops and chords, harmonics, passages of *pizzicato* and *arco,* and so on. In this arrangement the piece gained warmth and depth of feeling. It was given its first performance by David Oistrakh and Lev Oborin on June 17, 1944. Since then it has won a place in the repertory of many violinists both in the Soviet Union and abroad. Shostakovich hailed the Sonata as a "perfectly magnificent work."[21]

In late March of 1944 the Organization Committee of the Composers' Union held a plenary session in Moscow to evaluate the development of Soviet music during the war years. The work of Prokofiev was the subject of a special report by S. Schlifstein, and in the opening address, Shostakovich spoke very warmly of Prokofiev's creative activity: "Sergei Prokofiev occupies an important place in contemporary Soviet music. His talent has unfolded marvelously in our days. Unfortunately, he does not engage in pedagogical activity. He cannot be called a teacher and guide of our young generation in the literal sense of the word. Nevertheless, his influence on many composers is very great."

Shostakovich spoke favorably of the opera *War and Peace,* the Seventh Sonata, and the Flute Sonata, but made a number of critical observations concerning the *1941* suite and the *Ballad of an Unknown Boy.* Prokofiev devoted his speech to matters of composition. He reminded his listeners that it was impossible to write good music without creative imagination, without inventiveness: "To compose means to put together, to invent," he said. In discussing the new works of Shostakovich, Miaskovsky, Khachaturian, and Popov, he made special mention of the importance of polyphony. "Where, if not in polyphony," he asked, "can one find the path to the new?"

In the spring and summer of 1944 Prokofiev orchestrated *Cinderella,* hurrying to prepare the full score for the forthcoming production at the Bolshoi Theater. At the same time he composed the music for the film *Ivan the Terrible,* accumulated thematic material for the Fifth Symphony, made new piano transcriptions from *Cinderella* (Six Pieces, Op. 102), and prepared the Third Suite of the ballet *Romeo and Juliet.*[22]

Prokofiev spent the summer of 1944 at the Composers' House near the city of Ivanovo. Life in the quiet surroundings there was conducive to intensive creative work, and many other composers were then in residence at the House, including Glière, Miaskovsky, Khachaturian, Shaporin, Kabalevsky, and Muradeli. Among the works composed at Ivanovo were Glière's Concerto for Voice and Orchestra, Miaskovsky's Cello Concerto, Shostakovich's Trio, and Khachaturian's Second Symphony. The composers often played their new works for each other, engaged in heated discussions, relaxed together, and took long walks through the neighboring woods.

"At Ivanovo, Sergei Sergeyevich worked with amazing regularity," Khachaturian wrote in his memoirs. "Every morning he would go to the nearby village where the Composers' Union had rented rooms for the composers to work in. It was there, in a modest little house at the far end of the village, that the Fifth and Sixth Symphonies, the Eighth Sonata, a set of piano pieces from *Cinderella,* and many other works were written. From time to time, other musicians would gather there to listen to his latest works."

In his leisure time, Prokofiev would go mushroom picking with his friends or amuse himself with a game of volleyball. His colleagues were pleased to notice several striking changes in his character in recent years—greater sociability, simplicity, and gentleness. According to Khachaturian, during the period immediately following his return from abroad, Prokofiev seemed "curt, businesslike, and at times even a bit haughty. He saw few people other than a handful of old friends. And now, in the space of a few years under the influence of a different social environment, his attitude toward people had changed noticeably. He was drawn more and more into the life of the community, the life of the Soviet people, and the work of the Composers' Union. He became friendlier and more considerate, and his face more often shone with a bright smile."

The film *Ivan the Terrible* was supposed to have been finished in 1944, but Prokofiev did not want to leave Ivanovo. "Eisenstein has been trying to lure me to Moscow," he wrote Atovmyan on July 17, "but I would like to stay on here longer . . . as I have begun a symphony, and my work is going quite well."

Early in September 1944 the press reported that both the Fifth Symphony (in piano score) and the Eighth Sonata had been finished. In October the composer played both of these works in the Central House of the Composers. On December 30, Emil Gilels performed the Eighth Sonata successfully in the Great Hall of the Conservatory.

❦ ❦ ❦

The Eighth Sonata in B major is the third in the series of piano sonatas which Prokofiev had begun in 1939. Work on these sonatas (Op. 82, 83, and 84), which extended over a period of five years, ushered in a new stage in the development of the composer's piano style.

This cycle of three monumental sonatas clearly demonstrated the dualism of the composer's artistic aims. On the one hand, these later sonatas were more profound in conception, more dramatic, and on a grander scale than the earlier ones. On the other hand, the expressionistic tendencies that he had shown earlier he now indulged to an even greater extent. This can be seen in the exaggeration, lack of restraint, and harsh dissonance in certain passages (development sections of the first movements of the Sixth and Eighth Sonatas, first movement of the Seventh Sonata); in the rather enigmatic, bizarre quality of the lyrical themes (second themes of the first movements of the Sixth and Eighth Sonatas); and, occasionally, in the predominance of pure rhythm and motion over the melodic element (beginning of the Sixth Sonata, finale of the Seventh, middle section of the finale of the Eighth). While compositional techniques of this kind were interesting to seasoned professionals, they were not always easily grasped by the average listener, who had come to love the best examples of Prokofiev's piano style—for example, the Second, Third, and Fourth Sonatas, *Fugitive Visions, Tales of the Old Grandmother,* and the piano transcriptions from *Romeo and Juliet.*

Judging from the sketchbooks that have been preserved, the main themes of the Eighth Sonata were composed in 1939. Among these sketches we find two themes later used in the first movement, the principal minuet theme of the second movement, and the two opening themes of the finale. In the final writing, however, the composer revised his original plan considerably. New, sharply contrasting themes appeared (second theme of the first movement, middle episode of the finale), the tonality was changed from the original C major to B-flat major, and the number of movements was reduced from the projected four to three.

The opening material of the first movement is unusual in Prokofiev's instrumental writing. Here we find neither the terrifying exclamations of the Sixth Sonata and the Kabardinian Quartet nor the nervous frenzy of the opening of the Seventh Sonata. The first movement begins with a tender, melancholy theme, filled with vague yearning. The wanderings through different keys suggest complex and subtle emotion, but these wanderings are always resolved in firm, full cadences (Fig. 43).

The first theme, with its flowing melody and complicated harmonic digressions, calls to mind the love themes of *War and Peace.* This theme actually has a large three-part structure, with two new themes serving as its middle section. One of these, according to the composer, had originally been written as Liza's theme for the score for the film *The Queen of Spades,* which had been planned but was never made.

*351*

The bridge passage presents even more refined harmonic effects, such as the colorful interplay of pure triads and the strange modulations in the style of Rimsky-Korsakov's *Kaschei the Immortal.* The placid, flowing motion gives way to restless passage work, which provides the background for a restatement of the first lyrical theme, this time in the bass.

The second theme is also unusual. Following a passage containing somber, muted descending ninths in the bass, there appears a sad phrase, like a mournful lamentation, which reminds one of the troubled recitatives in Prokofiev's operas; indeed, the fragmentary nature of this theme does make it sound like a bit of operatic recitative. It is not unlikely that themes of this sort grew out of the experience Prokofiev gained while working on symphonic suites from his operatic music, such as those from *The Gambler* and *Semyon Kotko.*

Different, fantastic images appear in the development section of the first movement. Complicated running passages create an ever-increasing whirling energy, while the familiar first and second themes are sharply altered, becoming coarsened and elemental in form. The clash of these altered themes in sharply dissonant combinations creates the impression of a violent storm of emotions. This music has the same extremely exaggerated quality as that of the development section of the first movement of the Sixth Sonata. After the hurricane of emotions subsides, the tender first theme returns, sounding even more delicate, almost submissive. Only in the swift runs of the stormy coda does the seething dynamism of this work again reveal itself.

The more traditional second movement, *Andante sognando,* is a lyrical, dance-like miniature in the rhythm of a minuet with typical modulations (from D-flat to D) and comparatively uncomplicated variation development. The musical imagery of this movement is very similar to that of the slow movements of the Sixth and Seventh Sonatas.

The finale, on the other hand, contains much that is new and boldly dramatic. True, the opening material, with its fast triplet passages, resilient tarantella rhythm, and playful, spirited themes, is in the typical style of Prokofiev's early piano compositions; all this recalls the gay, "athletic" images in the First Piano Concerto, the *Études,* Op. 2, and the finales of the Second and Fourth Sonatas. The virtuoso aspect of Prokofiev's piano style is also richly represented here in the complicated technique of *perlé* runs, double notes, leaps, toccata-like passages, and sharp, biting staccato.

But in the middle section of the finale, the carefree running passages are suddenly interrupted by an agitated, almost visually dramatic scene. A mechanical, measured *ostinato* motion gradually develops. Sharp accents and incessant repetition of the same rhythmic figure evoke an image of heroic troops resolutely marching ahead, ready to crush anything in their path. The melodic element—terse, continuously repeated phrases—gives way to the mounting sonorities and the relentless power of the rhythm. Like the finale of the Seventh Sonata, this music calls to mind images of Russian armed might, but here, too, these images are presented in a highly stylized manner. Finally, at the climax of this "heroic" episode, an even more realistic dramatic conflict takes place. Over a persistent *ostinato,* the mournful phrase of the second theme of the first movement is stated several times. The image of war becomes even clearer, but then it gradually fades, as though receding into the distance. At this point one of the opening themes of the finale returns, hesitantly and imperceptively (marked *Ir-resoluto*). From here on nothing holds back the impetuous race of the swift and jubilant melodies. Just as in the finales of the Seventh Sonata and the Flute Sonata, Op. 94, the joy of living and the buoyant strength of the human spirit are once more affirmed.

The Eighth Sonata is one of Prokofiev's finest virtuoso piano works and it demands the highest technical skill of the performer. At the same time, it also abounds in variety, for alongside the swift runs and contemplative, lyrical passages, both quite typical of Prokofiev's instrumental music, there appear themes of an epic character, which convey suggestions of a hidden program. Such are the mournful "recitative" theme of the first movement and the "heroic" episode in the finale. These images, which were new for Prokofiev, bear a resemblance to some of his operatic themes and are to a certain extent connected with his impressions of the war years.

The Eighth Sonata is less dissonant than the Seventh, and its thematic material is clearer and warmer. Like the Sixth and Seventh Sonatas, it attracted the interest of Soviet pianists (Gilels, Richter, and Zak, for instance), but it never gained wide popularity. Prokofiev's early sonatas and the later Flute Sonata, Op. 94, with their more direct emotional communicativeness, proved more accessible and satisfying to the average audience.

❦   ❦   ❦

The year 1945 was one of great happiness for the Soviet people. Each day the radio brought news of the glorious victories of the Soviet Army. The feeling of pride in our country and the realization that ultimate victory was near found vivid reflection in the best Soviet music.

This period was very eventful in Prokofiev's creative life. The musical season 1944–45 saw the premières of his Fifth Symphony and Eighth Sonata, as well as the first concert performance of his opera *War and Peace*. In addition, the composer wrote two sets of arrangements of Russian folk songs, and Part I of the film *Ivan the Terrible* was completed and released.

Prokofiev was now settled in a new apartment at No. 11/13 Mozhaisk Road. During the fall he orchestrated the Fifth Symphony, completing the full score in November, and also worked hard with Eisenstein to complete the score for Part I of *Ivan the Terrible*.

At Eisenstein's invitation he visited the Mosfilm Studios, where he viewed completed sequences of the film. He carefully timed each episode that required musical characterization, at the same time outlining the plan of the music. The notes he made during these showings have been preserved. One section of them reads: "Tatars enter, 15 seconds; Tartar's speech, $31\frac{1}{2}$ seconds; the people see the Tsar (tense fade-out), $27\frac{1}{2}$ seconds; the Theme of Ivan (erratic, undulating, recurring), $154\frac{1}{2}$ seconds. The composer created the film score on the basis of such preliminary notes, in strict conformity with the timing of the film shots.

Prokofiev found working with directors and executing precise assignments very exciting. "I like a playwright or director to tell me exactly what he needs in terms of music," he said. "In other words, it is very helpful when they tell me, 'Here I need a minute and a quarter of music,' or 'Give me sad and tender music here.' "[23] Eisenstein was extremely precise in his demands, and he knew how to excite the composer's imagination with vividly pictorial descriptions.

But the main stimulus to Prokofiev's creativity was the dramatic intensity of the filmed portions of the movie and the magnificent performances of the actors—N. Cherkasov, S. Birman, A. Buchman, M. Nazvanov, M. Zharov, and others. Some of the musical sketches sprang from no more than the composer's first impression of the projected sequences and his meager notes on timing. Eisenstein spoke enthusiastically of Prokofiev's amazing ability to translate visual impressions quickly and exactly into the language of music. "I have always been astonished, for example, that after viewing a sequence two or at most three times (and given the time in seconds), the composer Sergei Prokofiev, with whom I worked, was able to write on the very next day such magnificent and flawless music, which in all its articulations and accents blended perfectly not only with the over-all rhythm of the action on the screen, but also with every subtle detail and nuance of the scenic sequence."[24]

On January 18, 1945, almost simultaneously with the première of the Fifth Symphony, the first part of *Ivan the Terrible* was released. Once again Eisenstein excited audiences with the panoramic scope, powerful imagery, sculpturesque form, and visual expressiveness of his art. The rather slow tempo, the unhurried majesty of the film action, which at times suggests a painting in motion, was in many respects complemented by the intensely forceful and dramatic music of Prokofiev.

❋ ❋ ❋

In the score of *Ivan the Terrible*, Prokofiev once more revealed with great power the national character of his art.[25] As in *Alexander Nevsky*, one is startled here by the almost visual concreteness of the musical images. The composer's fondness for character depiction, as well as for portraying battle, ceremonial, and genre scenes, did not prevent him from composing music on an epic and lyrico-dramatic plane. While musical portraits of groups predominated in *Alexander Nevsky*, here one finds a much broader representation of the personal emotions of the leading characters: the wide range of Ivan's feelings, from youthful vitality to acute suffering; the pitiful anguish of the young Tsarina Anastasia; and the treachery and malevolence of the boyarina Yefrosinia Staritskaya. Along with these characterizations the composer conveyed the historical atmosphere of sixteenth-century Muscovite Rus: on the one hand, the growing might of young Russia, united by Ivan's mighty will, and, on the other, the evil intrigues of the traitorous boyars.

The film opens with a brief and awe-inspiring overture which includes the chorus, "On the bones of the enemy, on the smoldering ashes, Rus stands united." Against a background of whirling passages in the violins appears a sharply defined theme in the trumpets and French horns, the theme of

355

Ivan. It is set forth in heavy unisons like the heroic themes of **Borodin**, and its Russian song quality is complicated by ponderous accents and somber harmonic shifts (FIG. 44).

FIGURE 44

The middle section of the overture consists of a short but dramatic male chorus, "The Black Cloud Is Gathering," which tells of the boyars' treachery and the intrigues of Ivan's enemies. The chorus continuously repeats a sharp phrase of warning, reminiscent of the theme of national disaster in the opera *War and Peace*. The theme of Ivan, first heard in the overture, is repeated many times like a leitmotiv and subjected to various modifications.

A different world of musical ideas, one associated with ancient Russian ceremonies, unfolds in the episode of the young Ivan's coronation. To the festive pealing of the bells the chorus sings "Long Live," which Prokofiev freely stylized in the manner of Russian liturgical chant. The scene of the wedding feast contains two short wedding songs, which are reminiscent of Glinka in their charming lyricism—one a eulogy to the young Tsar ("Like Young Oaks on a Hillock"), the other a lyrical female chorus, praising the beauty of the bride ("The White Swan Is Swimming"). The composer highlighted the light, exuberant coloring of both these songs, giving the first to the altos and tenors and the second to female voices alone; their transparent, joyous character is also sustained in the orchestral accompaniment. The grandeur of the ceremony and the beauty of the Russian melodic style are conveyed in both songs with extraordinary depth and national flavor.

The episodes of the people's rebellion and Ivan's encounter with the Tatar ambassadors are accompanied by brief but trenchant musical sketches. Prokofiev found apt, well-defined musical means to characterize the rebellious rabble who burst into the Tsar's chambers and to express the heart-rending wails of the saintly fool. (The theme of the fool, found in Prokofiev's manuscripts, was not used in the film score, however.) The music portraying the Tatar ambassadors who come to the palace to declare war on Russia ("Kazan is big, Moscow is small!") is unusually graphic. Their fierce strength is expressed by wicked, guttural shrieks in the orchestra. The composer's ability to portray by instrumental means not only the intensity of the action but also the intonations and timbres of human speech is striking.

Equally vivid and pictorial is the music of the battle episodes, depicting the march of Ivan the Terrible's forces against Kazan. As the enormous cannons are being dragged slowly up the mountain, a ponderous theme is heard in the low basses over a muffled rumble in the kettledrums. From somewhere far away comes the song of the Russian warriors, "Oh, Thou Bitter Sorrow, Tatar Steppe."

357

Next Tsar Ivan is shown in his headquarters pondering his plan for the next day's battle. His themes, heard in the music for this scene, express his wisdom, composure, and spiritual strength. Finally, the Moscow gunners burst into a valiant song as they are about to storm the impregnable walls of Kazan. Despite the economical means employed, this song grips one with its heroic power. Everything in it—the heavy accents, the severity of the harmony with its emphasis on the augmented fourth, and the manly vigor of the deep tone colors—is directed toward a single purpose, that of conveying the intrepid and formidable strength of the Russian warriors (FIG. 45).

FIGURE 45

In contrast to this theme are the shrieking grace notes in the woodwinds over the monotonous rhythm of the drums, which express the terror and pain of the captured Tatars put to torture. At the climax of the entire battle episode one hears the music of the storming of Kazan. In this, the powerful sonorities of the brasses predominate, in a continuous triplet motion with sharply accented chords and soaring scale-like passages; the images of Prokofiev's furious scherzos here acquire local, concretely descriptive features.

The musical episodes depicting Ivan's illness and the poisoning and death of Anastasia are completely different in character. The composer strives to penetrate the complex world of his heroes' emotions by utilizing orchestral leitmotivs in the manner of his operatic characterizations. The young, pure-hearted Anastasia, who is murdered by evil conspirators, is portrayed with true compassion. Her themes are permeated with elements of the Russian folk lament and mournful lyrical song.

One of the most eloquent musical passages of the entire film is the episode depicting the agony of the dying Ivan as he implores the boyars to recognize his infant son Dmitri as Tsar. The poignant theme of Ivan's suffering, given in the contrabasses *divisi,* has the ring of human speech; one hears in it the intonations of supplication, bitter moans, and sobbing.

Prokofiev employs his customary vivid, poster-art effects to characterize the Tsar's enemies. Particularly notable is the predatory, crow-like figure of Princess Yefrosinia Staritskaya, whose appearance on the screen is accompanied by sinister, "cawing" timbres in the strings *sul ponticello.* The themes of the reactionary boyars and those of the Tatars constitute a novel counteracting force in the complex musical dramaturgy of *Ivan the Terrible.*

Regrettably, the music for this film was never arranged for concert performance. As early as the beginning of the forties Prokofiev had thought of writing an opera on the subject of Ivan the Terrible; had he done so, he probably would have used the principal themes of the film music as the basis for his operatic score. He subsequently abandoned the idea of an opera, however, and instead incorporated a number of the film's themes into other works.

✳  ✳  ✳

Late in 1944 the distinguished folklorist Yevgeni Gippius suggested to Prokofiev that he make a set of arrangements of Russian folk songs for voice and piano, for a competition announced by the Committee on the Arts. Gippius selected a number of fine old songs which he and Z. Evald had recorded during the twenties in the northern regions of Russia, in the Onega, Pinega, and Vologda areas. The Moscow folklorist A. Rudneva also gave Prokofiev several songs which had been collected in the thirties in the Voronezh region.

Prokofiev was immediately impressed by the severe beauty of the old peasant melodies and their distinctive poetic character. He was also attracted by the idea that none of the songs chosen had ever been used by Russian composers.

*359*

Thus in the winter of 1944 the list of Prokofiev's works was augmented by the twelve arrangements of Russian folk songs, Op. 104. Seven of these were taken from Gippius' collection: *The Little Green Grove, Brown Eyes, Beyond the Woods, I Nowhere See My Love, Sashenka, Dunyushka,* and *The Monk.* Three were from Rudnev's collection: *Guelder-Rose in Summer, Katerina,* and *The Dream.* To these ten arrangements were added *Guelder-Rose on the Hill* and *White Snowflakes,* which had been published in Paris in 1931. The entire set was completed by the end of December 1944; on December 31 Miaskovsky noted in his diary, "Prokofiev played some excellent arrangements of folk songs."

Perhaps the least successful of these arrangements were the two that Prokofiev had made in Paris. Unlike those of the other songs, the original melodies of the fast round-dance *Guelder-Rose on the Hill* and the slow *White Snowflakes* are well known. The composer added to these very simple tunes a complex, harmonically sophisticated accompaniment with sudden, artificially refined modulations. This is true of the first song, with its *gusli*-like strumming and delicate, impressionistic chordal superimpositions, but even more so of the second, in which one clearly feels a discrepancy between the broad singing melody and the measured rhythm of the "verbose" piano part.

The arrangements made in 1944 are much richer and more profound in conception. In fact, one can hardly call them "arrangements" in the customary sense of the word, for the composer freely used the folk-song melodies and texts to create artistic works of his own. In each case he developed and expanded the melodies of the old songs, enriching their original texture and harmony and subordinating the folk material to his own aesthetic purposes. One example of his refashioning is the way in which he combined either two different lyrical tunes in a single work (*Little Green Grove*) or the melody of one song with the text of another (*Dunyushka*). Russian composers have often reshaped folk-song material, but usually for the purpose of using it in large symphonic or operatic works. Prokofiev boldly applied this method to the miniature form of solo folksong arrangement.

Not all the composer's experiments proved successful, however. The chief failings occur in those arrangements in which he disregarded the poetic content of the original folk material and overemphasized certain superficial aspects of it. For example, in the song *Katerina,* his interest in the round-dance character of the melody and in certain playful turns of phrase in the text resulted in a semicomic miniature with a dance-like accompaniment. But the text of the song tells of a "young girl who was given in marriage to an older man"; thus the underlying theme is rather sad, and not at all gay. In *Brown Eyes,* the excessively complicated piano part, with its deliberately discordant "hurdy-gurdy" harmonies and sudden modulations, is hardly suited to the very simple lyrical tune of the original folk song. In a number of instances the composer disregarded the broad and flowing coloratura quality of the slow songs and set them to vigorous, rhythmically incisive accompaniments. This is quite noticeable in songs with such charming melodies as *The Dream* and *Sashenka.*

However, when Prokofiev correctly perceived the poetic meaning and character of a song, when he understood its true beauty, he invariably found the proper means for setting it. One of the real masterpieces is *The Little Green Grove,* which expresses the unbearable grief of an abandoned girl.[26] Here the alterations introduced by the composer are so slight and so natural in character that one could hardly imagine this music in any other setting. The spare chordal texture, the expressive bass moving in unison with the voice part, and the sighing grace notes at the ends of the phrases—all this, together with the touching melody, creates a classical picture of a young girl's anguish (Fig. 46).

FIGURE 46

The profound simplicity of this melody was closely akin to the composer's own style, and thus it is hardly surprising that it recalls the deeply tragic and equally unaffected melody of the song "The Field of the Dead" from the *Alexander Nevsky* cantata.

*The Little Green Grove* is in three-part form. In the middle section the composer used the words and melody of another lyrical song taken down by Evald in the Vologda area, *They Said He Will Not Come,* which also treats of the theme of separation and unrequited love. The two women's songs are so successfully combined that the whole work impresses one as a single artistic entity.

No less interesting is the men's dance-song *Dunyushka,* which describes a young village boy's love for a beautiful girl. The text was taken from one source, *Russian Songs of the Vologda Region,* edited by Gippius, and the melody from another, *Songs of Pinega.* The composer reshaped the original melody, which he derived from a slow lyrical song entitled *There Is a Nightingale in the Green Garden,* giving it the character of a fast dance. The elaborate and very original piano part contains amusing and playful descriptive effects that seem to imitate a rooster's crowing. The combination of the merry text, the altered melody, and the sharply rhythmical accompaniment creates a little genre scene full of lusty humor. The listener is presented with a vivid portrait of a dashing youth expressing his passionate feeling for the "pale dove," Dunya. The music of this song was later used for the wedding dance of Danila's friends in Scene 2 of the ballet *The Stone Flower.*

The final song of this set, *The Monk,* also has a vigorous dance-like character. This entertaining piece, about a young monk who falls madly in love with a "darling girl" and in a rage tramples his black cowl under his feet, conveys superbly the ringing laughter and exuberance of the Russian dance.

The composer also displayed a fine feeling for style in the festive wedding song, *Guelder-Rose in Summer,* in the lyrical *Sashenka,* and in other songs in this collection. His experiments in the sphere of Russian harmony are interesting. In striving to find severe harmonic colors that would correspond to the character of the old melodies, he used such devices as open fifths, pedal point, and basses duplicating the melody in unison at the fourth or fifth below.

*Guelder-Rose in Summer* and *Little Green Grove* were awarded first and second prizes in the contest for concert arrangements of Russian folk songs, and *Little Green Grove* became one of the most frequently performed of Prokofiev's vocal works.

In the spring of 1945 Gippius suggested that Prokofiev arrange some songs for another competition announced by the All-Union Radio Committee. This time the composer expressed a desire to arrange songs of an epic character rather than ones in a popular or humorous vein. "I would like to find something in a narrative vein," he told Gippius. Writing for two male voices and piano, Prokofiev produced the two very original duets, Op. 106—*Famed Moscow Road* and *Every Man Takes a Wife.*

The first song, as sung by the Zakharov brothers, was taken down in 1900 by Ye. E. Lineva in Vladimir Guberniya and later transcribed by Gippius. It is a typical soldier's song, about military campaigns and the "renowned Preobrazhensky Regiment" pitching its white tents. The melody expresses Russian might and daring. Prokofiev accentuated the song's march-like rhythm and sharpened its melody in several places with repeated, stressed cadences. The setting of this song is enlivened by rich modulations and colorful harmonies.

Unfortunately, the composer did not avail himself of the authentic polyphonic devices of these Russian peasant songs. (Gippius advised him to write a vocal trio which would make use of their complicated contrapuntal texture.) Nevertheless, the polyphonic means employed here are quite original and interesting, for the composer used both imitation and simple instrumental accompaniment, as well as some two-part writing similar to that found in folk songs. Thus, without quoting the folk material but using it only as a thematic basis, Prokofiev created a dashing song of heroic infantrymen, reproducing in his own style a typical picture of Russian life.

He was particularly attracted by the stateliness and severity of the melody of the *bylina* about Dobrynya and Alesha, *Every Man Takes a Wife,* which Gippius and Evald had recorded in the Onega region in 1926. This is a story about the unhappy fate of a Russian youth forced to marry a girl he does not love. According to Gippius, Prokofiev became excited about the melody when it was sung for him and decided to write an extended vocal duet based on it. He was not deterred by the fact that the *bylina* was by nature a solo song and that two-part singing was not typical for this genre. The result was not an arrangement but a completely original work, in which only the two opening melodic phrases were taken from the original folk song. Here Prokofiev made extensive use of such techniques as imitation, tonal shifts, and exclamations akin to operatic recitative. Without duplicating the recitative devices of the *bylina,* he used the techniques of expressive Russian declamation. The entire piece sounds like a brilliant sketch for a big operatic scene in the style of the *bylina.*

The fourteen Russian songs in Op. 104 and Op. 106 represent an important aspect of Prokofiev's creative work. The folk melodies and texts directed his imagination toward an earnest search for new expressive means in the Russian national vein. Particularly significant was his interest in the lyrical Russian folk song and the *bylina.* A number of his later works, from *Ivan the Terrible* and the Violin Sonata, Op. 80, to *The Stone Flower,* contain rich and vivid evidence of this interest.

Despite the fact that some of these arrangements were experimental, certain discrepancies that appear between the folk melodies and the composer's harmonizations, on the whole these songs constitute one of the most original contributions to the new Russian music.

✹ ✹ ✹

The first performances of Prokofiev's opera *War and Peace,* which were given in concert form, were important events in the musical life of Moscow. The work was introduced, with piano accompaniment only, in October 1944 at the Moscow Actor's Club by the Soviet Opera Ensemble of the All-Russian Theater Society. Somewhat later, in June 1945, it was performed by artists of the Moscow Philharmonia with the State Symphony Orchestra under the direction of Samuel Samosud. Both performances, especially the second one, evoked great interest and were widely discussed in the press.

The interpretation by S. Samosud, one of the most ardent advocates of Prokofiev's music, brilliantly revealed the opera's most impressive features— the richness and originality of the melodic characterizations, the inspired quality of the lyrical episodes, and the sharpness of the dramatic contrasts. Much of the success of the concert presentations on June 7, 9, and 11 in the Great Hall of the Conservatory was due to the gifted soloists, among them A. Ivanov as Andrei Bolkonsky, A. Pirogov as Kutuzov, the young singer M. Nadion as Natasha Rostova, and N. Panchekhin as old Prince Bolkonsky.

Some critics acclaimed *War and Peace.* Kabalevsky, writing in *Pravda,* valued it "not only as an artistic work, but also as a monument to the strength and grandeur of the soul of the Russian people."[27] He praised particularly the lyrical opening scenes and the scene of the last meeting between Natasha and Andrei. On the other hand, the composer V. Shebalin drew attention to certain dramaturgical defects in this first version of the opera. "We find here an incredible number of characters, some of them totally superfluous; a general looseness of structure; a wearying preponderance of dialogue; lack of stage action; and episodes so fragmented that they sometimes completely destroy the sense of unity," he wrote.[28]

The controversy continued during the following years. The charges that the composer had underestimated the importance of well-developed vocal melody and that the opera contained an excessive number of unmelodic recitatives were unquestionably justified. Between 1950 and 1952, after having weighed this criticism, Prokofiev made a new version of the work.

On January 13, 1945, the composer participated in a concert of his works in Moscow. Along with such old favorites as the *Classical Symphony* and *Peter and the Wolf,* which were conducted by N. Anosov, the program included the première of the Fifth Symphony under the baton of Prokofiev. This was his last appearance on the podium.

The performance of the new symphony had special significance for Prokofiev. "Work on this symphony was very important to me, since it marked my return to the symphonic form after a long interval," he wrote. "I regard the Fifth Symphony as the culmination of a long period of my creative life. I conceived it as a symphony of the grandeur of the human spirit."[29]

The new work marked not only Prokofiev's return to the symphonic genre after a sixteen-year interval but also a new stage in the development of his orchestral writing. With few exceptions, his previous orchestral compositions had been based on material from his music for the theater. This was true of the Third and Fourth Symphonies, which incorporated themes from *The Flaming Angel* and *The Prodigal Son,* of the *Alexander Nevsky* cantata, and of the suites from *Romeo and Juliet, The Buffoon,* and *Lieutenant Kije,* among others. This time he undertook to write a non-programmatic symphony, and even though the music itself is strikingly dramatic, it is not directly connected with the theater. The experience he had gained from working on his later instrumental compositions (the three Piano Sonatas, the Second String Quartet, and the Sonata, Op. 94) undoubtedly contributed to the great success of the new symphony.

❧ ❧ ❧

The Fifth Symphony is a work of exceeding importance in the realm of recent Russian symphonic writing. Here, as in the later Sixth and Seventh Symphonies, the composer chose the epic, objective approach as his means of expression. Listening to this Symphony, one naturally visualizes real images of the theater—the epic canvas of a historical drama or the flowing action of a ballet. Thus in the majestic themes of the first movement, one senses a certain kinship to the musical portraits of Field Marshal Kutuzov in *War and Peace,* to the heroic warriors of *Alexander Nevsky,* and to the themes of armed might in *Ivan the Terrible.* On the other hand, the lyrical themes of the Symphony, which are melodious but also restrained and meditative, suggest similar operatic themes from *War and Peace* (such as the lyrical theme of Andrei Bolkonsky) or *Semyon Kotko.* And finally, the merry, exuberant dance-like themes of the second and fourth movements catch the spirit of the youthful amusements and gay carnival scenes in the ballet *Romeo and Juliet* and the opera *The Duenna.*

The very way in which the musical material is developed is more theatrical than symphonic: it is the shifting of various moods and scenes that predominates here, rather than the development and modification of themes. In most cases, the themes are not subjected to any substantial transformation, but simply painted in different tonal colors, varied, or set forth in new combinations. At times the work seems to be not so much a traditional symphony as an exciting symphonic drama.

This is in no way intended to disparage the composer. Along with the lyrico-philosophic genre, this style of symphonic exposition has long attracted Russian composers. The meager symphonic development is compensated for by the abundance and richness of the musical material and an amazing wealth of melody.

The Fifth Symphony is one of those late Prokofiev works in which inexhaustibly rich melody plays the leading role. Almost all of the melodies are impressive for their strong, confident tone. The composer shunned the emotional tension and thick sonorities he had used so shortly before in the Sixth and Eighth Sonatas and in the first movements of the Seventh Sonata and Kabardinian Quartet. A deep love of life and faith in man predominate in this music.

The heroic character of the Symphony is clearly revealed in its first and principal movement, which has much in common with the epic pages in the music of Borodin and Glazunov. The first two themes—the main theme and that of the bridge passage—are strong, resolute, unhurried, and characterized by a plastic flow of thought reminiscent of Glazunov. The use of the low register, the statement of the melody in open octaves, and the predominance of thick, bass colors are in the traditional manner of Russian epic themes.

This movement is noteworthy for its slow, flowing melodies, set forth in a free contrapuntal manner, the dominance of lofty reflection over vigorous action, and, finally, the method of development—the calm alternation of expressive instrumental phrases. The sober, lyrical second theme, which is restrained and free of any trace of sentimentality, is also distinctive. Even though the clarity of its idea seems somewhat obscured by an abundance of subtle modulations, this melody is tender, broad, and singing. The playful theme of the concluding section forms a fine ending for the exposition. Here sparkling phrases in the flutes and violins alternate with mysterious chords in the brasses to create an enchanting, elusive image.

In the modest development section, all four themes succeed each other kaleidoscopically in a new and unexpected order, undergoing scarcely any change. And except for the thicker and denser orchestration, the principal themes of the first movement remain unaltered throughout the somewhat abbreviated recapitulation.

Finally, in the coda, the composer brings the entire movement to a magnificent conclusion by presenting the epic opening theme in the ever-mounting, triumphant sonorities of an orchestral tutti (Fig. 47).

FIGURE 47

This is perhaps the most impressive episode of the entire Symphony, for it embodies with the greatest clarity the work's highest purpose—glorification of the strength and beauty of the human spirit.

The Scherzo which follows the towering first movement presents several completely different and varied moods. In this captivating movement, images of joy and anxiety, sun and shadow, bright poetry and grotesquerie come and go in fantastic interplay.

Listening to the opening theme of this movement, one recalls the charming scherzando moods of Prokofiev's lyrical comedies and instrumental pieces in the classical style. This melody, carried by the solo clarinet over a measured staccato accompaniment in the first violins, has a Mozartean transparency and grace, and at the same time an engaging roguishness. But this theme seems gay and carefree only in its first appearance, for with each new statement its hidden dramatic qualities are more clearly revealed; the orchestral colors become thicker and darker, the harmonies and rhythm more uneasy. This is particularly noticeable when the theme is given to the bassoons, in augmented form over heavy staccato figures in the bass. Snatches of this theme, heard in various instruments of the orchestra, often sound tense and tragic, and its initial carefree humor assumes an aspect of sadness and anxiety.

But just at this moment the almost idyllic middle section is introduced by an artless theme in the woodwinds, which is colorfully harmonized by an alternation of tonic chords and augmented sixth chords. The pastoral character of this theme recalls the love of nature and fresh perception of the world found in certain pages of Prokofiev's *Music for Children*. This simple woodwind tune twice gives way to enchanting dance sections which call to mind the "Dance of the Five Couples" from *Romeo and Juliet*. These passages seem like a recollection of a happy and peaceful life in a time of deep distress.

This bright, sunny episode is followed, quite unexpectedly, by a dark and sinister reprise, in which the Scherzo's opening theme appears in a new guise. The orchestral texture is thickened by the introduction of accented, staccato figures in the brasses, and the harmony is larded with blocks of dissonant chords. It is as though some evil freaks and monsters had suddenly broken out in a fiendish, mocking dance. This is the only moment in the Symphony when sinister images emerge before the listener.

The chiaroscuro of contrasting images appears also in the reprise. Here the grotesque dance once again gives way to the roguish opening theme. It is this colorful interplay of moods—infectious humor, anxiety, idyllic serenity, and grotesquerie—that makes this second movement so captivating. These dramatically heightened contrasts present a rich and varied picture of life.

The restrained and melodious Adagio opens with a profoundly lyrical theme, which progresses calmly against the background of measured triplet figures. This broadly phrased, sweeping melody, characterized by singularly charming harmonic transitions, wide intervals, and flights into the higher registers, is expressive and poetic. As the movement unfolds, the main theme is presented in different tonalities and is complemented by a declamatory phrase reminiscent of an expressive operatic recitative. This somewhat melancholy phrase serves to introduce the dramatic middle section of the movement, in which the rhapsodic dream gives way to mature reflection. The "theme of reflection," which sounds heavy and sad in the low basses in unison, is answered by agitated phrases suggestive of bitter moaning. Once again, as in the dramatic episodes of the Scherzo, images of mass suffering arise. These themes, so Russian in flavor, combining sublime lyricism and expressive recitative, have much in common with the melodic style of Moussorgsky. After an intense climax, the tragic middle section is followed by a restatement of the serene opening theme, this time enriched with embellishments. Here again bright, tranquil, noble meditation prevails.

The Finale of the Symphony begins with a slow introduction in which the main theme of the first movement reappears like a reminiscence; here the composer once more reminds the listener of the principal idea of the Symphony—the theme of man's spiritual grandeur and heroic strength. After this, the main theme of the Finale introduces a colorful, festive picture. While in certain melodic details and in its confident ascending motions this theme bears a certain resemblance to the first theme of the first movement, a completely different mood now prevails—a mood of intoxicating gaiety expressed in the infectious rhythm of a fast mass dance. Now and then the opening theme is interrupted by the careless laughter of fast running passages in the violins. The buoyant new dance theme of the bridge passage which follows, set forth in the high woodwinds staccato and violins *pizzicato,* is also permeated with a lively humor that has no trace of buffoonery. This theme leads into the lyrical second theme, a broad, flowing melody, which in its pensive character and its tonality (F major) is very close to the Adagio's opening theme. But here the lyrical monologue, heard over a soft dance rhythm, reminds one of an operatic love episode presented against the background of a distant carnival. The middle section presents much more of a contrast. This time the gay dance is interrupted by a slow Russian theme, which emerges in the basses like the "theme of reflection" in the middle section of the Adagio. But, as before, the contemplative mood proves to be rather short-lived, for it gradually gives way to the dance themes. Finally, in the recapitulation and the boisterous, jubilant coda the mood of joyful merrymaking and festive dances, seemingly accompanied by peals of hearty laughter, is utterly triumphant.

The Fifth Symphony proclaims a firm faith in life and human happiness. This music could have been created only by an artist who fully sensed the healthy, vibrant tone of the life of his country, the inexhaustible energy and strength of its people.

The form and style of this work merit special consideration. Of particular interest is the composer's attempt to unify the thematic material, to create melodic continuity between the movements. This can be seen not only in the exact repetition of the main theme of the first movement in the introduction to the Finale, but also in the definite melodic resemblance of the lyrical themes (the F major themes of the first, third, and fourth movements) and the swift-moving dance themes. The dominance of the virile B-flat major in both the first and last movements relates this work to the finales of the Seventh and Eighth Sonatas, the epic overture to *War and Peace,* and Part I of *Ivan the Terrible.* These diverse works of the 1941–44 period are characterized by certain kindred images, all inspired by the majestic epos of Russian history, past and present.

The harmonic idiom of the Symphony is characterized by thick chordal superimpositions and unusual suspensions (particularly in the first movement). The same severity of style and concentration of colors can be seen in the orchestration, which provides for an abundance of heavy, low timbres and massive combinations of instruments (with frequent use of the piano). In episodes of this kind, the composer achieves the kind of bold relief found in sculpture characterized not by carefully polished lines but by the unfinished texture of the raw stone. This endows the heroic pages of the Symphony with a special earthy power and epic sweep.

❉ ❉ ❉

The première of the Fifth Symphony, in Moscow on January 13, 1945, took place in an atmosphere of elation and pride. Just before the concert began, the audience received news of the great victory which the advancing Soviet Army had just won on the Vistula. The opening bars of the Symphony were heard against the thunderous background of an artillery salute. Prokofiev's compelling music perfectly suited the mood of the audience. The critics commented on this in their glowing reviews of the new composition. Kabalevsky, extolling the symphony as the embodiment of man's courage, energy, and spiritual grandeur, also made special note of its profoundly national character.[30] Later, M. Druskin spoke of the natural link between this work and present-day life.[31]

The Fifth Symphony was performed again on June 24, 1945, by the Leningrad Philharmonic Orchestra under the direction of Ye. Mravinsky. In the fall of the same year, it was played for the first time in Paris during a special Prokofiev festival. On November 9 and 10, it was given its first performance in Boston by the Boston Symphony under the baton of Serge Koussevitzky.

"The eagerly awaited Fifth Symphony of Prokofiev burst like a bomb-shell over the musical horizon of New York," wrote the critic of the magazine *Musical America* [reviewing the first New York performance]. "It is difficult, without understating, to describe a work so beautifully orchestrated, so cleverly linked together, so packed with wit and invention."* Another critic writing in the same magazine linked the impression of grandeur created by the Symphony to the historic events which had taken place in Russia during the past year. At the same time, music experts with aesthetic pretensions deplored the "retrospective quality" of its musical language and the fact that it "too openly appeals to the masses" (review in *Music News,* January 11, 1946). The latter charge was actually the highest praise that could be paid the Symphony.

Shortly after the Moscow première of the Fifth Symphony [January 13, 1945], Prokofiev suffered an accident which was to have disastrous effects upon him for the rest of his life. An accidental fall gave him a severe brain concussion which became the prelude to a serious illness. This illness, probably complicated by the effects of nervous fatigue, incapacitated the composer for several months. Accustomed to working continuously, Prokofiev found this extremely trying. "The doctors have absolutely forbidden all work for the time being," his wife reported in a letter. "He is longing to work and feels wretched over this enforced inactivity."[32]

Prokofiev was given expert care in one of the best sanatoriums near Moscow. "We loll around and stroll about here, and on the whole we feel fine," he reported at the end of April.[33] It was while he was in the sanatorium that he received the joyous news of the victory over fascism. The general rejoicing throughout the country could not have failed to raise his

---

* TRANSLATOR's NOTE: In its original English form, this passage reads as follows: "The eagerly awaited Fifth Symphony of Prokofiev burst more like a bon-bon than a bombshell upon the musical horizon of New York at the Boston Symphony's first visit of the season. This is not written to disparage a work so beautifully orchestrated, so cleverly linked together, so packed with wit and invention."

spirits. At the beginning of June, he attended the concert performances of *War and Peace,* where he received a tremendous ovation.

The four-year war period, from 1941–45, had been a wonderfully productive one for Prokofiev. The opera *War and Peace,* the Fifth Symphony, two Piano Sonatas, the Second String Quartet, the Flute Sonata, music for *Ivan the Terrible* and other films, the completion of the ballet *Cinderella,* the *Ballad of an Unknown Boy,* the suite *The Year 1941,* arrangements of Russian folk songs, the marches and mass songs—this is only a partial list of the works he composed during these unforgettable forty-six months. As an expression of its appreciation for his selfless work, the government had awarded him the Order of the Red Banner of Labor and a number of prizes.

Prokofiev's achievements were also noted abroad. In the fall of 1945 progressive musicians in France arranged a festival of his works. The British Royal Philharmonic Society awarded him a gold medal, a mark of the highest esteem given only to the greatest musicians in the world. In the middle of June 1945, in a festive atmosphere, the Ambassador of Great Britain presented the composer with this honorary award. In his acceptance speech Prokofiev spoke of the prospects for friendly cultural relations with the peoples of Europe, united by their victorious struggle against fascism.

# ELEVEN

# DIFFICULT YEARS

URING THE WAR YEARS Prokofiev's prestige in Soviet musical circles had grown tremendously. In one year alone, from November 1945 to December 1946, the theaters of Moscow and Leningrad staged four of his works. *Cinderella* and *Romeo and Juliet* were produced by the Bolshoi, the first part of *War and Peace* by the Maly, and *The Duenna* and *Cinderella* by the Kirov. The first three productions were awarded Stalin prizes. Prokofiev's cherished dream was being realized—his works were beginning to be performed on the opera and ballet stages of Russia. On his fifty-fifth birthday, in the spring of 1946, one cartoonist pictured him crowned with laurels and sagging beneath the weight of new scores.[1] So it was that many of the projects he had undertaken immediately before and during the war began to bear fruit.

During these four years the composer's interest in Russian history, in the majestic epos of Russia, had grown markedly. *Alexander Nevsky* and *Zdravitsa* had been followed by the epic scenes of *War and Peace,* the music for *Ivan the Terrible,* the heroic Fifth Symphony, and the Violin Sonata in F minor, Op. 80. One could now speak of the growing patriotic tendency in Prokofiev's work, of his increased striving to sing of the valor, daring, and spiritual strength of his countrymen. This could not have been said of the works written during the period of *The Buffoon* and *Le Pas d'acier.*

Also new for the composer was his increased interest in Russian, Kazakh, and Kabardinian folk material, which manifested itself in the interesting arrangements of Russian folk songs, the Kabardinian Quartet, and other compositions undertaken during the war.

Evident as well was Prokofiev's more frequent recourse to purely instrumental music, both symphonic and chamber—a turn possibly influenced by the work of Miaskovsky and Shostakovich. But, to be sure, influences of his ballet and operatic music could still be seen in the ever-present descriptive and declamatory elements and in the preponderance of vividly

*373*

dramatic passages over the abstract development characteristic of most instrumental writing.

One can observe, too, a further development of both the humorous element so dear to him and the lyrical strain, which had been brilliantly revealed in *Romeo and Juliet.*

The composer's progress from *Romeo and Juliet, Alexander Nevsky,* and *Zdravitsa* to new achievements was not smooth and direct, however, but beset by a number of new difficulties. Both during and after the war Prokofiev more than once succumbed to the temptations of expressionistic excesses. At times, echoes of the old "diabolic suggestions" could again be heard in this infinitely warmer and more profound music. The classical balance he had achieved in his best works was sometimes upset, with mechanical rhythms and dissonant harmonies or deafening tonal effects once again assuming primary importance.

As in his earlier works, there remained a certain constraint in the composer's vocal writing, a predominance of instrumental melody or excessively declamatory devices over natural tunefulness. On the other hand, in his striving for greater clarity and comprehensibility, he sometimes lapsed into oversimplification or abstractness. It was this which accounted for the failure of most of the mass songs written before and during the war, the suite *The Year 1941,* and the *Festive Poem,* Op. 113, composed in 1947. In these cases, the artistic intuition which usually served him unerringly in works based on concrete themes failed him, and cold, inexpressive images appeared in place of real and vibrant ones.

During the years 1945–47 these contradictions were not resolved, but instead became more serious. Continued success, the sweet words of praise showered on him by the press, the Committee on the Arts, and the Organization Committee of the Composers' Union stifled Prokofiev's sense of self-criticism and thus proved harmful to him. Even he himself subsequently acknowledged this, ascribing the failure of some of his works of the forties to a "certain complacency."[2] Together with such brilliant works as the Violin Sonata in F minor, there appeared such indifferent, superficial compositions as the *Festive Poem* and the Sonata for Unaccompanied Violins, Op. 115. His last opera, *The Story of a Real Man,* was not favorably received. Furthermore, he began to return to his works of the twenties (such as the Second and Fourth Symphonies and the Fifth Piano Sonata) with a view toward revising them and having them performed, and this did nothing to fix his realistic tendencies. There was even some danger that Prokofiev might lose contact with the Soviet audience which had grown to love the music of *Romeo and Juliet, Alexander Nevsky,* and several of his other compositions of past years. This danger was pointed out in the Party resolution of 1948 entitled "On the Opera *The Great Friendship,* by V. Muradeli." But let us return to a survey of Prokofiev's creative activity during the postwar years.

Prokofiev spent the summer and early fall of 1945 at the Composers' House in Ivanovo. After his illness the doctors strictly limited his work schedule, for from time to time he still suffered from severe congestion and headaches. But dedicated artist that he was, he tried not to waste a single minute. Every morning at a fixed hour he was at the piano, and any attempts to disturb his regular routine or interfere with his work infuriated him. While in Ivanovo he saw a great deal of his old teacher Glière and his dear friend Miaskovsky. Here, too, he formed close friendships with Shostakovich, Khachaturian, and Kabalevsky and often discussed his musical plans with them. In his leisure hours he readily joined the group in walks or volleyball.

During this summer Prokofiev composed and orchestrated the *Ode to the End of the War,* sketched out the Sixth Symphony (the themes of which had been partially conceived earlier, even before the Fifth Symphony), outlined the Ninth Piano Sonata, wrote two duets on Russian folk song themes (Op. 106), and corrected numerous proofs. He also resumed work with Eisenstein on the production of Part II of *Ivan the Terrible.* By the end of 1945 he had completed the music for it, and in February 1946 he happily informed Eisenstein that "everyone praises *Ivan.*" His work was facilitated partly by the fact that he had already composed some of the musical episodes for this part of the film. The manuscript of the magnificent chorus "The Vow of the Oprichniki," for example, is dated 1942 (Alma-Ata).

In Part II of *Ivan the Terrible,* Prokofiev once more displayed his brilliant sense of the theater and his deep understanding of the Russian spirit. As in Part I, this music is quite operatic in character. Evidence of this can be seen in the stirring chorus "The Vow of the Oprichniki," in the majestic song "The Ocean," in the "Song of the Beaver" for mezzo-soprano and orchestra, in the vocal-symphonic scene of the murder of Prince Vladimir, and in the two frenzied dances of the Oprichniki. According to the composer, one of these dances is "chaotic," that is, constructed on the persistent repetition of a single archaic melodic figure, whereas the other is "organized," with a refrain reminiscent of a traditional *chastushka* tune. The dances are accompanied by the lusty song of Fedor Basmanov, in fast tempo with typical choral *glissandi* ("They swarmed into the boyars' courtyards, smiting the boyars with their axes"). Both the music and words of this episode are permeated with the reckless daring characteristic of the songs of the Russian freemen (Fig. 48).

FIGURE 48

Here again Prokofiev's vividly graphic music blends organically with the film action. In a number of scenes with choruses, songs, and dances, the musical action even assumes the leading, determining role. Because of severe criticism of its basic ideological conception, Part II of *Ivan the Terrible* was not released, and thus Prokofiev's music was not heard. Later, Eisenstein planned to revise it substantially, but his untimely death in February 1948 prevented his plan from being realized.

On November 12, 1945, the *Ode to the End of the War* was given its first performance by the State Symphony Orchestra of the U.S.S.R. under S. A. Samosud, in the Tchaikovsky Hall in Moscow. On November 21, the ballet *Cinderella* had its première at the Bolshoi Theater; for this production the choreographer was R. Zakharov, the scenic artist P. Williams, and the conductor Yuri Faier. Both the *Ode* and *Cinderella* were widely commented on in the Soviet press.

Prokofiev's symphonic *Ode*, which was completed in full score late in September 1945, was the first significant attempt in Soviet music to celebrate the end of the war. Its two principal themes, the broad "theme of joy" and the gay, vigorous *Allegro energico,* were taken from the orchestral interludes of the *Cantata for the Twentieth Anniversary of the October Revolution,* which had never been performed.

The *Ode to the End of the War,* Op. 105, is a one-movement piece for orchestra with three sections: a solemn introduction; an extended middle section in a lively, exultant vein ("These are images of reconstruction, of creation," noted the composer); and a dazzling, joyous conclusion, for which the composer furnished the epigraph, "Strike the Bells and Timpani."

In writing this work, Prokofiev was particularly interested in the problem of its orchestration. The majestic theme of victory, he felt, required stunning colors and augmented sonorities. Accordingly, he enlarged the wind section, doubled the contrabasses, and added four pianos. In addition, he made wide use of timpani and bells, treating them like solo instruments. On the other hand, he eliminated almost the entire string section—the violins, violas, and cellos. He did this, he said, in order to achieve the severest tone color possible. As a result, the climaxes acquired a thunderous timbre with the sonorities of the deep basses predominating, recalling the tonal effects of the *Scythian Suite.*

Because brilliance and novelty of orchestration became ends in themselves, the melodic content of this piece was all but lost. Stunned by the exaggerated, unusually thick sounds of the orchestra, which lacked the singing tones of the strings, most listeners could not perceive the inner meaning of the music.

One cannot but agree with the newspaper *Trud* which characterized this piece as a "work glittering in form and pictorially descriptive, in which surface illustration and effect predominate over deep and meaningful content."[3] Performance of the *Ode* required an unusual combination of instruments and proved to be too difficult for most of the country's orchestras.

Thus it remained a purely experimental work and did not win a permanent place in the repertory.

❇ ❇ ❇

The ballet *Cinderella* is one of Prokofiev's most felicitous works for the theater. It was produced a comparatively short time after its completion and won unanimous approval. At a discussion in the Committee on the Arts, Shostakovich, Glière, Khachaturian, Mikhoels, Okhlopkov, and others paid glowing tribute to the work of both the composer and choreographer. They also spoke warmly of the masterful performances of Cinderella by Galina Ulanova and Olga Lepeshinskaya, and of R. Zakharov's staging and P. Williams' sets.

The story of Cinderella, which is known throughout the world, has more than once attracted the interest of musical theaters. As far back as the early nineteenth century, Rossini and Steibelt had written operas on this theme. As we know, in 1870 the Bolshoi Theater had suggested to Tchaikovsky that he write the music for a ballet entitled *Cendrillon,* an idea that was not carried out. In the 1890's the Maryinsky Theater produced the ballet *Cinderella* with music by B. Schell. According to the memoirs of the ballerina A. Vaganova, this production lacked artistic unity, for it contained many dances taken over in their entirety from other ballets.[4]

In his unpublished memoirs Asafyev states that at the beginning of the century, V. V. Stasov urged him to write a ballet on the Cinderella story. "Using all of his powers of persuasion to induce me to compose, the confirmed realist Stasov suggested as a theme the fairy tale *Cinderella,*" Asafyev writes. "He envisioned the treatment of it in human terms, as a reflection of reality, though he would still retain the element of fantasy. He collected for me all sorts of illustrations of Perrault's tales, and with childish naïveté the two of us found amusement in the ingenuity of the illustrators." Stasov later presented Asafyev with four volumes of his own works, inscribed "To the future composer of the future *Cinderella.*"[5]

Stasov's suggestion of a Russian ballet on the Cinderella story was carried out, forty years later, by Asafyev's friend Prokofiev. The great critic's idea of emphasizing the reality, humanity, and profound meaning of the folk tale finally found its realization in N. Volkov's libretto and Prokofiev's music.

As in the old tale, the underlying idea of the ballet is the superiority of Cinderella's modesty, industry, and spiritual purity over the greed, heartlessness, and crass arrogance of her stepmother and stepsisters. Following the original story, the cruel characters are derided and humbled, and the

*378*

good Cinderella is chosen by the Prince. Pure love is the central theme of both the libretto and the music of the ballet. "We did not want the audience to remain indifferent to the joys and sorrows of the humble dreamer Cinderella, the ardent Prince, the timid father, the wicked stepmother, and the coquettish sisters. We wanted the characters to seem like real people with real feelings and emotions," wrote the composer.

In *Cinderella* Prokofiev drew on the traditions of the classical ballet, with its many set numbers and its emphasis on the dance rather than on free pantomime. "I wanted this ballet to be as danceable as possible," wrote Prokofiev. "*Cinderella* is written in the tradition of the old classical ballet. It contains numerous variations, *pas de deux,* three waltzes, an adagio, a gavotte, and a mazurka."[6]

This adoption of the classical ballet form proved fruitful. Three marvelous waltzes, Cinderella's love adagio with the Prince, and the colorful dances of the fairies constitute the basis of this enchanting choreographic work. In its rhythmic variety, dynamic quality, and eminent danceability, the music of *Cinderella* approaches that of the best classical ballets.

It is interesting to recall that even before the outbreak of the war, when Prokofiev first began working on *Cinderella,* he had in mind writing a ballet that would be specifically national and Russian in character. In the spring of 1941 he wrote that he would like to take as his subject a traditional theme common to many peoples and present it "as a truly Russian fairy tale." He mentioned specifically his desire to use the motifs of the Russian tale *Masha Chernushka* from Afanasyev's collection.

However, in the process of composition this conception gradually changed. The music, especially in the traditional, set episodes, is for the most part written in a stylized manner more closely related to the fantasy of Charles Perrault than to a Russian folk tale. The mocking irony, so vividly embodied in the music, also derives from Perrault. In portraying Cinderella's haughty, wicked sisters and in the ball scene of Act II, the composer used the rhythms and texture of seventeenth- and eighteenth-century European dances. His long-standing love for classical forms, previously reflected in the piano pieces of Op. 12 and the First Symphony, stood him in good stead. The ironic quality of his "classical style," the comic ceremoniousness with which he endowed the gallant past, manifests itself more clearly and concretely here than anywhere else. Only the lyrical passages of the ballet, those connected with the portrayal of Cinderella and her love for the Prince, are tinted with the Russian warmth and tenderness which characterize Prokofiev's later lyricism.

Of course, alongside the majestic epic *War and Peace* and the tragic canvases *Romeo and Juliet* and *Semyon Kotko,* the simple tale of Cinderella was something of an interlude, a lyrical relief for Prokofiev. What drew him to Perrault's tale was its profound humanism: its love for ordinary human beings, modest and hard-working; its glorification of man's noble qualities and ridicule of his malice, vulgarity, and greed. This is unquestionably the pervading spirit of the ballet. The drama is based on the clash of two radically different spheres—the lofty sphere of love, honor, and goodness represented by Cinderella and her fairy protectors, and the base world of gaudy vulgarity. Here again lyricism is opposed to grotesquerie, poetic dreams to life's sordidness, and romantic impulses to stinging derision.

Prokofiev's characterizations of the greedy stepmother and her two cantankerous daughters are particularly apt and telling. In the libretto the sisters are called Kubyshka (Dumpy) and Khudyshka (Scrawny), and in the Leningrad version of the ballet Zlyuka (Furious) and Krivlyaka (Affected). The composer's trenchant humor and unfailing sense of character type here reveal themselves with great power and freshness. The music alone conveys the atmosphere of bickering, quarreling, capricious spitefulness, and black envy. One can almost hear the shrill screeching of the empty-headed "mother's darlings" fighting over a shawl and angrily stamping their feet, or visualize them striking all kinds of poses as they feverishly prepare for the ball. The caricatural quality of these musical portraits is heightened by the sprightly rhythm, the tersely graphic and occasionally sharpened orchestration, and the subtly employed dissonant harmonies. Thus, music and stage action are blended into a single comic image.

Touches of irony and withering mockery color most of the aristocratic dances in the ball scene (Act II): the dance of the courtiers in the rhythm of a pavane, the passepied, bourrée, gavotte (Prokofiev's fifth gavotte), and slightly caricatured minuet (Kubyshka's variation). With an arch smile, the composer draws a series of amusing portraits of the old fairy tale's characters—the arrogant, swaggering guests, the overdressed cavaliers and envious beauties—pointing up the degeneracy of some, the pomposity and affectedness of others.

Even the first musical sketch of the Prince has a faint touch of mockery. He enters the ball to the mock thunder of a fanfare, and according to the composer's stage direction, "seats himself on the throne as though he were mounting a horse."

But as soon as Cinderella appears on the stage, the music becomes tender and lyrical. Cinderella's themes seem to radiate warmth and beauty. They are characterized by a sweet melancholy and the freshness of a girl's first awakening to love. Cinderella moves in an emotional world similar to the one surrounding Rimsky-Korsakov's Snow Maiden and Prokofiev's own Juliet. Particularly notable in her characterization are the two principal leitmotivs, which appear first in the introduction to the ballet and are often repeated later. The first one, brooding and wistful, suggests her abasement and lowliness. An abundance of colorful modulations and delicate chromatic turns endow this theme with a tinge of yearning and weariness (Fig. 49).

FIGURE 49

Cinderella's second theme, which later becomes one of the themes of her love for the Prince, is quite different. This broad, impassioned melody over a pulsating tremolo is filled with radiant ecstasy. Thus, the music suggests Cinderella's changing fortunes—from joyless youth and poverty to later happiness.

The music for Cinderella's *pas de deux* with the Prince in the second and third acts is also lyrical and romantic. Particularly noteworthy is the C major adagio in Act II, with its soaring, passionate theme in the cellos. The portrayal of the Prince changes radically after Cinderella makes her appearance. From an almost toylike character, reminiscent of the comical Prince in *The Love for Three Oranges,* he is suddenly transformed into a living person seized with a lofty passion.

Finally, the group of lyrical themes includes the three symphonic waltzes—the Grand Waltz and Waltz-Coda of Act II and the slow waltz in Act III. In style they somewhat recall the popular waltzes of the nineteenth century; this is particularly true of the twice-repeated G minor waltz. These episodes endow the music of the ballet with warmth, simplicity, and charm.

The secondary contrast in the ballet, that between reality and fantasy, is less sharply defined. The creatures of fantasy—the good fairies and merry gnomes—do no evil; they only protect Cinderella and the Prince and help to promote their happiness. Accordingly, the music portraying this fairy world is soft and delicate. Here there are neither the frightening barbarisms of the *Scythian Suite* and *Seven, They Are Seven* nor the parodied devilry of the *Three Oranges*. The element of fantasy harmonizes excellently with the world of lyrical love themes, for the good fairies personify the forces of nature which help ordinary people in work as well as in love. The tremulous theme of the Fairy Godmother exudes a feeling of venerable goodness. The colorful scene which takes place as the clock strikes midnight, with the toylike tap dancing of the gnomes, is drawn with brilliance and inventiveness.

There is a certain artless spontaneity in the way Prokofiev sketched the scenes of nature in the dances of the four fairies called Spring, Summer, Autumn, and Winter. This music variously suggests the noisy bustle of spring, the blissful lassitude of summer, the murky, misty fall, and the snow-clad Russian winter. In these episodes the composer employs such typically impressionistic devices of tone painting as pungent, vivid harmonies, descriptive passage work, *fioriture,* and colorful modulations. Nevertheless, one can discern Prokofiev's characteristic manner throughout, especially in the harmonies and rhythms. Some parts of the ballet, such as the "Dance of the Grasshoppers and Dragonflies," are reminiscent of his children's music, conveying the same wide-eyed astonishment, the same fresh perception of the world.

Prokofiev was especially successful in depicting the swift-moving adventure episodes at the beginning of Act III, in which the Prince, burning with passion for the unknown beauty, journeys through the world in search of the owner of the magic slipper. The Prince's lively galop and the fiery dances of the Spanish and oriental beauties are among the ballet's most winning pages.

The enchanting blend of fantasy and irony, of lively humor and tender lyricism, relates *Cinderella* to *The Love for Three Oranges*. Evidence of a certain stylistic resemblance between these two fairy tales appears in the rather unexpected introduction of the famous March from *The Three Oranges* at the point in Act II where the Prince's guests are served oranges. It is as if one thread of living music here stretches between Prokofiev's two theatrical tales, spanning the twenty-five years that separate them. But how far Prokofiev had moved from the paradoxical eccentricity of *The Three Oranges*! In *Cinderella,* poetically inspired lyrical episodes predominate, the humor is more meaningful and purposeful, and even the fairy folk are humanized.

In his last ballet, *The Stone Flower,* Prokofiev took still another step toward a realistic treatment of the ballet genre. In doing so, he finally succeeded in realizing his old dream of creating a fairy-tale ballet in the Russian national style.

※　※　※

Virtually every Moscow newspaper carried an account of the première of *Cinderella* which acclaimed both the music and the production. *Pravda,* for example, found it an outstanding work, "worthy of the glorious traditions of the Russian ballet." Shostakovich, who wrote the review, declared that "with this work the art of the ballet has taken a step forward."[7]

Prokofiev, too, was enthusiastic about the production of *Cinderella.* He had great admiration for the artistry of Ulanova and was delighted with the details of the production, especially with his favorite scene in which the clock strikes. He did have some reservations about the excessively lavish sets, however, which at times clashed with the subtle irony of the music. And while acknowledging the artistic ability of the conductor, Yuri Faier, he could not accept certain arbitrary changes in his orchestration, introduced because of the theater's belief that the original scoring was "too transparent" and that the tradition of the classical ballet demanded thicker and louder sonorities. The later production by the Leningrad Kirov Theater, which retained the original orchestration, proved that conformity to poor traditions was not a sufficient reason for violating a composer's score.

*Cinderella* entered the repertory of the Bolshoi Theater, where it has enjoyed great popularity. Early in 1953, after a two-year absence, it was revived with some changes in the direction and staging.

Early in April 1946, five months after the Moscow première, *Cinderella* was presented at the Kirov Theater in Leningrad with N. Dudinskaya in the leading role. In this production, the choreography was by K. Sergeyev and the décor by B. Erdman. The Leningraders justly took a paternal interest in this work, since it had been originally commissioned by the Kirov Theater and written in close collaboration with it. Sergeyev succeeded in creating a completely original and very elegant version of the ballet, which in no way duplicated the Moscow production.

During the years following its première *Cinderella* was performed in Kiev and Riga, as well as in Poland, Czechoslovakia, and the German Democratic Republic. It has everywhere met with a warm reception from both the public and the press.

Despite his continuing serious illness, Prokofiev worked indefatigably during the winter of 1945–46. After completing Part II of *Ivan the Terrible*, he created three symphonic suites from *Cinderella*, basing them on his earlier piano transcriptions of the work. "These suites are not simply a collection of numbers mechanically taken out of the ballet," the composer wrote. "Much has been reworked and put into more symphonic form." The three suites include almost all of the music of the ballet. They were performed in concerts during 1946 and 1947 but did not win a permanent place in the repertory.

Throughout the winter Prokofiev kept in close contact with the Leningrad Maly Opera Theater, where the first eight scenes of *War and Peace* were being strenuously rehearsed. In the conductor S. A. Samosud he found an enthusiastic admirer and intelligent interpreter of the opera. It was at Samosud's suggestion that Prokofiev introduced the scene of the nobleman's ball (Scene 2), in which Natasha Rostova and Andrei Bolkonsky first meet. By the spring of 1946 Prokofiev had composed and scored this new scene, which contains several ballroom dances (a polonaise, a mazurka, a waltz, and an écossaise) and two short choruses to words by Batyushkov and Lomonosov. The music of this sumptuous ball serves as the background for the recitative of the principal characters as well as for the laconic dialogue between Natasha and Andrei, which ends with Andrei's ecstatic words "The wine of her charm has gone to my head!" The best episode in this scene, the B minor waltz, is especially captivating in its elegant lyricism and the singular charm of its harmony. In both mood and tonality it recalls Glinka's Valse-Fantaisie.

By the beginning of June, after long and painstaking preparation, the production of *War and Peace* was finally ready. It was billed as "Lyrico-Dramatic Scenes after L. Tolstoi's novel *War and Peace*." Prokofiev, who had attended the dress rehearsal, approved both the musical interpretation and the staging of the work. He remarked on the unusual sensitivity of Samosud's interpretive conception, the masterly work of the stage designer V. Dmitriev, and on the superb performances of the leading roles, particularly by T. Lavrova as Natasha, L. Petrov as Andrei, and the Leningrad composer Oles Chishko, who had been enlisted for the role of Pierre Bezukhov.

The fashionable balls (Scenes 2 and 4) were brilliantly staged, as was the monumental scene on the field at Borodino, in which something like two hundred artists participated. B. Arapov in *Pravda* and V. Bogdanov-Berezovsky in *Leningradskaya Pravda* acclaimed both the music and the production of the opera. Shortly after the première, the theater began work on the second part of the opera, which consisted of the five remaining scenes.

In the spring of 1946 Prokofiev's fifty-fifth birthday was celebrated by a series of concerts of his works. Sviatoslav Richter performed the Sixth, Seventh, and Eighth Piano Sonatas in the October Hall of the House of the Trade Unions. During the same season, Yakov Zak played the First, Second, and Third Piano Concertos with the State Symphony Orchestra of the U.S.S.R. These performances clearly demonstrated that Prokofiev's works had become part of the regular repertory of the best Soviet pianists.

Throughout 1946 Prokofiev carried on his work in defiance of the doctors' insistence that he shorten his work day. Even while in the Kremlin hospital during a period of acute attacks, he continued to compose, jotting down new themes in his notebooks without his doctor's knowledge. One of Prokofiev's friends related how the composer, after persuading him to stand guard at the door, snatched a notebook from beneath his pillow and hastily wrote down a new melody. It was impossible for him not to compose; new themes were constantly suggesting themselves to him.

In view of the increasing seriousness of his illness, Prokofiev decided to settle permanently in the country. In June of 1946 he settled in the picturesque forest hamlet of Nikolina Gora near Zvenigorod, sixty kilometers west of Moscow. Henceforth this country house, set in a large garden, became the composer's permanent home. Here, with rare interruptions, he spent the last years of his life.

During the summer of 1946, in Nikolina Gora, Prokofiev completed the Violin Sonata, Op. 80, sketched before the war, and composed the Sixth Symphony. He also finished writing the additional music for the Moscow production of *Romeo and Juliet* and worked out a plan for a new scene, "War Council at Fili," for the second part of *War and Peace*.

❄ ❄ ❄

The Violin Sonata in F minor, Op. 80, is one of the most powerful and original of Prokofiev's instrumental chamber works. His first sketches of it (beginning of the first movement, exposition of the second, and themes of the third) had been made eight years before, in 1938, between the writing of *Alexander Nevsky* and the opera *Semyon Kotko*. For this reason the composer called it Sonata No. 1, even though it was completed two years after Sonata No. 2 (Op. 94-bis). "In mood it is more serious than the Second," Prokofiev wrote. "The first movement, Andante assai, is severe in character and is a kind of extended introduction to the second movement, a sonata allegro, which is vigorous and turbulent, but has a broad second theme. The third movement is slow, gentle, and tender. The finale is fast and written in complicated rhythm."[8]

Indeed, the two violin sonatas represent two very different artistic tendencies in Prokofiev's work. While the second is transparent, cheerful, and permeated with genial humor and naïve lyricism, the first is dramatic, full of sharp contrasts and powerful, gloomy, tempestuous emotions. While in the Second Sonata Prokofiev adhered more closely to the "classical line" which had manifested itself in the First Symphony, he also revealed his new leaning toward a style inspired by heroic Russian epics. This Sonata has much in common with *Ivan the Terrible* and *Alexander Nevsky*, with the Russian songs, Op. 106, and in some respects with *Semyon Kotko*.

The Sonata's four movements present four sharply contrasting scenes, which might have been inspired by Russian epic poetry. The first movement is a compact *bylina*-like melody, suggesting the meditation of an ancient bard on the fate of the motherland; the second presents a scene of brutal encounter between warring forces; the third creates a poetic image of a young girl's lament; and the finale is a hymn to the might of Russia in arms, a paean to the people's freedom and strength. At the very end of the finale, material from the opening Andante returns, underscoring the basic epic-narrative quality of the work.

The music of the Sonata has something of the quality of a narrative poem and seems to contain a hidden program. Many of its pages, especially the warlike episodes of the second and fourth movements, evoke in the listener's mind almost visual scenes of national disasters and heroic deeds. This pictorial quality of the musical material relates the Sonata to examples of the Russian epic style in symphonic writing.

The main theme of the first movement—a contemplative melody stated in the piano in bass octaves—is a typically Prokofievan theme of profound meditation. We have noted the presence of similar themes in several of the composer's prewar works, such as the Andante of the First Quartet and *Thoughts,* as well as in the more recently composed Fifth Symphony. The Russian character of this theme in the first movement is underscored by both its tonal structure, with its emphasis on the subdominant, and its metrical scheme, which consists of an alternation of 3/4 and 4/4. In the middle section of this movement, the violin in double-stops introduces more restless, troubled phrases in the spirit of a Russian lament. The recapitulation is particularly interesting. Here the theme is harmonized in a new way, appearing as a succession of minor seventh chords against which the violin *con sordino* plays running scale passages (marked *freddo*). This music calls to mind the distant past; as if through the haze of centuries, there were arising stern visages of antiquity, darkened by time. The terseness of the melodic phrases emphasizes the introductory character of the movement, which is like a storyteller's prologue, a prelude to the action. It concludes with an unusual tonal effect, achieved by an alternation of arpeggiated chords in the piano and in the violin *pizzicato,* which remind one of the closing chords of a *gusli* player's prologue.

Now the epic tale gives way to the heavy, abrupt phrases of the Sonata's second movement, marked *brusco*. These march-like phrases, with their rigid, clipped cadences and strident harmonies, create an image of brutal military power. This has much in common with the music of the Teutonic invasion in *Alexander Nevsky,* with the most dissonant pages of the Sixth, Seventh, and Eighth Piano Sonatas, and perhaps with the "fascist march" in Shostakovich's Seventh Symphony. But later these coarse, mechanical images give way to a rich, soaring theme (marked *eroico*) sung out by the violin, which sounds particularly appealing after the harmonic and tonal harshness of the opening phrases. In both the development and the recapitulation, the hostile images appear alternately with those of a heroic nature. The mounting polytonal harmonies concentrated at the opening of the development section seem to embody a recollection of terrifying and dramatic events. One cannot but draw attention to the expressionistic excesses found in the closing episodes of this movement. Unlike the dramatically tense moments of *Alexander Nevsky,* these lack the justification of a plot and thus sound somewhat forced.

After all the fury of the Allegro, the sometimes plaintive, sometimes rhapsodic lyricism of the third movement sounds warm and appealing. The very tender, singing theme of the violin, which rises over softly rippling piano figurations suggestive of a peaceful spring scene, is the most felicitous melody in the entire Sonata. In its delicate chromatic turns and charming harmonic contrasts it resembles the lyrical, fairy-tale images of Rimsky-Korsakov's operas. This broad melody is followed by passages suggesting a restless recitative. There is an obvious relationship between the musical ideas found here and the portraits of the sad young girls in Prokofiev's cantatas and operas—the sweetheart in *Alexander Nevsky,* Lyubochka in *Semyon Kotko,* and Natasha in *War and Peace.*

The fourth and final movement of the Sonata reveals a very close kinship to the epic music of the Five. This can be seen both in the melodic structure of its first theme, which is in the manner of Borodin's *Song of the Dark*

*Forest,* and in its traditional mixed meter (the alternation of 5/8, 7/8, and 8/8). However, Prokofiev charged this epic theme with a propulsive energy, which endows it with new and modern features. In this respect the music of the finale bears a likeness to the titanic finale of Prokofiev's Seventh Sonata and the rigidly rhythmic episode in the finale of the Eighth. Here, too, the impelling dynamism of the first theme is juxtaposed with the restrained lyricism of the second. Both of these themes are interesting for their tonal structure, a combination of elements from the Lydian and Mixolydian modes, which reinforces the national color of the music. In the dynamic development section, the first theme is skillfully contrasted with the radically transformed second theme, which has been made subservient to the momentum of the dominating mixed meters. A large role is also played by heavily accented octaves in the lower registers of the piano, which recall the opening theme of the second movement. Thus in the development of the finale, the explosive fury of elemental conflict flares up once again.

The recapitulation of the fourth movement is unusual. It serves as both a recapitulation and a coda which combines the two themes of the finale with the melancholy, narrative music of the first movement. Again we hear the quiet running passages of the muted violin and the succession of colorless piano chords of the first movement's recapitulation. This reminiscence emphasizes, as it were, the retrospective quality of all that was stated before; here again an ancient chronicler seems to be calmly recalling images of the past, and then, for the last time, the second theme of the finale is heard, gradually fading away.

The Sonata contains many novel coloristic effects. Once again, as in the early First Violin Concerto, Prokofiev made use of colorful violinistic techniques, from harsh *sul ponticello* and *pizzicato* to muted running passages. But most important, he succeeded in filling the modest framework of a violin sonata with epic content of truly symphonic proportions.

※ ※ ※

The first musician to perform the F minor Sonata was David Oistrakh, a great admirer of the work, to whom it was dedicated. The première took place on October 23, 1946, in the Small Hall of the Moscow Conservatory, with Lev Oborin at the piano. The Sonata was acclaimed by many musicians. Miaskovsky noted in his diary: "Heard Prokofiev's new violin sonata in its entirety—a work of genius. (Oistrakh's playing was inspired.)" The newspaper *Pravda* hailed the Sonata, noting the "Russian national spirit" and "stern, epic grandeur" of the work, as well as the fresh and interesting way in which it exploited the expressive resources of the violin.[9] Oistrakh has since played this Sonata many times, both in the Soviet Union and abroad. It has been hailed by music critics in France, England, Italy, Poland, Czechoslovakia, Sweden, and other countries.

Shortly after the première of the Violin Sonata in Moscow on the eve of the October celebrations, another Prokofiev work, *The Duenna* (*Betrothal in a Monastery*), was given its first performance in Leningrad. It was presented by the Kirov Theater, with B. Chaikin as conductor and I. Shlepianov as producer.

This opera, written in 1940 for the Stanislavsky Theater, had awaited its first performance for about six years. As we know, it was almost ready for production in the summer of 1941, but the outbreak of the war had prevented its presentation at that time. In 1943, while living in Alma-Ata, Prokofiev had gone over the score and introduced a number of changes designed to make the recitatives more melodic.

Finally, on November 3, 1946, this sparkling comic opera had its first performance in the very hall where *The Gambler* had once been rehearsed and the sensational première of the *Scythian Suite* had taken place. The theater took extraordinary pains with the production. The leading roles were performed by B. Freidkov (Don Mendoza), A. Khalileyeva (Louisa), N. Velter (the Duenna), and V. Ulyanov (Don Jerome). I. Shlepianov and T. Bruni very tastefully recreated the atmosphere of everyday life in eighteenth-century Seville. The composer was particularly pleased with the fact that seven Duralumin cups tuned to various pitches were specially ordered for the finale, in which Don Jerome sings a drinking song while accompanying himself on glasses.

*   *   *

The English playwright Richard Sheridan, who had written *The Duenna* in 1775, had intended it for operatic presentation. With airs based on popular tunes of the day, this work enjoyed an unprecedented success in London, where it ran for seventy-five successive performances. Sheridan's contemporaries, enchanted with his sparkling wit, skillful handling of intrigue, and brilliant, polished dialogue, called him "the English Beaumarchais." "There is no pause, no softening; sarcasms fly like pistol shots," wrote Hippolyte Taine of Sheridan's comedies.

It is not surprising that of all Prokofiev's operas, *The Duenna* proved to be the best constructed. Unlike *The Gambler, The Flaming Angel, Semyon Kotko,* and *War and Peace,* it was not based on a story or novel, but on a skillfully wrought libretto intended specifically for the operatic stage. Although he was attracted by the comic aspects of *The Duenna*, Prokofiev relegated the satire and burlesque to second place and sought above all to give musical expression to the lovers' feelings. "I did not think that it would be a mistake to emphasize the romantic element in *The Duenna* rather than to concentrate on its comic element," he said.

Scarcely altering Sheridan's witty text, Prokofiev created a modern version of the *opera buffa*. Among the leading characters we recognize the traditional *buffo* types, treated in the composer's inimitable manner: the cantankerous father; the amorous old man, duped by an ingenious soubrette; the overripe virgin in search of a rich husband; and the two pairs of lovers, joining their fate after many tribulations. Such features of the old English play as the comic situations, tinged here and there with biting satire, the charming lyrical scenes, and the bright, pleasure-bent tone of the festive episodes, were perfectly suited to Prokofiev's talent.

The plot of the opera presents the typical situations of the eighteenth- and nineteenth-century *opera buffa*. The Seville nobleman Don Jerome wants to marry his daughter Louisa to the elderly fish merchant Don Mendoza. But Louisa is in love with the young Antonio and refuses to submit to her father's wishes. Her companion and confidante, the Duenna, brilliantly frustrates the plans of Don Jerome and Don Mendoza. She artfully spins a web of intrigues which result in the rich Don Mendoza marrying her (in the belief that she is the beauty Louisa), while the real Louisa, after tricking her father into giving his blessing, marries her beloved Antonio. Meanwhile, the fate of the other young lovers is also decided— Louisa's brother Ferdinand marries the beautiful Clara. The next to last scene takes place in a monastery, where a drunken orgy of the monks is interrupted by the arrival and betrothal of the two pairs of lovers.

*The Duenna* was Prokofiev's second comic opera, but in his handling of the comic genre he made it quite different from his earlier *Love for Three Oranges*. In *The Three Oranges*, the characters are stylized grotesques; in *The Duenna* they are real human beings. In *The Three Oranges* there are deliberate eccentric effects and parody for parody's sake; in *The Duenna* there is only witty satire. The lyrical element, almost completely lacking in *The Three Oranges*, plays a considerable role in *The Duenna*; along with the scenes of biting satire and gentle humor, an important place is given to romantic episodes filled with genuine emotion. In this respect *The Duenna* bears a certain resemblance to *Romeo and Juliet,* in which the composer also sought to blend the humorous and the lyrical, the commonplace and the lofty, the frivolous and the poetically moving.

The musical satire in *The Duenna* is directed mainly at the leading comic characters—the old rogue and lecher Don Mendoza, and the greedy, cantankerous Don Jerome. These are mercenary men, dreaming of a mutually beneficial marriage deal. The black-bearded Don Mendoza, a dealer in rotten fish who pictures himself as a Don Juan, is almost a carica-ture. In his predominantly declamatory vocal part, the composer employs pointedly mocking devices: the conceited remark, "Mendoza is a very cunning lad," which is repeated as a kind of leitmotiv; the playful exclama-tions, "You little rogue!"; the joyful, breathless patter in the duet with Don Jerome; the inane, fawning phrases in the scene with the Duenna. Don Mendoza's rather overdrawn recitative is combined with a derisively grotesque orchestral accompaniment.

The portrait of Don Jerome is somewhat kinder. He is not truly repul-sive like Don Mendoza, but instead simply ludicrous, with his tedious grumbling and senile irascibility. His lugubrious arioso, "If you have a daughter," and quite realistic, petulant "Su-u-perb" are extremely funny. His elated hopping about in the finales of the first and second scenes, and his drinking songs in the fourth scene (with Don Mendoza) and in the final scene (with the chorus) are also amusing.

One of the most brilliant and ingenious humorous touches in the opera is the "music-making" trio which Prokofiev introduces in Scene 6, where Don Jerome and his two partners perform a courtly minuet with mock-seriousness. The very composition of this amateur trio—clarinet, cornet, and bass drum—is comical. Now and then the musicians come in off-key, which increasingly irritates Don Jerome. The trio's ironic music is repeated like a refrain throughout the entire scene. Just as in *Cinderella,* the eighteenth-century dance forms which had so long intrigued Prokofiev are here subjected to a fresh and characteristically comic treatment.

Scene 8, laid in a Catholic monastery, is pervaded with an anti-clerical feeling. Here the composer employs some very effective techniques of musical caricature. The bravura chorus of the carousing monks ("The bottle's the sun of our life") is followed by a decorous, ascetic chant, which is interrupted by the drunken exclamations of Father Elustaph. The some-what coarse, grotesque character of the music heightens still more the effect of this bitingly satirical scene.

While the scene in the monastery calls to mind the acerbity of Boccac-cio's anti-clerical tales, the carnival and feasting scenes pulsate with the merrymaking of the gay Spanish crowd, full of exuberant playfulness and ecstatic love of life. The nocturnal carnival at the end of Scene 1, with its bacchanalian dances and prankish masks taunting the peevish Don Jerome, almost transforms the stage action into a ballet. This has much in common with the carnival episodes in *Romeo and Juliet.*

The portrait of the Duenna is drawn with strokes of subtle humor. Her scenes with Don Jerome and later with Don Mendoza, whom she adroitly dupes into marrying her, are full of action, wit, and chicanery. A good example of her characterization can be seen in her lyrical song in Scene 4, which combines sensual yearning, mincing manners, and a roguish smile. The characterization of Louisa, the opera's heroine, also has a trace of roguishness and youthful zest. She is a direct descendant of the coquettish heroines of Mozart and Rossini.

Contrasted to the sordid world of aging voluptuaries, greedy merchants, and hypocritical clerics is the world of the young lovers, filled with noble and lofty feelings. This contrast is clearly brought out in the music. Especially effective, after the caricatural episodes, are the lyrical themes associated with Louisa and Antonio, Ferdinand and Clara. Just as in *Romeo and Juliet,* Prokofiev unfolds a whole chain of instrumental leitmotivs to express the lovers' amorous reveries and ecstasy. The voice parts also contain fragments of these themes, set forth in his typically colorful intratonal development. On the whole, however, the composer makes sparing use of closed vocal forms, for the most part confining himself, as in the love scenes of *Semyon Kotko,* to brief but expressive lyrical dialogue.

Here, as in Prokofiev's other operas, a dominant feature of the score is the flexible recitative combined with a continuously developing orchestral part which illustrates the stage action. Of particular interest in certain scenes is the unerring realism of the musical characterization in the orchestra; for examples of this one need only recall the lively and expressive music accompanying the Duenna and Don Mendoza in Scene 4, Louisa and Don Mendoza in Scene 5, or the comic scene in which the disguised Louisa is driven from her father's house (Scene 2). Of no small importance is the role played by the independent orchestral episodes: the brief overture based on the wedding chorus in Scene 9, the mirthful dances of the masks in Scene 1, the amateur trio in Scene 6, the episode of Clara's amorous reveries in Scene 7, and the vigorous passage depicting the duel between Ferdinand and Antonio in Scene 8.

But let us repeat that it is recitative which holds the decisive place in the musical fabric of the opera. Prokofiev's declamation, based as it is mainly on a prose text, grows out of the varied inflections of the human speaking voice. At different moments in the opera we hear faint notes of anger or irritation, teasing jeers, sentimental outcries, excited chatter, stuttering prattle, and even purely onomatopoeic effects bordering on the burlesque. Quite different are the recitatives of Louisa and Clara, in which a mood of poignant lyricism prevails. It is this distinctiveness in the vocal characterizations which helps to individualize the opera's romantic characters—the daring, scheming Louisa, the pensive and modest Clara, the derisive Ferdinand, and the ardent Antonio.

Both in ingenious use of orchestral effects and in experimentation with declamatory devices, Prokofiev's imagination literally knew no bounds.* However, the abundance of recitative, particularly where it assumes distinctly grotesque features, can sometimes weary the listener, who begins to long for a simple, tuneful melody. It was not by chance that the composer tried to offset the continuous declamation with melodically well-defined episodes. One such episode is Antonio's moving serenade in the first scene, later repeated many times as one of the principal motivs of the love of Antonio and Louisa (Fig. 50).

К те-бе в ок_но гля-дит лу_на  и  ве_лит  о _ на  со _

_рвать по_ско_рей с тво-их дрем_лю-щих о _ чей по_вяз_ку сна

FIGURE 50

Other melodic passages are Clara's two ariosos, the Duenna's song, Don Jerome's arioso, and the rapturous, lyrical quartet at the end of Scene 5 (one of the very few examples of a completely worked-out ensemble in a Prokofiev opera). To this list one might add the already mentioned instru-

---

* Examples of this include the use of various groups of strings off stage at the end of the first scene, the comic trio in the sixth, and the playing on glasses in the final scene.

mental dance episodes. Even though they do not entirely compensate for the predominance of vocal declamation, all these melodic episodes unquestionably enrich the music of the opera.

❦ ❦ ❦

*The Duenna* had its première at the Kirov Theater on November 3, 1946. Although illness prevented Prokofiev from going to Leningrad to attend it, he had kept in close touch with the producers, especially with the conductor, B. Khaikin, while the opera was in rehearsal.

Shostakovich's warm review of the opera, which appeared in *Sovetskoye Iskusstvo,* made the composer very happy. "*The Duenna* is in all probability one of Prokofiev's most radiant and buoyant works," he wrote. "There is the freshness of spring and youth in this opera. . . . It is a superbly integrated, organic work, full of spontaneous humor and broad, good-natured, roguish laughter. Listening to *The Duenna,* one is reminded of Verdi's *Falstaff,* for it has the same spontaneity of feeling enriched by the wisdom of a great master."[10]

The year 1946, a successful one for Prokofiev, culminated on December 22 with the Bolshoi Theater's first performance of the ballet *Romeo and Juliet.* This was a somewhat enriched and more dramatic version of the Leningrad production of 1940, although the choreography and décor, by Lavrovsky and Williams respectively, remained largely unchanged. Juliet was again performed by Galina Ulanova, the creator of the role. But the distinguished ballerina said that the Moscow production, which took place almost seven years after the one in Leningrad, to some degree reflected the deep emotional exprinces of the war years. "I saw in the new Juliet the same spiritual qualities which, under other circumstances, would have impelled Shakespeare's heroine to a great deed of national significance," Ulanova wrote.[11]

In the Moscow production both the cruel, arrogant Tybalt (A. Yermolayev) and the jaunty Mercutio (S. Koren, who had also performed this role in Leningrad) were magnificent. In the scenes of Mercutio's death, the funeral cortege bearing Tybalt's corpse, and other episodes, truly Shakespearean passions were given full expression. *Romeo and Juliet,* especially with Ulanova, has become the pride of the Bolshoi Theater, one of its finest ballet productions.

Prokofiev spent almost the entire winter of 1946–47 and the summer and fall of 1947 in Nikolina Gora. On February 18 he completed the orchestration of the Sixth Symphony. In addition to this, he composed and orchestrated the scene "War Council at Fili" for *War and Peace,* sketched a cello sonata, and put the finishing touches on the symphonic suite *Waltzes,* which contained three waltzes from *Cinderella,* two from *War and Peace,* and the *Mephisto Waltz* from the music for the film *Lermontov.*[12] It seemed as though the composer were hurrying to bring all his creative plans to completion; only concern for his orchard lured him from his manuscript paper. Along with matters pertaining to scores, his business letters of this period contain references to posts and rails for the garden fence.

Early in the fall of 1947 Prokofiev completed the Ninth Piano Sonata, which he had begun a year and a half before, and dedicated it to S. Richter. He also wrote the short sonata for unaccompanied violin, Op. 115, orchestrated the symphonic suite *Summer Day* (based on material from the piano pieces *Music for Children*), and composed some works for the thirtieth anniversary of the Revolution. In September he heard the first performance of the third suite from *Cinderella* played on the radio by the All-Union Radio Orchestra conducted by A. Stasevich.

*   *   *

The Ninth Sonata in C major, Op. 103, was Prokofiev's last piano composition, his swan song in this genre. Unlike his three monumental and complicated sonatas (Op. 82, 83, and 84), the new work was characterized by a certain lightness of style and emotional serenity. Here the composer returned to the intimate style he had loved since his youth. In this Sonata, which contains neither violent outbursts nor complicated technical effects, bright pastoral images and intimate lyricism are mingled with playful and amusing fantasy. Many familiar techniques, such as tonal digressions, unexpected and deceptive cadences, and typically clear-cut rhythms, are employed here. At times one senses a relationship between this Sonata's musical material and that of the operas and ballets of the forties, such as *War and Peace* and *Cinderella.*

The Sonata is in four movements, the first and third predominantly lyrical, and the second and fourth fast and lively. On hearing the main theme of the first movement, one is strongly reminded of Andrei Bolkonsky's tender lyricism in *War and Peace.* The mood of this theme is a combination of bright reverie and sober contemplation (FIG. 51).

The refined harmonic texture, with its abundance of accessory chords and constantly moving chromatic inner voices, is typical of Prokofiev's later writing. The bridge passage and second theme are quite different, however,

FIGURE 51

containing gay, dance-like motivs which recall the ludicrous courtiers in *Cinderella.* The first movement, like the others, is miniature in form, modestly developed, and devoid of dramatic conflicts.

The second movement, a scherzo, opens with an impetuous running theme containing sharp rhythmic effects. This gives way to a soft, graceful dance reminiscent of the nocturnal dances in *Romeo and Juliet* and *The Duenna.* In the middle section there emerges a clear, singing melody which is one of the best lyrical themes of the Sonata. While the second movement is constructed like a scherzo with a lyrical middle section, in the third movement a song-like melody akin to the lyricism of *Romeo and Juliet* predominates, alternating with a vivacious theme.

The finale is the gayest, most lighthearted movement of the Sonata; we can sense behind it the young Prokofiev of thirty years before, still fond of tricks, enchanted with the joys of life, and laughing infectiously. As in most of Prokofiev's finales, the form here is that of a rondo-sonata. Its active themes—running passages and march-like figures—are restated in the exposition and the recapitulation, but in the middle episode, as a contrast, a tender, languid theme appears.

At the end of the finale, the pensive main theme of the first movement returns over softly murmuring runs, bringing the Sonata to a quiet close. This conclusion seems almost like a preliminary sketch for the fantasy-like coda of the finale of the Seventh Symphony.

This Sonata contains many interesting and novel coloristic effects. The use of a thematic link between the movements is very original: in the codas of the first, second and third movements, the main themes of the following movements appear, like heralds.

The Ninth Sonata failed to achieve acceptance. It remained unpublished for eight years and is seldom performed. Compared to Prokofiev's earlier sonatas, it seems on first acquaintance to be somewhat anemic and emotionally pallid, but after getting to know it better, one becomes aware of the modest charm of its lyricism and the inexhaustible vitality of its humor.

❋　❋　❋

The Sonata for Unaccompanied Violins, Op. 115, was something of an experiment. Its composition was prompted by the practice of groups of Soviet violinists playing in unison certain works by Bach, Handel, and other composers. Such ensembles of twenty to thirty young artists often performed at special concerts given on festive occasions at the Bolshoi Theater. From this Prokofiev derived the idea of writing a contemporary Soviet piece for violins played in unison. Consisting of a sonata allegro, slow variations, and a fast finale, this work is miniature in scale and technically simple in style, within the reach of young musicians. It was intended to be played in unison by twenty violinists.

The Sonata approaches the kind of classical style so brilliantly embodied in the Second Violin Sonata. The structure of the principal themes, the character of the figurations, and the method of strict variation are in many respects tied to the traditions of the Viennese classics, although the typical outlines of the melody and the modulations betray Prokofiev's hand. Particularly characteristic in this respect are the dance themes—for example, the mischievous second theme of the first movement, with its accordion-like refrain (the Sonata's best theme), and the bravura main theme of the finale, in mazurka rhythm, with sharp accents and brilliant leaps in double stops.

This Sonata bespeaks Prokofiev's intense quests in the realm of pure melody, his search for lyricism strong enough to stand without complex harmonic support. Here the composer seems to delight in the clarity and expressiveness of modest, single-voice melodies. Examples of this are the already mentioned second theme of the first movement, the bright, flowing Russian theme of the variations in the second movement, and the pensive second theme of the finale. This concentration on melody as the basic component of music is quite characteristic of Prokofiev's last works. In this Sonata the melodies are seldom adorned with countervoices, ornaments, or full chords, but the composer enriched his themes by employing novel tonal digressions and skillfully making use of concealed two-part writing.

The Violin Sonata, Op. 115, was never performed. Despite the charm of some of its themes, it sounds unusually thin when played by unaccompanied violin alone. Only if it were possible to hear this composition played by an ensemble of violinists in unison, as the composer intended, could one properly evaluate it.

✻   ✻   ✻

The Leningrad Philharmonic Orchestra opened its 1947 season on October 11 with the première of Prokofiev's Sixth Symphony. On this occasion the conductor was Ye. A. Mravinsky, one of the most active proponents of Soviet symphonic music. This was the first time he had conducted the première of a new work by Prokofiev. The Symphony was performed on two successive evenings in a festive atmosphere, with the composer attending. The newspapers *Sovetskoye Iskusstvo* and *Vecherny Leningrad* hailed the new work as an outstanding event, noting in it no contradictions whatever. But shortly afterward this evaluation was substantially revised.

The Sixth Symphony in E-flat minor, Op. 111, is perhaps the most difficult and complex work Prokofiev composed during his Soviet period. In it two contradictory tendencies clash—on the one hand, a tendency toward clear and meaningful themes, toward the expression of profound human emotions, and on the other, a tendency toward extremely thick, at times artificially intensified expressive means, aimed at stunning the listener with startling effects of harmony and orchestration. It seems as though the two Prokofievs, the old and the new, were engaged in a struggle with each other, revealing in the course of this struggle both powerful, genuine lyricism and sudden outbursts of unrestrained expressionism utterly incomprehensible to the listener.

It is quite possible that the general trend toward a complex, extravagant symphonic style, which had begun to be followed by a number of Soviet composers, had something to do with Prokofiev's reversion to his old expressionistic tendencies. In this atmosphere of what might be called a contest for complexity, Prokofiev, who had achieved new, beautiful, and profound simplicity in *Romeo and Juliet, Alexander Nevsky,* and the Fifth Symphony, once again began to speak in a very difficult and at times esoteric language. We have observed this tendency before in the harshest episodes of the Sixth, Seventh, and Eighth Piano Sonatas, in the massive sonorities of the *Ode to the End of the War,* and in other works. In the Sixth Symphony it can be seen in the contrived quality of certain themes (the introduction to the second movement, for example) and in the excessive accumulations of sound in the climactic episodes.

But at the same time, in the Sixth Symphony as in the last sonatas, one's interest is stirred by the intense drama built on a succession of sharply contrasting images and moods—searching reflection, mournful recitative, violent outbursts of rage, and at the end, boisterous mirth. These emotions are expressed in fitting, melodically well-defined themes, but unfortunately these themes are sometimes drowned in the deliberately complicated orchestration.

Just as in the F minor Violin Sonata, one can sense an underlying epic theme, even though the composer has not provided us with an explicit program. "The first movement is agitated, at times lyrical, at times austere; the second movement, *Largo,* is brighter and more tuneful; the finale, rapid and in a major key, is close in character to my Fifth Symphony, save for reminiscences of the austere passages in the first movement." This is all that the composer himself had to say about the content of the Sixth Symphony.

In a conversation with the present author in October 1947, he added that the main musical ideas of the Symphony, which had taken shape in 1944–45, had to some extent been inspired by the war years. "Now we are rejoicing in our great victory," he said, "but each of us has wounds which cannot be healed. One has lost those dear to him, another has lost his health. This must not be forgotten."

Troubled echoes of the war more than once burst into the musical narrative—in the deafening, battle-clamor of the orchestral *tutti,* in the powerful rumble of the timpani, in the doleful sound of a funeral procession, in the plaintive melody of a Russian lament. The heroic lyricism of the Symphony is presented against the somber background of the war just past.

The composer considered dedicating this Symphony to the memory of Beethoven. It bears the same opus number (111) as Beethoven's last piano sonata, which was a great favorite of Prokofiev's. Of course, what he had in mind was not the chance symbolism of the numbers, but rather a desire to carry on the tradition of lofty intellectualism and profound tragedy that characterized Beethoven's later works.

The most tragic of the Symphony's three movements is the first. Its two basic themes—the melancholy first and the pensive second, reminiscent of the mournful tune of a shepherd's pipe—do not contrast but rather complement each other (FIG. 52).

FIGURE 52

But at points between the statements of the themes and in the complicated development section, the din of war's fury prevails. In the middle of the development (marked *Lugubre*), a mighty funeral procession is introduced. This majestic, poignant episode is one of the most stirring passages in the entire symphony.

The themes of the slow second movement are also devoid of contrast. Both of them are serene and flowing; both, especially the first, abound in unusual, difficult turns. But here, too, the sober reflection is interrupted by ominous sounds which seem to symbolize the specters of war. The middle section of this movement (*Largo*) is a tender serenade sung by four French horns.

The main themes of the finale, a rollicking, athletically vigorous *Vivace,* are characteristically Prokofievan. Such, for example, are the gay, Mozartean first theme (FIG. 53) and the dance-like second theme, which recalls the carnival dances of *Romeo and Juliet.*

FIGURE 53

In the development these two themes are masterfully combined. A virile, frequently repeated "fanfare" in the basses, which suggests the military marches of Beethoven's time, plays an important role in this movement.

In the coda of the finale, however, the composer once again suddenly interrupts the gay dance motion with a rapid succession of contrasting episodes—the sad pipe-like melody of the first movement, the ominous image of war's fury, and at the very end, the dry, restless march figures. "I did not want the finale to be regarded merely as a gay appendage to the preceding movements," said the composer. Hence the troubled reminiscences in the coda, evoking, as it were, the unsubdued forces of evil.

The scoring of the Sixth Symphony, in which a wide range of coloristic effects are employed, is particularly noteworthy. Pure timbres (the oboe duet in the pipe-like theme of the first movement, for example) alternate with the massive sounds of various instrumental sections. Prokofiev deliberately upset the usual distribution of the voices, entrusting to the flute tones which lie below the oboe and clarinet, or combining the first violin with the tuba, two octaves apart. At rehearsals he called particular attention to the effect of the asthmatic "wheezing" of the French horns in the development of the first movement, and to the English horn, which plays above the oboe at the end of the finale. Throughout the Symphony, as in the *Ode to the End of the War,* it is the low, dense, metallic sonorities which predominate, intensified by the piano and percussion.

The Symphony was performed in Moscow on December 25, 1947, but it did not secure a place in the repertory. Its unusual orchestration and harmonic complexities made it difficult to grasp. Even seasoned musicians failed to understand this music at once. As Miaskovsky wrote in his diary, "I began to understand the Prokofiev only on the third hearing, and then I was won over: profound, but somewhat gloomy, and harshly orchestrated."[13]

The Symphony has been frequently performed abroad and has been recorded by several orchestras. To the foreign modernist critics who had hoped to find unusual complexities and dissonance in this music, much of it proved to be surprisingly traditional. The French critic René Dumesnil drew particular attention to the Symphony's clarity of thought and classical form. "Its transparent instrumentation, its melodic elements," he wrote, "were an unexpected surprise for all those who were expecting a new *Scythian Suite.*"[14]

Be that as it may, it is clear to us that despite certain stylistic incongruities, the Sixth Symphony is not only an important event in the creative history of an outstanding musician, but also a unique artistic monument of its time.

❋   ❋   ❋

Soon after he had completed the orchestration of the Sixth Symphony, Prokofiev revised the Fourth Symphony, which he had composed in Paris in 1930. He liked this symphony very much and regretted that it had not been successful in the Soviet Union. In the new version he tried to apply the experience he had gained from working on the Fifth and Sixth Symphonies. The first movement was radically reworked and considerably extended. "The previous material has been preserved to some degree, but I have added so much that is new that this work could actually be called my Seventh Symphony," he reported to the press.[15]

The new version of the Fourth Symphony was included in the list of Prokofiev's works as Op. 112. This version has not been performed, but the piano score indicates that except in the charmingly lyrical third movement, based on the music of the "Beautiful Maiden" from *The Prodigal Son,* the composer did not overcome the cold, abstract speculation found in most of his works of the Paris period.

In November 1947, the Soviet people celebrated the thirtieth anniversary of the Revolution. On November 5, just before the celebrations, the Soviet government conferred on Prokofiev the honorary title of People's Artist of the R.S.F.S.R.

For this anniversary Prokofiev wrote the *Festive Poem* for symphony orchestra (A major, Op. 113) and the cantata for mixed chorus and orchestra *Flourish, Mighty Land* (D-flat major, Op. 114), to words by Yevgeni Dolmatovsky. He also composed a number of mass songs for a contest organized by the Composers' Union. Only one of these—*To the Motherland,* with words by Mira Mendelson—was published; its broad, flowing melody was later used as Katerina's "theme of fidelity" in *The Stone Flower.*

The *Festive Poem,* which was performed by the State Symphony Orchestra on October 3, 1947, under the conductor K. Ivanov, proved disappointing. In this superficial, melodically pallid work, it is difficult to recognize the hand of the great master. The music of the cantata *Flourish, Mighty Land,* which was performed on November 12 under N. Anosov, is much fresher and warmer. Here the themes, especially the first melody of the orchestral introduction, are full of lyrical charm, and in their brightness they bear a resemblance to certain themes of *Zdravitsa.* On November 14 Miaskovsky noted in his diary, "Anosov played Prokofiev's cantata for the thirtieth anniversary—spirited, gay, and quite fresh." The effect of the cantata is weakened, however, by Dolmatovsky's cold, trite text and the inexpressive climactic episode "Glory."

During 1947 the Maly Opera Theater in Leningrad prepared the second part of *War and Peace.* It consisted of the following five scenes: Napoleon's headquarters at the Shevardino redoubt; the War Council at Fili; the burning of Moscow; the scene of Andrei Bolkonsky's death; and the Smolensk road—the ignominious retreat of Napoleon's defeated troops and the triumph of the victors. The new scene "War Council at Fili," which Prokofiev wrote at the suggestion of S. A. Samosud, presented aptly drawn portraits of the Russian generals—the cold, stiff Bennigsen, the vacillating Barclay de Tolly, the courageous Yermolov, and the wise Raevsky. The central figure in this scene is the Russian hero Field Marshal Kutuzov. Despite the economy of the expressive means, each character is distinguished by well-defined individual traits.

In the summer and fall of 1947 the opera was given at private hearings, but owing to a number of weaknesses in the dramatic conception, it was not shown publicly. Later the composer substantially revised the entire opera, consolidating the principal material of the extended two-part work in a single, unified version.

The production of *The Duenna* and the first part of *War and Peace* did not appease Prokofiev's desire to write another opera. From time to time he worked on the comic opera *Khan Buzai,* based on Kazakh folk material, but he still felt the need to treat a contemporary subject. With his wife and constant collaborator Mira Mendelson, he looked through a huge number of books in search of an interesting subject. They considered dramatizing N. Ostrovsky's *How the Steel Was Tempered* or A. Fadeyev's *Young Guard,* but Prokofiev decided that neither subject was suitable for operatic treatment.

A suitable subject was eventually found in B. Polevoi's wonderful *The Story of a Real Man,* which had just been published. The Kirov Theater enthusiastically encouraged the idea of an opera based on the heroic deed of the flier Meresyev, the hero of Polevoi's book.

During the fall of 1947, Mira Mendelson and the composer prepared a libretto in four acts and ten scenes, incorporating the principal dramatic situations of the novel and preserving Polevoi's original text. Prokofiev later stated that his aim was to saturate the opera with clear, melodic episodes. "In the above-mentioned opera, I intend to introduce trios, duets, and contrapuntally developed choruses, for which I am making use of extremely interesting authentic folk songs of the Russian north. Clear melodies and the simplest harmonic language possible—these are the other elements which I shall strive for in this opera."[16]

The opera was completely written and orchestrated by August 11, 1948. Included in it were certain episodes from the music for the film *Ivan the Terrible* (the song *The Young Oaks* from the wedding scene of Part I) and also *The Little Green Grove* and *Sashenka,* from the arrangements of Russian folk songs, Op. 104. At the beginning of the new season the company of the Kirov Theater, with B. Khaikin as conductor, began to rehearse it and on December 3, 1948, it was given a private run-through with the orchestra.

The discussion which followed this preview was not favorable. Those who had been present drew attention to the excess of minor details in the libretto and to the failure of the music to convey a real sense of the people's life during the war. It was noted that the great heroic theme was overshadowed by naturalistic details, by a conventional portrayal of everyday life. *The Story of a Real Man* was not produced and has remained in manuscript.

Thus by 1948, despite the intensity of Prokofiev's creative activity, his work began to show signs of becoming obscure to the general audience. This was what had caused the failure of the *Festive Poem* and the very cold reception of the Sixth Symphony, which most of the audience could not understand. Furthermore, expressionistic complexities made it difficult to grasp the Sixth and Seventh Piano Sonatas, the Second String Quartet, and other works. And at the other extreme, traces of a certain forced and artificial simplification appeared in his songs and choruses to texts by contemporary poets.

Since the critics had failed to point out these shortcomings, apparently content to praise every new work by a leading Soviet composer, the time had come for the Soviet public to make a serious critical evaluation of the work of the Composers' Union. It was necessary to help highly gifted artists overcome the errors into which they were falling, to bring their work closer to the demands of the people.

In the middle of January, a three-day conference of leaders of Soviet music was held at the Central Committee of the Communist Party. Among those present was Prokofiev, who listened with deep attention to the speeches, especially to the one by A. A. Zhdanov which raised a number of pointed questions about recent musical works. He himself did not participate in the discussions, but Zhdanov's speech and the Party's resolution "On the Opera *The Great Friendship,* by V. Muradeli," issued a month later, led him to ponder and re-evaluate his own aesthetic principles.

The resolution of February 10, 1948, severely criticized the creative errors of certain Soviet composers, among them Prokofiev. A number of sharply critical articles on the shortcomings of Soviet music also appeared at the time in the newspapers. A week later, on February 17, Prokofiev's Sixth Symphony, the *Ode to the End of the War,* the *Festive Poem,* the most recent piano sonatas, and some of the arrangements of Russian songs were subjected to criticism at a general meeting of composers in Moscow. Of his earlier works, the following were cited as examples of undesirable tendencies: the ballets *The Buffoon, The Prodigal Son, Sur le Borysthène,* and *Le Pas d'acier*; the opera *The Flaming Angel*; the Third and Fourth Symphonies; and the Fifth Piano Concerto.

A letter from Prokofiev was read at the meeting, in which he set forth his thoughts on the Party resolution and his own artistic views. "The Party resolution has separated the decayed tissue from the healthy," he said. "However painful this may be for a number of Soviet composers, including myself, I greet the Party resolution which creates the conditions for restoring to health the entire organism of Soviet music."

Reviewing the course of his career, Prokofiev noted that "elements of formalism" had manifested themselves in his music as far back as fifteen or twenty years before, owing to "contact with certain Western trends." He pointed out, however, that in such works as *Alexander Nevsky, Zdravitsa, Romeo and Juliet,* and the Fifth Symphony, he had striven to free himself from these elements, adding that he thought he had succeeded "to some degree" in doing this.

He then discussed the most difficult task facing a composer—creating clear and forceful melody, which he called "the most important element in music." He wrote: "To find a melody that is immediately understandable even to an unschooled listener and at the same time original—this is the most difficult thing for a composer. Many dangers lie in wait for him here. He is liable to fall into triviality or banality, or into repeating what has already been done before. In this respect, it is much easier to compose more complicated melodies. Sometimes, in working over a melody for a long time, the composer himself will not notice that he is making it over-refined or complicated, that he is moving away from simplicity. Undoubtedly I, too, fell into this trap in the process of my work. A composer must be particularly careful to keep the melody simple without allowing it to become trivial, saccharine, or imitative. This is easier said than done, and I shall bend every effort toward making this more than a precept, toward putting it into practice in my future work."

After noting that atonalism had no future and pointing to the decline of the Schoenberg school, he added, "Instances of atonality can be found in some of my compositions of recent years. Without feeling particularly sympathetic to this method, I nevertheless used it, mainly for purposes of contrast and to throw the tonal passages into relief. In the future I hope to rid myself of this method." A later portion of the letter contained Prokofiev's ideas on contemporary operatic style, in which was stated the need for making greater use of vocal melody while keeping the dramatic action dynamic and intense.

In conclusion he wrote, "I would like to express my gratitude to our Party for the clear directives set forth in the Resolution, which are helping me in my quest for means of expression that will be comprehensible and close to our people, for a musical language worthy of our people and our great country."

# TWELVE

# THE LAST FLIGHT

*Whence this unaccountable springtime*
*feeling of joy and renewal?*
The opera WAR AND PEACE, Scene 1

THE LAST FIVE YEARS of Prokofiev's life (1948–53) were filled with fruitful new quests. He strove to give his works greater simplicity and clarity without losing the freshness and individuality of his own style. He reached a much deeper understanding of the noble aims of the Soviet artist, whose obligation, he felt, was to fight with his art for a better future for mankind.

"Can an artist possibly stand aloof from life?" he asked in an article in 1951. "Can he lock himself up in an ivory tower, confine his art within the narrow limits of subjective emotions, or must he be where he is needed, where his work, his music, his chisel can help the people to live a better, brighter life?"

He recalled the great humanist artists who had served the people with their art—Beethoven and Shakespeare, Mozart and Tolstoi, Tchaikovsky and Dickens. "I firmly believe," he wrote, "that it is the duty of the composer, like the poet, sculptor, and painter to serve Man, the people. He must beautify human life and defend it. He must above all be a citizen in his art, glorifying life and leading man toward a radiant future. This I believe to be the immutable code of art."[1]

A brilliant expression of the increased social orientation of Prokofiev's art was his oratorio *On Guard for Peace,* which rang out like a fervent call in defense of peace and the happiness of peoples. In the ballet *The Stone Flower,* he sang for the first time of the beauty of human labor, creating music in a distinctly Russian folk style. The theme of childhood—poignantly naïve and joyful, undarkened by life's tribulations—became richer and more varied than in previous years. This joyous theme captivates the listener in the suite *Winter Bonfire* and in the best episodes of the oratorio *On Guard for Peace*. Many pages of the Cello Sonata, Op. 119, and the wonderful Seventh Symphony, his last orchestral score, are permeated with the poetry of youth. In these youthful images the composer achieved a lofty simplicity, a classical finish of style, and an inexhaustible richness of melody.

Critical opinion was sharply divided over the success of this last period of Prokofiev's creative work. Some critics and musicologists abroad—Olin Downes in the United States and Gerald Abraham in England, for example—maintained that his turn toward gentle lyricism and simplicity and his rejection of tonal excesses were signs of deterioration, impoverishment, and loss of creative individuality. This is what these critics saw in the music of the Seventh Symphony and the lyrical episodes of the Second Cello Concerto. According to them, Prokofiev had to write such music in order to comply with the Party resolution. The absurdity and falseness of this opinion is obvious.

At the other extreme is the idea that during his last five years Prokofiev reached the zenith in his search for a realistic, generally comprehensible musical style. Those who held this point of view considered the Seventh Symphony his consummate achievement, a work surpassing all his previous accomplishments. But such an opinion sets too low a value on such brilliantly realistic works as *Romeo and Juliet* and *Alexander Nevsky,* which remain unsurpassed in expressive power and the range of human experience they embody.

In fact, Prokofiev's work during the years 1948–53 showed neither a decline nor a triumphant ascent to unscaled heights. It would be more accurate to say that these years were simply the beginning of a new stage in his creative evolution, but years distinguished by works of very special value. His striving for serenity, contemplativeness, clarity of expression, and a predominance of lyricism and gentle humor in a number of his last compositions was not at all surprising. These traits had appeared repeatedly in his earlier works; it was only that they were now revealed with greater power. And yet even in his last works, Prokofiev did not forego creative experimentation, as we can see, for example, from the very interesting score of the Second Cello Concerto.

Prokofiev's last years were externally uneventful. He seldom left his country house or his Moscow apartment in Proyezd Khudozhestvenogo Teatra. He no longer experienced either sensational triumphs or sharp conflicts with his artistic opponents. Illness severely restricted his activities:

He neither visited the Composers' Union nor attended concerts; he no longer conducted and almost never played the piano; he did not go to the telephone; he even gave up chess, which he had loved since childhood. Everything was subordinated to his work. As before, he refused to abide by his doctors' orders. "The doctors really do not understand," he said, "that it is easier for me to jot down a melody than to keep it in my head." He found disruptions in his routine distressing. In 1949 he became so ill that he almost died. Once again he was put on a "starvation diet" of work —one hour a day—but no restrictions could curb his imagination.

The quiet life at Nikolina Gora conserved Prokofiev's strength and benefited him both physically and creatively. Nikolina Gora, one of the most picturesque spots in the Moscow suburbs, is a stretch of woodland surrounded by low hills and the capriciously winding Moscow River. At one time Taneyev, Chekhov, and I. I. Levitan had stayed in this vicinity, near Zvenigorod. Now Miaskovsky regularly spent his holiday at Nikolina Gora—as did V. I. Kachalov, N. S. Golovanov, A. V. Nezhdanova, S. A. Samosud, P. A. Lamm, and other figures in the art world. Prokofiev loved his rural seclusion. In summer and winter he wandered through the woods, pondering new melodies, details of texture, or orchestration. He often walked as far as the neighboring sanatorium, The Pines. He had favorite spots in the woods, to which he would sometimes take his friends to point out an oddly shaped tree or a scene which had caught his fancy. And he devoted a great deal of attention to his garden. He enjoyed growing flowers and was proud of his fruits and vegetables. This most probably reflected the love for the soil he had drawn from his father back in the days at Sontsovka.

It was only with reluctance that Prokofiev would leave Nikolina Gora for business trips to Moscow. But while driving through the city's suburbs, he took pleasure in noting the new buildings and apartment houses, the new ways people worked and lived. "The road which runs from the center of Moscow through the outskirts and into the country, along old and new forests, across rivers and past wheat fields I know very well," he wrote in an article. "There is a field. A new automotive combine is harvesting the tall rye. Dozens of kilometers farther on we pass a group of rosy-cheeked children from the kindergarten of a Moscow factory, playing on a green lawn under the watchful eye of their teachers."

Everything interested the life-loving artist—the planting of lime trees, the new Moscow University building, the scaffolding of new apartment houses. And we can see direct reflections of all these impressions in the oratorio *On Guard for Peace,* the suite *Winter Bonfire,* and many of his other late works.

The composer had a phonograph and radio in his country house. He listened intently to broadcasts of Soviet music written after February 1948, such as Shostakovich's *Song of the Forests,* Miaskovsky's Twenty-Seventh Symphony, Arutunian's *Cantata for the Motherland,* and Kabalevsky's Violin Concerto. He was delighted with the success of these works, and his friends often brought him new music and records.

As before, Prokofiev maintained his close ties with Miaskovsky; he was also on friendly terms with many other musicians and composers, among them Shostakovich and Kabalevsky. Shostakovich visited him in the summer of 1949, after returning from the United States; somewhat later, following the first performance of the Seventh Symphony, he wrote Prokofiev a very enthusiastic letter about the new work. Among the other friends and colleagues whom Prokofiev saw during this period were Atovmyan, who prepared all of his later works for publication, and the conductor Samosud, an ardent advocate of his music who conducted the premières of nearly all of his late works, from the *Ode to the End of the War* to the Seventh Symphony. Prokofiev loved to be with young people, especially the cellist Rostropovich, the pianists Richter and Vedernikov, and with his sons Sviatoslav and Oleg. His wife Mira read books and papers to him and also took care of his business correspondence and telephone calls, sparing him all unnecessary worry.

The loss of his closest friends, Asafyev, Miaskovsky, and Lamm, was a severe blow to Prokofiev.\* But despite these losses and the increasing seriousness of his own illness, he faced the future courageously, without fear or anxiety. Shortly before his death he put his manuscripts in order and sent them in installments to the Central State Archives of Literature and Art.

The musical organizations of the Radio Committee, and especially the editorial staff of the Children's Radio Division, gave the composer friendly help and encouragement in realizing his last creative plans. The suite *Winter Bonfire,* the oratorio *On Guard for Peace,* and the Seventh Symphony were planned in close collaboration with the Children's Radio Division. On the other hand, the theaters displayed an incomprehensible indifference toward Prokofiev's music. *The Stone Flower* was ignored for five years before being produced at the Bolshoi, and the composer did not live to see the new production of *War and Peace.* After listening to a radio

---

\* TRANSLATOR'S NOTE: These friends died in 1949, 1950, and 1951, respectively.

broadcast of a concert performance of Wagner's *Meistersinger* (an opera he regarded highly), he asked Samosud sadly, "There you are—performing Wagner. But when is *War and Peace* going to be put on?"

But even loss of friends, separation from active musical life, and thoughts of the approaching end of his life's journey did not alter the general character of Prokofiev's music. Right up to its last notes, it remains charming in its youthful freshness, optimism, and love of life. It bespeaks no gloomy presentiments or morbid fears. But more and more frequently, its former mischievousness, exuberance, and audacity are replaced by gentle humor combined with serene and wise contemplation. The years will pass and Prokofiev, like his teacher Rimsky-Korsakov, will be remembered above all as a troubador of happiness, an artful storyteller, a poet of sunlight and joy.

*   *   *

February 1948 found the composer working intensely on the opera *The Story of a Real Man* for the Kirov Theater. He devoted all the spring and summer to it, firmly believing that this opera, written on a contemporary subject, would be a real answer to the criticism leveled against him. But his expectations proved wrong. A private performance at the theater met with sharply unfavorable criticism, and for all practical purposes the work was a failure. Naturally this was a tremendous blow to the composer, who was present at the performance. He had expended a great deal of effort on the opera and he first ascribed its failure to the performers, who had prepared it hurriedly and indifferently. However, with his characteristic strength of will, he overcame the shock and began working with enthusiasm on an interesting new project—a ballet based on the tales of Bazhov.

Prokofiev and Lavrovsky had been planning to collaborate on a new ballet for a long time. At first they had thought of taking a libretto from Pushkin's play *The Stone Guest*. There was much in this classical subject that was tempting—the wonderfully vibrant characters of Don Juan and Leporello, the sharply contrasting scenes of love trysts and bloody duels, Don Juan's wild debauchery and violent end. The collaborators already had in mind possible performers for the future ballet, among them Ulanova for the role of Donna Anna.

The idea of *The Stone Guest* was soon dropped, however, because of Prokofiev's interest in writing a Russian national ballet. With this in mind, he reread almost every one of Pushkin's works. However, all of the works that would lend themselves to musical treatment for the stage had already been used by other composers. Ostrovsky's *Snow Maiden* was considered, but Prokofiev was so enamoured of Rimsky-Korsakov's *Snow Maiden* that he felt it would be impossible to match it.

The theme for the ballet was found unexpectedly. Mira Mendelson brought Bazhov's *The Malachite Box* from the library and read several of the tales to her husband. He was captivated by the original folk style of the Ural storyteller. He immediately began to visualize as ballet characters the imperious Mistress of the Copper Mountain, the craftsman Danila in love with his work, the faithful Katerina, and the "murderer" Severyan. Lavrovsky was also taken with the idea, and soon afterward he and Mira Mendelson drew up the libretto for the future ballet *The Stone Flower*.

Prokofiev was so excited by this project that he completed the piano score, begun on September 18, 1948, on March 24, 1949. While working on it, he studied Ural folk songs and later incorporated one of them as a dance theme in the fair scene (Scene 6). In addition he included two of the Russian songs, *Dunyushka* and *The Monk*, from his Op. 104; the wedding song, *The White Swan Is Swimming*, from Part I of *Ivan the Terrible*; and the mass song *To the Motherland*. The charming lyrical piece *Evening*, from the *Music for Children*, became one of the love themes of Danila and Katerina. These old themes were used judiciously. The wedding song from *Ivan the Terrible* formed the basis of the round dance of the girls in Scene 2, while the gay song *The Monk* provided the material for a riotous dance in the fair scene. This ballet, in four acts and eight scenes, also contains a huge quantity of new music; for the most part, the music is vividly national in character, depicting scenes ranging from everyday life in the old Urals to the fantastic world of the Mistress of the Copper Mountain. It is not unlikely that the best of this music—particularly the majestic, moving themes of the Mistress—reflected the composer's impressions of the Ural landscape, which had so captivated him while he was living in Molotov.

When the piano score of *The Stone Flower* was performed at the Bolshoi Theater in June of 1949, it was immediately acclaimed. Those who heard it pointed out the originality of its Russian style and even compared it with Rimsky-Korsakov's *Sadko*. Stimulated by this praise, Prokofiev spent the following months working hard on the orchestration (the score came to almost six hundred pages!). But the theater did not hurry to produce the ballet; the score lay untouched for about four years and the ballet was not presented until February 1954, after the composer's death.

In the spring of 1949, while working on *The Stone Flower*, Prokofiev also composed the three-movement Cello Sonata in C major, Op. 119, from sketches he had made two years before. M. Rostropovich helped him tremendously with the editing of the cello part. At the end of June, Rostropovich and Richter played the new Sonata for the Committee on the Arts.

The enormous strain of working on these two large-scale compositions led to a serious complication in Prokofiev's illness—an increase in his blood pressure, severe headaches, and a partial impairment of speech. On August 27, Miaskovsky anxiously noted in his diary, "Pr. has been seriously ill. Nevertheless, he has written the ballet *The Stone Flower*—enormous, with superb music."

In 1949 the Radio Committee asked Prokofiev to compose some popular dance pieces. He complied with the two lyrical waltzes, Op. 120 (in F major and C-sharp minor), written in a gentle style recalling Glinka. In this year the Soviet Union commemorated the 150th anniversary of Pushkin's birth, and as Prokofiev was rereading his favorite poet's works, he hit upon the idea of calling his two new pieces the "Pushkin Waltzes." These pieces were performed on the radio that year, under the conductor Samosud, and were also recorded.

In October 1949, having scarcely recovered from his serious illness, Prokofiev began to write a symphonic suite for children called *Winter Bonfire*. He worked closely with the poet Marshak, who wrote the text which serves as the program for the suite's eight small scenes. Corresponding sections of Marshak's poem, which relates the experiences of a group of Pioneers on a Sunday trip to the country, were to be recited between each of the musical numbers. The score was delivered to the Radio Committee in January 1950, exactly on time. Shortly afterward the suite was performed on the air by the Radio Symphony Orchestra, again under Samosud, and a boys' choir of the State Choir School. Miaskovsky's diary for April 10, 1950, contains the following entry: "Recently heard Pr's charming children's suite to verses by Marshak on the radio. Very imaginative and witty."

In its general musical color, its youthful clarity and sunny mood, *Winter Bonfire* closely resembles such works of the thirties as the *Music for Children*, Op. 65, and *Peter and the Wolf*. Here we find the same pure and polished harmonic style, the same simple, tuneful melody, and the same genuine feeling for the natural beauties of Russia. But while the *Music for Children* presents scenes of the summertime around Moscow (moonlit meadows, rain, a rainbow), *Winter Bonfire* depicts happy scenes of the Russian winter—a snow-covered forest, a group around a bonfire, bright dreams on a quiet winter evening. The boys in this suite strike one as more mature and more real than the rather stylized Pioneer, Peter. They ride on a train, march, skate to the strains of a waltz, and hold a gathering around a forest bonfire. Marshak's graphic, ringing verses lend the work the quality of a true story about the life of Soviet children.

The opening bars of the first movement, "Departure," are well conceived to arrest the young listener's attention. In this little scene depicting an onrushing train, the composer cleverly employs such descriptive effects as measured tapping of the timpani, a thundering roll of a snare drum, mechanically precise figurations in the strings, and shouts from the muted trumpets. These effectively create images of the metrical clatter of wheels and the blasts of a whistle of a train flying past snow-covered woods. However, these descriptive devices serve only as the background for a very gay and distinctly accented melody, full of youthful zest; here one is almost inevitably reminded of Glinka's *Song of the Road,* with its lively melody over a rhythmical accompaniment.

The second movement, "Snow Outside the Window," conveys the serene mood evoked by a quiet winter landscape:

> From the sky the snowflakes fall,
> In a boundless shroud,
> And, aflutter, cheer the heart,
> With their whiteness pure.

The principal melody, in a pensive vein, is like a flowing Russian song. The tone colors employed here—solo oboe, solo clarinet, and French horn —are spare and pure.

The third movement, "Waltz on the Ice," is in the manner of the lyrical Russian waltzes found earlier in *Cinderella* and *War and Peace.* This movement is constructed in the form of a rondo with the traditional contrasts, such as a brilliant ballroom waltz followed by a tender, slightly sentimental waltz.

The very short fourth movement, "The Bonfire," is purely descriptive in character. A thick tremolo in the low strings, in pungent diatonic harmony, draws the picture of a blazing fire. This is the only place in the entire suite where description becomes an end in itself and forces melody into the background.

"The Bonfire" is followed without pause by the fifth movement, "Pioneer Gathering." This, the only vocal movement in the suite, is a very simple song for boys' choir. Unfortunately, its effect is weak because its melody is naïve, lacks sweep, and sounds more like a nursery song than a song of the Pioneers. Still, the fresh sound of children's voices heightens the realism of the work. The descriptive music of the blazing bonfire returns as the coda of this movement.

The sixth movement, "Winter Night," is one of the most charming episodes of the suite. Once again, as in the second movement, the composer gives himself up to a serene and thoughtful mood, with two alternating themes creating an atmosphere of gentle repose. This music might have been inspired by a walk through a snow-covered forest.

The last two movements, which also proceed without pause, depict the happy ending of the Pioneer outing. The seventh movement is a march, with clipped accents on the weak beats of the measure, teasing grace notes, and *tirate*. Here, elements typical of "Pioneer music"—the rhythmical roll of the snare drum, signals of the muted trumpets—play an important role. Finally, in the brief eighth movement, "The Return," we hear once again the familiar music of the rushing train, which forms a coda to the entire suite.

The work is carefully constructed and symmetrical in form. The lively rhythmical episodes depicting Pioneer life ("Departure," "The Waltz on Ice," the Pioneers' song, and "March") alternate with those in a lyrical vein ("Snow Outside the Window," "Bonfire," and "Winter Evening"). The composer gave the work a certain unity by restating the opening episode, "The Train," at the end of the suite, as well as by organizing the tonal plan of the work so that it opens in Prokofiev's favorite key of C major, passes through other major keys (B flat, F, and G) in the middle movements, and ends again in C major. He also made an interesting attempt to achieve unity of timbre by using the bright, pastoral color of the French horn as a kind of "leit-timbre." Thus, the first and fourth movements open with a tune played by four horns, and these instruments are also given an important role in the second movement and the waltz.

The entire suite is suffused with the genial smile of its creator and reflects his great love and understanding of children. *Winter Bonfire* ranks with the best poetry of Marshak, Chukovsky, and Barto as one of the most brilliant examples of Soviet art intended for the very young.

❋   ❋   ❋

Prokofiev' Cello Sonata, Op. 119, was completed several months before *Winter Bonfire,* and its images have something in common with those of the scenes from childhood found in the suite.

This Sonata belongs to that group of unaffected lyrical compositions characteristic of Prokofiev's last period. As in the Ninth Sonata and the Seventh Symphony, contemplative themes predominate. Completely absent are the bold excesses, dissonances, and "barbarisms" heard not long before in the climaxes of the Sixth Symphony and in the second movement of the F minor Violin Sonata. The gentle lyricism and graceful humor which characterize this work are beautifully expressed by the warm, singing tones of the cello.

The Sonata has only three movements, the first and third of which are tranquil and lyrical, while the second, in contrast, is lighthearted and gay. The charm of this work lies in the wealth and variety of its melodies, which range from narrative to romantic, from sad and flowing to mirthful and dance-like. The composer subjects them to comparatively little development, preferring instead to continuously unfold new melodies before the listener.

The opening of the first movement (*Andante grave*) has the quality of a somewhat mysterious tale. Here the composer employs many of the traditional descriptive techniques found in Russian "fantastic" music—expressive, recitative-like phrases, fanciful passage work, restless *pizzicato* chords, and constantly changing harmonies. One is reminded of the gentle fantasy of *Tales of the Old Grandmother*. The first subordinate theme, a serene classical melody set forth in a free polyphonic manner, establishes a brighter, lyrical mood. The lyricism of the second subordinate theme is different, having a somewhat doleful character. This theme occupies the central place in the development section of the first movement. Later, when played by the cello over agitated, soaring arpeggios in the piano, it acquires a more dramatic hue; this is, in fact, the most dramatic moment in the entire Sonata.

Perhaps the most memorable movement in the work is the second movement (*Moderato*), a sparkling scherzo in the manner of Prokofiev's *Music for Children*. The main theme, a roguish little dance-like tune, closely resembles that of a children's game song (Fig. 54).

It is interesting to note the kinship between this melody and the popular "Pioneer" theme in Shostakovich's *Song of the Forests*. (The resemblance is, of course, fortuitous; the two works were composed at approximately the same time.) The second theme of the scherzo, also in 4/4 time and built on the F major triad, is broad, flowing, and graceful. Finally, like an echo of a joyous, festive dance, the gay third theme appears over a well-defined organ point, calling to mind the laughter of Mercutio in *Romeo and Juliet*.

FIGURE 54

The humor is heightened throughout by piquant harmonic details, clear-cut rhythms, and clever timbre effects achieved by the use of staccato, leaps, and alternations of *pizzicato* and *arco*. After this gaiety and mischievousness, the middle section (*Andante dolce*) unexpectedly presents suggestions of a beautiful love scene, portrayed in the passionate lyricism found in the love music of *Romeo and Juliet* and *The Duenna*. Here we recognize the characteristic devices of Prokofiev's later period: the alternation of wide intervals and colorful chromatic turns, beautiful modulations, and the general romantic color of the melody, heightened by the singing timbre of the cello. In the concluding section, as in a ballet, the infectiously laughing and lighthearted main themes of the scherzo gaily flit by.

The finale of the Sonata (*Allegro ma non troppo*) brings back the romantic lyricism found in the main themes of the first movement and middle section of the scherzo. This lyricism can be heard in the first theme, a broadly developed cantabile melody with typically Prokofievan harmonic twists, and in the new lyrical episode which appears in the middle of the development section. In contrast to this mood, the second theme again presents suggestions of a rather amusing dance. The gently humorous second part of this theme, which is akin to the main theme of the scherzo but more subtly harmonized, is especially appealing.

As in most of Prokofiev's cyclical compositions, the coda of the finale, in which the principal musical material of the first movement is restated, acquires a special significance. The composer reintroduces the main theme of the first movement in expanded form, with rhythmic alterations, accompanying it with one of the scherzo-like elements of the finale's second theme. Thus, at the conclusion of the sonata the opening material returns again, charged with energy, enforced by thicker chordal texture, and richly embellished.

As he had done in the First Violin Sonata, Prokofiev here created a real instrumental duet, with the piano as an equal partner of the cello. He displayed great inventiveness in his use of the cello, treating it not only as a singing instrument of very wide range but also as an instrument rich in virtuoso resources.

Collaboration with Rostropovich, who introduced the Cello Sonata, stimulated Prokofiev's interest in writing for this instrument. The Sonata, Op. 119, was followed by the Second Cello Concerto (*Sinfonia Concertante*), Op. 125, the Concertino for Cello, Op. 132, and the unaccompanied Cello Sonata, Op. 134. The last two works remain unfinished.

The Sonata, Op. 119, was given its first performance on December 6, 1949, at a private concert presented by the board of the Composers' Union at its third plenary session. Early in March of 1950 it was played at public concert in the Small Hall of the Moscow Conservatory. Miaskovsky commented in his diary: "Yesterday Rostropovich and Richter gave a public performance of Prokofiev's Cello Sonata—an amazing, first-class work." Not long afterward the Sonata was also performed abroad by Gregor Piatigorsky and Raya Garbousova.

☙ ☙ ☙

During his work on *Winter Bonfire* and the Cello Sonata, Prokofiev nurtured a fervent desire to write a vocal-symphonic work on the theme of the struggle for peace. The success of Shostakovich's *Song of the Forests* and several other works prompted him to turn his thoughts once again toward the oratorio form. In the last months of 1949 he gave considerable thought to planning the program of the oratorio and to finding a suitable coauthor for it.

Prokofiev was closely assisted in his planning by the writer Alexander Fadeyev, whom he had met in the spring of 1950 at the Barvikha Sanatorium. I. G. Ehrenburg and N. S. Tikhonov were considered as possible collaborators, but the choice finally fell on Marshak, with whom the composer had worked before. Fadeyev continued his participation in this project, reading preliminary drafts of the text and following with keen interest the composition of the music. Marshak approached the oratorio with unusual seriousness and wrote a very expressive text for it; shortly afterward this poem was published independently in the literary magazine *Novy Mir.*

By the fall of 1950 the new oratorio, entitled *On Guard for Peace,* Op. 124, was completed in full score and delivered to the Radio Committee. Also composed in 1950 were the short mass song, *Soldiers' Marching Song,* Op. 121 (to words by V. Lugovskoi), in the style of the military choruses of *War and Peace,* and the symphonic suite *Summer Night,* Op. 123, from the music of *The Duenna.* This suite consisted of five movements: (1) Introduction; (2) Serenade; (3) Minuet; (4) Dreams (Nocturne); and (5) Dance.

During the summer Prokofiev's beloved friend Miaskovsky became gravely ill while in Nikolina Gora. His friends were grieved to see the swift deterioration in his health. During his last days in the country, Prokofiev visited him almost every day. Whenever someone came from Moscow to see Miaskovsky, Prokofiev would warn him, "For heaven's sake, don't show that you notice a change in him!" Early in August Miaskovsky was taken to Moscow, where he died shortly afterward. His passing was a severe loss for Prokofiev, who had maintained an intimate friendship with him for forty-four years. The sympathetic mutual understanding of these two great composers and the strict standards by which they judged each other's work present a noble example for our young musicians.

In his last years, Prokofiev kept hoping for a new production of the opera *War and Peace*; his letters contain repeated references to it. "Have you seen E. P. Grikurov?" he wrote L. T. Atovmyan. "I would very much like to find out from him whether *War and Peace* is to be included in the schedule for the coming season. Samosud told me that in the spring Malegot had asked the Committee again for permission to produce it."[2]

In response to the theater's wishes, the composer prepared a new version of the opera, designed to be performed in one performance. Much of the score was substantially revised.[3] Of the thirteen scenes in the first version, only ten were retained. Those eliminated were the seventh, Pierre Bezukhov's study; the ninth, Napoleon and the Marshals on the Shevardino redoubt; and the eleventh, the burning of Moscow. In almost all the scenes, the minor episodes which had slowed the action were condensed. In addition, the composer wrote a great deal of new music for this version. He rewrote both Andrei's monologue in the opening scene, "At Otradnoye," and Kutuzov's aria in the scene "Before the Battle of Borodino," and composed a long monologue for Kutuzov in the climactic scene "War Council at Fili." He also added a duet for Natasha and Sonya (to verses by Zhukovsky) to enliven the opening scene. These additions and changes strengthened the melodic element of the opera. This can be heard in the considerably more natural and melodic new version of Andrei's monologue, which replaced the former unmelodic prose recitative. An even more striking example is Kutuzov's new aria, which is broadly conceived in the great tradition of Russian classical opera. According to Samosud, Prokofiev struggled for a long time with this aria and achieved the desired result only in his eighth draft. These labors were crowned with brilliant success, for Kutuzov's aria became one of the musical highlights of the opera. It enhances the patriotic tone of the work and also enriches the musical characterization of the illustrious general.[4] A more detailed comparison of the two versions of the opera would reveal the high standards Prokofiev set for himself and the evolution of his operatic principles toward a stronger melodic element, the need for which he had underestimated in former years.

＊　＊　＊

The first performance of the oratorio *On Guard for Peace,* which took place on December 19, 1950, in the Hall of Columns in the House of the Trade Unions, was an important event in the musical life of Moscow. On the same evening the suite *Winter Bonfire* was also given its first concert performance. Marshak's text for this suite was recited by the Pioneers Lyuda Pirogova and Natasha Zashchipina, and the austere Hall of Columns rang with the clear, eager voices of the boys' choir of the Moscow Choir School, which also participated in the oratorio. Despite the difficulties of the oratorio, the orchestra and chorus of the All-Union Radio Committee, under the conductor Samosud and the choral director K. B. Ptitsa, gave a superb performance. Much of the success of this première was due to the gifted singer Zara Doloukhanova, who sang the "Lullaby," and to the young singer Eugene Talanov, who performed the difficult solo part.

The new oratorio stirred the audience with its vital and timely significance. The poet and composer treated its central theme—the struggle for peace— in an original fashion, embodying it in happy images of childhood. Realistic sketches from the life of Soviet children form the basis of both the music and the text. The collaborators rejected abstract statements in favor of vivid, concrete images taken from everyday life. Even the dove,

the traditional symbol of peace, is portrayed quite realistically as a children's
pet from a nearby dovecot:

> 'Tis our Moscow lad
> Who has tossed the young
> Dove from the attic window
> Into the skies, like a ball,
> And reminded us that children
> In the towns and villages
> Demand peace in the world
> On this glorious summer's day.

"I did not seek this theme, nor did I select it from a number of others,"
Prokofiev wrote. "It sprang from life itself, from its turmoil, from everything that surrounds and stirs me as well as others . . . I have sought to
express my ideas about peace and war, my firm belief that there will be
no more wars, that the peoples of the world will defend the peace, save
civilization, our children, our future."[5]

The oratorio may be divided roughly into three main sections: the first
four movements, which tell of the last war; the middle three, which describe
the present peaceful life of Soviet children; and the concluding three, which
celebrate the mighty movement of the fighters for peace. The composer
was particularly successful with the middle three movements, in which
bright images of carefree children are presented, chiefly by children's voices,
both solo and chorus.

In setting the text, Prokofiev followed two very different compositional
procedures. The first, found also in his earlier cantatas *Seven, They Are
Seven* and *Ballad of an Unknown Boy,* is purely descriptive; it consisted of
writing an uninterrupted succession of musical scenes to illustrate the development of the subject matter. In such scenes the music follows the text,
accompanying it like the musical background of a film. Hence the im-
provisatory nature of form and tonal structure and the reduced role of
melody. This procedure is the one followed in the first, third, fourth, and
part of the eighth movements.

The second procedure proved considerably more effective; it dictated
the use of rounded-out melodic episodes with clear-cut forms and tonal
schemes. The music composed on this plan no longer simply accompanies
the text, but plays the leading role. Such are the oratorio's best numbers:
"A Lesson in the Mother Tongue" (in the fifth movement), "Dove of
Peace" (sixth movement), "Lullaby" (seventh movement), and the tenth
movement, in which the composer repeats and contrasts some of the
themes of the preceding movements.

Following these two procedures, Prokofiev created a work which skill-fully combines three different musical styles. The first style is used in the purely illustrative orchestral episodes, which depict scenes of war, labor, and demonstrations for peace. Here the vocal parts play only a declamatory role or are altogether replaced by the recitation of a narrator against the musical background. The second style is used for the melodic episodes in a gay or lyrical vein; in these episodes the chorus and soloists do not declaim but sing, assuming the decisive place in the musical action. Finally, the third style consists of leitmotivs symbolizing specific elements of the narra-tive, which are repeated alternately in the orchestra and the chorus. Thus the majestic "theme of peace," is heard first in the orchestra (in the introduc-tions to the third and fourth movements) and later also in the chorus (in the eighth and tenth movements). The same treatment is given to the tender, reflective second "theme of peaceful daily life," which appears in the third, seventh, and eighth movements. The "theme of the dove," heard first in the sixth movement and later in the finale, the "theme of the peace procession" in the eighth movement, and the "theme of joy" in the finale also acquire the character of leitmotivs. In most of these leitmotivs—both those in a festive, march-like vein ("theme of the procession," "theme of joy") and those in a solemn, majestic vein ("theme of peace")—one per-ceives a resemblance to the style of the Soviet mass song.

The contrast between the boys' choir and the mixed and male choruses, as well as the charming combination of the boy alto and mezzo-soprano (in "Lullaby"), add special color to the oratorio. In all likelihood, it was Shostakovich's *Song of the Forests* that prompted Prokofiev to use a chil-dren's choir. But while acknowledging Shostakovich's artistic ability, Pro-kofiev felt that the boys' choir had been used too sparingly in the *Song of the Forests*. Further elaborating Shostakovich's interesting idea, Prokof-iev entrusted three entire movements (the second, fifth, and sixth) to the children's choir and also used it, in combination with the mixed chorus, in the third, eighth, and tenth movements. Unfortunately, in certain epi-sodes (in the second movement, for example) the music for the children's choir is complicated by constantly changing harmonies and angular melodic lines, which are distinctly instrumental in character. This produced a certain emotional coldness in these episodes.

Although the text is generally fresh and appropriate for musical treat-ment, it suffers from occasional wordiness. For this reason, the composer assigned certain portions of it to a narrator, who recites them sometimes with orchestral accompaniment and sometimes unaccompanied (as in the ninth movement). Even so, the composer's adherence to the text, which is overloaded with descriptive details, led him into a certain looseness of form, especially in such predominantly narrative movements as the first, third, and eighth. It is not these passages which remain most vividly in one's memory, however, but the inspired music of the middle movements, the best in the work.

Prokofiev intended all of the oratorio's ten movements to proceed without interruption. The first, "Scarcely Had the Earth Recovered from War's Thunder," is a short dramatic introduction recalling the Second World War. The highly expressive opening phrases of the orchestra and chorus at once project the listener into the midst of terrible and nerve-racking events. In the episode that follows, the orchestral background to the narrator's part is suffused with a feeling of grief and anguish.

An unusual and complex image takes shape in the second movement, "To Those Who Are Ten Years Old." Here, even though the music of the children's choir is in the rhythm of a lively staccato march, certain details in the harmony give it a gloomy, troubled quality. This opening section is followed by a brief and poignant dialogue between the alto solo and the choir.

The third and fourth movements, "Stalingrad, City of Glory" and "May Indestructible Peace Be the Heroes' Reward," are constructed as continuous successions of scenes. Each of these movements opens with an orchestral introduction based on the leitmotiv of peace; in both, the choral part, which is heard against the background of a kaleidoscopic orchestral part, is declamatory in character (especially in the third movement).

The fifth movement, an engaging march-scherzo with sharp accents and simple, graceful harmony, may be counted with Prokofiev's best music about children. Here the alto solo tells of little schoolboys writing the simple words "We Do Not Want War." The inexpressible charm of the gay, naïve melody, the transparency of the orchestration, and the skillful juxtaposition of the alto and choir combine to create a warm, realistic portrait of our happy children.

The sixth movement, "Dove of Peace," is also a scherzo, more playful than the preceding one, with a lively, dance-like accompaniment. The boys' choir sings a joyous little song about a white dove flying in the peaceful sky above Moscow.

The deep tenderness of a mother's love for her child pervades the seventh movement, "Lullaby," which contains one of the most felicitous melodies of Prokofiev's later years. This broad, flowing theme, with its

FIGURE 55

range of about two octaves and its wide intervals, sounds particularly impassioned when sung by the mezzo-soprano (FIG. 55). The alternation of the mezzo-soprano and alto voices (as if the child were repeating its mother's loving words as it falls asleep) gives this aria-like song a special lyrical flavor. The suggestion of a quiet night and peaceful sleep is heightened by the soft, colorfully harmonized refrain of the women's chorus. The music of this simple scene conveys the serene joy of motherhood; in it, the composer poetically expressed the dream of a peaceful future shared by millions of mothers.

A completely different scene is presented in the eighth movement, a festive march of the fighters for peace of different nationalities. This entire episode is unified by the "leitmotiv of the march," which is repeated in various forms, ascending and descending. In the concluding measures the chorus sings the two "peace themes" from the third movement.

After the ninth movement, "A Talk on the Air," recited by the narrator without music, the oratorio concludes with a gala finale, "The Whole World Is Poised to Wage War on War." Here three themes appear in alternation—the principal "theme of peace," a new, triumphant "theme of joy" (recalling one of Dunayevsky's popular songs), and finally, the joyous melody of the sixth movement ("Dove of Peace"), representing the theme of happy childhood.

The oratorio *On Guard for Peace* was hailed by both the press and the Composers' Union.[6] In the spring of 1951, together with *Winter Bonfire,* it was awarded the Stalin Prize, second degree. Shortly after this the oratorio was recorded and began to be performed regularly on the radio and at concerts. A recording released in Paris by the French firm Chant du Monde was enthusiastically received; the critics pointed out that this work helped to "destroy the wall of distrust between West and East."

On April 21, 1951, music circles in Moscow celebrated Prokofiev's sixtieth birthday (April 23). The Composers' Union held a gala evening to mark the occasion, with M. I. Chulaki delivering the main address. There were greetings from the Secretariat of the Composers' Union and the Bolshoi Theater. Yu. A. Shaporin presented interesting reminiscences about Prokofiev's days at the St. Petersburg Conservatory. Illness prevented the composer from attending, but he listened to the congratulatory speeches over a two-way radio connecting his Moscow apartment with the Central House of the Composers and later replied with a speech of his own. Among those who participated in the program was S. Richter, who gave the first performance of Prokofiev's Ninth Piano Sonata.

On the whole, the year 1951 was not an auspicious one for Prokofiev. Illness more than once interrupted his work. More and more frequently one finds in his letters the brief remark, "I'm not well just now. I've been ordered to bed and forbidden to work."[7]

Nevertheless, even during this difficult year he continued to work every day and added several new titles to the list of his compositions. Among other things, he made three symphonic suites from *The Stone Flower—Wedding Suite*, Op. 126, *Gypsy Fantasy*, Op. 127, and *Ural Rhapsody*, Op. 128, which together incorporated a considerable part of the music of the ballet. The first suite had its première on December 12, 1951, at a concert presented by the board of the Composers' Union at its fifth plenary session, but it passed unnoticed.

In 1951 Prokofiev was principally occupied with the Second Cello Concerto, Op. 125, to which he devoted a great deal of effort. In addition, he worked on a dance suite for the light-music orchestra of the All-Union Radio Committee, and toward the end of the year he wrote a Festive Poem for the forthcoming opening of the Volga-Don Canal. "At present I am concentrating on a large symphonic poem for orchestra entitled *The Volga Meets the Don*," he reported to the press. "I am striving to make the music melodic and expressive of the joy of creation with which all our people are presently inspired."[8]

In November 1951 news reached Moscow that in Salt Lake City, in the United States, an attempt had been made to prevent a performance of Prokofiev's Fifth Symphony. A group of reactionaries had threatened to kill or injure Maurice Abravanel, the conductor of the symphony orchestra there, if he dared to perform the Soviet symphony.* Ill as Prokofiev was at

---

* TRANSLATOR'S NOTE: The Fifth Symphony was performed in Salt Lake City on November 10, 1951. On November 11, the following item appeared in *The New York Times*: "Maurice Abravanel conducted the Utah Symphony through Prokofiev's Fifth without any disturbance tonight, although he had been warned by an anonymous telephone caller that if he started he would 'never finish it.' Mr. Abravanel indicated he felt the call the work of a 'crank.'"

the time, he wrote an angry letter to the Moscow *News,* in which he denounced the "knights of the cold war" across the ocean.

"Why should a conductor be threatened with death for planning to perform my Fifth Symphony?" he asked. "Can it be because it extols the freedom of the human spirit? . . . This music—or is it its idea?—is distasteful to certain people in the State of Utah. Most probably they like music that maligns man, dulls his senses, and stultifies his feelings." Prokofiev concluded his letter with the following forceful affirmation of the noble ideas of Soviet art: "I consider the strange incident in Salt Lake City a confirmation of the correctness of the path we have chosen. Our music strives to give man a feeling of assurance, to inspire him with confidence in his strength and his future. It is for this reason that it is so abhorrent to those who are plotting to destroy this future and plunge humanity into bloody new wars. But they are powerless to silence the sound of our songs, our symphonies of peace and labor—I am convinced of this. For the Fifth Symphony was performed in Salt Lake City after all." This letter castigating the enemies of culture gives evidence of Prokofiev's sharpened political consciousness.

Early in January 1952 the press reported that the Second Cello Concerto had been completed. The new work was dedicated to Rostropovich, who, while a guest of the composer at Nikolina Gora, had helped edit the solo part and had assembled the full score on the basis of the composer's markings. According to *Sovetskoye Iskusstvo,* Prokofiev's collaboration with the gifted cellist "helped to bring out more fully the richest melodic and technical possibilities of the instrument."[9] On February 18, 1952, Rostropovich introduced the Concerto with the Moscow Youth Orchestra under the direction of S. Richter, who was making his first appearance as a conductor.

Even though its principal lyrical themes were warm and moving, the Concerto was not well received. Some of the composer's close friends advised him to lighten the orchestration somewhat and improve the form. During 1952 Prokofiev continued to rework the Concerto. In its final version it was renamed *Sinfonia Concertante* because of the independent character of its complicated orchestral part.

❋   ❋   ❋

The *Sinfonia Concertante,* the last of Prokofiev's completed instrumental works in the concerto form, is of great artistic interest. The composer incorporated in it, in radically altered form, a certain amount of material from the First Cello Concerto, which he had composed between 1934 and 1938. Once again he created a large-scale virtuoso work with a varied, original solo part and unusually inventive orchestration. The *Sinfonia* is in three movements: a lyrical, dramatic *Andante*; an extended *Allegro giusto;* and an *Andante con moto-Allegro* in variation form.

The first movement is a kind of lyrical introduction to the whole work. The two principal themes of this unpretentious three-part movement are fine examples of the pensive but singing lyricism so typical of Prokofiev's later writing. One can easily recognize the composer's manner in the softly tinted modal shifts and the bold, distinctive progressions—from broad, singing sixths, sevenths, and even ninths to insinuating chromatic inflections. The first theme, the more vigorous of the two, has a fervent, impassioned quality, while the second is noble and tender, recalling one of the Cinderella's leitmotivs. A purely coloristic supplementary episode of descending chords in the muted strings creates the atmosphere of a strange, shadowy dream.

The second movement is the most important, for it is here that the main musical ideas of the work are concentrated. From the moment the cello enters with an introductory cadenza, it is clear that it will play the protagonist's role in this movement. The compelling and dramatic opening theme, which first appears in angular, instrumental form, suddenly assumes the character of a transparent Russian melody. Another sharp contrast occurs in the bridge passage, where unadorned epic lyricism is replaced by a comic, semifantastic dance. In this episode, with its stressed accents and piquant orchestration, Prokofiev's long-familiar grotesquerie once again makes its appearance. But the beautiful Russian melodiousness reveals itself again, this time even more clearly, in the magnificent second theme, which is the finest theme of the *Sinfonia*. In this endlessly unfolding E major theme, one senses a heroic sweep, a passionate love for life, an ecstatic abandon to melody. Indeed, it would be difficult to find another melody of such unusual breadth and emotional power in all of Prokofiev's music. The development section is elaborately worked out and full of dramatic contrasts. It contains a very difficult cadenza based on material from the main theme and the bridge passage, a thematically enriched statement of the singing second theme, and an effective combination of the second theme with elements of the grotesque bridge passage. Immediately preceding the shortened recapitulation, an ominous, harsh-sounding episode, marked *più animato,* is introduced. After appearing even more prominently in the extended coda, this episode is superseded by a powerful restatement of part of the first theme, which brings the classically worked out sonata allegro to a close.

The finale is written in an interesting form—a three-part variation move-ment containing two themes. The first of these is a slow instrumental melody; not satisfied with strict variation techniques, the composer later transforms it into a playful dance with amusing accents and humorous orchestration. The second theme is in the style of a rhythmic folk dance and is thematically related to the familiar Belorussian song *Good Health to You,* but in varying it, the composer gave its simple melody a slight trace of irony. This can be seen in both the "moaning" harmonies and the stylized orchestration, which recall the music played by village wedding bands (the composer jestingly called this episode "poor relations"). On the whole, the second theme and its variations convey an amusing picture of everyday life similar in quality to the one found in the *Overture on Hebrew Themes,* Op. 34. After another set of variations on the first theme, there follows a dramatic coda in which elements of the second movement's grotesque theme appear in substantially altered guise. Once again the familiar rhythmical folk theme is heard in the mounting tremolo of the strings, but owing to the ringing timbre of the trumpet, it loses the slightly ironic quality it had before. Finally, the soaring energy of the closing pas-sages brings the *Sinfonia* to a brilliant conclusion.

In the *Sinfonia Concertante,* just as in the Sixth Symphony and the last piano sonatas, the old and the new in Prokofiev stand side by side. The old manifests itself chiefly in the harshness of timbre and harmony and in the deliberately disjointed character of certain passages. We find examples of this in the brief orchestral openings of the first and second movements, and in the strange, ominous theme which appears in the development sec-tion and coda of the second movement. But these particular passages, which displeased some members of the audience at the première of the work in Moscow, must not be construed as the predominant stylistic elements of the work. On the contrary, it is the broad and idiomatic singing themes, with their distinctive interval structure and fresh-sounding modulations, that are the most prominent features of this composition. The two themes of the first movement, the second theme of the second, and the first theme of the finale belong in this category. The sublime nobility and soaring romanticism which prevail in this work are perfectly suited to the tradi-tional role of the solo cello. In contrast to the leading lyrical themes, there are numerous dynamic running passages and humorous episodes, which are sometimes grotesque, as in the bridge passage of the first movement, but more often gay and dance-like in character.

For the novelty and inventiveness of its solo part, the *Sinfonia Con-*

*certante* might be ranked with the brilliantly original First Violin Concerto. Prokofiev did not confine himself to the customary cello writing, but boldly enriched the treasury of cello techniques. He wrote for the full range of the instrument, at one moment compelling the soloist to plunge into the lowest registers, and at another to ascend to the violin range. By virtue of the variety and complexity of its technical devices, such as leaps, shifts from *arco* to *pizzicato,* double stopping, chordal writing, and fast passage work, the *Sinfonia* belongs among the most difficult works in cello literature. At the same time, the composer treated the instrument's artistic resources in a very interesting and unusual way; he assigned to the soloist not only the broad, flowing themes but also some that are brittle, angular, and fantastic in character and others that in their lightness and range are quite violinistic. Finally, the originality of the work is enhanced by its orchestration, in which many ingenious combinations of timbres are employed.

When Rostropovich introduced this new version of the Second Cello Concerto in a number of European and American cities a few years later, the critics unanimously acclaimed it. "This is a magnificent score, humming with life and variety, compactly put together, and a gold mine of precious themes and episodes," said Louis Biancolli in *The New York World-Telegram and Sun.* "It retains a rather youthful spirit expressed in a romantic Russian tone," wrote Paul Henry Lang in *The New York Herald Tribune.* "The *Sinfonia Concertante* will take its place among the best of Prokofiev's works," asserted the critic of the Danish Communist newspaper *Land og Volk.*[10]

❦　❦　❦

Toward the end of 1951 Prokofiev reported to the press that he contemplated writing a simple symphony, intended for young listeners, for the Children's Radio Division.[11] The plan of the work gradually took shape and by March 20, 1952, the new Seventh Symphony was completed in piano score. The composer devoted the spring and early summer to orchestrating it. On July 2nd he wrote to Atovmyan: "I am finishing the symphony, and after that I'm planning to make some small changes in *The Stone Flower* in accordance with the request of the Bolshoi and Kirov Theaters, which seem ot be planning to produce it. Lavrovsky and Sergeyev visited me about this. I'm also making a few revisions in the Cello Concerto." The full score of the Seventh Symphony was finished on July 5, 1952.

The original conception of the Symphony changed in the course of its composition. Instead of a light "symphony for children," what emerged was a very lyrical work, profound in both feeling and thought. Although the composer's favorite "theme of youth" appeared only in certain scherzo-like moments in the finale and in the narrative section which concludes the first movement, this theme determined to some degree the Symphony's clarity of melody, modest scale and form, and unusually transparent orchestration. In the second movement Prokofiev used a lovely waltz which he had written the year before.

The pianist Anatoly Vedernikov played a large part in bringing the new symphony before the public. He drew up the full score according to the composer's detailed sketches, made a four-hand piano arrangement of it, and played it at the Composers' Union, where it was enthusiastically received. Kabalevsky wrote a brilliant article on the Symphony even before its public performance.[12] The reception of the new work was almost unanimous: musicians of all artistic views were charmed by its tenderness and emotional warmth.

After completing the Seventh Symphony, Prokofiev continued to work on the score of *The Stone Flower,* which was scheduled for production at the Bolshoi Theater. While the ballet was in rehearsal, he patiently complied with Lavrovsky's requests for additional music. During 1952 he wrote a new dance for the fair scene (Scene 6) and considerably expanded the last adagio of Katerina and Danila. He also made some changes in the orchestration but flatly refused the theater's request that he completely revise the score to make it more elaborate and full-bodied.

In August, during the celebrations attending the opening of the Volga-Don Canal, Prokofiev's Festive Poem *The Volga Meets the Don* was played on the radio; it was the only symphonic work dedicated to this historic event.

At the beginning of the concert season, on October 11, 1952, the première of the Seventh Symphony took place in the Hall of Columns at the House of the Trade Unions; it was played by the All-Union Radio Orchestra with S. A. Samosud conducting. This was the last time Prokofiev attended a concert performance of his own music. Listening to this youthfully exuberant music glorifying the joy of living, it is difficult to believe that it was written by a composer in the very last year of his life.

✷　✷　✷

The Seventh Symphony is one of those works of art which are difficult to describe in words; it is so classically simple, so transparent, so finely worked out, and so artistically perfect that the workmanship as such is imperceptible.

It is charming, first of all, for its wealth of melody, which flows forth freely and naturally throughout the entire work—in every transition, bridge passage, introductory section, and development section. As in several of Prokofiev's other late works, one is struck by the inexhaustibility of the composer's melodic invention. New themes pour forth continuously, as if from a horn of plenty. The composer seldom employs the usual methods of thematic development, preferring instead to introduce a new melody or a substantially altered version of a familiar one.

Certain musicians with a narrow conception of symphonic writing have noted an "absence of conflict" in the work, a lack which has led some to call it a "non-symphony" because it contains no well-defined clash of positive and negative images, no dramatic struggle ending in the traditional triumph of good over evil. But the lack of these important though by no means exclusive traits of the symphonic genre is wonderfully compensated for by the Symphony's philosophical depth, vivid contrasts, and vital imagery. The swift succession of pensive, optimistic, capricious, and rollicking moods, which alternate as naturally as in real life, is genuinely moving in itself, even without the contrast of the terrifying and harshly expressionistic images so frequent in Prokofiev's earlier works. We hear the pulse of our time in the Symphony's main themes—particularly in the second theme of the first movement (the principal one of the entire work, which is restated in the final coda). This theme, which expresses the courage and limitless strength of the human spirit, radiates a love for life, that "serenity and confidence in man's strength and his future" of which the composer wrote in his last article.

The Symphony contains themes expressive of more than the immediate present, however. At times the composer's reflections on the present and future seem interlaced with touching reminiscences of childhood and memories of well-loved tales that long ago nourished his artistic imagination. With the composer we observe scenes from life, such as the waltz in the second movement, and we delight in a somewhat droll but not alarming world of fantasy, as in the concluding theme of the first movement. Vivid images of childhood rise before our eyes as we hear the frolicsome, elegant dance in the manner of Haydn which forms the main theme of the finale. Similarly, the rather toy-like little march in the middle of the same movement evokes an image of little boys with wooden sabers marching valiantly to the roll of a Pioneer's drum.

Perhaps these vignettes stemmed from distant memories of Sontsovka, of the merry games the fair-haired little boy, the future celebrated musician, played with such abandon. Throughout his life Prokofiev retained loving memories of his childhood, and this can be felt not only in his memoirs but also in his charming musical reminiscences.

But, we repeat, the Symphony's principal themes, those which endow it with truly symphonic sweep—the themes of bright affirmation (the second theme of the first movement, which reappears in the coda of the finale) and genial philosophical reflection (the opening of the first movement and the principal material of the third)—predominate over the genre and fairy-tale images. With this music the composer seems to be saying, "The world is beautiful, and life will improve and flourish, even though all of us will not live to see it."

The charm of the Symphony lies not only in the beauty of its principal themes but also in the novel way in which they are set forth. For all the simplicity of their exposition, Prokofiev's distinctive manner is easily discernible in almost every way he handles them: in the melodic turns, the mischievous rhythmic accents, the freely flowing Russian polyphony, the characteristic modulations and digressions, and the transparent orchestration with its touches of subtle color.

The first movement (*Moderato*) opens with an expressive, flowing melody in the manner of a meditative Russian song. The national flavor of this theme is heightened both by its typical singing melodic line and its tuneful accompanying voices. At the same time, it is a completely Prokofievan theme, calling to mind the wistful lyricism of Cinderella and Juliet. Suddenly there appear restless running passages in the strings, which for a time create a feeling of mounting tension. But once again the soulful Russian melody returns, accompanied now by swiftly moving figurations. This first theme, like some of those in Tchaikovsky's symphonies, is constructed in three-part form. It gives way almost without preparation to the second theme, the most important theme of the first movement, which is introduced by the bassoons and horns against the background of a muffled tremolo in the upper strings. This is one of those noble, soaring melodies which, like the theme of the Mistress of the Copper Mountain in *The Stone Flower* and the opening of the Adagio in the Fifth Symphony, enrich Prokofiev's later instrumental lyricism. Virile coloring, austere background, and broad intervals endow this lyrical theme with power, beauty, and grandeur. When it reappears in the upper registers, it sounds even more majestic (Fig. 56).

Finally, as a sudden contrast to this powerful melody, a strange new theme appears, like the echo of a fairy tale. The angular shape and naïve

Prokofiev with members of the cast and orchestra after the first production of his *War and Peace*, in the Grand Hall of the Moscow Conservatory (1946)

The last photograph of Prokofiev (1952)

FIGURE 56

character of the melody, the charming harmony, and the transparent orchestration, with its harp and glockenspiel, give it a fantastic coloring. The basic motiv of this theme brings to mind the tunes of children's play songs.

When everything is enveloped in this pleasant and dream-like atmosphere, there begins a simple development section, the only one in the entire Symphony. Only at the beginning of this development does the composer attempt to modify the material (the first and concluding themes), presenting it in new tonal and orchestral guise. No sharp conflict occurs here; the principal ideas of the exposition are simply given a different treatment. The recapitulation presents no new material but merely restates the familiar themes in somewhat abbreviated form.

The second movement (*Allegretto*), an extended waltz, serves both as a scherzo and a lyrical interlude. There is much in it that recalls the fervent lyricism of the symphonic waltzes of Glinka, Tchaikovsky, and Glazunov. Despite the fact that the entire movement is set forth in a very simple formal pattern (A-B-A-B-A), the treatment of the material is quite symphonic. This is apparent in the subtly worked-out bridge passage and transitions, in the rich tonal development of the middle sections, and most of all in the diversity of moods and emotions presented. The waltz genre is here treated in a variety of ways. The whirling motion of the introductory passages gives way to the tender swaying of the main theme, after which a sharply accented, scherzo-like bridge passage leads into a new, rather melancholy waltz. Later these themes are repeated and subjected to various alterations.

The third movement (*Andante espressivo*) is marked by lofty inspiration. It opens with an austere, profound, Brahmsian theme in the singing tones of the strings, which in its gentleness and nobility calls to mind the venerable Friar Laurence in *Romeo and Juliet* or the reflective Andrei Bolkonsky in *War and Peace*. The cantabile element is skillfully blended with expressive, recitative-like phrases, which are set forth in the form of a quiet dialogue between the various instruments. The three-part form is combined with a strict, classical variation technique. But after the theme and two variations, the mood suddenly changes. We hear, as if in the distance, a rather fantastic march, which has a lyrical and even plaintive quality despite the persistent beat of its rhythm. It sounds like the echo of a sorrowful tale. But this image soon disappears, giving way to a restatement of the tranquil first theme, which is varied before the movement comes to a close.

The swift and excited opening of the finale (*Vivace*) bursts in with the sound of pranks and fun, as though a band of frolicsome children had burst merrily onto the stage. A combination of various elements contributes to the jocose quality of the first theme (in D-flat major), particularly the crisp, dance-like rhythm, the jaunty melody, and the general shape of the theme itself, which is akin to the humorous themes of Haydn and Beethoven (the latter's *Rage Over a Lost Penny,* for example). On the other hand, the second theme (in C major) bears a clear resemblance to the marching songs of the Pioneers, as well as to the youthful images of Kabalevsky's music, as in the third movement of his Violin Concerto. Unlike most of Prokofiev's finales, this movement is not a rondo-sonata but is constructed in an involved three-part form. The middle section contains two new themes. The first, rather fragmentary, is song-like and lyrical, while the second, which occupies a more important place, is a witty, spirited march. With the opening theme's reappearance in the recapitulation, this gay little scene from childhood is brought to a close.

In the coda, however, the jubilant, life-affirming second theme of the first movement returns with heightened emotional power. It is now stated in massive orchestral sounds, like an inspired hymn to happiness in the world. And when this majestic theme subsides, we hear once again the concluding fairy-tale theme of the first movement, this time in considerably expanded form over a measured ostinato figure in the piano, harp, and percussion. It is tinged with sadness, as though the composer, with a sigh of regret, were taking leave of his long-beloved realm of fantasy.

This was how the Symphony ended in its first and principal version. During the rehearsals, the opinion was expressed that this uncommon, contemplative ending lacked a feeling of finality. After considering this, Prokofiev provided an alternative ending, in which the final restatement of the main theme was treated differently. This revision ended the Symphony on a bright and cheerful note, but it lacked the inexpressible charm of the contemplative lyricism with which it had ended originally. Subsequently, it was the original and better version of the finale that was performed.

The Seventh Symphony was warmly received in the press. "It is truly joyful, lyrical, and delightful in its clear and bright content and its unusually fresh harmonic language," wrote Shostakovich in *Sovetskoye Iskusstvo*.[18]

Many speakers at the sixth plenary session of the Board of the Composers' Union, held in February 1953, spoke of the new symphony. Almost all of them commented on the consummate beauty of its music. However, some objected to the composer's ascribing to the Symphony a specific programmatic meaning associated with the theme of Soviet youth.* Four years later, in April 1957, the Seventh Symphony was awarded the Lenin Prize. This posthumous honor to the composer was greeted with satisfaction by all his admirers.

❧ ❧ ❧

In view of the serious condition of Prokofiev's health, the musical organizations proposed that the government grant him a special pension. On April 22, 1952, the Council of Ministers of the U.S.S.R. passed a resolution to this effect, thus once again demonstrating the Soviet government's concern for one of the most gifted Russian composers.

In 1952 Prokofiev turned his attention to interesting new projects. After completing his radical revision of the Second Cello Concerto, he wrote a substantial part of the music for the Concertino for cello and orchestra in G minor, Op. 132. In its general lyrical tone and melodic clarity, this simple, transparent work in three movements is stylistically related to the Seventh Symphony. Let us cite as an example the stirringly romantic main theme of the first movement (FIG. 57). The slightly humorous, dance-like

**Andante mosso**

FIGURE 57

* The performance of the Seventh Symphony in the United States after the composer's death left certain critics disappointed and displeased. The noted Olin Downes, who had once hailed the leftist excesses of the young Prokofiev, condemned the Symphony for the clarity and simplicity of its language, calling it an example of "bourgeois music." Downes' statement was sharply criticized by Shostakovich in *Sovetskaya Muzyka*, No. 8, 1953.

main theme of the finale is also in Prokofiev's typical style.[14] This concertino was subsequently completed by Rostropovich after the composer's sketches, and it soon entered the concert repertory.

In 1952 the composer also made substantial revisions in the Fifth Piano Sonata. Entire sections, such as the bridge passage and development of the first movement and the bridge passage of the finale, were completely rewritten. A comparison of the old and new versions of this work clearly reveals the composer's striving for greater clarity of thought, for heightened melodic expressiveness. The over-all conception and main themes of the Sonata remained essentially unaltered, however.

During these last months of his life, Prokofiev also thought of revising the Second Symphony; although he was unable to realize this plan, he entered the revision in the list of his compositions as a new opus, Op. 136. It was characteristic of Prokofiev to retain his interest in earlier compositions which had not won recognition when they were first written. He had that special tender feeling for them which parents sometimes have for an unfortunate child. He sought to find the reasons for their failure and to breathe new life into them. This is how new versions of the Fourth Symphony, the Fifth Sonata, the Cello Concerto, and others came to be written. However, it is quite impossible for an artist at an advanced stage of his creative development to change the basic idea and artistic character of earlier works born under completely different conditions. Therefore Prokofiev's new versions of old, unaccepted works remain compromises which cannot stand comparison with his best realistic works of the Soviet period.

In the summer of 1952 the composer was happy to learn that the State Music Publishing House intended to publish a three-volume edition of his selected piano works. "I am very pleased with this plan," he wrote Atovmyan.[15] "Muzgiz had the same idea ten years ago, but, unfortunately, it vanished into thin air. I should like to believe that this time they really mean it."

He painstakingly went through all his piano works of the past forty years, carefully selecting those which he considered worthy of inclusion in such a collection. Thus, of the four pieces, Op. 3, he retained only *Fairy Tale*; of the four pieces, Op. 4, only *Despair* and *Diabolic Suggestions*; of the four pieces, Op. 32, only *Dance* and *Gavotte*; of the ten pieces of Op. 12, only six; of the twenty *Fugitive Visions, Op. 22,* only ten; and so on. At the same time he asked that all but three of the pieces from the *Music for Children—Tarantella, Parade of the Grasshoppers,* and *Tag*—be included.

This process of selection indicates the severe standards to which the great artist held himself in judging his own works.

The January 1953 issue of *Sovetskaya Muzyka* carried a short statement by Prokofiev on his creative plans. He spoke of the Cello Concertino, Op. 132, and of an interesting idea for a three-movement concerto for two pianos and string orchestra. "I was prompted to turn to this form by Bach's Concerto for Two Pianos and Strings," he said. This Sixth Piano Concerto, listed as Op. 133, unfortunately remained only in the form of sketches. Other compositions also remained uncompleted: the unaccompanied cello sonata, Op. 134 (with remarkably beautiful melodies), and two piano sonatas—the Tenth, Op. 137, and the Eleventh, Op. 138.

"I am eagerly looking forward to working with the companies of the Bolshoi Theater and the Stanislavsky and Nemirovich-Danchenko Theater in 1953 on *The Stone Flower* and *War and Peace*," Prokofiev wrote in his last note. But this hope was not destined to be fulfilled.

During the first months of 1953 Prokofiev worked without ceasing. He completed the one-evening version of *War and Peace* and orchestrated the newly written parts, fully satisfied that the new version of the opera was ready for production. The title proposed for it was *Natasha Rostova,* or so the composer referred to it in one of his letters.

Early in 1953 Prokofiev also completed the additional parts he had written for *The Stone Flower*. The Bolshoi had already begun rehearsing the ballet, and the choreographer Lavrovsky often visited the composer with requests for additions or changes in the score. While working on the ballet, Prokofiev considered using some of the music for a cycle of piano pieces. For example, he planned to use material from the scene of Severyan's pursuit of the Mistress of the Copper Mountain as the basis of a virtuoso toccata.

In January Prokofiev was invited to serve as a judge in the Queen Elizabeth International Composers' Competition in Brussels. Because of the serious condition of his health, he declined this honor in a letter to the director of the competition (dated January 28, 1953). This letter, the composer's last one to be sent abroad, was carried in the foreign press.

March 5, 1953, began in Prokofiev's Moscow apartment as any other day, with intense work. The concertmaster S. K. Stuchevsky arrived, and Prokofiev gave him the completed lyrical adagio "Katerina's Joyous Meeting with Danila" (Scene 9) of *The Stone Flower*. Another batch of manuscripts was put in order and packed for delivery to the Central State Literary Archives. In the afternoon, after several hours of work, Prokofiev went out for his usual stroll. At six o'clock in the evening he suddenly found it extremely difficult to breathe. By the time the doctor arrived it was too late. Death had come almost instantly.*

Within three hours the small apartment on Proyezd Khudozhestvennogo Teatra was crowded with relatives, friends, and admirers of the composer, among them Kabalevsky, Knipper, P. A. Lamm's relatives, and Miaskovsky's family.

On the following day Prokofiev's body lay in state in the Central House of the Composers. Funeral services were held there, in the Small Hall, on the afternoon of March 7. The services were opened by Kabalevsky. Others who spoke included Shostakovich, Shaporin, Lavrovsky, Karen Khachaturian, and V. Stroyeva. The speeches were charged with deep emotion. "I am proud that I had the good fortune to live and work with such a great musician as Sergei Prokofiev," said Shostakovich. In addition to the addresses there was also music. S. E. Feinberg played Bach, and Oistrakh played the first and third movements of Prokofiev's F minor Sonata. There were many young people present in the hall.

The day was raw and dreary, and a wet snow fell as the funeral cortege moved slowly through the streets of Moscow to the Novo-Devichy Cemetery. Prokofiev was buried near his old friends and colleagues Miaskovsky and Asafyev.

The great composer's death caused profound sorrow among his many admirers in the Soviet Union and abroad. "With the death of Prokofiev, Soviet music has lost one of its most gifted, most brilliant representatives," said Kabalevsky.[16] The French, Japanese, and British radios broadcast the news of Prokofiev's death. Articles on his life and work appeared in scores of publications abroad.[17] The critics expressed deep reverence for the memory of the distinguished Russian composer. Memorial evenings were held in many musical centers of the world—from Paris to Prague to Montevideo.

At the end of 1953, the Bonn journal *Musik der Zeit* issued a special number dedicated to Prokofiev. It carried statements about him by the leading musicians of the West, including Arthur Honegger, Darius Milhaud, Gian Francesco Malipiero, Ralph Vaughan Williams, Jacques Ibert, and Benjamin Britten. It also contained reminiscences by well-known musical figures in Germany, France, and England who had met Prokofiev

* TRANSLATOR'S NOTE: A Moscow dispatch to *The New York Times* dated March 8, 1953, gives cerebral hemorrhage as the cause of his death, stating further that "Prokofiev's health had not been good in recent years, and he had suffered previously from a heart ailment."

abroad. "The death of this composer who possessed such wonderful vitality, such daring, such optimism, is a great loss to the entire world," wrote the English composer Benjamin Britten. "All his works give evidence of a tremendous musical temperament which refused to be bound by any theoretical dogmas. He will remain for us the greatest figure of contemporary music," wrote Arthur Honegger.

In June, three months after the composer's death, the Soviet Opera Ensemble of the All-Russian Theater Society gave a concert performance of the one-evening version of *War and Peace*. Shortly after this, newspapers reported a successful première of the opera in Florence. In October 1953 Samosud conducted a performance of the Fifth Symphony, which had not been played for a long time.

On February 12, 1954, *The Stone Flower* was given its première performance at the Bolshoi Theater, with a cast which included the theater's finest artists: Ulanova in the role of Katerina, A. Yermolayev as Severyan, M. Plisetskaya as the Mistress of the Copper Mountain, and V. Preobrazhensky as Danila.

*    *    *

*The Stone Flower* is one of the body of beautiful works that worthily concluded Prokofiev's creative career. It represents a very interesting summation of the composer's earnest quests for a Russian national style, a lifelong search beginning in the days of his youth with the Second and Third Piano Concertos and *The Buffoon* and continuing through his Soviet years. During the thirties and forties the composer had turned more than once to Russian folklore. Work on the *Russian Overture* and the folk song arrangements enriched his musical language with melodic, harmonic, and rhythmic elements of a vividly national character. We have already mentioned that when he undertook *Cinderella* at the beginning of 1941, Prokofiev expressed a desire to write a Russian national ballet. In Bazhov's tales he finally found a subject for the realistic Russian ballet he had dreamed of for so many years.

This ballet was the last of Prokofiev's musical fairy tales, bringing to a close the long series of his works in this vein. Almost thirty-five years separate it from *The Buffoon*. And what a sharp contrast these two works present! In *The Buffoon* we find the malicious antics of a jester, eccentric masks, and caricatured folk themes. *The Stone Flower* tells of the beauty of nature and the glory of man's labor, presents living people filled with noble aspirations, and ennobles folk material.

Although a fantasy, *The Stone Flower* is earthly and real, free of mystical overtones. It is firmly rooted in the simple, true-to-life story of the stone carver Danila's relentless striving for artistic perfection and the faithfulness and courage of his beloved Katerina. In Bazhov's tales, the creatures of fantasy—the Mistress of the Copper Mountain and Ognevushka (the Flamelet)—are quite lifelike. The Mistress is not a magic fairy, but a shapely young girl, "rather short," with a "raven black braid." This realism is also present in the music, for the themes of the Mistress and her spells symbolize not the magic of supernatural powers but rather the natural strength and beauty of the North.

The libretto is based on two of Bazhov's Ural tales, *The Stone Flower* and *The Craftsman of the Mountains*. To these were added motifs from two other tales—*The Steward's Shoes* (the character of the steward Severyan Kondratyevich) and *The Leaping Flamelet.*

The hero of the ballet is the young craftsman Danila, who has been taught to carve stone by the old man Prokopyich. Danila, the personification of the folk artist earnestly seeking true perfection in his art, dreams of making a malachite vase of matchless beauty. He sets out for the realm of the Mistress of the Copper Mountain to see the magic stone flower, in which, according to the old adage, "true Beauty is revealed." Danila disappears into the Mistress' mountain chambers. His beloved Katerina, who embodies woman's constancy, honor, and courage, waits long and patiently for him. She bravely withstands poverty and loneliness, and rejects the insolent advances of the steward Severyan. In her hour of need the Mistress of the Copper Mountain saves her from him by inflicting an agonizing punishment on him. With the aid of Ognevushka, Katerina finally makes her way into the Mistress' realm and frees Danila from captivity.

The writers of the scenario added certain details to the ballet's plot, such as the motif of Severyan's pursuit of Katerina, which became the virtual mainspring of the dramatic intrigue. They also found opportunities for introducing divertissements, such as the series of Russian wedding dances at the betrothal of Danila and Katerina (Scene 2), the extended fantasy-wrought divertissement in the Mistress' domain (Scene 4), and finally the Russian and gypsy dances at the colorful Ural fair (Scene 6). The dramatic structure of *The Stone Flower* proved far from perfect. By not placing Danila and Katerina in truly dramatic situations, the scenario writers failed to develop them as characters, and they also permitted the secondary conflict between Severyan and Katerina to overshadow somewhat the theme of Danila's creative labor.

Prokofiev's special interest in character delineation is revealed in his handling of the solos, duets, and solo scenes. The protagonists of *The Stone Flower*—Danila, Katerina, Severyan, and the Mistress—are worthy additions to the gallery of realistic musical portraits drawn in *Romeo and Juliet* and *Cinderella.* Here, as in *Romeo and Juliet,* the emphasis is on the inner feelings and emotions of the leading characters, and these are revealed in the composer's moving and uniquely expressive music.

Dramatically the ballet is based on a conflict between socially opposed forces: on the one hand, gifted working people, aspiring to use their talents for the benefit of mankind, and, on the other, cruel masters and their underlings, standing in the way of free and inspired creativity. Undoubtedly the characters Danila, his teacher Prokopyich, and the pure-hearted Katerina strongly appealed to Prokofiev, who had himself displayed since childhood a searching mind and a strong will united in a ceaseless striving for perfection.

The melodious themes of Danila and Katerina, of their mutual love and of Katerina's faithfulness, are permeated with noble feeling. While close in character to the Russian folk song, they by no means repeat familiar folk patterns. One can easily recognize the typical Prokofievan manner in the clear-cut rhythms and in the interval writing, with its wide skips and subtle use of chromaticism.

No less characteristic of Prokofiev's style are the themes of the inimical forces which stand in the way of the young lovers' happiness. Many such images of evil are to be found in the composer's works—from the pagan monsters of the *Scythian Suite* to the crusaders in *Alexander Nevsky* and the vengeful knights in *Romeo and Juliet.* Here the evil element is realistically embodied in the typical hireling Severyan, who, whip in hand, wanders with his henchmen through the village like a ferocious beast. In this musical characterization it is coarseness, inhumanity, and rowdiness that are emphasized. Here the composer once again employs harsh timbres, coarsely stomping *ostinato* basses, and sharply accented dissonant harmonies. At the same time, the themes and dances associated with Severyan are marked by a devil-may-care abandon. This is achieved by the use of material similar to that of boisterous Russian folk songs and by special orchestral effects, such as accordion-like accompaniment. Thus Severyan is presented not merely as an abstract embodiment of evil forces but as a full-blooded national type, closely related to such heroes of Russian classical opera as Vladimir Galitsky in *Prince Igor* and the Streltsi in *Khovan-*

*shchina.* The incidental figure of Barin in the second scene is more conventionalized; in this portrayal the composer uses highly stylized, grotesque, dissonant devices to emphasize the serf owner's cruelty.

The episodes depicting the dramatic encounters between Severyan and the workers, and especially his conflict with Katerina, which ends in his death, contain the most effective music of the ballet.

The relationship between the Ural craftsmen and the Mistress' fantastic world constitutes a subplot. The Mistress is not an enemy of the workers, but as the personification of the beauty and stern power of the mountains, she protects the strong and honest and punishes the wicked and greedy. Moreover, she possesses almost irresistible feminine charms. It requires great firmness to resist her allurements, but the steadfast Danila stands the test with honor, and for this he is freed and generously rewarded by the good enchantress. In his musical characterization of her, Prokofiev remained faithful to the dramatic conception of the Mistress. He did not differentiate her sharply from the ordinary people, but, on the contrary, portrayed her as profoundly human. Her themes occupy a leading place in the ballet, especially her principal leitmotiv, which serves as the opening theme of the introduction and appears repeatedly throughout the entire work. This broad, flowing melody with its typically Prokofievan, colorful modal shifts within the key, expresses the invincible power of nature, inspiring man to creative labor (FIG. 58). The Mistress' second theme, a

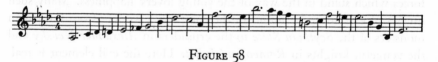

FIGURE 58

lyrical one expressing her kindness, femininity, and engaging maidenly charms, is equally inspired.

Prokofiev portrayed the ballet's leading characters, Danila and Katerina, with deep feeling. Like the Mistress' two leitmotivs, their themes have a captivating warmth, freshness, and melodic sweep. It was not by chance that the composer chose the melody of one of the children's pieces, Op. 65 (*Evening*), as the love theme. The simplicity, purity of feeling, and Russian tunefulness of this piece perfectly suited the characterizations of Bazhov's noble, pure-hearted heroes.

The girlishly fragile portrait of Katerina has a special charm. When drawing it, the composer had in mind the wonderful Ulanova, who had already created similar heroines in *Romeo and Juliet* and *Cinderella*. The characterization of Katerina is considerably more national in flavor than those of her predecessors Juliet and Cinderella, however. How natural, how like a Russian folk lament is the theme of her yearning for her lost sweetheart ("Where, oh where are you, my Danilushka?"). Song-like and declamatory elements of this kind enrich the music of the ballet, just as elements of the dance had served to enrich some of Prokofiev's operas.

Prokofiev's Katerina is more tender, more poetic than the fearless girl portrayed by Bazhov ("a buxom wench with broad shoulders, a steady eye, and seemingly capable of handling an axe"). Her themes are enchantingly feminine, at times tinged with a trace of longing. At the same time, her music also contains stronger and more majestic themes, such as the leit-motiv of her fidelity, which the composer borrowed from his mass song *To the Motherland*.

Ensemble dances play an important role in *The Stone Flower*, heightening the national color of both its real-life and fantastic episodes. Never before had Prokofiev used folk dance material so generously. (We know, for instance, that he refused to introduce folk dance episodes in the opera *Semyon Kotko* where the very nature of the action called for it.) *The Stone Flower* contains so many dance episodes that the composer constructed three symphonic suites from them. (A fourth, entitled *The Mistress of the Copper Mountain*, was included in the list of his compositions as Op. 129, but it was never completed.)

Russian dance themes drawn from folk sources occupy an important place in the ballet. Examples of them are the "Dance of the Unmarried Men" (Scene 2), derived from the song *Dunyushka*, the Ural dance, and the fair dance (Scence 6), based on the humorous song *The Monk*. Two contrasting types of Russian dances are represented here: sedate, flowing, or comic wedding dances in the betrothal scene, and rakish, drunken dances in the fair scene. In the latter category might also be included the subtly stylized gypsy dances.

The best of the wedding dances are the transparently serene round dance of the young girls, based on the music of the chorus *The White Swan Is Swimming* from *Ivan the Terrible,* and the comic "Dance of the Unmarried Men" with its amusing "cackling" accompaniment. The composer transforms one of the women's stately wedding dances into a kind of "leit-motiv of joy," repeating it in the finale as the theme extolling Danila.

The dances in the fantastic scenes of the Mistress's realm play a less important role. They are the least national in flavor of all the dances in the ballet, and have the character of inserted numbers. The most impressive of these are the sparkling "Waltz" (also borrowed from the *Music for Children*) and the graceful scherzo-like "Dance of the Semi-Precious Stones," which recalls the semi-ironic images of Prokofiev's early "classicism." In the group of fantastic dances may also be included the charming portrayal of the tiny Ognevushka. Her merry dance in Act IV is engaging in its childish mischievousness and guileless humor.

The Bolshoi's production of *The Stone Flower* proved disappointing to the audience in many respects. Because of its sumptuous and overly ornate conception, the simplicity and wisdom of Bazhov's folk material were all but obscured. What is more, the choreographer Lavrovsky failed to achieve an organic synthesis of classical ballet and Russian folk dance. Consequently, Prokofiev's magnificent work awaits a more daring and original interpretation.

The score of *The Stone Flower* contains a great deal of splendid music that treats Russian folk material in a delightfully fresh way. Its best melodies clearly demonstrate the flowering of Prokofiev's melodic gifts, the triumph of the realistic folk element in his art.

❦ ❦ ❦

A whole series of Prokofiev's works had their premières between 1954 and 1956, both in the Soviet Union and abroad. After the production of *The Stone Flower,* the pianist A. Vedernikov gave the first performance of the new version of the Fifth Sonata. Rostropovich played the *Sinfonia Concertante* in Denmark in December 1954 and in the United States in April 1956, both times with great success. At the beginning of the 1954–55 season, the orchestra and soloists of the Radiodiffusion Française, under Charles Bruck, gave a concert performance of *The Flaming Angel* at the Théâtre des Champs Elysées in Paris. Thus this opera, which Prokofiev had completed about thirty years earlier, was at last given its first performance, after the score had lain for many years in the Koussevitzky publishing house in Paris. A year later the same theater presented *The Gambler* in concert form, under the same conductor.

In March of 1955, L. Arnshtam's film of *Romeo and Juliet* was released in the Soviet Union. In this color version, the Bolshoi Theater production of the ballet, with Ulanova as Juliet, was filmed in a natural Crimean setting. The music, conducted by G. Rozhdestvensky, sounded all the more expressive when heightened by the dynamic film treatment. In the spring of 1955 this film was awarded a prize at the Cannes International Film Festival. The press reported new productions of the ballet in France (at the Paris Opéra), Italy, Poland, the German Democratic Republic, and other countries. The Italians presented it in the square in Verona, the very city where the action of Shakespeare's immortal tragedy is laid.

On March 31, 1955, the long-awaited première of *War and Peace* in its final, one-night version, took place in the Leningrad Maly Opera Theater.* The performance was dedicated "To the fond memory of the distinguished Soviet artists S. Prokofiev and V. Dmitriev." This was actually the first complete stage representation of Prokofiev's favorite work, and the first time that the Soviet public had an opportunity to hear it in its entirety. The new production, under the baton of Ye. Grikurov (staged by B. Pokrovsky with excellent sets by V. Dmitriev), brought out the many fine qualities of Prokofiev's opera.

※　※　※

*War and Peace* is the fruit of Prokofiev's many years of experience in the operatic genre. On no other composition had he labored so long with such persistence and enthusiasm.

For many years Prokofiev's work in this genre was constricted by his nihilistic views, his rejection of the principles of classical operatic form. While in his instrumental works, such as his sonatas, symphonies, and concertos, he adhered to classical principles of composition, in his operas he almost always rejected the traditional ensembles, arias, and choruses. He firmly believed that vocal "numbers" destroyed continuity of action and had long since become obsolete. In striving for this narrowly conceived "naturalness" of action, he also turned his back on the established procedures of libretto writing, choosing instead to construct his operas on the unaltered texts of his literary sources. This was the method followed in *The Gambler, The Flaming Angel, The Love for Three Oranges,* and to a considerable extent *Semyon Kotko.*

The first version of *War and Peace* was also constructed according to this principle. Tolstoi's text was followed almost exactly. The composer set it mostly as recitative over a continuously flowing symphonic background, avoiding finished vocal forms. This version proved unsatisfactory to many who heard it, including the composer himself.

During the years between its original and final versions (1941–52), *War and Peace* underwent substantial revision. The addition of new scenes ("The Nobleman's Ball" and "War Council at Fili") and the condensation and radical reworking of what had already been written led to changes in the music itself. In the process of this work, Prokofiev continued perfecting

* TRANSLATOR'S NOTE: Schlifstein (*S. S. Prokofiev: Materials, Documents, and Reminiscences,* Moscow, 1956) gives the date as April 1.

445

the opera's musical structure, giving more importance to expressive, clear-cut melody and limiting the role of unmelodic prose recitative.

Studying the history of the opera and tracing the evolution of its form from the first to the final version, we can clearly see that Prokofiev was moving with more and more assurance toward a mastery of operatic realism, that he was overcoming his narrow, naturalistic views toward opera.

The structure of *War and Peace* is unusual and original—a combination of lyrico-psychological drama and heroic-epic narrative. The opera falls into two parts, the first dealing with the personal lives of Natasha Rostova and Andrei Bolkonsky and the second with the events of the War of 1812. The first six scenes, all of which are lyrical in character, set forth the story of Natasha's love for Andrei and her infatuation with Anatole Kuragin. Scene 1, night at Otradnoye, portrays Andrei's awakening love for Natasha; Scene 2, the nobleman's ball, their growing love; Scene 3, Prince Bolkonsky's mansion, Natasha's encounter with the old Prince Bolkonsky, who opposes her marriage to Andrei; Scene 4, Ellen Bezhukhova's ball, Natasha's infatuation with Antole Kuragin; Scene 5, Dolokhov's study, Anatole's plan to abduct Natasha with Dolokhov's help; Scene 6, Maria Dmitrievna Akhrosimova's mansion, the failure of the plan and Natasha's despair.

Beginning with Scene 7, the events of the patriotic War of 1812 move into the foreground and the personal drama of Natasha and Andrei is all but supplanted by the monumental episodes of the historical chronicle. Scene 7, before the battle of Borodino, contains songs of the peasant militia and Russian soldiers, Andrei's reflections about Natasha's faithlessness, and Kutuzov's review of the regiments. Scene 8, on the Shevardino redoubt, shows Napoleon's headquarters during the battle of Borodino;* Scene 9, the war council at Fili, Kutuzov decides upon the temporary surrender of Moscow; Scene 10, a dark hut in Mytishchy, depicts Andrei's deathbed delirium and last meeting with Natasha. Finally, the triumphant epilogue celebrates the victory of the Russian army and the wisdom of Field Marshal Kutuzov.

A dramatic structure of this kind is not without flaws. The relationship between the various episodes is not always clear, and the transitions between them are abrupt and unmotivated. An example of this can be seen in the

---

\* The scene in Napoleon's headquarters was omitted from the final version of the opera. It is worth noting, however, that when this tense scene was included in the Leningrad Maly Theater production, it proved to be extremely convincing and added immensely to the work's dramatic effect.

transition from the intimate scene depicting Natasha's despair (Scene 6) to the mass scene which follows. There are times when the opera seems to be merely a series of unrelated illustrations for Tolstoi's novel. In order to understand them, the audience has to be thoroughly familiar with all of the particulars of the novel's plot. Here and there the text contains complicated prose constructions, transferred bodily from Tolstoi's book, which encumber the verbal fabric of the opera. These, then, are the basic flaws of the libretto of *War and Peace*.

However, the history of opera has proved that in the last analysis, the effectiveness of a work in this genre depends primarily on the vividness, profundity, and artistic expressiveness of the music. If a composer succeeds in making the music convey the innermost essence of a given plot, his opera will live regardless of its dramaturgical defects. On the other hand, if the drama is not adequately expressed in the music, the most admirable libretto is worthless.

There is no question that in the best scenes of *War and Peace,* Prokofiev's music has convincing power, charm, and originality and that the serious shortcomings of the libretto become secondary in importance. The more we listen to the music, the more we can forget the defects in dramatization. Prokofiev's brilliant music compels us to believe in the reality of Tolstoi's characters and stirs us with its portrayal of the basic themes of the novel— the love story of Natasha and Andrei and the epic struggle waged by Field Marshal Kutuzov and the people.

Most of the music of *War and Peace* is made up of two basic components: the symphonic fabric, which almost continuously comments on and fills in the emotional details of the action; and the vocal element, which is either tuneful and close to arioso style or purely speech-like recitative. Various types of genre music constitute the opera's third element. These genre elements occupy a subordinate place, even though their importance increased noticeably in the final version of the opera.

The orchestral part is based on several leitmotivs, which express either the protagonists' love or their patriotic thoughts and aspirations. In some cases these leitmotivs are thematically rounded-out melodic periods; this is the case with Natasha's inspired theme (Fig. 59), the love theme of Natasha and Andrei, Andrei's theme, and Kutuzov's theme. Because of their tunefulness and genuine emotional quality, the composer was also able to employ them in the vocal parts. At other times, these leitmotivs amount to no more than brief symphonic formulas, as is the case with the themes of Natasha's despair, of victory, of the people's tribulations, of Andrei's delirium,

FIGURE 59

and the theme expressing the tension of battle in the scene in Napoleon's headquarters. These have a more decidely instrumental character.

Just as in Prokofiev's ballet *Romeo and Juliet,* the orchestral leitmotivs are repeated in various combinations and in different tonal and textural modifications. They also shift from one character to another or return like reminiscences. At times the specifically instrumental quality of these themes leaves a definite imprint on the character of the vocal parts, marring their natural lyricism. But in the best lyrical episodes of the opera, such as Scene 1 (at Otradnoye) and Scene 10 (Andrei's death), the charm and warmth of the music is captivating. In these, as in the most successful of the other scenes, the composer organically combines a continuously developing orchestral fabric with profoundly expressive recitative, which at times assumes a flowing arioso character.

In the final version of the opera, the genre episodes—which convey the atmosphere of the action, the spirit of the epoch, and provide a rich emotional background for the unfolding of the thoughts and feelings of the leading characters—acquired great importance. The tender, slightly sentimental duet between Natasha and Sonya in Scene 1 (to words by V. Zhukovsky) harmonizes excellently with the poetic setting of the spring night and the presentiments of the love between Andrei and Natasha. The rather stiff and formal polonaise at the beginning of Scene 2 suggests the callousness and rigidity of aristocratic society, which are contrary to Natasha's ideals and aspirations. The two glittering waltzes—the B minor waltz of the New Year's ball in Scene 2 and the G minor waltz in Scene 4 at Ellen Bezukhova's—play an important, meaningful role. While the first provides a poetic background for the lofty romantic impulses of Andrei and Natasha, the second, with its bewitching, gypsy-like sensuality, conveys the seductive atmosphere which prevails in Ellen's salon. The themes of these waltzes appear later as musical reminiscences: the B minor waltz theme returns twice in Andrei's part (in Scenes 7 and 10) as the expression of his happy recollections of lost love, and the G minor waltz theme is repeated in the scene at Dolokhov's when Anatole, aflame with passion, recalls the love letter he sent Natasha. Both the majestic, epic theme of Kutuzov's monologue, which is repeated in the scene on the Shevardino redoubt when the invincibility of the Russian forces is mentioned, and the beautiful, flowing Russian theme of Kutuzov's aria are treated as leitmotivs. The latter is one of the highlights of the opera (Fig. 60).

Ве_ли_ча _ ва_я, в сол_неч_ных лу_чах, ма_терь рус _ ских го _ ро_

_дов, ты рас _ ки_ну_лась пе_ред на _ ми, Моск _ ва.

FIGURE 60

Another distinctive feature of the opera is the skillful and varied treatment of recitative. It would be incorrect to regard the composer's keen interest in enriching operatic recitative as a departure from the principles of realism. In persistently cultivating various forms of "melodic speech," and in the novel ways in which he set living Russian speech to music, the composer was unquestionably continuing the operatic experiments of such nineteenth-century realists as Dargomyzhsky and Moussorgsky. Of course, the declamatory element in *War and Peace* differs greatly from that of *The Stone Guest* and *Boris Godunov*. Prokofiev's recitative, which is based entirely on Tolstoi's prose, is much closer to everyday speech. In this lies both its strength and its weakness. The extreme difficulty of setting certain bits of the original prose to music sometimes led to contrived, unmelodic phrases in the score.[18] Occasionally the composer had to abandon melody altogether and simply set rhythmic prose to an orchestral accompaniment.

On the other hand, in the opera's best lyrical and dramatic scenes Tolstoi's prose, with its amazing precision, simplicity, and emotional richness, proved wonderfully adaptable to a natural musical setting. Natasha's remarks, for example, express the most varied shades of feeling, from pensive, naïve ecstasy in the first scene to dejection in the scene at Prince Bolkonsky's and nervous excitement and despair in the scene at Akhrosimova's. In this last-mentioned scene Natasha's part contains a great many subtle dramatic nuances: angry exclamations, tragic whispering, phrases broken off by repressed sobbing. These nuances are excellently conveyed in the heroine's vocal part.

The many minor characters in the opera are portrayed chiefly by means of distinctly individualized recitative. Ellen's insinuating, affected speech, Akhrosimova's blunt, cutting remarks, Anatole's boasting, and old Bolkonsky's nervousness and petty tyranny remain indelibly imprinted in the listener's memory. Here and there the composer skillfully introduces elements of genre music into the recitatives. One hears suggestions of a rakish Russian song in the boastful phrases of the coachman Balag, and of a sensual, languid *romance* in the remarks of the gypsy woman Matresha. In the scene of the war council at Fili, the characters of the generals—Bennigsen, Rayevsky, Yermolov, and Barclay de Tolly—are sketched with spare but telling strokes.

Some of the arias of the central characters—Natasha, Andrei, and Field Marshal Kutuzov—also grow out of the recitative. Here "musical speech" gives way to a more melodic arioso style. Examples of this are Andrei's aria in the scene at Otradnoye, Natasha's aria in the scene at Prince Bolkonsky's and her solo episodes in the scene at Akhrosimova's, Kutuzov's monologue in the scene before the battle of Borodino, and finally, the long scene of Andrei's deathbed delirium. The orchestral leitmotivs mentioned above, skillfully interwoven into the vocal parts, play a large role in the musical construction of these episodes.

Of course, the general audience was not accustomed to operas consisting primarily of recitative or even more melodic semi-aria forms. Therefore it was natural that the composer should enrich the melodic element by introducing a few more rounded-out, song-like vocal episodes. Accordingly, he added the poetic duet between Natasha and Sonya (Scene 1), the stylized choruses (Scene 2, to words by Batyushkov and Lomonosov), and Kutuzov's wonderful aria. Along with the waltzes, the polonaise, the mazurka, and the military march (in the scene of Kutuzov's review of the troops), these melodic numbers create a realistic atmosphere for the action.

Melodious choral episodes of this kind were especially needed in the scenes dealing with the events of the War of 1812, for in such scenes, recitative alone would have been inadequate. The most impressive of these choral episodes are the peasant militia's patriotic chorus "How our Kutuzov came to the people," the valiant soldiers' song heard off stage in the scene of the war council at Fili, and the triumphal choruses with which the opera ends. These choruses, as we have already noted, were another expression of that folk-epic element which was represented so powerfully in Prokofiev's music for *Alexander Nevsky* and *Ivan the Terrible*. On the other hand, some of the folk song episodes, such as the Cossacks' chorus and the women's song of welcome, have a certain stylized quality and lack the sweep of truly Russian choral folk music.

The central figures of the opera—Natasha, Andrei, and Kutuzov—proved to be the most vivid and realistic, primarily because in their musical characterizations recitative, tuneful arioso style, and orchestral means are successfully combined.

The portrait of Natasha—the "slender, dark-eyed little girl," engagingly ingenuous, full of life, and always singing—is particularly varied, human, and truthful. It is not surprising that Prokofiev thought of calling the final version of the opera *Natasha Rostova,* for in terms of both dramatic motivation and musical characterization, she is the most fully drawn figure in the opera. In this heroine, Prokofiev's exquisitely pure and delicate lyricism, known to us in his early songs of Op. 27 and later in the wonderful portraits of Juliet and Cinderella, once again found full expression. Even though not every facet of Tolstoi's Natasha is revealed in the opera (her courage during the war, her close ties with the people, and her infectious gaiety, for example), the composer does achieve a touching and truthful portrait of her.

The musical portrayal of Andrei also contains much that is appealing. His impassioned aria in the first scene and, more particularly, the powerfully dramatic scene of his deathbed delirium, over a monotonous chorus issuing from the darkness, are among the best pages of the opera. It is regrettable that after Scene 3, Andrei does not participate in the action until near the very end of the opera. His aria in the scene before the battle of Borodino sounds somewhat cold and unemotional.

Field Marshal Kutuzov is shown as a good man and a wise military leader, with a deep affection for the Russian people. His noble aria, newly written for the opera's final version, adds stature to his portrait, endowing it with features of epic grandeur. The music vividly brings out the truly Russian character and democratic spirit of Kutuzov, the soldier's idol, the "representative of the people's war." His strong ties with the people are underscored by the marked similarity between his musical themes and those which characterize the people and the soldiers. Time and again his themes are transferred to the people's chorus or (as at the end of the overture) contrapuntally combined with the chorus's own theme.

Prokofiev's creative originality is evident in the bold and novel construction of the through-composed scenes, which are based on a fusion of the music and the stage action. Examples of this method are the scenes in Napoleon's headquarters and in Dolokhov's study. Even though they contain neither arias nor melodic "numbers," these scenes are gripping for their swift pace, pointed recitative, and tensely pulsating orchestral background. The feeling of a mad gamble already lost pervades the scene on the Shevardino redoubt. Here the nervous *ostinato* theme in the orchestra, Bonaparte's hysterical exclamations, and the chain of anxious military commands create the atmosphere of a feverish game of chance, a spirit reminiscent of the roulette scene in *The Gambler*. The same mood of recklessness characterizes the equally dynamic scene in Dolokhov's study. Both these scenes and the highly dramatic scene at Akhrosimova's are charged with that swiftly paced action so typical of Prokofiev's operatic style. These tense episodes serve as an excellent contrast to the more static scenes, such as the lyrical nocturne "At Otradnoye" and the concluding scene with its triumphal choruses.

The richness of the score is revealed in the intricately interwoven threads of contrasting musical material. Two parallel sets of conflicting musical images stand out in the opera. The first of these is associated with the personal drama of Natasha and Andrei and includes, on the one hand, the impassioned themes of love and youthful hopes (Scenes 1 and 2), and on the other hand, images of deceit and worldly temptations (Scene 4), of vulgar cynicism (Scene 5), and finally, of death and love's shattered hopes (Scene 10). The second set of images, in which the antithesis is even more sharply defined, is associated with the events of the war. In this case, the patriotic pride of the Russian soldiers and Kutuzov's wisdom and serenity are contrasted with Napoleon's blind passion and nervous hysteria.

These two lines of the music and plot, the lyrical and the epic, are developed independently; they scarcely meet. While sharply contrasting, they also complement each other in certain ways. The images of war are perceived as an ominous evil force which causes Andrei's death just at the moment he and Natasha are reconciled. But the people's celebration, with which the opera concludes, reminds us of the might of Russia and the glory of victory achieved through common struggle and painful sacrifice.

*War and Peace* is a complex work, not without its shortcomings. Nevertheless, it is the climax of Prokofiev's operatic quest. The composer's achievements in this work have enriched contemporary operatic literature and advanced creative thought. The finest passages of *War and Peace* are worthy additions to the gallery of Russian operatic music.

# THIRTEEN

# STYLISTIC FEATURES

*The good master has gone, with his*
*precious eye and golden hand.*

P. Bazhov: THE MALACHITE BOX

S ERGEI PROKOFIEV'S creative activity spanned more than half a century, beginning in 1902 with the piano *Ditties* and the G major Symphony and ending in 1953 with several unfinished compositions. The list of his works runs to more than one hundred and thirty *opera,* not counting numerous arrangements and transcriptions, and it embraces almost every genre of musical composition: symphonies and cantatas; operas and ballets; concertos for piano, violin, and cello; sonatas; songs and romances; choruses; marches; music for children; folk song arrangements; music for the theater and films; and smaller instrumental forms. Prokofiev wrote seven symphonies, eight operas, seven ballets, seven vocal-orchestral works, nine piano sonatas, nine instrumental concertos, more than one hundred and twenty pieces for piano, and about sixty songs and romances.

Throughout his career as an artist, Prokofiev's tastes and artistic tendencies followed a clearly discernible evolution, a progress closely bound up with the changing social conditions of the complex times in which he lived. In tracing his development as a composer, we have attempted to divide his creative life into three periods: the very productive if somewhat contradictory period of his youth (1907–1918), vestiges of which remain in the works he composed between 1918 and 1921; the difficult foreign period, ending in 1933, which was in many respects intellectually detrimental to him; and finally, the Soviet period (1933–53), the most valuable and productive period of his work, during which he overcame many of his past errors and took his stand for musical realism.

Nevertheless, as we come to know the best of Prokofiev's works from both his youthful and most mature periods, we can distinguish in both certain common stylistic features, certain unique and expressive ways of handling melody, harmony, rhythm, and orchestration. In his maturity, to be sure, he abandoned some of the stylistic excesses that characterized the music of his youthful and foreign periods; but in such later compositions as *Cinderella, Winter Bonfire,* and the Seventh Symphony, we can easily discern the inimitable manner of the composer of *The Ugly Duckling,* the *Classical Symphony,* and the early piano sonatas.

Prokofiev's artistic ideas changed radically; they became more profound, meaningful, and purposeful. With increasing frequency, he abandoned the formal experimentation of his earlier days for serious efforts at achieving a realistic treatment of both the past and the present. But while his artistic direction changed, he retained many of the novel methods he had discovered in his youth until the very end of his life, continually perfecting them and adapting them to the expression of new ideas.

*❋ ❋ ❋*

Prokofiev was one of those pragmatic artists with little interest in theorizing—indeed, he nourished a genuine contempt for it. Time and again he ridiculed the efforts of musical prophets who tried to devise a universal key to the composition of new music. The twelve-tone system of Schoenberg left him cold, and he scornfully rejected the rationalistic, mathematical music of the dodecaphonists. He was not the least interested in Georgy Conus' theory of metric analysis, and severely criticized Conus at a musical conference.[1] Although he respected B. Yavorsky as a fine musician, he cared nothing for Yavorsky's tonal and rhythmic theories. Before and during the twenties, the general enthusiasm for the harmonic innovations of Scriabin left him unmoved. "Scriabin cannot have disciples. Scriabin must stand alone—he is a solitary genius," he declared in an interview.[2] And although Prokofiev responded warmly to Stravinsky's early music and was noticeably influenced by him, he clearly understood the limitations of Stravinsky's aesthetic views. "He is rather an observer and a composer absorbed in his own music than a man of deep feeling," he said of Stravinsky.

"I have no theories," Prokofiev once replied when asked about the basis of his musical innovations. He believed that a theorizing composer who sets up artistic dogmas thereby constricts his creative thought. "From the moment an artist formulates his own 'logic,' he begins to limit himself," he stated in an interview abroad. He went on to explain that his art did not stem from any rationalistic system, but simply from a desire to find the most fitting means of expressing his own artistic ideas. "I have always felt compelled to do my own thinking, to follow out my own ideas. . . . I was never satisfied to do things merely because the rules said so," he asserted. "When I first left the Conservatory, I had too many ideas and not enough technique to express them as I wished. But I decided this was better than the reverse." He worked out his own artistic style, he said, in the process of independent composition. "I am not ashamed to say that essentially I am a pupil of my own ideas. In all that I write, I have two leading principles—clarity in the presentation of my ideas and economy of expression, the avoidance of everything superfluous in expressing them."[3]

Not all the artistic ideas which stirred Prokofiev, especially in his early years and those abroad, were related to the advanced social tendencies of the time. Sometimes the only results of these ideas were superficial, formal experiments. But when he drew his inspiration from reality, from penetrating observations of life about him, he created brilliant and original works.

❊　❊　❊

One cannot speak of Prokofiev's philosophy of life and his aesthetic attitude toward reality without noting the strain of joyful optimism that runs throughout his music. It is the prevailing mood in many of his compositions—from the First Piano Concerto, the early sonatas, and the finales of the *Scythian Suite* and the First Violin Concerto to *Alexander Nevsky, The Stone Flower,* and the last symphonies. Faith in life, in man's strength, and in the creative power of labor permeate both his program works and his own utterances. Neither personal misfortunes nor severe illness could shake this faith or weaken his ceaseless drive to create. He often scolded his friends for complaining about approaching old age. "It is a waste of time to contemplate one's aging body. One must be able to understand the unreality of this aging," he wrote Asafyev.[4]

Prokofiev's optimism was not at all in tune with the decadent tendencies of bourgeois art in his time. His creative career began in a period of social stagnation. He was surrounded by an atmosphere of death, will-lessness, and a cynical lack of faith in man. The modernist poets were glorifying ugliness and evil, extolling the "black plague, leprosy, gloom, murder, and misfortune" (Balmont). But Prokofiev went his own way, resolutely transcending the unwholesome influences of decadence. His best works captivate the listener with themes of strength and aspiration, of inspired young love, of life's ecstasy and nature's beauty. His humanistic tendencies, obscured in his earlier works by either sarcastic grimaces or nervous distortions, triumphed completely in his music of the Soviet period. With Andrei Bolkonsky, the hero of his favorite opera, he might well have exclaimed, "To achieve happiness one need only believe in the possibility of happiness, one need only believe in spring and joy."[5]

A characteristic manifestation of the deeply human quality of Prokofiev's art is the ever-recurring theme of childhood, with all its guileless spontaneity and purity of feeling. Prokofiev was one of those pure-hearted artists who, as Gorky put it, had a vivid, uncanny remembrance of childhood. Images of childhood are to be found in many of his works—from the pieces of Op. 12 and *The Ugly Duckling* to *Peter and the Wolf, On Guard for Peace,* and the Seventh Symphony. These images are delightful in their simplicity and clarity, in the aptness of their tone painting, and in their charming romanticism and tender lyricism. In his touching concern with the world of childhood, Prokofiev continued in the tradition of Moussorgsky (in his cycle *The Nursery*), Tchaikovsky (in *Kinderalbum*), Lyadov, and other outstanding Russian masters.

Along with the world of childhood, Prokofiev also evokes a world of fantasy. His interest in the fanciful manifested itself throughout his life—from such early piano pieces as *Fairy Tale* and *Legend* to *Cinderella* and *The Stone Flower*. He was very much attracted by myths, tales, *bylini,* and fantasies of all kinds. He conjured up in his music, with a youthful spontaneity, images from such wonderful storytellers as Andersen and Gozzi, Perrault and Bazhov, as well as from ancient Slavic mythology and Russian, French, and Kazakh folk tales. Not infrequently, suggestions of a narrative quality—sometimes lofty and epic, sometimes amusingly ironic—can be discerned in his instrumental works.

Fairy-tale subjects served Prokofiev as a basis for creating a stylized, specifically theatrical atmosphere in which reality is interwoven with the most extraordinary and wondrous fiction. This naïve stylization with its exaggerated images somewhat resembles that of the ballet, puppet theater, and animated cartoon—art forms in which realistic situations are often refracted through the prism of bold fantasy, of artistic "magic." It should be added that in most cases Prokofiev's fantasy was no pretext for withdrawing from the realities of life. The best of his works, such as *The Ugly Duckling* and *Cinderella,* reveal in allegorical form the complex problems of human relationships. The conventions of fantasy were used in some cases to depict the beauty of nature, in others to draw portraits of good, simple folk and lovable animals, and in others to embody the dark, evil forces hostile to man. In his predilection for revealing the repellent and brutal aspects of life he at times approached such masters of the fantastic as Goya and Poe.

Though for the most part he sang of the joys of living, the beauty of nature, and the poetry of childhood, Prokofiev did not hesitate to present the ugly, horrible, and ludicrous sides of life. In his works he often mercilessly laid bare banality and mediocrity, cruelty and stupidity, envy and greed. His favorite means of exposure was laughter—either the stinging laughter of the nihilist, the violator of tradition (as in *The Gambler, The Buffoon,* and *Sarcasms*) or the triumphant laughter of the strong man who hates evil (as in *Cinderella* and *The Duenna*). At times he depicted the forces of evil as fearsome monsters, repellent in their inhumanity (the *Scythian Suite* and *Seven, They Are Seven*). In such cases his music became harsh, coarsely mechanical, and devoid of all human warmth. Echoes of these terrifying barbarisms are also to be found in his later works.

In his affirmation of human virtue and his exposure of negative forces, Prokofiev was not always equipped with clear ideological aims. He never gave enduring expression to the heroism and pathos of the people's life in the period of the victory of socialism. He was more successful in depicting the past (though he worked in a completely modern idiom) than in portraying revolutionary struggle and socialist creation.

Still, his art did reflect in its own way those great days when the world of truth and justice triumphed for the first time over the world of coercion and falsehood. And in this Prokofiev was a worthy son of our epoch.

❋   ❋   ❋

One cannot speak of Prokofiev's approach to art without noting his strong sense of national pride and, stemming from it, his increasingly serious quest for a Russian national style. He proudly identified himself with Russian culture and asserted "Russia's leading role in contemporary music." On his trips abroad he repeatedly proclaimed a great future for music in Russia, at the same time stressing the fact that the new Russian music was completely independent of contemporary Western influences. "Though Debussy's music is much loved by Russian musicians," he said, "I do not think that it has influenced them. German music, which rose to such heights with Wagner, and later declined with Richard Strauss and Reger, has certainly not influenced us."[6] Unfeeling cosmopolitanism was alien to Prokofiev from his very youth. In his letters and articles he severely criticized certain Russian musicians "who love to ape the French," men obsequiously bowing down before the idols of contemporary Western art.

Through the mouths of Babulenka in *The Gambler* and Maria Dmitrievna Akhrosimova in *War and Peace,* he hurled stinging ridicule at the snobbish cosmopolites who shunned their native land: "Their feelings are French; their dress is French. The women are half undressed, like those you see on the signs of public baths, if one may say so. . . . Their gods are French, their kingdom of heaven—Paris."[7]

His many years abroad did not affect Prokofiev's love of Russia. In his letters he spoke of his "irrepressible longing for Russia" and said that he would gladly exchange all the beauties of foreign lands for those of his native Russia. Fortune took him to the far-flung corners of the earth— to Canada and Japan, Mexico and Norway, Spain and North Africa. He saw the great expanses of the Atlantic, the mountain scenery of Bavaria, and the riotous verdure of the tropics. But he found the modest landscape of Central Russia, with its pine forests, mushroom glades, and quiet meandering streams far more charming. It is not surprising that many of his best works were written in the woodland quiet of Polenovo and Nikolina Gora.

The Russian character of Prokofiev's music is revealed in his melodic and harmonic idiom, which is tied by many threads to folk and classical traditions, as well as in his distinctive musical images, which range from the epic to the lyric to the derisive. In the Third Piano Concerto, *Alexander Nevsky,* and *Ivan the Terrible,* in the Fifth Symphony and *War and Peace,* Prokofiev comes forth as a poet of Russia, extolling her vast spaces, the expanse of her fields, and the might of her people. He perceived Russia differently from some of his gifted contemporaries; his work is free, for instance, of the profound melancholy which disturbs us in Miaskovsky's Sixth Symphony and Rachmaninov's Third Symphony. In Prokofiev's music vigor, exuberance, and unrestrained motion predominate over tragic complexities and spiritual confusion. A whole gallery of vividly portrayed national characters are presented in his operas and ballets on Russian themes. Be they men of towering strength, warm-hearted and gentle girls, or typical, everyday people, they are convincing and well-integrated. As examples we might mention Kutuzov and Ivan the Terrible; Natasha Rostova, Katerina, and the young girl from *Alexander Nevsky*; the steward Severyan from *The Stone Flower*; the coachman Balaga from *War and Peace*; and Babulenka from *The Gambler.*

The national basis of Prokofiev's artistic approach is clearly evident in his choice of subjects for musical treatment: works from classical literature (by Pushkin, Dostoyevsky, and Tolstoi); historical episodes from the thirteenth, sixteenth, eighteenth, and nineteenth centuries (*Alexander Nevsky, Ivan the Terrible, Lieutenant Kije,* and *War and Peace*); Russian folk tales (*The Buffoon, Tales of the Old Grandmother,* and *The Stone Flower*); folk song (the Russian Overture and the twelve arrangements, Op. 104); and finally, themes from contemporary Russian life (*Zdravitsa* and *Winter Bonfire*). This national element revealed itself in the composer's interest in the epic history of his motherland; in his tendency toward a profoundly lyrical melodic style, simple and free from excessive emotionalism; and in his characteristically cutting irony, mockery, and wit, which were applied mercilessly to enemies and good-naturedly to friends. It also manifested itself in his constant striving to capture the intonations of the human voice, in his careful attention to the sound of Russian speech in its most varied aspects.

Prokofiev's typically Russian traits are revealed in yet other ways: in his use of the variation technique of inner-thematic development, which is characteristic of slow Russian folk songs (for example, the first theme of the Third Piano Concerto); in his preference for a transparent diatonic style, which contains elements of the alternating modes found in the folk song; and in his tendency toward a free polyphony, at times close to that used in folk singing.

But as it was with the greatest Russian composers of the past, Prokofiev's interests were not limited to purely national subjects and musical materials. He was also attracted by the art of other peoples and countries; he composed works based on an Italian comedy by Gozzi, a French fairy tale by Perrault, and English plays by Shakespeare and Sheridan. Kazakh and Kabardinian materials, Ukrainian motivs (in *Semyon Kotko*), and Hebrew folk tunes are to be found in his works as well. But even when Prokofiev treated non-Russian material, his music retained a distinctly Russian flavor. *Romeo and Juliet, Cinderella,* the *Classical Symphony,* and *The Duenna* were written by a Russian artist with great talent for projecting images derived from foreign sources through the spectrum of his own national sensibilities.

Sometimes, especially in his early years, the national element in Prokofiev's works was subjected to an overly refined stylization—as in *The Buffoon,* for example. In such cases he was striving not so much to reveal folk characteristics as to display his own creative originality, and the results unquestionably reflected the influence of the modernist approach to art.

The composer's spiritual and intellectual growth in the Soviet period led him to a more natural treatment of Russian folk material. It was along this course that Prokofiev advanced toward realism and more truthful expression.

❈ ❈ ❈

It is important to trace the connection between Prokofiev's art and classical musical traditions. In some of his early works, and particularly in those of his foreign period, Prokofiev was more interested in upsetting traditions than in developing them creatively. In those years, when he did turn to the great composers of the past, it was usually to take from them what most closely corresponded to his own tendencies: striking descriptive means, such as sinister effects, impudent mockery, and delicate fantasy. He was attracted by the prose recitatives of Moussorgsky's *The Marriage,* by the rich, colorful harmonies of Rimsky-Korsakov's *Kashchei,* and by the humor of some of Greig's instrumental pieces (note the echoes of Greig's *March of the Dwarfs* in the scherzo of the First Violin Concerto). But the more mature and serious Prokofiev's art became, the more thoroughly he assimilated the noble traditions of the past, grasping not only individual details, but catching their very essence.

Prokofiev had an enormous respect for the Russian classical composers, most notably Glinka, Borodin, Moussorgsky, and Rimsky-Korsakov; and with each passing year, this respect increased. Among his favorite works were Borodin's *Prince Igor* and *To the Shores of My Distant Fatherland,* and Rimsky-Korsakov's *The Snow Maiden, Sadko,* and *The Legend of the Invisible City of Kitezh.* His concert programs included Moussorgsky's *Pictures at an Exhibition* and Rimsky-Korsakov's Piano Concerto. He felt rather uncomfortable when Asafyev compared his *Scythian Suite* with the great works of the Five: "You flattered me when, in speaking of Borodin and Rimsky-Korsakov, you made some reference to the *Scythian Suite.* It was pleasant and made me feel like a child put at the table with the grownups," he wrote to Asafyev.[8]

Of the European composers, Prokofiev particularly esteemed Beethoven as a bold innovator who revitalized musical forms. His admiration for Haydn, Mozart, and Scarlatti found expression time and again in his works which display features of eighteenth-century classicism. Prokofiev also loved the music of Schumann and Brahms, and among the later composers, of Ravel. The driving rhythms and Hoffmannesque quality of Schumann, the fiendishness of Liszt and Scriabin, and the fantasy of Greig were variously reflected in Prokofiev's works, especially those of his earlier years. But, of course, the traditions of the Russian classical composers, first

*461*

and foremost Glinka and the Five, had the greatest influence on his art, particularly in the most important of his mature works. It was from these men that Prokofiev inherited his flair for graphic instrumental writing, for music that evokes concrete, almost visual images of nature and life—what Asafyev called, not very precisely, the "symphonic style that creates illusions."

As we know, Glinka created unexcelled examples of vividly pictorial music, among them the sketches of nature in the orchestral episodes of *Ivan Susanin* and *Ruslan and Ludmila,* the colorful landscapes and scenes from everyday life in the Spanish overtures, and the sharply delineated, almost caricatural portraits of Naina and the dwarf Chernomor. One can trace a direct line from the famous march of Chernomor, with its abrupt, angular lines and sharply accented rhythm, to Prokofiev's fantastic marches and processions.

From Glinka, too, came Prokofiev's liking for majestic Russian choral episodes and for rapid and joyous themes, which we hear in the choruses of *Alexander Nevsky, Ivan the Terrible,* and *War and Peace.*

We also find in Prokofiev's vocal compositions a continuation of those tendencies toward the declamatory style which originated in Russian music with Dargomyzhsky. We know that Prokofiev made a careful study of Dargomyzhsky's *Stone Guest* and was impressed by the creative techniques of this innovator, that is, by his method of translating into music the intonations of human speech, his way of making "the sound exactly express the word." Admiration for this achievement also led Prokofiev to attempt to compose music on unaltered literary texts (as Dargomyzhsky had done in *The Stone Guest*) and to place greater emphasis on the details of recitative than on broadly conceived melodies. The abundance of speech-like recitative and the rather sparse use of flowing melodies unquestionably limited the comprehensibility and popularity of Prokofiev's vocal works (just as it had done to such purely declamatory Russian operas as *The Stone Guest, Mozart and Salieri,* and *The Covetous Knight*). But despite the limitations of this approach, one cannot ignore its objective: the subordination of vocal melody to the demands of dramatic realism. Without Dargomyzhsky's *Stone Guest* there probably would never have been the scene of Boris's death in *Boris Godunov* or the scene at the Countess' in *The Queen of Spades.* In the same manner, Prokofiev's innovations —as represented, for example, in the vocal writing in *War and Peace*— cannot but affect the future creative endeavors of our operatic composers.

It was probably his three brilliant predecessors, Rimsky-Korsakov,

Borodin, and Moussorgsky, who most strongly influenced the formation of Prokofiev's style.

Prokofiev spoke of his teacher Rimsky-Korsakov with tenderness and affection, and he deeply regretted that because of his youth he had failed to appreciate fully the opportunity of close contact with this composer. "An amazing genius!" he called Rimsky-Korsakov in an interview abroad. It was from Rimsky-Korsakov that he inherited his interest in the epic and the fantastic, in the humorous Russian fairy tale, and in the use of novel harmonies and orchestration for the purpose of vivid tone painting. To verify this, one need only to recall the many diverting scenes in Rimsky's operatic fantasies, with their amusing processions and comical characterizations of such personages as Bobyl (the poor peasant) in *The Snow Maiden,* Saltan and his entourage, and Dodon and Polkan in *The Golden Cockerel.* Other favorite theatrical devices of Rimsky's come to mind—the toy-like marches and the orchestral vignettes, with their stylized fanfares in the manner of a village puppet show. Surely it was these same devices that Prokofiev employed in the comic episodes of such works as *The Buffoon, The Love for Three Oranges,* and *Lieutenant Kije.* One can easily find in Prokofiev echoes of Rimsky's strangely harmonized music which deals with the world of fantasy (the Wood Spirit in *The Snow Maiden,* a great part of *Sadko, Mlada,* and especially in *Kashchei the Immortal*). We have already remarked upon the obvious relationship between some of Prokofiev's lyrical episodes and the delicate lyricism of Rimsky's fairy-tale heroines.

Even more apparent are Prokofiev's spiritual and stylistic ties with another great Russian composer of epic music—Borodin. Asafyev had noted this even in the pre-revolutionary years, when describing his first impressions of the *Scythian Suite*: "Not since the death of Borodin have we heard a voice singing so appealingly of the free and untrammeled life."[9] Indeed, one senses something of the primitive, pagan quality of Borodin's Polovtsian dances in the elemental power of Prokofiev's barbaric images. But the stylized *Scythian Suite* was fundamentally different from the realistic music of Borodin, which was based on the magnificent folk music of Russia and the East. It was not until the thirties and forties, when he turned to themes drawn from Russian history, that Prokofiev developed the stylistic ideas of the composer of *Prince Igor* and the "Bogatyr" Symphony with any great depth and naturalness. That he eventually succeeded in this can be clearly seen in the epic pages of *Alexander Nevsky,* the music for *Ivan the Terrible,* and much of *War and Peace.* Other examples of Borodin's influence can be found in the severe tonal texture and heavy unisons of the first movement of the Fifth Symphony, and in the heroic Russian images in the First Violin Sonata and the finales of the Seventh and Eighth Sonatas. Here the attentive listener will inevitably think of Borodin's Second Symphony, *The Song of the Dark Forest,* and *Prince Igor.* He will note as well the undeniable kinship with the vividly national style of Borodin's works, a kinship evident even in such basic elements as the typically Russian rhythms, textures, and accentuation. And the lively humor in the mischievous songs of Skula and Yeroshka, with their distinctive drone-like *ostinatos* and tart intervals of the second, appears again in many of Prokofiev's characterizations, from *The Buffoon* to *Alexander Nevsky.* This was not actual borrowing or direct influence, of course, but the creative continuity of a tradition. Borodin's style might well have become much like Prokofiev's had he lived into our times.

Prokofiev had a special reverence for Moussorgsky, whom he admired above all as one of the greatest innovators, one who defied academic rules and blazed new trails. He once observed, for example, that since Moussorgsky's time the Russian audience has become more receptive to musical novelty and bold invention, and that controversies between the public and musical innovators have often culminated in complete victory for the composers.[10] When one French musician proudly demonstrated to him the intricacies of his own contrapuntal technique, such as choruses with double counterpoint and so on, Prokofiev commented sharply, "Give all this back to your students and write, instead, like Moussorgsky."[11]

It would be going too far to say that what appealed to Prokofiev in Moussorgsky's music were the themes of the people's sorrow and revolutionary fervor. What Prokofiev inherited from Moussorgsky was, above all, his gift for bold description, his interest in the typical and comic aspects of life, and his ability to portray a man's appearance and the intonations of his speech in a few deft strokes. Prokofiev also fell heir to Moussorgsky's amazing command of declamatory recitative, his interest in prose texts and themes from everyday life, his liking for satire, and his ability to construct forms freely on the basis of content rather than according to ready-made academic formulas. One can easily trace a connection between the vividly pictorial episodes of *Pictures at an Exhibition* and a whole series of Prokofiev's program and non-program works, including *The Ugly Duckling, Tales of the Old Grandmother, Fugitive Visions,* and many parts of the piano and violin concertos. The hero of *The Gambler,* some of the satirical songs (such as *The Wizard*), and the comic characters in *The Love for Three Oranges, The Duenna,* and *Cinderella* owe much to the composer of

ROGER WOOD

ROY ROUND

CINDERELLA, as produced by The Royal Ballet, London. *Above*: Kenneth MacMillan and Frederick Ashton as the Ugly Sisters. *Left*: Svetland Beriosova as Cinderella.

ROMEO AND JULIET, as produced by the Bolshoi, Moscow. *Right*: Raissa Struchkova as Juliet. *Below*: the outbreak of fighting between the Montagues and Capulets.

WAR AND PEACE. *Above*: Helena Scott as Natasha, Gloria Lane as Ellen, and Davis Cunningham as Anatole in the NBC Opera Company production. *Left*: scene from a production in Florence, Italy. *Below*: scene from a production by the Stanislavsky and Nemirovich-Danchenko Music Theater in Moscow, with G. Zenkova as Natasha and V. Radzievsky as Anatole.

THE LOVE FOR THREE ORANGES, produced by the New York City Opera Company. *Above*: the Prince, the King, and the princess Ninetta. *Below*: John Tyers as Pantalon and Carlton Gould as Leandro.

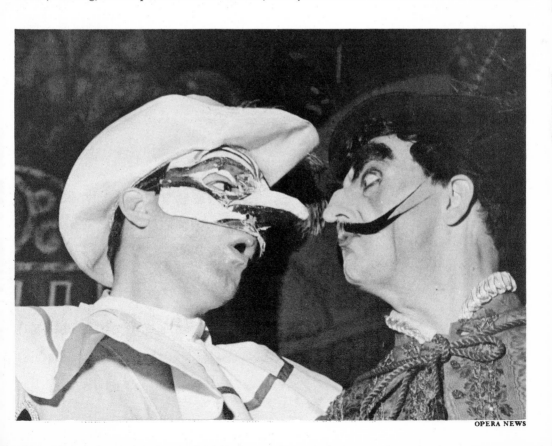

THE FLAMING ANGEL, as produced by the La Scala Opera, Milan. *Above*: Act I, scene 1. Ruprecht hears Renata explain her mystical relation with the Flaming Angel. *Middle*: Act V. The Inquisitor comes to visit Renata's cell in the convent.

THE DUENNA. *Left*: Act I. The carnival scene from a production in Brno, Czechoslovakia.

*The Urchin, The He-Goat, The Peep Show,* and *The Marriage.* In the grotesque images of Prokofiev's *Diabolic Suggestions,* the Second Piano Concerto, and the *Scythian Suite,* we find again the fantasy of *A Night on Bald Mountain* and Baba Yaga. The sweet and amusing children of Moussorgsky's *Nursery* come to life again in the music of Prokofiev. But one could draw dozens of analogies of this kind.

It is also interesting that contemporary critics who disapprove of Prokofiev's music sometimes repeat almost verbatim the criticisms once leveled against Moussorgsky. César Cui, for example, once declared that *Boris Godunov* contained "very little music" and that its recitatives were "not melodic." The opera's chief flaws, he wrote, were its "clipped recitatives and the disconnectedness of its musical ideas."[12] The very same words have been uttered about *War and Peace.* The question of Prokofiev's relationship to Moussorgsky is one of considerable interest, and merits scholarly inquiry.

Prokofiev's attitude toward the lyrical-psychological element found in the music of such composers as Tchaikovsky, Rachmaninov, Medtner, and Scriabin was considerably more critical. In his younger days he often expressed disapproval of the "out-and-out emotionalism" of Tchaikovsky and Rachmaninov, considering it a manifestation of "bad taste." But as he gradually freed himself from the nihilism of his youth, he overcame his former disdain for these wonderful Russian composers.

In many of his works, particularly those composed during the last years of his life, one can even detect echoes of the Tchaikovsky tradition. These resulted in part from his growing interest in romanticizing the popular Russian waltz by emphasizing its lyrical element. Brilliant examples of this are represented in *Cinderella, War and Peace,* and the Seventh Symphony. The fantasy of the *Nutcracker Suite,* with its striking orchestral effects and varied combinations of toyland and grotesque images was also undoubtedly congenial to Prokofiev. Finally, Tchaikovsky's elegant Mozartean quality, found in such works as his interlude "The Faithful Shepherdess" in *The Queen of Spades* and the orchestral suite *Mozartiana,* is also present in Prokofiev's ingenious "classical" pieces—from the piano pieces of Op. 12 to the Flute Sonata.

Prokofiev elaborated the musical traditions of the eighteenth and nineteenth centuries as a twentieth-century artist who had thoroughly assimilated everything new that the best modern composers had introduced into music. To a great extent, this explains the special qualities of his style. He was thoroughly familiar with the harmonic, coloristic, and polyphonic innovations introduced by Richard Strauss and Reger, Scriabin and the young Stravinsky, Debussy and Ravel, and he adapted them to his own needs. Although he questioned much in the work of these composers, he could not disregard their important contributions, particularly a considerable enrichment of the harmonic idiom, a broadening of the orchestra's expressive possibilities, and a general enhancement of music's descriptive means. While he did not fully share the artistic ideals of the French impressionists, he incorporated into his own music some of their colorful harmonic devices; examples of this can be seen in one of the variations of the second movement of the Third Piano Concerto and in the scenes in *Cinderella* where the Fairies of the Seasons appear.

It is common knowledge that although the music created by the Five was profoundly Russian, they also availed themselves of the techniques of such Western masters as Schumann, Berlioz, and Liszt. It was much the same with Prokofiev, whose individual style took shape as he boldly combined the latest coloristic harmonies with the simplest, most traditional devices of cadential writing.

✸　✸　✸

Prokofiev strove throughout his life to revitalize the expressive means of music, and this aspiration became one of the basic tenets of his artistic credo. He refused to compose music according to dogmatic precepts or canons of the craft. He regarded passive imitation and conformity to ready-made patterns in art a "deadly sin." "The cardinal virtue (or sin, if you wish) of my life has been the search for an original musical language, a musical language of my own," he wrote. "I detest imitation; I detest hackneyed methods. I do not want anybody else's guise. I always want to be myself." He scoffed at pseudo-romantic posing, at humoring Philistine tastes (or, as he put it, a composer's "coquetting" with the public). Hence his undeviating aversion to clichés, to vulgar imitations of romanticism and impressionism. He had no patience with cloying diminuendos, sensuous harmonies, and extravagant orchestral effects designed to tickle the ear.

At times his abhorrence of traditional techniques verged on eccentricity. For example, for a long time he could not endure sequences: "After all, sequences are cheap, and soon become boring," he wrote in a letter.[13] "Excellent material and, thank goodness, no augmented triads," he wrote of Miaskovsky's Third Sonata. In another letter he ridiculed Szymanowski's ability "to linger over 6/4 chords, and to fade out with muted passages and harmonics."[14] Certain saccharine passages in a song by his good friend Miaskovsky threw him into a frenzy. "One feels like running out of the room and hiding in shame in some dark corner. How dare Miaskovsky write such a page?!"[15]

Prokofiev considered all imitation an admission of failure, no matter who was being imitated—Tchaikovsky, Medtner, or Stravinsky. He repeatedly ridiculed helpless imitators "who reach down into the graves of dead composers." Even when there was a rationale for imitation, as in the neo-Bachian classicism of Stravinsky, Prokofiev could not accept it. From this point of view he was even willing to question the validity of his own very successful experiment in the *Classical Symphony,* which was a deliberate stylization of Haydn.[16]

On the other hand, as we noted earlier, Prokofiev did not entirely break with the classical past or try to throw it "overboard the ship of modernity." In revitalizing the musical language and thereby occasionally defying traditions, Prokofiev did not indulge in an indiscriminate repudiation of musical principles, as some of his contemporaries thought. He flatly disagreed with the pseudo-Marxist position of certain theoreticians of the Association for Contemporary Music, who maintained that the socialist revolution was supposed to bring about a complete change in the contemporary musical idiom. He considered this leftist thesis "unconvincing and unscientific." "There is no causal relationship between musical techniques and a world war or labor's struggle against capitalism," he asserted. "War can produce a revolution in surgery or revolution can start a war over factory architecture, but neither war nor revolution will overthrow the subject of a fugue or overturn harmonic structure."[17]

The overwhelming majority of Prokofiev's works are based on clear, sound harmonic principles. He spurned the anarchic, alogical harmony of the atonalists and the hazy, overrefined play of colors cultivated by the impressionists and their imitators. On the contrary, he vividly demonstrated the principles of tonality in his own full and perfect cadences. Even when he used the most dissonant harmonies for purposes of description or contrast, they were almost always conceived as purely functional and inevitably gave way to clear and accepted harmonies. The same is true in regard to form. No matter how unusual his musical idiom was, he remained loyal to such time-honored classical forms as the sonata allegro, the rondo sonata, the variation, and several kinds of three-part forms.

Prokofiev's experimentation was by no means always aimed at conveying a realistic portrayal of the objective world. Sometimes his innovations were clearly contrived, most noticeably in a number of his works of the foreign period. Constructivist tendencies can be seen in the artificial way in which melodic material was combined, either by stringing together musical episodes instead of developing them naturally, or by employing mechanical counterpoint. These tendencies also gave rise to the composer's predilection for percussive effects and relentless "motorism," which sometimes, as in the mechanistic episodes of *Le Pas d'acier,* assumed out-and-out urbanistic features.

In other cases the composer yielded to expressionism, displaying his originality at the expense of artistic truth. In his reaction against glib and characterless eclecticism, he sometimes went to the other extreme—portrayals of horror and ugliness, full of nerve-wracking exaggerations. These images were usually conveyed by harsh harmonies and timbres.

In Prokofiev's youth, these two tendencies—the constructivist and the expressionist—were considered ultra-revolutionary, ultra-experimental, and ultra-modern. But it was not long before their lack of substance was demonstrated. The principle of Socialist Realism, put forward by the leading Soviet ideologists, helped many honest artists, including Prokofiev, to follow a course of truly progressive innovation. Now Prokofiev's search for new means of expression was no longer based on the cold calculation of the constructivist, or on the desire for self-display, but was prompted by a determination to reflect reality truthfully. And when the old expressionist tendencies occasionally reappeared in certain works of the forties, they were more or less in the nature of a bow to the past; by then, what had triumphed in Prokofiev's music was the spirit of truth, a love for man and nature, and a realistic portrayal of Russia's past and present.

❧ ❧ ❧

How, then, did Prokofiev's new contributions to Russian music manifest themselves? When Prokofiev created new forms not as ends in themselves but as media for embodying new ideas and subject matter, he naturally enriched the expressive means of music. He was not given to psychological probing and abstract speculation. As we have seen from the piano pieces *Thoughts* and *Things in Themselves,* abstract philosophizing was not his forte. On the other hand, when he turned to concrete themes in his descriptive, program, or theater music, his music became vibrant and exciting. "Always and everywhere it is the same—feeling and character— without embellishment, without ostentation," wrote Asafyev of his music. "In Prokofiev the natural impulse is always present as the stimulus, the wellspring, the force that gives birth to the ideas and the musical material itself."[18]

Prokofiev loved to travel, to wander through the woods and commune with nature, to take note of the beautiful, the typical, and the comical aspects of life. All this is reflected in his music. A painter, *régisseur,* and eager observer, he knew how to find the exact means for portraying a man's characteristic traits, the beauties of nature, the ludicrous, the poignant, and the tensely dramatic moments of life.

It is not only Prokofiev's operas, ballets, and program works that evoke visual images. Listening to some of his non-program compositions, one can easily see fantastic creatures or lovers dancing, sinister forces of destruction or a gay carnival crowd. Many performers and critics of Prokofiev's works have remarked on this. Thus, on hearing *Diabolic Suggestions,* Asafyev visualized "dread horsemen of the steppes." To Richter the third movement of the Second Piano Concerto suggested the horrifying picture of a "dragon devouring its young." K. Igumnov proposed the following program for *Sarcasm* No. 5: "This is the image of a reveler. He has been up to mischief, has broken plates and dishes, and has been kicked downstairs; he lies there and finally begins to come to his senses; but he is still unable to tell his right foot from his left."[19] Prokofiev invariably found economical and striking tonal means for conveying the ideas and subjects that attracted him. As examples of this we might cite the themes of duels and mortal combat in *Romeo and Juliet,* of enemy invasions in *Alexander Nevsky,* and of ludicrous bickering and quarrels in *Cinderella.* Other examples are the realistic scenes from the life of Soviet children in *On Guard for Peace* and *Winter Bonfire,* and the amusing pictures of the animal kingdom in *The Ugly Duckling* and *Peter and the Wolf.*

The composer's most ingenious instrumental writing often grew from his direct observation of human speech, movements, and gestures. It was only his unique and resourceful imagination that enabled him to translate these impressions from life so brilliantly into apt and well-defined musical themes.

Prokofiev, like the Russian composers who preceded him, boldly revitalized the vocal element in opera—the aria, by broadening its range to the utmost limit and introducing colorful modulatory effects, and the recitative by making extensive use of prose texts.

Prokofiev introduced much that was new into the realm of Russian vocal lyricism. He realized that the overwrought, sensuous emotionalism of the nineteenth-century romantics, such as Liszt and Wagner, would not sound natural coming from the lips of present-day characters. However much we may admire the impassioned music of the romantic composers, we cannot express our feelings in their language—in our time, it seems somewhat pompous, even affected. Prokofiev's lyricism has a completely different character; it is restrained, pure, and devoid of overt sentimentality. This is true even of the most tender, romantic pages of his music. Sometimes, in fact, these lyrical pages may seem almost too spare and reserved. But on listening to them more attentively, we become aware of their deep feeling and genuine warmth.

Asafyev had a penetrating and perceptive understanding of Prokofiev's lyricism. "Behind the arsenal of lances, javelins, cross-bows, and other weapons of irony," he wrote, "I caught a glimpse of a secluded garden of lyricism with a spring of pure, bubbling water, cold and crystal clear, free of the scum of 'isms'. . . . One cannot but love these laconic wonders hiding shyly behind the arsenal's formidable walls."[20]

These lyrical ideas are very often expressed in bright diatonic sonorities (C major, "the white key"), in soft, delicate timbres, and in a specific type of melodic line, very broad in range and changing frequently from wide leaps to a subtle, chromatic motion. Many of Prokofiev's early works contain stretches of pure lyricism, at times intimately contemplative (as in the slow passages of the Second, Third, and Fourth Piano Sonatas), at times poetically fanciful (as in the *Tales of the Old Grandmother*). They appear even in his most audacious, barbaric works, such as the *Sarcasms* (in the middle sections of Nos. 1 and 3) and the *Scythian Suite* (the third movement). In his later music the lyrical element, once considered untypical, and long unnoticed, came into full bloom.

The best and most admired passages in his later ballets and operas, even in such works as *Semyon Kotko* and *War and Peace,* in which one might expect the heroic element to predominate, are those in a lyrical vein. The lyrical portraits of sad young girls—Sonya in *Semyon Kotko,* Natasha in *War and Peace,* and the grieving maiden in *Alexander Nevsky*—advance the magnificent tradition of realistic portraiture represented in Russian opera by Yaroslavna, Liza, Marfa, and the Snow Maiden.

Lyricism also plays a prominent role in a number of Prokofiev's instrumental works, among them the Seventh Symphony, the Second Violin Concerto, the Flute Sonata, and the openings of the Eighth and Ninth Piano Sonatas.

Prokofiev considerably enriched the musical means of representing both the repellent and the humorous aspects of life. For this purpose he employed vividly expressive harmonies, broken melodic lines, incisive rhythms, and harsh tonal effects. His music can express not only tenderness and innocent musing, but also anger, frenzy, terror, and impudent laughter. Together with moving lyrical passages, his works almost invariably contain cruel, evil images that are startling in their mechanical coarseness and diabolic sarcasm. This reflected not only the perversity of a violator of traditions (as his opponents regarded him), but also a natural desire to extend the boundaries of musical expressiveness. At times harsh and sardonic images seemed to predominate in Prokofiev's early compositions. This caused some of his contemporaries to regard him as a poet of fury and scathing laughter. "Prokofiev is the psychologist of loathsome emotions—hatred, contempt and anger—primarily anger, disgust, despair, mockery," commented a foreign critic. The composer's subsequent development clearly proved the one-sidedness of this criticism, however. For in later years, tragic expressiveness, grotesquerie, and mockery ceased to exist in Prokofiev's music as ends in themselves, and gave way instead to bright optimism and a vigorous affirmation of life. And when the powerful effects, the fury and anger did appear, it was for a more specific and meaningful purpose: to expose the enemies of mankind, the misanthropes who murder and destroy. No longer were Prokofiev's musical canvases filled with abstract "phantoms," "diabolic suggestions," and legendary Scythian gods. Instead, they presented realistic portraits of Teutonic crusaders (*Alexander Nevsky*), haughty, vengeful knights (*Romeo and Juliet*), the Kaiser's invaders (*Semyon Kotko*), and Napoleonic conquerors (*War and Peace*).

Much of Prokofiev's finest music is tinged with humor. Few of the great composers of the past have introduced so many subtle and original nuances of musical humor, humor ranging from good-natured smiles to biting sarcasm. We hear Prokofiev's impudent laughter in his early piano pieces, in the ballets *Romeo and Juliet* and *Cinderella,* in the comic operas *The Love for Three Oranges* and *The Duenna,* in the symphonic scherzos, and even in vocal compositions such as *The Ugly Duckling* and the children's songs.

In his early works the humor was at times merely playful and mischievous, with no apparent point, or it resulted from the caricaturing of lyrical or narrative themes, as in the development of the first movement of the First Violin Concerto and in many parts of the Second Sonata. A faint tinge of irony can be found in the composer's "classical" compositions, from the First Symphony to the court dances in *Cinderella*.

During the Soviet period, however, Prokofiev's humor took on a more meaningful tone. Sometimes, as in *Lieutenant Kije* and *The Duenna,* it amounted to social satire. Laughter for the sake of laughter, as found in the *Scherzo* for four bassoons and *The Buffoon,* ceased to interest the composer. The operas and ballets present an entire gallery of gay and amusing characters, whose gestures, speech, and infectious, ringing laughter demonstrate Prokofiev's keen powers of observation, his ability to point up, good-naturedly, people's individual traits. We are thinking now of Frosya and Mikolka in *Semyon Kotko,* Mercutio and the Nurse in *Romeo and Juliet,* the coachman Balaga in *War and Peace,* Don Mendoza and Don Jerome in *The Duenna,* and the swaggering courtiers in *Cinderella.* And finally, there is the true apotheosis of exultant laughter in the finale of the Fifth Symphony. As a poet of the comic, an observer of life, and a master of satiric portraiture, Prokofiev continued in his own distinctive way the traditions of Russian realistic art.

The historico-epic themes so strong in Russian art were also treated in a fresh manner in Prokofiev's music. The composer in many respects "modernized" the approach to the musical depiction of Russia's past. The mind and temper of a twentieth-century Russian artist can certainly be felt in the battle scenes of *Alexander Nevsky* and *Ivan the Terrible,* as well as in the finest epic pages of *War and Peace*; for other examples one need only recall the stirring chorus "Arise, Ye Russian People" or the gripping scene of "The Battle on the Ice," with its sharp clashes and graphic action. This music unquestionably has much in common with the epic pages of nineteenth-century Russian music, but at the same time the rhythms, the formal structure, and the approach to the past are quite different. This probably reflects the era of the motion picture, the era of swift tempos and new techniques. Despite the more resilient and incisive rhythms, the new methods of orchestration, and the distinctive harmonic idiom, however, one can always recognize a modern artist who is continuing the traditions of the Five.

In a number of his works Prokofiev displayed the special skill of a painter-historian, the ability to bring to life various periods of the past. In this he elaborated to some extent the favorite tendencies of the World of Art movement. His music reproduced scenes of ancient Rome (*Egyptian Nights*), thirteenth-century Novgorod (*Alexander Nevsky*), Renaissance Italy (*Romeo and Juliet*), the St. Petersburg of Tsar Paul I (*Lieutenant Kije*), and the life of a Ural stone-cutter in the early nineteenth century (*The Stone Flower*). But at the same time, in his depictions of the past, Prokofiev shunned the approach of an antiquarian. He neither hid behind a screen of musical quotations, nor reveled in archaism and simulated the styles of the past; he recounted the past as a modern artist, re-creating from a twentieth-century point of view. This was how he portrayed the sanctimonious Teutonic knights in *Alexander Nevsky*—without actual musical quotations, but with the utmost expressiveness and vividness. As a result of this, in Prokofiev's best works the spirit of the past seems to come alive in the present, and characters from the past (Juliet, Natasha, and the warriors in *Alexander Nevsky,* for example) seem to become people of our own time.

₩ ₩ ₩

Although Prokofiev never formulated a particular system, his music unquestionably has its own laws, its own specific logic. His expressive means were extremely individual and original. It is no easy task to analyze Prokofiev's musical style, and probably only a great collective effort will make possible a thorough and comprehensive analysis.[21] We shall endeavor to confine ourselves to a few very brief observations.

Many features of Prokofiev's style grew out of his rejection of the musical trends which had preceded him, as a protest against moribund clichés and uninspired imitation. To counteract the overrefined and vacillating harmonies, the nervous, capricious rhythms and diffuse colors, he created music that was clear, restrained, straightforward, and vigorous. To counteract the empty philosophizing, intellectual abstractions, and psychological haziness, he strove for vivid description and realistic, almost visual musical images.

Both in his early and later years, Prokofiev's themes were often derived from his own direct observation of life. In his music, we hear the inflections of human speech in cries of indignation, entreaties, and sneers; we find the rhythms of vigorous movement, a fierce scuffle or a swift chase, and portrayals of characteristic gestures and dance steps. All of Prokofiev's impressions from nature, skillfully translated into music, entered into the fabric of his works, "ponderous, rock-rough, age-grim"—as real as life itself. A sudden rush or outcry in the melody, spare but clear-cut beats of rhythm, brilliantly pictorial patches of tone color, or an unexpected change of harmony frequently communicate more than a long array of pretty ornaments and embellishments.

Prokofiev's response to the world of reality also manifested itself in his lifelong inclination toward dynamically saturated musical forms, in which he attempted to capture the tempo of contemporary life. This accounts for his striving after brevity, economy, and terse musical expression. In his music there is no redundancy, no emotional diffuseness. Each thematic idea is set forth concisely and firmly rounded out with a distinctly stated cadence. Prokofiev disliked drawn-out endings and lengthy codas. The finales of his operatic scenes and instrumental pieces are always charged with action.

473

He maintained that "the end of a movement is as important as its themes or its development section."[22]

Prokofiev's pursuit of dynamic musical forms can also be seen in his use of extremely sharp contrasts. In his compositions, images of bright dreams and romantic transports at times clash violently with images of wild rage or impudent mockery. The juxtaposition of tender lyricism and tense, passionate drama, which characterizes many of Prokofiev's non-program pieces, enables us to distinguish the dualism in his personality, the Eusebius and Florestan come to life in the musical soil of the twentieth century. Similar emotional contrasts were also typical of Mayakovsky's early poetry:

> If you like—
> I'll be furious flesh elemental,
> —or changing to tones that the sunset arouses,—
> if you like—
> I'll be extraordinarily gentle,
> not a man, but—a cloud in trousers!

There is much in Prokofiev's musical language that sounds simpler, clearer, and more straightforward than the refined, elegant language of the impressionists. But this simplicity is of a special kind. He aimed at expressing his ideas in a way that would be not only simple but original.[23] And it is for this reason that we find the unusual combination of extremely simple and extremely complex elements in his music. For example, he often combined deliberately simplified, clear-cut rhythms with unusually pungent harmonies. On the other hand, if using a harmonic structure that was simple and classically clear, he would introduce unexpected modulations, sometimes to distant keys. He would sometimes enliven an extremely simple, almost schematic form with original combinations of harmonies.

Throughout his life Prokofiev worked hard and persistently to revitalize the melodic structure of contemporary music. "I love melody very much. I consider it the most important element in music, and I have been striving to improve its quality in my works for many years," the composer asserted.[24] It was particularly in the realm of melody that he had a fear of banality and passive imitation. "A composer must be careful to keep the melody simple and comprehensible without permitting it to become imitative or trivial," he wrote.

In the best of Prokofiev's early works, one can see evidence of an interest in returning to the clarity and precision of classical melodic writing. This concern doubtless grew in reaction to the ruinous "overwhelming of melody by harmony," which characterized, for example, the later music of Scriabin. The most important element in most of Prokofiev's large instrumental works is the well-defined melodic line, which, just as in eighteenth-century music, is often constructed on the elementary foundation of simple major and minor triads. But for all their outward "classicism," one almost invariably finds in these themes unexpected melodic turns and harmonic modulations which immediately reveal the composer's distinctively modern touch.

In the realm of melody, just as in rhythm and harmony, Prokofiev often juxtaposes the simplest and most traditional classical patterns with the sharpest, most angular ones. Who is not familiar with his typically broken themes with their sudden leaps, which at times seem unmelodic? Distortion and exaggeration of the melodic line were used either to mock and caricature or to emphasize powerful emotions. Thus, the eerie-sounding interval of the ninth is found in many themes connected with grief and despair (such as the death theme in *Romeo and Juliet,* the funeral theme in *Semyon Kotko,* and so on).

Fear of lapsing into either triviality or sentimentality sometimes led the composer to concoct melodies that were complicated with artificial chromatic progressions, as in certain works of the foreign period, or melodies that were deliberately over-simplified but not logically developed, as in some of the mass songs. In such cases Prokofiev obviously indulged his desire for originality at the expense of any natural development of melodic ideas.

Although he possessed a surperb ability to create broad and sweeping melodies (for example, the opening theme of the First Violin Concerto and the Andante of the Fourth Sonata), in his youth Prokofiev seldom made use of flowing melodies, but confined himself instead to brief and succinct melodic formulas. The complexities and contradictions of his experimentation with melody are particularly evident in his vocal music. His operas contain a great deal of interesting and original vocal writing—especially of dynamic and novel recitative, based almost entirely on conversational prose texts. Yet Prokofiev's deliberate rejection of the natural song forms, his inclination toward an instrumental type of melody, and his preference for keen and pointed declamatory details over broadly conceived melody detracted considerably from the melodic richness of most of his operatic works.

During the Soviet period Prokofiev's interest in lofty subjects and themes in a lyrico-romantic or epic vein made it necessary for him to give greater attention to melody, to a more natural and truthful embodiment of human emotions. It was during these years that his rich melodic gifts found full expression and won him recognition as one of the most prolific melodists of our day. Melodies of a highly lyrical or epic character play a noticeably larger role in *Romeo and Juliet, Alexander Nevsky, Cinderella,* the Seventh Symphony, and *The Stone Flower.*

When using natural, song-like themes, Prokofiev often enhances them by introducing wide intervalic leaps (sixths, sevenths, ninths, and even elevenths) or by reducing them to smoothly flowing chromatic lines. These themes are enriched by syncopated rhythms and also by novel modulations, which do not upset the original tonality but merely give it a more varied character. Tonal shifts to a half tone above or below, to a minor third or an augmented fourth, are also distinctive features of Prokofiev's themes. It is by these shifts that he creates sudden changes of color, from the dark tonalities to the bright, and it is this color transformation that gives his melodies their singular charm.

An equally important characteristic of Prokofiev's melodies is their very wide range, which sometimes extends from the middle registers of an instrument to its highest, most transparent sonorities. Examples of this exist in the themes of the third movement of the Fifth Symphony, and the second theme of the first movement of the Second Violin Concerto, which covers a range of two octaves. Placed as they are in delicate, flute-like registers, these melodies acquire a tender, feminine quality.[25]

At times such themes are stated in spare unisons or entrusted to solo instruments. They have scarcely any chordal support, and sound thin and fragile over a modest accompanying voice or a faint tremolo. This is typical, particularly of themes expressing the first awakening of a girl's love (Cinderella's first leitmotiv, for example).

Prokofiev seldom employed the whining chromaticism, melodic embroidery, and drawn-out, endlessly repeated sequences so typical of romantic music. His melodies more often contain intervals of the third and the sixth, and sometimes even the circle of fifths and pentatonic formulas. In other cases he employed techniques typical of classical vocal writing, such as the embellishment of his melodies with trills. Because Prokofiev avoided the melodic turns common to the music of Liszt, Tchaikovsky, and Rachmaninov, many of his melodies at first seem too restrained and have no immediate appeal for the listener. But greater familiarity with the music can make this lack of appeal seem relatively unimportant. Those innovations in melody that were not contrived but inspired by genuine feeling proved to be of lasting value. This is true above all of Prokofiev's lyrical melodies.

In Prokofiev's later works, alongside themes of an intensely lyrical nature, one encounters an increasing number of contemplative themes associated with ideas of meditation and deep reflection. In his works for the theater, such themes directly express a character's state of mind, his thought, or his temperament. We find examples of this in Semyon Kotko's theme of reflection and Friar Laurence's theme in *Romeo and Juliet*. To the same category belong analogous themes in the instrumental works, beginning with *Thoughts* and the Andante of the First Quartet and ending with the middle episodes in the Adagio and the Finale of the Fifth Symphony. These themes are characterized by measured rhythm and modest movement in unison or parallel octaves without harmonic support, and they are mostly entrusted to the lower voices. Their harmonic coloring is also simple and straightforward, with clearly stressed supporting major and minor tonalities (or their alternate keys).

The abundance of pure, singing melodies, mostly Russian in style, which appeared in his later works, was also a new thing for Prokofiev. However familiar the melodic turns of these clear, predominantly choral themes may be, they clearly reveal the composer's distinctive manner. Wide intervals of the sixth, octave, and ninth serve to heighten even more the free-flowing quality of the slow, sustained Russian song. The simple and unassuming melodic material is sometimes reinforced by novel harmonic treatment in the various verses or other parts of a song. We find examples of this in the choruses from *Alexander Nevsky, Ivan the Terrible,* the principal melody of *Zdravitsa,* and the second theme of the *Russian Overture.* Traditional, typically Russian melodic figures also appear in the most important themes of the later instrumental works, such as the Fifth, Sixth, and Seventh Symphonies, the Violin Sonata, Op. 80, and *The Stone Flower.*

A distinguishing characteristic of many of Prokofiev's melodies is their sharpness of contour, in which the most typical features of a given image are deliberately exaggerated. Like a caricaturist, Prokofiev deftly captured the essence of whatever he was portraying—for example, the dull, automaton-like character of the Teutonic knights (the theme of the Crusaders' invasion in *Alexander Nevsky*), the cold formality of the barracks drill (the march in *Lieutenant Kije*), and recklessness and drunken daring (Severyan's theme in *The Stone Flower*).

Many themes of this type grow out of Prokofiev's caricatural treatment of the inflections of the human voice or the melodies of a song (the themes of Don Mendoza and the coachman Balaga, for example). We also find exaggeration of typical melodic figures in most of Prokofiev's dances, such as the "Dance of the Masks" in *Romeo and Juliet* and the waltz in the fourth scene of *War and Peace*. In the former case, the exaggeration serves to make the dance sound jaunty and grotesque, and in the latter to enliven the typical features of an old-fashioned waltz.

Prokofiev was no less an innovator in the sphere of harmony. His unique harmonic idiom is a particularly distinctive feature of his style, albeit a somewhat difficult one for the uninitiated to understand. Prokofiev enriched the expressive possibilities of modern harmony with such valuable innovations as unusual modulations, skillful, effective use of cadences (deceptive cadences, unexpected transitions to distant tonalities), fresh chordal combinations of a descriptive character, and a subtle use of diatonic harmony. In contradistinction to the infatuation with the "harmonic vertical," he boldly brought out the melodic nature of harmony; hence the spare and ascetic harmonic texture, the inner activation of the vocal lines by mobile basses, the incidental emphasis on leading tones, etc.

It goes without saying that not all of Prokofiev's harmonic innovations have withstood the test of time. Some of his attempts proved to be little more than interesting experiments. But the features that became firmly fixed in his harmonic idiom, especially in the last two decades of his creative life, constitute a valuable contribution to contemporary harmonic language.

Many elements in Prokofiev's harmonic idiom are striking in their deliberate simplicity. He did not hesitate to use the most ordinary and commonplace harmonies, but he always treated them in a new way, presenting them in unusual combinations. After the unprecedented, complex harmonies of the impressionists, Prokofiev demonstratively returned to the simplest and clearest tonalities, to the transparent C major (one of his most frequently used keys), to B-flat major, D major, and the commonest minor keys. But these clear and simple basic tonalities are always combined with strikingly unusual incidental and transitional chord combinations, and given rich modulatory development. Sometimes in his use of the familiar C major, we come upon so many transitions to distant keys and so many fresh harmonies that it appears as an entirely new and enriched tonality.

Unlike the atonalists, who seek to destroy the tonal foundations of music, Prokofiev consistently advocated clear-cut, functional harmony.

"The construction of a composition on a tonal basis may be compared to building on rock, whereas construction without a tonal basis is like building on sand," he maintained. "Tonal and diatonic music has much greater possibilities than music that is atonal and chromatic."[26]

Still, Prokofiev deliberately used dissonant harmonies, especially when they seemed necessary for descriptive purposes. We are familiar with Prokofiev's characteristically dissonant harmonic clusters, consisting of combinations of discordant sounds. Chord combinations of this kind are employed chiefly in episodes depicting the terrible, cruel, and ugly sides of life. In many cases these instances of atonality and polytonality comprise only relatively short episodes which are superseded by clear diatonic music.

Polyphony plays an important role in Prokofiev's harmonic style. Many dissonant harmonies emerge from the crossing of two or more horizontal lines and sometimes even of two different successions of chords. Side by side with the coarse-sounding harmonic clusters, we find pure diatonic harmonies, which are very refined in sonority but which have their deepest roots in Russian folk song.

During the Soviet period Prokofiev evolved a lighter harmonic style. As the melodic element became more important, the composer's interest in vertical harmony waned. His richly tonal melodies no longer needed complicated chordal support. The texture was reduced to unisons, to modest two-voice writing, or to a transparent, freely interwoven polyphony in which the bass and inner voices acquired independence of movement.

Prokofiev's typical combinations of harmonies took on a clearly defined function; they acquired an associative meaning. There was nothing new in this. Contrasting harmonies had long been employed for descriptive purposes in Russian music (for example, in *Ruslan and Ludmila, Sadko,* and *The Queen of Spades*). The bewitching harmonies of the "underwater kingdom" and the spellbinding whole-tone formations of Kashchei's sorcery are quite different from the pure major-minor harmonies employed by Rimsky-Korsakov in his genre and lyrical scenes. The same use of contrast can clearly be seen in many of Prokofiev's concert and theatrical works. Different types of dramatic action, different aspects of life are expressed by different harmonic means.

Prokofiev, as a rule, employs a firm tonal structure both in genre and lyrical images inspired by everyday life (songs and dances) and in depicting the emotions of real people. Time and again such pages are written in the composer's bright diatonic harmonies—in his favorite key of C major, enriched by digressions to distant keys, reinforced and "seasoned," as it

479

were, by pungent harmonies foreign to the tonic key. Sudden shifts to any degree of the scale (for example, chords of D-flat major, C-sharp minor, D minor, E-flat major, G-sharp minor, F-sharp major, all within the key of C major) only sharpen and add color to the tonality without robbing it of its character. After these wanderings to distant keys, the return to the tonic has a special, colorful charm.

The typically Prokofievan chains of parallel triads and unresolved seventh chords are in the nature of chordal scales, formed as a result of the independent harmonization of each note of the melody. The tonal digressions most frequently used to enrich otherwise harmonically colorless episodes are those to the augmented fourth and the diminished second, as well as the juxtaposition of major keys a major third apart. We repeatedly find juxtapositions of similar major and minor tonalities. In his lyrical themes, this sort of chiaroscuro is marked by the subtlest nuances.

Prokofiev had other favorite means of enriching his harmony. An example of this is his frequent use of incidental, unrelated tones, which add color and sharpen the sound of ordinary triads; by the addition of these tones the independent chromatic movement of each voice is strengthened in every possible way. "Each and every voice is considered a distinct tonal center, around which is grouped one or another of the tones related to it," Asafyev noted.[27] Sometimes the composer uses these means of harmonic alteration to make the repetition of a musical section more dynamic. If, for example, the theme is first stated in pure, major harmonies, these harmonies are later altered by means of added accidentals (see the beginning of the return of the first section in the second movement of the Fifth Symphony). This endows the repeat with a new emotional meaning. What sounded the first time like the expression of natural human emotion, when repeated, sounds distorted. Certain harmonically altered chords, such as the tonic triad with the addition of an augmented fourth, were used by Prokofiev time and again as a variant of the tonic. This typical device appears particularly in his gay, carnival dance themes. Sometimes the tonic chord includes the leading tone as a kind of "sticking" grace note.

It is more difficult to analyze the harmonies which Prokofiev used to portray somberly expressive or coarsely archaic images. These harsh and terrifying "polytonal" episodes cannot always be analyzed by conventional standards. In these cases we find, for example, major triads joined at the interval of an augmented fourth, or major and minor triads at the interval of an augmented or diminished second. It is more correct to regard such harmonies merely as coloristic, descriptive "chordal clusters."

In other cases polytonal devices are used for purely pictorial purposes, to create the effect of distance by presenting its rather distorted sound perspective. There is no doubt that diatonic chords built at intervals of the fifth acquire a polytonal character. When they include almost all of the tones of the diatonic scale, such chords sound barbaric and harsh (see, for example, the opening theme of the Kabardinian Quartet). Therefore, it is possible to establish two types of diatonic writing in Prokofiev's music: gentle, bright "Russian diatonicism," formed by alternating harmonies; and harsh diatonicism, formed by multiple layers of fifths (or fourths).

With respect to the purely coloristic aspect of Prokofiev's harmony, we might point to his frequently unusual placement of the tones in a chord. Open chords, made up of widely spaced intervals, with a vast expanse between the lower and upper voices, create a somber, desolate atmosphere.[28] On the other hand, when the tones of a chord are very close together, almost fusing it into a compact blotch, a ringing, metallic effect results. Here, just as in the previously mentioned use of the very high and very low registers to extend the range of the melodic line, purely acoustical effects are created.

Prokofiev's sharply expressive and fantastic images at times contain elements of amplified tonality. Especially characteristic here is the cult of the tritone: as a sustained harmony in the bass; as "sound that is stuck" in a tonic major triad; and as a succession of sounds in an *ostinato* figure. Finally, there are frequent juxtapositions of tritones, including imitation of voices at the distance of a tritone (as in the development section of the first movement of the Sixth Piano Sonata).

When episodes are harmonically complicated, Prokofiev almost invariably simplifies the other musical elements—rhythm, texture, and the melodic structure. This combination of complex and extremely simple means is very effective—as in the main theme of the first movement of the Seventh Sonata, for example. Its harmonic complexity is relieved by its modest two-voice texture, clear-cut tarantella rhythm, and persistently repeated melodic motivs. Here propulsive rhythms and pungent phonic effects are the principal expressive means, with melody relegated to a secondary role. This combination of expressive means is the one that Prokofiev uses mainly in episodes depicting sinister, mechanical images.

Certainly we should mention Prokofiev's distinctive, varied, and expressive rhythms. In many of his early works, the composer attached a great deal of importance to sharp, resilient rhythms and swift tempos. His love for rectilinear, rough-hewn rhythms and chiseled march time was particularly noted by his contemporaries. At that time the composer believed that, unlike music of the past, modern music could best express the spirit of the times in vigorous rhythms and fast tempos. "While 100 to 150 years ago our predecessors were attracted by merry pastorals and the music of Mozart and Rameau, and in the last century they admired slow, serious tempos," he wrote, "in our time, in music as in everything else, it is speed, vigor, and dash that are preferred."[29] In accordance with this urbanist notion, the young Prokofiev was often drawn to propulsive rhythms as ends in themselves. In his more mature years, however, he himself called this the least important element in his music.

There is much in Prokofiev's rhythms that strikes one as a bold challenge to the rhythmic anemia of the impressionists. Prokofiev turned from the ultrarefined, vacillating rhythms of the impressionists and the late Scriabin to accented, well-defined rhythms. His partiality for 4/4 time (marches and gavottes), 6/8 time (tarantella-like themes), and various kinds of triple meter and basic rhythms is generally known. In using the traditional, clear-cut dance patterns and the ceaseless motion of the *perpetuum mobile,* it is as if he were deliberately returning to the stock devices of the classical period.

But as in the case of other elements of his style, the young Prokofiev's rhythms are, at times, a combination of quite opposite extremes: the most simplified patterns, crudely archaic or primitive in the manner of children's games, and sharply accentuated, nervous rhythmic figures, abounding in spasmodic dashes, *tirate,* and sudden splashes of motion.

During the last twenty years of his career, as the lyrical and melodic elements in his music became enormously enriched, Prokofiev less often gave primary importance to purely rhythmic effects. Rhythm played a much less important role in the lyrical, contemplative themes. On the other hand, in the terrifying, grotesque episodes incisive rhythms still predominated, sometimes seeming almost hypnotic in their relentless persistence, at other times captivating for their playful mischievousness. Very often a modest melody and complex harmonic texture are accompanied by vigorous, straightforward rhythms. Predominance of the rhythmic element is clear in the finales of Prokofiev's Seventh and Eighth Piano Sonatas and in such purely descriptive episodes as the "Battle on the Ice" in *Alexander Nevsky* and in "Alarm" in *Egyptian Nights.*

Dance rhythms continued to play a large role in Prokofiev's later works —2/4 and 4/4 time (marches, gavottes) and 3/4 and 6/8 time (waltzes and tarantellas). It is not only in his ballets that Prokofiev used dance rhythms; they also predominate in the portrayals of some of his operatic characters, such as Truffaldino in *The Love for Three Oranges,* Frosya and Mikola in *Semyon Kotko,* and the dancing Don Jerome in *The Duenna.* The intoxicating atmosphere of festive ensemble dances also pervades his instrumental works, notably in the finales of some of the symphonies and concertos.

As the melodic element assumed more importance, polyphony also began to play a more important role in Prokofiev's music. His polyphony has distinctly individual features, however. The composer by no means adhered to the strict rules of classical counterpoint—hence his disagreement in principle with Stravinsky's neo-Bachism.

Prokofiev was not interested in pure, vigorous linear writing with its prevalence of absolute melos. His polyphony was derived to some extent from the method of contrapuntal improvisation found in Russian folk music. He often employed simple auxiliary voices, which spring forth freely and spontaneously, to strengthen or enhance the harmonic structure of the melody. This explains the predominance in Prokofiev's music of elements of free, contrasting polyphony over strict, imitative polyphony.

Prokofiev's style of polyphonic writing was often dictated by the peculiarities of his piano texture, and sometimes even of his orchestral texture, which in many instances is reduced to the simplest two-part writing, in the style of early classical music. The mobility and rhythmic freedom of the bass voice and the frequent use of a sustained *ostinato* movement combine to form a flexible polyphonic fabric.

In his instrumental and operatic works Prokofiev often combines the most important themes and musical ideas contrapuntally. At times such counterpoint acquires an almost visual expressiveness somewhat reminiscent of film montage. Numerous examples of this kind of interweaving of themes are to be found in *Alexander Nevsky* ("The Battle on the Ice" and the Finale), as well as in *Peter and the Wolf* (the final procession). In his sonatas and symphonies these techniques serve to dramatize the development sections or to make the recapitulations more powerful. The finale of the Fifth Symphony is a brilliant example of this.

The *basso ostinato* is another typical polyphonic device that plays an important role in Prokofiev's music. However, he never employs the *basso ostinato* as a sustained foundation for strict variations (as in the passacaglia, a form repeatedly used by Shostakovich). Prokofiev's manner of employing ostinatos has its roots in national tradition, particularly in the droning organ points so typical of Borodin. The endlessly reiterated pattern in the bass serves to brighten the harmony and give continuous support to the rhythmic pulsation. In the operas the *ostinato* patterns not only enliven the musical texture with their pulsating movement, but also serve a meaningful contrapuntal function in entire episodes (the episode of the mad Lyubka in the third scene of *Semyon Kotko* and that of the drunken monk in the eighth scene of *The Duenna*).

The classical quality of Prokofiev's music is clearly evident in his choice of form. The most widely used classical forms—the sonata, the one-movement symphonic poem, the rondo-sonata, variations, complicated three-part forms—are generously represented in his instrumental music. Throughout his life, Prokofiev was especially interested in the perennially vital, classical sonata allegro form. In an interview in 1918, he called sonata form "the most flexible musical form." In using this established form, however, he always filled it with fresh, original content, charged with emotion and action and free of the clichés of externally decorative ornamentation.

While he preserves the basic properties of the classical forms, Prokofiev often modifies some of their characteristic features. Examples of this are the methods he almost invariably employs to alter the recapitulation. He may conceive the recapitulation as a continuation of the development section (as in the Third Sonata), or he may combine the themes contrapuntally (as in the Andante of the Fourth Sonata and the Finale of the First Violin Concerto). In other cases, by sharply condensing it, he may transform it into a sort of recapitulation and coda rolled into one. Sometimes he follows the example of the romantics and either reduces the sonata cycle to one movement (as in the First Piano Concerto) or treats his themes as leitmotivs (reminiscences of themes from the first movements in the finales of the Second and Sixth Sonatas and the Seventh Symphony). And even when he does adhere strictly to the sonata form, he enlivens it with unusual tonal relationships, such as digressions to the augmented fourth or the minor second above or below.

Prokofiev constructs his vocal works very freely, completely subordinating their form to the demands of the text. He only rarely attempts to achieve a formal unity, as he did by using the principal theme as a refrain in *The Wizard* and *The Ugly Duckling*.

In Prokofiev's early instrumental pieces, such as the First Piano Concerto and the Second Sonata, one notes a tendency to construct "composites" from a series of individual musical episodes. This cinematographic technique of development is particularly apparent in his instrumental compositions for the theater (such as *The Buffoon*). In such works the fragmentary nature of the form, with its excessive dependence on the program, is to some degree compensated for by the vivid characterizations and dynamic flow of the music. The best of Prokofiev's later works (the Second Violin Concerto, the Fifth and Seventh Symphonies) reveal an organic formal unity based on the principle of development rather than the mechanical combination of contrasting fragments.

Prokofiev's frequent use of traditional forms, however, did not prevent him from searching for new and effective means of expression. During his last creative period he composed, in addition to sonatas and symphonies, a vocal-symphonic cycle which is structurally quite original (*Alexander Nevsky*); a children's symphonic tale, a new genre calling for the participation of a narrator (*Peter and the Wolf*); and large-scale instrumental works based on folk themes (the *Russian Overture* and the Kabardinian Quartet). This same creative search is clearly demonstrated in the field of opera, where Prokofiev persistently attempted to enrich traditional forms.

A few words should be said about some of the basic features of Prokofiev's orchestral and piano style. The most original of Prokofiev's early scores were the *Scythian Suite* and *The Buffoon*. In these works the composer definitely rejected the techniques employed by the academic composers, with their emphasis on orchestral balance and careful voice-leading. Here Prokofiev's music is distinguished by its unusually exaggerated orchestral sonorities, which are strident and thick and almost always used for descriptive purposes. What stands out in these scores is their density and complexity, their innumerable organ points, long-drawn *ostinato* sonorities, and percussive, onomatopoeic sound effects.

Prokofiev's orchestration is as colorful as his harmonic texture. His scores abound in harsh instrumental combinations, mixtures of tone colors used to achieve various dramatic or grotesque effects. "What difference does it make how the composer creates the impression of horror, whether by two blows on a drum, three notes of a clarinet, or a prolonged melody played by the violins? If it conveys horror, there is nothing more to be said," wrote one foreign critic about Prokofiev's orchestration.

In rejecting the soft colors of the impressionist orchestra, Prokofiev often employed deliberately coarse and harsh sonorities. The metallic timbres of the brasses (the high-pitched brasses in the finale of the *Scythian Suite*), a very complex array of percussion instruments, the dry, brittle sonority of the piano, and graphically descriptive devices in the strings (*col legno, sul ponticello, pizzicato*)—these are the effects he repeatedly used in his scoring.

Great contrasts in method are as characteristic of Prokofiev's orchestration as of all the other aspects of his style. Thus, along with the compli-

485

cated conglomerations of tone color in the *Scythian Suite,* he also created the transparent score of the *Classical Symphony,* constructed on pure solo timbres. The tendency toward pure timbres, toward an economical and even sparse use of orchestral color became more marked in Prokofiev's later works. Grotesque, eccentric orchestration gave way with increasing frequency to refined, transparent scoring. *Romeo and Juliet, Cinderella,* the Seventh Symphony, and other works that are among his finest scores contain many charming solo passages (tenderly singing flute, clarinet, and cello solos). On the other hand, many of his works of an epic nature reveal a continuing predilection for severe, thick timbres and overemphasized bass sonorities.

Prokofiev's piano writing reveals a similarly strong reaction against the refinements of impressionism. After the very delicate, filmy timbres which characterized certain pieces by Debussy and the late Scriabin, he returned demonstratively to the piano style of the classical epoch, accentuating the instrument's percussive qualities. Unlike the no less substantial but richly ornamented and sumptuous piano style of Rachmaninov, Prokofiev's piano style is spare and economical. While Rachmaninov's piano writing is colorfully baroque in texture, Prokofiev's is simple and pure, often with only two or three voices or parallel movement in octaves.

The technique of skips and hand-crossings in his pieces is strongly reminiscent of the tradition of Domenico Scarlatti; his light scale passages spring from the piano style of Haydn and the early Beethoven. Prokofiev very often used such toccata-like effects as alternating chords between the right and left hand (examples of which are found in Liszt and Balakirev), accentuated nonlegato passages, and so on. In contrast to the typically pianistic "urbanistic" elements of his style, we encounter beautiful and very natural lyrical cantilena, and sometimes even unexpected echoes of the impressionist style in blurred, vaporous runs and richly sonorous chords.

Prokofiev's declamatory vocal style and the idiosyncrasies of his operatic dramaturgy are of special interest. Here, too, he avoided the beaten path; he tirelessly invented and experimented in an effort to broaden the expressive possibilities of the operatic genre. His recitative, based on a flexible reproduction of the natural inflections of Russian speech, represents a new departure in our national music. Of considerable interest are his attempts to create through-composed operatic scenes, built on continuous and swift musical and dramatic action. Many of his experiments in this sphere suffered from nihilistic extremes. His quest for realistic and dynamic operatic action often led him to ignore the essentially lyrical nature of opera and avoid the traditional vocal forms. The result of this was a certain musical formlessness, of which we have cited many examples in the individual analyses of Prokofiev's operas.

The evolution of Prokofiev's operatic style from *The Gambler* and *The Love for Three Oranges* to the new version of *War and Peace* shows that he gradually overcame the excesses of his attempts at operatic "reforms" and turned to combining natural vocal declamation with finished, melodically integrated episodes. This was the path from naturalistic experimentation to a genuine operatic realism.

☙ ☙ ☙

There was a time when Prokofiev's early style was likened to the leftist trends in the plastic arts between 1910 and 1930. It was said that his incisive rhythms, the marked materiality and harshness of his harmonic and orchestral means, and his deliberate rejection of romantically "beautiful" lines were related to the latest tendencies in modern painting, sculpture, and architecture. There was unquestionably some truth in this parallel.

But those who believed that Prokofiev's antiromanticism was the basic element of his style were mistaken. Actually, behind the stunning constructivist innovations that astounded listeners in the *Scythian Suite* and the first piano concertos, one could also discern charming lyrical melody, original and fresh harmonic thought, skillful characterization, and telling descriptive devices. It was these qualities, so strikingly displayed in Prokofiev's early piano music, that later became firmly established in his work, almost entirely crowding out the earlier leftist excesses.

The effect of a different life in different social conditions helped the composer to revise substantially his artistic credo and expressive means. The former rebel, who had once preferred swift rhythms and teasing, pungent harmonies to openly expressed emotion, now turned to the portrayal of real human emotions, to scenes from nature, life, and history, and to glorification of the beauty and majesty of the real world.

Everything that was most natural and alive in the lyrical and humorous pages of his early music flourished brilliantly and was wonderfully enriched. The sharply expressive effects of a grotesque image or a tense and tragic character, which had at times been only ends in themselves, were now employed to depict various aspects of reality. Utterly new musical means of a specifically national character, so unusual in the music of the young Prokofiev, were richly used in the epic pages of his music.

It is still too early to speak of Prokofiev's works as classics; his music is too firmly rooted in the present. There are still many heated discussions about the composer in both professional and amateur circles. His compositions have not yet taken their place on the shelves among the collections of universally accepted and revered works. Many of them must be played again and again, heard and evaluated anew from the perspective of our day. Only then will it be possible to define more precisely which of the compositions born of passing fashion will be relegated to obscurity, and which will rightfully become part of Russia's immortal classical heritage.

Unfortunately, there are musicians among us who even now are afraid of the "unusualness" of Prokofiev's music, who appreciate only what has long been accepted and unchallenged. Without taking the trouble to look carefully into the rich world of Prokofiev's lyricism, they try to convince us that Prokofiev is too cold, too matter-of-fact, too unemotional. They frown; they are pained by the unusual twists of the melodies and the biting harmonies. They forget that other musical conformists once turned away just as scornfully from the music of Moussorgsky and Borodin, Liszt and Wagner, Scriabin and Ravel.

The best of Prokofiev's music should be performed more often, more widely, and with keener interest. Then its beauty will become more comprehensible, and the number of its admirers and adherents will grow immeasurably. The experience of the ballet and opera companies in preparing *Romeo and Juliet, Cinderella,* and *War and Peace* has proved that the more performers delve into this music, the more enamored they become of it, the more aware they become of its vibrant human qualities. The dedicated performer who gives a vital interpretation of an accomplished new work conquers his audience and inspires it with a love for new art. Thus it is that through the efforts of the outstanding artists of the Bolshoi Theater *Romeo and Juliet* is becoming one of the favorite ballets in the modern repertory.

Prokofiev's music belongs to our epoch and not only to posterity. Let us study it more carefully, play it more widely, and make it accessible to the millions of ordinary people for whom this great Russian musician worked so selflessly. And the more fully we comprehend Prokofiev's masterpieces, the clearer will it become that a great artist lived and worked among us, an artist of whom Soviet culture can be justly proud.

# NOTES

# NOTES

CHAPTER ONE

1. A bound edition of the piano score with a printed inscription *"The Giant,* Opera in Three Acts. Composed by Seryozhenka Prokofiev" is in the Central State Archives of Literature and Art [Moscow], Collection of 1929.

2. Communicated to the present writer by G. B. Beriandt.

3. April 11, 1903.

4. These songs are among Prokofiev's childhood manuscripts preserved in the Central State Archives of Literature and Art.

CHAPTER TWO

1. From B. V. Asafyev's unpublished book, "Thoughts and Reflections."

2. *Sovetskaya Muzyka,* No. 4, 1941.

3. V. Walter, "Lyadov as Teacher," in *A. K. Lyadov* (Petrograd, 1916).

4. L. Saminsky, "On Lyadov," *Muzyka,* No. 204, 1915.

5. Three *Ditties* of Series IV and V (*Scherzo, Minuet,* and *Waltz*) were published by the present author in a music supplement to the magazine *Sovetskaya Muzyka,* No. 12, 1954.

6. "Thoughts and Reflections," Chapter 1.

7. Materials from the archives of the St. Petersburg Conservatory, now in the State Historical Archives of Leningrad Oblast.

8. For a more detailed discussion of the activities of the Evenings of Modern Music, see the following chapter.

9. N. Ya. Miaskovsky, "Autobiographical Notes on My Creative Path," *Sovetskaya Muzyka,* No. 6, 1936.

10. V. Walter, "Lyadov as Teacher," in *A. K. Lyadov* (Petrograd, 1916).

11. The manuscript of the third and fourth acts of *Undine,* dated March–July 1907, is in the Prokofiev archives in the Central State Archives of Literature and Art.

12. From unpublished notes.

13. *Rech,* July 22, 1915.

14. *Muzyka,* No. 53, 1911.

15. *Muzyka,* No. 151, 1913.

16. From unpublished notes.

17. V. Kamensky, *Life with Mayakovsky.*

18. *Novy Den,* April 19, 1918.

19. *Rech,* Jan. 4, 1909.

20. *Slovo,* January 2, 1909.

21. Music note signed "M." in *Muzyka,* No. 94, 1912.

22. April 4, 1912.

23. *Rech,* June 11, 1915.

24. December 19, 1915.

25. Letter to Asafyev, May 23, 1925.

26. Music note signed "A. Versilov" in *K Novym Beregam,* No. 3, 1923.

27. *Russkoye Slovo,* March 8, 1910.

28. *Rech,* No. 339, 1912.

# Notes

### CHAPTER THREE

1. Letter to Derzhanovsky, August 17, 1914.
2. Letter to Derzhanovsky, February 10, 1915.
3. Letter to Derzhanovsky, August 25, 1913.
4. Letter to Derzhanovsky, July 15, 1913.
5. Entry of March 22, 1904. Quoted from M. Yankovsky, *Rimsky-Korsakov and the Revolution of 1905* (Moscow, 1950), p. 24.
6. Letter to Derzhanovsky, November 27, 1911.
7. Letters dated December 18 and 24, 1911.
8. On January 12, 1911.
9. Letter to Jurgenson, May 14, 1915.
10. *Golos Moskvy,* August 3, 1911.
11. Letter of October 11, 1911.
12. See M. Lieven, *Collected Plays—Astorre Trinci, Merry Friend, and Maddalena.* (St. Petersburg, published by the author.)
13. Letter of October 9, 1911. This comment was reprinted almost in full in *Muzyka,* No. 44, October 14, 1911.
14. In 1916 the Zimin Theater in Moscow considered producing *Maddalena,* but the composer was then immersed in work on *The Gambler* and no longer wished to return to his earlier opera. For a long time the manuscript of *Maddalena* was considered lost, but in 1954 it was discovered in the files of the Russian Music Publishing House in Paris.
15. Letter to Derzhanovsky, October 8, 1911.
16. Letter to Derzhanovsky, December 18, 1911.
17. *Golos Moskvy,* No. 173, 1912.
18. *Russkiye Vedomosti,* No. 173, 1912.
19. *Peterburgskaya Gazeta,* No. 213, 1912.
20. *Peterburgskiye Vedomosti,* August 18, 1912.
21. *Utro Rossii,* No. 173, 1912.
22. *Rech,* No. 212, 1912.
23. *Peterburgsky Listok,* August 18, 1912.
24. *Russkiye Vedomosti,* August 9, 1912.
25. "I laughed heartily at Sabaneyev's convolutions," he said in a letter to Ye. Zvyagintseva dated March 7, 1914.
26. Music note signed "M." in *Muzyka,* No. 94, September 21, 1912.
27. Music note signed "N.M." in *Muzyka,* No. 151, October 25, 1913.
28. *Muzyka,* January 9, 1915.
29. "From a Recent Experience," *Muzyka,* No. 249, March 25, 1916.
30. *Muzyka,* February 27, 1915.
31. *Muzyka,* October 4, 1913.
32. The manuscript of this note is in the Derzhanovsky archives (Central Museum of Musical Culture). The editors of *Muzyka* apparently decided not to publish the review because they did not want to become involved in a conflict with their regular contributor Sabaneyev. This refusal made Prokofiev angry and resentful, and almost led to a break with the editors of the magazine.
33. "Borovsky established a speed record with my Scherzo," Prokofiev remarked in a letter to Ye. Zvyagintseva, February 22, 1916.
34. From Asafyev's unpublished notes.
35. Sudden transitions of this kind from lyrical episodes to unexpected jests and whimsies are to be found later in Prokofiev's opera *The Love for Three Oranges.*

36. Letter to Derzhanovsky, March 8, 1914.
37. *Rech,* December 12, 1916.
38. Letter to Derzhanovsky, April 16, 1913.
39. Article signed "Chernogorsky" in *Teatr i Iskusstvo,* September 14, 1913.
40. Ten years later, in 1923, Prokofiev had to reorchestrate the Second Concerto, since the original manuscript of the score was lost. At the same time he also revised the piano part.
41. Letter to Derzhanovsky, September 6, 1913.
42. Feuilleton signed "Non-Critic" in *Peterburgskaya Gazeta,* September 7, 1913.
43. *Petersburgsky Listok,* September 6, 1913.
44. *Peterburgskaya Gazeta,* September 7, 1913.
45. *Novoye Vremya,* September 7, 1913.
46. N. Shebuyev in *Zritel,* December 15, 1916.
47. *Rech,* September 7, 1913.
48. Music note signed "B.AS." in *Muzyka,* February 20, 1915.
49. The charmingly graceful theme of the Second Movement of the Third Concerto, likewise composed in 1913 as "raw material" for a large-scale work, also belongs to this group of Prokofiev's lyrico-dance themes.
50. Letter to Jurgenson, May 14, 1915.
51. This letter is in the files of A. V. Ossovsky.
52. Another harp piece, which remained unpublished, was also dedicated to Eleanora, later known as the Leningrad harpist E. A. Damskaya-Tontegoda. Prokofiev's correspondence with her has been preserved.
53. *Russkiye Vedomosti,* February 7, 1914.
54. *Moskauer Deutsche Zeitung,* February 7, 1914.
55. *Muzyka,* No. 125, 1913, and No. 178, 1914.
56. Letter of April 9, 1914.
57. A friend and fellow student, V. Dranishnikov, accompanied Prokofiev at the second piano.

CHAPTER FOUR

1. Letter of November 11, 1914.
2. The facts concerning Bashkirov-Verin's salon have been drawn from E. A. Damskaya-Tontegoda's unpublished memoirs, and also from a conversation with her sister, V. A. Damskaya.
3. Letter to Derzhanovsky, November 7, 1913.
4. "Thoughts and Reflections," Chap. 12.
5. Letter to Derzhanovsky, May 24, 1914.
6. "The art of the word has, of late, discredited itself and must be assigned to the ash heap. . . . Instead, long live unthinking silence, the sacred rite of the dance," wrote Benois. (*Book on the New Theater,* published by "Shipovnik," St. Petersburg, 1908.)
7. The new version was played at a Siloti concert the following year.
8. Gorodetsky took the name Veles from mythology. "Chuzhbog" he fabricated from "Dazhdbog" [Sun God].
9. Letter to Derzhanovsky, January 25, 1915.
10. K. Chukovsky, *The Futurists* (Petrograd, 1922).
11. Quoted from A. Volkov, *Russian Literature of the Late Nineteenth and Early Twentieth Century.*

12. Letters to Derzhanovsky, June 7 and July 3, 1913.
13. A. Ostroumova-Lebedeva, *Autobiographical Notes* (Leningrad, 1935).
14. "Notes in Brief," February 6, 1916.
15. *Rech,* December 11, 1916.
16. "Notes in Brief," *Muzykalny Sovremennik,* December 22, 1916.
17. From Asafyev's unpublished notes.
18. "Thoughts and Reflections," Chap. 7.
19. January 25, 1915.
20. At the Evenings of Modern Music on January 30, 1915, with Zherebtsova-Andreyeva as soloist.
21. Letter to Derzhanovsky, February 5, 1915. By "modernists" Asafyev meant the leaders of the Petrograd magazine *Muzykalny Sovremennik,* which began to appear in 1914.
22. Letter to Derzhanovsky, February 9, 1915.
23. Review by B. Tyuneyev, February 7, 1915.
24. *Muzyka,* February 20, 1915, and *Teatr i Iskusstvo,* February 21, 1915.
25. On February 6, 1915, under the direction of N. Malko.
26. Letter to Derzhanovsky, February 8, 1915.
27. Review by Yu. Kurdyumov in *Peterburgsky Listok,* February 7, 1915.
28. Review by S. Rozovsky in *Den,* February 9, 1915.
29. *Muzyka,* No. 208, 1915.
30. Letter to Ye. Zvyagintseva, March 31, 1915.
31. *Il Messaggero,* March 6, 1915.
32. *Il Messaggero,* March 9, 1915.
33. Letter to Derzhanovsky, March 22, 1915.
34. *Muzyka,* May 1, 1915, No. 219.
35. Letter from Mayakovsky to the editor of *Nov* (*Collected Works,* I, 409).
36. A. N. Afanasyev, *Russian Folk Tales* (State Literary Publishing House, 1940, III, 206).
37. On May 2, 1915.
38. Letter of May 14, 1915.
39. *Rech,* No. 186, 1915.
40. Letter to Derzhanovsky, July 24, 1915.
41. Letters to Ye. Zvyagintseva, May 30 and July 2, 1915.
42. Letter to Derzhanovsky, July 22, 1915.
43. For many years *The Wizard* has been brilliantly performed by A. L. Dolivo.
44. Letter to Ye. Zvyagintseva, September 24, 1915. The "Little Girl" refers to *The Gray Dress.*
45. *Rech,* No. 330, December 12, 1916.
46. *Utro Rossii,* February 20, 1917.
47. Lenin, *Imperialist War* (*Collected Works,* XVIII, 96).
48. *Petrogradsky Listok,* May 17, 1915.
49. Albert Coates, the son of an English businessman, was born in St. Petersburg and was closely connected with Russian music.
50. *Vecherniye Birzheviye Vedomosti,* May 25, 1916.
51. Interview in *Vecherneye Vremya,* May 26, 1916.
52. Letters to Ye. Zvyagintseva.
53. *Vecherniye Birzheviye Vedomosti,* May 25, 1916.
54. *Teatr i Iskusstvo,* December 5, 1915.

28. Letter to Derzhanovsky, May 8, 1927.

29. In January 1956 a group of French artists presented this opera on the radio.

30. Letter to Derzhanovsky, October 26, 1927.

31. See his "Notes" in *Sovetskaya Muzyka*, No. 3, 1933.

32. "First in Philadelphia, where it failed, and later in New York with extraordinary success. There they considered it one of my important works and found that at last they had seen Prokofiev's serious side," the composer wrote Asafyev on April 9, 1932.

33. Letter to Derzhanovsky, February 12, 1929.

34. The *Divertissement* was first performed in Paris in December of 1929, with the composer conducting.

35. Review signed "K. Sh." in *Proletarsky Muzykant*, No. 1, 1929.

36. *Sovremennaya Muzyka*, No. 31 (May), 1928.

37. *Proletarsky Muzykant*, No. 6, 1929.

38. Letters to Derzhanovsky, February 18 and April 21, 1930.

39. Not having a large collection of original scores in its archives, this library, one of the most important in the United States, specially commissioned new works from noted modern composers. The Quartet received its first performance in Washington on April 25, 1931, at a special festival.

40. This work was performed in Moscow in October 1931 by the visiting Budapest String Quartet.

41. From letters to Asafyev dated October 20, 1931, and April 6, 1932.

42. Letter of September 14, 1931.

43. Letter to L. Atovmyan, November 7, 1932.

44. On November 19, 1931.

45. Letter to Asafyev, February 6, 1932.

46. Letter of April 9, 1932.

47. From an article by S. Moreux, "Through the Eyes of a Friend," published in *Musik der Zeit*, No. 5, Bonn, 1953.

48. To Derzhanovsky, September 12, 1929.

49. Letters to Derzhanovsky, August 29, 1923, and September 12, 1924.

### CHAPTER EIGHT

1. *Sovetskoye Iskusstvo*, December 3, 1932.

2. See his interview in the French journal *Comédie française* January 1933.

3. *Sovetskoye Iskusstvo*, No. 1, 1933.

4. From entries in Miaskovsky's diary, March 22, 1935, and March 9, 1941.

5. To L. T. Atovmyan, March 15, 1933.

6. *Sovetskaya Muzyka*, No. 3, 1933.

7. *Sovetskoye Iskusstvo*, November 27, 1932.

8. *Vechernaya Moskva*, December 6, 1932.

9. V. I. Lenin, *Collected Works*, Vol. IV, Book 2, p. 97 (New York: International Publishers, 1929).

10. Letter to Derzhanovsky, August 22, 1934.

11. Letter of July 31, 1932.

12. Letter to Derzhanovsky, February 8, 1934.

13. *Essays on Soviet Musical Works* (Moscow, 1947) p. 286.

14. *Teatr i Dramaturgiya*, No. 8, 1936.

55. *Vecherniye Birzheviye Vedomosti*, January 29, 1916.

56. On January 31, 1916.

57. Letter to Ye. Zvyaginsteva, January 30, 1915.

58. January 31, 1916.

59. February 1, 1916.

60. "Notes in Brief," *Muzykalny Sovremennik*, February 6, 1916.

61. *Rech*, November 13, 1916.

62. "Notes in Brief," *Muzykalny Sovremennik*, November 26, 1916.

63. *Rech*, January 31, 1916.

64. *Muzyka*, March 25, 1916.

### CHAPTER FIVE

1. *Vecherniye Birzheviye Vedomosti*, May 25, 1916.

2. *Petrogradskaya Gazeta*, April 28, 1916.

3. This concert was warmly reviewed in *Musical News* and other British publications. At that time the English musicologist M. Montagu-Nathan published a sympathetic article on Prokofiev in the magazine *The Musical Times* (London, October 1916).

4. December 15, 1916.

5. Yu. Engel in *Russkiye Vedomosti*, February 23, 1917.

6. Igor Glebov (Asafyev) in the brochure "S. Prokofiev" (Leningrad: Triton, 1927).

7. *Russkaya Muzykalnaya Gazeta*, No. 11–12, 1917.

8. Quoted by Igor Glebov in the brochure, "S. Prokofiev."

9. "Notes in Brief," *Muzykalny Sovremennik*, November 26, 1916.

10. *Novosti Sezona*, December 26, 1916.

11. Letter to Derzhanovsky, February 28, 1917.

12. The first issue appeared at the end of 1917. The second (and last), published in 1918, carried Asafyev's monograph on Prokofiev entitled "The Road to the Future."

13. *Iskusstyo*, No. 1, 1917.

14. *Russkiye Vedomosti*, February 23, 1917.

15. "Notes on Music" signed "Andrei Versilov," in *K Novym Beregam*, No. 3, 1923.

16. From a letter to Derzhanovsky, January 8, 1917.

17. On February 6, 1917.

18. See Glebov's (Asafyev's) brochure, "S. Prokofiev."

19. Asafyev, from unpublished notes.

20. *Nash Vek*, April 19, 1918.

21. *K. Novym Beregam*, No. 1, 1923.

22. Letter of April 11, 1917.

23. Letter of April 2, 1917.

24. V. Kolomyitsev in *Novy Den*, April 19, 1918. (An article on the *Classical Symphony* and other new works written in 1917.)

25. *Vecherniye Birzheviye Vedomosti*, May 10, 1907.

26. *Russian Music from the Beginning of the Nineteenth Century* (Ann Arbor, Michigan: American Council of Learned Societies, 1953).

27. Music note signed "Andrei Versilov," in *K Novym Beregam*, No. 3, 1923.

28. To Derzhanovsky, September 12, 1924.

29. *Essays on Soviet Music* (Moscow, 1947).

30. As told to the author by Prokofiev.

31. Concerning this article, see B. Asafyev, "The Symphony," in *Essays on Soviet Music* (Moscow, 1947).

32. As told to the author by Asafyev.

33. See Asafyev's article "The Symphony."

34. K. Balmont, *Voices of Antiquity: Hymns, Chants, and Invocations of the Ancients* (St. Petersburg: Pantheon, 1908).

35. December 29, 1924.

36. Igor Glebov, *Russian Music from the Beginning of the Nineteenth Century.*

37. V. Kamensky, *Life with Mayakovsky* (Moscow, 1940).

38. April 16, 1918.

39. *Vecherneye Slovo,* April 22, 1918.

40. *Novy Den,* April 19, 1918.

### CHAPTER SIX

1. The Japanese author probably drew the data for this chapter from Montagu-Nathan's article in *The Musical Times.*

2. See Prokofiev's letter to the editor in *K Novym Beregam,* No. 2, 1923.

3. *The New York Times,* September 19, 1918.

4. *Brooklyn Daily Eagle,* October 30, 1918.

5. *The World,* November 21, 1918.

6. From unpublished notes.

7. In 1952, on looking through pieces for an edition of selected piano works, Prokofiev excluded the *Waltz* and *Minuet,* Op. 32, evidently considering them less successful.

8. "Notes on Music," *K Novym Beregam,* No. 3, 1923.

9. See the magazine *The Love for Three Oranges,* No. 1, 1914. Prokofiev retained the plot and cast of characters in full but abridged the text considerably.

10. One can easily detect a certain relationship between the main theme of Prokofiev's *Overture* and the theme of the finale of Shostakovich's Piano Trio. But whereas in Prokofiev it is a scene from life drawn with a faint smile, in Shostakovich it is a *danse macabre* with a tinge of the grotesque.

11. *Musical Courier,* February 20, 1919.

12. The first complete performance of the opera was given posthumously in concert form at the Théâtre des Champs Elysées in Paris, November 1954. A year later, in Italy, the opera was staged for the first time at the Venice Music Festival (September 1955).

13. *Pacific Coast Musician,* January 1, 1921.

14. S. Prokofiev, "Maurice Ravel," *Sovetskoye Iskusstvo,* No. 1, 1938.

15. An example of parodied quotation, rare in Prokofiev. The composer probably wanted to call attention to the similarity of the situations. The words to the Tchaikovsky song are: "If I'd only known, if I'd only known / I wouldn't have looked out of the window / At the bold lad / As he went down our street . . ."

16. N. Zborovsky in *Posledniye Novosti,* May 1921.

17. *Zhizn Iskusstva,* No. 19, 1928.

18. *Sovremennaya Muzyka,* No. 28, 1928.

19. Letter of August 14, 1925.

20. *Zhizn Iskusstva,* No. 22, 1926.

21. The quartet had originally been conceived as a two-movement work. Fearing that the sustained diatonic style might prove monotonous, in 1921 the composer dis-

persed the thematic material of the quartet, using part of it in *The Flaming Angel* and part in the Third Concerto.

22. To Derzhanovsky, March 20, 1925.

23. *Sovremennaya Muzyka,* No. 10, 1925, and No. 19, 1927.

24. Asafyev, from unpublished notes.

25. From the brochure *The Love for Three Oranges,* published by the Leningrad State Theater of Opera and Ballet, 1934.

26. From a letter to Derzhanovsky, January 27, 1923.

27. Most of the files, which had remained in his Petrograd apartment, were burned during the civil war. Attempts by Asafyev to save the manuscripts were unsuccessful because of the criminal neglect of Arthur Lourie, who was in charge of the Music Division of the Commissariat of Education. However, thanks to the efforts of the staff of the former Papern Hospital, located in the same building, some of the manuscripts were preserved, among them the childhood *Ditties* and the piano score of the opera *The Giant.*

28. From a letter to Asafyev, February 8, 1925.

29. V. Mayakovsky (*Collected Works,* VII, 258).

### CHAPTER SEVEN

1. "Russian Productions in Paris," in *Teatr i Revolutsiya* (Petrograd, 1924).

2. Postscript from his letter to Asafyev, May 23, 1925.

3. Letter from France, August 9, 1926.

4. Letters to Asafyev, March 26 and August 9, 1926.

5. From a letter dated "Paris. Spring Season, 1925," published in the Le[?] collection *De Musica,* No. 1, 1925.

6. August 6, 1924.

7. "A Conversation with Stravinsky," *Zhizn Iskusstva* (Leningrad), Jun[?]

8. Letter to Derzhanovsky, September 30, 1925.

9. Letter to Asafyev, June 24, 1925.

10. N. Malkov in *Zhizn Iskusstva,* No. 21, 1926.

11. March 21, 1925.

12. January 21, 1926.

13. Letter to Derzhanovsky, September 30, 1925.

14. At various times Prokofiev used such assistants as P. Lamm, V. [?] L. Atovmyan, and A. Vedernikov.

15. Letter from Frankfurt, March 26, 1926.

16. Letter to Derzhanovsky, December 20, 1926.

17. Quoted from *Muzyka i Revolutsiya,* No. 1, 1927.

18. No. 10, 1926.

19. In 1928 the Overture was scored for a large orchestra.

20. From introductory remarks before a concert by I. Elins[?] *Zhizn Iskusstva,* No. 22, 1926.)

21. K. Kuznetsov in *Sovremennaya Muzyka,* No. 20, 1927.

22. *Muzyka i Revolutsiya,* No. 3, 1927.

23. *Sovremennaya Muzyka,* No. 19, 1927.

24. Review by M. M. Greenberg in *Muzyka i Revolutsiya,* N[?]

25. *Muzyka i Revolutsiya,* No. 2, 1927.

26. P. Lalo in *Comédie française,* June 1927.

27. *Théâtre et Comoedia illustrée,* June 4, 1927.

15. "Juliet's Variation," No. 14; "Romeo's Variation," No. 20; the servants' street fight at the beginning of Act I; the scene of Juliet and Paris in Act III; the episode of Romeo's death, and several others.

16. Concerning this, see the article by G. Ulanova, "A Ballerina's Schooling," in *Novy Mir,* No. 3, 1954.

17. From Prokofiev's article "In a Land of Friends," *Sovetskoye Iskusstvo,* No. 45, 1936.

18. Prokofiev also used this type of harmonic intensification in the finale of the Third Piano Concerto and in the finales of his later piano sonatas.

19. Asafyev, "Letters on Music" (MS., 1928).

20. See articles by M. Druskin in *Sovetskaya Muzyka,* No. 3, 1940; by I. Sollertinsky in *Iskusstvo i Zhizn,* No. 1, 1940; and V. Bogdanov-Berezovsky in *S. Prokofiev's Ballet "Romeo and Juliet"* (Leningrad, 1940).

#### CHAPTER NINE

1. *Sovetskaya Muzyka,* No. 1, 1948.
2. *Essays on Soviet Musical Works,* p. 77.
3. *Vechernaya Moskva,* June 22, 1936.
4. Entry in Miaskovsky's diary, June 12, 1936.
5. Entries of November 17 and 24, 1936.
6. The first performance of the Overture, in its original version, took place on October 29, 1936, at a concert of the Moscow Philharmonic Orchestra under Eugen Szenkar.
7. *Sovetskoye Iskusstvo,* October 29, 1936.
8. *Izvestia,* April 3, 1937.
9. Prokofiev later used one of the themes of Part Seven in *Ode to the End of the War.*
10. *Essays on Soviet Musical Works,* pp. 230–31.
11. *Pravda,* December 31, 1937.
12. "Eisenstein shot certain episodes of the film to fit my musical score," Prokofiev stated in an article in *Literaturnaya Gazeta,* September 20, 1938.
13. *Literaturnaya Gazeta,* September 20, 1938.
14. See G. Khubov's article, "Confusion Instead of Criticism," *Sovetskaya Muzyka,* No. 3, 1939.
15. *Sovetskaya Muzyka,* No. 3, 1939.
16. This identical "harmony of grief" appears in a similar theme of *Semyon Kotko* —the mournful tune of the minstrel at the beginning of Act. V.
17. *Essays on Soviet Musical Works,* pp. 77–78.
18. *Literaturnaya Gazeta,* September 20, 1938.
19. *Musical America,* September 28, 1918.
20. A. Solovtsov in *Essays on Soviet Musical Works,* p. 189. See also the article by G. Edelman in *Sovetskaya Muzyka,* No. 8, 1940.
21. From Prokofiev's article, "What I am Working On," in VOKS, 1947.
22. *Kurortnaya Gazeta* (Sochi), March 29, 1941.

#### CHAPTER TEN

1. Prokofiev, "My Wartime Work," VOKS, 1945.
2. Among those evacuated were V. Nemirovich-Danchenko, V. Kachalov, and O.

# Notes

Knipper-Chekhova (members of the company of the Moscow Art Theater); the writer V. Veresayev; the artist I. Grabar; the architects, the brothers Vesnin; and the musicians Miaskovsky, Shaporin, Anatole Alexandrov, S. Feinberg, A. Krein, A. Goldenweisser, and P. Lamm.

3. S. Schlifstein in *Sovetskaya Muzyka,* No. 5, 1946.

4. In a report entitled "Creative Results of 1943," given at a plenary session of the Organization Committee of the Union of Soviet Composers.

5. *Admiral Trash* and *Song of the Brave* remained unpublished. The other five songs were published in mimeographed form by *Muzfond* in the summer and fall of 1942.

6. Letter to Derzhanovsky, February 21, 1942.

7. Letter of March 29, 1942.

8. Letter to Derzhanovsky, June 27, 1942.

9. In conversation with the author.

10. *Essays on Soviet Musical Works,* p. 13.

11. Letter of July 18, 1942.

12. B. Borisov, "The Feat of Sevastopol," *Znamya,* No. 4, 1950.

13. Letter to Derzhanovsky, September 14, 1942.

14. From Prokofiev's article "My Wartime Work," in VOKS, 1945.

15. The Cantata was performed on February 21, 1944, by the soloists N. Spiller and F. Fedotov, the Leningrad State Choir, and the State Symphony Orchestra of the U.S.S.R. under the direction of A. Gauk.

16. From a letter to Ye. Koposova-Derzhanovskaya, September 4, 1943.

17. *Literatura i Iskusstvo,* April 1, 1944.

18. Letter to L. Atovmyan, April 24, 1943.

19. Letter to Ye. Koposova-Derzhanovskaya, September 4, 1943.

20. Letter of September 3, 1943.

21. Handbook of the Union of Soviet Composers, No. 7–8, 1945.

22. The Suite contains six parts not included in the first two suites: (1) "Romeo at the Fountain," (2) "Morning Dance," (3) "Variations of Juliet," (4) "The Nurse," (5) "Morning Serenade," and (6) "Juliet's Death." For this Suite the composer reorchestrated "Morning Serenade" and expanded the form of the episode "Juliet's Death." It was in this expanded form that the latter episode appeared in the final version of the ballet.

23. *Teatr i Dramaturgiya,* No. 8, 1936.

24. From an article by Sergei Eisenstein in "Problems of Motion Picture Dramaturgy" (published by *Iskusstvo,* 1954), p. 138.

25. An unpublished work by the young musicologist T. Korganov contains a number of valuable observations on the music for the film *Ivan the Terrible* (1952).

26. The principal melody of this song was taken down in 1916 by M. Ye. Piatnitsky, in Usman, Voronezh Guberniya. Piatnitsky's phonographic notes were transcribed by Hippius.

27. *Pravda,* June 14, 1945.

28. *Literatura i Iskusstvo,* October 28, 1944.

29. From Prokofiev's article "My Wartime Work," in VOKS, 1945.

30. *Sovetskoye Iskusstvo,* No. 5, 1945.

31. *Leningradskaya Pravda,* June 30, 1945.

32. Letter to Eisenstein, August 3, 1945.

33. Letter to L. T. Atovmyan, April 27, 1945.

# Notes

CHAPTER ELEVEN

1. See B. Yefimov's friendly caricature in *Vechernaya Moskva*, April 1946.
2. *Sovetskaya Muzyka*, No. 1, 1948.
3. November 16, 1945.
4. *Leningradskaya Pravda*, April 14, 1945.
5. B. Asafyev, "Thoughts and Reflections."
6. From Prokofiev's article "My Wartime Work," in *VOKS*, 1945.
7. *Pravda*, November 29, 1945. See also the reviews by V. Potapov in *Literaturnaya Gazeta*, M. Sokolsky in *Izvestia*, Ye. Grosheva in *Trud*, and T. Tsytovich in *Sovetskoye Iskusstvo*.
8. From Prokofiev's article, "What I Am Working On," *VOKS*.
9. *Pravda*, November 21, 1946. Several months later, in March 1947, the Sonata was awarded the Stalin Prize, first degree.
10. *Sovetskoye Iskusstvo*, January 17, 1947. In 1947 *The Duenna* scored a success at the Prague Opera House, and in 1956 at the Brno Opera House. In February 1956 portions of the opera were presented in concert form by members of the Moscow Philharmonia under the direction of B. Khaikin.
11. *Novy Mir*, No. 3, 1954.
12. Each waltz was given a title: (1) *Since We Met*; (2) *Cinderella in the Palace*; (3) *Mephisto Waltz*; (4) *End of the Fairy Tale*; (5) *Waltz for the New Year's Ball*; (6) *Happiness*. This suite was given its first performance on May 13, 1947, in the Great Hall of the Conservatory with the composer attending.
13. Entry of December 25, 1947.
14. *Le Monde*, March 10, 1953.
15. *Sovetskoye Iskusstvo*, January 1, 1948.
16. *Sovetskaya Muzyka*, No. 1, 1948.

CHAPTER TWELVE

1. *News* [Moscow], No. 10, 1951.
2. Letter of July 4, 1950. E. P. Grikurov is the principal conductor of the Leningrad Maly Opera Theater.
3. The composer completed the major work on the new version in 1950, but certain finishing touches, such as the middle section of Kutuzov's aria, were not completed until shortly before his death in 1953.
4. Prokofiev used as the basic theme of this aria the song, "Oh, Thou Bitter Sorrow, Tatar Steppe," from the music for Part I of *Ivan the Terrible*.
5. *News* [Moscow], No. 10, 1951.
6. See M. Sabinina's article in *Sovetskaya Muzyka*, No. 5, 1951.
7. Letter to L. Atovmyan, October 4, 1951.
8. *Sovetskoye Iskusstvo*, November 17, 1951.
9. January 12, 1952.
10. The *Sinfonia Concertante*, Op. 125, was not given its première in Moscow until January 1957. Rostropovich was the soloist and K. Zonderling conducted.
11. *Sovetskoye Iskusstvo*, November 17, 1951.
12. *Sovetskaya Muzyka*, No. 11, 1952.
13. November 12, 1952.
14. This theme repeats, with some modifications, the melody of the middle episode of the finale of the Second Cello Concerto.

15. July 22, 1952.

16. *Sovetskoye Iskusstvo,* March 18, 1953.

17. Among these were articles by René Dumesnil in the French newspaper *Le Monde*; Olin Downes in *The New York Times*; H. H. Stuckenschmidt in the West German newspaper *Die neue Zeitung*; M. Montagu-Nathan in the English journal *The Musical Times*; R. Hoffman in the French *Le Journal musical Français*; M. Zambrini in the Italian journal *Record* (Milan); N. d'Urbano in the Argentinian journal *Buenos Aires musical*.

18. For example, Pierre Bezukhov's words in Scene 6: "I seem to have a deeper feeling for her than a married man should have for the fiancée of a friend."

CHAPTER THIRTEEN

1. Letter to V. Derzhanovsky, September 12, 1924.

2. *Boston Evening Transcript,* September 26, 1918.

3. *The Musical Observer,* November 1918.

4. Letter of October 3, 1931.

5. From Scene 1 of *War and Peace.*

6. *The Musical Observer,* November 1918.

7. From the opera *War and Peace,* Scene 6.

8. Letter of February 6, 1932.

9. Igor Glebov (Asafyev): "From Recent Experiences." *Muzyka,* No. 249, 1916.

10. From a conversation with the present author.

11. S. Moreux, "Through the Eyes of a Friend," in *Musik der Zeit,* No. 5, Bonn, 1953.

12. *Peterburgskiye Vedomosti,* No. 37, February 6, 1874.

13. To Derzhanovsky, November 23, 1922.

14. Correspondence in *De Musica,* Leningrad, 1925.

15. This is a reference to one of Miaskovsky's romances to words by Alexander Blok, Op. 20.

16. See the quotation from Prokofiev's letter to Asafyev on p. 203.

17. Letter to Derzhanovsky, September 12, 1924.

18. From unpublished notes.

19. From *Masters of the Soviet Piano School,* State Music Publishers, 1954, p. 67.

20. From the unpublished essay, "Prokofiev" (in "Sketches of Soviet Composers," 1942).

21. Valuable observations on Prokofiev's style are to be found in a number of reviews by Miaskovsky and Karatygin (see his *Collected Works,* Leiningrad, 1926, pp. 194–204), in the works of Igor Glebov (Asafyev), V. A. Zuckermann, Yu. V. Keldysh, A. A. Khokhlovkina, V. O. Berkov, M. D. Sabinina, S. I. Schlifstein, in lectures by B. L. Yavorsky, in a dissertation by N. V. Zaporozhets (*The Tonal Structure of Prokofiev's Music,* 1947), and in a number of theses by young musicologists of Moscow and Leningrad.

22. From an article on Miaskovsky's Sixteenth Symphony. *Sovetskoye Iskusstvo,* October 29, 1936.

23. See his statements concerning this in *Izvestia,* November 16, 1934.

24. *Sovetskaya Muzyka,* No. 1, 1948.

25. A perceptive analysis of the distinctive phonic aspect of Prokofiev's music can be found in V. A. Zuckermann's article, "Some Thoughts on Soviet Opera," *Sovetskaya Muzyka,* No. 12, 1940.

# Notes

26. *Sovetskaya Muzyka,* No. 1, 1948.

27. *Melos,* Book II, Petrograd, 1918.

28. This spacial effect, based on an extremely wide disposition of voices, was used by Moussorgsky (for example, the final chord in the ballad *Forgotten*). The seconds that Prokofiev so loved to use in his harmonies were anticipated by the typical seconds in the music of Borodin.

29. Interview in the Riga newspaper *Sevodnya Vecherom,* January 1927.

# CATALOGUE OF PROKOFIEV'S WORKS

*giving for each opus the opus number, title,
date of composition (date of original form
in parentheses), and—when possible—first
publisher and date and place of first performance*

1 Piano Sonata No. 1 in F minor. One movement. 1909 (1907). Jurgenson, 1911. Moscow, March 6, 1910.

2 Four *Études* for piano: (I) D minor, (II) E minor, (III) C minor, (IV) C minor. 1909. Jurgenson, 1912. Moscow, March 6, 1910 (only three performed).

3 Four Pieces for piano: (I) *Story,* (II) *Badinage,* (III) *March,* (IV) *Phantom.* 1911 (1907–8). Jurgenson, 1911. St. Petersburg, April 10, 1911.

4 Four Pieces for piano: (I) *Reminiscence,* (II) *Élan,* (III) *Despair,* (IV) *Diabolic Suggestions.* 1910–12 (1908). Jurgenson, 1913. St. Petersburg, December 31, 1908.

5 Sinfonietta in A major, for orchestra. Five movements. 1914 (1909). Unpublished. Petrograd, November 6, 1915.

6 *Dreams,* symphonic poem for orchestra. 1910. Unpublished. St. Petersburg, December 5, 1910 (student performance).

7 Two poems for women's voices and orchestra, to words by K. Balmont: (I) *The White Swan,* (II) *The Wave.* 1909–10. Unpublished; MS. lost. (Shortly before his death Prokofiev reconstructed *The White Swan* chorus from surviving voice parts, writing a version for three female voices; MS. in Central State Archives.) St. Petersburg, 1910 (only *The White Swan* was performed).

8 *Autumnal Sketch,* for orchestra. 1910 (new version, 1934). Unpublished. Moscow, August 1, 1911.

9 Two songs for voice and piano, to words by A. Apukhtin and K. Balmont. 1910–11. Gutheil, 1917. St. Petersburg, March 28, 1914 (only one performed).

10 Concerto No. 1 in D-flat major for piano and orchestra. One movement. 1911–12. Jurgenson, 1913. Moscow, August 7, 1912.

11 *Toccata* in C major for piano. 1912. Jurgenson, 1913. Petrograd, December 10, 1916.

12 Ten pieces for piano. 1913 (1906–13). Jurgenson, 1914. Moscow, February 5, 1914 (only three pieces performed).

12-bis *Scherzo,* for four bassoons (transcription of No. 9 of Opus 12). 1912. Jurgenson, 1915.

OPUS

13 *Maddalena,* opera in one act. Libretto by M. Lieven. 1913 (1911). Unpublished.

14 Piano Sonata No. 2 in D minor. Four movements. 1912. Jurgenson, 1913. Moscow, February 5, 1914.

15 *Ballade,* for cello and piano. 1912. Jurgenson, 1915. Moscow, February 5, 1914.

16 Concerto No. 2 in G minor, for piano and orchestra. Four movements. 1923 (1913). Gutheil, 1925 (composer's arrangement for two pianos, four hands). Pavlovsk, September 5, 1913.

17 *Sarcasms,* five pieces for piano. 1912–14. Jurgenson, 1916. Petrograd, December 10, 1916.

18 *The Ugly Duckling,* for voice and piano. Based on Andersen's fairy tale. 1914. Gutheil, 1917. Petrograd, January 30, 1915.

19 Concerto No. 1 in D major, for violin and orchestra. Three movements. 1916–17. Gutheil, 1924. Paris, October 18, 1923.

20 *Scythian Suite (Ala and Lolli).* Four movements. 1914–15. Gutheil, 1923. Petrograd, January 29, 1916.

21 *The Buffoon (Chout),* ballet in six scenes. Scenario by S. Prokofiev. 1920 (1915). Gutheil, 1921. Paris, May 17, 1921.

21-bis *The Buffoon (Chout),* symphonic suite from the ballet. Twelve movements. 1922. Gutheil, 1924. Brussels, January 15, 1924.

22 *Fugitive Visions,* twenty pieces for piano. 1915–17. Gutheil, 1917. Petrograd, April 15, 1918.

23 Five songs for voice and piano. 1915. Gutheil, 1917. Petrograd, December 10, 1916 (only one song performed).

24 *The Gambler,* opera in four acts, six scenes. Libretto by S. Prokofiev, based on the story by Dostoyevsky. 1927 (1915–16). Russian Music Publishers, 1930 (piano score only). Brussels, April 29, 1929.

25 *Classical Symphony* (No. 1), in D major. Four movements. 1916–17. Russian Music Publishers, 1925. Petrograd, April 21, 1918.

26 Concerto No. 3 in C major, for piano and orchestra. Three movements. 1917–21. Gutheil, 1923. Chicago, December 16, 1921.

27 Five songs. To poems by Anna Akhmatova. 1916. Gutheil, 1917. Moscow, February 18, 1917.

28 Piano Sonata No. 3 in A minor. One movement. 1917 (1907). Gutheil, 1918. Petrograd, April 15, 1918.

29 Piano Sonata No. 4 in C minor. Three movements. 1917 (1908). Gutheil, 1918. Petrograd, April 17, 1918.

29-bis *Andante* from Piano Sonata No. 4, transcribed for orchestra. 1934. Unpublished. Not performed.

30 *Seven, They Are Seven,* cantata for tenor, chorus, and orchestra. To a poem by K. Balmont. 1917–18. Gutheil, 1925. Paris, May 29, 1924.

31 *Tales of the Old Grandmother,* four pieces for piano. 1918. Gutheil, 1922. New York, January 7, 1919.

32 Four pieces for piano. 1918. Gutheil, 1922. New York, March 30, 1919.

33 *The Love for Three Oranges,* opera in four acts, ten scenes with a prologue. Libretto by S. Prokofiev after the play by Carlo Gozzi. 1919. Gutheil, 1922 (piano score only). Chicago, December 30, 1921.

33-bis *The Love for Three Oranges,* symphonic suite from the opera. Six movements. 1924 (1919). Gutheil. Paris, November 29, 1925.

33-ter March and Scherzo from *The Love for Three Oranges,* transcription for piano. Gutheil, 1922.

34 *Overture on Hebrew Themes,* for clarinet, piano, and string quartet. 1919. Gutheil, 1922. New York, January 26, 1920.

34-bis *Overture on Hebrew Themes,* for symphony orchestra (new version of Opus 34). 1934 (1919). Gutheil, 1935. Prague (performance date unknown).

35 Five songs without words, for voice and piano. 1920. Gutheil, 1922. New York, March 27, 1921.

35-bis Five melodies for violin and piano (arrangement of Opus 35). 1925. Russian Music Publishers, 1925.

36 Five songs for voice and piano. Words by K. Balmont. 1921. Gutheil, 1923. Paris, June 14, 1928.

37 *The Flaming Angel,* opera in five acts. Libretto by S. Prokofiev after the story by V. Bryusov. 1919–27. Gutheil, 1927 (piano score only). Paris, November 25, 1954 (complete concert performance); Venice, September 1955 (first stage performance).

38 Piano Sonata No. 5 in C major. Three movements. 1923. Gutheil, 1925. Paris, March 9, 1924.

39 Quintet for winds and strings, in G minor (incorporating music from the unpublished ballet *Trapeze*). Six movements. 1924. Gutheil, 1927. Moscow, March 6, 1927.

40 Symphony No. 2 in D minor. Two movements. 1924. Russian Music Publishers, 1925. Paris, June 6, 1925.

41 *Le Pas d'acier,* ballet in two scenes. Scenario by G. Yakulov and S. Prokofiev. 1925. Russian Music Publishers, 1928. Paris, June 7, 1927.

41-bis *Le Pas d'acier,* symphonic suite from the ballet, in four movements. 1926 (1925). Russian Music Publishers, 1927. Moscow, May 27, 1928.

42 Overture in B-flat major, for 17 performers (first version). 1926. Unpublished. Moscow, February 7, 1927.

42-bis Overture in B-flat major, for full orchestra (second version). 1928 (1926). Unpublished. Paris, December 18, 1930.

43 *Divertissement,* for orchestra. Four movements. 1925–29. Russian Music Publishers, 1930. Paris, December 22, 1929.

43-bis *Divertissement,* transcription for piano, in four movements. 1938 (1925). State Music Publishers, 1940.

44 Symphony No. 3 in C minor. Four movements. 1928. Russian Music Publishers, 1931. Paris, May 17, 1929.

45 *Things in Themselves,* two pieces for piano. 1928. Russian Music Publishers, 1928. New York, January 6, 1930.

46 *The Prodigal Son,* ballet in three scenes. Scenario by B. Kokhno. 1928. Russian Music Publishers, 1929 (piano arrangement only). Paris, May 21, 1929.

46-bis *The Prodigal Son,* symphonic suite from the ballet. Five movements. 1929. Russian Music Publishers, 1930. Paris, March 7, 1931.

47 Symphony No. 4 in C major (first version). Four movements. 1930. Unpublished. Boston, November 14, 1930.

48 Sinfonietta, in A major, for orchestra (third version). Five movements. 1929. Russian Music Publishers, 1931 (piano arrangement only). Moscow, November 18, 1930.

49 *Portraits,* symphonic suite from the opera *The Gambler.* Five movements. 1930–31. Gutheil. Paris, March 12, 1932.

50 String Quartet No. 1 in B minor. Three movements. 1930. Russian Music Publishers, 1932. Washington, April 25, 1931.

50-bis *Andante* from Quartet in B minor, arranged for string orchestra. 1930. Unpublished. Not performed.

51 *Sur le Borysthène (On the Dnieper),* ballet in two scenes. Scenario by S. Lifar and S. Prokofiev. 1930. Russian Music Publishers, 1932 (piano arrangement only). Paris, December 16, 1932.

51-bis *Sur le Borysthène,* symphonic suite from the ballet. Six movements. 1933 (1930). Russian Music Publishers, 1930 (composer's piano arrangement only). Paris, 1934.

52 Six transcriptions for piano. (From Op. 46, 48, 35, 50.) 1930–31. Russian Music Publishers, 1931. Moscow, May 27, 1932.

53 Piano Concerto No. 4 in B-flat major, for left hand alone. Four movements. 1931. Unpublished. West Berlin, September 5, 1956.

54 Two Sonatinas for piano: (I) E minor, three movements; (II) G minor, three movements. 1931–32. Russian Music Publishers, 1932. London, April 17, 1932 (only the second one performed).

55 Concerto No. 5 in G major, for piano and orchestra. Five movements. 1932. Russian Music Publishers, 1933. Berlin, October 31, 1932.

56 Sonata for two violins, in C major. Four movements. 1932. Russian Music Publishers, 1932. State Music Publishers, 1947 (mimeograph). Moscow, November 27, 1932.

57 *Symphonic Song,* for orchestra. 1933. Unpublished. Moscow, April 14, 1934.

58 Concerto for cello and orchestra in E minor. Three movements. 1933–38. Anglo-Soviet Music, 1951. Moscow, November 26, 1938.

59 Three pieces for piano. 1934. Russian Music Publishers, 1935. Moscow, 1935.

60 *Lieutenant Kije,* suite based on the film score. Five movements. 1934. Gutheil, 1935.

60-bis Two songs from the film *Lieutenant Kije:* (I) *The Little Gray Dove is*

OPUS

*Cooing*; (II) *Troika*. 1934. Russian Music Publishers. "Iskusstvo" Publishers (No. 1), 1938.

61 *Egyptian Nights,* symphonic suite from the incidental music to the play. Seven movements. 1934. Gutheil, 1934. Moscow, December 22, 1938.

62 *Thoughts,* three pieces for piano. 1933–34. Russian Music Publishers, 1935; State Music Publishers, 1940. Moscow, November 13, 1936.

63 Concerto No. 2 in G minor, for violin and orchestra. Three movements. 1935. Gutheil, 1937. Madrid, December 1, 1935.

64 *Romeo and Juliet,* ballet in four acts, ten scenes. Scenario by S. Radlov, A. Piotrovsky, L. Lavrovsky, and S. Prokofiev. 1935–36. Muzfond, 1944 (mimeograph), State Music Publishers, 1946 (piano arrangement only). Brno, Czechoslovakia, December 1938.

64-bis *Romeo and Juliet,* first symphonic suite from the ballet. Seven movements. 1936. State Music Publishers, 1938. Moscow, November 24, 1936.

64-ter *Romeo and Juliet,* second symphonic suite from the ballet. Seven movements. 1936. State Music Publishers, 1938. Leningrad, April 15, 1937.

65 *Music for Children,* 12 easy pieces for piano. 1935. State Music Publishers, 1936. Moscow, April 11, 1936.

65-bis *Summer Day,* symphonic suite for small orchestra (transcriptions of Nos. 1, 5, 6, 9, 10, 11, and 12 from *Music for Children*). 1941. State Music Publishers, 1947. Moscow, 1946 (radio performance).

66 Six mass songs for voice and piano: (1) *Partisan Zheleznyak,* (2) *Anyutka,* (3) *My Country is Growing,* (4) *Through Snow and Fog,* (5) *Beyond the Hills,* (6) *Song of Voroshilov.* 1935. State Music Publishers, 1935 (Nos. 1, 2); "Iskusstvo" Publishers, 1939 (Nos. 3–6).

67 *Peter and the Wolf,* symphonic tale for narrator and orchestra. Text by S. Prokofiev. 1936. State Music Publishers: 1937, piano arrangement; 1940, score. Moscow, May 2, 1936.

68 Three children's songs, for voice and piano: (1) *The Chatterbox,* (2) *Sweet Melody,* (3) *The Little Pigs.* 1936–39. State Music Publishers: 1937, Nos. 1, 2; 1946, No. 3. Moscow, May 5, 1936 (*The Chatterbox* only).

69 Four marches for brass band. 1935–37. State Music Publishers, 1937 (first march only).

70 *The Queen of Spades,* music for the film. 1936. Unpublished.

70-bis *Boris Godunov,* music for the drama by Pushkin. 1936. Unpublished.

71 *Eugene Onegin,* music for the play after Pushkin. 1936. Unpublished.

72 *Russian Overture,* for symphony orchestra (two versions). 1936. Gutheil, 1936; State Music Publishers, 1946 (first version). Moscow, October 29, 1936 (first version).

73 Three romances, for voice and piano: (1) *Pine Trees,* (2) *Roseate Dawn,* (3) *In Your Chamber.* Words by Pushkin. 1936. State Music Publishers; in *A. S. Pushkin in Romances and Songs by Soviet Composers* (1937). Moscow, April 20, 1937 (radio performance).

74 *Cantata for the Twentieth Anniversary of the October Revolution,* for symphony orchestra, brass band, orchestra of accordions, percussion, and two

choirs. Ten parts. Text from writings and speeches of Marx, Lenin, and Stalin. 1936–37. Unpublished. Not performed.

75 *Romeo and Juliet,* ten pieces for piano. 1937. "Iskusstvo" Publishers, 1938. Moscow, 1937.

76 *Songs of Our Days,* for soloists, chorus, and orchestra. Nine parts. 1937. State Music Publishers, 1939 (Composer's piano arrangement only). Moscow, January 5, 1938.

77 *Hamlet,* music for the play. 1937–38. Unpublished. Leningrad, May 15, 1938.

77-bis *Gavotte* No. 4 from the music for *Hamlet,* for piano. 1938. Gutheil, 1939; State Music Publishers, 1940. Moscow, November 22, 1939 (radio performance).

78 *Alexander Nevsky,* cantata for mezzo-soprano, chorus, and orchestra. Seven movements. Words by V. Lugovskoi and S. Prokofiev. 1938–39. State Music Publishers, 1941. Moscow, May 17, 1939.

78-bis Three songs from *Alexander Nevsky.* 1939. State Music Publishers, 1939.

79 Seven mass songs for voice and piano. 1939. State Music Publishers, 1940.

80 Sonata No. 1 in F minor for violin and piano. Four movements. 1938–46. Muzfond, 1947 (mimeograph); State Music Publishers, 1951. Moscow, October 23, 1946.

81 *Semyon Kotko,* opera in five acts, seven scenes. Libretto by V. Katayev and S. Prokofiev, after a story by V. Katayev. 1939. Unpublished. Moscow, June 23, 1940.

81-bis *Semyon Kotko,* symphonic suite from the opera. Eight movements. 1941. State Music Publishers, 1947. Moscow, December 27, 1943.

82 Piano Sonata No. 6 in A major. Four movements. 1939–40. State Music Publishers, 1941. Moscow, April 8, 1940 (radio performance).

83 Piano Sonata No. 7 in B-flat major. Three movements. 1939–42. State Music Publishers, 1943. Moscow, January 18, 1943.

84 Piano Sonata No. 8 in B-flat major. Three movements. 1939–44. State Music Publishers, 1946. Moscow, December 30, 1944.

85 *Zdravitsa (Hail to Stalin),* cantata for chorus and orchestra on folk texts. 1939. State Music Publishers, 1941. Moscow, December 21, 1939.

86 *The Duenna (Betrothal in a Monastery),* opera in four acts, nine scenes, after the play by Sheridan. Libretto by S. Prokofiev, verses by Mira Mendelson. 1940. Muzfond, 1944 (piano score, mimeograph). Leningrad, November 3, 1946.

87 *Cinderella,* ballet in three acts. Scenario by N. D. Volkov. 1940–44. Muzfond, 1945 (piano score, mimeograph). State Music Publishers, 1954 (piano arrangement). Moscow, November 21, 1945.

88 Symphonic march in B-flat major for orchestra. 1941. Unpublished.

89 (I) Seven mass songs for voice and piano; (II) March in A-flat major for band. 1941–42. Muzfond, 1942 (mimeograph; Nos. 3–6). Nalchik, November, 1941 (Nos. 3, 4 only).

90 *The Year 1941,* symphonic suite for orchestra. Three movements. 1941. Unpublished. Sverdlovsk, January 21, 1943.

91 *War and Peace,* opera in five acts, thirteen scenes, with a choral prologue (first version). Libretto by S. Prokofiev and M. Mendelson-Prokofieva. Final version contained 11 scenes only. 1941–52. Muzfond, 1943 (two-volume piano score, minus *The Noblemen's Ball,* scene 2, and *War Council at Fili,* scene 9; mimeograph). Leningrad, June 12, 1946 (first version, first eight scenes only); Leningrad, March 31, 1955 (second version, eleven scenes).

92 String Quartet No. 2 in F major (Kabardinian Quartet). Three movements. 1941. State Music Publishers, 1944. Moscow, September 5, 1942.

93 *Ballad of an Unknown Boy,* cantata for soprano, tenor, chorus, and orchestra. Words by P. Antokolsky. 1942–43. Unpublished. Moscow, February 21, 1944.

94 Sonata for flute and piano in D major. Four movements. 1943. Unpublished. Moscow, December 7, 1943.

94-bis Violin Sonata No. 2 in D major (transcription of Flute Sonata, Opus 94). 1943–44. State Music Publishers, 1946. Moscow, June 17, 1944.

95 Three pieces for piano, from *Cinderella.* 1942. State Music Publishers, 1943.

96 Three pieces for piano (transcriptions from *War and Peace* and the film *Lermontov*). 1941–42. State Music Publishers, 1943.

97 Ten pieces for piano, from *Cinderella.* 1943. State Music Publishers, 1944.

97-bis *Adagio* from *Cinderella,* for cello and piano. 1944. Muzfond, 1945 (mimeograph). Moscow, April 19, 1944 (radio performance).

98 Sketches for National Anthem of the Soviet Union and National Anthem of the R.S.F.S.R. 1943. Unpublished.

99 March for band, in B-flat major. 1943–44. State Music Publishers, 1946. Moscow, April 30, 1944 (radio performance).

100 Symphony No. 5 in B-flat major. Four movements. 1944. State Music Publishers, 1947. Moscow, January 13, 1945.

101 *Romeo and Juliet,* third suite for orchestra. Six movements. 1946 (1935–36). Muzfond, 1947 (mimeograph); State Music Publishers, 1949. Moscow, March 8, 1946.

102 Six pieces for piano, from *Cinderella.* 1944. Muzfond, 1944 (mimeograph).

103 Piano Sonata No. 9 in C major. Four movements. 1947. State Music Publishers, 1955. Moscow, April 21, 1951.

104 Arrangements of Russian folk songs for voice and piano, in two volumes (Volume One, six songs; Volume Two, six songs). 1944. Muzfond, 1945 (mimeograph). Moscow, March 25, 1945.

105 *Ode to the End of the War,* for eight harps, four pianos, brass, percussion, and double basses. 1945. Unpublished. Moscow, November 12, 1945.

106 Two duets, arrangements of Russian folk songs for tenor and bass with piano. Folk texts taken down by Y. Hippius. 1945. Muzfond, 1946 (mimeograph).

OPUS

107 *Cinderella,* first suite for orchestra. Eight movements. 1946. Anglo-Soviet Music, 1949. Moscow, November 12, 1946.

108 *Cinderella,* second suite for orchestra. Seven movements. 1946. Unpublished.

109 *Cinderella,* third suite for orchestra. Eight movements. 1946. State Music Publishers, 1954. Moscow, September 3, 1947 (radio performance).

110 *Waltzes,* suite for orchestra (from *War and Peace, Cinderella,* and *Lermontov*). Six movements. 1946. Muzfond, 1947 (mimeograph). Moscow, May 13, 1947.

111 Symphony No. 6 in E-flat minor. Three movements. 1945–47. Leeds Music Corporation, New York, 1949. Leningrad, October 11, 1947.

112 Symphony No. 4 in C major (second version). Four movements. 1947. Unpublished. Not performed.

113 *Festive Poem ("Thirty Years"),* for orchestra. 1947. Muzfond, 1947 (mimeograph). Moscow, October 3, 1947.

114 *Flourish, Mighty Land,* cantata for chorus and orchestra for thirtieth anniversary of October Revolution. Text by Y. Dolmatovsky. 1947. Muzfond, 1947 (piano score only, mimeograph). Moscow, November 12, 1947.

115 Sonata for Unaccompanied Violins in unison, in D major. Three movements. 1947. Muzfond, 1947 (mimeograph); State Music Publishers, 1952. Not performed.

116 *Ivan the Terrible,* music for the films: Part I, 1942–44; Part II, 1945. Unpublished.

117 *The Story of a Real Man,* opera in four acts. Libretto by M. Mendelson-Prokofieva and S. Prokofiev, after the novel by Boris Polevoi. 1947–48. Unpublished. Leningrad, December 3, 1948.

118 *The Stone Flower,* ballet in four acts. Scenario by L. Lavrovsky and M. Mendelson-Prokofieva, after the story by P. Bazhov. 1948–50. State Music Publishers, 1956 (piano score only). Moscow, February 12, 1954.

119 Sonata for cello and piano in C major. Three movements. 1949. State Music Publishers, 1951. Moscow, March 1, 1950.

120 Two "Pushkin Waltzes" for orchestra. 1949. Unpublished. Moscow, 1952 (radio performance).

121 *Soldiers' Marching Song.* Words by V. Lugovskoi. 1950. Unpublished.

122 *Winter Bonfire,* suite for narrator, boys' chorus, and orchestra. Eight movements. Text by S. Marshak. 1949. State Music Publishers, 1951 (piano score only). Moscow, December 19, 1950.

123 *Summer Night,* suite for orchestra from the opera *The Duenna.* Five movements. 1950. Unpublished. (Nos. 2, 3, radio performance).

124 *On Guard for Peace,* oratorio for narrator, mezzo-soprano, mixed chorus, boys' chorus, and orchestra. Ten movements. Text by S. Marshak. 1950. State Music Publishers, 1952. Moscow, December 19, 1950.

125 *Sinfonia Concertante,* in E minor, for cello and orchestra. Three movements. 1950–52. Unpublished. Moscow, February 18, 1952 (in original form, as "Second Cello Concerto").

OPUS

126 *Wedding Suite,* for orchestra, from *The Stone Flower.* Five movements. 1951. Unpublished. Moscow, December 12, 1951.

127 *Gypsy Fantasy,* for orchestra, from *The Stone Flower.* 1951. Unpublished. Moscow, November 18, 1951.

128 *Ural Rhapsody,* for orchestra, from *The Stone Flower.* 1951. Unpublished. Not performed.

129 *The Mistress of the Copper Mountain,* suite for orchestra, from *The Stone Flower.* This work was projected, but never realized.

130 Festive Poem, *The Volga Meets the Don,* for orchestra. 1951. State Music Publishers, 1956 (piano score only). Moscow, February 22, 1952 (radio performance).

131 Symphony No. 7 in C-sharp minor. Four movements. 1951–52. State Music Publishers: 1953, arrangement for piano, four hands; 1954, score. Moscow, October 11, 1952.

132 Concertino for cello and orchestra in G minor. Three movements (unfinished). 1952. Unpublished.

133 Concerto for two pianos and string orchestra. Three movements (unfinished). 1952. Unpublished.

134 Sonata for unaccompanied cello, in C-sharp minor. Four movements (unfinished). Unpublished.

135 Piano Sonata No. 5 in C major (second version). Three movements. 1952–53. State Music Publishers, 1955. Alma-Ata, February 2, 1954.

136 Symphony No. 2 in D minor (second version). Three movements. This work was projected, but never realized.

137 Piano Sonata No. 10 (sketch only). The sketch for this sonata was Prokofiev's last work. 1953.

138 Piano Sonata No. 11. This work was projected, but never realized.

Piano Pieces                OTHER WORKS

Sixty *Ditties* (five series of piano pieces written between 1902 and 1906).

Waltzes by Schubert, transcribed and combined into a suite for piano, two hands. 1920. Unpublished.

Waltzes by Schubert, transcribed and combined into a suite for two pianos, four hands (revision of the earlier suite). 1923. Gutheil, 1923.

Organ fugue in D minor by Buxtehude, arr. for piano. 1920. Gutheil, 1923.

Incidental Music

*Partisans in the Ukrainian Steppes,* music for the film. 1942. Unpublished.

*Kotovsky,* music for the film. 1942. Unpublished.

*Lermontov,* music for the film. 1941–42. Unpublished.

*Tonya,* music for the film. 1942. Unpublished.

*Lieutenant Kije,* for small orchestra, music for the film. 1933. Unpublished.

*Egyptian Nights,* incidental music for the play. 1933. Unpublished.

*Alexander Nevsky,* for mezzo-soprano, chorus, and orchestra, music for the film. 1938. Unpublished.

# INDEXES

# GENERAL INDEX

Abravanel, Maurice, 425
Academy of St. Cecilia (Rome), 256
Acmeist group, 47, 90f, 129
Afanasyev, A. N., 100f, 379
Afinogenov, Alexander, 238, 258
Agnivtsev, N., 109
Akhmatova, Anna, 81, 128ff, 182
Akimenko-Stepovy, Y., 22
Alchevsky, I., 51, 124f
Alexandrov, Alexander, 257, 344
Alexandrov, Anatole, 258, 329
All-Russian Theater Society, 364, 439
All-Union Radio Committee, 249, 266, 291, 309, 363, 413, 419f
All-Union Radio Orchestra, 395, 413, 425, 430
Alma-Ata, 331, 339, 342ff, 348, 389
Andersen, Hans Christian, 16, 95
Anisfeld, Boris, 169, 176, 195
Ansermet, Ernest, 180
Antokolsky, P., 331, 340f
*Apollon* (St. Petersburg), 58, 77, 82
Apukhtin, A., 43
Arensky, Anton, 9, 13, 63
Artemyeva, Z., 125, 129
Arutunian, Alexander, 410
Asafyev, Boris (Igor Glebov): works mentioned, 245, 276, 319; career as music critic, 53, 55, 126f; comments on musical figures, 87ff, 125, 378; on Prokofiev's music generally, 148f, 221, 245, 468, 470, 480; on Prokofiev's piano pieces, 34, 42, 67, 72, 78, 93f, 97, 130, 132; on Prokofiev's sonatas, 31, 68, 139; on Prokofiev's concertos, 64, 75, 98, 193; *Scythian Suite,* 121f, 463; *The Love for Three Oranges,* 199f, 217; on other works, 59, 103, 282, 306, 334
Aslanov, A. P., 61, 76
Association for Contemporary Music (ACM), 204, 221f, 233f, 240, 245, 467
"Ass's Tail" group, 101
Atovmyan, L. T., 344, 348, 350, 410, 419, 429, 436
Auer, Leopold, 17, 144
Auric, Georges, 207, 209, 214

Bach, Johann Sebastian, 7, 20, 22, 84, 177, 203, 397
Balakirev, Mily, 35, 50, 332, 333, 486
Balanchine, George, 229

Balmont, Konstantin: poems and songs mentioned, 42f, 108f, 150f, 193f; mentioned, 81, 129, 132
Barcelona, 201, 263
Barto, A., 280, 282, 415
Bashkirov, Boris (Verin), 87, 108, 113, 144
Bazhov, P., 411f, 439f, 443, 457
Beethoven, Ludwig van: *Contredanses,* 177; *Egmont* overture, 26; piano sonatas, 22, 24, 399; symphonies, 22, 40, 336; influence on Prokofiev's music, 235, 399f, 434, 461, 486
Belyaev, Mitrofan, 54, 83
Belyaev, Viktor, 40, 48
Benois, Alexander, 40, 50f, 87ff, 114, 158
Berg, Alban, 221
Berlin, 203; Berlin State Opera, 217, 225
Berlioz, Hector, 80, 142, 266f, 466
Bernhard, A., 17, 19
Bernstein, N., 63, 76
Birman, S. G., 308, 313, 355
Black Hundreds, The, 77
Bolm, Adolph, 168f
Blok, Alexander, 48, 81
Bolshoi Theater (Moscow), 5, 137, 218, 234, 257, 261f, 349, 373, 377f, 383, 394, 397, 410ff, 425, 429f, 437ff
Borodin, Alexander: and "The Five," 50; influence on Prokofiev's works, 336, 356, 483; works mentioned, 5, 22f, 106, 121, 304, 387f, 441, 463f, 469
Borovsky, Alexander, 53, 67, 233
Bosse, G., 124, 217
Boston Symphony Orchestra, 54, 202, 216, 235, 371
Boult, Sir Adrian, 338
Brahms, Johannes, 41, 264, 433, 461
British Royal Philharmonic Society, 372
Brussels, 201f
Bryusov, Valery, 48, 177, 202
Buxtehude, Dietrich, 8, 181
*Bylina,* 296, 363f, 386

Campanini, Cleofonte, 173, 176
Central House of the Composers (Moscow), 324, 350, 438
Central State Archives of Literature and Art, 410, 437
"Change of Landmarks" group, 46

# INDEX OF PROKOFIEV'S WORKS